THE CITIZENSHIP LAW OF THE USSR

LAW IN EASTERN EUROPE

A series of publications
issued by the
Documentation Office for East European Law
University of Leyden

General Editor

F.J.M. FELDBRUGGE

No. 25

SPRINGER-SCIENCE+BUSINESS MEDIA, B.V.

THE CITIZENSHIP LAW OF THE USSR

by

GEORGE GINSBURGS
Distinguished Professor of Foreign and Comparative Law
Law School, Rutgers University (Camden)

SPRINGER-SCIENCE+BUSINESS MEDIA, B.V.

Distributors

for the United States and Canada: Kluwer Boston, Inc., 190 Old Derby Street, Hingham, MA 02043, USA
for all other countries: Kluwer Academic Publishers Group, Distribution Center, P.O.Box 322, 3300 AH Dordrecht, The Netherlands

Library of Congress Cataloging in Publication Data

Ginsburgs, George.
The citizenship law of the USSR.

(Law in Eastern Europe ; no. 25)
Bibliography: p.
Includes index.
1. Citizenship--Soviet Union. I. Title.
II. Title: Citizenship law of the U.S.S.R. III. Series.
LAW 342.47'083 83-22040
344.70283

ISBN 978-94-015-1186-5 ISBN 978-94-015-1184-1 (eBook)
DOI 10.1007/978-94-015-1184-1

TABLE OF CONTENTS

TO HERTA

FOREWORD

In 1968, the predecessor of this volume was published as Number 15 of the *Law in Eastern Europe* series, under the title "Soviet Citizenship Law". The decision to put out a new version of that study was prompted by the enactment in 1978 of the current Law on the Citizenship of the USSR and the various changes in Soviet practice in this domain which occurred in the intervening decade. I have drawn on the earlier work for background material and in order to make comparisons between the previous record here and the substance of the latest statute. However, the present monograph is not a second edition in the sense of being an expanded and updated revision of the original, but stands as an independent piece of research and analysis. Thus, three of the chapters (out of a total of six) featured in the 1968 volume — citizenship and state succession, state succession and option of nationality, and refugees and displaced persons — have now been omitted for the simple reason that the situation in these areas has remained virtually static during the past ten years so that the initial treatment requires no significant alteration. On the other hand, fresh problems have meantime arisen — such as, for instance, the connection between citizenship and emigration, and the relationship between citizenship status and the international protection of human rights — which called for attention and are dealt with in this book. In short, for complete coverage, both monographs should be consulted: the first one providing additional historical perspective, its successor focusing more on today's issues.

I gratefully acknowledge my indebtedness to the National Endowment for the Humanities for an award to pursue research on the development of Soviet constitutional and administrative institutions after Stalin of which the present study is a by–product, and to the FASP Grants Committee of Rutgers University for financial assistance that allowed this project to be completed. Special thanks are also due to Henn–Juri Uibopuu, Ger P. van den Berg and William B. Simons for supplying me with the texts of several pieces of recent local legislation and thus sparing me some embarrassing lapses.

G.G.

ACKNOWLEDGMENTS

This monograph is the culmination of an enduring research interest in various aspects of Soviet policy on citizenship law. In order not to overload the bibliography, I have decided to list separately my previous publications on the subject and, in that context, to express my gratitude to all people concerned for permission to draw on these materials in the preparation of the present work.

"The Soviet Union and the Problem of Refugees and Displaced Persons, 1917–1956", *American Journal of International Law*, 1957, No.2, pp.325–361.
"Option of Nationality in Soviet Treaty Practice, 1917–1924", *American Journal of International Law*, 1961 No.1, pp.53–75.
"Option of Nationality in Soviet Treaty Law: The War–Time and Post–War Record", *Iowa Law Review*, 1964, No.4, pp.1130–1176.
"Soviet Citizenship Legislation and Statelessness as a Consequence of the Conflict of Nationality Laws", *International and Comparative Law Quarterly*, 1966, No.1, *pp.1–54.*
Soviet Citizenship Law (No.15 in *Law in Eastern Europe* series, ed. by Z. Szirmai), Leyden: Sijthoff, 1968, 270pp.
"Nationality and State Succession in Soviet Theory and Practice: The Experience of the Baltic States", in A. Sprudzs & A. Rusis, eds., *Res Baltica*, Leyden: Sijthoff, 1968, pp.160–190.
"Soviet Law and the Acquisition of Citizenship At Birth", *University of Toronto Law Journal*, 1970, No.1, pp.71–80.
"The Soviet Union and International Cooperation in Legal Matters: Criminal Law — The Current Scene", *International and Comparative Law Quarterly*, 1970, No.4, pp.626–670.
"Soviet Citizenship Law: New Light on Administrative Procedure", *Osteuropa–Recht*, 1971, No.1, pp.1–6.
"Soviet Law and the Emigration of Soviet Jews", *Soviet Jewish Affairs*, 1973, No.1, pp.3–19.
"The Citizenship Status of Koreans in Pre–Revolutionary Russia and the Early Years of the Soviet Regime", *Journal of Korean Affairs*, 1975, No.2, pp.1–19.
"The Citizenship Status of Koreans in the USSR: Post–World War II Developments", *Journal of Korean Affairs*, 1976, No.1, pp.1–16.

"Current Legal Problems of Jewish Emigration from the USSR", *Soviet Jewish Affairs*, 1976, No.2, pp.3–13.
"The Citizenship Status of Soviet Koreans, 1945–1975", in L. Lipson & V. Chalidze, eds., *Papers on Soviet Law*, New York, 1977, No.1, pp.143–166.
"Emigratsiia koreitsev iz SSSR", *Khronika zashchity prav v SSSR*, 1977, vyp.25, pp.65–71.
"Citizenship Questions in Postwar Sino–Soviet Relations", *A Chronicle of Human Rights in the USSR*, 1977, No.26, pp.67–75;
"Problema grazhdanstva v poslevoennykh kitaisko–sovetskikh otnosheniiakh", *Khronika zashchity prav v SSSR*, 1977, vyp.26, pp.66–72.
"The New Soviet Citizenship Law and the Universal Declaration of Human Rights", *A Chronicle of Human Rights in the USSR*, 1979, No.33, pp.47–53;
"Novyi Sovetskii zakon o grazhdanstve i Vseobshchaia Deklaratsiia Prav Cheloveka", *Khronika zashchity prav v SSSR*, 1979, vyp.33, pp.62–71.
"Substantive Aspects of the 1978 Law on Soviet Citizenship: First Impressions", *Review of Socialist Law*, 1979, No.4, pp.381–407.

INTRODUCTION

1. Constitutional Basis

Like its predecessor, the 1977 Constitution of the USSR contains several provisions dealing with citizenship questions. An innovation of the latest Fundamental Law is the inclusion of the item "USSR Citizenship" in the title of chapter 6 (along with "Equality of Citizens") which, in turn, appears in the section devoted to the theme of "The State and the Individual". These stylistic changes have some interesting implications. In the 1936 federal charter, the main reference to the topic of citizenship — Article 21 — was featured in the chapter on the "State Structure" of the USSR. The location left no doubt that citizenship was then considered the exclusive affair of the state, whereas the present formulation tends instead to emphasize the relationship between the state and the individual in this connection. Or, as a Soviet author prefers to put it,

> "the prescriptions on Soviet citizenship in the aforecited constitutions [i.e., those belonging to the 1936 generation] figured in the sections on the state structure of the USSR and union republics. Thereby, citizenship as an institution defining the legal ties between the individual and the state ended up isolated from the fundamental rights and duties of citizens which formed the basis of their legal status.
>
> In the 1978 BSSR Constitution, just as in the 1977 USSR Constitution, the seminal prescriptions on Soviet citizenship are set forth in the same section as the fundamental rights, freedoms and duties of citizens. In this manner, there has been achieved a comprehensive enunciation of the bases of the legal status of the citizens of the Belorussian SSR."[1]

Such portrayal of the individual as a partner in the matter fits, of course, the regime's current desire to project a more "democratic" image of the workings of the Soviet system and to advertise the Soviet state's "abiding respect" for the position of the person. The mention of "USSR Citizenship" in a chapter heading also amounts to a technical promotion in that the step serves officially to elevate the artifact to constitutional rank. In terms of these kinds of "symbols", the previous Constitution had treated the business of citizenship in much more modest fashion.

The 1977 Constitution's substantive precepts regarding citizenship are set forth in Article 33, according to which:

> "A single union citizenship is established in the USSR. Every citizen of a union republic is a citizen of the USSR.

> The grounds and the procedure for acquiring and losing Soviet citizenship are defined by the Law on Citizenship of the USSR.
>
> Citizens of the USSR abroad enjoy the defense and protection of the Soviet state."

Since these postulates are reproduced virtually verbatim in the body of the 1978 statute on USSR citizenship, their concrete meaning will be fully analyzed in that latter context as the occasion arises. Here, a few general observations will suffice, aimed primarily at spotting elements of difference and similarity between the language of this passage and that of its earlier counterpart.

Although the first sentence of Article 33 closely resembles its opposite in Article 21 of the 1936 charter, the wording has been slightly altered and the change, one gathers, is intentional. The former version read: "A single union citizenship shall be established for the citizens of the USSR". For many years, the phrasing attracted no attention, but toward the end of the sixties and in the beginning of the seventies some Soviet scholars were at last moved to account for the apparent tautological quality of that clause which, taken literally, seemed to be saying that "for citizens of the USSR is established citizenship of the USSR". The explanation that was offered was to look at the expression "single" not as the equivalent of "common", but as evoking instead the concept of "united", i.e., in the sense of "unified" in lieu of "singular", which suggests a spiritual rather than a quantitative yardstick.[2]

This line of reasoning relies on the following points. Reference was made, for example, to the fact that the corresponding entry in the 1924 federal Constitution had directed that "for citizens of the union republics there shall be established a single citizenship". The 1936 revision which here skipped mention of the union republics and replaced "single citizenship" with "single union citizenship" consequently pursued a dual objective: 1) to ratify the existence of a separate phenomenon of "union citizenship"; and, 2) to recognize the principle of "union citizenship", but not draw any connection with the union republics. The shift presumably marked the achievement of a new synthesis in this area, with the institution of "union citizenship" incarnating the superior communion now attained by Soviet society. Or, to let a Soviet commentator articulate the thought in his own way, "the unity of socialist nations and peoples within the framework of the Soviet federation and autonomy thus also lies at the root of unity of Soviet citizenship".[3] Notwithstanding how intellectually fuzzy the argument might sound, the practical message is quite clear, namely, that the USSR had by then reached a stage of historical development where the level of internal cohesion required a country-wide citizenship to match the progress already registered by the community en route to final unification. Such a scenario summoned the vision of further expansion of federal powers in this sphere, meaning that the union republics might ultimately find themselves stripped of what little authority they were still officially endowed with in these affairs.

That prospect may, indeed, explain why these views did not go entirely unchallenged, since the criticism revolved essentially around how jurisdiction over these matters should be apportioned between the central and republican apparatus. Strong objection was voiced to the claim that "in the USSR there is a single union citizenship and that citizens of the USSR possess this citizenship" and the contrary thesis was propounded maintaining that there ought not to be citizens of the USSR in "pure" form, independent of the citizenship of a particular union republic (even though conceding that such a situation could in fact arise under current legislation). On that note, preference was expressed for the "more felicitous" formula featured in the 1924 Constitution on the grounds that speaking of "the principle of unity of Soviet citizenship does not reflect the presence of republican citizenship" and that the designation of that principle must reflect "the federative elements in Soviet citizenship".[4]

Enthusiasm for the cause of the union republics has since faded and, while the terminology of the applicable provision in the 1977 charter does manage to cure the semantic tautology that afflicted its predecessor, the union republics have not recovered their pre–1936 role in handling citizenship questions. The proposed roll–back of the federal government's precedence in this domain and simultaneous restoration of a fair equilibrium between the center and the republics in dealing with these items did not occur.

Formally, of course, the first paragraph of Article 33 in the latest federal Constitution strives to perpetuate the concept of the duality of citizenship in the USSR predicated on the concurrent existence of federal and republican citizenships. We will return to this topic later in discussing the relationship between citizenship status and the USSR's federal structure and look at the record in greater detail. Nevertheless, inasmuch as the new federal and republican charters also shed light on the subject, a preliminary survey of the relevant terrain as mapped in those documents may be warranted at this juncture.

No matter how much the Soviet regime would like to cultivate the image of a two–tier citizenship operating in the conditions of the USSR, the actual evidence leaves no doubt that federal citizenship figures far ahead in the pecking order. The substance of the next paragraph confirms that impression. The clause has no analogue in the 1936 version (or its subsequent republican replicas). Thus, the importance of the fact that the authors of the 1977 edition now chose to spell out that the grounds and procedure for acquiring and losing Soviet citizenship are defined by the Law on Citizenship of the USSR resides not in the tenor of the message (which is predictable), but in the underlying decision to grant express constitutional imprimatur to said statute. The move lends an aura of prominence to the legislation concerning USSR citizenship that further eclipses whatever meaning still attaches to any corresponding republican regulations and, coincidentally, the phenomenon of republican citizenship itself.

The tone of the republican constitutions strikes the same key.[5] For example, the 1978 Fundamental Law of the RSFSR (just as its 1937 antecedent) echoes the proposition that every citizen of the RSFSR is a citizen of the USSR and, revealingly, adds the federal Constitution's latest pronouncement that the grounds and procedure for acquiring and losing Soviet citizenship shall be defined by the Law on Citizenship of the USSR. Observe that the supreme law of the USSR's principal republic relies on the federal statute pertaining to citizenship questions, but never ventures to sanction the enactment of similar legislation on the local level to outline the mechanics of entry into RSFSR citizenship, even while publicizing such an identity. The RSFSR charter likewise indicates (thereby continuing a well–established tradition) that the citizens of the associated union republics enjoy on the territory of the RSFSR equal rights with citizens of the RSFSR. What this signifies is that a citizen of a sister–republic is not an alien or foreigner under the provisions of RSFSR law and his or her possession of another republican citizenship makes no difference in terms of capacity to exercise the ensemble of political, social, and economic rights vested in RSFSR citizens by dint of either federal or republican legislation. Hence, with rare and marginal exceptions (arising out of special circumstances of sojourn abroad), the individual's life is in no material sense affected by the republican citizenship he/she happens to hold.

In short, one is fairly safe in concluding that, as in the recent past, the role of the republics in this area will be limited to the performance of certain ancillary administrative chores involving the ad hoc implementation of germane federal directives. The arrangement has the advantage of fulfilling the regime's cosmetic exigencies for improving the looks of the Soviet federal model, while leaving real power to run this department in the hands of the central government.

The last paragraph of Article 33 (RSFSR, Article 31) which commits the competent authorities to the protection of USSR (RSFSR) citizens abroad enunciates a stock rule, but, once again, elevates it to the grade of a constitutional norm. Since the statement recurs in the 1978 citizenship act, its relevance to the technical aspects of citizenship will be analyzed in that context.

The second article to mention the subject of citizenship (USSR 59; RSFSR 57) does so in proclaiming the duty of every USSR (RSFSR) citizen to "bear with dignity the high calling of citizen of the USSR" (Soviet citizen). At first blush, the pitch sounds as a familiar sample of rhetorical bombast. However, to the extent that the formula suggests that a Soviet citizen may be called upon to meet certain standards of "moral excellence" in order to "deserve" full membership in Soviet society, failure to "pass the test" is apt to have adverse repercussions and, as the record shows, in fact is often cited as the official rationale for decreeing the "misfit's" exclusion from the community. The mere incident of the clause being so vaguely worded that it cannot possibly afford intelligent guidance on the manner of its prospective interpretation and enforcement in all likelihood only enhances the scheme's attractiveness in the eyes of the local officialdom. At any rate, Soviet legal spokesmen do not seem in the least troubled by such details and frankly invoke the language of Article 59 to justify the position that "acts discrediting the high calling of Soviet citizen, incompatible with it, can serve as reason for adopting a decision to deprive a person of Soviet citizenship".[6]

Several changes may also be noted on the organizational front. For instance, Article 14 of the 1936 federal Constitution which listed the items that fell within the jurisdiction of the USSR, as represented by its highest organs of state power and organs of state administration, numbered among them the adoption of "legislation on union citizenship". The phrase is missing from the corresponding rubric in the 1977 USSR Constitution (Article 73), perhaps because the authors of the document felt that it would be redundant given the earlier reference to the Law on Citizenship of the USSR in Article 33 (which, as previously indicated, is not encountered in the 1936 federal charter). Thus, they may just have assumed that such an express mandate for the enactment of a national citizenship statute obviously confirmed the power of the central agencies to engage here in appropriate legislative activity and so might have seen no need to feature an analogous formula elsewhere. A somewhat similar situation can be observed in the case of the new RSFSR Fundamental Law, where the general sanction to "grant rights of citizenship of the RSFSR" that figure in Article 19 of the 1937 RSFSR Constitution is now omitted from the contents of matching Article 72 in the 1978 version. The stylistic consideration that might explain the procedure at the federal level does not, however, apply in this instance, for Article 31 of the RSFSR charter (otherwise patterned on Article 33 of the federal Constitution) contains no primary provision recognizing the right of the competent republican institutions to issue legislation concerning RSFSR citizenship and, hence, the problem of repetition would not arise. Blind imitation of the federal script without taking these differences into account is conceivably responsible for this drafting slip in the RSFSR text. Or, the move may have been prompted by the realization that talk of authority to "grant rights of citizenship of the RSFSR" was too grand for the kind of administrative routine in these affairs that the republican apparatus was destined to handle in the future and the clause was then dropped to avoid creating a false impression.

On the other hand, neither the old USSR Constitution nor its RSFSR counterpart said anything about which specific state organ was going to be in charge of the practical traffic related to Soviet citizenship (the enactment of a formal Citizenship Law was, of course, always the sole prerogative of the Supreme Soviet, according to the letter of the Constitution). That secondary piece of business had been taken care of by statutory means, and the union and republican Presidia had been picked for the job. Nevertheless, in recent years scholarly attention had been drawn to the constitutional lapse, resulting in recommendations that the forthcoming charters rectify the omission.[7] The 1977 federal Constitution duly corrects the technical oversight by including a clause to the effect that, inter alia, the Presidium of the USSR Supreme Soviet "admits persons to citizenship and decides questions of the renunciation and deprivation of citizenship of the USSR ..." (Article 121[10]). Reflecting the republics' more restricted agenda in this sphere (they can only admit individuals to their citizenship and play no role in actions ensuing in exit from Soviet citizenship), the 1978 RSFSR charter follows suit (Article 115[12]) by conferring on the Presidium of the RSFSR Supreme Soviet the power to admit persons into the citizenship of the RSFSR. Thus, the designated modus operandi has won constitutional approval (thereby lifting the status and prestige of the whole enterprise) and, by the same token, the move to have the Fundamental Law identify by name the competent offices and supply a few functional details has managed to make the entire affair sound quite professional.

To sum it up, the current generation of Soviet constitutions puts more symbolic accent on the theme of Soviet citizenship than had the previous one and purveys some practical tips formerly buried in subordinate legislation, but introduces no substantive innovations in this domain.

2. Historical Background

The need for a fresh set of regulations on Soviet citizenship had long been recognized in Soviet circles. The latter openly admit today that the 1938 law

> "did not encompass anymore many relations pertaining to questions of citizenship which now arose in practice. To supplement it there were issued various normative acts, including instructions by ministries and departments regulating certain important relations which must be regulated by statute. In elaborating the new Law on Citizenship of the USSR the objective was to encompass all questions of citizenship that required legislative regulation".[8]

Work on such legislation had been initiated some years ago, but then hung fire pending the adoption of the oft–promised (and much delayed) Constitution. The machinery was set in motion back on June 25, 1973, when, at a session of the Presidium of the USSR Supreme Soviet, I.G. Kebin, chairman of the Commission on Legislative Proposals of the Soviet of Nationalities, acting in the name of the commissions on legislative proposals of both chambers, submitted a recommendation for the drafting of a new law on the citizenship of the USSR. One of the reasons he gave in this connection was that "the current law was adopted in 1938 and now did not regulate all the questions that arose in practice". The Presidium concurred in the suggestion and charged the commissions to start work on drafting the projected statute and attract representatives of the interested ministries and departments to take part in the job.[9] On July 13, 1973, a joint session of assorted standing commissions of both houses of the legislature heard a progress report by I.G. Kebin and approved the membership of a delegates' preparatory commission for drafting a law on the citizenship of the USSR.[10] Next, on October 24, 1975, a joint session of the commissions on legislative proposals of the two houses examined the question of the draft law on the citizenship of the USSR following a report on the subject by deputy V.I. Prokhorov.[11] At that point, the project was apparently put aside, to await the completion of the editing of the new Constitution for purposes of textual synchronization and to schedule its debut as part of the package of legislative reforms marking the occasion of the entry into force of the country's latest charter.

The promulgation of the present Fundamental Law again focused attention on the business of bringing order to the mass of accumulated legislation which cluttered the Soviet scene and rendered difficult the task of all concerned in figuring out the current status juris, which rules still applied and even where the pertinent information could be located. Or, in the words of a Soviet spokesman, the event accelerated the process "of further strengthening of the legal bases of state and social life of the country, of active improvement of our legislation".[12] Accordingly, a detailed plan for squaring the salient features of the nation's corpus of laws with the postulates of the most recent charter was enacted on December 12, 1977,[13] which, inter alia, ticked off a list of legislative measures slated for early completion. The roster included a statute on USSR citizenship, assigned for October 1978: pursuant to the Resolution of the Presidium of the USSR Supreme Soviet of June 25, 1973, the matter of drafting the text was entrusted to the commissions on legislative proposals of the two chambers of the USSR Supreme Soviet, in consultation with the USSR Ministry of Justice, the USSR Ministry of Internal Affairs, the USSR Ministry of Foreign Affairs, the Committee of State Security attached to the USSR Council of Ministers, the USSR Supreme Court, and the USSR Procuracy. Reportedly, representatives of civic organizations, specialists and scholars also took part in this activity, and the preliminary version was discussed in the Presidia of the republican Supreme Soviets.[14] Indeed, Soviet commentators choose to emphasize the magnitude of these research operations and the fact that the authors of the bill took into account the observations and recommendations received from the republican Presidia, deputies of the USSR Supreme Soviet and central organs of social organizations.[15] Despite the strictly intramural nature of the "dialogue", the scope they attribute to the affair lets them claim that "the preparation of the draft law was effectuated on a wide democratic basis".[16]

On the eve of the date fixed for the convocation of the session of the USSR Supreme Soviet on whose agenda the topic of the planned citizenship law was featured, the federal Presidium issued a resolution confirming that the item would be sponsored by the Presidium itself.[17] Finally, on December 1, 1978, the bill was submitted to a joint session of the legislature. V.V. Kuznetsov, first deputy chairman of the Presidium of the USSR Supreme Soviet, acted as the official rapporteur.[18] Delegates V.I. Prokhorov, V.I. Terebilov, V.S. Paputin, D.Iu. Banionis, and A.V. Gitalov mounted the rostrum to express their enthusiastic support for the proposed law,[19] whereupon the congregation voted unanimously in favor of the motion[20] and simultaneously approved a resolution defining the procedure for the law's entry into force.[21]

The lack of appropriate legislation dealing with the whole range of issues related to Soviet citizenship policy has, of course, been felt for many years. The previous statute, dating from 1938, was both badly inadequate and largely obsolete;[22] not only did the measure fail to address several important aspects of the problem, but in other cases where it did stipulate the relevant rule, subsequent administrative practice sometimes took a different tack, often without benefit of a corresponding adjustment in the established norms. Thus, a major survey of the state of Soviet legislation conducted in the sixties with a view to laying the groundwork for its eventual systematization, concluded that the future Law on Citizenship would, after the necessary revision, have to incorporate all the norms contained in various acts referring to citizenship questions. Positive mention was made of the fact that in "the countries of people's democracy there have been adopted laws on citizenship which regulated in detail all the relations connected with that institution". Recommended for inclusion in the local version were: 1) norms regulating the procedure of acquisition of USSR citizenship, restoration of and exit from Soviet citizenship; 2) norms defining the procedure for evaluating and accepting applications for admission to, exit from and deprivation of Soviet citizenship; and, 3) norms defining the civil rights of political emigres, etc.[23]

Nearly every Soviet scholar who looked at the situation here had his own slate of indispensable additions. One, for example, singled out such items as the conditions and procedure for restoration of Soviet citizenship, indications concerning the citizenship of Soviet children adopted by foreigners, and instructions regarding recognition of Soviet citizenship "by virtue of birth".[24] Occasionally, even more elaborate lists were drawn up, which tried to anticipate all likely contingencies.[25] In each case, though, the obvious message was that the 1938 statute was much overdue for a complete overhaul.

Still, technical lapses were only part of the total picture. The social environment itself had changed significantly in the intervening period and these developments, in turn, produced novel phenomena which called for proper legal solution. Soviet sources claim, for instance, that

> "the growth of economic, political and cultural ties between the USSR and other states leads to the increase of the number of foreign citizens located on its territory. For the last two years alone, around 8 million foreign tourists visited our country. More than 55 thousand students from 139 countries are studying in the USSR. A considerable number of foreign scientists visit us to take part in assorted congresses, conferences, symposia, to engage in joint scientific research. On the basis of inter–state agreements on scientific–technical cooperation that have been signed, foreign specialists work in the Soviet Union. Citizens of Bulgaria, Hungary, the GDR, Poland, Romania and Czechoslovakia have worked on the construction of a series of objectives; foreign specialists are assembling the equipment at the Kama automobile plant ... Annually, approximately 150 foreign artistic ensembles and artistic groups come here, over 200 soloists, dozens of exhibitions are staged."[26]

The record further shows, according to them, that

> "foreign tourism and travel, trips for rest and medical treatment to neighboring countries have become a common occurrence. Such dynamism of international intercourse has meant the expansion of contacts between the Soviet people and the peoples of other countries, primarily those of the socialist commonwealth. During a ten–year span, 13 million of our people visited the socialist states. Just in 1977, 2.7 million Soviet citizens went abroad on service and personal matters. Millions of foreigners visit the Soviet Union each year. Marriages between citizens of different states are no longer rare."[27]

Not all of these activities, of course, automatically affect the citizenship status of the individuals concerned. Nevertheless, experiences of this kind often plunge people into situations which can lead to a modification of their legal position. Greater freedom of movement, for example, can entail a decision to establish residence abroad, a step which, under the terms of Soviet law past and present, does not per se have any effect on a Soviet citizen's legal affiliation with the USSR. On the other hand, once a Soviet citizen succeeds in emigrating, he or she now has an opportunity to get naturalized in the new homeland and the conversion will undoubtedly have certain legal consequences of which the state whose nationality the subject previously possessed must henceforth also be cognizant. Aside from the problems raised by the current exodus of members of particular ethnic groups from the USSR which is the result of special policy considerations (and will be examined in a later context), people have been trickling out of the Soviet Union on an individual basis over the years who then set up domicile elsewhere and, in due course, seek to acquire local citizenship.

Estimates of the size of the traffic vary, but probably several thousand souls have left the USSR by this route in recent decades, headed in every direction. Here is a random sample. Between 1960 and 1971, the Ukrainian and Russian population in Czechoslovakia registered a net increment of 2,545, thanks to a "favorable migration balance".[28] Or, take the following figures on applicants processed for emigration from the USSR to the United States: 1972 — 494; 1973 — 758 (400 during the first 8 months of 1973, mostly Jews and Armenians); 1974 — 1,029; 1975 — 1,162; 1976 — 2,574; 1977 — 2,047. The drop recorded in 1977, after the steady upswing noted in the preceding years, was attributed to a decline in requests for entry visas from Armenians who were responsible for 69% of the petitions filed in 1976. The statistics on Soviet citizens documented for emigration to the United States in 1978 indicated 1,709, or 15% less than in 1977, and on this occasion the decrease was reportedly caused by a reduction in the number of passports issued by Soviet authorities to Armenians: only 1,123 Armenians were allowed to emigrate to the United States in 1978, compared with 1,370 in 1977. Meanwhile, the Jewish share of the efflux remained relatively stable at about 25% of the total, although the headcount fell from 493 in 1977 to 439 in 1978. In 1979, however, the trend was again reversed. First, in the six-month period ending September 30, 1979, the U.S. Embassy in Moscow documented a total of 1,233 Soviet citizens for emigration to the United States, against a total of 1,089 during the previous six-month span: of the former, 76 received visas to join family in the U.S., and 1,157 qualified as refugees (Armenians constituted 90% of that category). Then, from October 1, 1979, through March 31, 1980, the U.S. Embassy in Moscow issued 85 immigrant visas to Soviet citizens for the purpose of joining their families in the United States and another 3,713 Soviets were documented for immigration to the U.S. as refugees: a total of 3,798 3,581 of them Armenians) compared with 1,233 for the preceding six-month period. Thus, "the number of Soviet citizens processed by the U.S. Embassy in Moscow for immigration was higher in 1979 than for any previous year", due to a marked increase in Armenian emigration from the USSR to the U.S.[29]

In the aftermath of marriage to a foreign citizen, a similar pattern tends to emerge. When B. Shumilin, USSR Deputy Minister of Internal Affairs, granted an interview (published in 1976) to a Novosti correspondent concerning the mechanics of emigration from the USSR, he took pains to explain that marriages with foreigners routinely serve as a motive for emigration. By his computation, "5,500 Soviet citizens, i.e., all those who wished to do so, left with their families for 110 different countries in the past few years" on those grounds. "Among them were 544 men. About 2,000 Soviet citizens, married to foreigners, have so far not expressed any wish to emigrate, although they have every opportunity to do so". By the middle of 1980, the figures had risen dramatically. A fresh interview with K. Zotov, the head of OVIR, elicited the information that "during the last few years more than 15,000 Soviet citizens married foreigners and 10,500 of them left the USSR to reside in more than 100 countries".[30]

The fact itself that marriages between Soviet citizens and foreigners today occur quite frequently is not open to dispute. The enlarged scope of contacts with all kinds of visitors from abroad and the presence of a growing foreign community in the USSR whose members are there on a variety of assignments act as a natural spur to "mixed" marriages. The sizable contingent of Hungarian men studying in the USSR on scholarships offers a case in point in that in 1972 alone 273 of the lot married Soviet citizens.[31] Similarly, a survey of the situation in Kiev indicates that, whereas "international" marriages once happened very seldom, 31 such incidents were recorded in 1962, 33 in 1963, 37 in 1964, 42 in 1965, 57 in 1966, 60 in 1967, 76 in 1968, 78 in 1969, and 82 in 1970, while the number of children born in these households reached 80–100 per annum.[32] Generally, logistics favor the citizens of fellow socialist states in this respect, but matrimony with citizens of capitalist countries also no longer ranks as an exceptional event. Thus, according to U.S. sources, 19 binational (Soviet–American) marriages were registered between April and September 1979.[33]

Much less credible, however, is our official's assertion that marriage with a foreigner enables the Soviet spouse to leave the USSR virtually at will, that all requests for an exit permit under these circumstances have been duly honored by the Soviet authorities, and that only those partners in "mixed" marriages who desire to live in the USSR have stayed. Ample evidence attests to the contrary, in the sense of the competent agencies unilaterally determining in these instances as well who will be allowed to get out of the country and when. On several occasions, the regime has arbitrarily refused to sanction the departure of Soviet husbands or wives (and children) seeking to be reunited with the foreign spouse (and parent) waiting abroad to be joined by the rest of the family. Some of these episodes have caused quite a bit of diplomatic furor, the separations have dragged on for years, and the end is yet nowhere in sight. At the close of 1979, for example, the U.S. State Department let it be known that, despite all its efforts, many longstanding cases still remained unresolved, including one which had been active since 1956 involving American citizen Anatoly Michelson cut off from his wife and daughter in the USSR. As of May 31, 1980, the same source revealed that 102 divided family cases numbering 306 individuals and involving spouses and their minor children were long pending; with reference just to the October 1 — March 31 period, it was estimated that 10 exit or entry visas had been delayed more than six months for spouses and fiancés and that at least six Soviet spouses of American citizens had meantime received formal refusals of exit visa applications.[34]

Hence, without denying that emigration does take place under these conditions, the claim that marriage to a foreigner is tantamount to freedom to quit the USSR must be treated with a hefty pinch of scepticism in light of empirical data concerning the Soviet government's performance in these matters. Calls by Soviet authors for certain modifications in Soviet legislation to reflect the socialist community's initiatives at the Helsinki Conference aimed at fostering contacts between citizens of the attending countries and especially the proposals submitted by Poland and Bulgaria "to consider in a spirit of good faith and humaneness on acceptable terms the questions of reunion of families and conclusion of marriages between citizens of the participating states"[35] must be greeted with equal caution as long as administrative practice fails to match the high–flown rhetoric.[36]

Two last items round out the picture, the first related to ideology, the second to foreign policy. Since the 1977 Constitution marked the completion of the building of a "developed socialist society" in the USSR, legislation befitting the latest stage in the country's upward progression seemed in order and, in fact, Soviet commentators now refer to the 1978 citizenship statute as "already the Law on Citizenship of a state of developed socialism".[37] Next, when the 1938 statute was enacted, reliance on international law procedures in connection with citizenship problems was viewed as an extraordinary remedy, sparingly used on an ad hoc basis. The 1938 law thus eschewed any reference to the applicable international legal norms, even in the guise of the Soviet Union's own treaty repertory that featured citizenship themes. Such neglect does not square with the public image the Soviet regime is trying to project today as a fervent champion of international law and steps have been taken to correct the defective style of the 1938 law by including in the 1978 text appropriate allusions to the role here of international legal artifacts. Again, Soviet spokesmen seek to capitalize on the editorial change by spreading the word that "all the provisions of this Act fully correspond to the obligations assumed by the USSR under relevant international treaties, agreements, and conventions".[38] Not surprisingly, the new law is also said to "be directed ... at establishing good–neighborly relations with other peoples and nations".[39]

For all those reasons (technical and historical), a bid at extensively recasting the format of the old law sounded like a foregone conclusion and the physical difference between the 1938 and 1978 version is indeed startling. The 1938 statute boiled down to a mere 8 articles; by comparison its successor consists of 29 articles. Despite a certain element of continuity, the 1978 piece of legislation obviously contains a great deal of additional material. Or, to quote the bill's official sponsor on that score, the latest statute is "substantially richer in terms of its contents" than the earlier law in that:

> "The provisions of the legislation currently in force that had proved their vitality are fully preserved, the practice which evolved and the commonly accepted norms of international law have been taken into account. By the same token, the Law fills the gaps which exist in this branch of legislation."[40]

Finally, some aspects of the procedural side of the story warrant a quick glance. First, in the course of discussion of the 1938 bill on the floor of the legislature, two amendments were suggested. One was rejected. The other, aimed at eliminating the original version of an end clause, Article 9, officially repealing all anterior laws that, with the approval of the current act, lost force, was accepted. The extra provision was dropped and, instead, it was simply agreed that "the question of previous laws be entrusted to the Presidium of the USSR Supreme Soviet for solution in accordance with set procedure".[41] By contrast, the passage of the 1978 draft law was a completely tame affair, with several speeches lauding the virtues of the proposed statute, no motions for revision, and a unanimous vote in favor of the measure. Even the kind of limited "debate" which was staged on the previous occasion was omitted this time and the routine evinced all the signs of a rubberstamp operation. A plausible explanation, of course, for the starkly mechanical handling of the whole business at this point is that the initial text of the 1978 citizenship act had been the object of extensive study by interested institutions and individuals before being put on the legislative calendar and, hence, already reflected a consensus when it was submitted for formal endorsement. The 1938 statute had not so much as the benefit of an analogous "mini–referendum" and in its case live proof of parliamentary "review" was not amiss.

Second, on June 15, 1979, the Presidium of the USSR Supreme Soviet issued a special edict spelling out the mechanics of entry into force of the new citizenship law.[42] The decree established detailed technical guidelines for the manner of implementation of various clauses of the parent statute, particularly in terms of their retroactive effect, prescribed cut–off dates, the competent administrative authorities, etc. By comparison, the 1938 law which, given its meager substance, would have greatly profited from supplementary elaboration, never received such treatment and the job of adding flesh to its bare bones was left to be managed by the expedient device of ad hoc practice. The change in style is significant in that it denotes a switch to a markedly more legalistic approach to the task of both composing the 1978 citizenship statute and defining the method of its subsequent application, whereas the rudimentary quality of the 1938 law bespoke an absence of concern for legal niceties and a preference for letting executive and administrative policy take care of the many difficulties that were bound to arise once the attempt was made to use these general propositions to solve concrete problems.

Third, the decision to delete, as just mentioned, the last clause from the original edition of the 1938 law that would have summarily rescinded all earlier legislation dealing with citizenship themes made good sense, for it is hard to believe that the regime ever could have seriously meant the 1938 statute as a complete restatement of the law on the subject. At best, that terse document could only convey the highlights of official thinking on the matter, even if Soviet authors did then occasionally indulge in the claim that, despite its brevity, the 1938 act disposed of all the principal issues relating to Soviet citizenship.[23] Thus, where the established precedent ran counter to the new law, the latter presumably prevailed, in line with the well–known maxim lex posterior derogat priori. On the other hand, in those numerous instances where the latest enactment offered no answer to a particular legal question, the information had to be sought in the prescriptions of the last relevant piece of legislation to have been adopted previous to the promulgation of the 1938 law. In short, the initial scheme calling for the blanket annulment of the entire accumulation of directives extant in this sphere was rejected outright — and understandably so. In lieu thereof, the Presidium was instructed to ascertain which of the older laws had in fact been superseded in whole or in part by the new statute and formally remove the offending regulations from the books.

The Presidium soon complied and in its decree of June 2, 1939,[44] identified past laws which were forthwith pronounced to have expired due to the publication of the most recent set of rules. Included in the list were: 1) the Regulation on the citizenship of the USSR of April 22, 1931; 2) the Resolution of November 13, 1925, depriving of Soviet citizenship former prisoners of war and interned servicemen of the tsarist and Red armies and participants in counter–revolutionary uprisings, who had been granted amnesty and had failed to register by the designated deadline; 3) the Resolution of May 27, 1933, "Concerning former Russian subjects who had gone abroad prior to October 25, 1917, and had accepted a foreign citizenship or have applied for a foreign citizenship"; 4) the Resolution of November 1, 1930, "concerning the transfer to district organs of rights in determining citizenship ...";

and, 5) the Resolution of July 7, 1932, "On the procedure for issuing papers certifying possession of foreign citizenship". In closing, the edict recommended to the Presidia of the union republics that they set aside all republican legislation dealing with citizenship matters.

The five items which now were said to have lapsed obviously did not represent the entire contents of the cupboard and what remained on the shelves was clearly intended to rctain its normative function. Soviet sources have noted, for instance, that the 1938 statute featured no provisions governing the legal status of Soviet citizens located abroad. As a result, the responsible agencies continued to rely here on the resolution of the Central Executive Committee and Council of People's Commissars "Regarding the procedure of application by USSR consuls of the law of the union republics on marriage, divorce and acts of civil registry in respect to USSR citizens located abroad" (1928), as well as the corresponding chapters of the "Consular charter of the USSR" (1926). The latter, in particular, specified the duties of consular personnel to make sure that USSR citizens abroad could fully enjoy all the rights granted them by the laws of the host country, by international treaties and agreements to which the USSR was a party, and by international custom. Whenever any violation of such rights occurred, the local consul was required to take steps to obtain proper redress.[45]

On balance, then, the conclusion is inescapable that much of the earlier law was expected to and did stay in effect, except where its substance had been overruled, either tacitly or expressis verbis, by the terms of subsequent statutory enactments (incidentally, this basic concept, as will be shown later, was not consistently adhered to in practice either). The foregoing observation holds true even for the Regulation on the citizenship of the USSR of 1931, despite its official abrogation. The record indicates that only those of its elements which were definitely supplanted by the provisions of the act of 1938 and later directives henceforward were not deemed valid. As for the other clauses of the 1931 law, they still served to fill many of the interstices left, either deliberately or by oversight, in the text of the successor–statute in the guise of long–recognized general principles that, presumably, just found formal confirmation in that piece of legislation, but did not really amount to a unique and organic fixture of the latter and consequently survived intact its eventual repeal.

In the case of the 1978 statute, the approach to this problem has certainly been more cautious: no public talk was heard of cancelling at a single stroke the backlog of rules pertaining to the subject of citizenship and the text of the new law contains no suggestion that such a course was ever contemplated. On the contrary, one senses a commitment to a policy of careful selectivity on that score. Thus, the Resolution of December 1, 1978, which announced the schedule for putting into effect the latest citizenship law, let it be known that the 1938 act would become null once the 1978 law entered into force, i.e., on July 1, 1979.[46] Then, on June 15, 1979, the Presidium of the USSR Supreme Soviet approved a decree listing the federal legislative acts which had lost validity in connection with the adoption of the 1978 citizenship statute.[47] The roster comprised 24 items, namely: the decree of September 7, 1940, on the acquisition of Soviet citizenship by citizens of the Lithuanian, Latvian and Estonian SSRs; the decree of March 8, 1941, on the restoration of Soviet citizenship to the residents of Bessarabia and the acquisition of Soviet citizenship by the residents of Northern Bukovina; the decree of July 14, 1944, extending the decree of June 22, 1944, on the right of transfer to Polish citizenship of servicemen in the Polish army in the USSR and persons aiding it in the struggle for the liberation of Poland, as well as members of their families, to the residents of the areas ceded by the Soviet Union to the Lithuanian SSR; the 14 decrees dating from the period 1945–1947 which sanctioned reinstatement in Soviet citizenship of nationals of the former Russian empire and persons who had lost Soviet citizenship residing on the territory of Manchuria, in the province of Sinkiang and the cities of Shanghai and Tientsin, in France, Yugoslavia, Bulgaria, Japan, Czechoslovakia and Belgium (including decrees prolonging the duration of the original edicts); the decree of October 19, 1946, on the procedure of acquisition of Soviet citizenship by persons of Armenian nationality returning from abroad to their homeland in Soviet Armenia; the decree of October 31, 1946, on exit from Soviet citizenship by persons of Czech and Slovak nationality resettling from the USSR to Czechoslovakia and acquisition of Soviet citizenship by persons of Russian, Ukrainian and Byelorussian nationality resettling from Czechoslovakia to the USSR; the decree of December 16, 1947, on the procedure of acquisition of Soviet citizenship by persons of Lithuanian nationality, native residents of the city of Klaipeda and the Klaipeda, Śilute and Pagegiai districts of the Lithuanian SSR, and the two decrees of July 20, 1948, and July 2, 1949, extending the deadline for such individuals located abroad to register as Soviet citizens; and, the decree of March 30, 1948, on the procedure of acquisition of Soviet citizenship by citizens of the Lithuanian, Latvian and Estonian republics and natives of Bessarabia residing in Latin American countries.

Note that each of these measures qualified as a lex specialis designed to take care of a specific situation and that, with the exception of the 1946 decree governing Armenian "repatriates", all of them no longer applied pursuant to their own terms (i.e., they had lapsed as prescribed, but had never been formally pronounced void because that step had rightly been considered superfluous and was probably taken now just for the sake of officially emptying the files). No reference was made in this context to the prospect that any general legislation enacted earlier which also dealt with citizenship matters would automatically be terminated in view of the adoption of the latest rules and, in fact, the federal Presidium's companion decree of June 15, 1979, on the mechanics of entry into force of the 1978 Law on Citizenship of the USSR,[48] expressly confirmed that until the legislation of the USSR and the union republics was brought into line with the new statute, the existing legislative acts of the USSR and union republics remained in force insofar as they did not run counter to said statute. The situation here was thus left up in the air since neither edict provided further information on how the job of ironing out potential divergences was going to be performed or, indeed, when. Even when a manifest discrepancy occurred, as, for example, between the wording of paragraph 2 of Article 12 of the current citizenship law and paragraph 2 of Article 30 of the Bases of legislation of the USSR and union republics on marriage and the family of 1968, the phenomenon prompted no immediate move to correct the aberration: only on October 9, 1979, did a decree of the Presidium of the USSR Supreme Soviet extensively recast, inter alia, Chapter 5 of the federal guidelines on marriage and the family, dropping former Article 30 from the text and henceforth leaving Article 12 of the citizenship statute in sole possession of the field.[49] The reason for this modus operandi may lie in a desire on the part of the people in charge of sorting out the data to proceed in an organized and structured manner instead of responding to each inconsistency they discover in random, piecemeal fashion. To the extent that the business of synchronization of legislative norms in this sector is but one item on the grand agenda of systematization of the entire corpus of Soviet law on which work is presently being pursued in the USSR, this deliberate and "conservative" approach fits well the prevailing style on the local jurisprudential scene.

NOTES

1. V.A. Kuchinskii, *Osnovnye prava i obiazannosti grazhdan Belorusskoi SSR*, Minsk 1978, p.74.
2. V.S. Shevtsov, *Grazhdanstvo v sovetskom soiuznom gosudarstve*, Moscow 1969, p.69; *idem*, *Citizenship of the USSR (A Legal Study)*, Moscow 1979, pp.73–74.
3. V.S. Shevtsov, *Grazhdanstvo* ..., p.64.
4. N.V. Vitruk, in *Pravovedenie*, 1971, No.6, p.106.
5. For an English–language translation of the text of the 1978 RSFSR Constitution and a concordance with the 1978 Constitutions of the other union republics, see W.B. Simons, in F.J.M. Feldbrugge, ed., *The Constitutions of the USSR and the Union Republics: Analysis, Texts, Reports*, Alphen aan den Rijn & Germantown, Maryland 1979, pp.263–342. For an analysis of the general principles of the 1977 USSR Constitution, see G. Ginsburgs & S. Pomorski, "A Profile of the Soviet Constitution of 1977", *ibid.*, pp.3–67.
6. E.g., V.S. Shevtsov, *Sovetskoe gosudarstvo i lichnost'*, Moscow 1978, p.23.
7. For instance, V.S. Shevtsov, *Sovetskoe grazhdanstvo*, Moscow 1965, p.51, fn.1. *Idem*, *Grazhdanstvo* ..., p.137, fn.1.
8. G.I. Tunkin, "Zakon o grazhdanstve SSSR", *Sovetskoe gosudarstvo i pravo*, 1979, No.7, pp.22 (hereafter abbr. as *SGiP*).
9. *Vedomosti Verkhovnogo Soveta SSSR*, 1973, No.26, p.396 (hereafter abbr. as *VVS SSSR*).
10. *VVS SSSR*, 1973, No.29, p.449.
11. *VVS SSSR*, 1975, No.44, p.738.
12. Speech by V.V. Kuznetsov, *Pravda*, December 2, 1978 (hereafter abbr. as *Pr.*); *Izvestiia*, December 2, 1978 (hereafter abbr. as *Izv.*).
13. *VVS SSSR*, 1977, No.51, Art.764. Also *VVS SSSR*, 1978, No.49, Art.794.
14. V.V. Kuznetsov, *loc. cit.* (note 12 above).
15. N. Salishcheva, E. Koveshnikov, "Novyi zakon o grazhdanstve SSSR", *Sotsialisticheskaia zakonnost'*, 1979, No.3, p.9 (hereafter abbr. as *SZ*).
16. G.I. Tunkin, *op. cit.*, p.22.
17. *VVS SSSR*, 1978, No.19, Art.792.
18. See note 12 above.
19. *Izv.*, December 3, 1978.
20. For the text of the 1978 Law on Citizenship of the USSR, see *Pr.*, *Izv.*, December 2, 1978; *VVS SSSR*, 1978, No.49, Art.816. For the text in English, see *International Affairs*, 1979, No.1, pp.141–144, and W.B. Simons, trans., in *Review of Socialist Law*, 1979, No.4, pp.463–467.
21. *Pr.*, *Izv.*, December 2, 1978; *VVS SSSR*, 1978 No.48, Art.817. English text in *International Affairs*, 1979, No.1, p.145.
22. V.S. Shevtsov, *Grazhdanstvo* ..., p.164; R. Kulik, "Pravovye nachala sovetskogo grazhdanstva", *Sovety narodnykh deputatov*, 1979, No.2, p.33.
23. V.A. Pertsik, in S.N. Bratus', I.S. Samoshchenko, eds., *Teoreticheskie voprosy sistematizatsii sovetskogo zakonodatel'stva*, Moscow 1962, p.278.
24. V.S. Shevtsov, *Grazhdanstvo* ..., p.103. *Idem*, *Citizenship* ..., p.87.
25. E.g., B.V. Shchetinin, *Problemy teorii sovetskogo gosudarstvennogo prava*, Moscow 1974, p.184.
26. A. Arbuzkin, "Pravovoe polozhenie inostrantsev v SSSR", *Chelovek i zakon*, 1979, No.6, pp.12–13.
27. R. Kulik, *op. cit.*, p.33.
28. Radio Free Europe *Research*, Czechoslovakia/4, January 24, 1973, p.7.

29. *Khronika zashchity prav v SSSR*, 1973, vyp.4, p.33 (hereafter abbr. as *Khronika*); *ibid.*, 1977, vyp.28, p.37; U.S. Department of State, Bureau of Public Affairs, "Implementation of the Helsinki Accord, 6th Semiannual Report, December 1, 1978–May 31, 1979", *Special Report No.54* (July 1979), p.14; *ibid.*, 7th Semiannual Report, June 1–November 30, 1979, *Special Report No.62* (January 1980), p.13; *ibid.*, 8th Semiannual Report, December 1, 1979–May 31, 1980, *Special Report No.73*, p.14.
30. *Soviet News*, January 27, 1976, No.5819, p.35, and June 17, 1980, No.6024, p.183.
31. Radio Free Europe *Research*, Hungary/3, January 15, 1974, p.2.
32. G.K. Matveev, "Voprosy sovetskogo kollizionnogo semeinogo prava", *Pravovedenie*, 1972, No.2, p.99, fn.2.
33. *Special Report No.62* (note 29 above), p.15.
34. *Ibid.*, p.13, and *Special Report No.73* (note 29 above), pp.14, 16.

Of course, the phenomenon is by no means new and, in fact, predates the Second World War. See, for instance, M.M. Whiteman, *Digest of International Law*, Department of State Publication 8290, Washington, D.C. September 1967, Vol.8, p.657. For early post-war diplomatic contacts between the United States and the USSR concerning, inter alia, more than 250 "wives of American citizens who have been denied exit visas from the Soviet Union", although they had "for many months, and in several cases years, ... sought permission to leave the Soviet Union in order to join their husbands in the United States", see *ibid.*, pp.637–639. At one point, the U.S. State Department officially informed the Soviet embassy in Washington that "the continued refusal of the Soviet authorities to permit the departure of these wives of American citizens is incomprehensible to the Government and the people of the United States" (p.638).

The Chilean delegation to the 3rd session of the UN General Assembly (1948) protested against the refusal of the USSR to permit the Soviet wives of foreigners to join their husbands abroad (including the wife of the son of the Chilean ambassador in Moscow). Other states joined the chorus of denunciations and in 1949 the General Assembly adopted a resolution calling on the USSR to "withdraw the measures of such a nature which have been adopted". In the course of the debates, the U.S. government revealed that from the time of recognition of the Soviet government in November 1933 to 1948 only about 50 of the Soviet wives of American citizens have been permitted to leave the USSR. There were still 350 Soviet wives and 65 Soviet husbands of American citizens who had applied for permission to depart from the USSR without success and "the Soviet Government has been adamant in refusing to permit them to leave" (pp.657–658).

35. *Pr.*, July 8, 1973.
36. G.K. Matveev, in *SGiP*, 1974, No.5, p.151.
37. G.I. Tunkin, *op. cit.*, p.23; R. Kulik, *op. cit.*, p.33.
38. V. Shevtsov, *Citizenship ...*, p.88.
39. G.I. Tunkin, op. *cit.*, p.23.
40. V.V. Kuznetsov, *loc. cit.* (note 12 above). Likewise, V. Shevtsov, *Citizenship ...*, p.88.
41. V. Durdenevskii, "Zakon o grazhdanstve Soiuza Sovetskikh Sotsialisticheskikh Respublik", *Problemy sotsialisticheskogo prava*, 1938, No.6, p.61. Cf., "Closing word by deputy N.A. Bulganin", *Pr.*, August 20, 1938.
42. *VVS SSSR*, 1979 No.25, Art.436.
43. E.g., M. Shafir, *Grazhdaninom byt' obiazan*, Moscow 1972, p.23.
44. *VVS SSSR*, 1939, No.22; *Sbornik zakonov SSSR i ukazov Prezidiuma Verkhovnogo Soveta SSSR (1938g.–noiabr 1958g.)*, Moscow 1959, p.76.
45. M. Shafir, *op. cit.*, pp.23–24.
46. *Pr.*, *Izv.*, December 2, 1978; *VVS SSSR*, 1978, No.48, Art.817. Also, *International*

Affairs, 1979, No.1, p.145.

47. *VVS SSSR*, 1979, No.25, Art.437.
48. *VVS SSSR*, 1979, No.25, Art.436. English translation by W.B. Simons in *Review of Socialist Law*, 1979, No.4, pp.468–469.
49. *VVS SSSR*, 1979, No.42, Art.696.

SOURCES. FEDERAL CITIZENSHIP AND REPUBLICAN CITIZENSHIP

In the thirties, when the previous citizenship statute was promulgated, preambles to legislative acts were not in fashion and, true to pattern, the 1938 law did not feature an introductory statement. Today, of course, the pendulum has swung in the opposite direction and elaborate prefatory pronouncements are again in vogue. Accordingly, the present edition boasts a formal prologue declaring that the citizens of the USSR enjoy the totality of socio- economic, political, and personal rights and freedoms proclaimed and guaranteed by the USSR constitution and Soviet laws. The Soviet socialist all- people's state, the preface continues, protects these rights and freedoms and ensures the rights of USSR citizens in all areas of economic, political, social and cultural life. The overture then sounds a theme borrowed from the 1977 constitution to the effect that every citizen of the USSR is obliged to observe the constitution and Soviet laws, bear with dignity the high calling of citizen of the USSR, safeguard the interests of the Soviet state, contribute to the enhancement of its power and authority, and be loyal to his socialist Motherland. The concept of the interdependence of the individual's share of rights and duties, enunciated in the Fundamental Law, thus recurs, albeit in somewhat attenuated form, prompting speculation on whether failure to perform designated duties might, in the absence of any specific sanction, by itself serve as grounds for retaliation through curtailment of the "offending" party's assorted rights. The answer is by no means clear at this juncture, except that most analysts have tended to conclude that the dictum formulates a moral/ political instead of a legal imperative. Worth noting, however, is the fact that public utterances on this occasion took a lot of care to emphasize the point of the indivisibility of rights and duties accorded a proper citizen in the conditions of the socialist system,[1] which suggests that even if an organic linkage does not yet function, a scheme may be afoot to cultivate a popular climate which would make a positive move in that direction in the near future feasible.

1. Sources

The overwhelming majority of Soviet authors treat citizenship in general as an institution of state law and Soviet citizenship in particular as one of the most important institutions of Soviet state law, with the applicable norms being essentially of internal state provenance and, hence, set by the terms of Soviet legislation.[2] The most extreme advocates of this version maintain that, by virtue of its sovereignty, the USSR possesses the exclusive right to regulate its citizenship relations, which is to say that Soviet legislation operates on the principle that Soviet citizenship relations are determined only by Soviet law. Soviet diplomats make the same pitch in an effort to establish the precedence of national over international law in regulating citizenship questions. For instance, the Ukrainian delegate to the committee charged with drafting the Universal Declaration of Human Rights saw fit to object to the idea of incorporating nationality rights in that document on grounds that

> "the question of nationality — by which was meant a special relationship between a state and the individual — fell entirely within the internal competence of each state. To grant nationality or to take it away was a prerogative of sovereign states".[3]

Even in conflict situations, we are told, the practical monopoly remains unimpaired and, at least where Soviet policy is concerned, the rationale is that "insofar as pursuant to the USSR constitution the conditions for and procedure of acquisition of Soviet citizenship are prescribed by the Law on citizenship, i.e., by Soviet law, it follows from that proposition that the norms of law of foreign states can have no relevance to the solution of these questions".[4]

However, the most diehard champions of the primacy of domestic law in these matters[5] cannot totally ignore the role of international law here either and ultimately must admit that "the state cannot arbitrarily postulate any norms regarding citizenship, paying no attention to the universally recognized principles and norms of international law, international customs and international treaties to which the given state is a party".[6] The problem is that, despite the professed expectation that the salient aspects of the international law repertory will be taken into account in such cases, the state is thereby allowed to retain a great deal of latitude on how it chooses to accommodate itself to these rules and, in the last analysis, domestic priorities still come first in settling the issue. The pecking order in that respect is quite clear. In the words of a leading Soviet expert on the subject:

> "Citizenship has primarily an intra–state significance. In considering citizenship on the international law plane one must also start from the basic premise that only state sovereignty determines the existence of citizenship itself as well as the method of its regulation. Only then is the state itself competent to establish, alter or terminate that specific legal relation with a physical person which constitutes citizenship proper. For, in the final reckoning the existence of citizenship as a legal phenomenon becomes possible only in the presence of a plainly indicated and suitably formalized expression of will by the state, legally embodied in the competence to decide questions of citizenship. This competence represents the sovereign rights of the state."[7]

The logical consequence of this scenario is that its proponents end up in a position to resist attempts to invoke external standards for judging the validity of national practices pertaining to citizenship status. In light of the modern trend toward expanding the scope of international law to include various activities over which the appropriate state had hitherto exercised full control, finding ways and means of blocking this type of "intrusion", whether pursued under the guise of interest in the protection of human rights or desire to promote more liberal policies in the field of citizenship stricto sensu, has certain very definite political objectives. A run–down of the kind of developments in this sphere against which the Soviets have sought to raise the defense of domestic jurisdiction will show what is at stake.

The Swedish courts' resort to the so–called concept of "redifinition of citizenship",[8] for instance, has met with bitter criticism from Soviet sources. The formula is invoked in marriage–family and inheritance cases where Swedish law refers to the attribute of citizenship in order to ascertain the applicable law and to determine whether or not the local courts have jurisdiction over the matter. The practice originates in several judgments rendered by the Supreme Court of Sweden and, in particular, its decision of December 16, 1948, in a divorce case in which the Court recognized that, under Soviet law, the plaintiff had not lost the citizenship of the USSR, but nevertheless declared that the plaintiff was considered a stateless person for the purposes of the business at hand. In its decision of February 25, 1949, in another divorce suit the same Court admitted that the parties retained Soviet citizenship and then found that their citizenship was "purely formal".[9] These conclusions have been justified by claiming the need on humanitarian grounds to allow the settlement of such disputes in Sweden.

To Soviet spokesmen, the argument sounds unpersuasive and they maintain that the interests of the respective parties would be equally well served if the Swedish courts were to treat Soviet citizenship properly. The approach, they charge, is politically motivated and to prove the point they cite the decision of the Supreme Court of Sweden and the appellate court of Stockholm in the matter of the inheritance of R. Evelson. Her estate was located in Sweden and the deceased was a Soviet citizen living in the Latvian SSR where she was killed in 1941 by the German invaders. According to Soviet sources, no "humanitarian rationale" figures in the case since all the heirs resided outside Sweden. Even so, the courts disregarded the evidence of Soviet citizenship. In their opinion, the deceased had not possessed Soviet citizenship long enough and, furthermore, at the time of death was residing in the zone of the Soviet Union occupied by the Nazis. The courts of Sweden declared the deceased to have been a citizen of bourgeois Latvia and divided the estate under the terms of bourgeois law.[10] The courts of West Germany have also been denounced for following the Swedish example on frequent occasions, as witness the decision of the federal administrative court of July 7, 1959, in which the court established that the party to the hearing possessed Soviet citizenship, but still recognized him as a citizen of the late bourgeois Baltic republic.[11]

More pernicious yet, in the estimate of Soviet legal specialists, is the theory of "functional citizenship" which often underlies such decisions. Essentially, we are told, it asserts that in addition to regular citizenship there exists an ad hoc citizenship, depending on the circumstances of the specific case. Soviet observers contend that widespread reliance on this doctrine can inflict considerable harm on the regulation of relations not only in the realm of private international law, but in the domain of relations between states as well. Thus, they note that in recent years an increasing number of norms featured in international treaties of a general character bracket certain important consequences in the field of inter–state relations with the attribute of citizenship. For example, the 1972 Convention on international liability for injury caused by cosmic objects is keyed to the criterion of citizenship[12] and Soviet authors complain that, in light of the recorded trend here, any further spread of ambiguity in connection with citizenship is likely to have an adverse effect on the prospects for international cooperation among states.[13]

Soviet opposition to attempts to "dilute" the state's sole discretion to determine title to its citizenship by sanctioning the right of individual states to judge the validity of a fellow–state's policy on that score by some common standard also extends to organized efforts by the world community to enunciate such rules or "codify" the applicable principles on which sufficient international consensus is assumed to exist. In short, "interference" here in the private affairs of the state, whether by other states acting singly or collectively and through resort to administrative or judicial "review" or a joint bid to "enact universal legislation", elicits an equally negative reaction from Soviet circles and brusque condemnation as an unwarranted derogation of a state's inherent prerogative to define the terms of membership in its constituency. For instance, the line of reasoning in the advisory opinion of the International Court of Justice of April 11, 1949, which formulated the concept of "functional defense" by the United Nations of its personnel is unequivocally rejected by Soviet analysts as infringing the rights of the state with regard to its citizens and violating the basic precepts of international law.[14]

In similar vein, Soviet spokesmen have relied on the proposition that "no international body or agency is authorized to deal with citizenship matters as they are in the exclusive competence of the sovereign state" to argue that the projected texts of the Convention on the elimination of statelessness which were discussed in 1953 at the 5th session of the UN International Law Commission grossly ignored this fundamental postulate and so lacked legitimacy. Or, to quote directly,

> "In starting from the fallacious idea of priority of international over national law, the authors of the drafts put the emphasis on setting up a special tribunal within the framework of the United Nations, empowered to deal with matters concerning citizenship of different persons.
>
> When the convention was in its drafting stage, a Soviet and a Czechoslovak delegates — members of the Commission — spoke against the idea itself of such conventions and stressed that citizenship and statelessness were matters in the internal jurisdiction of sovereign states."[15]

On the other hand, a minority contingent of Soviet jurists who have had occasion to write on citizenship problems take a less dogmatic position on this issue and evince a more realistic appreciation of the fact, as they phrase it, that "questions of citizenship refer principally to the sphere of intra–state law, but at present their international law significance is growing".[16] The members of this group, consisting largely, albeit not exclusively, of individuals with a primary interest in the discipline of international law, thus adopt an essentially dualistic view of citizenship as a phenomenon governed by both national and international law. Even then, however, the scales are heavily tipped in favor of the former by virtue of a widely shared interpretation according to which "it is a basic and universally recognized principle of international law on questions of citizenship that these questions are mainly decided by the internal legislation of each state".[17] In short, although the function of international law here is duly acknowledged, its role is ranked a poor second to that played by municipal law in managing citizenship affairs.

Of course, to the extent that two sets of criteria are now said to apply to the institution of citizenship, the business of how to reconcile their respective provisions in the event that they differ also enters the picture. The standard response is that domestic law on the subject of citizenship must not run counter to the norms of international law and, not surprisingly, the world is forthwith informed that the "new Law on Citizenship of the USSR fully takes into account the norms of international law regarding citizenship questions that are currently in force".[18] The task of Soviet lawyers in effecting such reconciliation is rendered markedly easier, one might add, by their espousal of the thesis that the amount of customary norms of international law pertaining to citizenship is very small and they have little practical importance.[19]

Clearly, congruence between domestic legislation and international agreements is a separate issue in that both activities involve the exercise of state will and the operation lets the state concerned make up its mind and register its choice of what rules it will henceforth follow. By contrast, customary international law does not call for the expression of individual preference, but rather envisions acquiescence in an already established consensus and leaves the latecomer on the world scene with hardly any alternative. To avoid having to resolve the difficulty of which would have precedence in case of conflict between Soviet municipal law and international customary law on some aspect of citizenship policy, Soviet lawyers simply cast doubt on the existence of a special body of international customary law relating to citizenship matters and claim instead that it makes more sense to invoke the generally recognized principles of international law in order to settle an occasional dispute over citizenship than to try to induce from the random, and often mutually contradictory, record of state behavior in this domain a code of conduct binding on all.[20]

The attitude plainly stems from apprehension that a portion of the international community, relying on superior numbers, might attempt to "legislate" rules that the rest of the membership would then be expected to observe. These fears seem to have prompted at least one Soviet source to insist that "international law ... cannot and must not affect the particular features of citizenship of various states connected with the specific nature of their social–economic structure".[21] Needless to say, such a formula guarantees ample room for polemics over what rates as a peculiar attribute of the local political system and therefore qualifies for immunity from evaluation pursuant to international law indicia. The depth of Soviet suspicions here is well illustrated by the fact that even a document as widely accepted as the Universal Declaration of Human Rights is not spared. A premier Soviet international legal scholar has recently seen fit to remind us that "a declaration of the UN General Assembly is not equivalent to an international treaty and like other similar resolutions of the UN General Assembly represents a recommendation which is not legally obligatory for states".[22] On a technical level, the author has an arguable point, but to dismiss the Universal Declaration which now enjoys virtually unanimous support in this summary fashion and without exploring several subsidiary grounds on which the act may be said to possess normative potency betrays a remarkably narrow vision of the current array of sources of international law tantamount to adherence to an obsolescently conservative formalism on that score.

For all their talk about how free each state is to define the terms of its citizenship status, Soviet spokesmen are nevertheless forced to admit that in practice incidents do occur when one state will proceed to find fault with the record of another state in the treatment of citizenship questions because the latter's policies allegedly violate the applicable norms of international law. While prepared to concede that this sort of infraction must entail non–recognition by the rest of the states of the offending measure, Soviet commmentators are quick to add that the position of governments on these occasions is determined by their "general political line". The assessment allows them to fend off criticism aimed at Soviet experience in this field by charging that in the case of imperialist states refusal to acknowledge the validity of foreign legislation concerning citizenship is often motivated solely by hostile feelings toward the political systems of other countries.

Not unexpectedly, objections to certain features of the Soviet record in this sector are routinely ascribed to such animus. West Germany again figures prominently as the villain of the piece, incurring intense Soviet wrath by dispatching a letter from the Ministry of Internal Affairs in Bonn to the International Refugee Organization on August 3, 1951, with the explanation that, in the opinion of the West German government a regime of military occupation operated in Lithuania, Latvia and Estonia and, consequently, the citizenship of these countries had undergone no change.[23] According to this version, then, the citizens of these states retained their former nationality and did not acquire Soviet citizenship, whereas, of course, Soviet legal experts consider the whole idea absurd: the concept of some kind of military occupation of the Baltic states, they claim, is utter nonsense, the local population voluntarily opted to join the Soviet Union and thus settled the issue of its citizenship affiliation. In that context, we are told, the extension of Soviet citizenship to the Baltic territories did not run counter to international law, leading to the conclusion that the proposed non–recognition constituted not just an unfriendly act, but an intervention in the domestic business of the USSR since a foreign state thereby presumed to pass judgment on the propriety of Soviet laws.[24]

The connection between the question of recognition of foreign laws on citizenship and the question of their validity from the standpoint of international law is fairly obvious. When Soviet jurists write that the recognition of an invalid act on citizenship and the non–recognition of a valid one are equally illegal, they are merely expressing conventional wisdom. However, the real difficulty lies in the mechanics of the formula's subsequent implementation: when Soviet spokesmen insist that recognition cannot serve as the index of the validity of laws on citizenship and maintain instead that the validity of such legislation serves as the basis for its lawful recognition, they fail to carry the analysis a step further and specify what standards are to be consulted if two states disagree over the nature of the evidence. True, demanding that a state clear its citizenship legislation in advance by obtaining the approval of its fellow states for the projected regulations smacks of curtailment of its "sovereign rights" in this sphere; conversely, letting each state assert the validity of its own citizenship practices and expect the rest of the international community to defer to its judgment would effectively deny all opportunity for an outside "review". Resort to a common "code" offers the one reasonable answer, but that is precisely what the Soviets, with their commitment to the principle of state supremacy in shaping the respective institutions of citizenship, have so far proved unwilling to accept. The result is a vexing dilemma from which the only escape route is the invocation of subjective values. The Soviets have not hesitated to avail themselves of that tactic, while denouncing the competition for doing likewise.

The double–standard ploy is used as both a defensive and an offensive weapon. While the Soviets look askance at any bid by another state to criticize their performance on the citizenship front by reference to some external criteria, they have no compunctions against assigning poor grades to other states on that count in the light of their own desiderata. Note, for instance, the violent tone of Soviet condemnations of various earlier attempts by certain West German circles to win international backing for the theory that persons of German nationality residing on the territory of Poland, East Germany and other "socialist" states had kept their "former German citizenship". These efforts were branded by the Soviets as "rubbish in the scientific sense and frankly revanchist in essence". The Basic Law of the FRG of May 23, 1949, was attacked for arbitrarily enlarging the concept of German citizenship and the Law on universal military service of July 1956 fared as badly for purporting to apply to all Germans living on the territory of Germany as defined by the frontiers that existed in 1937.[25]

A similar pattern may be observed in the procedure followed in the USSR in dealing with "conflicts–in–law" cases, namely, a policy mix in which firm intent to guard the home ground from "invasion" by foreign law is coupled with definite interest in not slamming the door on prospective opportunities for "exporting" local normative prescriptions designed for such contingencies. As previously mentioned, Soviet practice here abides by the principle that "all questions of Soviet citizenship are governed exclusively by Soviet law", which, in turn, means that "resolution of a collision between Soviet citizenship and a foreign one falls solely within the competence of Soviet law" and leads to the corollary proposition that the norms of the foreign law involved in the collision never enter the adjudicative picture.[26] The reverse, however, does not hold true. Take, for example, the situation where a conflict arises between the norms of Soviet law regarding the modus operandi for establishing the fact of a particular person's entitlement to the citizenship of a foreign state and the norms of the corresponding foreign legislation elaborating the terms for proving possession of the citizenship of that foreign state. Oddly enough, Soviet sources indicate that in such instances Soviet legislation spells out the procedure for deciding the issue and regulates all questions related to the matter: even though most foreign states have their own set of rules concerning certification of the fact of possession of their citizenship, we are told that "in general, these norms of foreign legislation on citizenship are not applied by the competent Soviet organs".

Instead, Soviet, and not foreign, law specifies what information and documents will be considered by the proper Soviet institutions as evidence in order to ascertain ownership of a foreign citizenship. The same goes for deciding the probative force of the documents submitted in this context, with Soviet law once again designating which foreign document provides the basis for reaching the conclusion that the claimant does or does not have a valid right to the citizenship of a foreign state.

Lastly, Soviet law alone establishes the procedure for arguing the case, especially with respect to assigning the burden of proof. To be sure, Soviet jurists admit that ad hoc exceptions sanctioning resort to the norms of foreign law are possible, usually through the phenomenon of renvoi. The question of the term of validity of a foreign passport presented to a Soviet agency to demonstrate the bearer's possession of a foreign citizenship is cited as an item on which the relevant foreign law can be allowed to have the final word: the gesture of accommodation marks a positive contribution to the furthering of international cooperation among states (never mind how slight), without inflicting doctrinal malaise on any of the parties.

Still, such individual and discretionary exemptions which recognize the role of the foreign partner's law for certain limited purposes do not significantly detract from the overall picture keyed to the theme of the essential primacy of Soviet law in resolving technical problems stemming from competing jurisdictional claims. Trying to justify the "monopoly" by attaching the label of procedural to the operative rules has little persuasive effect since it is plain that pre–selection of the applicable rules is apt to dictate the substantive outcome of the inquiry. When Soviet lawyers fail to note this causal relationship, the omission is not due to unawareness on their part that the connection indeed exists, but to conscious intention to devise a scenario that will let them maximize the scope of Soviet law while curbing the effective range of rival legal systems.

No matter how peripheral the role which the Soviets ascribe to international law as a source of norms concerning citizenship, the fact remains that the Soviet Union has had occasion to enter into general and special agreements dealing with citizenship issues and these documents certainly feature rules that create rights and duties for the signatories. Under such circumstances, a situation can obviously occur where a material discrepancy develops between these two sets of prescriptions and a decision must then be made as to whether treaty law or municipal law here enjoys precedence. The 1978 citizenship statute tackles the problem (Art.29) by mandating that "if an international treaty to which the USSR is a party establishes rules different from those which are contained in the present Law, the rules of the international treaty apply". The formula is, of course, helpful and it is good to have official assurance that the Soviet Union intends to honor its international obligations in this area, even if they reflect an approach unlike the one that figures in the domestic legislation. Nevertheless, questions about how the proposed scheme is expected to function persist and need further elucidation.

Remember that Soviet doctrine does not treat international agreements that are in force as an integral part of the law of the land in the sense of equating their normative status with that of domestic enactments.[27] The postulates of international agreements operate on home ground only after undergoing the additional process of reception or transformation and the mere act of publication of the text of a treaty in the governement gazette does not elevate its contents to statutory rank so as to let its terms henceforth directly regulate the conduct of the interested citizens. In short, unless national law intervenes by medium of express reference or incorporation, the provisions of an international agreement have no way of affecting conditions on the Soviet internal scene and a valid international agreement meanwhile continues to shape relations solely between the participating states. To be sure, the latter may be called upon to adapt their national law to the treaty's requirements and failure to make that accommodation would entail liability vis–à–vis the respective partner on an inter–state level, but the citizens of the delinquent state would still be left with no viable means of redress against their own government for depriving them of the benefits promised by the treaty.

In case of such divergence, the individual would have access to domestic law alone, regardless of charges of incompatibility with the provisions of a treaty, and the language of Article 29 does nothing more than instruct the competent officials what rules they must choose to enforce where the relevant prescriptions of treaty law and national law do not match. The collision is "resolved" by ordering the responsible personnel to give preference to international law on these occasions, and not by sanctioning the private party's right to invoke the appropriate rule on his own behalf, thus maintaining intact the individual citizen's essential dependence on the good faith of authorities in this domain. Whether or not the regime's practical performance complies with the standards set by the treaty can be an object of discussion between the signatory states, but the available evidence is far from clear that in the USSR the person himself is effectively in a position to impugn the government's record on that score by pressing a claim that the stipulations of an international treaty are either not being applied at all or are being applied wrongly by the agencies vested with jurisdiction over the corresponding piece of business.

Soviet experts in the field of citizenship law have never wavered in their contention that "an international treaty confers on a state definite obligations, but this does not affect in the least the state's sovereign right to determine and regulate its citizenship".[28] The norms of international law regarding the status of individuals, according to them, are intended to be implemented through the domestic law of states and, consequently, are slated in each case to acquire the "proper social coloration". By then, they will have been converted into prescriptions of national law and function in the latter capacity. The pacts on human rights are said to operate in similar fashion in that they require the contracting parties to take suitable steps at home, including the enactment of enabling legislation. In this version, neither the Universal Declaration nor the covenants confer rights squarely upon individuals, although they establish reciprocal duties between states to grant such rights.[29] While Soviet authors concede that the experience represents in a sense an "intrusion" by international law into a sphere which traditionally had belonged to the domestic jurisdiction of each state, they still insist that the current situation does not mean that human rights are directly regulated by international law or that they have ceased to be in the main an internal affair of the respective states.[30]

Where the USSR is concerned, the official pitch is always the same, to wit, that the Soviet government scrupulously fulfills its international commitments and, in that context, also makes sure that its domestic legislation comports with its international legal repertory since a single standard must in fact prevail. The Law on Citizenship of the USSR, for instance, is constantly praised for how well its contents integrate the norms of international law to which the Soviet Union has subscribed. Until recently, the general task of devising a satisfactory synthesis was entrusted to the executive and administrative apparatus and the competent organs, in discharging their assigned duties, would routinely decide how each problem should be managed. Reportedly, the job was done right, but in any event these matters were settled intramurally and strictly by virtue of executive and administrative fiat. The adoption of the 1977 Constitution and the accompanying program of legislative reform wrought some noticeable changes here.

For example, the statute on the Supreme Court of the USSR of November 30, 1979, now features a novel clause (Art.5) stating that "the Supreme Court of the USSR decides within the limits of its competence questions arising from international treaties of the USSR".[31] The latest law on the Procuracy of the USSR, passed on November 30, 1979, follows suit (Art.11) by indicating that "the organs of the procuracy within the limits of their competence and pursuant to the established procedure decide questions arising from international treaties of the USSR".32 The formula sounds as if both institutions would engage in this type of activity at their own discretion or in response to initiatives from other branches of government or perhaps even in the wake of inquiries from ordinary citizens, but the impression one gets is that the mechanism cannot be unilaterally set in motion by an aggrieved individual with a stake in availing himself of the practical benefits accruing from a rule embedded in a treaty concluded by the USSR. On the other hand, letting two law–associated organs gain entrée into this field may bring an element of legal thinking into the picture, hitherto monopolized by policy considerations. The end result may be a difference in style rather than substance; yet, allowing the legal community a modest voice on the subject could, in the long run, lead to decisions on some of these issues prompted by a legal rationale instead of mere political convenience.

Next, there is Article 58 of the 1977 Constitution which proclaims, inter alia, that:

> "Citizens of the USSR have the right to address complaints against actions of officials and of state and social organs. Complaints must be considered in the manner and within the time–limits established by law.
>
> Complaints may be brought to a court, in the manner established by law, against actions which violate the law or exceed the authority of officials and which infringe the rights of citizens."

The trouble is that the up–dated legislation spelling out the procedure for examining proposals, statements and complaints of citizens[33] and the organization of people's control in the USSR[34] refers only to infractions of the law in this context and never names international agreements as a source of rights which the citizen may be entitled to defend through these channels. Since, as mentioned earlier, international treaties are not automatically considered "law" in the sense of forming part of the corpus of local legislation which applies to the circle of eligible individuals at first–hand, the technical term "law" ought once again to be construed narrowly in this case to signify just domestic enactments. The scenario thus does not seem to cover complaints by citizens against actions of officials felt to be improper in the light of rules contained in the international treaties to which the USSR is a party, except where they have been duly translated into or reincarnated as norms of municipal law.

The list of complaints which the citizen will be able to take to court (under the provisions of paragraph 2) has not yet been drawn up: in theory, private suits against officials charging violations of rights guaranteed by international agreements could figure in the final catalogue, but at this stage the chances of that occurring look extremely remote. The agenda here for the foreseeable future, then, calls for the apparatus to police its own operations and counts on the average citizen to alert the officialdom to lapses that it should take care to correct, but without affording him the formal means to bring the culpable party to heel in an adversary setting.

None of the above is convincingly disproved by occasional cryptic pronouncements by Soviet spokesmen who seek through recourse to elliptical diction publicly to create the opposite impression. An excellent sample of such tactics may be found in the answers furnished by the representative of the USSR to the Human Rights Committee some of whose members had requested further information on certain questions dealt with in the initial report filed by the USSR on its record of implementation of the clauses of the International Covenant on Civil and Political Rights. At one point, for instance, the Soviet delegate assured his interlocutors that "citizens of the USSR could invoke the provisions of the Covenant before State Authorities and courts if they so wished".[35] As far as it goes, the statement is accurate enough, but it really does not explain much: the citizen might indeed be free to cite the Covenant in these circumstances, but we are still not told that the referral will make any practical difference in the way the matter is handled by the administrative or judicial organ hearing the case. Will drawing the attention of the competent officials to the language of the Covenant cause them to refrain from applying the local law that is alleged to contravene the corresponding article of the pact or to reinterpret the municipal norm that has been challenged on these grounds in terms more compatible with the relevant postulates of the Covenant? On this critical issue, Soviet sources prefer to maintain a prudent silence, leaving one to infer that the reticence smacks of a negative connotation.

2. Federal Citizenship and Republican Citizenship

The adoption of a federal structure added a special dimension to Soviet citizenship policy. For ideological and logistical reasons, the local leadership has since insisted on the simultaneous operation of two (and sometimes three) layers of citizenship which, of course, raises some complex doctrinal problems. The present pattern here was set by the 1936 charter and 1938 citizenship law. Namely, "based on the provision of Article 21 of the Soviet Constitution of 1936, in fact repeating it to the letter, Article 1 of the new law preserved the old idea incorporated in the Statute of 1931 that in the Soviet Union there shall be a single Union citizenship and that each citizen of a Union Republic be also a citizen of the USSR".[36] More than that, in combination, the 1936 Constitution of the USSR and the Citizenship Law of 1938 marked the final triumph of the concept of federal supremacy and the virtual ouster of the union republics from an area in which, even after the instauration of the federal system, they had so far managed to retain extensive, indeed primary, powers. Except for the minor stylistic changes noted before that did away with the element of semantic tautology which afflicted the previous formulation, the script has been kept intact and Article 1 of the 1978 act opens once again with a reaffirmation of earlier statutory and recent constitutional precedent fixing a single union citizenship and determining that every citizen of a union republic is a citizen of the USSR. The language, we are told, vividly expresses "the state unity of the Soviet people — a new historic, social, and international community of men".[37]

Otherwise, the sole innovation in this context amounts to an extra paragraph spelling out that "USSR citizenship is equal for all Soviet citizens, regardless of the grounds for its acquisition". The item lets Soviet commentators dwell on the superiority of this feature of Soviet legislation compared to the record of discrimination encountered in the law of capitalist countries which, "in a variety of instances, circumscribes the rights of the individual depending on how and when he obtained his citizenship".[38] Interestingly enough, an analogous provision already figured in Hungary's Law on Citizenship,[39] from which it was very likely borrowed. The coincidence lends credence to a Soviet author's statement that the drafters of the 1978 statute took into account "the experience of the fraternal socialist states in questions of citizenship" as part of the general process of legal integration in this domain which has pursued two routes: 1) the conclusion of special bilateral conventions; and, 2) stock-taking of the norms of national legislation concerning citizenship matters found in the repertory of the different members of the socialist community.[40]

However, to return to the theme of the relationship between federal citizenship and republican citizenship, the point that now needs to be made is that, despite the federal government's obvious predominance in this field since the late thirties, the 1977 charter and 1978 citizenship act continue to refer to citizens of the respective union republics, mostly, one feels, still for symbolic reasons. If, as all Soviet spokesmen have over the years maintained, the union republics are sovereign states, then it logically follows that each must command its quota of citizens,[41] else what would state sovereignty signify were the state not to have its own citizens. In other words, the fiction of the sovereignty of the union republics underlying Soviet constitutional doctrine has inevitably led Soviet jurists to postulate, in turn, the existence of a republican citizenship,[42] further evidenced, inter alia, by the recognized right of every republic to admit individuals into its citizenship.[43] By the same token, the phenomenon of republican citizenship is often cited as proof positive that the union republics are in effect sovereign states — as claimed — because only such entities are entitled to have their own contingent of full-fledged citizens and the capacity to confer that status on persons wanting to join the constituency.[44]

The presence of a federal authority, together with a single federal citizenship, always complicated the picture though, keeping Soviet lawyers busy constructing elaborate theories explaining the dialectical relationship back home between republican and union citizenship predicated on the parallel operation in the Soviet political system of two separate, but interdependent, sovereign wills fully merged into a "higher unity".[45] The results have never sounded too convincing. Dogma, however, exacts its price and so it has become standard procedure in Soviet legal literature to treat the issue in this manner. Nevertheless, talk of "harmonious synthesis" does not mean unanimity of opinion on the subject of ranking the components in the final "alloy". The majority of Soviet writers prefer to skirt the topic of whether federal citizenship or republican citizenship enjoys precedence within the combination by pretending that "such an approach to the problem runs counter to the very idea of a single Soviet citizenship"[46] and that there are no grounds for opposing them to one another since they function in an "organic concordance".[47] Yet, occasionally a dissenting voice is also heard: either a more candid and realistic appraisal which, while paying lip–service to the "indivisibility of union and republican citizenship", concedes the former's "primacy";[48] or, a rare (and, in retrospect, quixotic) call for reform that claims pride of place in the equation for republican citizenship and insists on its priority within the diad (or triad, as the case may be).[49]

One can, in a way, appreciate the need experienced by Soviet law–makers on ideological grounds, even at this late date, to go on paying lip–service to the familiar theme of the acknowledged function of a distinct republican citizenship in Soviet public life. However, already from the terms of the 1938 edict, it was quite clear that republican citizenship in actuality now connoted little more than that a Soviet citizen was a regular resident of the corresponding union republic and, by virtue of that fact, also counted as a citizen of that republic. The previous statute on the citizenship of the USSR, that of April 22, 1931, admitted as much, except for allowing that when by his nationality or by his origin a person considered himself linked to one or another union republic he could select the citizenship of that republic. The 1938 law was silent on that score, casting some doubt on whether Soviet administrative policy still recognized this right, and indeed the likelihood is that it has since lapsed. Doctrine sounds equally sceptical of the further rationale of such practice and at least one Soviet author has taken the view that,

> "... at present, when there has arisen a new historical entity — the Soviet people, the choice by a citizen of one union republic of the citizenship of another union republic on national grounds loses its meaning. The reason for this is that the unshakable friendship of the people of the multinational Soviet state determines the unity of rights and duties of Soviet citizens regardless of their racial or national affiliation, religious denomination, education, sedentariness, social extraction, etc."[50]

In the final analysis, then, residency in a union republic and possession of that republic's citizenship are almost synonymous expressions in contemporary Soviet jurisprudence. First, we have the testimony of Soviet experts in this field who openly bracket the two items. Discussing, for instance, the mechanics of acquisition of union citizenship by a foreigner permanently residing abroad, a Soviet writer adds that such a person becomes a citizen of a union republic (and possibly an autonomous republic as well) on arrival for residence in the USSR, which a colleague amplifies with the revealing observation that, in this sequence, "the citizenship of a union republic cannot be refused to a citizen of the USSR".[51] On the domestic scene, similar indicia are applied in figuring what republican citizenship a particular individual possesses and the sole disagreement here among Soviet specialists is whether mere residence or permanent residence constitutes valid qualification for this purpose. Some local savants seem to consider extended physical presence in a given republic a sufficient condition, but, according to others,

> "the basic criterion for recognition by union republics of Soviet citizens as citizens of the respective union republic must be the citizen's permanent

> residence. A citizen of the RSFSR, for example, will be recognized as a citizen of the Ukrainian SSR only in case he has changed his place of residence and has permanently settled on the territory of the Ukrainian SSR. In those cases where a citizen of the RSFSR settles on the territory of the UkSSR only temporarily, he retains the citizenship of the RSFSR.
>
> The question of ASSR citizenship must be resolved in analogous fashion."[52]

From the technical standpoint, the latter version sounds more plausible. The proposed formula has the further advantage of precluding a citizen of the USSR from ending up with the citizenship of two or more union republics on the principle that "republican citizenship changes upon transfer to a permanent place of residence from the territory of one union republic to the territory of another", — the switch, by the way, ensues automatically in that "change of citizenship of a republic requires no petition to the organs of power of the union republic".[53] By contrast, if a brief sojourn on the soil of a union republic led to the acquisition of local citizenship, this could mean for a peripatetic person either a random accumulation of republican citizenships or a rapid succession of republican citizenships and a potential headache for officials charged with keeping track of the relevant statistics.

Second, legislative failure to identify the juridical attributes of republican citizenship leaves one with no practical alternative save to rely on the concept of residence to supply the missing answer. All local legislation defining the conditions for the acquisition and loss of republican citizenship lapsed pursuant to the directive contained in the federal decree of June 2, 1939, henceforth leaving domicile as the sole objective criterion for deciding the question of which republic's citizenship an individual was vested with. And, where subsequently some of the republics had occasion, in connection with the accession of territory to the USSR, to issue instructions on the acquisition of their citizenship by the inhabitants of these fresh increments to the Soviet domain, these measures confined themselves to verbal repetition of the corresponding stipulations of preceding federal legislation that had already finished converting these people into citizens of the USSR.[54] Thus, during the tenure of the 1938 citizenship act, a prominent Soviet constitutionalist was moved to observe that "the question of citizenship of a union or autonomous republic did not find appropriate legal regulation and has not been properly worked out by legal scientists" and note that "in the law on the citizenship of the USSR it is not even established who is a citizen of a given union or autonomous republic".[55] The 1978 statute has not filled this void, the situation here remains just as before and, through omission, the phenomenon of union republic (and autonomous republic) citizenship continues to inhere in the institution of (permanent?) residence.

Nor does legislative reference alone to republican citizenship prove very much. For example, the constitutional charter of each Autonomous SSR of the post–1936 generation talked of citizens of the respective ASSR. Yet, learned opinion on the subject was badly split at the time on whether the autonomous republics did indeed possess a genuine citizenship and the majority then seemed to share a negative view on that score.[56] In the mid–sixties and early seventies, a marked shift in attitude took place in favor of emphasizing the sovereign status of the component entities of the Soviet federal system, probably in reaction to the former Stalinist agenda that had given the matter short–shrift. In any event, a compromise theory was now formulated which confirmed that autonomous republics had no claim to sovereignty stricto sensu,[57] but since the official record attested to the existence of an ASSR citizenship the latter feature, "representing one of the most important means of realizing state self–administration by a nation, reflects, effectuates and guarantees the sovereignty of that nation".[58]

Fuzzy though the doctrine of "state self–administration by a nation" and "sovereignty of that nation" (not state sovereignty, mind you) may have sounded to outsiders, the die was cast and, for a while there, every Soviet scholar who wrote on citizenship echoed the theme and took care to mention all three versions of citizenship and, of course, their ultimate unity within the framework of a single USSR citizenship.[59] As one Soviet author put it:

> "Each autonomous soviet socialist republic also has its citizenship. The citizen of an autonomous republic is simultaneously a citizen of that union republic of which the given ASSR is a part, as well as a citizen of the USSR. All soviet citizens on the territory of the given autonomous republic are guaranteed legal equality with its own citizens.
>
> Let us illustrate this proposition with an example. A citizen residing on the territory of the RSFSR is a citizen of the RSFSR and the USSR. Each of these citizenships is quite real and entails specific consequences. In case a citizen resides, for instance, on the territory of the Tatar ASSR which is part of the RSFSR on an autonomous basis, he is concurrently a citizen of the USSR, a citizen of the RSFSR and a citizen of the Tatar ASSR. The same goes for the other soviet republics."[60]

Just like the citizenship of a union republic, citizenship of an autonomous republic was said to be determined by local residence.[61] A lame attempt was even made to explain how the citizenship of an autonomous republic can exist without being legally spelled out by insisting that the institution of citizenship arises together with the state and does not depend on legal formalization which can occur later. Mention was made in this connection of the experience of the RSFSR the citizenship of which allegedly emerged coincidentally with the inception of the state, i.e., on November 7, 1917, whereas special legislation on citizenship appeared only after a certain interval.[62] However, the account still begs the question in that it fails to: 1) indicate the legal grounds on which autonomous republics are entitled to stake out a separate citizenship; and, 2) what this citizenship amounts to in the absence of a legal document pinpointing its essential attributes.

Be that as it may, the practice of invoking the three–tiered arrangement became so common that a recommendation was made to amend the applicable legislation accordingly. Noting that all the ASSR constitutions (post–1936 vintage) contained articles stipulating that each citizen of the ASSR is a citizen of a union republic and a citizen of the USSR, the proposal called for supplementing "the law on citizenship of the USSR of 1938 with a reference to this norm".[63] Interestingly enough, the authors of the 1978 bill did not see fit to heed the suggestion and, indeed, the text's silence on this issue may have served as a signal that the advisability of continuing to subscribe to the concept of an ASSR citizenship was under study. Thus, mere oversight may not have been the reason why in a treatise on the latest citizenship statute sent to the printer before the law was enacted and relying on the draft edition, the leading local authority on Soviet citizenship policy managed to omit the usual discussion of the role of ASSR citizenship in the federal structure of the USSR.[64] In the end, though, any possible doubts were apparently resolved in favor of preserving the status quo in this area and the new charter of the Tatar ASSR, for example, which was adopted very soon after, once again explicitly spoke of the citizens of the Tatar ASSR (Art.28).[65] This should put the matter to rest and prompt Soviet sources to revert to the old routine of singing the virtues of the three–in–one package.

Notwithstanding the ideological and political constraints which leave them no choice but to endorse the public claim that the USSR's constitutional system features a triple–citizenship scheme, Soviet legal analysts are not unaware that the official picture of the simultaneous operation of two (or three) different citizenships on the national scene and the rapport between them is fraught with internal contradictions that can only be reconciled by appealing to the mysterious workings of the dialectical process. The following is a typical sample of resort to such artifice in an effort to match the pieces and convince the prospective audience that it all somehow makes sense:

> "However, if the very existence of citizenship depends on possession by the state of definite sovereign powers, then, on the other hand, one must explain the fact not only of the absence of these powers in the case of a nonsovereign state, which is what an autonomous republic is, but also the definite limitation of these powers in the case of a sovereign state (union republic). Does the absence of these rights in the case of an autonomous republic (the right of admission to citizenship, the right of deprivation of citizenship, etc.) and the limitation of rights in the case of a union republic (absence of the right to sanction exit from citizenship, to deprive of soviet citizenship) render nominal the very fact of existence of the citizenship of these states?
>
> Obviously not. In the conditions of the Soviet federation, there is a single Soviet state, and the simultaneous existence of union and republican citizenship is guaranteed by the effectuation of powers with regard to questions of citizenship belonging to the Union and the union republics.
>
> Admission to the citizenship of the USSR falls within the joint competence of the USSR and the union republics which compose it. Deprivation of Soviet citizenship and permission to leave it falls within the exclusive competence of the USSR. To the exclusive competence of the USSR in the person of the Presidium of the USSR Supreme Soviet is also assigned the admission into Soviet citizenship of foreigners residing outside the borders of the USSR."[66]

What we are asked to conclude, then, is that because total harmony marks the relations between these three tiers of the governmental hierarchy, no infraction of the sovereignty of a union republic is committed when the federal branch is vested with sole control, say, of the business of permitting individuals to shed Soviet citizenship since the central regime is simply presumed to act on behalf of its respective republican counterpart and, in so doing, cannot help but fully reflect the latter's interests. Whether anyone else except those who accept the Soviet credo will find the scenario persuasive is debatable.

To make a long story short, when one skips the fancy terminology, the status of the union and autonomous republics here boils down to the proposition that, within the scope of its constitutional rights, each of them exercises legal authority over a person residing on its soil. Labeling that person a "citizen" of that republic or autonomous republic adds nothing to the equation. In other countries as much is achieved via the commonplace formula of plain territorial jurisdiction. Just as a further indication of the relative weight attached in current Soviet legal philosophy to federal and republican citizenship within the framework of the Soviet government organization, every citizen of a union republic, according to the language of both the 1938 and 1978 acts, is automatically a citizen of the USSR, but, by the same token, not every citizen of the USSR must of necessity be a citizen of one of the component republics. Or, to phrase it differently, Soviet law eo ipso rules out the possibility of a republican citizenship existing apart from and unaccompanied by federal citizenship.[67] It openly puts the stamp of approval on the reverse situation. By comparison, the 1931 regulation at least went through the motions of ordaining that in all cases both citizenships be held concurrently, to such an extent that when a foreign citizen living abroad applied for naturalization to the Presidium of the USSR Central Executive Committee, the latter literally had to admit him "to the citizenship of one of the union republics and thereby also to the citizenship of the USSR".

The 1938 act dropped that condition and henceforth, to quote a Soviet source, practice followed the rule whereby "a person who has submitted a declaration on reception into the citizenship of the USSR is simultaneously received into the citizenship of a union republic only in the event the declaration is addressed to the Presidium of the Supreme Soviet of the union republic".[68] And even this was due strictly to a general constitutional mandate and administrative convenience and not to any statutory prescript: an individual could equally well petition the federal authorities for naturalization (regardless of whether he lived abroad or in the USSR at the time) and upon approval of his request routinely qualify for a republican citizenship on grounds alone of residence on the territory of a particular republic (union and, when pertinent, also autonomous). True, some of the republics reportedly took the extra step of issuing decrees officially conferring local citizenship on such individuals residing on their soil, but again the gesture only had symbolic meaning and certainly did not fulfill any statutory requirement, especially since the relevant republican legislation was formally repealed in the wake of the adoption of the 1938 federal law.[69]

As mentioned, the 1978 statute likewise recognizes the possibility of possession solely of federal citizenship — although, we are told, these cases are exceptional: the situation is apt to occur when a foreigner residing abroad applies for and gets Soviet citizenship and, as long as he does not establish residence in some union republic, he will not pick up the corresponding republican citizenship and count only as a citizen of the USSR. In one respect, however, the procedure here has undergone a stylistic change. Previously (i.e., pursuant to the 1938 version) a foreigner residing in the USSR could apply for naturalization either to the competent republican or federal institution: if he took the federal route and succeeded in his quest, he next collected the appropriate republican citizenship by medium of residence (or ad hoc decree). Now, the law reverses the order and provides that, in normal circumstances, a foreigner residing in the USSR will file a request for naturalization with the Presidium of the republic where he maintains permanent residence (Art.26): if his petition is approved, he will receive republican citizenship and concurrently gain the citizenship of the USSR. To be sure, the statute still keeps open the alternative channel by allowing the federal Presidium to render a decision concerning any question of citizenship it elects to include on its agenda and a direct application for naturalization from a foreigner residing on Soviet soil would fall under that heading if the Presidium opted to exercise its discretionary power to consider the case: nevertheless, willingness to "grant certiorari" in these instances would presumably be warranted by some special circumstances, else the interested party would be expected to observe the standard modus operandi and file his application forms with the right republican agency.

Where republican citizenship has practical implications is in determining what set of laws applies to a Soviet citizen abroad. Indeed, as long as Soviet codes are republican in origin, there is the item of figuring out which code's provisions should control the legal position of a Soviet citizen during his stay in a foreign country. For instance, Soviet citizens away from home have the right to be married in the local Soviet consulate. Articles 32 and 37 of the Fundamentals of legislation of the USSR and union republics on marriage and the family of June 26, 1968, as per the decree of October 9, 1979,[70] cover the various contingencies arising in connection with entry into matrimony or the performance of other acts of civil status on such occasions: if the parties are citizens of the same union republic, the legislation of the USSR and of that republic applies; if they are citizens of different republics or it is not established the citizens of what republic they are, they jointly decide which republic's law shall apply, and if they cannot agree, the official registering the act of civil status makes that decision. Even so, shopping among the codes can only produce marginal results. Soviet spokesmen themselves nowadays concede that "in reality we cannot note significant distinctions in the legal condition of citizens of the different union Soviet republics".[71] At an earlier stage of Soviet history, the opposite was true and, in fact, the divergences between republican legal inventories were then deemed sufficiently meaningful that they were cited as a further rationale for the role played by the concept of republican citizenship.[72] The absence of substantive incongruities makes that thesis no longer tenable at this point and, psychologically, the prospect of justifying the existence of republican citizenship by dwelling on chance disparities in their legislative repertory seems to leave Soviet analysts quite cold.[73] Yet, letting a phenomenon grandly designated as "citizenship" just operate in a few "conflicts–in–law" situations whittles the institution down to very modest proportions.

Considering how little Soviet policy here has changed since the thirties, a condensed review of the reforms proposed in this sector during a recent stretch of more "benign" weather in Soviet politics might be instructive in shedding light on which features of the agenda were felt in local circles to require improvement, which aspects of the current record attracted criticism and on what grounds, and what desiderata animated these projects. Published accounts reveal a remarkable consensus among those favoring revisions about what, in their opinion, needed to be done in this context. One of the first members of the legal community to take the plunge and, incidentally, set the tone for subsequent scholarly discourse on the theme zeroed in on the key element when he wrote that, "in order to strengthen the institution of citizenship of a union republic, it is mandatory to establish by legislative means who is a citizen of a union republic". Article 2 of the Regulation on Citizenship of 1930 impressed him as possibly offering useful guidelines on this score inasmuch as it had prescribed that a citizen of the USSR was a citizen of the union republic on the territory of which he ordinarily resided, unless by his race or origin he felt himself closely tied to another union republic, in which case he could choose the latter's citizenship instead. He also advocated the introduction of a definite rule whereby a person could not be admitted into the citizenship of the USSR without at the same time being admitted into the citizenship of a union republic, "as had taken place under the Regulation of 1931 (Art.12)". To that end, an individual lodging a request for naturalization with the Presidium of the Supreme Soviet of the USSR would be expected to state in his application which union republic he preferred to be a citizen of, while the federal Presidium would be empowered to accept people not just into the citizenship of the USSR but, with the concurrence of the interested republican Presidium, into the citizenship of the given republic as well.[74]

Logically enough, the idea of enlarging the rights of the union republics "in deciding questions concerning citizenship"[75] generated strong support in these quarters. Indeed, the point was then made that "the tendency toward the further expansion of the rights of the union republics and perfection of legislation at the contemporary stage of communist construction raises the question of granting rights of recognition , admission, exit and deprivation of its citizenship not only to a union, but also to an autonomous republic". A step in this direction was considered, of course, to have at this time both a theoretical and practical significance.[76] In order to guarantee the component units of the federation effective exercise of the aforementioned powers, the backers of this scheme envisaged a clear division of competence to issue acts pertaining to citizenship affairs, under the terms of which the federal authorities would be charged with establishing fundamental principles of legislation relating to citizenship policy and the jurisdiction of the union republics would simultaneously be broadened by assigning them the task of promulgating current legislation in this domain. Obviously, the republican edicts would deal solely with elements of republican (union and autonomous) citizenship, just as the respective federal acts, in addition to postulating the fundamental principles of Soviet citizenship, would regulate various concrete phenomena of USSR citizenship. Such a distribution of functions here reportedly would serve as "a major means toward the further development and refinement of socialist federation".[77]

In conjunction with plans to enhance the status of the union republics in this sector, preference was generally expressed for the "extremely important" 1931 formula that was not featured in the 1938 law which, it will be recalled, had required foreigners seeking admission into Soviet citizenship to indicate forthwith which union republic's citizenship they wished to acquire, otherwise they could not, stricto sensu, obtain the citizenship of the USSR either. Still, not everyone of the lot was ready to commit himself to the companion proposition that the applicant be formally instructed in each case to record explicitly his choice of union or autonomous republican citizenship since that issue would be duly taken care of when the interested person established a permanent residence within the confines of a particular union or autonomous republic.[78]

Even comprehensive models of union and republican statutes on citizenship were privately drawn up in those days. The only published sample happened to involve the Armenian SSR and represented the most ambitious project along these lines attempted by the pro-reform contingent. The scenario is clearly inspired by the desire to reassert the primacy of republican citizenship vis-à-vis union citizenship, to erase the utterly unwarranted restrictions imposed on republican legislative activity by past policy spawned by the now discredited "cult of the personality"[79] and to reassociate the republics with the management of all aspects of citizenship practice by giving them an equal (and sometimes slightly superior) stake in the exercise of the corresponding rights compared to the share here assigned to the federal branch. As one might expect, the topic of who was a citizen of a designated union republic received special attention and on this occasion the draft text offered an elaborate definition of those who qualified as citizens of the Armenian SSR. The passage is worth quoting at length because the contents show how far a few Soviet scholars were willing to go at this stage of the game to recapture for the union republics a role in full partnership with the federal apparatus in handling citizenship operations.

Thus, the category of citizens of the Armenian SSR was seen as comprising: 1) all Soviet citizens who permanently resided on the territory of the Armenian SSR and were not citizens of other union republics entering into the USSR; 2) Soviet citizens although not residing on the territory of the Armenian SSR but who considered themselves citizens of the Armenian SSR (the principle proposed in this instance was more "liberal" than the version which figured in the 1931 Regulation in that it no longer posited a kinship grounded in "nationality" or "origin" — concepts pronounced obsolete under contemporary Soviet conditions — and instead left the individual with complete freedom of selection); 3) children of Soviet citizens born on the territory of the Armenian SSR if at the time of birth at least one of the parents was a citizen of the Armenian SSR, as well as children born on the territory of the Armenian SSR whose parents were citizens of different union republics or one of whose parents was a citizen of a foreign state; 4) persons born on the territory of one of the union republics entering into the USSR if at the moment of birth both parents were citizens of the Armenian SSR; 5) persons born on the territory of the USSR if at the moment of birth one of the parents was a citizen of the Armenian SSR and the other a citizen of a foreign state, as well as persons even though born abroad if at the moment of birth one of the parents was a citizen of the Armenian SSR provided that the father at the moment of birth was living on the territory of the USSR. If one of the parents was a citizen of the Armenian SSR and the other a citizen of a foreign state and at the moment of birth both parents were living outside the territory of the USSR, the citizenship of the child was determined by agreement of the parents; 6) persons who acquired the citizenship of the Armenian SSR in the manner prescribed by law; 7) persons who opted for the citizenship of the Armenian SSR pursuant to the international agreements of the Armenian SSR and USSR.

The balance of the recommended legislation (and the accompanying analysis) was devoted to the business of spelling out in extenso what powers the union republics should be vested with in connection with the process of naturalization (1. both with respect to applicants living on Soviet soil and abroad; and, 2. contingent on mandatory conversion to a specific republican citizenship in order to obtain USSR citizenship), denaturalization, release from and deprivation of Soviet citizenship. (The technical terms proposed for exercising these rights will be discussed later under the appropriate headings.)

In the end, none of these schemes won official approval or affected the substance (as opposed to style) of the 1978 citizenship act. With Khrushchev's downfall and the growing conservative trend in Soviet politics over the last decade, these visions apparently lost their appeal and ceased reflecting the dominant strands of Soviet public thinking. It is therefore doubly ironic to run across a recent statement by a Soviet writer to the effect that, "in contrast to the law previously in force, the new law formulates more broadly the legislative rights of the union republics on questions of citizenship",[80] since the evidence plainly shows that nothing has changed in this respect and the claim thus rates as a piece of sheer unadulterated fantasy. As for the revisions that were advocated in that earlier period, although the issue is at present quite academic, the fact remains that many of these views seem to endure and, at some opportune moment, may well resurface, prompting the conclusion that they attest to certain deeply-rooted convictions within segments of the Soviet legal community about the proper nature of the federal system in the USSR unlike those espoused by today's ruling elite.

NOTES

1. V.V. Kuznetsov, *Pravda* and *Izvestiia*, December 2, 1978 (hereafter abbr. as *Pr.* and *Izv.*, respectively). Also, editorial, "Grazhdanin Sovetskogo Soiuza", *Pr.*, December 4, 1978.
2. E.g., S.I. Rusinova, "Zakon o Grazhdanstve SSSR", *Pravovedenie*, 1980, No.1, p.4; V.G. Butkevich, "Pravovye voprosy grazhdanstva i statusa inostrantsev v pervye gody sovetskoi vlasti", *Problemy pravovedeniia*, 1977, vyp.35, p.67.
3. *A/C.3/SR.123*, at 335, cited by H.–J. Uibopuu, "Soviet Nationality: Privilege or Burden? An International Lawyer's View", *Israel Yearbook on Human Rights*, 1977, Vol.7, p.55.
4. A.A. Rubanov, "Osnovnye kollizionnye voprosy sovetskogo zakonodatel'stva o grazhdanstve", *Sovetskoe gosudarstvo i pravo*, 1979, No.7, p.49 (hereafter abbr. as *SGiP*).
5. For example, V.S. Shevtsov, *Grazhdanstvo v sovetskom soiuznom gosudarstve*, Moscow 1969, p.56. Likewise, the Hungarian jurist V. Baiaki (Bajáki), "Obshchee i osobennoe v pravovom regulirovanii grazhdanstva v evropeiskikh sotsialisticheskikh stranakh", *SGiP*, 1976, No.11, p.81.
6. N.V. Vitruk, "Grazhdanstvo kak pravovaia sviaz lichnosti s gosudarstvom", *Problemy gosudarstva i prava,* 1976, No. 12, p.19.
7. V.S. Shevtsov, "Sovetskoe grazhdanstvo i gosudarstvennyi suverenitet", *SGiP*, 1970, No.6, pp.45–46.
8. Cf., H. Eek, "The Administration of Justice in Conflict Cases Involving Refugees", *Scandinavian Studies in Law*, 1959, Vol.3, p.35, cited by A.A. Rubanov, *op. cit.*, p.51.
9. Laurine c/a Laurine, *Zeitschrift für ausländisches und internationales Privatrecht* 145 (1951), cited by H.–J. Uibopuu, *op. cit.*, p.64.
10. A.A. Rubanov, *Zagranichnye nasledstva. Otnosheniia mezhdu sotsialisticheskimi i kapitalisticheskimi stranami*, Moscow 1975, pp.253–255, 269–270.
11. *Idem*, *op. cit.* (note 4 above), p.51.
12. See, A.A. Rubanov, *Mezndunarodnaia kosmichesko–pravovaia imushchestvennaia otvetstvennost'*, Moscow 1977, pp.108–122.
13. *Idem*, *op. cit.* (note 4 above), p.52.
14. V.S. Shevtsov, *op. cit.* (note 5 above), p.59. To the same effect, S.B. Krylov, "Mezhdunarodnyi Sud Organizatsii Ob"edinennykh Natsii", in *Voprosy mezhdunarodnogo prava i protsessa v ego praktike za desiat' let (1947–1957)*, Moscow 1958, pp.60–65, and O.V. Bogdanov, *Pravovye voprosy prebyvaniia OON v SShA (pri vilegii i immunitety OON)*, Moscow 1962, pp.54–57.
15. V.S. Shevtsov, *Citizenship of the USSR (A Legal Study)*, Moscow 1979, p.55. *Idem*, *op. cit.* (note 5 above), p.56, and F. Ivanov, S. Volodin, "Piataia sessiia Komissii mezhdunarodnogo prava OON", *SGiP*, 1953, No.7, pp.98–99.
16. S.V. Chernichenko, *Mezhdunarodno–pravovye voprosy grazhdanstva*, Moscow 1968, p.3. Likewise, G.I. Tunkin, ed., *Mezhdunarodnoe pravo*, Moscow 1974, p.216.
17. G.I. Tunkin, "Zakon o grazhdanstve SSSR", *SGiP*, 1979, No.7, p.23.
18. *Ibid.*
19. S.V. Chernichenko, *op. cit.*, p.36. Also, G.I. Tunkin, ed., *op. cit.*, p.217.
20. S.V. Chernichenko, *op. cit.*, pp.36–37.
21. See, G.I .Tunkin, ed., *op. cit.*, p.217.
22. G.I. Tunkin, *op. cit.* (note 17 above), p.29.
23. *American Journal of International Law*, 1957, No.1, p.126, cited by S.V. Chernichenko, *op. cit.*, p.90.
24. S.V. Chernichenko, *op. cit.*, pp.90–91.

25. V.S. Shevtsov, *op. cit.* (note 5 above), p.58, fn.2. Likewise, I.S. Rozanov, "Voennoe zakonodatel'stvo Federativnoi Respubliki Germanii — orudie remilitarizatsii i revansha (Obzor materialov opublikovannykh v Germanskoi Demokraticheskoi Respublike)", *SGiP*, 1959, No.7, p.163.
26. A.A. Rubanov, op. *cit.* (note 4 above), p.54.
27. Cf., the author's "The Validity of Treaties in the Municipal Law of the 'Socialist' States", *American Journal of International Law*, 1965, No.3, pp.523–544. A different interpretation has now been offered by E.M. Ametistov, "Mezhdunarodnyi dogovor i sovetskii zakon", *Problemy sovershenstvovaniia sovetskogo zakonodatel'* stva, 1979, Trudy 14, pp.152–166. He argues that the treaties and agreements entered into by the USSR acquire the force of law by the mere fact of ratification and are subject to internal execution upon subsequent publication in accordance with established procedures when their provisions are sufficiently specific to lend themselves to direct application. The examples he cites, though, involve either: 1) executive–administrative or judicial acts which give effect to the terms of an international treaty by virtue of the principle that the competent state organs will enforce the prescriptions of a treaty where they diverge from the corresponding stipulations of domestic law; or, 2) acts by the appropriate state and social organs adjusting the provisions of domestic law to match those of international treaties. No mention is made of what would happen when the required accommodation does not occur and an interested individual might seek to have the norm of an international agreement pronounced to be superior to the competing norm of domestic legislation, which in fact is the crucial test of the status of international agreements as a source of law in the national forum.
28. V. Shevtsov, *op. cit.* (note 15 above), p.37.
29. *Idem*, *Gosudarstvennyi suverenitet (Voprosy teorii)*, Moscow 1979, p.128.
30. E.g., G.I. Tunkin, *Teoriia mezhdunarodnogo prava*, Moscow 1970, p.93.
31. *Vedomosti Verkhovnogo Soveta SSSR*, 1979, No.49, Art.842 (hereafter abbr. as *VVS SSSR*).
32. *VVS SSSR*, 1979, No.49, Art.843.
33. Decree of the Presidium of the USSR Supreme Soviet of March 4, 1980, amending the Decree of April 12, 1968, *VVS SSSR*, 1980, No.11, Art.192.
34. Law on People's Control in the USSR of Nov. 30, 1979, *VVS SSSR*, 1979, No.49, Art.840.
35. Report of the Human Rights Committee, General Assembly Official Records, 33rd session, Suppl. No.40(A/33/40), New York 1978, p.72.
36. T.A. Taracouzio, "The Soviet Citizenship Law of 1938", *American Journal of International Law*, 1939, No.1, p.157.
37. Editorial, *Pr.*, Dec. 4, 1978. Also, V.V. Kuznetsov, *loc. cit.* (note 1 above).
38. V.V. Kuznetsov, *loc. cit.* In like vein, Terebilov, Banionis, Gitalov, *Izv.*, Dec. 3, 1978; Editorial, *Pr.*, Dec. 4, 1978, and V. Zenin, "Gromadianstvo SRSR — velika chest' i velika vidpovidalnist'", *Radianske pravo*, 1979, No.2, p.10.
39. Cf., V. Baiaki, *op. cit.* (note 5 above), p.81.
40. V.V. Polianskii, "Printsipy sovetskogo grazhdanstva", *SGiP*, 1980, No.5, p.124, and fn.5.
41. E.g., D.L. Zlatopol'skii, *Gosudarstvennoe ustroistvo SSSR*, Moscow 1960, p.247; M. Kirichenko, "Grazhdanstvo Soiuza SSR", *Sovetskaia iustitsiia*, 1972, No.11, p.9 (hereafter abbr. as *SIu*); V.S. Shevtsov, *op. cit.* (note 29 above), p.108; M. Shafir, in *Sotsialisticheskaia zakonnost'*, 1970, No.4, p.94 (hereafter abbr. as *SZ*).
42. For example, V.S. Shevtsov, *Sovetskoe grazhdanstvo*, Moscow 1965, pp.27–32; Report by N.A. Bulganin, *Pr.*, Aug. 18, 1938.

For earlier discussions of this complex problem, see S.S. Kishkin, "Sovetskoe grazhdanstvo", in M.O. Reikhel, ed., *Sovetskii federalizm, sbornik*, Moscow–Leningrad 1930, pp.62–65; S.A. Kotliarevskii, *SSSR i soiuznye respubliki*, Moscow 1924, pp.31–32; M.O. Reikhel, *Soiuz Sovetskikh Sotsialisticheskikh Respublik*, *Ocherk konstitutsionnykh vzaimootnoshenii sovetskikh respublik*, Kharkov 1925, Chast' I: Obshchaia, pp.128–147; V. Ignatiev, "Soiuznoe grazhdanstvo", *Sovetskoe stroitel'stvo*, 1930, No.3(44), pp.1–9; N.I. Palienko, "Pravo grazhdanstva v Soiuze SSR", *Vestnik sovetskoi iustitsii*, 1925, No.7(41), pp.270–273.

Republican citizenship (nationality) should not be confused with *natsional'nost'* which means something like ethnic affiliation; *natsional'nost'* is not a strictly defined legal concept (although a person's *natsional'nost'* is mentioned in most official documents). Viz., F.J.M. Feldbrugge, "Nationality", in F.J.M. Feldbrugge, ed., *Encyclopedia of Soviet Law*, Dobbs Ferry, N.Y., and Leyden 1973, Vol.2, pp. 463–464.

43. V.S. Shevtsov, *op. cit.* (note 7 above), p.46.

44. *Idem*, *op. cit.* (note 5 above), p.48; V.V. Polianskii, *op. cit.*, p.123. The literature on the status of the union republics and citizenship as a manifestation of their state sovereignty is vast. Suffice it to note the following works: S.Ia. Osherov, *Soiuznaia respublika v sotsialisticheskoi federatsii*, Moscow 1948, p.76; S. Radzhabov, *Tadzhikskaia SSSR — suverennoe sovetskoe gosudarstvo*, Dushanbe 1957, p.246; M.M. Faiziev, *Uzbekskaia SSR — suverennoe gosudarstvo*, Tashkent 1961, p.62; S.R. Vikharev, *Suverenitet Belorusskoi SSR v sostave Soiuza SSR*, Minsk 1958, p.124.

45. E.g., V.S. Shevtsov, *op. cit.* (note 42 above), pp.27–28; A.I. Lepeshkin, "Konstitutsionnoe razvitie sovetskogo soiuznogo gosudarstva", *SGiP*, 1962, No.12, p.31; M. Shafir, in *SZ*, 1970, No.4, p.95; *idem*, *Grazhdaninom byt' obiazan*, Moscow 1972, p.29.

Incidentally, a similar solution was adopted in Czechoslovakia where the constitutional Law of December 20, 1970, revising and supplementing the Constitutional Law on the Czechoslovak Federation of 1968, provides (Art.5, as amended), that: 1) there exists a single Czechoslovak citizenship; 2) each Czechoslovak citizen enjoys on the territory of the Czechoslovak Socialist Republic equal rights and owes equal duties; and, 3) each Czechoslovak citizen is simultaneously a citizen of the Czech Socialist Republic or Slovak Socialist Republic. See, *Biulletin' chekhoslovatskogo prava,* 1971, fasc.1–4, p.153.

46. B.V. Shchetinin, *Problemy teorii sovetskogo gosudarstvennogo prava*, Moscow 1974, p.183; V.S. Shevtsov, *Suverenitet sovetskogo gosudarstva*, Moscow 1972, p.235; N.V. Mironov, *Pravovoe regulirovanie vneshnikh snoshenii SSSR 1917–1970 gg.*, Moscow 1971, p.90.

47. For example, V.S. Shevtsov, *op. cit.* (note 7), p.44.

48. R. Kulik, "Pravovye nachala sovetskogo grazhdanstva", *Sovety narodnykh deputatov*, 1979, No.2, p.36.

49. Most notably, A.A. Esaian, *Nekotorye voprosy sovetskogo grazhdanstva (Voprosy naseleniia v praktike Sovetskoi Armenii)*, Erevan 1966, pp.86, 88.

50. S. Kosakov, "Konstitutsionnye osnovy kompetentsii soiuznoi respubliki po voprosam grazhdanstva", *Izvestiia Akademii nauk Kazakhskoi SSR*, 1980, No.5, seriia obshchestvennykh nauk, p.64.

51. V.S. Shevtsov, *op. cit.* (note 5 above), p.67, fn.1; R.I. Kulik, *Zakon o grazhdanstve SSSR*, Moscow 1980, p.33.

52. E.g., K. Kuznetsov, "Zakon o grazhdanstve SSSR", *Partiino–politicheskaia rabota v RKKA*, 1938, No.17, p.13. Per contra, V.S. Shevtsov, *op. cit.* (note 5 above), p.68; *idem*, *op. cit.* (note 15 above), pp.72–73; S. Kosakov, *op. cit.*, pp.63–64.

53. V.S. Shevtsov, *Sovetskoe gosudarstvo i lichnost'*, Moscow 1978, pp.16–17; R.I. Kulik, *op. cit.* (note 51 above), p.33.

54. Cf., Decree of the Presidium of the Supreme Soviet of the Lithuanian SSR of December 30, 1940, in G. Geilke, *Das Staatsangehörigkeitsrecht der Sowjetunion*, Frankfurt 1964, p.341; Belorussian Decree of February 6, 1945, *ibid.*, pp.366–367, citing *Sbornik zakonov Belorusskoi SSR i ukazov Prezidiuma Verkhovnogo Soveta Belorusskoi SSR za 1938–1955 gg.*, Minsk 1956, p.45.
55. D.L. Zlatopol'skii, *op. cit.*, p.249.
56. It is interesting to note that in a dissertation for the degree of candidate of legal sciences on the topic of "Soviet Citizenship" defended in 1950, the aspirant, T.I. Zhukova, reportedly formulated the thesis that the ASSRs possessed their own citizenship. Both official opponents, S.S. Studenikin and D.A. Gaidukov, took issue with that proposition, but the student maintained her original position and still got her diploma. For a brief account of the proceedings, see *SGiP*, 1951, No.1, pp. 76–77.
57. Cf., B.V. Shchetinin, *op. cit.*, p.172; V.S. Shevtsov, *op. cit.* (note 7 above), p.46.
58. V.S. Shevtsov, *op. cit.* (note 42 above), p.24. See, too, the discussion in D.L. Zlatopol'skii, *op. cit.*, pp.248–249.
59. M. Shafir, in *SZ*, 1970, No.4, p.95; V.S. Shevtsov, *op. cit.* (note 5 above), p. 47; S.M. Ravin, *Printsip federalizma v sovetskom gosudarstvennom prave*, Leningrad 1961, p.23.
60. M. Shafir, *Grazhdaninom byt' obiazan*, p.29.
61. V.S. Shevtsov, *op. cit.* (note 5 above), p.47; B.V. Shchetinin, *op. cit.*, p.172.
62. V.S. Shevtsov, *op. cit.* (note 5 above), p.70, fn.1, citing a candidate dissertation by M.M. Altman, *Institut grazhdanstva v sovetskom sotsialisticheskom gosudarstvennom prave*, Erevan 1955, p.13.
63. B.V. Shchetinin, *op. cit.*, p.184.
64. Viz., V. Shevtsov, *op. cit.* (note 15 above), pp.47, 49. The book was sent to the printer on May 5, 1978, whereas the Law on Citizenship of the USSR was enacted on December 1, 1978. The Constitution of the Tatar ASSR was adopted on May 31, 1978.
65. *Konstitutsiia (Osnovnoi zakon) Rossiisskoi Sovetskoi Federativnoi Sotsialisticheskoi Respubliki, Konstitutsii (Osnovnye zakony) Avtonomnykh Sovetskikh Sotsialisticheskikh Respublik, vkhodiashchikh v sostav RSFSR*, Moscow 1979, pp.469–470.
66. V.S. Shevtsov, *op. cit.* (note 7 above), p.46.
67. M. Shafir, *Grazhdaninom byt' obiazan*, p.30.
68. D.L. Zlatopol'skii, *op. cit.*, p.261.
69. See, H.–J. Uibopuu, *Die Völkerrechtssubjektivität der Unionsrepubliken der UdSSR*, Vienna–New York 1975, p.67, and fn.8.

For example the BSSR decrees of January 24, 1939, and July 10, 1939, in *Sbornik zakonov Belorusskoi SSR* ... (note 54 above), pp.44–45; the Kazakh SSR decree of August 20, 1939, *Sbornik zakonov Kazakhskoi SSR i ukazov Prezidiuma Verkhovnogo Soveta Kazakhskoi SSR (1938–1957)*, Alma–Ata 1958, p.75.

Indeed, one Soviet author went so far as to suggest that, after 1938, the enactment of legislation on citizenship fell within the exclusive competence of the federal branch. S.R. Vikharev, *Suverenitet Belorusskoi SSR v sostave Soiuza SSR*, Minsk 1958, p.125. Despite the effective absence of any republican legislation on citizenship since 1938, the opinion has nonetheless been expressed that, in principle, the existence of a single citizenship in the USSR does not constitute an obstacle to *granting* the union republics corresponding powers to issue legal acts on questions of republican (union as well as autonomous) citizenship. V.S. Shevtsov, *op. cit.* (note 5 above), p.95, fn.1. Note the use of the term "granting" which implies that the powers were not there at the time of writing (1969), but would have to be formally conferred on the union republics by suitable means. The latest generation of Soviet charters fails to feature such a mandate, but Art.2 of the 1978 citizenship statute does contain a paragraph stating that the "legislation of a union republic resolves questions of Soviet citizenship within its jurisdiction under the Constitution of the USSR, the Constitution of the union republic, and the present Law".

70. *VVS SSSR*, 1968, No.27, Art.241; 1979, No.42, Art.696.
71. V. Shevtsov, *op. cit.* (note 15 above), p.47; *idem*, *op. cit.* (note 7 above), pp. 41–42.
72. See, for instance, S.A. Kotliarevskii, "Voprosy soiuznogo grazhdanstva i grazhdanstva soiuznykh respublik", *Vestnik Verkhovnogo Suda SSSR i prokuratury Verkhovnogo Suda SSSR*, 1927, No.2(5), p.16.
73. E.g., V.S. Shevtsov, *op. cit.* (note 5 above), pp.49–50.
74. D.L. Zlatopol'skii, *op. cit.*, pp.260–261.
75. *Teoreticheskie voprosy sistematizatsii sovetskogo zakonodatel'stva*, Moscow 1962, p.278; N.V. Vitruk, in *Pravovedenie*, 1971, No.6, p.106.
76. V.S. Shevtsov, *op. cit.* (note 5 above), p.54.
77. *Ibid.*, pp.95–96, 165.
78. *Ibid.*, p.139.
79. A.A. Esaian, *op. cit.* (note 49 above), pp.86, 96.
80. R. Kulik, *op. cit.* (note 48 above), p.39.

LEGISLATIVE BASIS. RECOGNITION. MARRIAGE. RESIDENCE ABROAD. EXTRADITION

1. Legislative Basis

According to Article 2 of the 1978 citizenship statute, "the legislation of the USSR on Soviet citizenship consists of the present Law, defining in conformity with Article 23 of the USSR Constitution the grounds and procedure for acquiring and losing Soviet citizenship, and other legislative acts of the USSR". The reference to "other legislative acts of the USSR" is interesting because it implies the possibility that further legislation on the subject might be forthcoming: in fact, of course, some supplementary instructions intended to clarify the method of application of various provisions of the 1978 statute have already been issued. Whether the cryptic statement concerning additional legislative activity means a medley of such ancillary measures, ad hoc edicts dealing with special cases involving citizenship status, and occasional clauses in legislation addressed to different themes (e.g., the federal Fundamentals of legislation on marriage and the family), or more ambitious ventures into the field of citizenship regulation is not clear from the letter of the law. On the whole, the first alternative sounds likelier.

The next paragraph also invites speculation by declaring that "the legislation of a union republic resolves questions of Soviet citizenship assigned to its jurisdiction by the Constitution of the USSR, the Constitution of the union republic, and the present Law". The point worth noting here is the explicit mention of "legislation of a union republic" in connection with citizenship affairs. The words mark an increment to the language of the current republican charters which only sanction the right of admission into the citizenship of the republic (e.g., Art. 115–12 of the RSFSR Constitution) and feature no general mandate to adopt legislation regarding citizenship matters.

Indeed, common admission to citizenship does not require "legislation" stricto sensu, but a simple executive decision by the competent Presidium and certainly in the recent past the role of the republics in the area relating to citizenship affairs has been limited to the performance of assorted subsidiary administrative chores figuring episodic implementation of germane federal directives. The arrangement offered the advantage of fulfilling the regime's exigencies for improving the looks of the Soviet federal model, while leaving the real power to run this department in the hands of the central apparatus. Now, however, the 1978 statute muddies the waters somewhat by raising the prospect that the union republics might henceforth engage in full-scale legislation in this domain. As a Soviet source has observed, "the Law on Citizenship of the USSR of 1978 has for the first time precisely determined and solidified the right of the union republics to have their own legislation on questions of citizenship in accordance with the USSR Constitution, the constitutions of the union republics and the Law on citizenship".[1] To be sure, no one can yet tell if such legislation will materialize and, should that occur, what its scope will be and whether the contents will then warrant the impressive designation of "legislation" or remain at the prosaic level of routine translation of the relevant federal rules to treat incidental developments.

2. Recognition

The new citizenship statute emulates the example of its predecessor by including a primary description of who counts as a citizen of the USSR: Article 3 in the 1978 edition; Article 2 in the 1938 counterpart. The similarities and differences between the two versions deserve a moment's attention.

The 1938 specimen had posited that "the following are citizens of the USSR":

a. all those who on November 7, 1917, were subjects of the former Russian empire and who have not lost their Soviet citizenship;

b. persons who have acquired Soviet citizenship in a manner established by law.

Several aspects of the wording of the clause call for comment. To begin with, while Soviet spokesmen generally praised this provision as a lucid, concise statement of which people were at the passage of the bill deemed Soviet citizens by operation of the law, this is far from true. All that was thereby accomplished was to send a person back to the welter of laws, edicts, directives, instructions and ordinances circulated from 1917 on and to force him to grope his way through a bewildering thicket of disparate, often openly contradictory, regulations accumulated over a 20–year period in order to discover who was a subject of imperial Russia on the day the Bolshevik revolution erupted, became a Soviet citizen by "succession", as it were, and throughout managed to retain his or her Soviet citizenship and who had meanwhile entered into possession of Soviet citizenship in accordance with prescribed procedure, e.g. by formal naturalization, by executive decree, by legislative fiat. The net effect of the above formula was thus almost tautological, since all it really said was that those people presently qualified as Soviet citizens who at some point in the past obtained Soviet citizenship and never forfeited it. As before, the crucial questions of who did so and how and when were left to be answered by laboriously consulting the contents of the numerous pieces of legislation haphazardly collected over the preceding two decades.

In its latest incarnation, the pitch of the message has been noticeably altered and the current text identifies as citizens of the USSR "persons who had USSR citizenship on the day when the present Law enters into force" and "persons who have acquired USSR citizenship in accordance with the present Law". The shift to the present tense marks a significant departure from the tenor of the corresponding passage in the 1938 law: the reported reason for the change is that the previous norm was evidently obsolete and called for a replacement that would register the situation "as of this day".[2] Bear in mind that in 1938 thousands of Russian exiles remained scattered all over the world, their legal status still unsettled. Some territories which had managed to secede from the Russian empire in the wake of the revolution had so far not been "recouped". In 1917, the concept of Russian national applied to a larger human contingent than the population that lived under effective Soviet control in 1938. Hence, the regime was obviously interested in casting the net as widely as possible in order to round up the maximum number of specimens of "latent" Soviet citizenship, afterwards screening out on an ad hoc basis individuals who had officially been relieved of that title.

At this stage of the game, however, conditions have been stabilized and the authorities have a fairly precise picture of who qualifies as a Soviet citizen. To be sure, doubts persist concerning the legal position of many individuals originating from pre–1917 Russia or its successor states and currently residing abroad (emigrés, refugees, displaced persons, etc.), but the solid core of those owning Soviet citizenship has been plainly identified. Given that no wholesale increments to the Soviet population through a process of "recovery" are expected at the moment, the Soviet leadership can now afford to operate with the recorded inventory, allowing for occasional additions and subtractions, instead of, as hitherto, wishfully relying on the data computed for an optimal base year, gradually deflated by virtue of acquiescence in sporadic deductions dictated by hard experience. The stylistic switch offers graphic evidence that where the Soviet Union had formerly suffered from an unappeased appetite in these matters, the latest attitude smacks of satiety.

The second clause which talks of the segment of the Soviet constituency that comprises "persons who have acquired Soviet citizenship" also reads differently from its 1938 equivalent. Instead of the terminology "persons who have acquired Soviet citizenship in a manner established by law", we have the formula "persons who have acquired USSR citizenship in accordance with the present Law", which at least one local commentator considers "more precise".[3] The new phrasing may, indeed, seem technically superior to the old version and, by putting the spotlight here on the 1978 Law on Citizenship of the USSR, the intent could well have been to stake out the latter's monopoly in this area and avoid a repetition of the earlier the team. The process remains just as complicated as before and calls for thorough familiarity with the sources in order to retrace the genealogy and discover who legally rates as a member in good standing of the national collectivity and whose position is shakier and why. Second, since the latest citizenship law makes no attempt to resolve the recurrent ambiguities that marked past Soviet policy in this field, but simply proceeds ex nunc, a great deal of uncertainty persists concerning the citizenship qualification of various individuals both in terms of whether some tendency to let a random lot of special edicts usurp the field by reeling off a string of improvised solutions to an assortment of particular incidents in Soviet history that involved citizenship questions. Thus, an attempt to "codify" the law governing such activities is a commendable enterprise. On the other hand, focusing on the 1978 statute alone in this context sets a static tone which tends to undermine the scenario's credibility since the likelihood is quite high that additions to the legislative repertory will periodically occur and a few of them are apt to institute a different approach for treating some specific aspect of the problem from the standard procedure sanctioned by the parent statute.

How the business of certifying possession of Soviet citizenship would be handled was left to be elaborated by the federal Presidium (Art.28). The 1978 Law was signally remiss in not naming the agencies which would be competent to deal with such cases on the merits and the oversight was only corrected by the federal edict of June 15, 1979.[4] The latter confirmed that, in the event a question arises about whether a person belongs to the citizenship of the USSR, the determination of that fact is effectuated in accordance with rules established by the Presidium of the USSR Supreme Soviet. Next, the directive filled the statutory gap on the jurisdictional matter by indicating that the power to ascertain a person's entitlement to the citizenship of the USSR rested with the organs of internal affairs and, in regard to an individual residing abroad — with the corresponding diplomatic or consular mission of the USSR. Finally, the measure provided an extra safeguard by informing potential parties that complaints against decisions on questions of ownership of Soviet citizenship were to be submitted to the Presidium of the USSR Supreme Soviet. This took care of most of the administrative details, except, of course, that the procedures which the appropriate institutions are required to observe in considering if a person is vested with Soviet citizenship, when they are drawn up by the federal Presidium, will in all probability never be made public, allowing the officialdom complete discretion in reaching its conclusions: lack of knowledge about what criteria guide the apparatus in its deliberations successfully deprives the dissenting individual of practical grounds on which to challenge the findings.

As indicated, the 1978 statute recognizes as Soviet citizens two categories of people, the first of which consists of "persons who had USSR citizenship on the day when the present Law enters into force". The Resolution of the USSR Supreme Soviet of December 1, 1978,[5] settled on July 1, 1979, as the date on which the Law on Citizenship of the USSR would go into effect, at which time the Law of August 19, 1938, was slated to lapse. The implication, then, was that until July 1, 1979, the old norms would continue to apply and a certain number of people would be added to the rolls under the existing rules up to the scheduled deadline. However, nothing was explicitly said on that score at the time and formal instructions on the modus operandi to follow in this contingency again had to await the issuance of the federal decree of June 15, 1979. Article 7 of that edict now explained that, if the circumstances relating to the person's assignment to USSR citizenship transpired before the current Law's entry into force, the rules of the legislative acts of the USSR and the union republics operating when these facts arose had to be applied. One might further note that, in principle, the possibility of routine resort to the prescriptions of previous pieces of legislation dealing with citizenship policy was kept alive, at least provisionally, by virtue of the general dispensation extended in Article 1 of the federal decree of June 15, 1979. That clause stated that, until the legislation of the USSR and the union republics was brought into conformity with the 1978 citizenship statute, the existing federal and republic legislative acts on citizenship retained their validity insofar as they did not run counter to the latest law. In real terms, though, the formula is not likely to have much of an impact, even during the transition period.

The remark made earlier suggesting that Article 3 of the 1978 law was worded in a way designed to give its pitch a contemporary flavor and a sense of stability should not be understood too literally. First, despite the reference to the status quo memorialized on July 1, 1979, who counted as a Soviet citizen at that crucial moment can still only be determined by checking the historical records to see who once figured as a Soviet citizen and never lost that identity, who "inherited" the affiliation and then maintained it, who acquired that title by one of several means (some voluntary, others not) and thereafter had neither legally shed it nor been stripped of it, and, finally, who had at a particular point owned Soviet citizenship and had in due form subsequently won release from it or been "dropped" from the team. The process remains just as complicated as before and calls for thorough familiarity with the sources in order to retrace the genealogy and discover who legally rates as a member in good standing of the national collectivity and whose position is shakier and why. Second, since the latest citizenship law makes no attempt to resolve the recurrent ambiguities that marked past Soviet policy in this field, but simply proceeds ex nunc, a great deal of uncertainty persists concerning the citizenship qualification of various individuals both in terms of whether some had indeed properly joined the constituency and others had effectively left it. A few samples will demonstrate the kind of problems encountered in this area that continue to bedevil many people's relationship with the Soviet authorities and to cause intermittent diplomatic difficulties between the USSR and a fair number of foreign countries.

The experience of N.I. Budulak–Sharygin offers a convenient starting place for compiling a representative dossier. He was born in 1926 in the Ukraine and in 1941 was deported for labor in Germany. The end of the war found him in the American zone, from where he was transferred by the American authorities to the Soviet zone and took a job there. In 1947, he crossed into the British zone. Later, he was condemned in absentia to death by the firing squad for fleeing abroad. The sentence was subsequently rescinded. In 1948, Budulak–Sharygin moved to England where he received a technical education and began working for a company specializing in electronic equipment (eventually becoming co–owner). Business trips took him to different countries and in 1968 he went to the USSR. Persistent efforts were then made to recruit him for the KGB, all of which he rejected. On the twelfth day of his stay in the USSR — September 20, 1968 — he was arrested. One of the first interrogation sessions was attended by Andropov who, in reply to Budulak– Sharygin's demands to see the British consul, reportedly told him: "the British queen will not declare war on us because of you". The Russians were apparently encouraged in their attitude by the fact that the detainee had not had time to complete the formalities for obtaining British citizenship, although he had filed the necessary papers with the proper authorities. His foreign passport was thus "flawed" in that it did not guarantee the protection of his interests on the territory of the Soviet Union and the East European states.

The investigation lasted fourteen months. First, Budulak–Sharygin was charged with espionage, then with treason, and was finally sentenced to two years in jail (which he had already served almost in full while awaiting trial) and eight years in corrective–labor camp. After stints in various prisons and camps, Budulak–Sharygin was released in September 1978 and brought to live in the town of Kalinin. At the local district police headquarters, he was offered a Soviet passport and put on probation for one year: he refused the passport, declaring that he was not a Soviet citizen and intended to return to England as soon as he could. No pressure was exerted to get him to change his mind. In the beginning of October, his daughter (with whom he resided in Kalinin) visited the British embassy and heard the consul explain that completing the formalities for British citizenship on the basis of a ten-year old application was impossible and advise that Budulak-Sharygin accept a Soviet passport in order to begin proceedings to emigrate through the Department of Visas and Registration (OVIR). The embassy did issue an affidavit certifying that Budulak-Sharygin had been granted permission to immigrate to England. The Kalinin KGB officials, in turn, gave assurances that his desire to emigrate would meet with no obstacles. Toward the end of October, Budulak- Sharygin agreed to accept a Soviet passport and forthwith submitted an application for an exit permit. On November 13 he was issued a foreign passport and left for London on November 19.[6]

Obviously, when Budulak-Sharygin initially decided to go to the USSR, he operated on the erroneous assumption that: 1) through prolonged (21 years) disassociation from the USSR he had managed to rid himself of his former Soviet citizenship; and, 2) the Soviets recognized his "conversion" to another citizenship by letting him travel to the USSR on the strength of valid foreign documents (whatever the special limitations attached).[7] He was thus guilty of a common enough misapprehension of Soviet policy on both counts, although not many such cases fare as dramatically. Technically speaking, however, these episodes can occur quite easily, if the Soviet regime chooses to enforce a strict interpretation of its views concerning the nullity of any unilateral bid at denaturalization and the exclusivity of Soviet citizenship in situations marked by dual (or multiple) nationality.

On a bigger scale, the large community of Baltic emigrés has often featured as an object of contention occasioned by the unsettled citizenship status of its members. Soviet policy vis-à-vis this contingent on the issue of their citizenship denomination has oscillated over the years, but on one recent occasion at any rate it was reported that:

> "The Soviet Consulate General in Bonn has adopted a new procedure towards citizens of the Federal Republic of Germany applying for visas for the USSR who have previously resided in the Soviet Union. The applicants receive letters saying that the statements in their application forms give ground for the assumption that they are still Soviet citizens. They are offered the alternatives of keeping their Soviet nationality and applying for new Soviet passports, or of applying for release from Soviet citizenship. Application forms for release from Soviet citizenship are appended and an advance payment of DM 225,- — for administrative proceedings — is demanded."[8]

The account adds that similar procedures were followed in the USA in the early sixties.[9] According to the source, "the affected persons were, as a rule, born within the borders of the Soviet Union as they exist today" and "most of them had been living in the Federal Republic for over thirty years and some had visited the USSR in the last few years without any difficulties". The crucial question, of course, is whether these people had ever acquired Soviet citizenship at all, and there is a school of thought which maintains that "this point is doubtful at least with regard to the affected persons of Baltic origin". Furthermore, even accepting for the sake of argument that they did end up with Soviet citizenship, the fact remains that "all of them considered themselves not to be Soviet citizens, all of them had abandoned all personal links with the Soviet Union". As noted, "their German nationality was beyond doubt and in some cases the USSR had already implicitly recognized it by issuing tourist visas in their German passports".[10]

Here, what we have is a legal tangle stemming from a basic difference of opinion about whether this category of persons was actually entitled to be classified as Soviet citizens, followed by a secondary strain of disagreement over the propriety of continuing to assign valid possession of this putative Soviet citizenship to individuals who in practical terms had clearly recorded their lack of interest in either "retaining" or "reviving" that title. Consensus may be absent on who is right and who is wrong in the present controversy, but a lot of people possess this set of attributes and the Soviet government's perception of their citizenship status can, in certain circumstances, cause them a great deal of inconvenience, to put it mildly, by treating them as Soviet nationals despite vocal claims from the individuals concerned that no legal grounds exist for doing so.

Loss of Soviet citizenship is at stake in the third type of situation or, rather, the problem of being able in some instances to establish for sure that Soviet citizenship has truly been lost. For example, tens of thousands of Soviet citizens of Jewish origin have in recent years been allowed to emigrate, with Israel figuring as their official destination. The exodus has entailed prior surrender of Soviet citizenship. Yet, as an eyewitness recollects:

> "In 1973–1974, when I filed with OVIR a request for an exit visa the following procedure was in effect. Right after acceptance of my statement, I was warned that, if my request was approved, I would lose my citizenship upon crossing the Soviet frontier. When my request was approved, I was ordered to pay a tax for the right to quit Soviet citizenship, which I did. I do not exactly remember but it seems to me that in the exit visa which I was issued there was indicated that I was 'stateless'. One would think that everything is perfectly clear. The problem, however, is that OVIR which issued me the visa and concurrently took away the receipt concerning payment of the tax for exit from Soviet citizenship is not competent to decide questions of exit from citizenship. As regards the decision of the competent organ — the Presidium of the USSR Supreme Soviet — its decision was not communicated to me. Meanwhile, exit from citizenship represents a rather serious legal act and every Soviet emigrant has the right to count on receiving, at least in exchange for the receipt showing payment of the tax for exit from Soviet citizenship that is taken away from him, an official document stating when specifically the Presidium of the USSR Supreme Soviet authorized that release. I do not know if the procedure just described is still observed. ... In any event, today I do not possess any document confirming that the Presidium of the USSR Supreme Soviet permitted me to quit Soviet citizenship ..."[11]

In fact, none of these people can now formally prove that they duly relinquished

Soviet citizenship. Nor can their children born on Soviet soil. Indeed, even children born abroad of parents both of whom were Soviet citizens before leaving the USSR under these conditions might some day find themselves unilaterally identified as Soviet citizens and have no documentary means of demonstrating that the parents had shed Soviet citizenship in the prescribed manner early enough to immunize their descendants from "inheriting" that status.

Simply put, the formula on recognition of Soviet citizenship that appears in the 1978 statute may be better drafted than its 1938 equivalent, as Soviet authors contend, but like its predecessor, it neglects to dispel a wide legal penumbra that beclouds the citizenship title of a large number of individuals who happen to fall into that compartment and, as a consequence, cannot tell with confidence in which world they live.

3. Citizenship and Marriage

The precedent set here by the 1938 citizenship law is worth recapitulating in its essential details because, although the corresponding provision of the 1978 statute does feature some stylistic innovations, much of the old routine practiced in this domain still forms part of the current repertory. Thus, in the matter of the effects of marriage on the citizenship of the persons involved, the 1938 act faithfully adhered to the pattern established by earlier legislation in that it, too, denied that the accident of contracting a marriage affected in any way the nationality status of the parties to the ceremony. Article 5 made this very plain indeed, emphasizing that "matrimony by a citizen of the USSR with one not such a citizen entails no change of citizenship".[12] The basic rationale was still the same as before, stemming from certain key ideological premises and long–standing policy considerations on the parity of the sexes in Soviet society on which the regime has operated from the very outset: to underline that neither partner in marriage is legally subservient to the other and, especially, to do away with the notion that the woman occupies in the family relationship a position in any sense juridically inferior to that of the man; to demonstrate that in the eyes of the law the wife is not the possession of, or an appendage to, her husband and, of course, also the reverse.[13]

The difference between the 1938 statute and its predecessors lay in its not providing for the possibility of naturalization or denaturalization "in a simplified manner" in the wake of marriage upon the couple's express wishes to bring their citizenship into harmony. True, even under the previous regulations such a process was by no means automatic and the authorities could always turn down a request of this kind and advise the petitioners to go through the usual channels, but at least in the past the law had offered people an opportunity to try and find out if they might not perhaps succeed in getting or giving up Soviet citizenship in a hurry in conjunction with a "mixed" marriage. That principle was now abandoned because the political climate in the Soviet Union did not at the moment favor human rights. The interests of the state, questions of national security absorbed the regime's energies to the near exclusion of the individual's claim for public attention or administrative concern for private needs and aspirations. In other words, at this point the collective frankly came first and the ordinary person's convenience was largely forgotten, together with assorted concessions the law had hitherto seen fit to grant on that count.

To that extent, then, the formula of "speeded–up" naturalization or denaturalization schedules for married people belonging to different nationalities, formerly a standard feature of Soviet jurisprudence, simply fell victim to the tenor of the times. Besides, if the Soviet leadership really intended to enhance the prestige quality of Soviet citizenship, it would almost inevitably feel compelled to rid itself of those elements in the existing legislation that might tend to depreciate the worth of that commodity. In the popular mind, mechanical or unduly facile acquisition or loss of citizenship can imply and, in fact, is frequently associated with low regard for the item's value. So, this particular dimension also might account for Moscow's decision to adopt here a new line, which Soviet jurists thereafter assiduously defended by arguing that to obtain Soviet citizenship a person must desire it and deserve it and that the virtually extraneous phenomenon of matrimony did not per se constitute grounds enough for admission to the exalted calling of citizen of the USSR.[14]

In any event, the federal edict of February 15, 1947,[5] managed to render the issue more or less academic simply by henceforward prohibiting marriages between citizens of the USSR and aliens. The Presidia of the Supreme Soviets of the union republics were forthwith instructed to bring the local legislation in conformity with the present directive. And, on February 4, 1948, the national Supreme Soviet passed a law confirming the Presidium's decree and formally repealing Article 5 of the Citizenship Act of August 19, 1938.[16] On the face of it, the wording of both the initial decree and the companion statute seemed absolutely to preclude any prospect of a marriage between a Soviet citizen and a foreign national hereafter being celebrated on Soviet soil.

Yet, in practice that does not appear to have been the case, the letter of the law notwithstanding. For, while the policy was still in effect, a thoroughly informed Soviet jurist nevertheless thought it incumbent upon him to explain at some length that "the promulgation of the Decree of the Presidium of the USSR Supreme Soviet of February 15, 1947, on the prohibition of marriages between citizens of the USSR and foreigners, obviously in no way alters what was said above rthat marriage does not affect the nationality of the partiest since in the individual instances of possible permission for marriage between citizens of the USSR and foreigners the aforementioned principle of Soviet law concerning citizenship in marriage preserves, of course, its full force".[17] Concededly, under the new conditions a special dispensation from on high was required for that purpose, but once proper authorization was secured the old rules that matrimony did not interfere with the nationality status of the participants reputedly remained just as valid as in the past.

This situation did not last long, and on November 26, 1953, a further decree set aside the 1947 measure, restored Article 5 of the 1938 law and charged the republican Presidia again to rewrite their legislation accordingly. Rather shamefacedly, Soviet spokesmen then blamed the whole sorry affair on Stalin and the "cult of the personality". Belatedly, they admitted that thereby "were flagrantly violated the principles of socialist internationalism, was artificially restricted the civil capacity of Soviet people", and that "it was impossible to justify this edict by any practical or theoretical considerations", which is "why neither the text of the edict or any other official sources contained any motivation".[18] In all that, it sounds as if what irked them most about the entire unfortunate incident was that the language of the two pieces of legislation supposedly inspired by Stalin drew no distinction between the citizens of "capitalist" powers and those of the "socialist" countries, actually treating both with equally undisguised hostility. Coinciding as it did with the emergence of the "world socialist system", this lumping together by the Kremlin of its officially designated friends and enemies in order to discriminate against them both must have left a singularly bad taste in the mouth of all concerned.

Otherwise, few proposals for revision in this specific sphere of Soviet citizenship legislation were heard when the discussion unfolded about the desired contents of the projected statute to replace the 1938 edition. A solid consensus emerged in favor of retention of the norm postulating that the marriage of Soviet citizens with foreigners did not result in any alteration of the citizenship of the spouses. A wish was, however, expressed to supplement the corresponding article with a clause stating that the citizenship of one spouse would not be affected by change in the citizenship of the other spouse.[19] Interestingly enough, back on September 6, 1957, the Soviet Union affixed its signature to the Convention on the Nationality of Married Women and, by so doing, signified its acceptance, inter alia, of the provision recommending that a foreign woman married to one of its citizens be enabled to obtain at her request the citizenship of the husband "through specially privileged naturalization procedures",[20] subject to such limitations alone as are dictated by considerations of state security or public order. The occasion prompted some speculation that reforms were forthcoming in this area of Soviet law to accommodate the language of the Convention, leading to a return to expedited naturalization and denaturalization procedures in the context of "mixed" marriages, even though this device had never really met with the approval of most local lawyers when it was a fixture of the Soviet legal system.[21] At any rate, if hopes were stirred by these moves that a "restoration" might be here accomplished, they were soon dashed — as demonstrated by subsequent developments.

The statute just enacted (Art. 4) features a more elaborate phraseology than its antecedent, but in substantive terms, it sticks to recent tradition by pronouncing that the marriage of a USSR citizen (male or female) with a citizen of a foreign state or a stateless person does not alter the citizenship of the spouses, save to append a sentence indicating that the dissolution of such a marriage does not affect the citizenship of the ex–partners either. This last proposition (with no analogue in the 1938 law) presumably evokes a version of "mixed" marriage in which one spouse then formally converted to the citizenship of the other for purposes of clarifying that, in the event the marriage is terminated, automatic reversion to the previous citizenship does not occur. The policy in this sector is the same as before, except that henceforth an explicit norm covers the terrain. This is also true of the second paragraph which specifies that the acquisition or loss of USSR citizenship by one of the spouses entails no change in the citizenship of the other spouse (an addition advocated, as already mentioned, during the initial explorations of what to include in the text of the scheduled law). In this respect, too, contemporary practice has not varied, and statutory billing merely means legal certification of a familiar routine: for, to quote a Soviet source, this principle figures as an immutable norm of Soviet legislation, based on the premise of the equality of men and women, and bespeaks the fact that "indeed Soviet legislation paved the road for the norms of international law concerning the juridical equality of men and women in general, and further as pertains to questions of marriage".[22]

The stylistic innovations, though not terribly significant, are perhaps worth pinpointing for the sake of getting the record straight. Note, first, that the latest citizenship act takes special pains to refer to both male and female citizens of the USSR in discussing the consequences of marriage to foreign nationals in a bid formally to underline that they enjoy full parity in this regard: sex has no bearing on the status of a Soviet citizen who acquires a foreign spouse and identical treatment is accorded either the Soviet husband or the Soviet wife in such a contingency. Second, the current piece of legislation has the foresight to spell out (as its predecessor did not) that the concept of "mixed" marriage applies to Soviet citizens married both to citizens of foreign states and stateless persons — a minor, but useful, technical footnote. On the essentials, however, the Soviet position on these issues has stayed firm.

In particular, the 1978 law still makes no concession on the matter of priority handling of requests for naturalization or denaturalization motivated by entry into marriage, notwithstanding, inter alia, the Soviet Union's adherence in 1957 to the Convention on the Nationality of Married Women. For the man, the whole business is virtually irrelevant since rarely, if ever, is his citizenship status affected by matrimonial experience, while for the woman the absence of an auxiliary modus operandi sanctioning the possibility of a quick switch in citizenship affiliation following a marriage contract can cause serious difficulties. To be sure, the present formula effectively safeguards Soviet wives of foreigners and stateless persons from involuntarily incurring statelessness as an accompaniment to marriage. On the other hand, Soviet experts are quite aware that some countries continue to subscribe to the imperative of family unity, achieved by means of summary extension of the husband's citizenship to the wife and children. In fact, they take pleasure in denouncing the practice as contrary to the UN Charter's affirmation of the equality of men and women;[23] yet, Soviet law offers no sure cure for the occasion where a woman belonging to the citizenship of a state enforcing that principle marries a Soviet man, forthwith loses her old citizenship and meantime is not guaranteed that her application for Soviet citizenship papers will get preferential attention and meet with prompt approval. Statelessness may be the end result, thanks, at least in part, to Soviet insistence that the other party mend its ways and refusal to step in and provide the necessary relief.

Or, consider the reverse version in which a Soviet woman marries a man who is a citizen of a country that upholds a conservative view of family unity. Again, Soviet legal experts realize that the woman in question will then have a second citizenship thrust upon her. The problem has, of couse, been around for ages and, for that matter, Soviet writers now recall that the 1930 Hague Convention on dual citizenship had failed to deal with it adequately (citing Art. 11) because its authors had allegedly succumbed to the influence of proponents of the credo that men and women were not entitled to equal rights in citizenship affairs. The spectacle had even impelled the Soviet delegation which attended the conference in the capacity of observer to declare in one of its statements that such a situation was intolerable.[24] Nevertheless, Soviet law today proposes no ready remedy for a phenomenon that the regime's representatives had ample opportunity long ago publicly to castigate as inadmissible by modern standards.

A few general comments are in order at this point to put the picture in proper perspective. To begin with, when Soviet spokesmen currently refer to marriages between Soviet citizens and foreigners, they tend to make it sound like a fairly common occurrence. According to an offical account (reported earlier), as of 1976 "5,500 Soviet citizens, i.e. all those who wished to do so, left with their families for 110 different countries in the last few years" on those grounds. "Among them were 544 men. About 2,000 Soviet citizens married to foreigners, have so far not expressed any wish to emigrate, although they have every opportunity to do so." By the middle of 1980, the numbers had almost doubled and, we are now informed, "during the past few years more than 15,000 Soviet citizens married foreigners and 10,500 of them left the USSR to reside in more than 100 countries".[25] Local statistics are also adduced in an effort to show that the incidence of "mixed" marriages has recently been on the rise.[26] Indeed, the impression is created that such episodes have become so routine that some portions of the relevant legislation needed to be modified to deal with the growing traffic. The recommendations included revamping the Instruction of the RSFSR Ministry of Justice "On the procedure for registration of acts of civil status" of January 20, 1958, by supplementing its format with a section containing systematized information on the special conditions attaching to registration of marriages of foreigners with Soviet citizens, the principal legal consequences of conclusion of marriage envisaged by the legislation of foreign states (submission of requisite documents for conclusion of marriage, the rights and duties of the spouses, children, the procedure for dissolution of marriage, etc.). The reasoning behind these proposals was that if the applicable rules were not observed, a marriage entered into on the territory of the USSR might not be recognized in another country and, in that case, the interests of a Soviet citizen (male of female) and his (or her) children would suffer.[27]

A new set of instructions on the procedure for registration of acts of civil status in the RSFSR was approved on October 17, 1969,[28] and we are told that, for instance, owing to differences between the pertinent legislation of the USSR and foreign countries, marriages contracted on Soviet territory might not fulfill the expectations of the respective foreign law and be pronounced invalid in the latter jurisdiction. To protect the interests of citizens contemplating marriage, and especially Soviet citizens, the competent organs "must explain to them the possible consequences of registration of such a marriage".[29] Thus, where obtaining the prior permission of the state of which the prospective foreign spouse is a citizen is mandatory before the marriage can be celebrated, the office of registry of civil status must brief the parties on that country's legal requirements, warn the citizen entering into marriage with a foreigner that if the proper authorization is lacking the marriage will not be recognized as valid in the country concerned and indicate the consequences this may have, in particular on issues related to the birth of children, property and child support rights, the right of spouses to maintenance, and the like.[30]

Still, one should not get the false idea that marriages pairing Soviet citizens and foreigners verge on the habitual. True, the experience is not a rarity, as it once was, but neither has it reached flood level nor, in fact, is it likely that in the near future "mixed" marriages involving Soviet citizens are going to be handled as casually as this type of business is transacted in most countries or match the frequency with which people elsewhere commit matrimony with natives of other lands.

The evidence is, of course, intended to convey a positive image of the Soviet record here. Occasional remarks can be found in Soviet literature in favor of marriages between citizens of different countries.[31] Soviet diplomats have publicly assured their foreign colleagues that in the USSR "there were no prohibitions or restrictions as far as marrying foreigners was concerned"[32] and Soviet legal sources emphasize that Soviet "legislation features no additional conditions or restrictions whatever for the conclusion of marriage between citizens of the USSR and foreigners".[33] The numerous references to the provisions of the law are also meant to make it look as if the whole business is run in accordance with standard procedures, that these activities are governed by law alone and that, as distinct from Stalin's crude attempt to proscribe marriage between Soviet citizens and foreigners, the law today raises no egregious obstacles in the path of establishment of this kind of relationship. Formally speaking, the claim that Soviet law does not discriminate against marriage arrangements between aliens and Soviet nationals is accurate enough. The current Soviet leadership is too sophisticated to imitate Stalin's clumsy performance, at least in this case, and has preferred to maintain a benign legal facade on this stretch of road. The trouble is that behind the friendly legal exterior lies a vast expanse of administrative dominion where practice often succeeds in producing results contrary to those which reading the official script lets one anticipate.

To be fair, the point must first be driven home that Soviet conduct in this field has both its good and its bad moments. A recently published story tells how an American girl, who visited Moscow in the summer of 1979 and met her Russian husband–to–be during that trip, returned in 1980 to marry him: "When we walked into the Soviet wedding office speaking English, every conversation stopped and the people waiting all stared at us. But the officials working there took it all in stride." U.S. government sources estimate that about 60 Soviet–American marriages are registered annually — a major increase since the days before détente, although exact figures are not available.[34] A periodic State Department review, inter alia, of the USSR's compliance with the principles of Basket III of the Helsinki Final Act reported that the preponderance of binational marriages take place without incident, but added that in about 15% of the cases delays occur and can linger for years: thus, 19 binational marriages were logged between April and September 1979, while 5–10 projected marriages had been dragging for more than six months.[35]

For, one must remember that, the letter of the law notwithstanding, the Soviet regime has at its disposal a large assortment of practical devices that can make life difficult for a "mixed" couple wanting to marry and, by resort to these surreptitious methods, often even manages to derail such plans altogether. Among the bureaucratic pitfalls, the two–stage Soviet wedding process represents the initial obstacle:

couples register their desire to get married with the local authorities and then must wait 30 to 90 days for a wedding date. If the foreigner's visa is due to expire during that period, he or she must leave the country and reapply to come back for the wedding. In one case, Cathy Theimer, an American who became engaged to a Russian in 1972, tried in vain for years to return to Moscow to marry him, until in 1977 he finally received permission to emigrate himself.[36] Similarly, when Boris Spasskii, the former World Chess champion, decided to marry a French citizen, the Soviet government attempted to thwart him by refusing her an entry visa and denying him an exit visa and only later relented and allowed him to join her in Paris.[37] Many others have shared the experience of forcible physical separation that has prevented them from getting married either in the USSR or abroad.[38] And, in some instances Soviet officials simply invent new administrative requirements designed to prolong matters or scuttle the marriage on technical grounds.[39]

A balanced assessment of the track–record in the present sector should not omit to mention, however, that not just the Russians are capable of obstructionist tactics in this connection. The media has revealed, for example, that in June 1980, the U.S. Embassy in Moscow was expected officially

> "to restate its policy that American au pairs working for embassy families — whose visas to be here depend on embassy support — will lose that support within 48 hours if they marry a Russian.
>
> U.S. sources said the policy is being enforced with the goal of reducing marriages to Russians among embassy–related persons, and the complications that arise from them'."[40]

Ordinary desire to retain adequate control over how much fraternization takes place between the natives and foreign visitors accounts for many of the measures instituted by the regime to limit contact that might, inter alia, culminate in marriage plans being drawn up. An extra consideration, of course, is the fact that often the upshot of "mixed" marriage is a distinct interest in emigrating to the homeland of the foreign spouse and that, in turn, sets the stage for the eventual acquisition of a new nationality. Neither emigration nor denaturalization hold any appeal to the Soviet authorities, so to the extent that "mixed" marriages are very apt to increase the incidence of both phenomena, the concept itself ends up on the blacklist and the ruling apparatus is not about to encourage the practice by awarding the responsible parties instant exit visas. If the public claim that in the USSR marriages between foreigners and Soviet citizens meet with no official hindrance is shown on closer inspection to ring hollow, there is no reason to accept at face value local assertions that every Soviet citizen married to an alien has always freely exercised his or her option to go live abroad or continue to reside in the USSR either. Indeed, a very different picture emerges from the historical evidence.

Even when nothing untoward happens, a minimum of three to four months is bound to elapse before the Soviet partner receives an exit permit — and the American spouse may not be able to remain in the USSR for all of that period. Otherwise, the wait may last a long time. In 1979, for example, the U.S. State Department reported that during the preceding six months, at least four marriages had been blocked by Soviet refusal to give the American partner an entrance visa and in several instances travel permission for either the Soviet or American partner had been denied for more than six months. As of April 30, 1980, such problem cases officially numbered fifteen. With reference just to the October 1–March 31 period, it was estimated that ten exit or entry visas had been delayed more than six months for spouses and fiancés and American diplomatic sources now noted "an apparent tendency by the Soviet Government to delay entry visas to American fiancés of Soviet citizens".[41] In the most famous current case, Irina McClellan, a Russian who married an American professor in 1974, is still seeking Soviet consent to let her join him in America. Soviet citizens married to individuals from other countries do not necessarily fare better, as witness the experience of Iosif Kiblitskii whose efforts to be reunited with his German wife residing in Dússeldorf have met with no success for over a year and a half.[42]

The bitter irony of the situation is that, despite their government's soothing rhetoric, Soviet citizens are sufficiently aware of how unpredictable the process of emigration tends to be even when family cohesion is at stake that the officials sometimes can exploit these fears to induce people to change their mind altogether about undergoing the travails of the "mixed" marriage scene. According to reliable accounts, "Soviet authorities inform citizens that they will not allow them to leave the country in order to see their foreign spouses, and very often fulfill this threat". Episodes in which "a newly married husband or wife is not allowed to follow his or her foreign spouse to his or her home country, particularly if it is not a communist bloc country", are legion.[43] News of this type travels fast and a discreet hint from the proper quarters that an exit permit will not be issued following a "mixed" marriage has been known on occasion to have the effect of nipping such plans in the bud.

Finally, what are we to make, then, of the views expressed in a recently published piece rating "singleness of citizenship of members of a family"[44] as a keynote theme in this branch of Soviet jurisprudence — naturally, not in the sense of uniformity imposed by external fiat (whether executive, legislative or administrative), but a common affiliation reflecting the preference of the partners themselves. To discuss the matter intelligently, one has to disregard the record of so-called bureaucratic aberrations here the whole thrust of which serves to give the lie to that statement and concentrate instead on the formal indicia of the legal canon. However, at this level, too, the dilemma persists: How is one supposed to square the gist of the foregoing doctrinal pronouncement with the plain fact that, in practical terms, Soviet law does not provide any recognized means for people in such a position to convert readily into or out of Soviet citizenship with the object of gaining a shared status? The standard Soviet response to the query is to point out that local law subjects the process of acquisition or loss of Soviet citizenship to no special conditions or rigid time-limits: hence, we are told, in normal circumstances the rules are now applied so expeditiously that further relaxation would neither be warranted nor necessary. When the authorities are prepared to move quickly on these issues, the business can indeed consume very little time. Still, official generosity is not a fit substitute for hard legal assurance and when the government's attitude is less than benign, the lack of institutionalized avenues for obtaining relief puts the affected individual at a sore disadvantage in trying to get justice done.

The Stalinist xenophobia cited earlier as a likely reason for the abandonment in the late thirties of the concept sanctioning "simplified" entry into and release from

Soviet citizenship in connection with "mixed" marriages probably no longer accounts for the current leadership's aversion to the scheme. More plausible explanations for the persistence of that policy to date are: 1) the Soviet regime continues to be interested in making it look as if Soviet citizenship is a precious attribute that ought to be earned and not just picked up as part of some package deal; and, 2) the accent on juridical rectitude masks the reality of sweeping administrative discretion, combining to give the apparatus the best of both possible worlds — a good public image, but also full latitude to wreak its will sub rosa, and ample opportunity to discriminate in practice between fellow socialists and the class enemy without a shred of solid evidence in the legal repertory to impugn the propriety of the Kremlin's performance on that score.

4. Residence Abroad

The next item (Art. 5) poses a slight enigma. The cryptic statement that residence by a Soviet citizen abroad does not per se incur loss of Soviet citizenship is susceptible of two, equally plausible, interpretations. One can read the words as tacit confirmation of willingness by the regime to permit some of its citizens to emigrate without requiring that the decision cost the expatriates their Soviet citizenship. The dispensation might apply to particular categories of people, e.g., Soviet citizens of German descent lately being allowed to leave permanently for West Germany, or particular individuals (like the chess master Boris Spasskii, who lives in France) whose desire to live abroad the authorities find it advisable to humor but whom the Soviet government would prefer to keep on the official rolls out of sundry pragmatic considerations (e.g., national prestige). Or, the message perhaps boils down simply to saying in round–about fashion that a Soviet citizen who happens to set up residence on foreign soil should have no illusions that this circumstance alone will enable him (or her) unilaterally to shed Soviet citizenship, signaling that the consent of the Soviet state would still be necessary in such a situation. In the second case, nothing new will have been added to Soviet policy, except for the business of apparent legislative ratification of an established modus operandi.

As a matter of fact, the point is worth emphasizing that Soviet sources have consistently maintained that, where they are concerned, if a person resides abroad, the validity of that person's citizenship is in no way diminished by his refusal to exercise the rights granted by the legislation of his state and to fulfill the duties owed to his state. Regardless of how the individual living elsewhere elects to behave vis–à–vis his mother country, they claim, "the absence of de facto realization of rights and duties which enter into the concept of citizenship does not terminate their juridical effect" in that thereby "citizenship suffers no legal injury, it only suffers factual injury".[45] Given the attitude that even a person's express wish to disassociate himself from the state whose citizenship he is formally vested with cannot legally achieve the ends of denaturalization, a person's mere physical relocation from the Soviet Union to a different country logically cannot be expected to have a greater impact on the emigrant's citizenship designation.

The language of the 1978 statute thus clearly rejects the principle that an inherent juridical connection exists between the phenomenon of expatriation and citizenship status and, indeed, asserts the opposite view, namely, that these institutions are mutually independent. To the extent, then, that the current exodus of Jews or occasional egress of Koreans from the USSR is predicated on the prior surrender of Soviet citizenship by the members of either group when seeking exit permits, the practice runs counter both to the spirit and the letter of relevant Soviet legislation and represents an administrative departure from the prescribed norm that is presumably warranted because certain unique conditions distinguish these contingencies. (This side of the picture is examined in detail below in the chapter on emigration and citizenship.)

Otherwise, the act of duly relinquishing Soviet citizenship is neither a prerequisite for departure from the country nor a prologue to emigration. Many accounts have circulated in the west in the last several years of people who, driven to desperation by the regime's repeated rejection of their requests to leave the Soviet Union (or the general experience of repression), have resorted to the expedient of "voluntarily renouncing their Soviet citizenship and sending their Soviet papers back to the authorities".[46] Whatever symbolic or psychological value such gestures may have in dramatizing the determination of the people involved to win release from further sojourn in the USSR and persuading the local apparatus to let them go, the procedure itself has no legal meaning. In those instances where any of these individuals subsequently received exit visas from the competent organs, no public mention was made of their purported attempt single–handedly to waive Soviet citizenship and, for the record, their petitions were treated in routine style.[47] Legal subtleties notwithstanding, chances are good that the demonstrative impact of the "opt–out" has often proved sufficient to change the bureaucracy's mind and get it to disgorge the desired exit permit without ever admitting the true reasons for doing so: the rules remain the same, but on a completely ad hoc basis the party concerned is all of a sudden found to be eligible for the benefits that they feature. In the legal sense, the whole business is highly irregular and no viable precedent is set here to profit others; yet, insofar as the individual somehow succeeds by these devious methods to extract once in a while a tangible concession from his political custodians and substantially improve his position versus the state machine, these egregious devices for bypassing the rigid strictures of the written law and surmounting the attendant administrative hurdles hold out a measure of hope for bettering the individual's lot on the Soviet citizenship–cum–emigration scene.

At any rate, the wording of Article 5 is as close as the statute comes to formulating a general acknowledgment of the possibility of emigration from the Soviet Union and the potential effects of that phenomenon on the citizenship status of the expatriates. The actual terms controlling the exercise of these "exit rights" remain an administrative matter and habitually escape legislative attention. Thus, the statute sheds no light on the subject. Conscious of the gap in the script, the regime may have staged a token effort on the occasion of the parliamentary "debates" over the merits of the proposed legislation to erase the discrepancy by letting one of the scheduled speakers for the bill, associated (be it noted) with the top echelons of the department of internal affairs,[48] publicly assure the audience that, at the subordinate level, various steps had already been instituted to upgrade the quality of the work in handling applications for departure from the USSR. According to the source, "... the procedures for drawing up official papers for travel abroad have been simplified, the amount of time consumed in considering requests to leave the country have been reduced ..." Reportedly, the end result of all these initiatives is that:

> "The overwhelming majority of citizens who address themselves to the organs of internal affairs seeking visas to travel abroad with the aim of family reunification or out of other motivations — tourism, trips, cures — receive such permission in the prescribed manner."[49]

Needless to say, the authenticity of these claims cannot be independently verified, but the available data plainly favor the contrary conclusion.

Seeing how insistent Soviet spokesmen sound on the theme of the indissolubility of the ties that bind the Soviet citizen abroad to his home state and the array of reciprocal rights and duties that stamps the relationship, one would think that such close entente automatically assumed the right of the Soviet citizen living on foreign soil to return to his country at will. Elsewhere, this freedom is virtually taken for granted, even though local politicians may engage in less public fanfare than their Soviet counterparts about the total communion reigning between the individual and the state in their respective case. By contrast, although the topic is not often discussed in Soviet literature, when Soviet legal experts do venture to tackle its technical aspects, the results of their analysis verge on chaos. The mental confusion is not accidental and accurately reflects the glaring asymmetry that marks the Soviet government's treatment of its nationals abroad.

Typically, doctrinal assessment here starts from the proposition that international law does not require states to ensure their own citizens an unconditional right to return once they go abroad. Should a particular state choose to guarantee such a right, it must observe the commitment, but the duty then is not imposed by international law and owes its existence to municipal law alone. Noting that some bourgeois lawyers claim that international law mandates that each state accept its own citizens back and that the obligation operates between states independently of whether or not a norm to that effect figures in the corresponding domestic legal inventory, Soviet legal authors respond that this viewpoint cannot be accepted without reservation. While conceding that a state cannot burden other states with its citizens, they still try to avoid painting themselves into a corner by insisting that the state's duty to let its citizens enter its territory arises only in the event that the foreign state refuses to allow them to establish local residence. In this version, the individual ends up with considerably less than what is generally understood to be a "right to return" to his Motherland and the state retains a great deal more discretion in granting reentry permits to its citizens than is commonly deemed to be proper.

Now, on the matter of recognizing analogous rights for ex-citizens living abroad, the Soviet position can afford to be both quite unambiguous and uncompromisingly negative. Soviet legal specialists mince no words in criticizing those of their bourgeois confrères who consider that a state must admit to its territory former citizens currently without another citizenship if other states deny them the right to reside within their borders. Their first objection is that, in purely logistical terms, such a situation is not too likely to occur because it is difficult to imagine that not a single country can be found that will extend its hospitality to a person in that predicament. Next, they fault the excessively liberal scenario on the legal grounds that invoking an international law obligation to permit this class of people to return to the territory of the state whose citizenship they once possessed would infringe on the sovereignty of the state concerned since the latter would then be stuck with individuals who are no longer its citizens, — as, we are caustically reminded, the Soviet Union already had occasion to point out way back at the 1930 Hague conference.[50]

The question, as mentioned earlier, is not just an academic one, for history records that the Soviet authorities have in fact discriminated on that score against a sizable contingent of individuals residing abroad equipped with Soviet papers that do not automatically entitle their owners to travel to the USSR. In the immediate post-war years, for example, the Soviet government promulgated a series of decrees, virtually identical in content, mutatis mutandis, that enfranchised persons currently residing in Manchuria, the province of Sinkiang, the cities of Shanghai and Tientsin, in France, Yugoslavia, Bulgaria, Japan, Czechoslovakia, and Belgium who on November 7, 1917, were subjects of the former Russian empire, as well as persons who, having possessed Soviet citizenship, lost it, together with their children, to recover Soviet citizenship. Those among them who wished their Soviet citizenship reinstated had to submit an application to that effect with the local Soviet diplomatic mission, appending to it documents establishing their identity and the fact that they were at one time subjects of the old Russian empire or Soviet citizens. These papers would be examined on the spot and if they were found to satisfy the requirements of the law, a permis de séjour *(vid na zhitel'stvo* or *sovzagranvid)* would forthwith be delivered to the petitioner. Anyone else who could ask for the return of his or her Soviet citizenship pursuant to these regulations and did not do so in time could subsequently seek admission to Soviet citizenship in the ordinary fashion.[51]

Apropos the present discussion, these new or "revived" citizens of the Soviet Union could not assert the right to go and live in the USSR on the strength alone of the certificates issued to them, but had to secure separate authorization from the Soviet officialdom if they wanted to transfer their abode to the Soviet Union. Or, as an informed Soviet commentator preferred to put it:

> "The establishment of a new legal expression 'Soviet residence permit' meant that the corresponding category of persons was recognized as citizens of the USSR and, consequently, that they hereafter came under the legal protection of the Soviet Union.
>
> As regards their entry within the confines of the USSR, that question was decided specially in each single case independently of the admission of the given category of persons into Soviet citizenship. This was dictated as much by the interests of guaranteeing state security as by the imperativeness of proper resettlement of said citizens and their labor placement in the Soviet Union."[52]

A good illustration of how this approach sometimes worked is what happened in Yugoslavia after the war. Thus, it is reported that, when in 1948 an ideological dispute embittered relations between the USSR and Yugoslavia and Belgrade decided to rid itself of all Soviet nationals in the country (several thousand people most of whom had obtained Soviet citizenship in conformity with the decree of June 14, 1946), the Yugoslav government was finally compelled to resort to mass expulsion because Moscow would not give its consent to the repatriation of these individuals, despite the fact that they ostensibly held perfectly valid Soviet documents.[53]

The experiment in "group conversion" (or "re–baptism") has not been replicated since, but the practice of issuing *sovzagranvidy* on an individual basis is still part of the Soviet diplomatic repertory. (See Form No. 52 — Questionnaire to be filled by the person requesting the issuance or prolongation of a *sovzagranvid* and submitted to the local Soviet consulate.) One is fairly safe in assuming that a person who now acquires such a document occupies essentially the same position as those who availed themselves of the comparable opportunities offered by the 1945–1947 crop of edicts in that his admission to Soviet territory calls for extra approval by the competent Soviet agencies and possession of a Soviet "residence permit" by itself is not enough to enable its owner to exercise his "right to go home". In short, this procedure acts to create a separate category of Soviet "nationals" eligible to live abroad and, by virtue of their special identification papers, to count on receiving legal protection from the Soviet government. The regime is seemingly willing to sanction a juridical association of sorts with these expatriate elements as long as the individuals involved are content to maintain their foreign domicile, but insists on additional screening should any member of this emigré community express the desire to move to the USSR. In "exile", these people serve a certain purpose as far as the Soviet authorities are concerned and letting them have Soviet documents is the price the apparatus is prepared to pay to enable it to make proper use of these strategically placed human resources. The prospect of their presence on Soviet soil, however, is far less attractive and, confronted with that possibility, the Soviets have opted for a restrictive policy where further scrutiny of the aspiring immigrant's record must precede his or her relocation to Soviet soil. Going by the common concept of what constitutes a "right", the current version falls short of the acceptable norm by a wide margin.

Article 6 of the 1978 citizenship law also deals with the business of Soviet citizens outside their homeland and, following the language of Article 33 of the 1977 federal charter, declares that "citizens of the USSR abroad enjoy the defense and protection of the Soviet state". Taken literally, the formula contains nothing new and echoes a universal principle of contemporary international relations. Soviet commentary on the item's meaning is quite unenlightening and boils down to a string of general clichés. We are told, for instance, that defense by the Soviet state of USSR citizens abroad figures as a component of state sovereignty in matters of citizenship, that ensuring such defense is both the duty and the sovereign right of the state in that the Soviet state cannot leave its citizens without protection while no other state can on its own initiative take it upon itself to protect Soviet citizens. The fact that the norm features in the text of the latest Soviet constitution (for the first time in Soviet constitutional experience) and the current Law on Citizenship of the USSR testifies to the sovereign will of the Soviet state and, coincidentally, the recognition of its responsibility for the fate of its citizens. None of this, according to local exegesis, is contrary to international law or infringes on the interests and sovereignty of foreign states.[54]

The foregoing picture is fairly straightforward, but it fails to explain where lies the substantive connection between the gist of this constitutional and statutory pronouncement and the routine of citizenship practice. Two nexuses can be suggested. First, Soviet spokesmen have in the past had occasion to criticize some states for trying to usurp the right of certain fellow–states to protect their own citizens. West Germany's behavior vis–à–vis East Germany in this respect has been the object of frequent Soviet (and, of course, East German)[55] denunciation: thus, Bonn's attempts to arrogate itself stewardship of the citizens of the German Democratic Republic have repeatedly been branded as interventionistic and in flagrant violation of the latter's sovereignty. So, the move to assert that Soviet citizens abroad enjoy the defense and protection of the Soviet state could be aimed at preventing any other state from offering them similar services and thereby setting the stage for a de facto transfer of allegiance from the USSR to the new "bodyguard", with the probable idea of eventually consummating the switch in a juridical sense as well.

Second, the authors of the law may have been motivated by a negative rationale. As has been observed, since "... the granting of emigration permits to Israel (except for a few isolated earlier cases) started only after the Six Day War, when the USSR broke off diplomatic relations with Israel, it became arguable whether the USSR could 'protect', 'assist' or 'defend' its citizens in Israel, and therefore had to ask emigrants to Israel to surrender their citizenship".[56] In other words, given an overt commitment to defend and protect its citizens abroad, the USSR now adopted the position that whenever its citizens chose to go to a country with which the USSR did not maintain diplomatic relations and, hence, where it could not afford them direct legal protection and defense, the sole viable option then would be to require them to surrender their Soviet citizenship upon departure for such a destination. Remaining a Soviet citizen while residing in a country where the USSR could not exercise its rights and fulfill its duties to safeguard the expatriate's interests would thus not be considered an acceptable situation because the attributes of neither citizenship nor state sovereignty could be effectuated in full under these adverse circumstances, forcing the authorities to demand prior relinquishment of Soviet citizenship if the individual concerned nevertheless insisted on taking that awkward route. The fact that Jewish emigrés nominally heading for Israel and Korean emigrés with ties to South Korea have so far been singled out for this treatment lends credence to that interpretation.

One last comment is in order here. Despite references to the defense and protection of USSR citizens abroad being both a right and a duty of the Soviet state, the conclusion is inevitable that right it may indeed be, but that where duty is at stake, at best what is meant is moral obligation to rescue when trouble strikes. The affected soul is certainly without the practical means to compel the Soviet government to come to his assistance, so whatever "duty" the state owes him in this context ultimately just depends on its own discretion and, properly speaking, should not even be dignified by that designation. The next question, however, is what avenues of redress are open to the private party in the event his home state does not live up to its "obligation" and, to all intents and purposes, leaves him in the lurch. Logic suggests that the aggrieved person might in that case be free to discard the citizenship of the derelict state and seek a better sponsor elsewhere, except that Soviet authorities would be most unlikely to go along with this idea on the premise that: 1) they could never by guilty of that kind of failure; and, 2) denaturalization always requires the state's consent and the "divorce" cannot possibly be accomplished by the individual acting alone, no matter what the alleged grounds.

5. Extradition

The clause stipulating that "a citizen of the USSR may not be surrendered to a foreign state" (Art. 7) represents a novel feature of Soviet citizenship legislation. Soviet doctrine did not always subscribe to this principle and, indeed, earlier on the contrary thesis was vigorously propounded, namely, that "Soviet law, to which is alien the narrowly nationalistic outlook, does not prohibit the extradition of our own citizens, siding in this respect with the Anglo–Saxon system".[57] Subsequently, though, Stalinist dogma took its toll and Soviet sources now made the proposition sound self–evident that, "in view of the fundamental and essential differences between the character of Soviet legislation and the legislation of capitalist states, Soviet citizens who have committed crimes against the interests of foreign states are not subject to rendition and must bear responsibility in conformity with Soviet laws".[58] After Stalin's death, local scribes dropped the strident tone, but continued to preach the message that "the Soviet Union does not surrender its citizens who have committed crimes on the territory of other states to these states" and that, "in these circumstances, the question is resolved by Soviet judicial organs in accordance with operative criminal legislation".[59] The rule was confirmed in the series of bilateral treaties on legal assistance in civil, family and criminal cases which the USSR concluded with most of its "socialist" allies in 1957–1958, and with Yugoslavia in 1962, Iraq in 1973, Bulgaria in 1975 (replacing the 1957 accord), the German Democratic Republic in 1979 (superseding the 1957 agreement), Greece and Vietnam in 1981.[60] Thus, the script of Article 7 duly follows the pattern of recent precedent in this domain and, of course, thereby affixes to the policy a formal legislative cachet.

Otherwise, Soviet analysts add little to the picture. They claim, for instance, that the theme of non–extradition of one's own citizens is closely related to the concept of defense of one's citizens abroad in that both envisage the citizen's accountability to his state. Consequently, a citizen of the USSR committing a crime abroad is answerable under the laws of the Soviet state, unless the crime is of an international nature.[61] Neither insight is particularly earth–shaking.

At any rate, the linkage between extradition and citizenship is a tenuous one and my guess is that the reason the subject of extradition was brought up in the 1978 citizenship statute was simply in order to underline that a benefit associated with possession of Soviet citizenship was the inadmissibility of its owner's surrender to a foreign state: how much the object of this solicitude is apt to appreciate such a benefit is something the reader will have to decide for himself.

NOTES

1. V.V. Polianskii, "Printsipy sovetskogo grazhdanstva", *Sovetskoe gosudarstvo i pravo*, 1980, No.5, pp.126–127 (hereafter abbr. as *SGiP*). The author notes parenthetically that the USSR Constitution of 1924 might be viewed as having followed a similar principle of letting the union republics have their own legislation in the field of citizenship since the federal branch was only charged with promulgating "basic legislation in the field of union citizenship", (p.127, fn.13). Nevertheless, he says, the formula was not put into effect.
2. G.I. Tunkin, "Zakon o grazhdanstve SSSR", *SGiP*, 1979, No.7, p.24.
3. *Ibid.*, pp.24–25.
4. *Vedomosti Verkhovnogo Soveta SSSR*, 1979, No.25, Art.436 (hereafter abbr. as *VVS SSSR*); English translation in *Review of Socialist Law*, 1979, No.4, pp.468– 469.
5. *Pravda*, *Izvestiia*, December 2, 1978 (hereafter abbr. as *Pr.*, *Izv.*, respectively); *VVS SSSR*, 1978, No.48, Art.817. Also, *International Affairs*, 1979, No.1, p.145.
6. *Khronika tekushchikh sobytii*, 1979, vyp.51, pp.208–210.
   A somewhat different account of this episode appears in V. Bukovskii, *I vozvrashchaetsiia veter ...*, New York, 1978, p.364. It adds the interesting detail that during the interrogation session Andropov long studied the passport and other documents and then reportedly said to his assistants, poking a finger at Sharygin's passport: "Why do you keep repeating: Englishman, Englishman ... He was after all born here, in the USSR." On the other hand, this version omits to mention that Sharygin had not completed formalities to acquire British citizenship and had traveled to the USSR with British papers containing a specific reservation concerning the availability of diplomatic protection in the Soviet Union and the East European countries.
7. Technically speaking, even if the de cujus had procured a full–fledged British passport stamped with a Soviet entry visa, he might have met with the same fate given the Soviet regime's refusal to acknowledge the validity of a foreign citizenship where, in the opinion of the Soviet authorities, the bearer also possesses Soviet citizenship. In this case, the "defective" passport made the KGB's task easier, but it did not alter the basic situation.
8. H.–J. Uibopuu, "Soviet Nationality: Privilege or Burden? An International Lawyer's View", *Israel Yearbook on Human Rights*, 1977, Vol.7, p.61, and fns.37 and 38.
9. *Ibid.*, citing G. Geilke, *Das Staatsangehörigkeitsrecht der Sowjetunion*, Frankfurt am Main–Berlin, 1964, p.191.
10. H.–J. Uibopuu, *op. cit.*, p.62.
11. Iu. Lurii, "Sovetskii zakon o grazhdanstve i emigranty", *Russkaia Mysl'*, May 31, 1979, p.6.
12. V.S. Shevtsov, *Grazhdanstvo v sovetskom soiuznom gosudarstve*, Moscow, 1969, p.125, fn.3, points out that Article 5 of the 1938 citizenship statute "textually reproduced Art.7 of the Code on Marriage, Family and Guardianship of the Uzbek SSR".
13. E.g., B. Volin, *Grazhdanin SSSR*, Moscow, 1938, p.17. In the same vein, A.I. Lepeshkin, *Kurs Sovetskogo gosudarstvennogo prava*, Moscow, 1961, Vol.1, pp. 461, 469; F.I. Kozhevnikov, *Sovetskoe gosudarstvo i mezhdunarodnoe pravo, 1917– 1947 gg.*, Moscow, 1948, p.166; *Diplomaticheskii slovar'*, Moscow, 1960, Vol.1, p.405.
   For similar comments by non–Soviet authors, see D.V. Sandifer, "Soviet Citizenship", *American Journal of International Law*, 1936, No.4, p.624; T.A. Taracouzio, *The Soviet Union and International Law*, New York, 1935, pp.90–91; R. Dufour, "La Nationalité dans l'U.R.S.S.", *Revue Générale de Droit International Public*, 1930, pp.511, 516.
14. Cf., I. Trainin, "K voprosu o grazhdanstve", *Sovetskoe gosudarstvo*, 1938, No.5, p.70.

15. *VVS SSSR*, 1947, No.10; *Sbornik zakonov SSSR i ukazov Prezidiuma Verkhovnogo Soveta SSSR za 1947 god*, Moscow, 1948, p.36.
16. *VVS SSSR*, 1948, No.6; *Sbornik zakonov SSSR i ukazov Prezidiuma Verkhovnogo Soveta SSSR za 1948 god*, Moscow, 1949, p.17.
17. F.I. Kozhevnikov, *op. cit.*, p.167.
18. A.Ia. Berchenko, "Voprosy sovetskogo grazhdanstva", in *Torzhestvo leninskoi natsional'noi politiki*, Moscow, 1963, p.276.
19. Cf., V.S. Shevtsov, *op. cit.*, p.126.
20. Text in *VVS SSSR*, 1958, No.28, Art.373; *Sbornik deistvuiushchikh dogovorov, soglashenii i konventsii, zakliuchennykh SSSR s inostrannymi gosudarstvami*, Moscow, 1961, Vol.20, pp.438–442 (hereafter abbr. as *SDD*).
21. See, for instance, M. Rusakov, "Sovetskoe grazhdanstvo (Praktika RSFSR)", *Administrativnyi vestnik*, 1930, No.3, pp.18–20; *idem*, "Brak i grazhdanstvo po sovetskomu zakonodatel'stvu", *ibid.*, 1927, No.10–11, pp.104–109; N.I. Palienko, "Pravo grazhdanstva v Soiuze SSR", *Vestnik sovetskoi iustitsii*, 1925, No.7(41), p.272; S.S. Kishkin, *Sovetskoe grazhdanstvo*, Moscow, 1925, pp.44–47.
22. G.I. Tunkin, *op. cit.*, p.25. It must be admitted that the tone of the 1978 citizenship act matches that of the 1979 Convention on the Elimination of All Forms of Discrimination against Women insofar as the latter declares (Art.9) that:

    "State Parties shall grant women equal rights with men to acquire, change or retain their nationality. They shall ensure in particular that neither marriage to an alien nor change of nationality by the husband during marriage shall automatically change the nationality of the wife, render her stateless or force upon her the nationality of the husband.

    States Parties shall grant women equal rights with men with respect to the nationality of their children."

    The USSR signed the Convention on July 17, 1980, and ratified it on Dec.19, 1980. *VVS SSSR*, 1982, No.25, Art.464.
23. S.V. Chernichenko, *Mezhdunarodno–pravovye voprosy grazhdanstva*, Moscow, 1968, p.104.
24. *Ibid.*, p.117, citing *Mezhdunarodnaia zhizn'*, 1930, No.5, p.79.
25. *Soviet News*, 1976, No.5819, p.35, and 1980, No.6024, p.183.
26. See the figures for the city of Kiev reported in G.K. Matveev, "Voprosy sovetskogo kollizionnogo semeinogo prava", *Pravovedenie*, 1972, No.2, p.99, fn.2, reproduced on p.10 above (text accompanying fn.32 in Chapter I).
27. K.L. Emelianova, "Nekotorye voprosy sovershenstvovania deiatel'nosti organov ZAGS", *Pravovedenie*, 1968, No.4, p.102.
28. Approved by resolution of the RSFSR Council of Ministers of October 17, 1969, No.592, *Sbornik postanovlenii Pravitel'stva RSFSR*, 1969, No.22, Art.123. The Instruction entered into force on November 1, 1969.
29. *Kommentarii k zakonodatel'stvu o registratsii aktov grazhdanskogo sostoiania*, Moscow, 1977, p.186.
30. *Ibid.*, p.188.
31. E.g., G.K. Matveev, in *SGiP*, 1974, No.5, p.151.
32. Report of the Human Rights Committee, General Assembly, Official Records: 33rd session, Supplement No.40 (A/33/40), p.73.
33. *Kommentarii* ... (note 29 above), p.185. This principle has now been legislatively confirmed in the Law on the legal status of foreign citizens in the USSR of June 24, 1981 (scheduled to enter into force on January 1, 1982) — Article 17. Text of the Law and the Resolution putting it into effect in *Pravda* and *Izvestiia*, June 25, 1981.
34. Thomas Kent, "U.S., Soviets Create Own Detente", *The Korea Herald*, June 6,

1980, p.5.

35. U.S. Department of State, Bureau of Public Affairs, *Implementation of Helsinki Accord, June 1–November 30, 1979*, 7th Semiannual Report, Special Report No.62, p.15.

36. Thomas Kent, *loc. cit.*

37. Yu. Luryi, "Soviet Family Law", *Manitoba Law Journal*, 1980, No.2, p.129.

38. Note, for instance, the letter from Yelena Bonner Sakharov to the editor of the *New York Times*, July 25, 1980, p.A24, appealing on behalf of her son's fiancée for an exit permit to enable her to leave the USSR and go to the United States to be reunited with the man she wanted to marry.

39. Yu. Luryi, *op. cit.*, pp.129–130, mentions certain incidents where the authorities plainly tried to fabricate reasons to prevent the conclusion of particular "mixed" marriages. In one case, K. Fedicheva, prima ballerina of the Leningrad Ballet, managed to marry an American, but then was suddenly notified by the local procurator that her previous divorce was not valid and that therefore her latest marriage was null and void. Apparently, the entire affair was utter nonsense and had been manufactured whole–cloth for the occasion. "Only after great trouble and pressure from Western public opinion, was she able to exercise her right to enter into a marriage of her choice and to leave the U.S.S.R." In another case, a Canadian slated to marry a Soviet citizen was unexpectedly informed by the head of the office of registry of civil status that he needed special permission from the Executive Committee of the City Soviet in order to get married. Knowing that there was no legal ground for the demand, the Canadian citizen strongly objected and "the marriage was finally registered".

40. Thomas Kent, *loc. cit.*

41. U.S. Department of State, Bureau of Public Affairs, *Implementation of the Helsinki Accord*, 6th semiannual report, Dec. 1, 1978–May 31, 1979, Special Report No.54, p.16; *ibid.*, 8th semiannual report, Dec. 1, 1979–May 31, 1980, Special Report No.73, pp.15–16.

42. *Khronika tekushchikh sobytii*, 1980, vyp.53, pp.142–143.

43. Yu. Luryi, *op. cit.*, p.129.

44. V.V. Polianskii, *op. cit.*, pp.123, 125.

45. S.V. Chernichenko, *op. cit.*, p.25.

46. See, for instance, the report in Radio Liberty Research, RL 21/77, p.2, that G.D. Reimar was arrested on the grounds that he tried to renounce Soviet citizenship. "An additional 200 Germans living in Alma–Ata Oblast' also submitted their passports to city authorities, indicating a renunciation of their citizenship in protest against being refused permission to emigrate from the USSR." Also, A. Zariņš, "Latvian Dissident Renounces Soviet Citizenship for the Eleventh Time", RL 214/77, concerning the case of Gunars Rode, unusual in that while wishing to shed Soviet citizenship, the person indicated no interest in emigrating and apparently wanted to remain in the USSR in a stateless capacity.

For other such episodes: *New York Times*, February 8, 1979, p.A10, the case of Mustafa Dzhemilev; *Khronika zashchity prav v SSSR*, 1973, vyp.3, p.35, the case of Lev Eliashevich; 1973, vyp.4, p.34, the case of the Stezhko family; 1975, vyp.15, the case of Daniil Shumuk; 1977, vyp.27, p.15, "O presledovanii nemtsev v Litve", Dokument No.6; *Khronika tekushchikh sobytii*, 1976, vyp.42, p.57, the case of Vasilii Romaniuk.

47. The same is true where the request for emigration is turned down. In the case of V. Nekipelov, *Khronika tekushchikh sobytii*, 1980, vyp.53, pp.139–140, for instance, the federal Presidium formally rejected his application to emigrate to Israel and relinquish Soviet citizenship taking no notice of the fact that he had earlier written to that organ to renounce his Soviet citizenship and had mailed his Soviet passport along.

48. Lieutenant–General Viktor S. Paputin, later reported to have died in Afghanistan in the course of the operation to remove President Amin. See, David Binder, "U.S. Links Afghan Events and Soviet General's Death", *New York Times*, Feb. 3, 1980, p.10.
49. V.S. Paputin, Speech in *Izv.*, Dec. 3, 1978.
50. S.V. Chernichenko, *op. cit.*, pp.84–85, citing *Mezhdunarodnaia zhizn'*, 1930, No. 5, p.79.
51. *VVS SSSR*, 1945, No.78; 1946, No.2; 1946, No.21; 1946, No.36; 1946, No.37; 1947, No.18; *Sbornik zakonov SSSR i ukazov Prezidiuma Verkhovnogo Soveta SSSR (1938g.*–noiabr' *1958g.*), Moscow, 1959, pp.78–84.
52. A.I. Lepeshkin, *op. cit.*, p.478.
53. J. Vernant, *The Refugee in the Post–War World*, New Haven, 1953, p.55.
54. V.V. Polianskii, *op. cit.*, p.126.
55. E.g., G. Riege, "Die Staatsangehörigkeitsdoktrin der BRD — Interpretation und Konsequenzen", *Neue Justiz*, 1979, No.2, p.70.
56. S.J. Roth, "The New Soviet Citizenship Law and Jewish Emigration", Institute of Jewish Affairs *Research Report*, USSR/79/3, p.3.
57. V.V. Egor'ev, G.N. Lashkevich, M.A. Plotkin, B.D. Rozenblium, *Zakonodatel'stvo i mezhdunarodnye dogovory Soiuza SSR i soiuznykh respublik o pravovom polozhenii inostrannykh fizicheskikh i iuridicheskikh lits*, Moscow, 1926, p.90.
58. O.E. Polents, in E.A. Korovin, ed., *Mezhdunarodnoe pravo*, Moscow, 1951, p.254.
59. Cf., I.I. Solodkin, in M.D. Shargorodskii & N.S. Beliaev, eds., *Sovetskoe ugolovnoe pravo, chast' obshchaia*, Leningrad, 1960, p.191. *Idem*, in N.A. Beliaev & M.D. Shargorodskii, eds., *Kurs Sovetskogo ugolovnogo prava, chast' obshchaia*, Leningrad, 1968, Vol.1, p.143; M.A. Gelfer, in V.M. Chkhikvadze, ed., *Sovetskoe ugolovnoe pravo, obshchaia chast'*, Moscow, 1959, p.80.
60. See the author's "The Soviet Union and International Co–operation in Legal Matters: Criminal Law — The Current Phase", *International and Comparative Law Quarterly*, October 1970, pp.626–670. For text of the treaties with Iraq and the GDR, *VVS SSSR*, 1980, No.35, Art.712, and *SDD*, Moscow, 1976, Vol.30, pp.91– 100; with Bulgaria, *VVS SSSR*, 1976, No.8, Art.133; and with Vietnam and Greece, *ibid.*, 1982, No.44, Art.827 and No.45, Art.839.
61. V.V. Polianskii, *op. cit.*, p.126. Also, V. Shevtsov, *Grazhdanstvo SSSR*, Moscow, 1980, p.41, fn.1.

DUAL NATIONALITY

I. General Principles

On the face of it, the Soviet position on the question of dual (or multiple) nationality sounds deceptively plain: within the frontiers of the USSR, the Soviet regime simply refuses to recognize the legal consequences of dual (or multiple) nationality in cases involving persons also in possession of a valid Soviet citizenship.

In the earlier legislation, this rejection was made explicit. The Decree of the Council of People's Commissars of the RSFSR of August 22, 1921, already featured a clause (Art. 8) to the effect that "persons residing within the territory of the RSFSR admitted to Russian citizenship and not having liquidated their relations derived from the citizenship (nationality) of a foreign state, are deprived of the right to appeal for protection of their interests to the government of the state whose citizens they formerly were". And, the Circular of the People's Commissariat for Foreign Affairs of the RSFSR of December 8, 1921, concerning the admission of foreigners to Russian citizenship further embroidered on that theme by directing that "persons admitted to Soviet citizenship are required to sign a statement, within a month from the date of receiving the notification rof admissionst, that they are familiar with the contents of Article 8 of the Decree of the Council of People's Commissars of August 22, 1921, whereupon their foreign passports are exchanged for the passports established for the citizens of the RSFSR".

The first federal enactment on citizenship followed a somewhat different course in this respect, neither going into any details regarding the status in Soviet law of a naturalized foreigner vested with two or more citizenships nor demanding an affidavit from the de cujus declaring that he fully comprehends and accepts these conditions. All it said on that score was that "foreign citizens admitted to citizenship of the Union of Soviet Socialist Republics enjoy no rights and owe no duties pertaining to citizenship of other states". The Regulations of 1930 and 1931 repeated the 1924 formula verbatim. As explained at the time by a leading Soviet legal specialist, "thereby was acknowledged the inevitability of dual citizenship in certain instances and was correctly understood that for persons with dual citizenship Soviet citizenship alone is recognized".[1] The observation is a true indication of how the statutory provision was interpreted and applied as a matter of policy. Technically speaking, however, the statement is inaccurate on two counts: first, legislation so far contained no reference to the concept of "non-recognition" of dual nationality stricto sensu; and, second, although administrative routine probably did extend the so–called "non–recognition" rule to all cases of dual nationality, the express language of the law still only concerned foreigners who may have gained entry to Soviet citizenship through the process of formal naturalization while purportedly retaining some connection with their former nationality.

Oddly enough, the 1938 Citizenship Act opted to maintain complete silence on the subject. Nonetheless, the incident marked no change in the official Soviet attitude toward this important issue, for Soviet commentators were quick to point out that the sole reason for the omission rested in the fact that the statute was "undoubtedly taking into account the principle firmly anchored in Soviet law that an individual with dual citizenship cannot claim the status of a foreigner if he is simultaneously a Soviet citizen".[2] The Soviet diplomatic record furnished added support for that proposition, as witness the report that "in the Note of the Ministry of Foreign Affairs [of the USSR] to the Government of the German Federal Republic of May 29, 1956, on the results of a check of the list submitted by the Embassy of the GFR in Moscow to the Soviet authorities of persons allegedly possessing German citizenship and situated on the territory of the USSR, it is indicated that the legislation of the USSR does not foresee dual citizenship".[3] Lastly, most of the pertinent Soviet sources chose to emphasize that "it is generally recognized in international practice that a person having double citizenship cannot, while on the territory of one State of which he is a citizen, cite his obligations to the other State of which he is also a citizen".[4] Ergo, runs the inference, the chance absence of legislative provisions announcing as much does nothing to alter the old familiar picture, since international law reputedly embodies an identical norm and that would suffice to achieve the selfsame objective.

So, the policy here remained precisely as before. As for the formal lacuna in the law, Soviet authors themselves characterized it as unfortunate and, especially in the sixties, the view was frankly being voiced that

> "the legislation on Soviet citizenship must, obviously, contain a general norm barring dual citizenship. In our opinion, the norm of Article 4 of the Regulations of 1930 and 1931 to the effect that citizens of the USSR do not enjoy rights and carry no obligations associated with belonging to the citizenship or nationality of another state should be reinstated."[5]

The realization must soon have dawned on the advocates of reform that bare reliance on the corresponding clause of the 1930/1931 statutes would not achieve the desired goal given the narrow scope of its wording. Thus, the perception prompted them later to switch in favor of featuring a provision analogous to the 1930/1931 version, but suitably adapted to endow its contents with a "universal character",[6] i.e., enunciated in terms designed to encompass every species of dual nationality instead of, as in the older model, just the sort begotten by the mechanics of naturalization.

The local solons have responded by including in the text of the 1978 Citizenship Act Article 8 postulating that "a person, who is a citizen of the USSR, is not recognized as having citizenship of a foreign state". The main stylistic differences between the latest formula and the earlier treatment are worth recapitulating. First, as already mentioned, the only dimension of dual nationality that Soviet legislation had dealt with in the past was the kind engendered on occasion by the acquisition of Soviet citizenship by an alien through normal naturalization channels, the regime apparently feeling called upon to warn any person contemplating such a step of the possible repercussions should he or she in the process incur dual or multiple nationality. Hence, where an act of will on the part of the interested individual lay at the bottom of his subsequent difficulties stemming from conflicting allegiances to two or more states, the Soviet government took the precaution of letting him know ahead of time that thereafter it would attach no legal significance to the ties binding him to a foreign country and that he would not be permitted to seek refuge in a foreign citizenship to evade his civic responsibilities to the USSR. Quite clearly, advance notice of this sort would serve no good purpose where a person ended up with dual or multiple nationality through no fault of his own which, presumably, is why no reference was made to that common contingency.

One result of the most recent change, of course, is the statutory affirmation expressis verbis of the concept of "non-recognition" of the phenomenon of dual (or multiple) citizenship — in the double sense that the present legislation addresses itself to the issue (in marked contrast to its 1938 predecessor) and adopts that particular terminology. Another is that, in its current incarnation, this rejection is not limited to dual nationality caused by the experience of naturalization — as was literally the case until 1938 — but applies to all instances of dual nationality regardless of how they happen to arise. To be sure, where the affected individual contracts this status through no decision of his own, telling him that the Soviet apparatus refuses to take cognizance of his "foreign" citizenship still has no practical value since the private party cannot control the scenario in order to avoid the predicament. Whether or not these formal revisions also warrant the conclusion that a "new"[7] norm has been forged here depends on the standard of measurement used: if one goes by the script, the element of innovation is evident; if, on the other hand, one looks at established practice, the latest law merely follows precedent and lends statutory authority to an old administrative modus operandi.

Second, up till now the successive Soviet citizenship enactments utterly ignored the reverse situation, where a Soviet citizen got himself naturalized abroad while retaining his Soviet citizenship. That occurred often enough. Yet, in all these years the Soviet regime responded to the phenomenon just once when, by the decree of May 27, 1933, it declared all former Russian citizens who had gone abroad before November 7, 1917, and had acquired a foreign citizenship or filed for a foreign citizenship to have forfeited their Soviet citizenship.[8] The measure elicited from at least one Soviet lawyer the comment that "this further underlined that the utilization of dual citizenship will not be tolerated".[9] Neither before nor since has any like solution been tried, again despite the fact that such incidents are far from rare and inevitably lead to international collisions over which state the individual so endowed shall fulfill his duties to when each of them asserts its rights to the exclusion of the rest.

True, under the circumstances the Soviet Union can do very little in any event, given the range of available choices. A feasible solution might be to defer to the opposite side's claim, which makes sense since that is what Moscow expects of everybody else when the tables are turned, but which really amounts to letting the individual renege on his debt to the Motherland through the mere subterfuge of assuming a second citizenship. The Soviet hierarchy has always branded the idea abhorrent by reason of a professed conviction that "any steps taken by a citizen to withdraw from Soviet citizenship without proper permission injure the sovereignty of the Soviet state".[10] Another alternative might be routinely to divest the offender of his Soviet citizenship, except that this too would imply tacit acquiescence in the individual's private decision to expatriate himself and switch citizenships and then his failure to obtain prior special sanction for the deed, as prescribed, would mean practically nothing. The same aversion to condoning an act perceived as detrimental to the sovereignty of the Soviet state would render this route unattractive.

The final approach would be to persist in demanding that the individual perform his role as a Soviet citizen, despite absence of any further means to compel him to obey orders from home. Even though the latter procedure smacked of futility, the Soviet Union consistently stuck to it,[11] probably because it preferred to argue its case in vain than encourage the notion that a Soviet citizen could on his own initiative legally sever his relationship with the USSR, leaving the government to accept the fait accompli as best it can. Note, however, that before 1978 the Soviet authorities pursued this line as a policy matter without bothering to put the operation on a legal footing. With the promulgation of the latest citizenship statute, the "oversight" has been corrected: in effect, no spatial restrictions can be read into the wording of Article 8 and the legislators clearly seem to have intended that its provisions apply around the world to incidents of dual nationality involving persons considered citizens of the USSR.

Third, informing all concerned that the Soviet regime will not, within its domestic jurisdiction, attach any legal validity to any foreign nationality to which a citizen of the USSR may also have title does not dispose of the matter. Soviet citizens nevertheless fall victim to dual and multiple citizenship, as do people everywhere else, and perhaps as frequently.[12] As long as they stay inside the borders of the USSR, only their Soviet citizenship will in effect apply. Still, that does not eliminate the foreign nationality; it renders the institution provisionally inoperative, and no more. In international law, however, the juridical superimposition survives unimpaired and no degree of domestic proscription can hope to settle the issue conclusively in favor of the home citizenship and against its competitors.

Whereas previously the USSR relied on ad hoc practice and scholarly exegesis to let it generally be known how Soviet law proposed to handle any case of dual nationality occurring on the local scene where Soviet citizenship was coupled with a foreign one, the regime's views on the subject have now been officially spelled out under the terms of Article 8. A source of potential confusion has thus been liquidated, at least as regards formal indication of the kind of treatment the Soviet authorities say they will accord the problem. Meantime, though, by clarifying its position here, the Soviet government has prompted other states to respond to its action where they feel that the announced policy is liable to infringe on their national interests or violate their rights under international law. For example, the United States quickly moved to counter the Soviet bid and stake out its own claim by notifying the Soviet side through proper channels that:

> "The United States, like the USSR, rejects the concept of dual nationality as a matter of policy. The United States does, however, acknowledge the

existence of dual nationality in individual cases as a matter of fact resulting from the conflicting laws of other countries. The conflicts exist since there is no uniform rule of international law relating to acquisition of nationality. Because of differences between the nationality laws of various countries, including the United States and the USSR, there are many persons on whom nationality is conferred by two or more countries. As a result, it is possible for a person to have a legitimate claim to United States citizenship under United States law while at the same time having a legitimate claim to USSR citizenship under USSR law."[13]

Whether or not such a protest is filed, it is quite evident that an individual's valid citizenship link with one state cannot be unilaterally sundered by virtue of the person's concurrent possession of the citizenship of another state, even where the physical setting enables the latter to maintain exclusive jurisdiction over the certified bipatride.

The American diplomatic démarche quoted above offers a sampling of the sort of difficulties that have arisen in trying to implement the general principle enunciated in Article 8 of the 1978 citizenship statute. In order to understand the record, we must look at the doctrinal motives that dictated the USSR's resort to "non–recognition" in dealing with the contingency of dual nationality and what the choice of policy implies for the methods likely to be used to resolve such practical problems that have been and will continue to be encountered on the foreign affairs scene. Analysis must start with the observation that Soviet spokesmen are unanimous in denouncing the status of dual (or multiple) nationality.

A fairly typical assessment concedes that international law contains no direct prohibition of dual citizenship, but adds that it is neither indifferent to nor recognizes the phenomenon. The reason given is that the experience undoubtedly represents a source of international conflict which states usually strive to avoid by various means because, inter alia, the relationship can easily hinder the realization of certain common principles of international law. For example, if an individual possesses the citizenship of two states and both therefore are entitled to exercise an array of sovereign rights with respect to that person, only one will in fact be able to do so and, consequently, the sovereignty of the other will suffer some injury.[14] The moral, then, is that from the standpoint of international law dual nationality is an "evil" which ought to be treated as a juridical anomaly,[15] or, in more sober tones, the condition is simply pronounced "wrongful",[16] "abnormal",[17] and so forth. Even the principle of "functional protection" by the United Nations of its personnel, sanctioned by the International Court of Justice in its 1949 advisory opinion, does not escape unscathed and is duly condemned for intruding on the rights of the state vis–à–vis its citizens and, hence, running counter to the canons of international law.[18] Since the policy of "non–recognition" expresses rejection of the status of dual nationality, the logical conclusion is that the formula fully complies with the generally recognized norms of international law.[19] Characteristically, the entire elaborate discussion focuses not on the adverse effects dual nationality has on the human being who contracts that affliction, but on the "loss" incurred by the state when thus denied sole control over its citizen's activities.

Emphasis on the negative aspects of dual nationality would suggest a matching interest in devising appropriate therapy, for, whatever its ostensible contribution here, the technique of "non–recognition" plainly offers no positive cure for the malady. Soviet legal experts are not unmindful of the connection between these two themes. Indeed, admitting that dual nationality will still occur as a result of the collision of the statutory prescriptions of different countries despite Soviet law's bid to ban the concept, one of them has ventured to recommend as a desideratum that the relevant Soviet legislation be supplemented with a rule "stipulating that if dual or multiple citizenship does in fact strike a citizen of the USSR, the question of his citizenship is determined in accordance with an international agreement".[20] In such a case, of course, the question can be decided with comparative ease.

The trouble with that scenario, as is often noted in Soviet literature and corroborated by the historical evidence, lies in the marked shortage of agreements of this kind. Soviet specialists claim that insuperable contradictions between the capitalist states have scuttled all earlier efforts to arrive at a consensus among them and further acknowledge that the ideological struggle between the capitalist and socialist systems rules out the prospect that they might manage to reconcile their differences and adopt common guidelines designed to deal with the problem in comprehensive fashion.[21] Taking pride in the proven ability of the socialist states to settle these issues inter se by means of a network of bilateral treaties and citing the achievement as an example of the socialist community's superiority over its capitalist rival in promoting international unity misses the vital point: in a comradely environment, dual nationality figures as a mere nuisance that can be tolerated without serious hardship; the acid test is how to surmount its aggravating qualities on occasions where the states whose interests are at stake do not share this close affinity.

What makes the whole business more intractable in the context of the Soviet Union's relations with the "non–socialist" world is the Soviet contention that international law features no universally accepted indicia for judging the substantive merits of a dispute between two states where each feels entitled to consider a particular individual its own citizen. To the extent, also, that Soviet jurisprudes and their colleagues in the other socialist countries maintain that citizenship is an institution of constitutional law and not of public or private international law, the thesis assumes every state's supremacy in defining its citizenship qualifications. With no state deemed accountable to its fellow on how it chooses to handle such "domestic affairs", the absence of a higher authority signifies that the impasse can be broken only by an agreement between the parties or, indeed, by the introduction of "independent" measuring devices for evaluating these citizenship claims and determining who has a better case. The Soviets have shown little enthusiasm for the latter alternative. Recent experimentations with the concept of "effective citizenship", for instance, have found no favor with Soviet legal scholars, although a few of them do mention, without actually committing themselves, that "in international practice, priority is, as a rule, granted to the citizenship of the state in which the bipatride resides or with which he is in fact primarily associated".[22]

Specifically, Soviet objections to the "effective citizenship" formula boil down to the following. To begin with, putting the accent on residence makes it sound as though territorial jurisdiction has precedence over personal jurisdiction, whereas the idea of ranking them does not appeal to the Soviet legal community. Next, opposition to letting the individual's preference dictate the outcome where the de cujus has indicated the desire to disconnect himself from the state the citizenship of which he hitherto possessed in favor of a de facto relationship with a different state is just as strong. Refusal by a national located abroad to avail himself of the protection of his old government or fulfill the duties owed to the state whose citizenship he formally retains is a practical matter which, according to Soviet spokesmen, does not affect the juridical puissance of the state's rights and obligations vis–à–vis the self–styled "apatride".[23]

Then, even the acquisition of a foreign citizenship is not recognized by Soviet sources as capable of terminating the newly naturalized person's previous citizenship affiliation or demoting it to some sort of secondary position. The state whose citizenship the bipatride originally owned is said to be fully entitled to count him as its citizen as long as he has not lost it in the manner locally prescribed and, more important, the contrary tendency to pronounce absolute freedom of expatriation the valid norm of international law is condemned as inconsistent with the principle of the sovereign equality of states and the principle of non–interference.[24] Finally, at the procedural level, Soviet authors charge that enforcement of the principle of "effective citizenship" by state courts is incompatible with international law in that, by deciding on the effectiveness of this or that citizenship, the domestic court assumes the role of a supranational organ.[25] No obstacles are raised to the use of that yardstick in international litigation or arbitration proceedings, but only because in those fora the parties jointly determine what standard shall be invoked and they are certainly quite free to be governed by the principle of "effective citizenship". Otherwise, Soviet analysts prefer the criterion of equality, which calls for similar weight to be assigned to the claim of both sides where each has legitimate grounds for ascribing its citizenship to the individual concerned. This modus operandi, in their view, fits better the requirements of contemporary international law and so must be applied to all controversies involving persons with dual citizenship that have not been submitted to international court or arbitration, unless the parties arrange differently. What is never explained is how this technique can help settle the argument since the initial premise here is that both sides are right.

In a sense, of course, this is the whole point of the exercise, namely, to establish that either the states agree on the terms for resolving their confrontation over a case of dual nationality or each remains at liberty to treat the bipatride as its citizen. The curious workings of this policy are amply illustrated by how the Soviet regime treats the problem of citizens residing abroad. Two propositions set the general tone. First, the postulate is framed that, from the perspective of Soviet law, "a person who is recognized as a Soviet citizen will be regarded exclusively as a Soviet citizen, even though, by the laws of another state, he may be reckoned among the citizens of that state".[26] The item of the individual's location does not feature in the script and no distinction is drawn between situations on the home front and "overseas". Second, a dissenting vote is cast against the notion that a state cannot afford protection to its citizen versus another state whose citizenship he likewise holds and, instead, Soviet legal specialists insist that either state, by virtue of its sovereign prerogatives, has that right vis–à–vis the other, except that each can also reject such an attempt by referring to its own citizenship title.[27] On the scale of legal doctrine, both sides are evenly matched.

Armed with these artifacts, the Soviet government has waged determined campaigns to assert jurisdiction over Soviet citizens living in other countries who have either made clear their wish to forget about their former Soviet citizenship or have acquired a foreign citizenship without bothering to request offical permission to quit their old Soviet citizenship. The experience of the Kuzmin family offers a prime example of Soviet conduct on these occasions. The child custody case involved four children of Mr. and Mrs. George Kosmin [Kuzmin], Soviet displaced persons, who came under the jurisdiction of the Chicago Family Court when the parents were placed in a mental institution. Three of the children were Soviet citizens born in a displaced persons camp in Germany and one an American citizen born in the United States in 1956. After release from the mental institution in 1954, the parents sought to regain custody of their children in order that the entire family might return to the Soviet Union. The parents left the United States for the USSR in June 1957, and their effort to obtain custody of the children was continued on their behalf by Soviet authorities. In its decision of August 19, 1959, the Family Court of Cook County, Illinois, declared that it was "satisfied that now the best interests of these four children ... would be served it they were given to the custody of their parents". The four Kosmin [Kuzmin] children subsequently departed from the United States to join their parents in the USSR.[28]

Whether the court's ruling was sound is open to reasonable debate. On the other hand, the propriety of the U.S. action in asserting a stake in the matter is beyond doubt since one of the children was an American citizen. The latter consideration did not, however, prevent the competent Soviet agencies from pressing their claim by all available means. Soviet commentators have gone even farther: while admitting that one of the children was assigned U.S. citizenship, they emphasize that all four children were vested with Soviet citizenship and denounce the incident as a case of "illegal detention" (omitting, rather conveniently, to mention that the children were eventually allowed to leave for the USSR).[29]

A similar mentality marks current Soviet policy toward the large Russian emigré community (estimated, by Soviet computations, to number 12 million expatriates from the USSR living outside their native country as of 1959). The earlier commitment to the mass repatriation of these "compatriots abroad" has been replaced by a show of acquiescence in these people's wish to remain in their adopted homelands. The pitch today is that such an expatriate can also be "a good Soviet patriot" on foreign soil as long as he maintains close ties with the "Mother country".[30] Citizenship status plays an important role in promoting the desired sense of identification in that the overwhelming majority of emigrés from the USSR have never formally shed their Soviet citizenship and therefore still qualify as Soviet citizens despite the foreign nationality they may have meantime acquired: thus, they either figure as dual citizens (with the Soviet regime making no secret of its belief in the primacy of Soviet citizenship in those situations) or, in extremis, they will find that the Soviet authorities only recognize the validity of the original Soviet citizenship and dismiss the relevance of the interim conversion to a foreign citizenship.

One can approve or disapprove of the Soviet record in this area, but the modus operandi does represent a logical extension of the doctrinal writ. The acid test, though, is how consistently the Soviets apply the same standards to other countries, i.e., measure their behavior by the rules they observe themselves and let them invoke vis–à–vis the Soviet Union the practices that the Soviet follow in dealing with them. By that count, the Soviet performance fails abysmally. Soviet authors have, for instance, been unsparing in their criticism of the motives they impute to Imperial Germany in featuring a clause in the 1913 citizenship law that sanctioned the retention of German citizenship by persons who petitioned for admission to a foreign citizenship. The provision, they are fond of pointing out, was taken over intact by the Hitler regime which otherwise extensively revised the 1913 statute to conform to its racist theories. Another favorite target is the Japanese law on citizenship which, in its 1924 edition, stipulated that a Japanese national who acquired a foreign citizenship lost his Japanese citizenship only upon his request and then solely with the consent of the Japanese Ministry of Internal Affairs.

According to the Russians, the goal in both cases was to create a vast espionage network manned by bipatrides, a huge "fifth column" ready to carry out the nefarious plans of its fascist masters. Today, the same accusations are hurled at Israel, resorting to the blatantly false charge that Israel ascribes "dual citizenship" to all Jews living "in exile".[31] The allegation is untrue: any person of Jewish origin living outside Israel is indeed entitled to ask for and obtain Israeli citizenship and also receives it upon settling permanently in Israel, but as a citizen of a foreign state he does not legally own Israeli citizenship just by virtue of a Jewish identity.

The singular irony, of course, is that while seeking to crucify their "enemies" for "the crass exploitation of the more unsavory aspects of dual nationality for their own selfish reasons", the Soviet authorities have behaved no differently themselves and certainly their record here is much worse than anything they have been able to prove against Israel. Soviet citizenship legislation, like that of Kaiser Germany's, assumes that a citizen residing "overseas" keeps his "native" citizenship (unless he is forced to surrender it upon emigration on orders of the government) even if he should subsequently become a naturalized citizen of his new homeland. Soviet citizenship legislation, like that of imperial Japan, mandates that a citizen abroad can win release from his citizenship by official dispensation alone. The current Soviet policy of cultivating the loyalty of the Soviet emigré community to the Mother country by, inter alia, treating its members as bipatrides who formally still owe allegiance to the USSR smacks of the subversive activities for which the Nazis are constantly flayed. Past schemes for the repatriation of Ukrainians, Belorussians and Armenians sound the theme of innate citizenship based on ethnic stock similar to what Israel practices with respect to Jewish "returnees". Why everybody else should be pronounced guilty on those grounds while the Soviets proclaim themselves blameless is hard for an ordinary mind to grasp. How ridiculous this double standard can be is evident from the following: Soviet scribes chastize Israel for disregarding the work of the UN International Law Commission in drafting conventions to prevent the incidence of dual nationality; it does not seem to have occurred to them to notice that the Soviet government never endorsed these treaties or that its routine in this domain runs squarely counter to the essence of the recommendations contained in these documents.

An equally schizophrenic pattern emerges when one looks at the picture of how the Soviet Union and its foreign competitors fare in the business of vindicating the right to provide diplomatic protection for dual nationals abroad. As previously mentioned, other states are constantly confronted with Moscow's efforts to intercede in "defense of the interests" of locally domiciled bipatrides whom it considers vested with Soviet citizenship. However, when the roles are reversed, the Soviet apparatus is quick to invoke the concept of "non–recognition" of dual nationality to bar an analogous mission on behalf of individuals residing in the USSR who are said to possess a foreign citizenship in addition to their Soviet one. The Kosmin rKuzmint episode and the comments it elicited in the Soviet media should be contrasted with the running battle the United States, for instance, has been forced to wage for years on end in a bid to extricate an assortment of individuals stranded in the USSR and entitled, in accordance with the respective legislation, to the citizenship of the U.S. or both the U.S. and the Soviet Union. Diplomatic materials reveal that it has been an uphill fight every step of the way, the results have been mixed and the successes few.

Thus, as far back as 1949, the U.S. State Department had occasion to communicate with its Soviet counterpart in an attempt, inter alia, to get the Soviet authorities to free from confinement a group of 31 persons "whose status as American citizens is not open to question" and permit their departure from the USSR. In subsequent correspondence, the American side was moved to complain that the Soviet officials ignored the U.S. Embassy's statements indicating that "the persons concerned had been documented as American citizens after careful investigation" and simply resorted, when they bothered to respond at all, to "assertions and reiterations of the Soviet citizenship, whether real or alleged, of these American citizens" as though that foreclosed further discussion. An aide–mémoire filed with the Soviet Ministry of Foreign Affairs as 1949 drew to a close recapitulated the developments to date and identified four different categories of cases. The first involved approximately thirteen American citizens who, despite their Soviet certification as stateless persons or as foreigners living in the USSR, had been unable to obtain exit visas. The second consisted of twenty or so American citizens who had been erroneously declared Soviet citizens by the Soviet Foreign Ministry. The third comprised 2,000 persons having claim to American citizenship, of whom 659 had been verified as American citizens and 112 were pending verification by the U.S. State Department. Among the former were some twenty minor children who desired to join their parents in the United States and a group of elderly women. The American Embassy had been unable to maintain communication with these people or verify their citizenship status definitively where any of them might have, in addition to U.S. citizenship, also possessed the citizenship of the USSR or another state. Many of these individuals, it was noted, were now confined in Soviet forced labor camps and others had been forcibly resettled in the northeastern region of the Soviet Union. The fourth included around 32 persons (the number had earlier been put at 31), several of them women, currently detained at forced labor in the Soviet Union, who had been arrested in Eastern Europe or elsewhere outside the USSR during or at the end of the late war by Soviet military or police authorities. Of these, circa fourteen were American citizens with claim to no other citizenship and the American citizenship of the remaining eighteen was unquestioned by the United

States, although a few of them might have simultaneously qualified as citizens of a third state.

On March 3, 1950, the State Department issued a statement to the press which cited a recent Soviet reply and assessed the existing situation. The review referred to the repressive measures instituted by the Soviet regime against American citizens attempting to arrange for departure from the Soviet Union. Of the thirteen Americans listed in the first category, one had by then been granted permission to leave; of the twenty Americans falling under the second heading, three had been allowed to depart; of the 2,000 in the third lot, only one woman had received an exit visa; and of the 32 United States citizens detained at forced labor, 23 had received approval to emigrate to Eastern Europe, although it was still uncertain that they would be able to travel on to the United States. The fate of the others remained unsettled. In particular, the legal argument continued unabated, with the American side prompted, inter alia, to protest in this connection that:

> "... the Soviet Government states that the 'decision of the question concerning the citizenship of Soviet citizens is the exclusive concern of Soviet authorities'. Nonetheless, ... it arrogates to itself the right to determine who is and who is not an American citizen.
>
> This Government cannot accept the assertion of the Soviet Government that it has the right to pass upon the American citizenship status of persons recognized by this Government to be American citizens."[32]

Lest this seem ancient history, consider that in its report for the second half of 1979 on the implementation of the Helsinki Accord, the State Department was finally in a position to announce that several longstanding cases involving individuals who held both American and Soviet citizenship were resolved during that period, including the case of the Kargol family that had been a subject of Embassy representations since 1947, and the Kachurak case that had been pursued by the Embassy since 1963.[33] The account added that the active file contained many other longstanding cases and, if precedent is any guide, these can last indefinitely. To be sure, even the foregoing evidence suggests that the Soviet regime is not completely impervious to diplomatic pressure from a foreign country exerted on behalf of an individual whom the latter carries on its citizenship rolls, though he may coincidentally be reckoned a bipatride. We know that energetic intercession by the U.S., for instance, following discovery that a party is entitled to American citizenship has occasionally had the desired effect of prevailing on the competent Soviet organs to let the subject leave the country. The experience of Simas Kudirka illustrates how the system sometimes functions: returned by the Coast Guard to the Soviet navy after jumping ship and requesting asylum on an American vessel in 1970, Kudirka was sentenced to ten years' loss of freedom; he was subsequently certified by the U.S. authorities as an American citizen by birth and the fact brought to the attention of the Soviet government; in 1974 Kudirka was pardoned, released from confinement and soon after emigrated to the United States.[34]

In the great majority of such instances, however, there is no happy ending and, indeed, the consequences for the person seeking to invoke his foreign citizenship in order to terminate his legal association with the USSR have often been tragic,[35] since these efforts usually meet with harsh reprisals by the local apparatus. The rate of success here is low and the result is a marked asymmetry in the performance of the USSR and much of the rest of the world when faced with this problem. No matter how emphatically most other states profess to reject the concept of dual nationality and refuse to recognize the phenomenon, few are totally insensitive to claims from fellow– states based on those grounds. The Soviet regime is well aware of this "weakness" and strives to take advantage of it whenever possible by vigorously lobbying for its rights in the hope of fanning the opponent's sense of malaise and thus increase his willingness to make concessions. Yet, when approached by a foreign government on similar business, the Soviets can be utterly intransigent just because they suffer from no moral qualms about denying the other side's valid interest in the "common product". Or, to paraphrase an old joke about the Kremlin's negotiating style, the pitch in this case sounds suspiciously like "My dual national is mine, and your dual national is also mine".

If and when the Soviet regime does choose to compromise in these affairs, then, its decision is dictated not by an instinct for fairness, but by perceptions of political expediency, and this tough pragmatism reduces the chance of influencing Soviet behavior on these issues since, given the technical parity of both parties' stake in a certified bipatride, in the final analysis the scales are often tipped by appeal to humanitarian values — charity, compassion, and so forth. In official Soviet circles, these commodities have always been in short supply and victims of dual nationality are apt to fare no better in terms of the brand of treatment they will be afforded by the Soviet administrative apparatus than the mass of their countrymen.

II. Conflicts–in–Law Portfolio

Having set the doctrinal stage, let us next look at the mechanics of inception of dual nationality through conflicts–in–law contingencies in which the principles of Soviet law are pitted against the norms prescribed by other legal systems. For, it is worth repeating, despite claims by Soviet spokesmen that "our state constantly takes measures to eliminate undesirable facts of dual citizenship",[36] these lapses continue to occur — on the Soviet scene just as elsewhere — and, of course, will never be wholly eradicated until a global consensus imparts uniformity to the applicable rules. Meantime, latent dual or multiple citizenship can supervene to afflict Soviet citizens as the product of the following chain of developments.

1. At Birth

A. Jus Sanguinis

In a "mixed" marriage, adherence by the states of which the spouses are respectively citizens to the principle of jus sanguinis is a frequent cause of the offspring incurring dual (or multiple) nationality at birth. The situation is aggravated in the Soviet case by the fact that, unlike many other states, the USSR does not discriminate between the sexes in this regard and its citizenship "descends" equally through the paternal and maternal lines, thereby doubling the chances of the children contracting that condition in the context of a binational (or multinational) household. Under the terms of Article 12 of the 1978 statute which deals with the procedures of acquisition of USSR citizenship at birth when one parent is a Soviet citizen and the other is a foreigner, several opportunities exist for overlapping claims based on the kinship criterion to produce dual citizenship ab ovo. For instance, the child born on Soviet soil of a mother who is a Soviet citizen and a father who is a citizen of another state which follows the rule that its citizenship is ipso jure transmitted by the pater familias will start life vested with both parents' citizenships.[37] In a parallel scenario, if the foreign state shares the Soviet Union's liberal view and allows its citizenship to devolve via the mother as well, a child born on Soviet soil of a father who is a Soviet citizen and a mother who is the citizen of such a state will also figure as a dual citizen from the outset. Similar consequences mark the birth abroad of a child of a Soviet parent and a foreign parent whose citizenship the offspring automatically "inherits" by virtue of the corresponding country's law, provided both parents maintain at the time a permanent place of residence on the territory of the USSR or either of them does so.

If, in addition, any of these occasions feature parents possessing more than one citizenship each that can all pass by succession to the offspring, the child will enter the world encumbered with multiple citizenship.

B. Jus Soli Versus Jus Sanguinis

According to the 1978 enactment, a child both of whose parents are Soviet citizens at the time of its birth (Art. 11) or one of whose parents is at that moment a Soviet citizen and the other is a stateless person or not known (Art. 12) counts as a Soviet citizen whether born on the territory of the USSR or outside its borders. In the latter event, if birth occurs on the territory of a state that practices jus soli, the child will be considered a dual citizen ab origine. The same results may be observed in the framework of a "mixed" marriage when the child is born on the territory of a state that embraces the concept of jus soli in circumstances where at least one of its parents is a Soviet citizen and both parents at the time maintain a permanent place of residence on the territory of the USSR or either of them does. In the above setting, if the child happens to receive a different citizenship from each parent through the operation of the doctrine of jus sanguinis and, furthermore, manages to be born on the territory of a third state applying the principle of jus soli, multiple citizenship ensues forthwith.

"Exotic" embellishments on this basic recipe readily come to mind. A child of Soviet parents or the kind of Soviet/foreign "alloy" just described, born on the high seas on a vessel flying the flag of a country which has elected to abide by the institution of jus soli and coincidentally treats its ships as "floating extensions of its territorial domain", will possess two citizenships from date of birth. Or, if a child with identical roots should see the light of day on board a ship while the latter is located in the territorial waters of a state which draws no distinction between the land realm and the territorial sea from the standpoint of upholding the principle of jus soli in both, the pattern will repeat itself. With a proper combination of these elements, the child can even join the company of mankind loaded down with three citizenships. Though not exactly ordinary, such complicated results are not altogether unheard of.

C. Agreement of the Parents Versus Jus Sanguinis and Jus Soli

Article 12 of the 1978 statute further provides that, in case the parents have different citizenships with one of them owning Soviet citizenship at the time of the child's birth and both of them maintain a permanent place of residence outside the USSR, the citizenship of the child born beyond the confines of the USSR is determined by agreement of the parents. However, as a Soviet jurist correctly noted on the occasion of the publication of the draft version of the Basic principles of legislation of the USSR and union republics on marriage and the family, in which an analogous clause appeared, the parents' choice in the matter did not preclude the intervention of foreign law(s). While effective as a means of guaranteeing the offspring possession of Soviet citizenship, the arrangement did not prevent the child from perhaps also contracting the citizenship of the country where it was born by virtue of the institution of jus soli or the citizenship of the state of which the foreign parent was a citizen through the operation of the doctrine of jus sanguinis and starting life saddled with dual or triple nationality.[38]

★ ★ ★

Now, with regard to all the above contingencies of dual (multiple) citizenship by accident of birth, international practice has developed certain palliatives and these are not unknown to members of the Soviet legal profession. In Soviet technical literature, for instance, mention is frequently made of personal option as a common device for solving dual nationality problems, visualizing, inter alia, a right to choose between the contending citizenships usually exercised by the de cujus upon attaining majority.[39] Nonetheless, Soviet law has never thought fit to adopt that method. Reluctance to countenance unilateral decisions by an individual concerning his national affiliation, or aversion to any automatic scheme of denaturalization depending wholly on the individual's inner volition may explain that state of affairs.

Finally, what has been said so far about the potential of the applicable norms of Soviet law to generate dual nationality at birth calls for a brief appraisal of how much more prone the relevant provisions of the 1978 statute are to induce that status than the system which functioned here in the past. The difficulty with attempting that kind of evaluation, of course, is that one is somewhat unsure as to what policy the Soviet authorities actually followed in this connection prior to 1968 since the 1938 citizenship law kept silent on the subject of the mechanics of acquisition of Soviet citizenship by descent. If one goes on the assumption that the regime abided by the previous formula which featured the radical strain of jus sanguinis whereby one Soviet parent was enough to relay Soviet citizenship to the offspring at birth under any circumstances, then, quite clearly, the current approach is bound to be less productive of dual citizenship incidents than its predecessor. If, however, one takes into account the fact that the administrative routine may have changed in the sixties and switched to the procedure which was eventually consecrated in the corresponding article of the 1968 federal "code" on marriage and the family, the magnitude of the most recent reform is either negligible or eludes precise measurement.

The difference between the 1968 and 1978 editions on this question is that the former summarily assigned Soviet citizenship to a child of "mixed" parentage born abroad if either parent resided at the time on the territory of the USSR and, alternatively, let the parents decide among themselves on the child's citizenship association if both parents resided at the time outside the borders of the USSR (Art.30) and the latter replaces in both contexts the word "resided" by the expression "had a permanent place of residence". Roughly put, more such offspring would be apt to inherit Soviet citizenship at birth via a parent fulfilling the bare "local residence" requirement of the 1968 model than would be true under the revised 1978 criterion of "permanent local residence" (the first being broader in connotation than the second), thus multiplying their chances of incurring dual nationality. Conversely, a larger sample of parents would in these instances be competent to exercise the right to pick the child's citizenship just because they "resided" abroad as per the letter of the 1968 scenario than would be the case under the tougher 1978 injunction that they maintain "a permanent place of residence abroad" in order to be so eligible. This means that the greater latitude sanctioned by the older rule could serve to reduce the statistical frequency of dual nationality by permitting proper selectivity when compared with the conditions today when that opportunity is strictly restricted to the fullfledged expatriates among Soviet citizens living "overseas", i.e., those who had established a permanent foreign residence and had no further imputable title to permanent residency in the USSR. Experience alone will show how these offsetting combinations of gains and losses from the perspective of inherent capacity to breed dual nationality affect the actuarial tables: a prognosis based on textual exegesis cannot anticipate the possibilities of certain situations conducive to the inception of dual nationality transpiring more often than those unpropitious to the occurrence of that phenomenon or vice versa.

2. Naturalization

A. Primary Naturalization

A citizen of the USSR can win release from Soviet citizenship solely by permission of the federal Presidium. Accordingly, where a Soviet citizen through naturalization acquires a foreign nationality without previously having shed his Soviet citizenship pursuant to regulations, he will discover himself in possession of two citizenships.[40]

The mechanism functions in the opposite sense as well. Should a foreigner who is a citizen of a state that, just as the Soviet Union, rejects the idea of freedom of expatriation and on each occasion requires prior official authorization for exit from its citizenship ask for and receive Soviet citizenship without having bothered to surrender his original citizenship through set procedures, he will henceforward sport two citizenships.

The Citizenship Law of 1938, unlike its predecessors, neglected to forewarn people falling into this category of the impending consequences of such a step. The 1978 enactment at least goes to the trouble of cautioning all potential candidates for Soviet citizenship, including those contemplating becoming naturalized Soviet citizens, that once a person qualifies as a citizen of the USSR the Soviet officialdom will not recognize any affiliation with the citizenship of a foreign state. Apart from that advance notice couched in the most general terms, current Soviet legislation features no practical safeguards against the likelihood of these "lapses" and essentially Moscow's attitude here seems to be that "a state is ... not obliged, when naturalizing some person, to pay attention to possession by that person of the citizenship of another state".[41] In line with this proposition, Soviet law–makers have betrayed no inclination to embark on the alternative course, favored by many countries, of demanding of a person aspiring to its citizenship either that the subject first produce proof of having relinquished his former nationality or confirm that he will be duly shorn of it upon being admitted to a new (Soviet) citizenship. Of course, given the broad language of the statute, the regime can always use its discretion and, if it should so please, impose that as a condition for naturalization, in purely ad hoc fashion or in anticipation of a specific class of cases.[42] There are no grounds for believing that the apparatus has so far found it necessary to invoke that power, apparently remaining quite content to deny the juridical viability of dual citizenship within the confines of the USSR instead of instituting prophylactic measures designed to curtail its actual incipience. The disparity between the vehemence of Soviet denunciations of the evils of dual citizenship and the failure to provide even minimal treatment of an obvious source of allegedly undesirable phenomena is striking.

Two last comments will help put the picture in a broader perspective and pinpoint an interesting recent development that seems to have modified the standard rules of the game pertaining to this item in the relations between the USSR and some of its close associates. First, the record shows a marked difference in the way the various European members of the socialist community have elected to tackle this important issue. Bulgaria's citizenship legislation stipulates that an individual possessing a foreign citizenship can acquire Bulgarian citizenship if he has lost his "former citizenship or will be released from it". The law further explains that this condition is deemed fulfilled if the person filing an application for admission to Bulgarian citizenship is a stateless person or shall lose his citizenship pursuant to the law of his homeland for reasons of naturalization abroad. In Poland, acceptance into Polish citizenship may be made dependent on submission of evidence of exit from foreign citizenship. In Yugoslavia, where the foreign state does not allow exit from its citizenship or imposes impossible conditions in that connection, it is enough that the party upon receiving Yugoslav citizenship declare that he waives his foreign citizenship. In short, "the legislation of Poland, Bulgaria, Romania and Yugoslavia envisages as a mandatory prerequisite for the acquisition of rtheir respectivet citizenship by foreigners the dissolution of legal ties with the state of which they were citizens".[43] By contrast, the USSR and the GDR do not make admission to their citizenship contingent on the prior loss of the competing foreign citizenship. In Hungary, no requirement to that effect exists either, except that when examining requests for admission to citizenship the circumstance that the petitioner is a stateless person or will lose his citizenship as a result of entry into Hungarian citizenship or will repudiate his foreign citizenship or will ask to be released from his foreign citizenship redounds in his favor.

Observing this array of practices, an East European analyst cites the need to bear in mind the "full and unlimited sovereignty of the state in questions connected with citizenship and, therefore, also its absolute supremacy in deciding applications for admission to citizenship ...".[44] The legal norms of Poland, Bulgaria, Romania and Yugoslavia, it is pointed out, sanction the possibility of viewing the refusal by a foreign state to permit exit from its citizenship as an "impracticable condition" and in that event approving a petition for admission to local citizenship despite the formal impediment. This procedure aims at curbing the frequency of dual citizenship occasioned by the mechanics of naturalization, while guaranteeing the receiving country adequate flexibility in these affairs and saving it from having to pay rigid deference to another state's potentially unreasonable policies in the matter of expatriation. The disadvantage of such an approach, we are told, is that it drags out the business of admitting a person to citizenship in each of these states. In principle, the USSR, the GDR and Hungary operate on a faster schedule because the foreign status of the candidate for naturalization is not an extra factor that can hold up the conversion, but the price exacted is the increased chance of precipitating cases of dual nationality. Second, one gets the net impression from random statements in Soviet and East European legal literature that among themselves the socialist countries now routinely follow the principle of not admitting each other's citizens to their citizenship unless the applicants have been properly authorized to relinquish their former citizenship.[45] Or, to quote directly:

> "There has been forged between the majority of socialist states an international legal custom (which figures, undoubtedly, as a norm of the developing socialist international law) according to which in principle not a single socialist state admits to its citizenship a citizen of another socialist state if he does not have the appropriate approval of the competent organs of the latter. This custom functions, for instance, between the USSR, Czechoslovakia, Romania, Poland, Bulgaria, the KPDR, the GDR. The existence of a customary norm on admission to citizenship does not preclude its incorporation in a treaty. On the contrary, it is affixed in the conventions on the prevention of occurrence of cases of dual citizenship between the USSR and Hungary of January 21, 1963, between the USSR and Poland of March 31, 1965, and between the USSR and Bulgaria of July 6, 1966."[46]

The setting leads local authors to conclude that in the intramural affairs of the socialist states the inception of dual nationality in the process of naturalization is "in a number of cases ... impossible"[47] or is flatly "excluded".[48] Apparently, the administrative format has been suitably adjusted and, again, it sounds like these new rules are at present being enforced vis-à-vis all the socialist states, although they originated in particular agreements entered into between the USSR and some of its allies with the intent of abating the incidence of dual citizenship in their mutual transactions. One Soviet scholar, for example, has written that "citizens of socialist countries petitioning for admission to Soviet citizenship must submit documents attesting to the attitude of the organs of state power of the corresponding countries toward the admission of these persons to Soviet citizenship" and, where they cannot provide such documents, they file a declaration to that effect.[49] The innovation is still credited, of course, to the tenor of the corresponding pacts between the USSR and its socialist friends, but the wording here implies a geographical scope broader than that of the initial treaty package.

Remember, too, that these regimes are well known for insisting that no denaturalization is valid without official sanction which puts most members of the partnership in the position of having to deny admission to their citizenship unless suitable permission has been obtained or being constrained to pronounce their associate's refusal to grant such approval "unreasonable" in order to license admission over the latter's demurrer — which cannot be an attractive prospect. Reluctance to refer to the behavior of a fellow socialist in those disparaging terms would also mean, even without resort to the fiction of an international legal custom, that denaturalization within the company would commonly either be coupled with loss of the previous citizenship — thus guaranteeing immunity from dual citizenship — or a request for naturalization would be summarily turned down if permission to leave the current citizenship were not forthcoming and then the incurrence of dual citizenship would equally be aborted.

B. Derivative Naturalization

Under the terms of the 1938 and 1978 statute alike, "in the event of a change of citizenship by both parents, when both become citizens of the USSR, or when both of them cease to be such, the citizenship of their children under fourteen changes correspondingly". Should the parents be citizens of a state which does not allow expatriation without official approval and that had not been secured before their admission to Soviet citizenship, the ensuing dual nationality of the parents is shared by their children under fourteen. By contrast, the change of the citizenship of children aged fourteen to eighteen in case of change of the citizenship of their parents may take place only with their consent, which the 1978 enactment amplifies with the provision that this acquiescence be expressed in written form. Assuming a state of affairs where the parents of a minor falling into that age group both leave Soviet citizenship and acquire the citizenship of a state which ipso jure confers its citizenship on the minor children of its newly naturalized citizens, but the child in question had not given due assurance that it concurred in its parents' decision, dual nationality will again set in. Or, should a minor between the ages of fourteen and eighteen possess the citizenship of a country in which the business of naturalization is surrounded by similar restrictions and the de cujus had failed to observe these regulations before assenting to the acquisition of Soviet citizenship by his parents, thereby precipitating his own conversion to Soviet citizenship, dual nationality henceforth becomes his lot.

In dealing with the status of minor children where only one parent enters or leaves Soviet citizenship, the present law departs from precedent and the current procedure can produce "secondary" specimens of dual nationality in a number of situations. Now, for example, if just one of the parents becomes a citizen of the USSR and the other remains a foreign citizen, the minor child can acquire the citizenship of the USSR at the request of the parent acquiring the citizenship of the USSR. Since many countries require both parents to approve the change of citizenship of their minor children or, in extremis, vest the pater familias with that authority, the move by one parent in the former case or by the mother in the latter case to convert the child to Soviet citizenship will simply add Soviet citizenship to the old citizenship and turn the offspring into a dual citizen. Or, when one parent becomes a Soviet citizen and the other continues as a stateless person, the minor child residing on the territory of the USSR is automatically assigned Soviet citizenship: however, if the child hitherto possessed the citizenship of a country whose law makes change of citizenship here contingent on agreement by both parents or at least affirmative action by one parent, the unilateral initiative of just one parent in the former case or the involuntary nature of the operation in the latter case will result in the acquisition of Soviet citizenship without attendant loss of the previous citizenship and, hence, infection with dual nationality. Given the same set of facts, except that the minor child resides outside the confines of the USSR, the latest rule is that the offspring can obtain Soviet citizenship at the request of the parent acquiring the citizenship of the USSR: again, lack of parental unanimity or an attempt by the mother to effect the child's conversion when by law the father alone is vested with that power might fail to terminate the child's original citizenship, though meanwhile succeeding in establishing title to Soviet citizenship, and the minor would then be stuck with dual citizenship.

A major innovation in Soviet citizenship law concerns the position of the child where one parent exits from Soviet citizenship and the other retains it: in that event, the child keeps the citizenship of the USSR. The absolute bar against the child's release from Soviet citizenship in these circumstances (even, be it noted, if both parents condone the move) is bound to occasion incidents of dual nationality since it is common practice for states to extend their citizenship forthwith to the minor children when a parent gets their citizenship by naturalization, especially when the bid emanates from the father.

Generally speaking, chances are that the revised norms in this area will be responsible for an increase in the frequency of dual citizenship through the route of derivative naturalization. The combination of eased access to Soviet citizenship or, in some instances, plain assignment to the offspring of Soviet citizenship by local fiat and the ban on expatriation of minor children as long as one parent remains a Soviet citizen creates more opportunities for minor children to contract dual citizenship by osmosis, as it were, than was true under the system applied during the past forty years (i.e. 1938 to 1978).

3. Marriage

A large number of countries unilaterally bestow their citizenship on alien women upon marriage to their citizens. The Soviet jurisprudential canon, on the other hand, attributes no special value to matrimony in that respect and maintains that both partners to a "mixed" marriage keep their erstwhile citizenship after the ceremony as well. Thus, where a female citizen of the USSR happens to wed a citizen of a state which adheres to the doctrine that the wife gains her husband's citizenship by "mechanical devolution", so to speak, the conflict of legal formulas will now cause her to have two citizenships.[50] On rare occasions, a male citizen of the USSR can run into a similar problem, if, for example, he should own immovable property in Brazil, be married to a Brazilian woman or have Brazilian children, and reside in Brazil he will, under Brazilian law, be considered a citizen of Brazil, unless he had announced the intention of not renouncing his old nationality. By contrast, a positive feature of the intra–socialist repertory here is that dual citizenship cannot be incurred as a result of citizens of the member countries entering into marriage since none of these states subscribe to the principle that "the wife follows the citizenship of the husband".[51]

Interestingly enough, up until 1938 Soviet legislation offered a simple solution for this routine contingency by authorizing naturalization or denaturalization "in a simplified manner" in such a context. Precisely what this "simplified manner" consisted of is a moot point and certainly it could not be claimed by the people involved as a matter of right, but depended essentially on administrative discretion. Nevertheless, individuals could at least hope to get out of an embarrassing position through this procedure whereas since 1938 that avenue has been closed to them. Remember, too, that in 1947 the regime went a step farther and altogether forbade marriages between Soviet citizens and aliens and only in 1953, at Stalin's death, was the prohibition repealed and the status quo ante fully restored. In short, with the introduction of rigid controls over the function of admission into and release from Soviet citizenship in the wake of the Stalinist purges, all regular channels of relatively "uncomplicated" acquisition or surrender of Soviet citizenship were hermetically sealed, including the one which had hitherto held out to married couples with an "international complexion" the promise that they might be able to synchronize their divergent citizenship affiliations with a minimum of bureaucratic fuss.

Although Soviet sources often refer to personal option as a useful tool for handling this issue,[52] government circles have as yet shown no signs of wanting to furnish persons placed in that unfortunate predicament with a convenient way out. In the thaw of the early sixties, a proposal was floated recommending that Soviet law be revised in order to facilitate transfers from the citizenship of the other socialist nations to that of the USSR, and vice versa.[53] Had the scheme been adopted, it would, of course, also have eased the difficulties that continue to be encountered in this sector — even if just in terms of preserving family unity in citizenship affairs, since the problem of dual nationality in connection with marriage no longer arises in local intramural relations. In any event, the law–makers did not incorporate the suggestion in the text of the 1978 statute which contains no hint that some sort of "accelerated schedule" may apply to certain classes of people for entering or leaving Soviet citizenship; however, from circumstantial evidence one does get the impression that administrative practice may lean in the direction of expediting such traffic between the Soviet Union and its comrades or other close tactical allies (to wit, in the Third World) when political considerations counsel the need to signal special treatment.

4. Minors

A. Adoption

Children possessing the citizenship of the USSR who are adopted by foreign citizens or by a couple of whom one is a citizen of the USSR and the other is a foreign citizen retain Soviet citizenship (Art.24). The law adds that at the request of the adopting parents the Presidium of the USSR Supreme Soviet may allow such a child to relinquish the citizenship of the USSR. Meanwhile, many states peremptorily assign their citizenship to children in conjunction with their adoption by their own citizens or even by a family in which only the head of the household is their citizen. So, where a minor deemed to be a Soviet citizen is legally adopted by citizens of or by a family unit whose pater familias is a citizen of a country subscribing to this rule, he is condemned to a career of dual nationality unless the competent Soviet organs decide to release the de cujus from Soviet citizenship.[54] To the extent that official loss of Soviet citizenship hinges on executive dispensation and is not a right legally guaranteed to the affected individual, no assurance exists that the federal Presidium will approve the application and, hence, dual nationality is always a distinct possibility in these conditions. Still, the language of the 1978 enactment marks a formal improvement over how the subject was handled the last time it was dealt with at the statutory level, namely, in the Citizenship Regulation of 1931. On that occasion, the pertinent clause (Art.11) simply decreed that "the children of citizens of the USSR adopted by foreign citizens retain their citizenship of the USSR" and doctrinal writings confirm that this pronouncement set the general tone for corresponding practice until the 1978 reform.[55]

Although the 1938 citizenship law said nothing regarding the citizenship status of foreign children adopted by Soviet parents, the initial consensus of Soviet legal opinion was that such adoption per se operated to impart Soviet citizenship and, indeed, the advisability was recognized of clarifying the position of children of foreign extraction adopted by Soviet parents by amending the statute to enunciate expressis verbis that adoption automatically earned them Soviet citizenship. The 1978 act meets the requirement and now spells out that a child possessing a foreign citizenship and adopted by citizens of the USSR or by spouses of whom one is a citizen of the USSR and the other is a stateless person qualifies ipso jure as a citizen of the USSR. If the minor was originally the citizen of a country which, like the USSR, insists that its citizenship remains unaffected by these developments, the end product will once again be double citizenship. Finally, where a child vested with foreign citizenship is adopted by a couple consisting of a citizen of the USSR and a foreign citizen, the child becomes a Soviet citizen by agreement of the parents,[56] except, of course, that their bare preference is not always enough to engineer loss of the previous citizenship and, in case it does not have that effect, dual citizenship will ensue from their desire to enroll the adoptee as a Soviet citizen.

The sentiment voiced earlier in Soviet legal literature that "a maximum mark of respect for international courtesy in this connection would be to grant the person so adopted a right to opt for his former citizenship upon attaining majority"[57] fell on deaf ears and was ignored by the drafters of the current piece of legislation.

B. Legitimation and Quasi–Legitimation

In outlining the mechanics of acquisition of Soviet citizenship by birth, the new statute refers to parenthood in biological and not in juridical terms, which signifies that Soviet citizenship may be inherited by descent irrespective of whether or not the infant's parents are matrimonially linked to each other. Thus, where both parents (or either parent) have (has) to fulfill certain attributes for the offspring to count as Soviet citizens, establishing the identity of the unwed parents by various ancillary means may prove crucial for determining the child's entitlement to the citizenship of the USSR and, if the discovery is accomplished in the prescribed manner, proper certification will in designated circumstances prompt the aforementioned eligibility.

Article 16 of the 1968 Basic principles of legislation of the USSR and union republics on marriage and the family stipulates that the provenance of a child from parents who are not married to one another is recorded through submission of a joint statement in that vein by the father and mother of the child to the appropriate state bureau of civil registry and, absent such a declaration, paternity may be settled by resort to the courts. The law which put the Basic principles into effect applied the procedure retroactively to children born out of wedlock before these regulations entered into force, i.e. prior to October 1, 1968.[58] Under those terms, several contingencies may be envisioned where the offspring will incur dual citizenship.

For example, the unwed mother is a citizen of a state which in these conditions extends its citizenship to the offspring, as, incidentally, many states do, the child was born on the territory of the USSR and the man then either voluntarily admits fatherhood by filing a suitable affidavit or the question of his liability is decided by the court and he turns out to be a Soviet citizen. The child now also figures as a Soviet citizen ex tunc and will henceforward suffer all the handicaps accruing from investiture with dual citizenship. Or, take the same set of facts, the single mother is a Soviet citizen and so the child immediately shares her Soviet citizenship; when the identity of the father is duly ascertained, he is found to be the citizen of a country which takes cognizance of legitimation procedures abroad and confers its citizenship on the offspring of its male citizens where the element of paternity has been legally established (as is the practice, for instance, in the socialist states of Eastern Europe where the attribution of citizenship in that event dates back to the moment of birth);[59] once again, the child is staked to two citizenships.

Or, the child of an unwed mother (not a Soviet citizen) is born outside the territory of the USSR and the mother communicates her citizenship to the child, but the father is officially revealed to be a Soviet citizen and either the mother or the father maintains a permanent place of residence on Soviet soil: the result is that the child is assigned Soviet citizenship in addition to the foreign citizenship transmitted by the mother. Or, the child is born out of wedlock outside the USSR to a woman who is not a Soviet citizen and does not maintain a permanent place of residence in the USSR and the child acquires foreign citizenship at birth either by virtue of jus sanguinis or jus soli; subsequently, it is formally disclosed that the father is a Soviet citizen who likewise maintains a permanent place of residence abroad, but the parents nevertheless agree to inscribe their child as a Soviet citizen: the child faces the future burdened with dual (or multiple) nationality.

The only "saving grace" where the outcome depends on the validity of proceedings instituted abroad involving litigation to fix paternity or legitimation through the medium of an administrative writ is that the child may be spared dual citizenship because the Soviet regime in principle can still refuse to recognize within its borders foreign judgments and, a fortiori, foreign administrative rulings, even if non-contentious in nature, in the absence of specific treaty arrangements envisaging cooperation across state lines on legal matters. By ignoring the determination of the primary affiliation, the Soviet authorities may avoid the further need to validate the findings in the sense of acknowledging the attendant claim to Soviet citizenship. The picture is different where international agreements on legal aid intrude. Since 1957, the Soviet Union has indeed signed pacts of that type with several states and vis-à-vis these countries it now carries definite obligations pertaining to overt recognition of their jurisdictional rights over various items and domestic enforcement of decisions duly rendered by their competent agencies on business falling within these areas.

Legitimation is one of the topics covered by most of these conventions, so that in an episode where a qualified local organ certifies a Soviet man as the father of a child born out of wedlock to a girl who is a citizen of that country, the child has excellent chances of starting life with two citizenships. An attempt has more recently been made to correct some of these defects through the parallel conclusion of bilateral accords aimed at preventing the inception of dual nationality (to be discussed below), but only one of these documents (the 1980 Soviet–Czechoslovak treaty) features a clause addressed explicitly to the prophylaxis of instances of dual nationality owing their existence to discrepancies in the statutory rules of the signatory nations devoted to the mechanics of legitimation. The relevant provision specifies that if in the case of a child of minor age, born to an unwed woman who is a citizen of one contracting party after the entry into force of the present agreement, there will be established the paternity of a citizen of the other contracting party, the parents can select for the offspring the citizenship of either signatory by filing a joint declaration not later than three months from the date of determination of fatherhood. In picking a citizenship for a minor child over the age of fourteen, the joint declaration of the parents is valid solely on the condition that it be accompanied by the written consent of the child. In the other countries concerned, practice may yet offer a similar measure of relief here if acquisition of dual citizenship by legitimation is analogized to bequeathal of dual citizenship at birth, a phenomenon which these compacts manage effectively to abort.

* * *

As the preceding tour d'horizon makes clear, dual citizenship is no stranger to the Soviet scene, passionate local denunciations of the experience notwithstanding. For that matter, a glance at the salient features of the 1978 citizenship law suggests that some of its novel provisions will cause the incidence of dual citizenship to increase in the years ahead. The only bright spot is the experiment to develop an impressive degree of immunity from dual citizenship in the relations between members of the socialist community by synchronizing their policies in a manner designed to reduce accidental bouts of dual citizenship through entrapment in one of the many specimens of the conflicts–in–law warp. The next step, then, is to see how the Soviets have fared in the bid to tackle the problem in their current diplomatic and treaty repertory both within the intimate circle of their class friends and in their dealings with the rest of the world.

NOTES

1. V. Durdenevskii, "Zakon o grazhdanstve Soiuza Sovetskikh Sotsialisticheskikh Respublik", *Problemy sotsialisticheskogo prava*, 1938, No.6, p.59.
2. *Ibid.*, p.65. In the same vein, V.N. Durdenevskii, in V.N. Durdenevskii & S.B. Krylov (eds.), *Mezhdunarodnoe pravo*, Moscow 1947, p.187; O.E. Polents, in E.A. Korovin (ed.), *Mezhdunarodnoe pravo*, Moscow 1951, pp.231–232; K.Ia. Chizhov, in F.I. Kozhevnikov (ed.), *Mezhdunarodnoe pravo*, Moscow, 1957, p.145; V.I. Menzhinskii, in F.I. Kozhevnikov (ed.), *Mezhdunarodnoe pravo*, Moscow 1964, p.288; N.T. Samartseva, in D.B. Levin & G.P. Kaliuzhnaia (eds.), *Mezhdunarodnoe pravo*, Moscow, 1964, p.159; D.L. Zlatopol'skii, *Gosudarstvennoe ustroistvo SSSR*, Moscow 1960, pp.258–259; A.I. Lepeshkin, *Kurs Sovetskogo gosudarstvennogo prava*, Moscow 1961, Vol.1, p.471; V.S. Shevtsov, *Sovetskoe grazhdanstvo*, Moscow, 1965, pp.25, 47; *idem*, in *Entsiklopedicheskii slovar' pravovykh znanii (Sovetskoe pravo)*, Moscow, 1965, p.91.
3. D.L. Zlatopol'skii, *op. cit.*, p.260, fn.1, citing *Izvestiia*, May 30, 1956. 1966 witnessed renewed controversy between the two capitals centering around the mailing of pension questionnaires by the Bonn Government to which the Soviet authorities objected on grounds that they sought secret data. The addressees could be the Soviet citizens of German origin whom the West Germans had attempted to locate through the Soviet officialdom on the earlier occasion and the rebuff may have prompted the West Germans to try to reach some of them by direct post or elicit information about them through personal contacts. See *New York Times*, June 29, 1966, p.12, and *Soviet News*, 1966, No.5291, pp.157, 159.
4. K.Ia. Chizhov, in F.I. Kozhevnikov (ed.), *International Law*, Moscow, 1957, tr. from the Russian by Dennis Ogden, p.149. Likewise, O.E. Polents, in E.A. Korovin (ed.), *op. cit.*, p.231; V.I. Menzhinskii, in F.I. Kozhevnikov (ed.), *op. cit.*, p.276; V.N. Durdenevskii, in V.N. Durdenevskii & S.B. Krylov (eds.), *op. cit.*, p.178.
5. V.S. Shevtsov, *op. cit.*, p.47, fn.1.
6. *Idem*, *Grazhdanstvo v sovetskom soiuznom gosudarstve*, Moscow, 1969, p.117.
7. L.B. Kuzmenko, "Razvitie pravovogo regulirovaniia statusa lichnosti v novom zakone o grazhdanstve SSSR", *Vestnik Moskovskogo universiteta*, 1980, No.4, seriia 11, Pravo, p.30.
8. *SZ SSSR*, 1933, No.34, Item 200. The text is also published in G.E. Vilkov (comp.), *Zakonodatel'stvo SSSR i mezhdunarodnye soglasheniia po voprosam grazhdanstva (sbornik)*, Moscow, 1964, pp.22–23.
9. I. Trainin, "K voprosu o grazhdanstve", *Sovetskoe gosudarstvo*, 1938, No.5, p.66.
10. V. Shevtsov, *Citizenship of the USSR (A Legal Study)*, Moscow, 1979, p.48.
11. Note that the 1933 decree that mandated the forfeiture of Soviet citizenship by all former Russian citizens who had gone abroad before November 7, 1917, and had acquired a foreign citizenship or applied for a foreign citizenship, does not contradict this observation since its terms dealt with Russian emigrés of the pre– Soviet period. Technically, they were eligible to succeed to Soviet citizenship, but had let the opportunity lapse by failing to take the necessary steps to register as Soviet citizens. The 1933 edict thus cancelled their potential title to Soviet citizenship and did not strip them of effective possession of Soviet citizenship.
12. This was noted earlier by B. Trachtenberg, "La Législation Soviétique sur la Nationalité", *Revue de Droit International Privé*, 1931, p.152, fn.1, in commenting on the provisions of the 1930 Regulations, where he disputes the opinion expressed by E.A. Korovine in his article "La République des Soviets et le droit international", *Revue générale de droit international public*, 1925, p.301, that "Soviet law repudiates the status of

dual nationality", based on the same evidence.

Today, Soviet legal writers openly concede that the fact of Soviet refusal to recognize the status of dual citizenship does not prevent the latter's actual occurrence. See, for instance, G.I. Tunkin, "Zakon o grazhdanstve SSSR", *Sovetskoe gosudarstvo i pravo*, 1979, No.7, pp.26–27 (hereafter abbr. as *SGiP*); V.M. Safronov, *Ty — grazhdanin Sovetskogo Soiuza*, Moscow, 1978, pp.29–30.

13. See, *American Journal of International Law*, 1979, No.4, p.678.
14. S.V. Chernichenko, *Mezhdunarodno–pravovye voprosy grazhdanstva*, Moscow, 1968, p.99. In similar vein, V.S. Shevtsov, *op. cit.* (note 6 above), p.55; *idem*, in *Konstitutsionnyi status lichnosti v SSSR*, Moscow, 1980, p.42; *idem*, "Sovetskoe grazhdanstvo i gosudarstvennyi suverenitet", *SGiP*, 1970, No.6, p.45; *idem*, *Gosudarstvennyi suverenitet (Voprosy teorii)*, Moscow, 1979, p.113.
15. S.V. Chernichenko, *op. cit.*, p.99. For a similar judgment by a Hungarian author, see V. Baiaki (V. Bajáki), "Obshchee i osobennoe v pravovom regulirovanii grazhdanstva v evropeiskikh sotsialisticheskikh stranakh", *SGiP*, 1976, No.11, p.83.
16. V.S. Shevtsov, *op. cit.* (note 6 above), pp.24–25.
17. B. Nepesov, "'Dvoinoe grazhdanstvo': chto eto takoe?", *Chelovek i zakon*, 1979, No.11, p.12.
18. V.S. Shevtsov, *op. cit.* (note 6 above), p.59.
19. Cf., V. Baiaki, *op. cit.*, p.84.
20. B.V. Shchetinin, *Problemy teorii sovetskogo gosudarstvennogo prava*, Moscow, 1974, p.184.
21. B. Nepesov, *op. cit.*, pp.16–17. Likewise, V.V. Polianskii, "Printsipy sovetskogo grazhdanstva", *SGiP*, 1980, No.5, pp.125–126, fn.8.
22. L.N. Galenskaia, in G.I. Tunkin (ed.), *Mezhdunarodnoe pravo*, Moscow, 1974, p.221.
23. S.V. Chernichenko, *op. cit.*, p.25.
24. *Ibid.*, p.78.
25. *Ibid.*, p.108.
26. V. Shevtsov, *op. cit.* (note 10 above), p.48. Also, G.I. Tunkin, *op. cit.*, p.26.
27. S.V. Chernichenko, *op. cit.*, p.110.
28. M.M. Whiteman, *Digest of International Law*, Washington, D.C., 1967 (Department of State Publication 8290), Vol.8, p.640. Per contra, in the Choolokian case, decided in 1947, the New York court ruled against the father, a native of Armenia and a naturalized citizen of the U.S., who sought to regain custody of his three minor children, native–born citizens of the U.S., with a view to removing them and himself to Soviet Armenia to which he was being repatriated. The Court reasoned that "if the father were permitted ... to take these three children to Soviet Armenia, it seems clear under present conditions that their right to avail themselves of the privileges of their American citizenship might be forever lost. It is unthinkable that an American court would permit this father to place his infant children in such an irretrievable position. While he may make that choice for himself, it will certainly not promote the interests of the children ... to permit the father or anyone to dissipate beyond redemption these priceless rights of the children. The exercise of these rights should not be left to the remote chance that they might some day before their twenty–third birthday be able to escape from Armenia and return to the United States" (pp.639–640). Soviet charges that the Choolokian children were held by "unlawful actions taken by the American authorities" and U.S. retorts that they were "protected from forced transfer" became the subject of heated diplomatic exchanges (p.656).
29. I.K. Gorodetskaia, "Grazhdanstvo detei", *SGiP*, 1971, No.4, p.38. These cases are again being rehashed with much vitriol in connection with the current Polovchak hearings.

See, I. Konstantinova, "Amerikanskaia femida protiv prav roditelei i detei", *Chelovek i zakon*, 1981, No.1, pp.120–123.

30. S. Voronitsyn, "New Approach to 'Compatriots Abroad'", Radio Liberty *Research* 348/76 (July 8, 1976), 4pp.

31. V. Semenov, "Solntsa pravdy ne zaslonit", in *Vot ona, ikh "pravda"*, Kharkov, 1972, pp.83–86. For more on the subject, see S.V. Chernichenko, *op. cit.*, pp.104–105; *Kurs mezhdunarodnogo prava*, Moscow, 1967, Vol.3, p.75, and B. Nepesov, *op. cit.*, p.14.

32. M.M. Whiteman, *op. cit.*, pp.649–657.

33. U.S. Department of State, Bureau of Public Affairs, "Implementation of Helsinki Accord, June 1–November 30, 1979", 7th Semiannual Report, *Special Report No.62*, p.13.

34. See *Khronika zashchity prav v SSSR*, vyp.10, p.50.

35. Compare the case of A.V. Malkin, reported *ibid.*, vyp.17, pp.47–53.

36. R. Kulik, "Pravovye nachala sovetskogo grazhdanstva", *Sovety narodnykh deputa tov*, 1979, No.2, p.37. See, too, V.S. Shevtsov, in *Konstitutsionnyi status lichnosti v SSSR*, p.42.

37. Cf., G.I. Tunkin, *op. cit.*, p.26.

38. S. Chernichenko, "Nash grazhdanin", *Izvestiia*, June 15, 1968.

39. E.g., V.I. Lisovskii, *Mezhdunarodnoe pravo*, Kiev, 1955, p.101; *idem*, *Mezhdunarodnoe pravo*, 2nd ed., Moscow 1961, p.113. Also V.N. Durdenevskii, in V.N. Durdenevskii & S.B. Krylov (eds.), *op. cit.*, p.176.

40. Vide B. Trachtenberg, *op. cit.* (note 12 above), p.156.

41. S.V. Chernichenko, *op. cit.*, (note 14 above), p.59.

42. N. Bar–Yaacov, *Dual Nationality*, London, 1961, p.124.

43. V. Baiaki, *op. cit.*, p.86.

44. *Ibid.*

45. *Ibid.*, p.83.

46. S.V. Chernichenko, *op. cit.* (note 14 above), pp.129–130.

47. *Ibid.*, p.129.

48. V.M. Safronov, *op. cit.*, pp.32–33.

49. S. Kosakov, "Konstitutsionnye osnovy kompetentsii soiuznoi respubliki po voprosam grazhdanstva", *Izvestiia Akademii nauk Kazakhskoi SSR*, 1980, No.5, seriia obshchestvennykh nauk, p.65.

50. V.S. Shevtsov, *Sovetskoe grazhdanstvo*, p.46; G.I. Tunkin, *op. cit.* (note 12 above), p.26.

51. S.V. Chernichenko, *op. cit.* (note 14 above), p.129; V.M. Safronov, *op. cit.*, p.32.

52. See, for example, the literature cited in note 39 above.

53. A.Ia. Berchenko, "Voprosy sovetskogo grazhdanstva", in *Torzhestvo leninskoi natsional'noi politiki*, Moscow, 1963, p.277.

54. With the further proviso, laid down in Article 25, that the change of the citizenship of the children between the ages of 14 and 18 in case of adoption can take place only with the consent of the children expressed in written form. See, too, V.S. Shevtsov, *Sovetskoe grazhdanstvo*, p.46.

55. V.N. Durdenevskii, *op. cit.*, p.64; *idem*, in V.N. Durdenevskii & S.B Krylov, eds., *op. cit.*, p.186.

56. Again, with the same qualification as mentioned in note 54 above relating to Article 25.

57. V.N. Durdenevskii, *op. cit.*, p.65.

58. *Vedomosti Verkhovnogo Soveta SSSR*, 1968, No.27, Art.241. The decree of the USSR Supreme Soviet Presidium of October 9, 1979, amplified these provisions by adding

that "where, in conformity with Soviet legislation, it is permitted to establish paternity in the organs of registry of acts of civil status, the parents of a child who reside outside the confines of the USSR, when at least one of them is a citizen of the USSR, have the right to file a statement concerning establishment of paternity with the consular offices of the USSR", *VVS SSSR*, 1979, No.42, Art. 696.

59. V. Baiaki, *op. cit.*, p.82. It is not clear whether this is also true of the Soviet Union. Note that Article 9 of the federal decree of September 20, 1968, on the procedure for putting into effect the Basic principles of legislation of the USSR and union republics on marriage and the family *(VVS SSSR*, 1969, No.39, Art.353) provides that in the event of recognition of fatherhood in the case of children born out of wedlock before the Basic principles went into force either by declaration or court order, the mutual rights and duties between a child born before October 1, 1968, and the father, as well as the father's relatives, are considered as arising from the date of the child's birth. Whether this procedure applies only to "private" rights or, by analogy, further extends to the public domain, such as citizenship law, remains uncertain.

DUAL NATIONALITY AND SOVIET DIPLOMATIC AND TREATY PRACTICE

The Soviet government has, from the outset, shown keen awareness of the grave tensions that disputes over dual nationality have habitually engendered on the diplomatic scene.[1] Typical responses from Soviet quarters range from sweeping assertions that Soviet law rejects the very notion of dual citizenship[2] to grudging admissions that "Soviet constitutional law takes the attitude that a person's concurrent possession of the citizenship of two states is abnormal and can only have a temporary character".[3] Or, in the same negative tone, "in contemporary international law the principle is generally recognized that each person must be the citizen of some state and, to boot, of one only; from that perspective, the statelessness of apatrides and dual or multiple citizenship are equally undesirable".[4] Or, again, "in contemporary international law it is generally recognized that every person must be the citizen of some one country. In the event a physical person has two or more citizenships, it must choose one."[5]

However, for all the brave words, Moscow has from the start done very little to help cure this major cause of serious friction between states. As previously observed, merely denying the existence of dual or multiple nationality at home is not a viable answer. Active treatment is required and yet, in its sixty plus year history, the USSR has but rarely evinced willingness to initiate positive steps to deal with that "endemic ailment". On the other hand, one must also concede that, save for a few signal exceptions, the Soviet leadership has ordinarily abstained from instituting measures that would directly increase the incidence of the "disease". By and large, its conduct here has been marked by apathy, if you will, in the sense that the regime has philosophically accepted the reality of dual nationality precipitated by the blind collision of disparate legal orders, without bothering to do anything about it beyond trying to minimize the chances of conflict between itself and other states arising on these grounds by announcing, a priori, that it will entertain no claims generated by competing citizenship interests. Meanwhile, the fate of the de cujus, in the process literally impaled on the horns of a dilemma, has seemingly left it completely cold.

There have been some detours from the main route, of course, going both ways: occasionally, the USSR has condescended to tackle the problem of dual nationality in a constructive manner; in a few instances, it has backslid and through its policies furthered the spread of dual nationality in the outside world.

For example, the series of "option" agreements concluded between the USSR and the Third Reich in the period 1939–1941 was definitely inspired, at least at the

Soviet end, by a resolve to prevent future difficulties with Berlin owing to the extension of Soviet citizenship in the wake of the incorporation of fresh lands on the USSR's western perimeter to a large segment of the local population to which, by ethnic standards, Nazi Germany unilaterally attributed its own nationality.[6] Prior to the Nazi–Soviet rapprochement (and the theme is now popular once again, with the cast of villains expanded and updated to include Imperial Japan, Israel, and the mainland Chinese regime), Soviet spokesmen had never missed an opportunity to denounce that particular practice in the most violent terms, branding it a plot against world peace and the security of other nations, a plan to organize "fascist fifth columns" abroad, an instrumentality for a campaign of mass treason and subversion wherever so–called volksdeutsch enclaves had put down roots. With that in mind, Stalin's administration must have been more than eager to settle that question permanently with its Nazi partner where, thanks to recent Soviet territorial gains, their jurisdictional circuits currently happened to overlap.

This is not to say, as has sometimes been done, that the Soviet government was unwilling, ex principio, to grant its citizenship to the German element in the newly annexed regions or that it automatically classified the German colonists in these areas as citizens of the Third Reich. Rather, aware of the fact that Nazi Germany laid specific demands on their obedience and, indeed, considered them fullfledged German subjects, the USSR was determined to get a commitment from Berlin that would finally clarify the status of this alien minority: either these people could leave for Germany and be solely German citizens; or, they could stay on Soviet soil, forget all about their "German blood" and become Soviet citizens exclusively. In other words, it was not their "Germanic ancestry" that rendered them suspect in the Kremlin's eyes, as has often been alleged, but the prospect of their continued juridical association with Germany, the latter insisting on treating them as its nationals and they perhaps behaving accordingly. That thought was unbearable to the Red hierarchy which, especially at this juncture, was using all the means in its power to monopolize the loyalties of every member of the Soviet body politic. However, as soon as this link with another state was broken, the inhabitants with a German background of the districts just absorbed into the USSR were as welcome to the title of Soviet citizen as their native neighbors.

No different was the situation with respect to Poland when, toward the close of the Second World War, the Soviet Union mounted a sustained effort to regularize the position of its citizens of Polish stock whom the Poles also regarded as citizens of Poland. The decrees of 1944 and the early bilateral treaties between the UkSSR, the BSSR, the Lithuanian SSR, the USSR, and Poland, aggregately pursued the single objective of annulling, again through the application of quasi–option techniques, one of the two citizenships these people were deemed vested with and ultimately producing individuals who were either citizens of Poland or purely citizens of the USSR, but not both simultaneously.[7] And, the two experiments conducted jointly with Czechoslovakia in the Transcarpathian Ukraine and the former province of Volhynia were likewise aimed at "sorting out" which person was the citizen of what country.

In some of these instances, bona fide dual citizenship was at stake, in the sense that both parties had valid jural claims to the individuals concerned. Elsewhere, the clash involved a legal relationship, on the one hand, and an "ethnic affiliation" symptomatic of latent citizenship ties or pregnant with potential citizenship bonds, on the other. Either spelled wide latitude for foreign intervention in defense of individuals purportedly identified with the self-appointed protector-power through racial kinship, and it sounds as though that is exactly what the Kremlin was attempting to guard itself against.

The desire to curb manifestations of dual nationality in the USSR also accounts for the adoption of decree No. 142/41 of August 30, 1956, which prescribed the procedure for the loss of Soviet citizenship by persons of Spanish nationality residing in the USSR since 1936-1940 and departing for Spain for domicile. For, as far as one can tell, these individuals, most of them minors when evacuated to the Soviet Union in the last stages of the Spanish Civil War, had retained their Spanish nationality intact and, in addition, had subsequently requested or accepted Soviet citizenship, thus incurring dual nationality. Those of them who took advantage of this offer were considered to have relinquished their Soviet citizenship upon leaving the USSR and so managed to shed one half of the citizenships with which they were encumbered. The status of those who stayed behind underwent no change, since the Soviet government could not alone resolve their predicament, except that, having taken this step, Moscow was certainly better equipped to argue that those who had chosen to remain in the USSR had conclusively demonstrated their preference for Soviet citizenship and that their erstwhile Spanish nationality was, to all intents and purposes, henceforth a dead letter.

Far less satisfactory from that point of view was the second portion of the enactment which recognized the right of Soviet citizens not of Spanish nationality married to Spaniards to emigrate together with their spouses and, in that connection, indicated that any such person preserved his or her Soviet citizenship if he or she had not submitted beforehand a special declaration renouncing it. In effect, this meant that where, under these circumstances, the non-Spanish wife of a Spanish exile decided not to discard her Soviet citizenship on embarking for Spain with her husband, she nevertheless was likely to find herself issued a Spanish passport upon arrival as the wife of a Spanish citizen and so discover that she now had two citizenships. Much of this was due to the simple lack of administrative coordination that marked the operation from start to finish: in the absence of direct diplomatic contacts between Moscow and Madrid, the business had to be arranged through their respective Red Cross Societies and that, in turn, led to a great deal of poor planning and legislative confusion. Had the program been synchronized a bit more carefully, many of its glaring defects and unfortunate repercussions could have easily been avoided. Still, one may want to give the interested parties credit for having had good intentions.[8]

On the opposite side of the ledger, one finds, to be sure, the collection of edicts promulgated shortly after the defeat of the Axis designed to enable persons who on November 7, 1917, had been subjects of the Russian empire and persons who had formerly had Soviet citizenship and had lost it, as well as their children, and who then resided in Manchuria, in the province of Sinkiang and the cities of Shanghai and Tientsin, in France, Yugoslavia, Bulgaria, Japan, Czechoslovakia and Belgium to recover their Soviet citizenship by filing petitions to that end with the local Soviet diplomatic mission, accompanied by documents establishing the applicant's identity and his past possession of the nationality of the old Russian empire or Soviet citizenship. Whether or not these individuals were at present endowed with another citizenship was apparently quite immaterial. They could obtain Soviet citizenship by this "speeded-up" process independently of whether they already owned a set of valid foreign citizenship papers or not, and, if they did, without having to relinquish it first. Such a scheme naturally entailed numerous episodes of dual citizenship, but the Soviet authorities must have judged the price not an unreasonable one to pay for the sake of the major propaganda victory represented by the well-advertised return to the fold of an appreciable quantity of individuals who had at one time openly repudiated the regime.[9]

By the same token, the assorted instructions which defined the conditions for acquisition of Soviet citizenship by permanent residents of the Baltic States, Bessarabia, the city of Klaipeda, Śilute and Pagegiai districts of the Lithuanian SSR following the absorption of these territories into the USSR had one feature in common in that, when dealing with the item of those individuals among the above who were abroad on the critical day, they called on the absentees to register immediately with the nearest Soviet diplomatic office and receive Soviet passports. The current citizenship status of these persons was ignored: even if they had in the meantime been admitted to a foreign citizenship, they could obtain Soviet citizenship virtually by asking for it and, ostensibly, could then hold on to both, unless the state whose citizens they had been up to this point cancelled their citizenship in the face of this evidence of their "renaturalization".[10]

A comparable experience befell a large contingent of Armenians who fled or were expelled from the Ottoman Empire (or its heirs) on the eve of, during and after the First World War and flocked by the thousands to settle in Russian (later Soviet) Armenia.[11] Many had no citizenship papers at all or possessed documents that had either expired or were no longer recognized by the country of origin or, in an number of cases, the successor state. Others could furnish some evidence of a connection with a foreign citizenship. The general policy of the authorities in Soviet Armenia was to recognize without further ado all Armenians within reach who were former subjects of Turkey (in its previous or present incarnation) as subjects of the Armenian SSR. However, while mechanically accepting Armenian refugees into Armenian nationality or treating them as nationals of the Armenian SSR, the competent local agencies overlooked the need for personal validation, even if only in simplified form, of the conversion of each Armenian refugee who was a past subject of Turkey and, of course, the absence of legal records eventually caused a great deal of confusion.

Twenty years elapsed before the regime finally moved to correct the anomaly. Following a report by the Commission of the Presidium of the USSR Supreme Soviet charged with examining questions of admission to, exit from and deprivation of USSR citizenship, the federal Presidium resolved at its session of August 8, 1940, to recommend to the Presidium of the Supreme Soviet of the Armenian SSR to expedite the formal inscription into Soviet citizenship of Armenian ex-refugees residing on the territory of Armenia and not duly registered as Soviet citizens. Complying with these instructions, the Presidium of the Supreme Soviet of the

Armenian SSR issued a resolution on December 26, 1940, mandating the application of the necessary procedures for certifying the Armenian citizenship of former Armenian refugees who had relocated to the USSR and resided on the territory of the Armenian SSR and did not possess a validated Soviet citizenship.[12] The bulk of the people caught in this police dragnet could not prove entitlement to any foreign citizenship and so, technically speaking, the issue of dual citizenship did not arise in their case (indeed, they were now officially rescued from statelessness and the operation will also be subsequently discussed under that heading). However, others in their midst did have such a claim and yet indications are that they, too, were not spared in the mass head–count and had Soviet citizenship summarily thrust upon them, thereby simply superimposing it on the earlier identity and thus creating at least a dormant condition of dual nationality.

Less chaotic was the second wave of migration to Soviet Armenia that gained momentum in the aftermath of World War II and witnessed the repatriation of around 100,000 Armenian "exiles" from the Middle East, France and the United States during 1945–1947 alone.[13] A much greater percentage of these "evacuees" already possessed a foreign citizenship than was true of their forerunners. Nevertheless, the Kremlin's policy here was still premised on the concept of the immediate integration of the "returnees" into Soviet citizenship, as attested to by the terms of the federal Presidium's edict of October 19, 1946, directing that persons of Armenian nationality coming "back home" to Soviet Armenia be recognized as Soviet citizens from the moment they entered the USSR.[14] The net effect of this collective baptism was once again to spawn many instances of dual citizenship since it was nowhere stipulated that the gift of Soviet citizenship to these immigrants had to be preceded by the proper surrender of their previous nationality. Soviet citizenship merely overlaid whatever nationality they had hitherto enjoyed, if they themselves had not taken the prior precaution of shedding it or had not been forced to do so by the country whose citizens they had been on the eve of the exodus or did not automatically forfeit it upon receiving Soviet citizenship. In 1962, a decision was made to put the program on a regular footing and the leading organs of Soviet Armenia forthwith instituted a permanent project of repatriation of "overseas" Armenians. The repeal of the decree of October 19, 1946 (effective July 1, 1979) in connection with the enactment of the 1978 citizenship statute marks the end of the venture — as far as the initial wholesale format and priority billing are concerned, at any rate.[15]

In fact, the flow of traffic has recently changed direction and, ironically, the dual nationality problem of many of the same people has now emerged in a reverse setting in that a growing number of the original post–war "repatriates" and their descendants are invoking the latent foreign citizenship as grounds for requesting permission to emigrate. In the event they manage to obtain an exit visa, they go abroad still vested with Soviet citizenship (as will be noted later in the chapter) and, by reviving their old citizenship or acquiring a different one in their new homeland, perpetuate their status as dual nationals (except that in the present context the Soviet strain is virulent, whereas while they were in the USSR their concurrent claim to a foreign citizenship in practice remained inactive).

* * *

Between 1956 and 1958, the USSR signed pacts, officially designated as conventions "to regulate the question of citizenship of persons with dual citizenship", with nine countries: Yugoslavia, on May 22, 1956;[16] Hungary, August 24, 1957;[17] Romania, September 4, 1957;[18] Albania, September 18, 1957;[19] Czechoslovakia, October 5, 1957;[20] Bulgaria, December 12, 1957;[21] North Korea, December 16, 1957;[22] Poland, January 21, 1958;[23] and Mongolia, August 25, 1958.[24] Reportedly, Communist China was also approached, for, according to Soviet sources, in 1960 Peking turned down a Soviet proposal that the two governments enter into an agreement concerning citizenship and the legal protection of citizens of both countries.[25] However, East Germany joined the company on April 11, 1969,[26] and a fresh treaty was concluded with Romania on June 28, 1978, which, inter alia, reverted to the matter of settling existing cases of dual citizenship.[27] This ensemble of agreements represents the first systematic attempt on the part of the Soviet government to solve outstanding issues of double citizenship affecting its interests by means of formal bilateral accords. So, before proceeding with a technical analysis of the contents of these documents, a closer look at the environmental factors which brought about this landmark development might prove worthwhile.

Soviet authors usually allude to this aspect of Soviet diplomatic policy in order to make the point that "the conclusion by the USSR of bilateral agreements on citizenship once more demonstrates that in our country dual citizenship is rejected".[28] Indeed, some go even farther and contrast the Soviet Union's accomplishments in this connection with the futility of past efforts of the "capitalist" world to find a workable answer to that objectionable phenomenon, explaining that "only with the evolution of international relations of a new type, relations between socialist states, did a clear possibility emerge of solving this problem successfully, in particular through the conclusion of bilateral agreements".[29]

That the negotiation of each of these conventions was dictated by a desire on both sides to liquidate recorded incidents of dual nationality involving their citizenship is self–evident. This simple observation does not, however, convey the whole picture and to grasp that one must try to understand what initially caused the situation to arise. In effect, as noted by a leading western authority on the subject,

> "the origins of all these cases of dual nationality can be very different. But one can suppose that, as a general rule, the genesis of these cases lies in the migrations after the first World War and during the second. These migrations resulted in naturalizations consummated outside the Soviet Union not entailing the loss of Soviet nationality under the legislation of the USSR, and vice versa."[30]

Several elements must be distinguished here.

To begin with, the accumulation of episodes of dual nationality the parties proposed to deal with in this manner must have contained a fair proportion of ordinary instances of dual nationality occasioned by the routine collision of the corresponding citizenship norms, many dating back to the immediate post– war years before the nationality statutes of the satellite countries had been thoroughly reorganized on the Soviet model. For that matter, the reforms themselves did not always turn out to be a panacea in this respect either. To cite just one example, the primary reliance throughout the "orbit" on the doctrine of jus sanguinis has since actively contributed to the frequency of dual citizenship at birth for children of local "mixed" marriages. In any event, the item of "involuntary dual citizenship" also needs to be taken into account for these purposes.

Next, the vast movements of population that accompanied the fighting in World War I, as well as in the Bolshevik Revolution and the ensuing civil strife, carried large numbers of former Russian and Soviet citizens into Eastern Europe and the Far East where thousands of these exiles gradually acquired permanent resident status together with the citizenship of the host country. Those of them who were not deprived of their Soviet citizenship by virtue of the various edicts issued by the regime in the meantime now found themselves with two citizenships. If they had managed to survive World War II, had not been caught in the dragnet cast by the Red Army in its sweep through these lands in pursuit of the retreating Wehrmacht and the defeated Japanese forces and summarily shipped off to the USSR by the Soviet military authorities, and at this juncture were still domiciled in their country of adoption with whom the USSR had signed such a treaty, the latter's clauses applied to them in full.

The same holds true for many of the prisoners of war interned in Russia at the close of World War I who joined the revolution and stayed in the USSR, ultimately receiving Soviet citizenship, often without having ever lost their original nationality, and leftist political refugees from these areas who fled from persecution at home and sought asylum in the USSR and were later admitted to Soviet citizenship, while keeping their old citizenship. If any among them currently qualified as citizens of both states and had the right combination of citizenships (within the present frame of reference), they were subject to the provisions of the appropriate agreement.

Added to that, every ex–Russian and ex–Soviet emigré who, in 1946 was living in Yugoslavia, Bulgaria, or Czechoslovakia and had accepted Moscow's invitation, extended through the two decrees of June 14 and the decree of October 5, 1946, respectively, to register as a Soviet citizen and, upon so doing, got a Soviet permis de séjour, but had not surrendered beforehand his local citizenship, since he was not expected to, was covered by the terms of the corresponding convention.

Again, the mass of people to whom the USSR had offered a haven in the course of World War II to a great extent consisted of individuals from many of these same countries who, while in the Soviet Union, either requested Soviet citizenship or were pressed into asking for it, simultaneously retaining their previous citizenship, and ended up with two perfectly valid citizenships. Subsequently, their ranks were swelled by hundreds of prisoners of war from the units dispatched by Nazi Germany's lesser allies to the Russian front who were not returned when the fighting in Europe stopped, put down roots in the Soviet Union and became naturalized Soviet citizens, but in the interim had not relinquished their former citizenship. The pacts were aimed at this species of bipatrides too.

Conversely, through deportation, evacuation, or escape, a host of Soviet citizens also wound up in these countries during the war and a few had somehow avoided repatriation to the USSR when peace was restored, had settled down and were now naturalized citizens of their new homeland, overlooking in the process the small technical detail that their Soviet citizenship always remained unimpaired. As persons officially vested with two citizenships, they came within the purview of the latest measures designed specifically to handle people in that ambiguous position.

Finally, and this is the most interesting facet of the entire experiment, there was a special category of individuals, natives of these lands or ethnically identified with them, who had made their way to the USSR over the years, had acquired Soviet citizenship and then were sent back to their homes to assist with the execution of Moscow's project for the political take–over of these countries. At this point, their erstwhile citizenship was either revived or refurbished, their Soviet citizenship did not lapse and they henceforth apparently performed as citizens of both nations. Nobody knows how many individuals were recruited in this manner to do the Kremlin's bidding in the territories which fell under its sway as a result of the military defeat of the Axis, although one suspects that the scheme involved a very appreciable contingent of persons carefully screened and deliberately equipped with dual nationality in order better to fulfill their assigned functions.

That their primary loyalty lay with the Soviet Union in those days is not seriously open to doubt. Indeed, the operation was conceived in precisely that spirit, as witness the following apt description of how these tactics were employed in North Korea — itself just a typical contemporary sample of such practices elsewhere in the emergent Soviet empire:

> "Most of the key positions of power rin North Korea after 1945t were entrusted to Soviet–Koreans who were selected from the Korean communities in the USSR and brought into North Korea after the close of the war with Japan for this special role. These men retained their Soviet citizenship and membership in the Soviet Communist Pary and generally remained in the background in the North Korean political arena, but they were infiltrated into, and dominated, the top levels of the party and the government. The general nature and importance of these quasi–Russian Koreans may be indicated by the case of Ho Kai, First Secretary of the North Korean Labor Party. Ho had formerly been a member of the Central Committee of a Soviet Central Asian Republic; in North Korea he was perhaps the most powerful official in the regime."[31]

The reverse side of this particular coin was represented by the human stream flowing in the opposite direction: deportees from the nations freshly integrated into the Soviet realm being scattered in the depths of the Eurasian continent to remove them from their natural political habitat, physically isolate them and ideologically disarm them, at least for the duration of the "class struggle" and until the safe consolidation of Communist rule in their countries. Ulteriorly, some won release from the camps in which they had at first been detained, were allowed to resume relatively normal life as alien residents of the USSR and succeeded in obtaining Soviet citizenship on top of the one they had hitherto possessed.

The complex of agreements intended to regulate the citizenship of persons with dual citizenship was organically concerned with both these groups as well. In fact, perhaps in a sense it is the unresolved status of these people that constituted the real rationale for drawing up all these elaborate plans.

For, when the events are thus put in proper perspective, it is easy to see that this affair marks a definite political setback to Soviet policy. An important concession wrung from the Kremlin by the disruptions within the camp triggered by the death of Stalin and the ensuing struggle for the vacant throne among his heirs, it wiped out a major element in the powerful apparatus of informal control so skillfully nurtured by Stalin to impose and perpetuate his domination of the satellite nations: dependable people in each of them trained to carry out his will, bound to the Soviet Union, inter alia, by the juridical ties of citizenship; a ready reserve of people in the USSR itself endowed with dual citizenship and prepared, if commandeered "home", to serve on the spot as the Soviet government's emissaries in lieu of unreliable indigenous cadres or any of their own predecessors who had become too thoroughly acclimatized and betrayed nationalistic inclinations.[32]

This also explains why the deal with Yugoslavia was plainly more favorable to the latter than were the comparable arrangements to the other states, notwithstanding attempts by Soviet sources to picture the situation as though "these differences are not a matter of principle and only emphasize the diversified approach to the solution of the question of individuals possessing dual citizenship":[33] Belgrade simply had more to bargain with and could name a higher price for what the Russians wanted in exchange than the rest who, though they likewise benefited from the transaction, did so more due to Moscow's desire to reach a modus vivendi with the centripetal forces loosed in the Communist world by the post–Stalin developments than because they were, as yet, genuinely able to set down conditions vis–à–vis the USSR.

As regards certain classes of individuals, the latitude for election was narrower in the case of Yugoslavia, which in effect meant that an assortment of persons whom the USSR heretofore had claimed as Soviet citizens suddenly saw their Soviet citizenship nullified, leaving them solely in possession of a Yugoslav citizenship. Their private preferences did not seem to count; Soviet diplomatic protection was publicly withdrawn from a local element with a past record of strong pro–Muscovite orientation and it was abandoned to its fate. Elsewhere, the outcome was far less drastic and an opportunity freely to choose cushioned the shock of transition for those individuals who, because of their earlier activities, thought they would feel more comfortable if they presently transferred and took up domicile on Soviet soil.[34]

In concrete terms, the scope of the accord with Mongolia was probably the most marginal of the lot. Many of the factors that helped create the problem in the other "people's democracies" were absent in this instance. For example, an effort was made at a very early stage to deal with the consequences of migration by certain Siberian nomadic peoples, notably the Buriats, across the border to Mongolia. Already in 1922, a congress of delegates from the local Buriat population which met in Urga adopted a resolution to petition the Mongolian government to accept into Mongolian nationality those among them who desired to convert. The application was approved, suitable directives were issued in the USSR and Mongolia sanctioning, respectively, the right of citizens of the USSR who had emigrated to Mongolia to transfer to Mongolian nationality and their entry into Mongolian nationality and, in 1923, after negotiations between the USSR and Mongolia, a special commission was appointed to regulate this question.[35]

At the Third Congress of the Mongolian People's Party, held in August 1924, it was disclosed that 3,000 Buriat households had by then asked for and received Mongolian nationality and that the immigration of Buriats into Mongolia was increasing all the time.[36] The phenomenon was, of course, well known to the Soviet authorities and, in fact, may even have been encouraged by them, since Soviet Buriats were extensively used by Moscow in consummating the "Sovietization" of Mongolia. To take care of the matter of the citizenship status of these resettlers, an option agreement was concluded on October 3, 1924, by which the parties confirmed that, in accordance with the lists appended thereto, Buriats who had duly filed a statement on exit from the citizenship of the USSR and admission to Mongolian nationality were forthwith considered to have switched to Mongolian nationality.[37] At the First Great Khuruldan of the Mongolian People's Republic, convened in November 1924, an official spokesman reported that a total of 4,360 Buriat yurt owners or households had transferred to Mongolian nationality, the number including 5,149 adult males, 5,296 adult females, 2,995 minors of the male sex, 2,683 minors of the female sex, or 16,093 mouths in all.[38]

Because the 1924 agreement treated only existing incidents of dual nationality occasioned by naturalization procedures, the signatories had to return to the subject twice more in order to dispose of successive accruals of such cases. Thus, a new accord was concluded on May 20, 1930,[39] which provided that each side would not on its territory admit into its citizenship persons belonging to the citizenship of the other without the consent of the latter's competent organs, to be communicated via its local diplomatic representative. The Soviet government reiterated its acceptance of the exit from Soviet citizenship of those Soviet citizens who were admitted into Mongolian citizenship on the territory of Mongolia prior to 1924 and figured on the lists drawn up in 1924 by officials of the two countries. In turn, the Mongolian government expressed its willingness to review, jointly with the Soviet envoy in Mongolia, the question of the citizenship status of individuals not named in the above lists but admitted by then into Mongolian citizenship. In this connection, the parties concurred that Mongolian citizenship would not be recognized as vesting in persons concerning whom information was available that they had engaged in crimes or political activities hostile to the USSR or Mongolia. Those persons who would not be allowed to retain Mongolian citizenship would be liable to expulsion to the USSR. The modus operandi prescribed by the present protocol was slated to apply for three years following the accord's entry into force, i.e., until February 28, 1934.

The arrangement effectively lapsed as scheduled and on April 24, 1937, Moscow and Ulan–Bator entered into a fresh agreement which repeated the clause about neither of them on its territory admitting into its citizenship the citizens of the other without proper acquiescence by that side.[40] However, the routine was now revised. Instead of the "naturalizing" state waiting to be notified by the original homeland of the petitioner that no objections existed to the transfer, henceforth the former's Ministry of Foreign Affairs would in every instance address an inquiry to the local diplomatic representative of the other partner asking if there was any opposition to the proposed switch: failure to answer within three months meant acquiescence. None of these considerations affected the freedom of either party to admit into its citizenship in the established manner persons who maintained that they were citizens of the other country but did not submit as proof a passport or some substitute document corroborating the statement. Conversely, the diplomatic or consular representative of one state could request the other's government to defer the final admission of such a person to its citizenship pending clarification by the diplomatic or consular mission of the issue of whether the de cujus was a citizen of its country. A four–month deadline was set for verifying these facts and, if the check revealed that the citizenship claim was indeed valid, the usual procedures were observed. As regards those people who had, in the period between February 28, 1934, and April 24, 1937, converted from the citizenship of one signatory to that of the other, their current citizenship was to be left undisturbed, and the contracting parties undertook to exchange lists of names of those who fell into this category. On being furnished the roster, the receiving side had three months to convey its reservations regarding any person appearing on it and get together with the other party to examine the decision taken with respect to this "dubious" contingent in order, if need be, to review the record. The accord was concluded for an indefinite term and is still in force.

All of these projects concentrated on a single source of dual nationality, namely, the mechanics of naturalization, and, as one Soviet writer points out, the 1937 treaty with Mongolia is the only agreement of this kind to which the USSR is a party that "deals exclusively with admission to citizenship".[41] The therapeutic effect of the entire experiment is thus quite limited owing to the specialized focus; even so, the likelihood of dual citizenship occurring here by virtue of the conflicts–in–law phenomenon was sensibly reduced as a consequence and, of course, valuable experience was gained on how to curb the frequency of these incidents in the relations between socialist states. The success of these measures in shutting the door on the inception of dual citizenship through naturalization notwithstanding, the species of dual nationality acquired at birth continued to accrete[42] and it was chiefly this item that must have convinced the participants of the advisability of a supplementary convention between them to fill the remaining interstices.

The spatial range of the agreements varied. The Soviet–Yugoslav text was to apply to persons whom both sides regarded as their citizens insofar as these persons permanently resided on the territory of either signatory. The Soviet–Hungarian, 1957 Soviet–Romanian,[43] Soviet–Albanian, Soviet–North Korean, Soviet–Polish and Soviet–Mongolian documents repeated that formula (the 1978 Soviet–Romanian version further explaining that its terms referred to overlapping claims extant on the date of the agreement's entry into force), except that they omitted the word "permanently" and spoke just of residence. The treaties between the USSR and Czechoslovakia, the USSR and Bulgaria, and the USSR and East Germany, on the other hand, covered more ground in that they encompassed all "persons whom both Contracting Parties on the basis of their legislation considered their citizens", irrespective of where they happened to be situated and, hence, made separate provisions for those among them who were located on the territory of third states. The 1978 Soviet–Romanian variant featured a lone clause à propos the status of certain minor children born and residing on the territory of third states, but elsewhere firmly maintained a territorial frame.

Then, as already mentioned, the circle of individuals to whom the right to "opt" was now guaranteed was not identical in every case. The Soviet–Yugoslav compromise explicitly barred from the enjoyment of its benefits persons who, while in possession of one country's citizenship obtained the citizenship of the other without having received permission to relinquish the citizenship they previously owned, if they permanently resided on the territory of the country whose citizenship they formerly had. This major restrictive clause is missing from the other agreements in the original series, plus the 1969 Soviet–East German offshoot, which extended the privilege of voluntary decision to all persons who duly qualified as dual citizens, independently of how they came by that status. The 1978 Soviet–Romanian edition occupies a position mid–way between these two models by mandating that the citizens of one signatory who, prior to the entry into force of the current convention, had received upon their request the citizenship of the other side without losing their existing citizenship kept the most recent citizenship.

Since the second Soviet–Romanian treaty was essentially designed to cure the fresh backlog of dual citizenship outbreaks recorded after the first accord lapsed, i.e., in the interval between March 3, 1958, and April 15, 1979 — cases routinely caused and devoid of any political history (quite unlike the initial package handled by its predecessor) — there was no reason at this stage to impugn the propriety of the naturalization operations performed during this period or question the preferences freely expressed by the individuals concerned on that score. However, in light of this acknowledgment that such transfers could until then take place in circumstances which produced dual citizenship casts doubt on the veracity of certain statements by Soviet and East European authors that a customary rule precluding that very possibility marked the intra–mural practice of the major segment of the socialist community without benefit of a corresponding treaty norm (in fact absent, one should note, from the 1957 Soviet–Romanian prototype). Or, the Soviet–Romanian experience may in this respect have simply differed from that of its sister–states functioning in a similar setting due to the less intimate rapport between the Soviet and Romanian regimes in the intervening years compared to the close ties maintained between the USSR and the other members of the cast.[44]

Otherwise, persons who were deemed eligible under the proposed program and who, living on the territory of one country, desired to stay with the citizenship of the other could, within a year of the entry into force of the corresponding convention, file a declaration of intent with the local embassy (diplomatic or consular office in the USSR–Czechoslovakia, USSR–GDR, and 1978 USSR–Romania treaties) of the state whose citizenship they had chosen. The USSR and Yugoslavia later prolonged the deadline an extra year;[45] the balance underwent no further revision. The Soviet–Polish, Soviet–East German and 1978 Soviet–Romanian accords specified that the request had to be submitted in duplicate. The Soviet–Czechoslovak, the Soviet–Bulgarian, and the Soviet–East German conventions adopted the same procedure for persons living in a third country who could register their preference with the proper diplomatic or consular mission accredited there (or, in the USSR–GDR case, also directly with the appropriate Ministry of Foreign Affairs).

Individuals who had reached majority could petition, i.e., persons eighteen and over, or younger than eighteen if married (the Soviet–Mongolian and 1978 Soviet–Romanian pacts say eighteen and make no special dispensation for young married people; oddly enough, the Soviet–East German version neither mentions nor defines majority in this context).

Minor children eo ipso shared the citizenship of the parents where both parents finished up with the same citizenship; the Soviet–Czechoslovak accord had the foresight to add that the same held true where only one of the parents was alive, and both the 1978 Soviet–Romanian and Soviet–East German specimens rephrased the proviso to include the contigency where the place of residence of one parent was not known by the last day set for submitting the declarations. In marked contrast, the Soviet–East German script here eschewed the automatic conversion route — save, as indicated, in special situations featuring a lone parent. First, if the minor child born before the present convention became operative did not itself qualify as a dual citizen, it retained whatever citizenship it had no matter which of the two citizenships the parents ended up with, even, in extremis, if both parents emerged from the "polling–booth" with the other of the duo of citizenships at stake: the negative by–product of that approach was the increased risk of family units split in terms of the citizenship affiliation of its members. Second, if the minor child was born before the treaty went into effect and was itself vested with these two citizenships, the parents could within the space of a year following the date of the treaty's entry into force jointly pick for the minor either of the twin citizenships (where such minors had already celebrated their fourteenth birthday, their consent was required). Again, the citizenship they thus selected for the offspring (with the latter's acquiescence if more than fourteen years old) did not have to coincide with their own and the same adverse consequences then awaited the family cell in the sense of internal division prompted by diverse citizenship identities: the compensating factor, of course, is room for choice (practically ruled out in the rest of the accords on analogous occasions where the parents managed to share a common citizenship).

Next, pursuant to the Soviet–Yugoslav scenario, if ultimately the citizenship of the parents still did not match, their minor children acquired the citizenship of that country on whose territory they permanently resided with their parents or one of them. The Soviet–Hungarian treaty embraced an alternative solution: in kindred circumstances, the citizenship of the minors would be determined by agreement between the parents, recorded at the time the adults exercised their right of "option", or, in the absence of any agreement, it would be the citizenship of the state on the territory of which they then lived. The Soviet Union's conventions with Romania (1957), Albania, Bulgaria, North Korea and Poland followed the Soviet–Hungarian example in this matter, but expressly limited the formula's application to minors who themselves were dual citizens, granted the parents a full year to make up their minds concerning the citizenship they wanted for their progeny and gave notice that, if the parents did not arrive at the required agreement, the minor children would keep the citizenship of the country on the territory of which they resided (presumably on the expiration of the "election" deadline). The Soviet– Czechoslovak, Soviet–Mongolian and Soviet–East German accords also guaranteed the parents one year, which the 1978 Soviet–Romanian version extended to eighteen months, to reach such an agreement and took care to spell out that, in the event the parents failed to agree on a choice, or else omitted to put in a petition (USSR–GDR, 1978 USSR–Romania) or ran into the dissenting vote of a minor over the age of fourteen (USSR–GDR), the minor children would indeed be assigned the citizenship of the country on the territory of which they resided when the prescribed period elapsed.[46]

The early conventions sanctioned the same routine for handling both petitions filed by adults on their own behalf and submitted by parents in the name of their minor children. In essence, the system called for eligible individuals residing on the territory of one contracting party and preferring the citizenship of the other to communicate that wish (for themselves or their children) to the designated agencies of the country to whose citizenship they wanted to "transfer": in principle, affirmative action was de rigueur only when the "outside" citizenship was selected (since the "home" state's citizenship could in due course be acquired passively or by default). The USSR– GDR and 1978 USSR–Romania scripts have devised a more elaborate procedure — the former as regards applications related to minor children, the latter for both adults and minor children involved in the "option" scheme. Thus, the USSR–GDR model recognizes that parents can decide explicitly to choose for their children the citizenship of the state on the territory of which they reside (and not just that of the "absentee" state) and lets them do so by filing a statement to that effect with the competent local government organs; if they desire the minor child to have the citizenship of the state on the territory of which the parents do not maintain joint residence, the corresponding petition must be filed with the latter's diplomatic or consular mission. The relevant forms had to be filled out in two copies and, if not filed in person, the signatures of the parents affixed thereto had to be properly authenticated. In roughly comparable terms, the latest Soviet–Romanian version specifies that, where the persons choosing a citizenship (for themselves or their minor children) reside on the territory of the state whose citizenship they seek to retain, they submit the necessary papers (again in duplicate) to the organs of the Ministry of Internal Affairs in the USSR or offices of registry of civil status at their place of residence in Romania; where they pick the citizenship of the country other than the one in which they reside, the applications must be submitted to the appropriate diplomatic or consular institution.

Similarly, the Soviet–Romanian (1957), Soviet–Albanian, Soviet–Czechoslovak, Soviet–North Korean, Soviet–Polish and Soviet–Mongolian documents directed that minors whose father lived on the territory of one signatory and whose mother lived on the territory of the other retained the citizenship of the parent by whom they were being reared, unless the parents had made arrangements to the contrary. The Soviet–Hungarian and Soviet–East German pacts simply refer in this connection to parents not living together, not necessarily in separate countries, but espouse a like remedy, while in the Soviet–Yugoslav, Soviet–Bulgarian and Soviet–Romanian (1978) cases this phenomenon is completely ignored. Then, under the agreements with Yugoslavia and Mongolia, minors without parents preserved the citizenship of the country on whose soil they permanently resided; the rest of the treaties uniformly postulated that under–age children whose parents were dead or could not be located (or else, in the 1978 USSR–Romania and USSR–GDR samples, had been deprived of parental rights) remained citizens of that country on whose territory they lived at the termination of the period scheduled for the completion of the respective "option" project.

The Soviet–East German text stands alone in anticipating two additional contingencies of this type and furnishing a suitable answer: 1) if the parents are not married or the marriage was dissolved or pronounced void before the treaty went into effect and the parents fail to submit by the appointed deadline a written statement or reach an agreement to pick a citizenship for the minor child, the latter will be vested with the citizenship of the parent to whose care it has been entrusted; 2) if, after the treaty has entered into force, the marriage is dissolved or pronounced void before the time set for the exercise of the "option" rights has run out and the parents omit to file a statement or cannot agree on a choice of citizenship for the minor child, the child will likewise share the citizenship of the parent to whose custody it has been assigned.

The proposed solution (for which the apposite clause in the Soviet–Hungarian accord can serve as a conceptual precedent, albeit couched in far more general terms) seems plainly superior to the method by which the problem was apt to be settled under certain conditions among most of the other partners (i.e., USSR v. Romania–1957, Albania, Czechoslovakia, North Korea, Poland and Mongolia). Indeed, here you had the prospect that if both parents were alive and accessible, resided in the same country, but elected different citizenships, either they had to agree on choosing a citizenship for their minor child or, if they did not, the children kept the citizenship of the country on whose territory they resided — even if this meant that they might now end up not having the same citizenship as the parent who was in charge of them. Where citizenship is attributed in these circumstances by fiat, adherence to the personal rather than the territorial principle has much to recommend it.

In order to compensate in part for the rather rigid system of ascribing a particular citizenship to minors, the Soviet–Yugoslav text further permitted any minor over sixteen who might like better the other citizenship, in place of the one mandatorily assigned to it under the preceding rules, to so indicate and hence have access to the regular channels open to adults for these purposes. The USSR's agreements with Romania (1957), Albania, Czechoslovakia, Bulgaria, North Korea and Poland enlarged the scope of the "dispensation" in two ways: 1) juniors were given the right to express an independent choice if they had reached their fourteenth birthday, a watershed consecrated by the Soviet legislative canon; and, 2) minors over fourteen were free to assert a personal preference not just where a designated citizenship was being conferred upon them by force of law, but also where their parents were entrusted with deciding the issue on their behalf. The USSR– GDR treaty followed a conservative policy here in that minors over fourteen were required to register their consent where they themselves possessed dual citizenship and their parents were called upon jointly to select from the pair for them: in this one setting, and only then, did the minors have to be affirmatively consulted (rather than, as in the foregoing cases, merely being allowed to speak their mind); on the other hand, a dissenting vote did not dictate the outcome and simply meant that the parents' choice was not enforced either, and the law now stepped in summarily to vest the minor with the citizenship of the party on whose territory it resided when the "option" deadline expired. For no known reason — except perhaps a more pronounced aversion on the part of these three associates of the Soviet Union to the concept of "mixed" families, especially along the lines of young children versus parents — the Soviet–Hungarian, Soviet–Mongolian and Soviet–Romanian (1978) conventions contain no such clauses.

Again, there are special sections in the USSR–Czechoslovakia, USSR–Bulgaria, USSR–GDR and 1978 USSR–Romania treaties devoted to the fate of minor children domiciled in third countries and entitled to the citizenship of each duo of interested parties. Under the terms of the Soviet Union's agreements with Czechoslovakia and Bulgaria, their citizenship would be picked by the parents and, lacking a decision, the offspring would retain the citizenship of that side where they or their parents had permanent residence before going abroad. The 1978 USSR–Romania version featured a similar formula — which applied, however, only where the child was both born and still resided on the territory of some third state. On all three occasions, no arrangements were made in the further event that no parental consensus was forthcoming and yet the parents had not maintained a joint permanent residence on the soil of either signatory prior to settling "overseas", and, technically, the 1978 USSR–Romania specimen also skipped the item of the child born on the territory of one signatory but at present residing abroad in the absence of parental unanimity on the subject of the child's future citizenship affiliation (unless fitted by analogy into the general rule). In that respect, the Soviet– East German script is better drafted. For, the latter provides that if the child was born or resides on the territory of a third state and either the parents have no common preference or the minor over fourteen refuses to endorse their choice, the child then counts as the citizen of the party on whose territory the parents had resided prior to leaving the country; and, if in these circumstances the parents had not established a joint place of residence on the territory of either party before moving abroad, the child keeps the mother's citizenship.

Those eligible to "opt" who availed themselves of that right and whose declaration was approved by the country in whose favor they pronounced themselves would thereafter be considered exclusively the latter's citizens (the 1978 USSR–Romania accord does not explicitly say so, but the premise inheres in the spirit of the enterprise). The process of endorsement was not always mechanical, though, and the Soviet Union's treaties with Yugoslavia, Hungary, Romania (1957), and Albania clearly stipulated that anyone whose petition met with rejection by the state whose citizenship was being sought was forthwith deemed to be solely the citizen of the country on whose soil he (she) resided ("permanently resided" in the phraseology of the Soviet–Yugoslav pact).[47] The companion agreements with Czechoslovakia, Bulgaria, North Korea, Poland, Mongolia, East Germany and Romania (1978) seemed to eschew this added complication, but one cannot tell from the bare letter of the documents whether this really reflected a change of policy or not: somehow, it is hard to imagine that the states involved would surrender so easily their sovereign prerogative of certifying who had a legitimate claim to their citizenship and who did not. Perhaps silence on this point merely acknowledged that residual right and, if the signatories assumed that their current experiments left it unimpaired, then indeed it would have been superfluous to spell it out at length in the body of the treaties themselves.

The one thing that can be suggested is that where the contracting parties put in an article overtly insuring them the privilege of refusing these "option" applications without listing the grounds for such action, the impression is created, correctly or wrongly, that any motive at all would do, since no explanation was called for. As against that, if the authority to turn down a request is tacitly construed from the innate sovereign power of every state to establish who does and who does not possess its nationality, it could be argued that, where nothing was said on that score, the participants did not intend to question each other's freedom to check and see if a candidate was in fact their citizen and, if not, to dismiss the case, but, by implication, effectively singled out this element as the only valid criterion for passing judgment.

In much the same vein, persons who neglected to submit a statement by the fixed deadline wound up as citizens of that country alone on whose territory they resided ("permanently resided" in the Soviet–Yugoslav agreement; resided at the time the designated option period lapsed — USSR–GDR). Such "conversion by default" was also sanctioned by the USSR–GDR and 1978 USSR–Romania conventions despite the fact that both these documents recognized that the persons entitled to "opt" could actively do so not only in favor of the "absentee" state (as prescribed by the rest of the agreements) but if their choice fell on the current "homeland" as well. Pursuant to the extra terms of the Soviet–Czechoslovak, Soviet–Bulgarian and Soviet–East German conventions, individuals with the corresponding combination of citizenships who, living in third states, did not lodge a declaration in time would henceforward count as citizens of that signatory on whose soil they had permanently resided (just "resided" in the USSR–GDR edition) before emigrating.

Within six months of the date set for the closure of the respective "option" operation, each side was to inform its opposite as to the petitions it had received asking for its citizenship, with the Soviet–Yugoslav, Soviet–Hungarian, Soviet–Romanian (1957) and Soviet–Albanian pacts requiring in addition that the accounting governments indicate which of these had been honored. The 1978 USSR–Romania project called for one copy of each declaration on choice of citizenship to accompany the list reporting the request; in the USSR–GDR case, such lists had to furnish the necessary data and addresses and, again, a copy of each application referred to had to be appended. The parties obligated themselves, in the preamble to the agreements or both in the preamble and the text, to guarantee full opportunity to those displaying the proper qualifications to exercise freedom of choice. To that end, the Soviet–Yugoslav accord provided for the publication of its contents in the press and their dissemination through other suitable mass media no later than thirty days from the date of its entry into force. In its fellow treaties, these instructions were less specific, the signatories simply pledging themselves to carry the official version in the newspapers after the agreement between them came into effect. The USSR–GDR model cryptically noted that the convention would be published and the theme does not figure in the 1978 USSR–Romania scenario.

Oddly enough, none of the older conventions took care to pinpoint the moment when the "uncoupling" was considered legally consummated. The more recent accords make an effort to correct that oversight. Thus, by virtue of the 1978 USSR–Romania arrangement, adults and minors born before the agreement went into effect were slated to "acquire" (sic) the citizenship of choice on the day when the list bearing their name was duly forwarded, but nothing was said about how the system worked in instances where the law decided the issue of the single citizenship and not the individual's own initiative (or, where appropriate, his or her parents'). The USSR–GDR sample used a different approach and covered more ground: the citizenship chosen by and for individuals born before the treaty became valid was recognized as "effective" from the day the corresponding statement was received by the competent organs and, where no application was filed by adult optants or by parents responsible to opt for their minor children, the day when the period set for recording a choice expired marked the "effective" date.

Next, the Soviet–Yugoslav compact took pains to emphasize that just because a person requested the citizenship of the other state was not sufficient reason to subject him to a special regimen and that once a person had acquired the citizenship he wanted, he could retain his former domicile and would be granted alien status and enjoy the same treatment as other aliens, including the unrestricted possibility of repatriation. The other documents did not go into such great detail — ostensibly, in the inner circle of "socialist" nations no need was felt for these elaborate precautions — and contented themselves with noting that people who found themselves in this position would fall under the usual regulations pertaining to foreign citizens (the 1978 USSR–Romania agenda does not mention the subject).

The process of "option" was in every instance exempt from any tax or levy. Rather surprisingly, only the Soviet–Bulgarian treaty saw fit to warn potential candidates that persons who, pursuant to its terms, chose the citizenship of one country were not as a result immune from settling any fiscal debts incurred vis–à–vis the other state prior to the moment of "election".[48]

In fine, two items invite brief comment. First, no data are available on relevant administrative practice which would shed light on the concrete manner of interpretation and implementation of the norms incorporated in this grid of closely related agreements: how many souls were affected thereby and in what way, what difficulties were encountered in the course of execution of these assorted principles and the legal techniques employed to overcome them, and similar issues. Second, the bulk of these conventions confined themselves strictly to dealing with already recorded episodes of dual nationality: they were designed to function retrospectively, to eliminate the existing backlog of incidents of dual nationality, and not to anticipate a fresh accumulation of such problems and prevent the latter from happening.[49] In this sense, the Soviet–Czechoslovak and the Soviet–Bulgarian treaties stood apart from the rest, in one area at least, in that they looked ahead and endeavored to handle some aspects of the situation by endorsing prophylactic measures, no matter how modest (i.e., for the future both concentrated exclusively on the strain of dual nationality incurred by children at birth), instead of being satisfied merely with advocating post hoc cures. They thus form a bridge, so to speak, between the Soviet–Mongolian accord of April 24, 1937, on the one hand, and, on the other, the current generation of conventions either principally or equally aimed at preventing the occurrence of cases of dual citizenship between the USSR and Hungary of January 21, 1963,[50] the USSR and Poland of March 31, 1965, [51] the USSR and Bulgaria of July 6, 1966,[52] the USSR and the GDR of April 11, 1969,[53] the USSR and Romania of June 28, 1978, and the USSR and Czechoslovakia of June 6, 1980.[54] Or, in the words of a Soviet author, the 1963–1966 agreements combined the provisions of the 1937 treaty with Mongolia and the 1957 convention with Czechoslovakia, while supplementing and simplifying some of the terms. Further worth noting in this connection is the fact that the same spokesman pronounced the initial trio of accords the most complete and successful in virtue of the precision of the formulations as well as the breadth of inclusiveness of all possible cases of inception of dual citizenship and claimed that a definite trend was then afoot to conclude analogous agreements between the USSR and the other socialist states: yet, as the record shows, only three such treaties have since been signed and neither is an exact replica of the original sampling.[55]

The Soviet–Mongolian pact, it will be recalled, focused exclusively on questions of dual nationality arising out of naturalization. The newer agreements have gone beyond that and, while this dimension of the phenomenon is by no means ignored,[56] the main emphasis has now shifted to the brand of dual citizenship precipitated by accidents of birth. To trace this progression, we will have to start by recapitulating the key postulates of the Soviet–Mongolian accord. On that occasion, the parties confirmed that on their territory they would henceforth not accept into their citizenship persons possessing the other's citizenship without the consent of the appropriate organs of the latter; to get it, the Foreign Ministry of the country whose citizenship was being solicited was then to contact the other's local diplomatic representative to inquire whether his state opposed the proposed transfer. If in three months no answer was vouchsafed, it would be taken as a sign of approval. Further, nothing was to prevent the signatories from granting their citizenship in accordance with their domestic legislation to individuals who insisted that they were citizens of the other country, but could not produce official papers in support of their claim. Still, the country whose citizenship was presently invoked could ask the other to postpone the decision on naturalization until the truth could be ascertained. A maximum of four months was allowed for that purpose. If the investigation showed that the candidate had a valid case, the usual rules were to be observed.

The Soviet–Polish text here adopted a somewhat different procedure, binding the signatories in the future not to entertain requests for acquisition of their citizenship from persons vested with the citizenship of the other side if the applicant could not furnish documents issued by the proper authorities of the home state certifying that no objections stood in the way of the desired change of citizenship. The Soviet–Hungarian, Soviet–Bulgarian, and Soviet– East German counterparts sounded a trifle enigmatic on that count since all they had to say on this topic was that after the respective agreement's entry into force each regime would not admit to its citizenship persons owning the citizenship of its associate except with the consent of that second country's competent institutions, but offered no clues as to how that was actually to be accomplished. However, a Soviet author comes to the rescue when he lumps the three conventions dating from 1963–1966 together (his analysis logically extends to the subsequent Soviet–East German item) in contrasting them with the 1937 Mongolian version to make the point that their innovative contribution in this sector boiled down to letting the person himself submit to the organs of the country whose citizenship was sought the required documents attesting that the organs of the other side condoned the switch.[57] While helpful, the appraisal is not entirely accurate, for a careful reading of the script would indicate instead the following spectrum of nuances: in the USSR–Mongolia (1937) venture, the responsibility for eliciting the relevant information fell on the interested agencies of the accosted state; in the USSR–Poland operation, the onus probandi is shifted to the individual concerned; and in the other three instances one is left with the impression that any partner in the triangular relationship can exercise the initiative to adduce the necessary data.

If they signify exactly what they say, the 1978 USSR–Romania and 1980 USSR–Czechoslovakia versions rank in this sense as the mavericks of the lot, for the signatories now pledged themselves not to accept into their citizenship persons possessing the citizenship of the other side if they did not supply evidence that they were no longer citizens of the contracting party whose citizenship they previously had. So far, the determinant assumption seems to have been that absence of any objection to the contemplated conversion meant that official approval for release from the original citizenship would be duly forthcoming, but in this case the wording suggests that full divestiture of the old citizenship had to precede acquisition of the next one. The added "safeguard" might be seen as reflecting the special quality of Soviet–Romanian relations in this department compared with the record of the USSR's analogous transactions with the "stalwart" members of the pack, but Czechoslovakia's entry into the picture suggests that politics may not be responsible after all since that country certainly ranks among the USSR's close friends within the community.

The language of the clauses designed to prevent the further inception of double citizenship in conjunction with naturalization leaves no doubt that reference is to adults availing themselves of the standard route for trading their current citizenship for a new one. An examination of the contents of the agreements reveals that they feature no instructions concerning the question of the citizenship status of children in the context of adoption. Yet, according to a Soviet writer, the formal commitment by the parties not to admit to their citizenship persons who are citizens of the other side without the consent of the latter's competent organs has in practice also been extended to adoption matters. As an illustration, the source cites the case of the Soviet married couple, M., who, while temporarily staying in Hungary, took from a children's home the girl Teresa M. — a Hungarian citizen — for upbringing and then sought to adopt her. The competent Hungarian organs responded favorably to the request of the spouses M. They gave the required permission for implementing the adoption and at the same time visaed the release of Teresa M. from Hungarian citizenship.[58] The administrative improvisation supplements in an important way the treaty network's coverage against the recurrence of dual nationality within the constituency and so fills a significant gap in the original agenda.

The Soviet–Mongolian, Soviet–Polish, Soviet–Bulgarian, and 1978 Soviet–Romanian agreements also addressed themselves retrospectively to the plight of individuals who, in the interlude between the two sets of treaties, had incurred dual citizenship through naturalization. The Soviet Union's accords with Romania (1978) and Mongolia directed that such persons would keep their latest citizenship. The Soviet and Mongolian governments further undertook to exchange lists of names of those who had obtained their citizenship during this period and, if either regime had any reservations concerning a person who appeared on the list, they could, within three months, jointly study the case and, if necessary, rescind the order. The Soviet–Polish and Soviet–Bulgarian conventions used a different criterion in deciding on the single citizenship in these circumstances — the citizenship of the country on whose territory the bipatride currently resided now prevailed — , but they reverted to the earlier norm (i.e., the citizenship most recently acquired) in resolving the status of individuals afflicted with dual citizenship who permanently resided on the territory of a third state (a contingency not dealt with in the USSR–Mongolia and USSR–Romania project).

Two aspects of the foregoing picture attract attention. First, the Soviet– Hungarian pact is missing from the scene. The omission intrigues because no artifact designed to prevent the future incidence of dual citizenship in connection with naturalization figured in the 1957 agreement and the available reference to the alleged existence of an intra–socialist custom mandating that a member–state shall not sanction the naturalization of another's citizen without the latter's consent did not explicitly mention Hungary either. Whatever the reason — whether technical negligence, lack of policy consensus, practical irrelevance, or something else —, the Soviet–Hungarian convention ignores the lag problem. Second, the same source does include Poland and Bulgaria in the practicing group[59] and yet in 1965 and 1966 the USSR and both these countries again had to tackle the job of "sorting out" individuals who meantime had managed to catch dual citizenship in the process of naturalization (a pattern which, as noted previously, marks the Soviet–Romanian repertory for the years 1957–1978 as well).

No explanation springs to mind to account for the obvious discrepancy and local spokesmen have not proposed one either, at least so far. Earlier, in focusing on the Soviet–Romanian incident, I had speculated that politics might have intervened to derail the scheme, but that consideration would not apply to the USSR's relations with Poland and Bulgaria; or, that the claim was spurious, and the Polish and Bulgarian experience would not contradict that interpretation and, indeed, tends to lend it greater credence; or, just to add a piece to the puzzle, that perhaps simple slippage in administrative routine caused this fresh increment of dual citizenship cases which required a fresh round of surgery. If, in fact, the unwritten system's past inefficiency is to blame for the "relapse", one is then entitled to wonder how "fail–safe" the performance of its treaty incarnation is apt to be. On the "plus" side of the ledger, though, be it noted that the 1980 Soviet–Czechoslovak agreement also omits to deal with any possible interim accumulation of dual citizenship cases spawned by naturalization proceedings despite the absence of any clause in the 1957 treaty designed to prevent such incidents in the future: however, Czechoslovakia (unlike Hungary) was listed among those abiding by the special "intra–socialist custom" in this matter and perhaps its example vindicates the effectiveness of the procedure. At any rate, from now on, everybody involved apparently felt that it would be best, for safety's sake, to have the policy reduced into writing rather than continue to rely on some vague consensus.

The status of children "inheriting" dual nationality at birth posed a graver challenge since in this case the range of variables is greater. The 1957 Soviet–Czechoslovak accord (since superseded) postulated in rather general terms that upon subsequent inception of the question of dual nationality of children the choice of citizenship of one of the interested parties fell to the parents who would let the conclusion they reached together be known at the time the child's birth was recorded. The Soviet–Hungarian, Soviet–Polish, Soviet–Bulgarian, Soviet–East German, 1978 Soviet–Romanian and 1980 Soviet– Czechoslovak versions followed the same basic method, but referred in this context to children whose father was the citizen of one side and whose mother was the citizen of the other. In practice, it amounted to the same thing, but this formulation described the events accurately, whereas the first one might convey the misleading impression that dual citizenship at birth could in that situation arise in other ways as well.

The Soviet–Hungarian, Soviet–Polish, Soviet–Bulgarian, Soviet–East German and 1978 Soviet–Romanian specimens all spelled out how the parents were to proceed at this juncture: if they chose the citizenship of the country on whose territory they lived, they could submit a written declaration to that effect to the competent agencies there — within one year of the child's birth in the USSR–Hungary, USSR–Bulgaria and USSR–GDR cases, within three months pursuant to the USSR–Poland and 1978 USSR–Romania scripts. (The 1980 USSR–Czechoslovakia version features no comparable clause defining the mechanics of option in favor of the local citizenship, i.e., that of the country of current residency, although such a right must be assumed to exist, in which event a modus operandi similar to the above probably applies.) In addition, the Soviet–Polish, Soviet–Bulgarian, Soviet–East German and 1978 Soviet–Romanian editions specified that the corresponding statement had to be filled out in two copies and both the Soviet–Bulgarian and Soviet–East German samples also stipulated that where the declaration was not lodged in person, the signature of the parents had to be notarized.

If, living on the soil of one treaty partner, the parents inclined toward the citizenship of the other (revised in the USSR–GDR case to read "if the parents choose for their minor children the citizenship of the contracting party on whose territory they do not maintain a joint residence"), or, if they had established domicile in a third state, then whatever their preference in this connection, they could in the same span of time, respectively, communicate their wish to the local diplomatic or consular mission (or Foreign Ministry in the matching USSR–GDR clause on third–state residents) of the country for whom they had "voted". In the 1980 Soviet–Czechoslovak version, the wording of this formula is substantially amended for it speaks instead of parents picking for their child *born on the territory* of one signatory the citizenship of the other as well as parents of a child *born on the territory* of a third state who can choose between the respective citizenships without ever taking notice of their present location. The parent's joint statement (in writing and in duplicate) had to be submitted to the diplomatic or consular institution of the country whose citizenship was selected no later than three months from the day of the child's birth, with the further proviso that if the papers were not handed in by the parents themselves, their signatures had to be authenticated by an appropriate agency. A receipt was to be issued to the petitioners by the diplomatic or consular office where the application was filed. (Incidentally, this portion of the latest USSR–Czechoslovakia scenario is again deficient in that it also does not refer to the parents' right to decide for the citizenship of the country where they currently reside, which one must yet presume to be a viable alternative.)

In the event the parents (the 1980 USSR–Czechoslovakia document is careful to explain that it means parents living together) do nothing, the citizenship of the child will be that of the signatory on whose territory it was born, according to the Soviet–Czechoslovak (both 1957 and 1980), Soviet–Polish, Soviet–Bulgarian and Soviet–East German agreements, but that of the signatory on whose territory it resided on the day of expiration of the deadline for filing the declaration, by virtue of the Soviet–Hungarian and 1978 Soviet– Romanian projects. If in these circumstances the child was born (was born or lives — USSR–GDR; was born and lives — 1978 USSR–Romania) in a foreign country (USSR–Czechoslovakia 1957 & 1980; USSR–Poland; USSR–Bulgaria) or currently resided in a foreign country (USSR–Hungary), it would keep the citizenship of the country where its parents had resided (USSR–GDR; 1978 USSR–Romania) or permanently resided (USSR–Hungary; USSR–Czechoslovakia 1957) or jointly resided (USSR–Poland; USSR–Bulgaria; USSR–Czechoslovakia 1980) prior to going abroad. The Soviet–Hungarian, Soviet–Polish, Soviet–Bulgarian, Soviet–East German and 1980 Soviet–Czechoslovak treaties further foresaw that, absent such permanent (joint) residence, the child would share exclusively the mother's citizenship. This extra detail apparently escaped the attention of the drafters of the 1957 Soviet–Czechoslovak and 1978 Soviet– Romanian documents.

The 1980 USSR–Czechoslovakia agreement inserts an interesting innovation at this point which significantly expands the coverage provided by the other texts so far. The improvement is designed to plug the hole created by legitimation proceedings by directing that if in the case of a minor child born after the entry of the treaty into force to an unwed woman who is a citizen of one signatory there will be established the paternity of a citizen of the other signatory, the parents can choose for the child the citizenship of one of the signatories by filing a joint declaration not later than three months from the date of determination of fatherhood. Where a minor child over fourteen years of age is involved the parents' statement is valid when accompanied by a written consent from the child, all the papers in fact being submittted in writing and in two copies with receipt acknowledged by the diplomatic or consular office concerned. Parents who picked for their child born on the territory of one contracting party the citizenship of the other contracting party and parents who selected for their child born abroad the citizenship of either contracting party filed a joint declaration to that effect with the diplomatic or consular institution of the state whose citizenship they favored. Failure to exercise a choice in the wake of an act of legitimation results in the child sharing the mother's citizenship.

Next, the Soviet–Hungarian, Soviet–Polish and Soviet–Bulgarian conventions envisaged the retroactive application of the foregoing regulations to children who, already on the date of their entry into force, possessed the citizenship of both interested parties (the corresponding prescriptions of the USSR–GDR and 1978

USSR–Romania models have previously been analyzed and only the appropriate provisions intended for prospective use will be noted below). In the Soviet–Hungarian instance, this was expressly understood to mean children born between January 15, 1959, when the year scheduled by the agreement of August 24, 1957, for conducting their reciprocal "option" operation ended, and the moment the present treaty acquired validity (i.e., August 18, 1963). Between the USSR and Bulgaria this interval spanned from March 28, 1959, to January 19, 1967. The Soviet–Polish venture left that issue vague, but its objective scope in this sector boils down to the same goal, mutatis mutandis.

On each occasion, the parents were allowed one year from the day the accord took effect in which to make their choice known to the authorities and, if they failed to do so, the child's citizenship would stay that of the country in which it resided when that period had drawn to a close. If that happened to be a foreign country, the child's citizenship would be fixed as that of the state in which he was born and, should that turn out to be a foreign country too, it would be the citizenship of the country in which the parents jointly resided before moving abroad or the mother's citizenship if even that criterion did not fit (USSR–Poland; USSR–Bulgaria); and, the citizenship of the country in which the parents had permanent residence before emigrating or the mother's citizenship if no such permanent residence could be discovered (USSR–Hungary).

On the matter of the future status of children living with just one parent, the texts diverged. Where the child's upbringing was entrusted to either parent, the child would henceforth have that parent's citizenship under the terms of the arrangement between the USSR and Poland. The conventions between the USSR and Hungary, Bulgaria, East Germany and Czechoslovakia (1980) let the parents jointly decide the business of the minor child's citizenship affiliation even where no common household existed (e.g., the parents were not married, or the marriage had been dissolved or annulled, or the parents were married but lived apart — in the USSR–GDR example), and only if the parents omitted to do so in the slated interval did they recognize that the citizenship of the parent who brought up the child preempted the scene. These four accords, plus their 1978 Soviet–Romanian counterpart (in its lone foray into this area), also follow the principle of automatically assigning the minor child the citizenship of the parent who rears it in those situations where the other parent is dead or his (her) whereabouts cannot be determined (1980 USSR–Czechoslovakia: dead, missing, or deprived of parental rights to the day the "voting" deadline expires).

A child whose parents were dead or could not be located was considered solely the citizen of the country on whose territory it resided when the allotted "grace period" had run, and the Soviet–Polish treaty extended this rule to children for whom a guardian had been appointed in the wake of the parents' deprivation of parental rights (as did the USSR–GDR and 1978 USSR– Romania versions, but without any express mention of an official wardship). In the 1980 USSR–Czechoslovakia specimen, the formula applies when the parents are dead, missing, or deprived of parental rights to the date when the three-month deadline lapses, but the parties drop the residency criterion in favor of the citizenship of the signatory on whose territory the child was born. The Soviet–Polish compact also faced up to the prospect of an "orphaned" child living in a foreign land: in that eventuality, the child would retain the citizenship alone of the country on whose soil it was born or, if it was born abroad, it would be the citizenship of the state in which its parents had maintained permanent residence before expatriating themselves and, lacking that, the mother's "late" citizenship prevailed. Given the 1980 USSR–Czechoslovakia treaty's predilection for the "place of birth" test, its solution to this problem is suitably adjusted as follows: if the "orphaned" child was born on the territory of a third state, it receives the citizenship of the contracting party whose citizenship the mother has or had. Oddly enough, the rest of the pack overlooked the "third–state" wrinkle.

Then, the Soviet–Polish convention filled a major gap left behind by its predecessor in expanding its coverage to include individuals with the proper technical qualifications who, because they resided on foreign territory, did not have a chance to participate in the first round of "voting" (how this new development affected unaccompanied minors living on foreign territory whose predicament had hitherto also been disregarded was noted a minute ago). To remedy the oversight, these people were now given the usual year's stint in which to announce their wish to the local diplomatic or consular mission of the state toward whose citizenship they leaned. If they expressed no desire, they preserved just the citizenship of the country where they had lived before going abroad. The Soviet–Hungarian and 1978 Soviet–Romanian blueprints again made no attempt to deal with that item.

For some obscure reason, neither the Soviet–Bulgarian nor the Soviet–Polish agreements bothered to nail down at which instant the acquisition of either citizenship by an adult "optant" (a retroactive theme not dealt with in the Soviet–Hungarian or 1980 Soviet–Czechoslovak accord at all) was deemed consummated (whereas, as noted earlier, both the 1978 USSR–Romania and USSR– GDR conventions did pay attention to that subject). Furthermore, of the 1963–1966 vintage, uniquely the Soviet–Bulgarian instrument had the foresight to pinpoint when a minor's "conversion" pursuant to its provisions became effective, which the USSR–GDR, 1978 USSR–Romania and 1980 USSR–Czechoslovakia models now do too. Thus, if the child was born after the entry into force of the accord, the status dated from the day of its birth, except that under the terms of the USSR–GDR agreement this formula applied just to children whose citizenship was affirmatively selected and when the upshot represented an ex parte assignment, so to speak, owing to failure or inability to register a choice, the deadline for casting the respective "vote" marked the "initiation". On the other hand, if the child was born before the corresponding convention assumed force (not applicable to the 1980 USSR–Czechoslovakia operation), the solo citizenship stretched from the date of the declaration or, if no declaration was submitted on the child's behalf, then from the time of its birth (USSR–Bulgaria), or from the day when the appropriate list bearing the name of the de cujus was duly forwarded through diplomatic channels (1978 USSR–Romania), or from the day the petition was lodged or, in a default situation, the last day of the period mandated for recording a preference (USSR–GDR). The 1980 Soviet–Czechoslovak edition had to cover extra ground in this context since it also sanctioned parental choice of citizenship for the minor child in the aftermath of an act of legitimation and elected to figure the child's possession of a single citizenship from the time the parents filed an appropriate statement in its name or, if they omitted to do so, from the date of the child's birth.

In line with set precedent, the process of "option" was exempt of all taxes and levies. The Soviet and Polish governments concurred that they would henceforth send each other through diplomatic routes data concerning the parents' choice of citizenship in favor of children infected with double citizenship at birth no later than six months from the day of each birth and that within eighteen months after the convention went into effect they would trade lists of children whose dual nationality antedated the agreement and of adults domiciled in third countries who had picked their respective citizenship. The USSR and Hungary arrived at a somewhat different solution: the rosters of children for whom the parents had during the previous calendar year elected one of the citizenships would be transmitted during the first quarter of the following year and the date of the declaration filed by the parents had to be indicated. The Soviet–Bulgarian accord borrowed the Soviet–Hungarian rule for handling future dual citizenships incurred at birth and the Soviet–Polish formula to chronicle the liquidation of the backlog.

The 1978 USSR–Romania, USSR–GDR and 1980 USSR–Czechoslovakia treaties essentially adopted the USSR–Hungary procedure calling for lists identifying minor children born after the treaty came into force for whom the parents had during the preceding calendar year picked one of the citizenships to be exchanged during the first three months of the next year (the 1980 USSR– Czechoslovakia sample adding that one copy of the parents' statement and, where a minor child over fourteen was involved, one copy of the child's written consent had to be appended to the roster). The 1978 USSR–Romania and USSR–GDR agreements further established that data concerning choice of citizenship by adults and by parents for children born before the treaty became valid would be transmitted no later than eighteen months in the case of adults and two years in the case of children from the day the treaty went into effect in the 1978 USSR–Romania context and eighteen months in both instances in the relations between the USSR and the GDR (the former repeating the Soviet–Polish modus operandi, but with a longer schedule; the latter squarely matching its format).

The Soviet–Polish pact emphasized particularly that all such decisions had to be voluntary and, while the rest of the lot did not think it necessary to put it in so many words, they were, quite obviously, based on the same principle. All questions that might subsequently arise in the course of interpretation and implementation of the language of the conventions were to be settled through diplomatic channels. The USSR and Czechoslovakia also undertook to work out a single type–form of a joint declaration on choice of citizenship.

Finally, the proposed duration of the agreements varied. The 1957 Soviet–Czechoslovak instrument said nothing about how long it was expected to remain in force. The Soviet–Polish and Soviet–East German treaties were to last indefinitely or until six months after formal denunciation by either side. By comparison, the Soviet–Hungarian, Soviet–Bulgarian, 1978 Soviet–Romanian and 1980 Soviet–Czechoslovak pacts were limited to an initial term of five years and, if not denounced at least six months in advance, would continue to function for successive five–year periods until notice of cancellation was duly served. The rationale of the whole project lies, of course, in the uninterrupted practice of these prophylactic methods and the lapse of any of these treaties would forthwith prompt the gradual build–up of a fresh dual citizenship deposit involving the citizens of the respective signatories. Indeed, the strange aspect of the foregoing picture of Soviet diplomatic activity in this domain is precisely the fact that such arrangements with North Korea and (in part) Mongolia, for instance, figure as a one–shot affair providing relief for past problems but oblivious of the need to apply preventive medicine in order to check a new outbreak of the disease.

* * *

Far more modest, on every count, were the accomplishments here of the Convention on the Nationality of Married Women, of February 20, 1957, which the USSR ratified. The step marked the Soviet Union's only excursion up till now into the realm of multilateral regulation of nationality problems, a departure from precedent that can readily be explained by the phenomenon that the treaty contained very little that in any way conflicted with the pertinent norms of Soviet legislation and the fortuitous circumstance that on virtually all key issues the former's substance actually coincided with the corresponding principles espoused in Soviet theory and experience. For that matter, the general attitude in local circles on this subject is that

> "socialist society ensures the true equality of rights of women with men and does not require for its realization the supplementary guarantees created by norms of international law. However, the Soviet Union, in unison with the other socialist countries, takes an active part in the international cooperation of states in defense of the rights of women, whose goal it is to attain equal rights throughout the world. Championing international, universal human interests, appreciating how much the achievement of equal rights for women means for the progressive development of the entire society, the socialist countries strive for the adoption of international acts reflecting the demands of women for equal rights. In this connection, the socialist countries consider that one of the most effective means of international defense of the rights of women is conventions establishing international law duties of states on particular issues."[60]

Because the USSR takes primary credit for the gains registered by the women's movement on the global scene, extravagant pronouncements are heard at times concerning this whole enterprise, as, for example, the claim that "the norms on the equal status of men and women are consecrated in the UN Charter in a categorical, imperative form that forbids states to refuse or avoid observing them", and, hence, that "in essence these are norms of *jus cogens*".[61] In view of the importance they attach to the role played by the USSR in advancing the universal cause of equal rights for women, it is not surprising to find Soviet commentators also accounting for the formulation of certain propositions enunciated in the 1957 Convention in terms of the decisive influence exerted on an international scale by the Soviet Union's performance in the field of citizenship law—especially as regards the Convention's adoption of the rule ordaining that entry into marriage shall entail no change in the citizenship of the spouses.[62]

Still, the praise Soviet spokesmen heap on the Convention is not unqualified and trenchant criticism is occasionally leveled at some of its aspects which fail to meet Soviet expectations — allegedly owing to the unwillingness of the bourgeois co-authors of the text to shed their old prejudices. One shortcoming, we are told, is the absence of a single provision requiring the state — in its legislation as well as its practice — to equalize the rights of women in respect to citizenship with those of their menfolk.[63] Then, Soviet analysts fault the treaty for addressing itself only to the narrow question of the citizenship of married women and yet falling short of fully vindicating the concept of equality of the spouses by sanctioning, for instance, a simplified procedure for acquisition by the wife of the citizenship of the husband which, in considerable measure, "confirms his supremacy in the family".[64] Or, to put it differently, without denying that the proposed modus operandi appears to offer the woman certain privileges, Soviet spokesmen nevertheless denounce the scheme for perpetuating discrimination on grounds that:

> "The Article [Art.3] functions on the assumption that in cases of conclusion of mixed marriages the citizenship of the wife, and not of the husband, is subject to change. In other words, to maintain unity of the family preference is given to the citizenship of the husband. One can say that this is privilege in inequality. As a result of this privilege, the more enslaved person becomes less enslaved, but not equal. It is precisely this principle that underlies the legislation on citizenship of all capitalist states which formally recognize the equality of the spouses."[65]

To be sure, despite these imperfections, the Convention still receives a positive appraisal in Soviet literature for its many other merits.[66] One should note, though, that, from the standpoint of reducing the frequency of occurrence of dual citizenship, the accord has but marginal importance, — indeed, in a sense, it even helps beget dual citizenship. Thus, the signatories resolved, inter alia, that the celebration of a marriage between one of their nationals and a foreigner would not ipso jure effect any change in the citizenship of the wife. That has always been the Soviet pitch and, as observed earlier, this policy had produced double citizenship whenever a Soviet woman married a citizen of a country that unilaterally imposed its citizenship on the alien spouses of its male citizens. Where today such a country adhered to this revised formula, the inception of dual citizenship under similar conditions would literally be nipped in the bud. As against that, however, the document further called on the High Contracting Parties to make possible for a woman wed to one of their citizens to acquire, at her request, the citizenship of the husband through "specially privileged naturalization procedures", and did not couple that recommendation with a desideratum that, in a case of the sort, the female applicant should also be able to divest herself as quickly and easily as possible of her old nationality. With one state complying with the above voeu and facilitating admission to its citizenship while the country of origin failed to match the gesture by assuring the synchronous release of the de cujus from its nationality, — and nothing in the text obliges it to guarantee such chronological concordance, — the outcome for the person concerned would be dual citizenship.

Interestingly enough, Soviet legal experts are quite aware of the predicament and its negative consequences, but insist that "these cases are possible relatively seldom" because, they claim, "as a rule, states which make loss of citizenship depend on getting special permission, if their female citizen goes abroad and acquires in a simplified manner the citizenship of her husband, will not deny her request to leave the citizenship".[67] These assumptions notwithstanding, the plain fact remains that Soviet law recognizes just one method (and tempo) of denaturalization, and a Soviet woman marrying a foreigner whose state hewed to the letter of the treaty could well, as a result, incur dual nationality faster than would otherwise have been true. Bear in mind, too, that when Soviet sources report that in recent years more than 15,000 Soviet citizens married foreigners and 10,500 of them left the USSR to reside in more than 100 countries, they make no reference to concurrent renunciation by these people of their Soviet citizenship.[68] A safe guess would be that the majority of this emigrant contingent consists of Soviet brides many of whom would then be entitled to preferential treatment in acquiring their husband's citizenship and, if official silence means that no arrangements have been made for prompt release of these individuals from Soviet citizenship, there is a high probability that a substantial proportion of the women in the group will end up as bipatrides.

A further point to be made in this connection is that the Soviet Union not only does not sanction "easy exit" from Soviet citizenship in these circumstances, but, in deviation from common usage which even self–styled socialist nations like the People's Republic of China follow,[69] local legislation does not so much as acknowledge that marriage to a foreigner constitutes a valid reason for the interested party to petition for routine release from Soviet citizenship (though the concept of family reunification is publicly recognized as grounds for seeking emigration). To be sure, telling the affected person that he or she can cite marriage to a foreigner as justification for wanting to be relieved of his or her citizenship neither guarantees the applicant that the case will be handled expeditiously nor, indeed, that success will ultimately crown these efforts. Nevertheless, the signal does convey a symbolic commitment on the part of the state and fans in the individual involved a sense of psychological comfort that, ceteris paribus, the request for denaturalization stands a fair chance of being approved. The language of Soviet law offers no such balm, no matter how ephemeral the gesture's practical effect.

So far, we have been discussing the Soviet government's neglect to bring its citizenship regulations in line with the 1957 Convention's tacit premise that the signatory countries would forthwith institute a relaxed procedure for renunciation of the married woman's old citizenship to accompany reforms designed to accelerate the pace of admission into the husband's citizenship and how the resulting lag increases the chances of a Soviet female entering into a mixed marriage to contract dual citizenship. Paradoxically, the same failure to simplify the mechanics of admission into Soviet citizenship in the reverse situation where a foreign woman marries a Soviet citizen has served to inhibit the occurrence here of dual citizenship by precluding rapid integration into Soviet citizenship without corollary loss of the existing citizenship. Should the Soviet regime decide to revise the corresponding provisions of its law to match the terms of the Convention, the immediate prospects, ironic as it may sound, are for a hike in the frequency of occurrence of dual nationality on these occasions owing to the prevailing asymmetry between the norms of national legal systems relating to timing, accessibility of license to transfer, etc.

One last comment is in order. Over the years, the level of incidence of dual nationality episodes figuring Soviet citizenship stayed, as best one can judge, rather constant. The curve did register a dramatic upswing in the early postwar period, but that merely reflected the sizable increment of deliberately induced instances of dual nationality stemming from the plethora of decrees published at the time aimed at "returning" Soviet citizenship to former Russian and Soviet citizens who had once had it and then lost it and granting it to absentee inhabitants of various lands recently incorporated into the Soviet domain, plus the corps of pre–fabricated double citizens earmarked for injection into the political fabric of the fledgling "people's democracies". The moment passed and conditions in this sector reverted to normal: dual nationality precipitated by the blind collision of divergent legal repertories still haunted the Soviet scene, to be sure, but the total volume of persons afflicted with that impediment remained largely stable.

At any rate, the sudden spurt just mentioned was more than offset by the bar to the marriage of Soviet citizens to foreigners maintained from 1947 to 1953 and, of course, by the impact of the treaty network assembled after 1956 focusing on the organized eradication of sundry existing manifestations of dual citizenship and the conscious prevention of further inception of that phenomenon. All other things being equal, that program, if it operates smoothly, can dry up many of the well–springs of dual citizenship between the USSR and the majority of the members of the Communist commonwealth and, in the long run, make dual citizenship of this type a rarity. In its present format, the project cannot eliminate the problem entirely: for example, almost none of these measures treat of dual citizenship caused by adoption or legitimation. These are secondary factors, however, minor sources of irritation, as it were, that cannot materially alter the over–all picture. Be that as it may, there is still room for improvement and, yet, one must also note that the momentum here seems to have gradually slackened. Thus, Soviet authors have always said that resort to universal conventions to deal with these issues was unrealistic in the context of a deeply divided world, singled out bilateral accords as a better medium for accomplishing the job, and added that, on occasion, reliance on multilateral treaties "in which would participate states whose legal systems were akin" would not be amiss either.[70] That next step toward closer rapprochement in this policy area and greater regional uniformity of procedures related to the institution of citizenship has not been taken up till today.

* * *

By a strange twist of fate, with the appreciable liberalization of the Soviet regime since the death of Stalin, this beneficial trend may now be facing a serious threat from an altogether unexpected quarter. The late Premier Kosygin's remarks during his visit to France calculated to convince his audience that the Soviet government would raise no obstacles in the way of the reunification of families separated by the last war, even if this meant allowing people to leave the USSR, heralded a radically new Soviet attitude toward the whole troublesome matter of expatriation.[71] By 1980, Soviet spokesmen were claiming that over the past few years around 300,000 people had quit the USSR to be reunited with their families, in the main, Jews, Germans, Spaniards and Greeks (and one should include Armenians who, for some reason, were omitted from the list).[72]

The Jewish element accounts for the bulk of the exodus and insofar as the members of this group are required to surrender their Soviet citizenship before leaving for their official destination — Israel — the question of potential dual citizenship does not intrude in their case. Some non–Jewish emigrants or exiles are also compelled to name Israel as their prospective homeland and must then go through the same routine of renouncing their Soviet citizenship, regardless of where they in fact intend to settle. Yet other emigrants and expellees are either stripped of their Soviet citizenship before departure from the USSR or deprived of it after they find themselves abroad. In both these situations, too, prior loss of Soviet citizenship — by voluntary or involuntary means — saves the people concerned from ending up as bipatrides. As far as one can tell, however, for the rest of them, — i.e. the ordinary emigrants headed for a country with which the USSR maintains normal diplomatic relations (unlike with Israel and South Korea, for instance)[73] — the formal abandonment of Soviet citizenship is not a prerequisite to departure. The result is that growing numbers of Soviet citizens, still in possession of valid Soviet documents, are leaving the USSR and resettling in foreign countries. Some of them will undoubtedly seek naturalization in their adopted homelands and, unless they first win release from Soviet citizenship in the prescribed manner, which hitherto most individuals placed in that position have not bothered to do, they will wind up with two citizenships. In purely technical terms, the "thaw" will here have had unfortunate consequences. Nevertheless, the human prize is well–worth the attendant legal inconvenience.

To be sure, nothing prevents the Soviet authorities from resorting to bilateral arrangements to untangle such complications. So far, however, precedent for this sort of accommodation has been both scant and inconclusive. Reference may be made to the exchange of notes between the USSR and Canada of July 14, 1967,[74] which, inter alia, provided that "the declarations of persons on exit from the citizenship of the USSR or Canada would be considered by the competent organs in accordance with the legislation of that state whose citizenship they wished to leave". The formula presumably confirmed the primacy of the law of the country of origin in deciding the issue of sanctioning denaturalization by a citizen now residing on the territory of the other contracting party — which, of course, is standard operating procedure and vindicates Soviet policy on the matter. The only hint of a shift comes from the accompanying clause to the effect that "in considering these declarations there will also be taken into account the place of permanent residence of the applicant", and this addendum clearly suggests that in studying requests for relinquishment of the first citizenship emanating from people who are currently expatriates with permanent roots in the other country, the latter factor ought to sway the responsible agencies in the old homeland in favor of letting the individual concerned officially quit his (her) former citizenship. Still, the proposition is couched in highly tentative terms and at best expresses a consensus over a desideratum and certainly does not establish a hard and fast rule on that score.

Somewhat more substantive is the meaning of a second paragraph in the same correspondence recognizing that "a person arriving on the territory of Canada with a Soviet passport featuring a Canadian visa or on the territory of the USSR with a Canadian passport featuring a Soviet visa will not be denied permission to leave Canadian or Soviet territory, respectively, on the sole grounds that the question of his citizenship is interpreted differently by the two Governments and that he is viewed as a citizen by the state which he is visiting". If properly adhered to, the pronouncement would at least safeguard binational persons from running into physical difficulties because of that status and would guarantee their right to indicate a preference between the rival claimants to their allegiance, that is, in the sense of freedom of corporal movement. A mere commitment to allow this species of bipatride "guest" to go abroad does offer minimum protection at the de facto level inasmuch as it enables the interested party to assert his choice of citizenship association by the expedient of returning to the sanctum of the country with which he presently casts his lot and where the paper jurisdiction stemming from past nationality connections cannot in practice be enforced against a recalcitrant subject.

Perhaps this largely "bromide" treatment will yet serve as a prototype for future efforts by the USSR and the rest of the world outside the circle of socialist intimates to deal with the more pressing aspects of dual citizenship collisions sparked by the mounting human traffic across international frontiers. To date, though, the record shows no rush to imitate the experiment with further partners and, one must emphasize, the proposed warranty scheme is indeed rudimentary.

NOTES

1. This is well illustrated by the discussions which unfolded already in connection with the passage of the RSFSR decree "On the Acquisition of Rights of Soviet Citizenship" of 1918, as reported in *Protokoly zasedanii Vserosiisskago Tsentral'nago Ispolnitel'nago Komiteta 4–go sozyva*, Moscow, 1920, 64–66, and the comments by Chicherin in his capacity as rapporteur on the draft Regulation on Union Citizenship of 1924 at the morning meeting of the 2nd session of the CEC of the USSR, 2nd convocation, on October 24, 1924, reproduced in S.S. Kishkin, *Sovetskoe grazhdanstvo*, Moscow, 1925, pp. 74–88, at 80–83.
2. V. Durdenevskii, "Zakon o grazhdanstve Soiuza Sovetskikh Sotsialisticheskikh Respublik", *Problemy sotsialisticheskogo prava*, 1938, No.6, p.65; *idem*, in V.N. Durdenevskii & S.B. Krylov, eds., *Mezhdunarodnoe pravo*, Moscow, 1947, p.187; O.E. Polents, in E.A. Korovin, ed., *Mezhdunarodnoe pravo*, Moscow, 1951, pp. 231–232; K.Ia. Chizhov, in F.I. Kozhevnikov, ed., *Mezhdunarodnoe pravo*, Moscow 1957, p.145; V.I. Menzhinskii, in F.I. Kozhevnikov, ed., *Mezhdunarodnoe pravo*, Moscow, 1964, p.288; N.T. Samartseva, in D.B. Levin & G.P. Kaliuzhnaia, eds., *Mezhdunarodnoe pravo*, Moscow, 1964, p.159; D.L. Zlatopol'skii, *Gosudarstvennoe ustroistvo SSSR*, Moscow, 1960, pp.258–259; A.I. Lepeshkin, *Kurs sovetskogo gosudarstvennogo prava*, Moscow, 1961, Vol.1, p.471; V.S. Shevtsov, *Sovetskoe grazhdanstvo*, Moscow, 1965, pp.25, 47; *idem*, in *Entsiklopedicheskii slovar' pravovykh znanii (Sovetskoe pravo)*, Moscow, 1965, p.91; L.D. Voevodin, in S.S. Kravchuk, ed., *Sovetskoe gosudarstvennoe pravo*, Moscow, 1980, p.215.
3. A.I. Lepeshkin, *op. cit.*, p.471.
4. E.Ia. Chernomordik, "K voprosu o dvoinom grazhdanstve v inostrannom i mezhdunarodnom prave", *Sovetskoe gosudarstvo i pravo*, 1947, No.1, p.57 (hereafter abbr. as *SGiP*).
5. V.I. Lisovskii, *Mezhdunarodnoe pravo*, Kiev, 1955, p.101.
6. These option experiments are analyzed in greater detail in my "Option of Nationality in Soviet Treaty Law: The War–Time and Post–War Record", *Iowa Law Review*, 1964, No.4, p.1130–1176, and *Soviet Citizenship Law*, Leyden, 1968, Chapter IV. See, too, the excellent work on the option experience of the Baltic states by D.A. Loeber, *Diktierte Option, Die Umsiedlung der Deutsch–Balten aus Estland und Lettland 1939–1941*, Neumünster, 1972.
7. For a fuller discussion of this series of measures, see my *Soviet Citizenship Law*, Chapter IV. Some new materials have now been released and published in the collections *Sovetskii* Soiuz — *Narodnaia Pol'sha 1944–1974, dokumenty i materialy*, Moscow, 1974, and *Dokumenty i materialy po istorii Sovetsko–pol'skikh otnoshenii*, Moscow, 1974–1976, Vols.8 and 9. Several extensive and detailed studies on the subject have also been published in Poland recently, with copious references to local literature and archival materials. See, for instance, M. Motas, "Niektóre kwestie dotyczace przesiedlienia ludności polskiej z USSR do Polski w latach 1944– 1946", *Z dziejów stosunków Polsko–Radzieckich, studia i materialy*, Warsaw, 1975, Vol.11–12, pp.221–234, and K. Kersten, *Repatriacja ludności polskiej po II wojnie światowej (studium historyczne)*, Wroclaw, 1974, and the sources cited therein.

   The number of individuals of Polish origin remaining in the USSR continues to be hotly disputed and considerable concern has been expressed as of late in unofficial Polish circles about their status and the lack of personal and social contact with members of the Polish community in the Soviet Union. Cf., Radio Free Europe *Research*, Poland/40, December 20, 1974.

8. D.L. Zlatopol'skii, *op. cit.*, p.264; A.I. Denisov & M.G. Kirichenko, *Sovetskoe gosudarstvennoe pravo*, Moscow, 1957, p.139; L.D. Voevodin, in S.S. Kravchuk, ed., *op. cit.*, p.223.
9. Texts in *Sbornik zakonov SSSR i ukazov Presidiuma Verkhovnogo Soveta SSSR (1938g.–noiabr 1958g.)*, Moscow, 1959, pp.78–84.
10. *Ibid.*, pp.76–77, 84–85.
11. See the author's "The Soviet Union and the Problem of Refugees and Displaced Persons, 1917–1956", *American Journal of International Law*, 1957, No.2, pp.325–361, and O.U. Meliksetian, *Deportatsiia zapadnykh armian i repatriatsiia zarubezhnykh armian v Sovetskuiu Armeniiu 1915–1940*, Erevan, 1975, in Armenian. The citizenship policy of the Soviet Armenian regime in the early years is analyzed by A.A. Esaian, *Nekotorye voprosy teorii i istorii mezhdunarodnogo prava*, Erevan, 1977, pp.265–271.
12. A.A. Esaian, *Nekotorye voprosy sovetskogo grazhdanstva (Voprosy naseleniia v praktike Sovetskoi Armenii)*, Erevan, 1966, pp.8–20.
13. *Ibid.*, p.20. Cf., Yaacov Ro'i, *From Encroachment to Involvement, A Documentary Study of Soviet Policy in the Middle East, 1945–1973*, Jerusalem, 1974, pp.45–46.
14. *Vedomosti Verkhovnogo Soveta SSSR*, 1946, No.39 (hereafter abbr. as *VVS SSSR*).
15. Decree of the Presidium of the USSR Supreme Soviet of June 15, 1979, *VVS SSSR*, 1979, No.24, Art.437.
16. *VVS SSSR*, 1956, No.16, Art.353; *Sbornik deistvuiushchikh dogovorov, soglashenii i konventsii, zakliuchennykh SSSR s inostrannymi gosudarstvami*, Moscow, 1960, vyp.18, pp.271–274 (hereafter abbr. as *SDD*); *United Nations Treaty Series*, Vol. 259, pp.155–167 (hereafter abbr. as *UNTS*).
17. *VVS SSSR*, 1958, No.1, Art.2; *SDD*, Moscow, 1961, vyp.20, pp.212–214, *UNTS*, Vol.318, pp.35–51.
18. *VVS SSSR*, 1958, No.5, Art.103; *SDD*, vyp.20, pp.224–227; *UNTS*, Vol.318, pp. 89–101.
19. *VVS SSSR*, 1958, No.9, Art.205; *SDD*, vyp.20, pp.205–208; *UNTS*, Vol.307, pp. 251–263.
20. *VVS SSSR*, 1958, No.17, Art.289; *SDD*, vyp.20, pp.227–230; *UNTS*, Vol.320, pp. 111–127.
21. *VVS SSSR*, 1958, No.7, Art.141; *SDD*, vyp.20, pp.208–211; *UNTS*, Vol.302, pp. 3–19.
22. *VVS SSSR*, 1958, No.4, Art.84; *SDD*, vyp.20, pp.215–217; *UNTS*, Vol.292, pp. 107–119; *Supplement to the Volume on Laws Concerning Nationality 1954*, New York, 1959, United Nations Legislative Series, ST/LEG/SER.B/9, pp.100–101.
23. *VVS SSSR*, 1958, No.9, Art.209; *SDD*, vyp.20, pp.221–224; *UNTS*, Vol.319, pp.277–289.
24. *VVS SSSR*, 1958, No.35, Art.426; *SDD*, vyp.20, pp.218–220; *UNTS*, Vol.322, pp.202–213.

    Concurrently, several such conventions were signed by the East European states between themselves. For an analysis of the provisions of the latter documents and the USSR's set of bilateral agreements with these countries, see I. Sipkov, "Settlement of Dual Nationality in European Communist Countries", *American Journal of International Law*, 1962, No.4, pp.1010–1019.
25. *Vneshniaia politika i mezhdunarodnye otnosheniia Kitaiskoi Narodnoi Respubliki*, Moscow, 1974, vol.1, p.232.
26. *VVS SSSR*, 1970, No.6, Art.50; *SDD*, Moscow, 1973, vyp.26, pp.96–99; *UNTS*, Vol.777, pp.144–167.

    Presumably, the tardiness in concluding the agreement with the GDR was occasioned by the latter's delay in enacting a citizenship law and reluctance to spell out its citizenship policy in light of the continuing controversy with West Germany over the issue. A statute defining the citizenship of the GDR was finally adopted on February 20, 1967. Text in English in *International Legal Materials*, 1967, No.3, pp.466–467.

27. *VVS SSSR*, 1979, No.18, Art.331.

28. D.L. Zlatopol'skii, *op. cit.*, p.260. Cf., A.I. Lepeshkin, *op. cit.*, p.473: "From what has been said, one can see that Soviet constitutional law considers the status of dual citizenship abnormal, temporary and transitional. Accordingly, our state, guided by humane and democratic aims, strives to solve the question of liquidation of that condition on the basis of strict respect for the principle of full freedom of will of the individuals in choosing their citizenship". See, too, L.D. Voevodin, in S.S. Kravchuk, ed., *op. cit.*, p.227.

For brief analysis of the main clauses of the treaties, see A.I. Lepeshkin, *op. cit.*, p.472; V.I. Menzhinskii, in F.I. Kozhevnikov, ed., *op. cit.*, pp.288–291; N.T. Samartseva, in D.B. Levin & G.P. Kaliuzhnaia, eds., *op. cit.*, p.160; *Kurs mezhdunarodnogo prava*, Moscow, 1967, Vol.3, pp.77–79; P.I. Savitskii, in G.V. Ignatenko & D.D. Ostapenko, eds., *Mezhdunarodnoe pravo*, Moscow, 1978, pp. 187–188.

29. G.E. Vilkov, "Mezhdunarodno–pravovoe regulirovanie voprosov dvoinogo grazhdanstva", *Sovetskii ezhegodnik mezhdunarodnogo prava 1959*, Mocow, 1960, p.360. Likewise, V.V. Polianskii, "Printsipy sovetskogo grazhdanstva", *SGiP*, 1980, No.5, pp.125–126, fn.8; B. Nepesov, "'Dvoinoe grazhdanstvo': chto eto takoe?", *Chelovek i zakon*, 1979, No.11, pp.16–18.

30. A.N. Makarov, "Le droit d'option en cas de double nationalité dans les conventions internationales", *Varia Juris Gentium*, Leyden, 1959, p.199.

31. *North Korea: A Case Study in the Techniques of Takeover*, Washington, D.C., 1961, Department of State Publication 7118 (Far Eastern Series 103), p.3.

32. See some of the revelations regarding the role of Soviet citizens in Yugoslavia and Yugoslav anti–Tito emigrés in the USSR in the course of the Soviet–Yugoslav dispute following Yugoslavia's expulsion from the Cominform, in *Livre Blanc sur les procédés agressifs des Gouvernements de l'URSS, de Pologne, de Tchécoslovaquie, de Hongrie, de Roumanie, de Bulgarie, et d'Albanie envers la Yougoslavie*, Belgrade, 1951, pp.110–131.

33. G.E. Vilkov, *op. cit.*, pp.370.

34. It is interesting to note that in all of these treaties, except the one between the USSR and Yugoslavia, the signatories heavily emphasized in the preamble that they were motivated "by the desire to liquidate possible cases of dual citizenship on the basis of free choice of citizenship by the persons involved". The preamble to the Soviet–Yugoslav agreement merely referred back to the Joint declaration signed in Belgrade on June 2, 1955, and confirmed the parties' desire to "liquidate unresolved questions of citizenship and repatriation". The relevant passage in the Joint declaration reads:

"6. The two Governments have agreed to take steps to conclude treaties with the aim of settling questions relative to citizenship or, correspondingly, relative to the repatriation of citizens of one Contracting Party who are located on the territory of the other Party. The two Governments agree that the treaties must be based on respect for principles of humaneness, as well as on generally recognized principles of freedom of choice by said individuals.

The two Governments also agree to guarantee the right to ensure protection to the citizens of the other side on their territory, understanding by that the right of citizens to retain the citizenship they had before arriving on the territory of the other Contracting Party too."

The text of the declaration may be consulted in *Izvestiia*, June 3, 1955, and *Deklaratsii, zaiavleniia i kommiunike Sovetskogo pravitel'stva s pravitel'stvami inostrannykh gosudarstv 1954–1957gg.*, Moscow, 1957, pp.297–302.

At the time of the Joint Declaration, the signatories made no reservations regarding "freedom of choice by the interested persons" and left the impression that the entire "option" program would be conducted in accordance with that formula. The decision to limit it and exclude a designated category of individuals from the "election proceedings" must then have come later.

35. *Novaia Mongoliia, Ekonomiko–politicheskoe i kul'turnoe sostoianie strany, Protokoly pervogo Velikogo Khuruldana Mongol'skoi Narodnoi Respubliki*, Ulan–Bator–Khoto, 1925, p.206.

36. *Tretii s"ezd Mongol'skoi Narodnoi Partii*, Urga, 1924, p.12.

37. V.V. Egorev, G.N. Lashkevich, M.A. Plotkin, B.D. Rozenblium, *Zakonodatel'stvo i mezhdunarodnye dogovory Soiuza SSR i soiuznykh respublik o pravovom polozhenii inostrannykh fizicheskikh i iuridicheskikh lits*, Moscow, 1926, pp.14–15.

38. *Novaia Mongoliia*, p.206.

39. Text in *Dokumenty vneshnei politiki SSSR*, Moscow, 1967, Vol.13, pp.276–277; *Sovetsko–Mongol'skie otnosheniia 1921–1974, dokumenty i materialy*, Moscow–Ulan Bator, 1975, Vol.1, pp.226–228.

40. Text in SDD, Moscow, 1955, vyp.10, pp.20–22; *Sovetsko–Mongol'skie otnosheniia 1921–1966, Sbornik dokumentov*, Moscow, 1966, pp.103–105.

41. S.V. Chernichenko, *Mezhdunarodno–pravovye voprosy grazhdanstva*, Moscow, 1968, p.123.

42. Mongolia operated till recently without a citizenship statute. However, B.V. Shchetinin, in I.P. Ilinskii & B.V. Shchetinin, *Gosudarstvennoe pravo stran narodnoi demokratii*, Moscow, 1964, p.192, indicated that: "In the Mongolian People's Republic a child becomes a Mongolian citizen if both parents are citizens of the MPR. In the event one of the parents is a foreigner, the child born to the couple may become a Mongolian citizen by agreement of the parents. In the absence of the parents' agreement, the child is assigned the citizenship of the mother." See, too, E. Tomson, *Das Staatsangehörigkeitsrecht der ostasiatischen Staaten*, Frankfurt– am–Main/Berlin, 1971, pp.285–289.

A Law on Citizenship was confirmed on Dec. 30, 1974, which revises the above formula on acquisition of citizenship by birth. According to Art.3(a), a child born on the territory of the MPR or on the territory of another state, one of whose parents is a Mongolian citizen shall be deemed a citizen of the MPR. The new rule enhances the chances of dual citizenship occurring at birth through conflict of Soviet and Mongolian citizenship legislation. For text, translated by W.E. Butler, see *International Legal Materials*, 1981, No.5, pp.1203–1206 (with instructions on application of the Law).

43. Hereafter, mention of the USSR–Romania treaty practice in this domain without indicating a date refers to both the 1957 and 1978 agreements.

44. Stranger still is the fact that S.V. Chernichenko, *op. cit.*, p.130, specifically lists Romania as one of the countries whose mutual relations with the USSR in citizenship matters were governed by this "custom". The statement was printed in 1968, i.e., eleven years after the signature of the 1957 convention which was silent on this point and ten years before a corresponding norm was enunciated expressis verbis in the 1978 convention, with a view to its *prospective* application.

45. Exchange of notes of August 22, 1957, and August 29, 1957, prolonging the deadline for submitting declarations until July 31, 1958.

46. S.V. Chernichenko, *op. cit.*, p.128, points out that the drafting of these clauses displays considerable stylistic differences. For example, in some of the conventions (with Yugoslavia, Poland, Hungary) a literal reading of the corresponding clauses might suggest that these rules would here apply to the children of just those persons who had dual citi-

zenship before the convention entered into force. In his opinion, "such an interpretation would be too narrow" and he considers the formulation editorially more felicitous in the conventions with Czechoslovakia, Bulgaria, Mongolia, etc., which, inter alia, allowed the parents with different citizenships (but not hitherto dual citizens) to exercise a choice on behalf of their minor children who did happen to be dual citizens.

47. Again, S.V. Chernichenko, *op. cit.*, p.127, considers that the corresponding clause was better drafted in the USSR–Hungary edition than in the USSR–Romania (1957), USSR–Yugoslavia and USSR–Albania versions in that the former left no doubt that only the requested state had the right to reject a petition, whereas the language of the latter could give the impression that both signatories had the right to do so — the result, according to him, of not "altogether successful" articulation.

48. In addition, the USSR–Bulgaria, 1978 USSR–Romania and USSR–GDR treaties contained a clause explaining that any questions arising in connection with the execution and interpretation of the respective convention would be resolved through diplomatic channels. The rest of the conventions do not feature a similar caveat — probably because that is the standard operating procedure anyway.

49. Cf., I.K. Gorodetskaia, *Mezhdunarodnaia zashchita prav i interesov detei*, Moscow, 1973, p.39.

50. *VVS SSSR*, 1963, No.30, Art.340; G.E. Vilkov, comp., *Zakonodatel'stvo SSSR i mezhdunarodnye soglasheniia po voprosam grazhdanstva (sbornik)*, Moscow, 1964, pp.111–114.

51. *VVS SSSR*, 1966, No.15, Art.225; *SDD*, Moscow, 1971, vyp.24, pp.73–76.

52. *VVS SSSR*, 1967, No.7, Art.78; *SDD*, Moscow, 1972, vyp.25, pp.122–125. A supplementary protocol to the convention repealed Art.5 of the treaty of December 12, 1957. The latter had dealt briefly with prospective cases of dual citizenship at birth; its substance was absorbed into the latest agreement.

53. *VVS SSSR*, 1970, No.6, Art.50; *SDD*, vyp.26, pp.96–99.

54. *VVS SSSR*, 1979, No.18, Art.331, and 1981, No.32, Art.950.

55. S.V. Chernichenko, *op. cit.*, pp.132–133.
The principal features of the USSR's latest agreements with Hungary, Poland, and Bulgaria, plus the accord with the GDR, are reviewed in I.K. Gorodetskaia, "Grazhdanstvo detei", *SGiP*, 1971, No.4, p.41.

56. Except, of course, that the provisions of the old Soviet–Bulgarian and Soviet–Czechoslovak conventions seeking to abort the future occurrence of dual citizenship between the parties involved concentrated exclusively on the type engendered at birth and paid no attention to the variety produced by naturalization.

57. S.V. Chernichenko, *op. cit.*, p.132.

58. I.K. Gorodetskaia, *op. cit.*, pp.45–46.

59. S.V. Chernichenko, *op. cit.*, p.130.

60. G.K. Dmitrieva, "Mezhdunarodnyi god zhenshchin", *SGiP*, 1975, No.3, p.7. For text of the Convention, see *VVS SSSR*, 1958, No.28, Art.373; *SDD*, vyp.20, pp. 438–442; *Supplement* ..., pp.91–99.

61. *Idem*, "O mezhdunarodnoi zashchite prav zhenshchin", *Pravovedenie*, 1975, No.6, p.7.

62. S.I. Rusinova, "Zakon o grazhdanstve SSSR", *Pravovedenie*, 1980, No.1, pp.6–7.

63. G.K. Dmitrieva, *Mezhdunarodnaia zashchita prav zhenshchiny*, Kiev, 1975, p.113.

64. *Idem*, "Nekotorye aspekty mezhdunarodnoi zashchity prav zhenshchin", *Pravovedenie*, 1969, No.6, p.114.

65. *Idem, op. cit.* (note 63 above), pp.114–115. The author then adds:
"Real equality is possible where are not only proclaimed the equal rights of women with

men to citizenship, but is also applied an identical procedure of naturalization for both spouses. The principle of equal rights of the parties to marriage, notes S.V. Chernichenko [*op. cit.*, p.104], is not contradicted by a relaxed procedure of naturalization of foreigners entering into marriage with citizens of the given state. However, it is necessary to stress that this proposition is accurate only in the event the relaxed procedure is applied uniformly both to the alien wife and the alien husband."
In that respect, the sense of Article 9 of the 1979 Convention on the Elimination of All Forms of Discrimination against Women, which the USSR ratified on Dec.19, 1980, is superior inasmuch as it mandates that:
"State Parties shall grant women equal rights with men to acquire, change or retain their nationality. They shall ensure in particular that neither marriage to an alien nor change of nationality by the husband during marriage shall automatically change the nationality of the wife, render her stateless or force upon her the nationality of the husband."
If a common citizenship for the family unit is still desired, presumably it can be attained by giving each partner the same opportunity to convert to the other's nationality, whether through regular or special privileged procedures. One also assumes that the bar against the woman's exposure to involuntary conversion and statelessness in connection with marriage enunciated in the second sentence is not meant in absolute terms, but only insofar as these handicaps affect only the wife and not the husband: as long as the consequences are identical for both spouses, the substance of the treatment here seems to be immaterial. By contrast, the 1957 Convention on the Nationality of Married Women sought to prevent certain negative results per se, without concerning itself with the problem of the equal status of the principals in a matrimonial setting or implying that these results might be acceptable if they were fully shared by the husband and wife.

66. *Ibid.*, p.115.
67. S.V. Chernichenko, *op. cit.*, p.125.
68. *Soviet News*, 1980, No.6024, p.183.
69. See the Nationality Law of the People's Republic of China, adopted on September 10, 1980, in *Beijing Review*, 1980, No.40, pp.17–18, and for comments on this point, Gong Qiuxiang, "On the Nationality Law", *ibid.*, 1980, No.45, p.24. For an analysis of the provisions of the latest law, see the author's "The 1980 Nationality Law of the People's Republic of China", *American Journal of Comparative Law*, 1982, No.3, pp.459–498.
70. S.V. Chernichenko, *op. cit.*, p.137.
71. *Pravda* and *Izvestiia*, December 5, 1966.
72. *Soviet News*, 1980, No.6024, p.183.
73. The legal connections between emigration, immigration and citizenship will be explored more fully below in the special chapter on the subject.
74. *SDD*, vyp.25, pp.78–80.

STATELESSNESS AS A CONSEQUENCE OF THE CONFLICT OF NATIONALITY LAWS (PART I)

As compared to the precedent set in this area by the earlier citizenship legislation of the Soviet Union, perhaps the single most distinctive element of the 1938 Law on the Citizenship of the USSR was its approach to the problem of statelessness. Indeed, as every Soviet source has dutifully noted since, its "final Article 8 introduces the new condition of statelessness, unknown to Soviet law before 1938".[1] Technically speaking, the claim crediting Article 8 of the 1938 law with engineering the debut of the concept of statelessness on the Soviet legal scene turns out, on closer inspection, to be a trifle exaggerated. Rather, the real innovation here consisted in that the 1938 act sanctioned statelessness as a discrete, third category of citizenship status, along with local citizenship and foreign citizenship, a recognition until then denied to it in the USSR by the workings of federal legislation.

Article 9 of the 1978 statute is a virtual replica of its predecessor, confirming that persons residing on the territory of the USSR who are not citizens of the USSR and have no evidence of possession of a foreign citizenship are considered stateless persons. The present formula thus retains the triumvirate of citizens of the USSR, foreigners, and apatrides — on the model pioneered by its 1938 antecedent. Of course, as Soviet commentators point out, what this also means is that the terms of the current piece of legislation make "it completely impossible for any stateless person to be automatically counted as a Soviet citizen"[2] — at least where adult individuals are concerned, since, for example, according to Article 13, the child of stateless persons maintaining a permanent place of residence in the USSR who is born on the territory of the USSR ipso jure figures as a citizen of the USSR.

In the Soviet Union, as everywhere else, a substantial proportion of the recorded instances of statelessness is today the outgrowth of a phenomenon best described as the blind collision of competing legal systems. The rest of the portfolio features samples of statelessness that represent the product of deliberate policies pursued by the regime, designed to reduce either certain individuals or selected groups of individuals to that status. Consciously induced statelessness is by no means a rarity in the Soviet legal inventory, but, to the extent that this species is the result of a calculated decision on the part of the proper authorities, its spread can easily be controlled and, in fact, its inception can be prevented altogether. Far more resistant to unilateral treatment is the common or unintended offshoot of statelessness, i.e., that engendered by the unpremeditated clash of nationality laws, and so this strain continues to recur.

The following section proposes to deal only with the latter aspect of the question, although, as will become apparent toward the end, the solutions to this problem which the Soviet government has experimented with at different times have rarely taken into account the underlying causes and have, as a rule, confined themselves to prescribing an ad hoc corrective to the immediate situation without delving into what had brought it about or drawing fine distinctions for therapeutic purposes between the two types of statelessness. The next step, then, is to: 1) examine the reasons for the incidence of this jural condition as they relate to the latest principles and norms of Soviet law pertaining to the subject; and, 2) survey the special remedial measures, if any, introduced into Soviet legislation to cope with such cases.

I. Conflicts–in–Law Varietals of Statelessness

1. Failure to Acquire Nationality at Birth

A. Jus Soli Versus Jus Sanguinis

It is a commonplace of international law that in the modern practice of countries "neither the doctrine of *jus soli* nor of *jus sanguinis* has been adopted to the exclusion of the other". Just as self–evident is the observation that, as a consequence, a state of affairs currently obtains in which "the very fact that both systems are contemporaneously employed may give rise to cases of statelessness".[3]

The language of the 1978 enactment leaves no doubt that the principle of jus sanguinis constitutes the prime criterion for determining the acquisition of Soviet citizenship at birth. In the normal course of events, therefore, statelessness at birth will happen whenever a child of parents who are nationals of a state subscribing exclusively to the rule of jus soli is born on Soviet soil. The parents' state does not confer its nationality on the child because it is born outside its territory, while, simultaneously, the Soviet authorities, adhering to the proposition that parentage is the deciding factor, likewise refuse to grant the child Soviet citizenship. Ergo, the child ends up stateless.

Further, one can visualize a variant on this basic theme, also producing the same consequences. Where, for example, a child is born on Soviet ground of foreign parents each with different citizenship, if the country of which the father is a national abides by the precept of jus soli, the child will be stateless, even though the mother may be a citizen of a country enforcing the rule of jus sanguinis. Indeed, "it is a generally accepted principle that the nationality of a legitimate child is determined by the nationality of the father".[4] Hence, unless the legislation of the state of which the minor's mother is a citizen contains an emergency clause extending its nationality where the child for some extraordinary reason does not inherit the citizenship of the father — and such prescience is not standard fare — the child, as suggested, incurs statelessness at birth.

Because of the heavy reliance in Soviet law on the institution of jus sanguinis to route how Soviet citizenship passes by descent, infants born to Soviet parents or even one Soviet parent are effectively safeguarded from lapsing into statelessness at birth. True, federal legislation now recognizes a lone exemption to this comprehensive immunity. Article 30 of the Principles of legislation of the USSR and union republics on marriage and the family of June 27, 1968, which were applied from October 1, 1968, provided, inter alia, that where the parents did not share the same citizenship and one of them at the moment of the child's birth was a citizen of the USSR, if both parents resided at the time outside the borders of the USSR the citizenship of the child would be settled by agreement between them.[5] These terms were later modified by the corresponding clause of the 1978 citizenship law (Art.12), which mandated instead that where the parents had different citizenships and one of them on the day of the child's birth was a citizen of the USSR, if at the time both parents had a permanent place of residence outside the borders of the USSR the citizenship of the child born outside the USSR would be determined by agreement of the parents.[6]

In the course of the public discussion of the merits of the marriage and family bill, the point was cogently made that in these circumstances the parents' choice was guaranteed to work only where they properly picked Soviet citizenship for their offspring and that otherwise the outcome would depend entirely on the operation of the relevant legal systems which, naturally, where in no way obliged to defer to the parents' preference in selecting a foreign citizenship for their progeny.[7] The upshot of all this discordance, as duly signaled by the critic, could well be a brush with statelessness. To be sure, the revised formula featured in the 1978 citizenship statute shifted to a more restricted scope in limiting the arrangement to bona fide expatriates in lieu of merely individuals physically located abroad on the occasion of their child's birth and, to the extent that this meant that Soviet citizenship would be summarily assigned to a larger number of children born abroad in a "mixed" marriage situation which involved a parent vested with Soviet citizenship, the chances of the child fetching up as an apatride were commensurately reduced. Even so, illustrations of how statelessness can occur in this setting readily spring to mind. A child is born to a couple maintaining a permanent place of residence on the territory of the mother's home state. The father is a Soviet citizen and the law of the country of which the mother is a citizen follows the doctrine of jus sanguinis in the sense that the offspring shares the father's citizenship. The parents opt for the mother's citizenship, the lex loci certifies the child as a Soviet citizen, Soviet law takes the attitude that the parents' will prevails, and the result is that the child ends up as stateless ab origine. Or, under similar conditions if a child only whose father is a Soviet citizen is born on the territory of a third state which adheres to the rule that the citizenship is transmitted via the father, the outcome is identical. Or, in each of these two contingencies, the parents either neglect to express a desire or fail to reach a consensus, and once again the child figures as a stateless person from date of birth.

Note, however, that this experience does not quite fit your stock conflicts–in–law scene where the individual is accidentally victimized by the random operations of an egregious mechanism. Here, an element of free will does enter the picture since the parents can always protect the child from contracting statelessness by the expedient of promptly registering it as a Soviet citizen. So, in practical terms, it is the parents' positive wish that the child have a citizenship other than a Soviet one, or, indeed, their resolve that the child definitely not have a Soviet citizenship no matter what the consequences, or plain dereliction on their part in enrolling the offspring as a Soviet citizen, or an insurmountable difference of opinion on that score which then rules out access to this solution, that sets these erratic forces in motion.

How novel this whole procedure was and whether it really led to a jump in cases of statelessness affecting children of Soviet–foreigner couples domiciled abroad is hard to tell. The uncertainty stems from the fact that the 1938 statute said nothing about the grounds for acquisition of Soviet citizenship at birth, Soviet authors made it sound as though, in line with precedent, the norm of jus sanguinis in its extreme version (i.e., bequeathal by either parent) still applied, and several of the republican family codes continued to display articles modeled on the matching clause in the 1924 federal citizenship act which endorsed the "agreement of the parents" routine with reference to the citizenship affiliation of children born into "mixed" expatriate families in which one parent retained Soviet citizenship. Not only does evidence indicate that the 1924 formula was sometimes used long after it was thought to be a dead letter owing to the contrary provisions of federal legislation, but in the 1960's administrative policy apparently reverted to the old practice in such instances without benefit of legislative sanction. Thus, the assessment of the magnitude of the "reform" largely depends on whether comparisons are drawn with the official script as expounded by the early glossators or the latter–day record which, according to other reports, foreshadowed the 1968 revisions in the script.

B. Child of Stateless Parents

After the promulgation of the 1938 regulations, a child born on Soviet soil of stateless parents was ipso jure deemed stateless, given the parents' inability to transfer any nationality to their progeny and premier Soviet commitment to the principle of jus sanguinis. The USSR thereby joined, as has aptly been put, the ranks of those countries "wherein, it would seem, statelessness is a disease that can be inherited".[8] What is more, whereas some states then try to offer a palliative and in these adverse circumstances grant their nationality unconditionally, the USSR was not among them, foresaw no special remedy, and merely let events take due course.

During the "liberal" 1960s, assorted suggestions cropped up in Soviet legal literature recommending that the existing modus operandi here be changed. One rather timid proposal favored an accommodation by virtue of which children of stateless persons who came of age during their stay in the USSR would receive Soviet citizenship independently of whether their parents acquired Soviet citizenship or not.[9] More straightforward in this respect was the position of a second Soviet spokesman who wanted to see "a norm established in accordance with which children of persons without citizenship, born and permanently residing on the territory of the USSR, would be considered Soviet citizens regardless of whether or not their parents acquired Soviet citizenship".[10]

These lobbying efforts were ultimately crowned with success and Article 13 of the 1978 citizenship act now proclaims that a child born on the territory of the

USSR of stateless persons who have a permanent place of residence in the USSR is a citizen of the USSR. The federal decree of June 15, 1979,[11] which detailed the mechanics of entry into force of the Law on the Citizenship of the USSR, explained that the system functions automatically as concerns such children born after June 30, 1979, when the new legislation had gone into effect. However, a different treatment was reserved for children with the same background born before that date who had not turned eighteen by July 1, 1979: they could acquire the citizenship of the USSR on the strength of a statement by their legal representatives which had to be filed at the place of residence with the nearby organs of internal affairs before the child attained majority, but in any event no later than July 1, 1980, with the further qualification that eligible children between the ages of fourteen and eighteen had to append their personal written consent to the proposed "conversion". Failure to avail oneself of this opportunity presumably meant that admission to Soviet citizenship would then have to be sought through regular naturalization channels and the common naturalization route is also the only one accessible to any person who fell into this general category except that he (she) had already reached adulthood by July 1, 1979.

Looked at prospectively, the terms of the 1978 statute are most generous in dealing with this problem and manage to rid the Soviet scene of one source of chronic statelessness. Although the Soviet government never ratified the 1961 Convention on the Reduction of Statelessness[12] and has been a consistent critic of its key features, the instant naturalization henceforth afforded children of locally domiciled expatriates meets the maximum standards prescribed by that document for handling this type of phenomenon — i.e., "At birth, by operation of law" (Art.1, para.1(a)) — and thus justifies Soviet claims that the language of the 1978 enactment takes into account the Convention's instructions in grappling with the question of stateless individuals[13] — at least on this particular issue. In tackling past occurrences of this sort, the mood is more restrained: stateless minors seemingly could receive Soviet citizenship by the expedient of a simple request, but stayed stateless if they neglected to take the initiative unless, as mentioned, they subsequently applied for admission to Soviet citizenship in the established manner; stateless adults with a like vita remained stateless until they succeeded in getting naturalized through the usual procedure. Relief in these cases is neither immediate nor assured, and, indeed, the stateless condition of many of these people can be expected to persist — perhaps even indefinitely — if, for instance, they had managed somewhere along the line to run afoul of the authorities, which is no difficult feat in the Soviet environment.

Note, too, that such "unilateral enrollment" into Soviet citizenship avails only a child born on Soviet soil to stateless parents who themselves have a permanent place of residence in the USSR. A child born in the USSR to a stateless couple on a visit or in transit would not be "bailed out" in this manner and would still incur statelessness at birth. Thus, the rescue mission here is predicated on the concept not of a random territorial connection at the moment of birth, but of a more enduring linkage combining jus soli and evidence of the family unit's local settlement. The "safety–net" turns out to be less than universal in scope and omits to rescue the offspring of "foreign" apatrides (as against "domestic" apatrides) from being precipitated into statelessness.

C. *Foundlings*

The Law on Citizenship of 1938 failed to regulate the matter of the status of foundlings discovered in the Soviet Union. In light of the official silence, a Soviet jurist posed a question in this connection as to whether "the minor children of unknown parents found on the territory of the USSR (so–called 'foisted children', homeless minors)" should be included in the category of stateless persons named in its Article 8. His own belief was that "in this — practically ever rarer — event was permissible ... a presumption of Soviet extraction and, consequently, of Soviet citizenship".[14] Many years later, a local colleague expressed the same view in a much firmer tone, declaring that "children found on the territory of the USSR whose parents are unknown are recognized as Soviet citizens on the strength of the presumption that they are born of Soviet citizens".[15]

Article 14 of the 1978 statute lays the matter to rest by stipulating that a child located on the territory of the USSR both of whose parents are unknown is a citizen of the USSR. However, the federal edict of June 15, 1979, is careful to indicate that this rule extends only to such individuals born after June 30, 1979. Otherwise, as in the case of children of stateless persons, those in their midst born before that date who had not turned eighteen by July 1, 1979, were given the right to acquire the citizenship of the USSR by virtue of a statement by their legal representatives filed at the place of residence with the vicinal organs of internal affairs before the child attained majority, but not later than July 1, 1980 (petitions relating to children between the ages of fourteen and eighteen had to be accompanied by written notice of acquiescence from the de cujus to the scheme). Adults in the group (i.e., anybody who had reached eighteen by July 1, 1979), again like their counterparts among the offspring of stateless persons, were left to resort to the device of ordinary naturalization if they wished to receive Soviet citizenship.

The treatment in store for foundlings located on Soviet soil after the new law went into effect would probably be pronounced fair by current international standards and certainly fits the desideratum enunciated in Article 2 of the 1961 Convention on the Reduction of Statelessness — adding another notch to Soviet claims of close rapport between the language of the treaty and that of the statute. What comes as a great surprise, though, is the sense of the decree's reference to the earlier crop of foundlings: inasmuch as the current script calls for these individuals to take positive steps in order to acquire Soviet citizenship (whether by plain request or by formal naturalization), the inevitable conclusion is that all or most of them hitherto did not figure as Soviet citizens. The resulting picture does not square with what Soviet authors have been telling us about the administrative record in this domain. While it is impossible to verify which of these versions is correct, considerable weight attaches to the argument that there must have been a practical rationale prompting the legislators to arrange for solutions designed to apply retroactively to unfinished business posted under this heading of the agenda.

Still unclear is the item of whether the initial premise is final or conditional, i.e., if once acted upon, it may not subsequently be refuted by fresh data as to the origins and/or locus of birth, or if it holds true only as long as the contrary has not been demonstrated. In the former case, foundlings in the Soviet Union never face the prospect of ending up stateless. In the latter, statelessness may very well arise in several ways. For example, should the foundling's parentage later become established and should the parents' citizenship be such that, had it been known all along, the previously described conflict of opposite systems of law based, respectively, on jus soli and jus sanguinis would have precipitated the child's statelessness at birth, this destruction of the raison d'être for the original presumption, inviting, in turn, withdrawal of Soviet citizenship, would forthwith transform the individual into a stateless person, with effect back to the presently revealed date of birth. Or, take the instance where a child of as yet unidentified parents thought to have been born in the Soviet Union is at some future date found to have been born abroad. The first presumption has been badly weakened. But, as distinct from the previous setting, here discovery of the real state of affairs does not altogether discredit the original inference since the subsequent presence of the child in the USSR could validly be construed as evidence that at least one of the parents was a Soviet citizen, (else why bring the child to the USSR), and therefore the child is too. What the authorities would do in such circumstances is a moot point. In all likelihood, they would not change their mind, but that is a guess at best.

D. Illegitimate Children

Quite complex too are the legal problems engendered by the birth in the USSR of an illegitimate child to a foreign mother. In an eventuality of this sort, "it is a generally accepted principle that the nationality ... of an illegitimate child ris determinedt by the nationality of the mother",[17] regardless of where it is born. Not all states, however, follow this policy and, if the mother should be a citizen of one of the latter, her country would now refuse to grant its citizenship to the child. With Soviet law concurrently maintaining that the citizenship of an illegitimate child is dictated by the citizenship of the mother and on these grounds withholding its citizenship from the offspring in question, the child again winds up stateless by virtue of having missed acquiring nationality at birth.

a. Paternity

Between 1944 and 1968, Soviet law offered no possible escape from the dilemma through the expedient of a paternity action. Repeal of the previous "right of a mother to sue in court to establish the fatherhood ... of a child born of a person with whom she had not contracted a registered marriage"[18] blocked every avenue hitherto available that sanctioned resort to adversary proceedings with the object of officially recording the name of the father of a child born out of wedlock, so that thereafter the status of such a child became totally dependent on the status of the mother. In the conditions described above, the child would be stateless at birth and the mother had no recourse in Soviet law during that interval to change this state of affairs except to rely on routine naturalization procedures on behalf of the offspring.

The reforms effected in 1968 in the field of family law afforded only slight relief to persons who had incurred statelessness in this fashion before the new law went into effect. Indeed, in approving the Principles of legislation of the USSR and union republics on marriage and the family on June 27, 1968, and directing that these federal guidelines be put into force from October 1, 1968, the legislators took care to explain that the revived rule which now let the courts hear cases seeking recognition of a person to whom the mother was not married as the father of her child referred to persons born after October 1, 1968.[19] "Regularization" of the position of similarly handicapped persons born before October 1, 1968, was essentially entrusted to the technique of joint declaration filed by both the mother and the "confessed" father or, as subsequently amplified by the decree of October 9, 1979,[20] by the putative father alone where the mother had died, was pronounced legally incapacitated, had been stripped of her parental rights, or her whereabouts could not be ascertained, the upshot of the "admission" then being entered by the organs of registry of acts of civil status in the child's birth certificate. The sole exception featured a situation where the man who had maintained the child and had acknowledged being its father had died and, in these particular circumstances, the courts were entitled to settle the paternity issue at the request of the mother or the child's guardian or the child itself upon attaining majority or other individuals that republican legislation chose to vest with this power, with an affirmative decision going to the organs of registry of acts of civil status for inscription in the child's birth certificate. Establishment of paternity affecting persons who had reached adulthood was permitted only with their consent.

In this special instance, the court's determination that a Soviet citizen had in fact been the father of an illegitimate child born to a foreign woman on Soviet soil would presumably constitute sufficient grounds for conceding the child's right to Soviet citizenship, marking its simultaneous release from statelessness. Whether the "enfranchisement" here operates ex nunc or ex tunc remains unclear. The solitary clue we have is Article 9 of the edict of the Presidium of the USSR Supreme Soviet of September 20, 1968, on the mechanics of entry into force of the federal guidelines to legislation on marriage and the family, which indicated, inter alia, that in the event of recognition of paternity by court decree in the case of children born before October 1, 1968, the mutual rights and duties between the child and its father, as well as the father's kin, were considered as arising from the date of the child's birth.[21] The clause says nothing about the nature of these rights—i.e., if they are limited to "private" rights or also include an automatic stake in the father's citizenship, accruing from the date of birth.

Of course, a negative ruling by the courts meant no change in the status quo and, hence, the perpetuation of the party's original stateless condition.

There is no reason to assume that the current dispensation which gave the courts jurisdiction over certain paternity cases involving persons born before October 1, 1968, applied solely to persons born on Soviet soil and, ceteris paribus, did not equally benefit the child born abroad where the individual competent to file suit decided to do so in a Soviet court. A judicial finding that the child's father was a Soviet citizen and the ensuing realization that if the relationship had been known from the beginning the offspring would have been duly assigned Soviet citizenship at birth (owing to one Soviet parent or owing to one Soviet parent residing in the USSR at the time — depending on one's sense of what the relevant practice was in those days) would probably combine to convert the child into a Soviet citizen and end its career as an apatride.

It is hard to tell what value, if any, this safety device had for a Soviet woman who gave birth to an illegitimate child abroad before October 1, 1968, and was eligible to submit her claim to court because the purported father was no longer alive. The trouble is that we are not sure how administrative policy handled this kind of problem. If one prefers to believe that up till then the script had called for rigid enforcement of the jus sanguinis principle by the terms of which even one Soviet parent (never mind whether the father or the mother) could transmit Soviet citizenship to the progeny regardless of place of birth, the point is academic because congenital statelessness could not occur in this frame. A different picture emerges if one accepts as accurate various local reports that already prior to the introduction of the 1968 reforms Soviet officials had switched to the formula which later became the legal norm, namely, that a child born abroad to parents of whom only one was a Soviet citizen ipso jure acquired Soviet citizenship if the father resided at the time on Soviet soil or, if neither parent did, the child's citizenship was left to be settled by agreement between the parents. In this setting, a child born abroad to a single Soviet woman with no man willing to identify himself as the child's father would presumably qualify at once as a stateless person either because no father could be relied upon to produce the necessary territorial connection or because the required parental consensus that could stage a rescue through option for Soviet citizenship for the offspring was not feasible under the circumstances. Resort to a Soviet court by virtue of the retroactive clause could have positive results if the court established that the child's father was: 1) a foreigner who resided in the USSR when the child was born; or, 2) a Soviet citizen, since a child born to two Soviet citizens counted as a Soviet citizen no matter where it was born.

Note, however, that even before the right to hear paternity suits was thus restored to Soviet courts (as an ad hoc emergency operation for certain past contingencies and standard fare for future mission) the illegitimate child of a foreign woman and a Soviet man born abroad and perhaps also the illegitimate child born abroad to a Soviet woman (if one accepts the diluted jus sanguinis model) stuck with statelessness at birth enjoyed an extra advantage in a bid to save them from that affliction thanks to the possibility of having a paternity action instituted on their behalf in the appropriate foreign court. What, one may ask, would in that instance be the effect of a foreign court order recognizing a Soviet citizen as the father of an illegitimate child born to an alien woman or establishing that a foreigner living in the USSR at the time a child was born to a single Soviet woman residing abroad was its father? Theoretically, of course, there would be nothing to prevent the Soviet authorities from duly recognizing and enforcing in the USSR a valid judgment of a foreign court in a case of this sort. Throughout most of the USSR's history, though, Soviet doctrine has tended to make such recognition and execution contingent on the existence of a valid treaty on the subject between the USSR and the foreign state, barring which execution would commonly be denied.[22]

On the other hand, one's attention is drawn to the fact that the tone here has softened somewhat in recent years. For example, Article 38 of the 1968 federal guidelines to legislation on marriage and the family (in the amended 1979 version) now provides that "documents issued by competent agencies of foreign states in authentication of acts of civil status performed outside the borders of the USSR under the laws of the corresponding states with respect to citizens of the USSR, foreign citizens and stateless persons shall be considered valid in the USSR given a consular legalization". To be sure, the business falls under the usual *ordre public* reservation, with Article 39 (in the 1979 edition) signaling in this connection that recognition of acts of civil status based on foreign laws on marriage and the family "cannot take place if such ... recognition would contravene the basic principles of the Soviet system".[23]

Clearly, the whole process is still far from automatic, but the language just quoted suggests an essential inclination to cooperate in these matters, except where a fundamental incompatibility of legal values intrudes and puts in question the propriety of extraterritorial application of a foreign judicial/administrative determination. If so, an indirect consequence of this more relaxed attitude might well be that a number of illegitimate children born abroad would be spared a stateless existence because Soviet authorities chose to give legal effect to foreign rulings in paternity cases which ascribed fatherhood to Soviet citizens in a context where that additional element spelled entitlement of the children concerned to Soviet citizenship by operation of the law.

Meantime, on the treaty front, a series of bilateral accords featuring a comprehensive legal aid package was concluded during 1957 and 1958 between the Soviet Union and Czechoslovakia, the German Democratic Republic, Bulgaria, the Korean People's Democratic Republic, Poland, Romania, Albania, Hungary, and Mongolia. A parallel agreement was signed in 1962 between the USSR and Yugoslavia and in 1981 between the USSR and Vietnam.[24] Each of these documents contained provisions dealing with reciprocal recognition and execution of court judgments in civil, family and criminal cases. Included were cases arising from court suits instigated to determine the fatherhood of a child, both born in and out of wedlock, a procedure then sanctioned by the law of all the contracting states save the USSR, but to which under the right circumstances the latter now bound itself to give effect on its own territory.[25] These clauses had no significant impact on the incidence of statelessness of the kind here depicted, though. For the conflicts–of–law principles which they enunciated applied solely to "mixed" events involving the citizens of the respective signatories, and the citizenship laws of the USSR's treaty partners were at this point sufficiently well synchronized with kindred legislation of the Soviet Union to all but preclude unintended "collisions" apt to produce this species of statelessness to begin with. A lone exception in that sense is the treaty on the mutual extension of legal aid between the USSR and Iraq of June 22, 1973, which mandates (Art.14) that the decisions of each party's courts or other competent institutions in family matters would be duly recognized and executed on the territory of the other. Since the citizenship legislation of these two states is not "integrated" — contrary to the case among the members of the "socialist community" — statelessness can occur in this relationship and a determination of paternity should on occasion play a practical role in alleviating that condition.

Even so, one possible departure from the general pattern should be mentioned. If prior to October 1, 1968, Soviet citizenship practice did, indeed, observe the rule that children born abroad to a "mixed" duo would acquire Soviet citizenship either if the father resided at the time on Soviet soil or, in the event he did not, if the parents jointly requested Soviet citizenship for their progeny, a child born to a single Soviet woman residing on the territory of some of the USSR's treaty partners could conceivably end up stateless at birth. (Note that this contingency was eliminated upon the entry into force on July 1, 1979, of the 1978 citizenship statute whose Art.12, para.3, henceforth provides that the child one of whose parents was a Soviet citizen at the time of its birth and the other a stateless person or was unknown is a citizen of the USSR regardless of the place of birth.) Since Soviet law did not sanction judicial proceedings for settling paternity issues at the time, the mother could only turn to the competent foreign court for relief in a contentious situation. However, the 1968 reform offered her the alternative of filing suit in a Soviet court where the child was born prior to October 1, 1968, and the putative father was no longer alive. A finding by the Soviet court that a citizen of one of these countries had been the father of the child, duly recognized by the proper agencies of the other party, would earn the child the citizenship of that country and cancel its stateless status.

Recovery by the Soviet courts of the primary right to decide paternity suits involving children born after October 1, 1968, has restored some symmetry in the relations between the USSR and its associates in this particular sector. Now, for example, an unwed Soviet woman who gives birth to a child abroad can also avail herself of the services of a Soviet court in order to establish the identity of the child's father. Should the Soviet court pronounce a citizen of one of these socialist countries to be the child's father, recognition of that decision by the father's home state under the terms of the treaty would function to confer local citizenship on the offspring and, up until July 1, 1979, served to remove the stigma of statelessness. (After that date, the child was spared statelessness by virtue of being assigned Soviet citizenship in accordance with the 1978 citizenship statute whenever one parent was a Soviet citizen at the time of birth and the other was unknown, irrespective of the place of birth.)

Even without benefit of special treaty arrangements, the fact that the courts in the USSR are once again granted full jurisdiction over paternity suits referring to children born after October 1, 1968, means that the system may impose additional curbs on the incidence of the phenomenon of statelessness. Consider the following examples: 1) an illegitimate child is born to a foreign woman on Soviet soil, fails to receive the mother's citizenship and is headed for statelessness, except that a Soviet court routinely determines that a Soviet citizen is the father of the child; 2) an illegitimate child is born to a Soviet woman residing abroad (before the 1978 citizenship act went into effect) and the Soviet court finds that the father is likewise a Soviet citizen or, 3) a foreign citizen who resided on that date on Soviet soil. In each instance, the court's ruling would operate to vest the child with Soviet citizenship.

Or, an illegitimate child is born to a foreign woman on Soviet soil and a Soviet court certifies a foreign man as the father — because the decision can be voluntarily recognized by the proper foreign authorities, the child may be saved from statelessness by virtue of eligibility to share the citizenship of the officially designated father. Or, an illegitimate child was born (prior to July 1, 1979) to a Soviet woman residing abroad and a Soviet court attributed fatherhood to a Soviet citizen or a foreigner also residing abroad — the two parents of record could then communicate their common desire in the legally prescribed manner that the child be a Soviet citizen and by this means prevent the child from possibly incurring statelessness.

One further point needs to be made here. Where establishment of paternity creates a stake in citizenship, the question of when the respective rights originate plays an important role. In the Soviet setting, the applicable norm is that the position of children born to unmarried persons upon the establishment of paternity is exactly the same vis–à–vis their parents and relatives as that of children born to persons married to each other (e.g., Article 50 of the 1969 RSFSR code on marriage and the family).[26] Though the wording does not indicate whether the proposition extends to "public" as well as "private" rights, the more plausible conclusion is that the rule covers both — so acquisition of Soviet citizenship by this route would be backdated to the day of birth.

b. Legitimation

The effects of legitimation on citizenship must next be assessed. Prior to the 1968 reforms, Soviet law did not, technically speaking, conceive of legitimation. However, a federal decree of March 14, 1945,[27] had introduced a rule which, while purporting to ignore the doctrine, in practice carried similar implications. Indeed, it stipulated (Art.3) that "in the event the mother enters into a registered marriage with the person by whom she has given birth to the child, and this person acknowledges that he is the father of the child, the child shall be considered in all respects on an equal footing with children born in a registered marriage".[28] While citizenship was not expressly referred to, duly affirmed fatherhood by a Soviet citizen could, in the various situations previously described in connection with court–determined paternity, ipso jure act to confer Soviet citizenship ab ovo, as it were, on the child so recognized. Hence, where the child, thanks to the factors enumerated above, would have been stateless from the time of birth, such belated registration would, it seems, intercede retroactively to wipe out that status and reinstate the de cujus as a Soviet citizen from date of birth.

The mechanism of "legitimation", in its Soviet version, was thus possible exclusively as an accompaniment to matrimony and no other form of acknowledgment of paternity was envisaged in those days by Soviet law. Elsewhere, though, it could often be achieved through an officially recorded declaration on the part of the man involved quite apart from any registered marriage. A Soviet citizen abroad could, then, through a simplified administrative procedure not available to him at home, identify himself as the father of a child born out of wedlock, with all the legal consequences attendant on such an admission. To be sure, in view of the past reluctance of the Soviet authorities to grant currency to foreign statutes inside the USSR, one had no guarantee that much would be accomplished thereby in terms of next securing the regime's consent to treat the child so legitimized as a citizen of the USSR in accordance with the relevant prescriptions of Soviet law governing acquisition of citizenship by descent.

It is to be noted that in the countries with which in 1957, 1958 and 1962 the Soviet Union entered into comprehensive agreements on "legal aid", as mentioned before, voluntary acknowledgment of fatherhood still constituted the normal procedure of legitimation.[29] And, a declaration properly certified by the organs of the other signatory could forthwith claim recognition in the USSR as well. Theoretically, this should have marked a major contribution toward the lessening of frequency of this variety of statelessness in the matrix of the relations between these nations. For, a Soviet citizen residing in one of the other contracting states and desirous of being identified as the father of a child born there out of wedlock could under local law do so with a minimum of formality and know that now the step taken by him would also carry validity in the USSR and act to confer Soviet citizenship on the offspring by right of descent, even though at home no such ready remedy was accessible to him.

Once again, however, only marginal significance attached to these measures since they were solely designed to solve conflicts–in–law cases to which the citizens of the signatory states were parties and the standardization of citizenship laws within the socialist Commonwealth plus Yugoslavia had already progressed so far that little room existed for discrepancy in this area between the legal systems of these countries to cause any significant amount of statelessness on such grounds in the first place. The occasional exception was the single Soviet mother residing abroad and giving birth to a child on the territory of the host country after Soviet administrative practice switched in the sixties from a strict concept of jus sanguinis to the compound formula in the case of "mixed" expatriate parents requiring a territorial additive or calling for parental consensus in favor of Soviet citizenship: the child could in fact be stuck with statelessness in these special conditions and legitimation certainly had the capacity to offer effective relief from that predicament by supplying the missing ingredient, — i.e., fulfillment of the jus sanguinis criterion by both parents, or the necessary dash of jus soli, or agreement by both parents to vest the child with Soviet citizenship.

(As regards Iraq, with whom a legal aid agreement was signed in 1973 that provided for the mutual recognition of decisions rendered by courts and other competent agencies dealing, inter alia, with family matters, the "neat fit" between respective citizenship legislations is missing, which means that statelessness due to the conflicts–of–law phenomenon can arise and the process of reciprocal recognition of legitimation acts could play a practical role in curtailing such incidents. However, the deterrent potential here of the Soviet– Iraqi document is a mystery to me since I have no inkling of how the subject of legitimation is handled in Iraqi law or even if the latter sanctions treatment of the problem in administrative proceedings.)

At any rate, the script was thoroughly rewritten in 1968. Article 16 of the federal guidelines to legislation on marriage and the family postulated, inter alia, that a child's descent from parents who are not married to each other is established by medium of submission of a joint declaration by the father and mother of the child to state organs of registry of acts of civil status. The procedure that applies in such contingencies, according to Article 17, is for the inscription of the child's mother to be effected on the strength of the mother's statement and the inscription of the child's father to be entered pursuant to a joint statement by the child's father and mother. However, in the event of the mother's death or the impossibility of ascertaining her whereabouts, the recording of the child's father could be performed following a declaration by the father alone. The law of June 27, 1968, which ratified the Principles of legislation of the USSR and union republics on marriage and the family, amplified these instructions by explaining that the device of joint declaration by the mother of an illegitimate child and the person admitting to being its father was equally available to straighten out the status of children born before the Principles went into force, i.e., October 1, 1968, and that determination of paternity in reference to adult individuals was only permitted with their consent. Next, the decree of the Presidium of the USSR Supreme Soviet of September 20, 1968, which spelled out how the Principles were to be put into effect, plugged yet another hole by prescribing that where recognition of paternity worked retrospectively in affecting a child born before October 1, 1968, the mutual rights and duties between the child and the father, and the latter's relatives, were considered as arising from the date of the child's birth.

Finally, the Principles were again extensively revised by virtue of the federal edict of October 9, 1979, which made a number of important stylistic and substantive changes in the contents of both the parent statute and some of the enabling legislation. First, the scope of the clause in Article 17 which dealt with the special circumstances where a father's sole acknowledgment of paternity was valid was enlarged to include cases where the mother was recognized as legally incapacitated or had been deprived of parental rights (the original formula had only envisaged death or location unknown). Second, the same section was supplemented with a new paragraph providing that a person entered as the father or mother of a child had the right to dispute the executed registration within one year from the time when he (she) learned or should have learned of the fact, except that if the person was a minor at the time, the year's duration was computed from the time he (she) turned 18.[30]

Third, Article 34 was added which specified that Soviet law governed the establishment of paternity in the USSR regardless of the citizenship of the parents or child or their place of residence and that where Soviet legislation sanctioned recognition of paternity in organs of registry of acts of civil status, a child's parents who resided outside the confines of the USSR and at least one of whom was a Soviet citizen had the right to file an affidavit of paternity with the consular offices of the USSR. Fourth, the wording of Article 3 of the law of June 27, 1968, which elaborated how the paternity procedures featured in the guidelines were to be applied to children born before October 1, 1968, was modified also to allow here paternity declarations by the father alone in cases where the mother was dead, certified as legally incapacitated, deprived of parental rights, or pronounced missing, in lieu of the initial requirement that all such declarations be jointly submitted by the parties concerned.[31]

The findings of the earlier analysis tracing the impact of court–designated paternity on the citizenship status of the affected child are fully relevant to the various situations where, instead, the item of voluntarily acknowledged paternity complements the interested child's vital statistics with data that now spawn a citizenship claim. The result is the same portfolio of scenarios in which the act of official identification of the illegitimate offspring's father has the potential to reverse the original verdict of statelessness by creating entitlement either to a Soviet or a foreign citizenship and thus operates as an ad hoc means of reducing the frequency of occurrence of that undesirable phenomenon or shortening its life–span subsequent to inception. The move to restore the institution of "legitimation by declaration" to the Soviet legal canon likewise meant achievement of a balance in this sector in the treaty relations between the USSR and the majority of its socialist allies on matters of legal aid where a certain degree of quid pro quo had so far been lacking owing to disparities in their respective policy on this issue. Lastly, to the extent that the Soviet legislators have openly elected to adopt a more benign tone in referring to the possibility of recognizing on home grounds acts of civil status based on foreign laws where the practice would not contravene the fundamental principles of the Soviet system, many instances of illegitimate children incurring statelessness at birth might henceforth be avoided through increased Soviet willingness to validate administrative certificates of filiation emanating from appropriate foreign agencies and reciprocal inclination on the part of the latter to afford such Soviet documents equal treatment.

2. Stateless Minors

A. Change of Nationality of Parents

Several possibilities must be considered in this connection, where expatriation by one or both parents involving either acquisition or loss of Soviet citizenship could lead to the statelessness of their minor children.

Perhaps the most common type of such case stems from the acquisition of Soviet citizenship by a foreign married couple through the ordinary process of naturalization or loss of Soviet citizenship by a Soviet married couple. The subject is dealt with in Article 20 of the 1978 statute which, like its immediate precursor, posits that in the event of a change of citizenship by the parents, when both of them become or when both of them cease to be citizens of the USSR, the citizenship of their children under fourteen shall change correspondingly. Article 25 of the new law, also closely patterned on a provision featured in the 1938 enactment, further explains that the change of citizenship of children between the ages of fourteen and eighteen in the event of change of citizenship of the parents can take place only with the children's consent, expressed in written form.

With respect to the acquisition of Soviet citizenship by the foreign parents of a minor, then, in principio statelessness can ensue just for those of their children between the ages of fourteen and eighteen. This may occur when under the law of the state of which the parents originally were citizens, minors (and that ordinarily includes the fourteen to eighteen bracket) automatically follow the citizenship of the parents, but coincidentally those of them required in the light of the above rule of Soviet law to register positive consent to acquisition by them of Soviet citizenship together with their parents fail or decline to do so. Having lost the old nationality of the parents and not obtained a new one, they end up stateless.[32]

Conversely, given the contents of Soviet citizenship legislation, where the Soviet parents of a minor cease to be Soviet citizens, only those of their children under fourteen may as a consequence unintentionally be afflicted with statelessness. They alone have no choice but to follow the nationality of the parents and, if the latter acquire the citizenship of a country that does not unconditionally or immediately extend its nationality to the children of its freshly naturalized subjects, they forthwith find themselves turned into stateless persons. The same result is to be anticipated should the two parents, once Soviet citizens, at some point both become apatrides.

To this it must be added that in like circumstances children of an ex–Soviet couple between the ages of fourteen and eighteen might ultimately also suffer that fate, but in their case the outcome would have at least in part depended on their own choice. Indeed, one can foresee a situation where a fourteen to eighteen year old offspring of Soviet parents acquiring another citizenship consulted, as required by Soviet law, as to his attitude would opt to accompany his parents and surrender his Soviet citizenship, only thereafter to discover that the law of the state the nationality of which his parents now held did not eo ipso grant it to the minor children of newly naturalized citizens. The minor would thus be precipitated into statelessness, if but temporarily.

As indicated, however, in the case of minors between the ages of fourteen and eighteen whose parents either enter or leave Soviet citizenship statelessness would not be the product of a conflict of laws stricto sensu, for the situation always envisages an initial causative decision by the de cujus predicated on a positive exercise of free will on the latter's part, and that despite the subject's youthfulness.

This takes care — and quite neatly, one might add — of the legal repercussions as regards minor children in the event of acquisition or loss of Soviet citizenship by both parents.

The 1978 statute fully observed precedent in its treatment of the question of the effect of entry into or exit from Soviet citizenship by both parents on the citizenship status of their minor children. Meantime, a very different picture emerges when comparing what the latest law has to say about how the citizenship status of a minor child is affected by admission or release from Soviet citizenship of just one parent with the matching provisions of its 1938 predecessor. Here, major changes have been wrought in the earlier routine. Under the terms of the previous modus operandi, in every instance where both parents of an under–age child did not simultaneously get admitted into or win release from Soviet citizenship, no matter what the reason for their failure to act jointly, a special request from the parents for naturalization or denaturalization had to be addressed in the name of the minor to the Presidium of the USSR Supreme Soviet or the Presidium of the Supreme Soviet of the union republic in which the party resided.[33] The approach to this problem is now much more diversified.

To begin with, according to the first section of Article 21, if one parent becomes a citizen of the USSR and the other remains a foreign citizen, the child can acquire the citizenship of the USSR at the request of the parent acquiring the citizenship of the USSR, with the standard extra proviso that children between the ages of fourteen and eighteen had to give their written consent to the proposed transfer. The fact that the desire of one parent and, to boot, that parent who is seeking admission to Soviet citizenship will today suffice to vest a child under fourteen with Soviet citizenship is bound to cut down on how often minors will incur statelessness on such occasions in contrast with past practice where both parents had to agree before the conversion could be effected. To be sure, statelessness can still happen under the revised system: if, for example, the parent applying for Soviet citizenship was the citizen of a country under whose law the child was expected to share that parent's citizenship, failure by the sole transferring parent to request Soviet citizenship for the child or rejection of that petition by the competent Soviet organs would leave the child stateless. The distinction, of course, is that under present circumstances the responsible parent must affirmatively fail to take the necessary precautions to cause the crisis, whereas the preceding format called for prior consensus by both parents — not as easily achieved — absent which statelessness would be visited upon the minor child in the setting just described. On the other hand, a similarity of the 1938 and 1978 scripts in this connection is that both make it possible for a child between the ages of fourteen and eighteen to wind up stateless by refusing to go along with the parents' or parent's decision concerning transfer to Soviet citizenship while confronted with the loss of the former citizenship on grounds that the switch was mandatory.

Next, by virtue of the second paragraph of Article 21, if one of the parents becomes a citizen of the USSR and the other remains a stateless person, the child residing on the territory of the USSR becomes a citizen of the USSR. The proposition marks a major innovation in Soviet citizenship repertory; how the scheme was supposed to work was subsequently clarified by the federal decree of June 15, 1979. First, the current arrangement extended only to persons born after June 30, 1979, i.e., the date when the new citizenship act went into force. Second, children in the same position who had not turned eighteen by July 1, 1979, could obtain the citizenship of the USSR by declaration of their legal representatives, duly filed at the place of residence with the nearby organs of internal affairs before the child attained adulthood, but in any event no later than one year from the time the law went into effect, i.e., before July 1, 1980. Eligible minors between the ages of fourteen and eighteen were required, as usual, to endorse in writing the petition for their naturalization.

For the future, therefore, the law automatically protects the minor child from catching statelessness in the wake of one parent's admission to Soviet citizenship in a context where the minor is especially vulnerable owing to the fact that the other parent is stateless and so unable to offer much help to the progeny in these matters. In tackling the backlog of such cases, the law is less generous — at least in terms of not granting immediate and guaranteed relief from the difficulty — but makes it sound as though a fairly simple show of initiative on behalf of the de cujus would do the trick. If the assumption that these petitions were indeed handled in a benevolent manner is warranted, the size of the local contingent of stateless individuals should promptly have shrunk further.

Then, the last portion of Article 21 instructs that where one of the parents becomes a citizen of the USSR and the other remains a stateless person, the child residing outside the borders of the USSR can obtain the citizenship of the USSR at the request of the parent acquiring the citizenship of the USSR (as long as the child between the ages of fourteen and eighteen properly concurs in the decision). The formula is identical to that which applies to a minor child when one parent seeks Soviet citizenship and the other retains foreign citizenship, except for referring strictly to minors residing abroad whereas in the latter situation the rule covers both the minors residing in and those living outside the USSR. Again, the prospects for reducing the number of children inadvertently stuck with statelessness as a result of this congeries of phenomena are perceptibly improved when stacked against the previous record: first, because only one parent's will can bring Soviet citizenship into the picture and thus interdict the advent of statelessness instead of the joint parental agreement that was formerly the norm; and, second, because the parent who wishes to become a Soviet citizen also has the power to perform that service for any minor child involved and, logically speaking, is prone to favor that solution anyway.

Finally, the real breakthrough on this front concerns minor children one of whose parents quits Soviet citizenship while the other retains it: Article 22 ordains that the child here keeps the citizenship of the USSR. Statelessness simply cannot occur under these conditions, which certainly was not true in the past on analogous occasions.

Undoubtedly, the net effect of these reforms is significantly to lower the chance of minors fetching up with statelessness in situations where only one parent enters or leaves Soviet citizenship compared to previous fare. The balance–sheet thus substantiates in essence the Soviet contention that "in regulating relations pertaining to the citizenship of children in connection with the change of citizenship of the parents ... the [1978 Citizenship] Law took steps to curb the growth of the number of stateless persons".[34] Judged solely by objective criteria of success in countering the incidence of statelessness in such instances, the policy is plainly praiseworthy. Note, however, that these gains have been achieved by means of expansion of the role of legislative fiat in solving citizenship problems matched by a proportionate decline in the space alloted to personal preference in these affairs. Stylistically, the technique of prescribing a cure for statelessness by medium of "peremptory operation of the law" fits, for example, the pitch of the 1961 Convention on the Reduction of Statelessness and, hence, does not per se deserve condemnation. Nevertheless, one must remember that the willingness to tolerate unilateral state intrusion to eradicate the plague of statelessness is generally coupled with the notion that the rescued individual retains the inherent right to alter the terms of the ex parte transaction at some future date, say, when he or she reaches majority. A combination of that sort is perceived as imposing no intolerable burden on the beneficiary of a government's desire to contribute to the fight against the spread of statelessness even when the initial response takes the shape of summary assignment of its citizenship to the individual otherwise poised on the verge of statelessness. The trouble with Soviet policy in this domain, of course, is that the key premise that the affected person can later reverse the verdict by his (her) own choice is not valid and the whole project then assumes a much less benign appearance.

B. Adoption

Under certain conditions, adoption can also generate statelessness on the part of the minor representing the object of the proceedings. For example, where the child does not acquire ipso jure the nationality of the adopting parents, but concurrently foregoes the nationality of origin, the end result as far as it is concerned is statelessness.

Appreciating the magnitude of the 1978 revisions in this area of Soviet law is a difficult task for the bare reason that the 1938 citizenship act said nothing of the effects of adoption on the nationality of the child affected thereby. To make matters worse, opinions on the subject within the Soviet legal community diverged on virtually every aspect of the problem, leaving the outside observer to wonder how these issues were in fact handled when they arose in practice, which cannot have been all that rare.

Let us take first the case of a foreign child adopted by Soviet parents. For many years following the promulgation of the 1938 citizenship statute, Soviet authors quite uniformly expressed the view that a foreign child adopted by Soviet citizens automatically acquired the citizenship of the parents,[35] occasionally tempered by a further recommendation that international courtesy would be nicely served by granting the person thus adopted a right to opt for his (her) former citizenship upon attaining majority.[36] In the mid–sixties, however, the old unanimity was no longer in evidence and a wide variety of new interpretations was making the local rounds. To be sure, a few exponents of Soviet policy continued to maintain that a child adopted by Soviet citizens automatically received Soviet citizenship,[37] but their claim was now increasingly being challenged by colleagues who painted a quite different picture.

According to some sources, for instance, if the child permanently resided on the territory of the USSR and had no citizenship, it acquired Soviet citizenship upon adoption and, if the child had a valid foreign citizenship, then in connection with its adoption the prior approval of the diplomatic mission of the corresponding foreign state was required.[38] And, at the opposite extreme from the veterans who argued for immediate conversion to Soviet citizenship coincidentally with adoption, a recently emerged faction contended that the act of adoption of a foreign child by Soviet parents per se entailed no change in the child's citizenship status and that the only way in which Soviet citizenship could be acquired in these circumstances was through the routine of naturalization.[39] The spokesmen for this position sought support both from the language of existing legislation — admittedly inconclusive on this point — by creative extrapolation from the general meaning of tangential provisions and the logistical complexity which cast doubt on the feasibility of applying the rival formula that treated naturalization as a staple by–product of adoption, referring here to the record which indicated that often one parent would adopt the child of the other parent who had a different citizenship than the adopter or a child would be adopted by parents with different citizenship.[40]

Interestingly enough, this version itself prompted objections on practical grounds. While conceding that a literal reading of the 1938 law did warrant the assertion that mere adoption did not alter the citizenship of the child, the critic took exception to the attitude which suggested the desirability of sticking with this procedure in the future as well and questioned the value of perpetuating a situation where, if the citizenship of both adopting parents or the adopter and the natural parent did not match the citizenship of the child, the child was nonetheless slated to keep its former citizenship. More à propos, the very effectiveness of the rule was disputed since current regulations in the USSR reportedly rendered the modus operandi technically unenforceable. To quote directly:

> "The fact of the matter is that in order to preserve secrecy of adoption, the adopters at their request are inscribed in the certificate of birth of the child as blood parents and from the documents issued it is impossible to determine whether the given child is natural or adopted. That is why if, for example, Soviet spouses adopt a foreign child and are entered as its parents, the child will de facto be considered a Soviet citizen and will be issued a Soviet passport, since proof will be lacking that the parents named in the documents are in reality adoptive parents. In light of the above, it appears advisable (by analogy with that provision of the law which envisions that in connection with change of citizenship of the parents as a result of which both parents become Soviet citizens or cease to be such, the citizenship of their children changes accordingly) to prescribe that when both adopting parents (or the adopting parent and natural parent) are citizens of the Soviet Union or both are foreigners, the adopted child acquires their citizenship (if the adopted child is over fourteen, then, obviously, subject to his acquiescence)."[41]

In any event, the drafters of the 1978 citizenship statute wound up devising their own mix. Thus, mandatory acquisition of Soviet citizenship lies in store for: 1) a child who is a foreign citizen or a stateless person, when adopted by citizens of the USSR; 2) a child who is a foreign citizen, when adopted by spouses one of whom is a citizen of the USSR and the other is a stateless person; and, 3) a child who is a stateless person, when adopted by spouses one of whom is a citizen of the USSR. On the other hand, a child who is a foreign citizen and is adopted by spouses of whom one is a citizen of the USSR and the other a foreign citizen, becomes a citizen of the USSR by agreement of the adopting parents — which, parenthetically, leaves unresolved the important question of the administrative feasibility of this approach in view of its potential incompatibility with the "secrecy of adoption" principle, since failure officially to choose Soviet citizenship for the minor may be practically negated by registration of the adopters as natural parents in circumstances that would entitle the offspring to Soviet citizenship from birth.

Exactly how the latest arrangement was intended to function was spelled out by the federal edict of June 15, 1979. Under the terms of this decree, the provisions of the law which establish that adoption coincided with conversion to Soviet citizenship affected only children born after June 30, 1979. Eligible minors who had not turned eighteen by July 1, 1979, could obtain the citizenship of the USSR by declaration of their legal representatives, from which one is free to deduce that in the past these individuals had not in fact been routinely assigned Soviet citizenship at the time of adoption. Such declarations had to be filed at the place of residence with the local organs of internal affairs before the child reached majority, but in any case within one year from the date of entry of the law into force, i.e., by July 1, 1980, and as usual, children between the ages of fourteen and eighteen could acquire Soviet citizenship in this manner only as long as the application was accompanied by their written consent. Finally, where admission to Soviet citizenship called for a joint decision by the adopting parents, the relevant agreement had to be submitted in written form to the organs of internal affairs or, if the adopting parents resided abroad, to the diplomatic or consular mission of the USSR within a year from the day of adoption.

For the future, then, the current set of rules is quite generous in unilaterally granting Soviet citizenship as a bonus, so to speak, to foreign children adopted by a Soviet couple or even a married couple with one Soviet partner. Children with a similar vita but born before June 30, 1979, are less fortunate in this respect since a formal petition for acceptance into Soviet citizenship had to be lodged on their behalf and, presumably, those among them who were already eighteen by July 1, 1979, had to resort to regular naturalization proceedings if they wished to receive Soviet citizenship. Most likely, the regime afforded such applications preferential treatment and, hence, the chances of any of these people still floating around as stateless persons appear rather slim. In individual instances, though, that possibility is by no means excluded. On the other hand, statelessness can, at least in theory, easily be occasioned where the foreign child is adopted by a binational couple featuring one Soviet parent: the law of the country of origin might here assume that the child will forthwith come into possession of Soviet citizenship, Soviet law lets the parents nominate the child's citizenship and, if they fail or are unable to make up their mind or select not the Soviet citizenship but a foreign one which is not available for the picking, the child will promptly lapse into statelessness. True, the denouement is not wholly accidental and, ultima analysi, the parents bear the responsibility for the crisis insofar as they omit to invoke Soviet citizenship in order to spare the child statelessness: the choice is very limited, yet because it exists the phenomenon does not rate as a classical conflicts–in–law experience.

Nevertheless, the new system is visibly superior to its predecessor in terms of lessening the opportunities for the occurrence of statelessness by virtue of adoption of foreign children by Soviet citizens and, by quantitative indicia, the experiment can be pronounced a success that might justify the Soviet claim that "in regulating the relations pertaining to the citizenship of children ... in connection with adoption the [1978 Citizenship] Law took steps to curb the growth of the number of stateless persons".[42] As previously mentioned, however, the cure is achieved through marked increase in the scope of state control over the individual's lot in the form of a more "liberal" policy of ex parte assignment of Soviet citizenship to an inflated constituency without the saving grace of a binding commitment to the proposition that the affected party retains the right to revise the arrangement at some future date through exercise, say, of the common freedom of expatriation. Indeed, even the cautious call by a Soviet legal specialist referred to earlier for allowing the adopted child to opt for his (her) former citizenship upon reaching majority as a token of respect for international comity fell on deaf ears and the designers of the 1978 citizenship statute plainly evinced no interest in equipping their model with such an escape–hatch, no matter how modest in scale.

In contrast to the doctrinal uncertainty that long surrounded the question of the impact on the citizenship status of a foreign child of its adoption by Soviet parents, no division of opinion marked the Soviet position on the issue of the relationship between adoption and citizenship in the reverse situation where a Soviet child was adopted by foreign parents. Both legislative practice and learned exegesis consistently purveyed the message that a child vested with Soviet citizenship retained it following adoption by a foreign couple. The policy harks back to the twenties and reportedly originated during the drive mounted in 1925–1927 for the registration of foreigners residing on the territory of the USSR. On that occasion, considerable difficulties were encountered in establishing the citizenship affiliation of various individuals and, in particular, some people who had been adopted by foreigners sought to take advantage of obvious lacunae in the 1924 Citizenship Regulation to claim foreign citizenship. The authorities responded by publishing instructions in 1928 to the effect that, in the event of adoption by foreigners of children of Soviet citizens, the adopted parties continued to be recognized as Soviet citizens, except that upon reaching majority such persons could obtain release from Soviet citizenship in a simplified manner.[43]

The subsequent record, we are now told, showed that no need existed for maintaining a special procedure for exit from Soviet citizenship in these cases and the citizenship enactments of 1930 and 1931 omitted reference to the device of "quick denaturalization" in connection with the adoption of Soviet children by foreigners.[44] Although the 1938 Citizenship Law shed no light on the theme of citizenship and adoption, the universal consensus among local commentators was that the old norm according to which no change of citizenship accrued as a result of this operation still set the tone for administrative routine. Nevertheless, the formal gap in the law gradually caused enough unease to prompt calls for correcting the deficiency: the recommendations that remedial action be instituted in the context of the project to synchronize the legislation of the union republics with the 1968 federal guidelines to the law on marriage and the family came to naught and another decade was allowed to elapse before the business was at last properly attended to in drafting the new citizenship statute.

Under present terms, a child who is a citizen of the USSR and is adopted by foreign citizens or is adopted by spouses of whom one is a citizen of the USSR and the other is a foreign citizen retains the citizenship of the USSR. At the request of the adopting parents, the child may be granted permission to leave the citizenship of the USSR by the Presidium of the USSR Supreme Soviet. A child who is a citizen of the USSR and is adopted by stateless persons or a couple of which one partner is a citizen of the USSR and the other is a stateless person keeps the citizenship of the USSR. Thus, precedent is essentially observed on that count and the possibility of a Soviet child incurring statelessness as a consequence of adoption by foreigners is virtually excluded: the sole exception is where the federal Presidium duly sanctions renunciation of Soviet citizenship on behalf of the adopted child and the latter then fails to acquire a substitute foreign citizenship. The chances of this happening are quite remote, however, for, given the regime's public commitment to shield Soviet children from succumbing to statelessness, the necessary permission to quit Soviet citizenship is not apt to be forthcoming until official quarters are satisfied that a smooth transition is in the offing here.

The general picture of how adoption can affect the citizenship status of the de cujus in the current Soviet legal repertory from the perspective of its potential to cause the interested party to experience statelessness would not be complete — and, indeed, would look badly distorted — if insufficient attention were paid to the ancillary fact that the whole process of transnational adoption is subject to extremely strict control by the Soviet side. For example, Article 34 of the 1968 Bases of legislation of the USSR and union republics on marriage and the family specified that the adoption of a child who was a Soviet citizen and resided outside the confines of the USSR was performed in the embassy or consulate of the USSR (as amended by the federal decree of October 9, 1979, the consulate alone). If the adopting person did not possess Soviet citizenship, adoption required the approval of the competent organ of the union republic.[45] The clause next provided that the adoption of a child who was a Soviet citizen performed in the organs of the state on whose territory the child resided was also recognized as valid on the condition that prior approval for such adoption be obtained from the competent organs of the union republic. The latter alternative constituted a departure from the primary route, allegedly added to the script in order to protect the interests of the child in those exceptional circumstances where the standard modus operandi was not feasible.[46] Then, the last paragraph determined that the rules for adoption of children who are Soviet citizens by foreigners on the territory of the USSR are established by the legislation of the union republics which, in almost every instance, again mandates preliminary acquiescence by the competent organs in the proposed transaction.[47]

Note, too, that in these latter cases Soviet law relies exclusively on the territorial principle, whereas, as has been pointed out, a common trend in recent international practice favors the recognition of the national laws of the adopting parents for defining the procedure and conditions of adoption as well as its revocation. Even among Soviet jurists, a few have pronounced the policy unduly conservative and ventured to predict that the further development of Soviet conflicts family law would be accompanied by increased accent on national legislation — as long, of course, as the practice did not contravene the conceptual underpinnings of the Soviet social and political system — on grounds that such an approach would successfully promote the growth of international cooperation in safeguarding the rights and interests of the upcoming generation.[48] Instead, however, the Soviet solons seem to be headed in the opposite direction. The federal edict of October 9, 1979, which, inter alia, extensively revised this particular section of Article 34 (now renumbered 35) took special care to spell out that adoption in the USSR by foreign citizens of children who are Soviet citizens and adoption of children who are foreign citizens and reside in the USSR takes place in accordance with Soviet legislation, leaving the territorial doctrine undisputed master of the field and giving the lie to the optimistic prognoses of the "progressive" element within the ranks of Soviet "conflicts" experts.

Between insistence that these matters be governed essentially by Soviet law and the dictate that "mixed" adoptions first receive official clearance, the Soviet apparatus enjoys ample opportunity to monitor the record and refuse to sanction the operation if, among other things, it should discover that the proposed act of adoption might plunge the affected child into statelessness. The elaborate machinery of supervision thus enables the Soviet authorities effectively to counter the conflicts–in–law phenomena that precipitate statelessness on such occasions. Given Moscow's professions of acute aversion to the thought of children suffering from statelessness, prophylactic intervention on its part in these circumstances ought to be expected and the occurrence of statelessness in the wake of adoption could be aborted even in those few instances where, today's tighter safeguards notwithstanding, the unimpeded collision of competing legal systems otherwise might still spawn a random sample of statelessness.

One related issue remains unresolved, to wit: inasmuch as Soviet legislation envisages that the courts have the right to recognize an adoption as void and to annul an adoption, the question arises as to the position of an adopted child who acquired a citizenship by virtue of adoption once the adoption proceedings are either found to have been invalid or are quashed. Strangely enough, neither legislative nor scholarly sources furnish an answer to a problem that is far from academic. Failure to retain the citizenship acquired by medium of adoption upon the latter's cancellation could, of course, easily spell coincidental lapse into statelessness.

NOTES

1. E.g., M.M. Avakov, "Oktiabr'skaia revoliutsiia i sovetskoe grazhdanstvo", *Uchenye zapiski* (Belorusskii gosudarstvennyi institut narodnogo khoziaistva im. V.V. Kuibysheva), Minsk, 1957, vyp.4, p.309. In the same vein, for instance, see *Bol'shaia Sovetskaia Entsiklopediia*, 2nd. ed., Moscow, 1950, Vol.2, p.550; *ibid.*, Moscow, 1952, Vol.12, p.421; A.I. Denisov, in A.I. Denisov & M.G. Kirichenko, *Sovetskoe gosudarstvennoe pravo*, Moscow, 1957, p.139; *Diplomaticheskii slovar'*, Moscow, 1960, Vol.1, pp.169–170; *ibid.*, Moscow, 1971, Vol.1, p.190.
2. V. Shevtsov, *Citizenship of the USSR (A Legal Study)*, Moscow 1979, p.103.
3. W. Samore, "Statelessness as a Consequence of the Conflict of Nationality Laws", *American Journal of International Law*, 1951, No.3, p.476; Harvard Research in International Law: Draft Conventions on Nationality, Responsibility of States, Territorial Waters, *ibid.*, 1923, Spec. Supp., p.29.
4. T.A. Taracouzio, *The Soviet Union and International Law*, New York, 1935, p.84.
5. *Vedomosti Verkhovnogo Soveta SSSR*, 1968, No.27, Art.241 (hereafter abbr. as *VVS SSSR*).
6. The edict of the Presidium of the USSR Supreme Soviet of June 15, 1979, Art.3, further explained that this agreement by the parents had to be submitted to the diplomatic or consular mission of the USSR in written form within one year from the day of the child's birth. *VVS SSSR*, 1979, No.25, Art.436.
7. S. Chernichenko, "Nash grazhdanin", *Izvestiia*, June 15, 1968, p.5.
8. W. Samore, *op. cit.*, p.477.
9. A.Ia. Berchenko, "Voprosy sovetskogo grazhdanstva", in *Torzhestvo leninskoi natsional'noi politiki*, Moscow, 1963, pp.277–278.
10. V.S. Shevtsov, *Sovetskoe grazhdanstvo*, Moscow, 1965, p.45.
11. *VVS SSSR*, 1979, No.25, Art.436.
12. For text see *Human Rights. A Compilation of International Instruments*, United Nations Publ. ST/HR/1/Rev.1, New York, 1978, pp.76–80.
13. S.I. Rusinova, "Zakon o grazhdanstve SSSR", *Pravovedenie*, 1980, No.1, p.8.
14. V. Durdenevskii, "Zakon o grazhdanstve Soiuza Sovetskikh Sotsialisticheskikh Respublik", *Problemy sotsialisticheskogo prava*, 1938, No.6, p.65. Also, *idem*, in V.N. Durdenevskii & S.B. Krylov, eds., *Mezhdunarodnoe pravo*, Moscow, 1947, p.187.
15. V.S. Shevtsov, *op. cit.*, p.50.
16. Technically speaking, the expression "illegitimate children" has no place in Soviet law. It is here used conditionally as a common term of description for children born out of wedlock, without necessarily any special legal implications.
17. T.A. Taracouzio, *op. cit.*, p.84.
18. Decree of the Presidium of the USSR Supreme Soviet of July 8, 1944, in *VVS SSSR*, 1944, No.37; extracts in *Kodeks zakonov o brake, sem'e i opeke RSFSR*, Moscow, 1961, as amended through February 1, 1961, pp.43–53.
19. *VVS SSSR*, 1968, No.27, Art.241.
20. *VVS SSSR*, 1979, No.42, Art.696.
21. *VVS SSSR*, 1968, No.39, Art.353.
22. "Reshenie inostrannogo suda", in *Iuridicheskii slovar'*, Moscow, 1953, pp.576–577, and *Iuridicheskii slovar'*, 2nd ed., Moscow, 1956, Vol.2, pp.339–340. See, too, P.N. Evseev, "Ispolnenie sudebnykh poruchenii i reshenii inostrannykh sudov", in L.A. Lunts, ed., *Problemy mezhdunarodnogo chastnogo prava*, Moscow, 1960, p. 190.
23. *VVS SSSR*, 1979, No.42, Art.696.
24. Texts of the 1957–1958 agreements in *Dogovory ob okazanii pravovoi pomoshchi po*

grazhdanskim, semeinymi ugolovnym delam, zakhliuchennye Sovetskim Soiuzom v 1957–1958 gg., Moscow, 1959; text of the agreement with Yugoslavia, *VVS SSSR*, 1963, No.21, Art.236. The texts of these agreements have now been assembled in *Dogovory ob okazanii pravovoi pomoshchi po grazhdanskim, semeinym i ugolovnym delam, zakliuchennye SSSR s drugimi sotsialisticheskimi gosudarstvami*, 2nd enl. ed., Moscow, 1973.

New treaties were signed with Bulgaria on Feb. 19, 1975, the German Democratic Republic on Sept. 19, 1979, and a protocol was concluded with Poland on Jan. 23, 1980, which do not, however, alter the original picture in this area. Texts in *VVS SSSR*, 1976, No.8, Art.133; 1980, No.35, Art.712; and 1980, No.50, Art. 1075. Agreements on legal aid were likewise concluded with Austria on Mar. 11, 1970, Finland on Aug. 11, 1978, and Greece on May 21, 1981, but none deals with the present problem. *VVS SSSR*, 1972, No.12, Art.96; 1980, No.34, Art.690; 1982, No.45, Art.839. The texts of the agreements with Iraq and Vietnam appear in *VVS SSSR*, 1974, No.19, Art.293; 1982, No.44, Art.827.

25. For a survey of the practice of some of the "people's democracies" in this sphere, see G.M. Sverdlov, *Semeinoe pravo evropeiskikh stran narodnoi demokratii*, Moscow, 1961, pp.174–184.

26. English text of the RSFSR Code on Marriage and the Family of July 30, 1969, as amended, translated by L.G. Robinson, in W.B. Simons, ed., *The Soviet Codes of Law*, Alphen aan den Rijn, The Netherlands, 1980, pp.761–819, *(Law in Eastern Europe* No.23).

27. Text in VVS *SSSR*, 1945, No.15; *Kodeks zakonov o brake, sem'e i opeke RSFSR* (1961 edition), pp.53–54.

28. For an analysis of the established practice in this matter, see G.M. Sverdlov, *Sovetskoe semeinoe pravo*, Moscow, 1958, pp.190–191.

29. Vide, G.M. Sverdlov, *op. cit.*, (note 25 above), pp.169–173.

30. Where the person thus identified as a parent knew or should have known of the executed registration before the entry into force of the Code of marriage and the family of the RSFSR, the statute of limitations tolled from November 1, 1969. However, it was considered to have expired if more than three years had elapsed from the time the person knew or should have known of the executed registration and no grounds could be shown for suspending, interrupting or restoring the prescribed duration (Decree of the Presidium of the RSFSR Supreme Soviet of October 17, 1969, on the procedure for putting into effect the Code on marriage and the family of the RSFSR, *Sovetskaia iustitsiia*, 1969, No.21, pp.30–31). For a case illustrating conditions under which even a five–year lapse was not found to bar suit, see *Biulleten' Verkhovnogo Suda RSFSR*, 1969, No.12, p.8.

31. Interestingly enough, the question of why the clause in Article 17 of the federal guidelines to legislation on marriage and the family which originally sanctioned the submission of a statement of paternity by the father alone when the mother was dead or missing was not given retroactive effect when the Principles were put in force in 1968 was raised in Soviet legal literature at the time. The answer then offered (long before the enactment of the decree of October 9, 1979) was that no express reference to such procedure was necessary because an analogous general norm already existed. Nevertheless, apparently the legislators later figured it was best to cover the point squarely. See, V.P. Shakhmatov, B.L. Khaskel'berg, *Novyi kodeks o brake i sem'e RSFSR*, Tomsk, 1970, pp.139–141.

32. B. Trachtenberg, "La Législation Soviétique sur la Nationalité", *Revue de Droit International Privé*, 1931, p.154, had already remarked on this contingency à propos the similar provisions of the 1938 Regulation; likewise, D.V. Sandifer, "A Comparative Study of Laws Relating to Nationality at Birth and Loss of Nationality", *American Journal*

of International Law, 1935, No.1, pp.248, 269.

33. V. Durdenevskii, *op. cit.*, p.65; D. Gaidukov, *Grazhdanstvo SSSR*, Moscow, 1940, p.31.

34. L.B. Kuzmenko, "Razvitie pravovogo regulirovaniia statusa lichnosti v novom zakone o grazhdanstve SSSR", *Vestnik Moskovskogo universiteta*, 1980, No.4, seriia 11: Pravo, p.33.

35. E.g. V.I. Menzhinskii, in F.I. Kozhevnikov, ed., *Mezhdunarodnoe pravo*, Moscow, 1964, p.285.

36. V.N. Durdenevskii, *op. cit.*, p.64. See, too, idem, in V.N. Durdenevskii & S.B. Krylov, eds., *op. cit.*, p.186.

37. *Kurs mezhdunarodnogo prava*, Moscow, 1967, Vol.3, p.85.

38. V.M. Safronov, *Ty — grazhdanin Sovetskogo Soiuza*, Moscow, 1978, p.24; M. Shafir, *Grazhdaninom byt' obiazan*, Moscow, 1972, p.31.

39. Cf., V.I. Menzhinskii, in F.I. Kozhevnikov, ed., *Kurs mezhdunarodnogo prava*, 2nd ed., Moscow 1966, p.294; I.K. Gorodetskaia, *Mezhdunarodnaia zashchita prav i interesov detei*, Moscow, 1973, pp.44–45; *Kommentarii k zakonodatel'stvu o registratsii aktov grazhdanskogo sostoianiia*, Moscow, 1977, p.185; *Kommentarii k kodeksu o brake i sem'e RSFSR*, Moscow, 1971, p.230.

40. I.K. Gorodetskaia, *op. cit.*, p.45.

41. A.Ia. Pergament, in *Sovetskii ezhegodnik mezhdunarodnogo prava 1974*, Moscow, 1976, pp.320–321.

42. L.B. Kuzmenko, *op. cit.*, p.33.

43. See, Resolution of the CEC and Council of People's Commissars of the USSR of March 21, 1928, "On the adoption by foreign citizens of children — citizens of the USSR", *SZ SSSR*, 1928, No.19, Art.162. Corresponding directives were issued in the union republics: e.g., *SU RSFSR*, 1928, No.117, Art.735; *SU UkSSR*, 1929, No.17, Art.162.

44. V.S. Shevtsov, *Grazhdanstvo v sovetskom soiuznom gosudarstve*, Moscow, 1969, p.127.

45. Namely: in the Lithuanian and Azerbaidzhan SSRs — the Presidium of the Supreme Soviet of the republic; in the Georgian, Armenian and Tadzhik SSRs — the Council of Ministers of the republic; in the RSFSR, UkSSR, BSSR, Estonian, Latvian and Uzbek SSRs — the Ministry of Education; in the Moldavian, Kirgiz and Turkmen SSRs — the Ministry of Public Education; in the Kazakh SSR — the executive committees of the respective oblast Soviets of people's deputies.

46. *Kommentarii k zakonodatel'stvu o registratsii aktov grazhdanskogo sostoianiia*, p.193.

47. I.e., in the Lithuanian SSR — the Presidium of the Supreme Soviet of the republic; in the Estonian, Armenian, Kirgiz, Tadzhik, and Turkmen SSRs — the Council of Ministers of the republic; in the Georgian and Azerbaidzhan SSRs — the Council of Ministers of the republic, the Council of Ministers of the ASSR or the executive committee of the Soviet of people's deputies of the autonomous oblast; in the RSFSR, UkSSR, BSSR and Uzbek SSR — the Council of Ministers of the ASSR or the executive committee of the krai, oblast, city (in cities ranked directly below republican level) Soviet of people's deputies; in the Latvian SSR — the Ministry of Education; in the Moldavian SSR — the Ministry of Public Education. In the Kazakh SSR, no special permission was required for adoption on the territory of the republic by a foreigner of a child possessing Soviet citizenship.

48. G.K. Matveev, in *Sovetskoe gosudarstvo i pravo*, 1974, No.5, pp.151–152.

STATELESSNESS AS A CONSEQUENCE OF THE CONFLICT OF NATIONALITY LAWS (PART II)

3. Statelessness as a Result of Marriage

A. At the Time of Marriage

From the very first, the official doctrine of the equality of man and woman has been a cardinal principle of Soviet law, and in Soviet citizenship legislation this ingredient has throughout found expression in the rule that matrimony by a citizen of the USSR with one not such a citizen entails no change of citizenship. Or, as the 1978 Citizenship Law (Art.4) puts it:

> "Entry into marriage by a male or female citizen of the USSR with a person who is a foreign citizen or a stateless person ... entails no change in the citizenship of the spouses."

The position of the Soviet regime on this item, it might be added, has always been a source of considerable pride to Soviet spokesmen — not altogether without reason. Accordingly, much is usually made of it in Soviet legal literature, and the following statement may be taken as typical of what is commonly said in that context:

> "Soviet law stands guard over the citizenship interests of the Soviet woman. The Great October socialist revolution has established, and the law on citizenship again confirms, that entry into marriage by a citizeness of the USSR with a person not a citizen of the USSR does not entail for her a change of citizenship, that exit of the husband from the citizenship of the USSR does not entail for her exit from the citizenship of the USSR."[1]

While such a policy incontestably has certain merits in terms of rendering it impossible for Soviet citizens inadvertently to blunder into statelessness as the aftermath of marriage to a foreigner, its very rigidity also produces markedly adverse effects which tend to offset much of the positive quality of the approach. Indeed, while fully protecting Soviet citizens from contracting statelessness through marriage to an alien, so to speak, it fails to make any allowance for the reverse situation in which, through blind collision of disparate legal systems, a foreigner may be precipitated into statelessness merely by virtue of marriage to a Soviet citizen, through no personal choice or desire on the part of the victim to suffer that fate. Examples of such results are legion, what with the large number of countries subscribing even today to the rule that their female nationals automatically forfeit their nationality by marriage to an alien, while other states, the Soviet Union among them, just as adamantly refuse to extend their citizenship to persons thus egregiously penalized for marrying one of their citizens.

True, for a while there the Soviet government did offer a remedy for these ills, except that most people would rate the cure it chose far worse than the original ailment. What the authorities did was to prohibit by the decree of February 15, 1947, marriages between foreigners and Soviet citizens.[2] This state of affairs lasted until the promulgation of the edict of November 26, 1953, which restored the status quo ante.[3]

To return to the central point, however, in this field Soviet law today is back on the main track and statelessness as a result of the marriage of a foreign woman to a Soviet citizen is therefore again a normal occurrence.

The other observation to be made in this connection is that from the outset the Citizenship Law of 1938 seemed to consummate a major break with precedent by eschewing all mention of special ways and means to counteract the ensuing difference in the citizenship status of the spouses and overcome the negative consequences of such an awkward situation to the unity of the family, and its 1978 successor follows in its footsteps. Prior to that, relevant federal legislation had always provided that in conditions of "mixed" marriage, a petition by one of the partners for a change of nationality in order to acquire that of the other was permitted to proceed in a simplified manner, thereby also allowing, at least in principle, a ready avenue for handling any threat of incipient statelessness due to matrimony. And, the sole reason ever given for the regime's failure to perpetuate this progressive rule was that

> "Soviet law is based on the full realization by the spouses of their responsibilities in regard to the family and as citizens of a socialist society. The law stimulates this consciousness as concerns citizenship. It considers that the citizenship of the USSR may be obtained not by contracting marriage, but by whether said person is deserving of being a citizen of the USSR."[4]

In any event, on closer inspection this departure from past practice turns out to be more a matter of form than of substance. In the first place, as the 1931 Regulation had made clear, the competent agencies could always refuse to apply this "simplified manner" and advise the petitioner to file for naturalization through the usual channels. Not only was such a decision not subject to appeal, but the law further omitted to specify on what grounds the request could be denied, apparently leaving it entirely to administrative discretion. In the second place, the idea had from the start met with considerable opposition within Soviet legal circles on the grounds that it served no good purpose and actually was only used by Soviet citizens married to foreigners and desirous of emigrating with their spouse so as to pass for foreigners and thus avoid having to pay the heavy duties levied on Soviet citizens applying for documents to travel abroad.[5] Aside from providing people in this position with a convenient escape clause permitting them to leave the country legally upon payment of just a nominal fee instead of the standard and much higher tax imposed on the average Soviet citizen seeking to go outside the USSR, critics of the measure argued that it never filled any real need and, they charged, managed from inception merely to provoke doctrinal controversy and sow bureaucratic confusion.

Moreover, it should be noted, from the standpoint of factors contributing to the incidence of statelessness, the rule was not an unmixed blessing either. Granted, it did offer foreign brides of Soviet citizens fearing to become stateless in the wake of marriage a relatively easy solution for their troubles. But, on the other hand, it likewise enabled Soviet citizens, both male and female, married to a foreigner to renounce Soviet citizenship in favor of acquisition of the citizenship of the alien spouse. If the latter were not forthcoming, statelessness was the result. That happened fairly often. Any number of states, for instance, do not automatically bestow their citizenship on a foreign woman upon her marriage to one of their citizens. And, few states have conferred their citizenship on a foreigner just because he married a woman possessing their nationality.

In short, while the current policy does work some hardship on the participants in "mixed" marriages, it does have certain compensations; conversely, though former practice in this area had several advantages, it too was not completely free of shortcomings. Yet, when all is said and done, the positive features of the earlier regulations here surely outweighed the negative aspects enough to make them still seem preferable to the norms now in force (even if neither would qualify as ideal), and particularly so when one remembers that, under the old regimen, where statelessness did set in, a good deal of the time it owed its genesis to the deliberate choice of a given course of action by the aggrieved party.

What is curious about the Soviet record in these matters is how widely the pendulum swung in the opposite direction in 1938 — from rather routine acceptance of the principle of "easy" entry into and exit from Soviet citizenship in the context of transnational marriage to doctrinaire rejection of any "soft" alternative to standard naturalization (denaturalization) procedures even on these special occasions. The leap from one extreme to the other is not the only possible solution to the problem, however, and both the pragmatic and philosophical rationale for the switch could have been substantiated by resort to a different, and less radical, technique. I am now referring to the type of compromise formula that commonly figures in the citizenship repertory of members of the international community and has also found favor with some "socialist" countries, such as the Democratic Republic of Vietnam and the People's Republic of China.

The former's legislation, for instance, lays down the conditions and procedure for choice of citizenship by persons married to foreigners and recognizes the right of foreigners married to Vietnamese citizens to receive Vietnamese citizenship.[6] The recently enacted statute on the citizenship of the PRC determines that having close foreign or Chinese relatives constitutes valid grounds for applying for loss or acquisition of Chinese citizenship, respectively, and secondary sources have explained that the spouse in a binational marriage meets this kinship criterion and offers an adequate alibi to sustain a petition for denaturalization or naturalization.[7] Note that the mechanism does not function automatically and that here, too, official approval is required to effect the desired conversion following the conclusion of the corresponding "mixed" marriage: nevertheless, the scenario has certain obvious psychological and cosmetic advantages over the dogmatic tone of the Soviet pitch on the subject, while at the same time not diminishing in any sense the amount of real control exercised by the state apparatus over the operation. Be that as it may, the Soviets seem unwilling to make even a symbolic concession on this issue — perhaps out of fear that by so doing they might impair the state's total freedom to decide when to sanction naturalization and, more important yet, denaturalization where matrimonial ties inject a foreign element into the picture.

B. During and at the Dissolution of Marriage

Whatever the faults of the contemporary Soviet legal view on the citizenship of the married woman, one point can safely be made in its defense, to wit, that once Soviet citizenship is duly acquired by a foreign woman following marriage to a Soviet citizen, she thereafter holds it in her own right and no action on the part of the husband can ever jeopardize her claim to that citizenship. Neither divorce, nor the death of the husband, nor his subsequent decision to expatriate himself and become the citizen of another state in any way affect the woman's status as a naturalized citizen of the USSR. To quote from Article 4 of the 1978 citizenship statute, dissolution of a marriage between a male or female citizen of the USSR and a foreign citizen or stateless person "entails no change in the citizenship of the spouses" and, in similar vein, "acquisition or loss of the citizenship of the USSR by one of the spouses entails no change in the citizenship of the other spouse". All this compares very favorably with the jurisprudential record of most other states which to a greater or lesser degree countenance the permanent dependence of the woman on the husband in matters of citizenship, often leading to her statelessness when her ties with the man are severed or, in turn, when the latter's association with the state is formally terminated. Because in these cases the grant of the state's citizenship to the woman in question is originally predicated on her marriage to a citizen of that country, it survives only as long as the marriage does or so long as the man whom she married and through whom she had literally by devolution obtained her current nationality preserves it himself.

An automatic extension of a country's citizenship to a woman solely by reason of marriage to a citizen of that nation thus oftentimes remains revocable on the plea that circumstances have changed. Since Soviet law never mechanically bestowed Soviet citizenship on either alien brides or bridegrooms of Soviet citizens, but always demanded of them that they show a positive will to acquire it, it also precludes the possibility of involuntary withdrawal of that citizenship once it is conferred on grounds alone that the matrimonial relations of the parties had altered.

By that token, the foreigner who, motivated by marriage to a Soviet citizen, applies for and secures Soviet citizenship for himself or herself henceforward stands protected from any unpleasantness over his or her title to Soviet citizenship if something should happen to the marriage or to the citizenship of the other spouse, judging at least by the letter of the law. Soviet citizenship is here held in a purely personal capacity and that possession is not open to challenge by collateral means, as it were. However, Moscow also expects others to see things in this light and that is seldom the case. Nevertheless, where a Soviet citizen has renounced Soviet citizenship in the prescribed fashion in order to acquire the citizenship of the alien spouse and, after a while, loses the latter citizenship due, for instance, to the marriage's dissolution, Soviet law recognizes no simplified procedure for the reversion of the ex–citizen to Soviet citizenship. True, as observed earlier, the edicts promulgated in 1945, 1946, and 1947 guaranteed that chance to certain former Russian and

Soviet citizens residing abroad, including, presumably, persons in this category as well, but that was by special dispensation alone and only for a brief duration. Nothing of the sort, though, has ever functioned as a regular mechanism in the Soviet legal system to ensure a relatively informal reintegration into the Soviet body politic of erstwhile citizens who at some point in life had for various good reasons elected to give up their citizenship and then sought to retrieve it.

Again, this is not to say that the Soviet government will not occasionally relent and introduce either through the medium of an international treaty or institute on its own a simplified scheme for entry into or exit from Soviet citizenship for designated groups of people that will also benefit all parties to existing "mixed" marriages in which one member of this type of household personally qualified for such a plan. In every instance so far, however, this special modus operandi has associated the "easy" change of nationality with the physical transfer of permanent residence from the state the citizenship of which was thus being surrendered to the country for the citizenship of which it was being exchanged.

For example, by the two decrees of June 22 and July 14, 1944, the Soviet authorities acknowledged the right of certain Soviet citizens of "Polish nationality" residing in the western districts of the Ukraine and Byelorussia, as well as in other areas of the USSR and of the Lithuanian SSR, to renounce their Soviet citizenship in favor of Polish nationality.[8] They simultaneously endorsed the right of members of the families of persons entitled "to opt" under this program to do likewise, regardless of whether they were of "Polish nationality" or not. Hence, both a Russian husband of a Polish woman who fell within the scope of either statute and the Russian wife of a Polish man who was eligible under the terms of one of the edicts could divest themselves of their Soviet citizenship and accompany their "ethnically alien" spouse to the latter's new homeland, through an arrangement closely reminiscent of the pattern which obtained in Soviet legal doctrine and administrative practice with respect to "mixed" marriages and expatriation prior to 1938.

This basic formula was repeated in the bilateral agreements on option concluded between Poland, on the one hand, and the Ukrainian SSR, the Belorussian SSR, the Lithuanian SSR, and the USSR, on the other, during 1944 and 1945.[9] The same procedure was followed in conjunction with the exchange of populations between the USSR and Czechoslovakia in 1946.[10] One finds it reappearing in the treaty signed in 1957 between the USSR and Poland concerning "the further repatriation of persons of Polish nationality from the USSR."[11] In all these cases, then, the contracting parties confirmed the right of kin of the "primary optants" to win release, inter alia, from Soviet citizenship so that here the regime's wish to forestall mass incipience of "mixed" households within its jurisdiction in fact operated to create for certain Soviet citizens a ready opportunity and legal avenue for expatriation which otherwise had one major advantage over earlier practice, namely, these negotiated solutions were so designed as to preclude any lapse into statelessness by the persons concerned in the course of their implementation.[12]

Much less satisfactory from this last standpoint was Decree No.142/41 of the Presidium of the USSR Supreme Soviet, dated August 30, 1956,[13] which defined the modalities for the renunciation of Soviet citizenship by persons of Spanish nationality living in the USSR since 1936–1940 and now leaving for Spain for permanent residence. Under the terms of the measure, these individuals

> "were considered to have relinquished their Soviet citizenship from the moment of their departure from the USSR. In this connection, Soviet citizens not of Spanish nationality married to Spaniards and leaving the USSR together with their spouse are considered as having lost their Soviet citizenship from the moment of their departure from the USSR on the condition that they first submit individual declarations renouncing the citizenship of the USSR."[13]

Upon contrasting these regulations with the relevant provisions of Spanish law the following peculiar picture emerges. In accordance with Spanish legislation,[15] a married woman shares the condition and nationality of her husband. Thus, a Soviet woman married to a Spaniard who, preparing to accompany him to Spain, waived her Soviet citizenship had nothing to fear since upon arrival she would collect papers identifying her as a Spanish citizen (assuming, of course, that her husband was still accepted as such by the Spanish government — a safe bet, else Madrid would not have been likely to cooperate in the repatriation scheme to begin with). Quite different was the situation as regards the family in which the husband was a Soviet citizen and the wife a former Spanish national. The enactment apparently permitted such households to emigrate to Spain too. However, when they did, the wife lost her acquired Soviet citizenship automatically upon leaving Soviet soil, but without thereby ceasing in the eyes of Spanish law to retain her husband's identity, and so seemingly ended up stateless. As for the husband, he could choose to keep his Soviet citizenship even abroad simply by refraining from filing a statement indicating a desire to give it up. If he did surrender it, though, he did not acquire Spanish citizenship merely by virtue of the act of emigrating to Spain with an ex-Spanish wife and therefore also became stateless.

On this occasion, poor coordination on the part of the two states involved, quite evident in the way the whole plan was worked out and carried out,[16] led to final results which in most respects can only be described as inferior, in the sense that throughout no proper solution was prescribed for assorted difficulties bound to arise from such a direct collision of the respective national legal systems.

Two reasons have prompted us to dwell on these historic episodes. First, the recital shows that, contrary to the clear intent of the law, the Soviet regime nevertheless has on numerous past occasions sanctioned procedures whereby Soviet husbands or wives of individuals of "foreign extraction" were enabled to divest themselves of Soviet citizenship on preferential terms upon emigration to their "foreign" spouse's homeland. What could happen before can happen again if the proper political animus exists, the express language of the 1978 citizenship statute to the opposite effect notwithstanding. Simply put, precedent counsels caution about relying on the formal strictures of the law in attempting to predict how the Soviet leadership will behave when tactical expediency renders a detour temporarily more alluring.

Second, the current exodus from the Soviet Union bears some resemblance to the operations just described and so deserves a quick glance to see whether its format squares with the legislative injunction against change in the citizenship of one spouse owing to loss of the citizenship of the USSR by the other. A closer look at the data elicits a negative answer. The bulk of today's emigrants consists of members of particular minority groups — Jews, Greeks, Armenians, Germans — who, for these purposes, are apparently classified as a "foreign element" and, hence, afforded an uncommon opportunity to return to the "country of origin": quite often, this privilege is shared by spouses who do not themselves belong to a stock designated as "alien" in this frame of reference and the marital partnership thus lets the latter leave the Soviet Union by special arrangement. Unlike the earlier experiments which involved a formal collective grant of the right to emigrate to specific ethnic entities, the present project practices favorable treatment of certain nationalities in regard to expatriation, but then handles the individual applications as mere requests wholly liable to administrative discretion. The "native" spouses not only do not by derivation earn a stake in an objective right, but even their access to the ad hoc dispensation is highly tentative since there is no official commitment to the principle that the approval of one partner's petition will eo ipso forward the other partner's suit: of course, chances are that the family unit will be kept intact — though the petitions are filed individually and allegedly processed on their own merits, and the people in charge are quite free to decide the cases differently.

With all these caveats, the fact remains that a "mainstream" Soviet citizen married to a representative of this "foreign stock" is in a much better position to apply for emigration than a compatriot without such an exotic profile and that, despite official pretense that the petitions are dealt with singly, the key ingredient of eligibility to submit a request for an exit visa here derives from the status of the other spouse and creates an extra benefit for the family member who would not personally be entitled to pursue this short–cut. In a nutshell, then, marriage between an "indigenous" Soviet citizen and one whose "extraction" now facilitates emigration from the USSR makes it possible, by a twist of reverse discrimination, for the "aboriginal" half of the "mixed" couple to qualify for the prized bonus of an exit permit and, by this means, to affect his or her citizenship status.

The subsequent itinerary depends on which of the two main categories the prospective emigrant fits into. If the primary candidate is of Jewish origin, for example, formal renunciation of Soviet citizenship must precede departure from the Soviet Union and the entire family lands on foreign soil technically stateless: if no foreign citizenship is immediately forthcoming, they all face the future as apatrides. If the primary candidate hails from a national group that is not required to renounce Soviet citizenship before going abroad, both that person and the rest of the family continue to count as Soviet citizens even when residing "overseas": they can still incur de facto statelessness by unilaterally repudiating Soviet citizenship prior to obtaining a valid replacement or de jure statelessness by duly winning release from Soviet citizenship while outside the country and not acquiring a foreign citizenship in lieu thereof.

To be sure, none of the preceding scenarios epitomizes the conflicts–in–law phenomenon since in each case a voluntary act by the afflicted party sets the mechanism in motion. On the other hand, the experience shows that, despite what the law says, loss of Soviet citizenship by one spouse can in certain circumstances have dramatic consequences for the citizenship status of the other spouse, a process punctuated, far too frequently, by encounters with statelessness.

Before leaving the subject, one final remark is in order. On September 6, 1957, the Soviet Union adhered to the Convention on the Nationality of Married Women, opened for signature on February of that year. By so doing, it officially obligated itself to respect and enforce the following packet of rules. First, it endorsed the proposition that neither marriage of a citizen to an alien, nor the dissolution of such a marriage, nor change in the citizenship of the husband during the lifetime of the marriage would automatically reflect on the citizenship of the wife. Second, it underwrote the idea that neither the voluntary acquisition by one of its citizens of the citizenship of another state, nor the renunciation by one of its citizens of its citizenship would serve as an obstacle to the wife of that citizen keeping it. Third, it acceded to the formula that a foreign woman married to one of its citizens could obtain at her request the citizenship of the husband "through specially privileged naturalization procedures", subject to such limitations alone as were dictated by considerations of state security or public order.

Of the trio, only the last clause added anything new to the existing Soviet law. The meaning of the provision is, of course, perfectly well understood by Soviet legal experts. As one of them explained the relevant passage, its terms did not signify

> "the duty of the states to simplify to a greater degree the procedure of naturalization of a foreign woman married to one of its citizens than the procedure of naturalization of a foreign man married to a citizen of that state. The state can establish an exactly identical procedure of naturalization for these persons. That is precisely the modus operandi envisaged in the legislation of the socialist countries. And it is the only one to guarantee the equality of spouses in questions of citizenship. What we are talking about is the duty of states to guarantee a more simplified procedure of naturalization for the foreign woman married to a citizen of that state as compared to the procedure of naturalization of a person who is not married or the foreign wife of a foreigner."[17]

Yet, neither the 1938 citizenship statute during the post–1957 phase nor its 1978 successor made any effort to bring the applicable domestic norm in line with the treaty's divergent stipulation so as to afford a foreign man or woman married to a Soviet citizen preferential treatment in transferring to Soviet citizenship or expedite exit from Soviet citizenship by a Soviet man or woman married to a foreigner.

Note, too, that the textual congruency between the other points of the Convention mentioned above and the corresponding prescriptions of Soviet law is not matched by practice. In particular, where men of Jewish origin apply for emigration, name Israel as their destination, as they are required to, and are next obliged to renounce Soviet citizenship before receiving an exit permit, the wives are likewise ordered to surrender their Soviet citizenship if they choose to accompany their husbands abroad. Thus, despite what the Convention calls for, they are not allowed to retain their Soviet citizenship. The routine refers not just to wives who themselves may be of Jewish origin, but also to non–Jewish wives of Jewish emigrants and even to non–Jewish wives of non–Jewish emigrants on occasions where leading dissidents subjected to virtual expulsion are compelled by the authorities to indicate that they intend to go to Israel thereby furnishing the officials with a convenient excuse to demand that they first formally quit Soviet citizenship on those grounds and so effectively spare the regime further notoriety accruing from resort to special edicts summarily stripping them of Soviet citizenship. In each instance, then, to the extent that the pater familias is penalized for his decision (voluntary or induced) to live elsewhere by mandatory loss of Soviet citizenship, the rest of the family is now forced to share his lot — the plain message of the 1957 Convention to the contrary notwithstanding.

II. Legislative and Diplomatic Practice

When the concept of statelessness was formally introduced into the Soviet legislative canon in 1938, the move coincided with and was attributed to the Sturm und Drang that then swept every aspect of Soviet life. Several specific reasons were offered at the time to account for this switch in Soviet policy and such explanations continued to be echoed in Soviet pronouncements on the subject until the end of the Stalin era. The principal theme here was increased concern for the national safety of the USSR which rendered it inadvisable automatically to assign Soviet citizenship to apatrides because the process of "mechanical" naturalization harbored excessive risk for the security interests of the country. Lax methods of admission of aliens to full membership in the Soviet polity allegedly facilitated the job of those who sought to penetrate the system in order to harm it and made it easier for external enemies to worm their people into local positions of responsibility where they could serve their "capitalist masters".[18] A second favorite leitmotiv was the need for greater centralized control over the operations of the USSR's administrative apparatus in light, inter alia, of the deteriorating international situation and, hence, concentration of authority in these affairs at the highest level of the government organization to put a stop to the fairly casual way in which Soviet citizenship had been awarded in the past.[19] Affirmative bureaucratic action superseded the "open enrollment" procedures that had hitherto been the practice in these matters. Finally, a combination of xenophobia and militant nationalism also played a role in the decision to revise the rules — a desire to monitor closely and contain the influx of "suspect" foreign elements into the Soviet community and to inflate the value of Soviet citizenship by making the applicants prove their worthiness to "earn that high honor".[20] The idea of having Soviet citizenship virtually thrust upon individuals just because they could not establish that they were foreign citizens or provided almost on request did not fit the Kremlin's new emphasis on the sovereign prerogatives of Soviet statehood.

The abnormal domestic circumstances that prompted the change in Soviet policy coupled with dramatic developments on the diplomatic scene shortly afterwards are reflected in the regime's erratic treatment of the problem of statelessness in those days. Some of the measures taken, for instance, generated numerous cases of statelessness. Two examples may be mentioned. First, even prior to 1938, the competent Soviet agencies had conceded to certain individuals residing on the territory of the USSR and unable to demonstrate possession of an effective foreign citizenship the right to have themselves inscribed pro tem as persons "having declared themselves foreigners" in the expectation that their status would soon be verified and they would eventually wind up certified either as legitimate foreigners or receive Soviet citizenship owing to failure to supply evidence of entitlement to a valid foreign passport.[21] Following official endorsement of the institution of statelessness in Soviet law, these people were routinely entered under that rubric, clearing the record, but saddling the USSR with a batch of freshly minted apatrides. Second, after the promulgation of the 1938 citizenship statute, the authorities launched a thorough review of the files of foreigners who had settled on Soviet soil on earlier occasions and at some point had been duly issued Soviet papers because they no longer qualified as foreigners although they had never expressly solicited Soviet citizenship. Soviet sources noted at the time that, as a result of the audit, "it became possible to get rid of quite a quantity of pseudo-citizens and formalize the Soviet citizenship of those who were recognized to be deserving of it".[22] The individuals who flunked the test presumably lapsed into statelessness — a sizable increment that further swelled the ranks of the fledgling colony of locally domiciled apatrides.

On the other hand, while busy manufacturing an assortment of stateless persons, the regime simultaneously took steps to eradicate manifestations of that phenomenon elsewhere. For example, reference was previously made to the big group of Armenian refugees who found a home in the USSR during the inter-war period. Although considered citizens of the USSR by the Soviet authorities, most of them had not actively requested Soviet citizenship and in 1940 the administration, eager to attend to this unfinished business, resorted to conversion en masse through the simple expedient of summoning the individual concerned to the nearest police station to collect documents identifying them as Soviet citizens.[23] In this case, several thousand souls were spared a stateless plight by executive fiat, in stark contrast to how the government had recently chosen to behave in comparable situations.

The same inconsistency marks the Soviet treatment of the problem of acquisition of the citizenship of the USSR by the population of large segments of territory adjacent to its western frontiers which the Soviet Union incorporated into its domain between 1939 and 1941. In so doing, Moscow did not bestow Soviet citizenship outright on all the permanent residents of the newly won provinces, but implemented a highly selective policy of assimilation in the context of state succession. Thus, diverse minority elements in the Baltic states — persons without citizenship belonging to ethnic entities who, in the conditions of the "reactionary political regimes existing in Lithuania, Latvia and Estonia formerly could not obtain the citizenship of these republics" (e.g., the Poles and Jews of the Vilna area) — were forthwith vested with Soviet citizenship.[24] However, fellow apatrides settled in the absorbed regions (and that included ex-Russian and ex-Soviet citizens who had been stripped of their erstwhile citizenship by earlier decrees of the Soviet government) did not fare as well and were expected to file for Soviet citizenship individually in the prescribed manner. Furthermore, the ethnic Romanian settlers in Bessarabia were likened to stateless persons after the USSR took the province back from Romania, and for a while so were the Polish refugees from the western half of Poland overrun by the Germans who had fled to Soviet soil.[25]

The "mixed" pattern recurs in the post–World War II era. The series of ad hoc edicts promulgated in 1945–1947 which offered easy restoration of Soviet citizenship to former Russian and Soviet citizens and their descendants who then resided in certain countries applied equally to those among them who were currently stateless and spelled quick relief for their present sorry state. Meanwhile, military victory meant territorial aggrandizement by the USSR at the expense of some of the Axis partners and renewed attention to the issue of the citizenship status of the local population: Soviet citizenship was not automatically extended to the indigenous occupants of the ground lost by Finland, Germany and Japan and, because their original citizenship became de facto inoperative, these people were now transformed into functional apatrides who could escape that fate only by petitioning for admission to Soviet citizenship. Thanks to mass repatriation, flight and expulsion, few of the native inhabitants remained in the conquered territories,[26] but the Soviet authorities still made no effort to engineer their smooth transition from a nationality that had effectively lapsed to the citizenship of the USSR and were content to let them travel the regular naturalization route or face the prospect of being in practice treated as stateless aliens in their latest homeland.

A closer look at the record shows, of course, that these acts were not random and that a definite rationale shaped the official agenda, prompting those in charge of the operations to draw invidious distinctions between "desirable" individuals who deserved to be rescued from statelessness by government intervention and their "undesirable" counterparts who were cast adrift. The important aspect of the picture, though, is not that a coherent explanation can here be mounted to account for Soviet conduct, but rather that, despite its oft–professed general aversion for the concept of statelessness,[27] the Soviet leadership was in reality motivated by specific political considerations in deciding whether and how to deal with the phenomenon. Another significant fact worth remembering is that, notwithstanding the post– war emergence of a clutch of fellow socialist regimes in Europe and Asia, Soviet citizenship policies remained locked even at this stage in the conservative mold forged at the time of the USSR's worst isolation on the international scene. No trace, for example, can be found of the old spirit of revolutionary solidarity that had once given foreign workers on Soviet soil the same rights and privileges as those enjoyed by their hosts[28] and Soviet behavior in this area continued to bear the stolid nationalistic imprint that bespoke its Stalinist origins.

The first tangible signs of change appeared in 1954. As reported by one Soviet writer:

> "On December 16, 1954, the Presidium of the USSR Supreme Soviet adopted a resolution "On persons who have long resided on the territory of the USSR and who have not formalized their citizenship". In accordance with that resolution persons who were born abroad and who arrived in the USSR at various periods (with the exception of political immigrants) and did not produce documents to show possession of a foreign citizenship (nationality), as well as their children, are citizens of the USSR. This resolution reinstated with minor revisions Article 3 of the Regulation on the Citizenship of the USSR of 1931, which in fact almost liquidated the institution of persons without citizenship."[29]

As far as can be ascertained, it was a secret decree, that is, it was never published in any of the regular outlets. Since the text cannot be consulted, one has to rely entirely on secondary sources and try to extrapolate from their summation what the edict proposed to accomplish. Actually, the best approach would be to begin by saying what it did not intend to achieve and thus set the record straight.

Despite the author's assertion, it is safe to conclude that the measure did not "reinstate with minor revisions Article 3 of the Regulation on the Citizenship of the USSR of 1931", which, one will recall, had stipulated that "every person on the territory of the USSR is recognized as a citizen of the USSR insofar as there is no proof of his being a citizen of a foreign state". First, the text of the Citizenship Law of 1938 was subsequently reprinted in several official compendia and nowhere did it appear with any alteration that would substantiate such a claim.[30] Second, even judging from the scanty information obtainable on the subject, the aim here of the 1954 resolution differed markedly from that of Article 3 of its 1931 predecessor in that the latter foresaw automatic naturalization *tout court* of individuals with no demonstrable foreign citizenship located on Soviet soil whereas the 1954 piece of legislation undertook to do that only for a special category of "persons who have long resided on the territory of the USSR". What was meant by "long" in this context remains unclear, but nonetheless this ingredient certainly added a new and material dimension as compared to the language of the 1931 statute. As a result, the two scripts were quite distinct in their conception of and solution to the problem of statelessness.

Now, what was the purpose of the 1954 decree? From what little one knows about it, the directive would seem to have represented an ad hoc enactment not calculated formally to supersede any provision of the 1938 Citizenship Law and not envisaged as a regular feature of Soviet citizenship legislation, but seen as a purely provisional arrangement designed to cure a specific existing situation and lapsing as soon as it succeeded in doing the job. The timing of its promulgation is à propos, for it indicates that it was part and parcel of the steps immediately initiated by Stalin's heirs in almost every field to curb the abuses and excesses associated with his name. The people whom the edict had in mind, who had for many years lived in the USSR and yet had not secured Soviet passports, were evidently those to whom the previous regime had refused to grant Soviet citizenship either on political grounds (the survivors, for instance, of the group deprived of Soviet citizenship in 1938 in conjunction with the passage of the new citizenship law; those members of the population of the territories seized by the USSR in 1939–1941 and possibly also in 1945 to whom Soviet citizenship was not extended ipso jure upon incorporation and who were instructed to apply for it on an individual basis) or out of ideological motivations (due to extreme suspicion of foreigners, feelings of militantly nationalistic exclusiveness, etc.).

The operation therefore consummated two major changes in the juridico– political fabric bequeathed by the Stalin era: one, it repudiated some of the worse idiosyncrasies of the preceding leadership which, inter alia, had expressed themselves in the systematic persecution of certain foreign Communist elements that had found asylum in the Soviet Union; two, it relaxed the rigid controls instituted under Stalin intended to transform the USSR into a closed society, uncompromisingly hostile to all outsiders, and dedicated to keeping the Soviet world immune from alien influences. Accordingly, many of Stalin's private prejudices and personal techniques for exercising dictatorial power which during his reign had stamped every facet of Soviet public life, including the sphere of law and, in turn, the subsidiary branch of citizenship legislation, were now quietly put to rest by those who followed him. The 1954 decree was just one manifestation of this desire to erase the more objectionable traits of the ancien régime. However, all it was expected to do was to rectify a long–standing injustice, not introduce (or reintroduce) a daring legal formula that henceforward would operate as a general rule.

Up to this point, one can only applaud the sentiments which inspired the adoption of the 1954 edict. But, as usual, there is another side to the story that makes one pause, for, going by the brief synopsis furnished by secondary sources, it would appear that the government alone determined which of "the persons who had long lived in the USSR and not formalized their citizenship" had resided in the country "long" enough forthwith to be summarily naturalized. The decision, then, lay entirely within the discretion of the authorities, so that the whole program was in actuality much less "automatic" than it at first sounded. Furthermore, the decree did not state expressis verbis that only those persons among the eligible sample who wanted Soviet citizenship but heretofore had been unable to obtain it would presently receive it. As a consequence, individuals who had perhaps during all these years resisted official pressure to ask for admission into Soviet citizenship now found themselves forcibly transformed into citizens of the USSR, in total disregard of their own feelings on the issue. Hence, the positive aspects of this scheme for rendering justice to some, for which the new leadership deserves due credit, may have been partially at least offset by evidence of the injustice which in the process was visited on others.

A Soviet spokesman has in fact tried to rebut this latter criticism by claiming that, "significantly, ... the resolution did not sanction the automatic enrollment in the ranks of Soviet citizens of all persons without citizenship living on the territory of the USSR".[31] The attempt is disingenuous, since anybody can figure out that not every stateless individual inside the USSR was thereby assigned Soviet citizenship: prima facie, political immigrants and apatrides who were pronounced not to have lived in the USSR the required duration or who had not been born abroad did not fall under the terms of the directive and so were spared such "instant conversion". The real question is whether those who in this instance were picked to get Soviet citizenship by executive fiat had a choice in the matter or not: our Soviet commentator manages to shed no light on that subject and odds are that the people concerned were indeed offered no chance to record a preference on this occasion.

The whole affair, be it further noted, does not quite square with the opinion enunciated in an officially approved textbook recently published in the USSR to the effect that:

> "Compulsory or automatic naturalization sometimes practiced with respect to a population that has long resided on the territory of a state runs counter to the principles of international law. In this case, citizenship is imposed against the will of the interested persons and, coincidentally, the sovereign rights of the state whose citizenship the naturalized persons have are infringed."[32]

Granted that, technically, the present project featured only individuals who could not prove possession of the citizenship of a foreign state and so, in theory, avoided the problem of violating a foreign state's sovereign rights. However, the crucial question of disregard for the will of the affected persons remains and one waits in vain for an answer that will here adequately bridge the gap between promise and performance, — except, perhaps, to imagine some lame explanation that the remark was addressed strictly to a situation where the "alien enclave" retained the valid citizenship of another state and that where a truly stateless component was involved even a unilateral attribution of its citizenship by the host country was better than the current status of juridical limbo.

One is hard put to guess at the magnitude of the impact of the 1954 decree. If the conclusion is warranted that most of the "permanently stateless" individuals in the USSR after 1938 were in that position because the regime rejected their applications for naturalization, then the edict must have succeeded in all but wiping out the phenomenon inside the Soviet Union. Local analysts certainly give the impression of a steady decline in the size of the apatride colony in the USSR, affirming that "from the date of passage of the Law on the Citizenship of the USSR of 1938 the number of persons without citizenship in our country has been reduced manifold and today they constitute a very insignificant fraction of the population".[33] In particular, the 1954 resolution is said to have made a major contribution to that trend by "bringing to a minimum the number of people without citizenship living in the USSR".[34] Of course, because the 1954 measure was both provisional and directed at past history, so to speak, a fresh accumulation of stateless persons was bound to build up in the USSR after the inventory, primarily due to the continued operation of conflicts–of–nationality laws.

Remember, too, that the "reform" still left a residue of "hard–core" apatrides living within the borders of the USSR. Political immigrants comprised a substantial proportion of that constituency, although it is impossible to estimate how many people fall into that category. In any event, the contingent was sufficiently large to move the authorities in various instances to issue extra regulations defining the treatment to be applied to designated sub– groups. For example, a decree of the federal Presidium of September 22, 1956, introduced special restrictions on choice of place of residence by former Greek and Turkish citizens and Iranian subjects who were stateless persons. An order of the Procurator–General of the USSR, dated November 9, 1972 (No.54), lifted the restraints and prescribed that henceforth these stateless elements enjoyed the same rights in this area as common apatrides in accordance with the existing legislation governing the procedures to be followed by foreigners and stateless persons for residence in the USSR.[35] In a somewhat different context, an underground report announcing the establishment of a dissident organization dedicated to the struggle for freedom of departure from the USSR listed as a corporate member a cluster of more than 200 Iranians living on the territory of the USSR with "residence permits" instead of passports and not considered Soviet citizens: apparently, they have been striving for years to go home, but the administration turns down all their requests.[36]

The game is, of course, played with specific tactical objectives in mind, namely, to keep alive the option of repatriating political refugees when they might prove useful in their native environment by citing the temporary nature of their sojourn in the USSR as indicated by failure to acquire Soviet citizenship and thus integrate into the Soviet community. Presumably, the calculus is that at least some of them will labor to further Soviet interests in their own land upon remigrating, despite their experiences during exile in the USSR. The pragmatic outlook means that not all political emigres in the Soviet Union are apt ipso facto to be consigned by the authorities to a life or even a stint of statelessness, but only those who are deliberately earmarked for this sort of mission. Other escapees who end up on Soviet soil may indeed be offered Soviet citizenship on preferential terms under certain conditions and in their case statelessness, if it occurs, is the sole result of a conscious decision on their part not to accept the proposed deal. How the system works can be glimpsed from the story of Ma Hun who fled from China to the USSR in 1968, was detained for illegally entering the country, but then the charges were dropped and he received a residence permit, was soon after infiltrated into China on an assignment for the KGB that failed and recrossed the frontier, was urged to accept Soviet citizenship in connection with the KGB's plans to train him for espionage activities against the PRC, demurred on both counts, was arrested in 1972, tried as a spy and served time in a forced labor camp until four years later a superior court reduced the original sentence and ordered him released, and was last reported to be living in the Khabarovsk region, forbidden, as a stateless person, to travel outside the local district.[37]

To be sure, not all political immigrants in the USSR have such checkered careers and most, one assumes, routinely agree to convert to Soviet citizenship if told to do so or settle down with mere "residence permits" that in practice relegate them to a status of functional statelessness where that is the sole available alternative. Nevertheless, as Ma Hun's case illustrates, occasional mavericks can also crop up in their midst who remain stateless by choice and contrary to official wishes, and yet manage to induce the authorities to let them stay in the country and eventually pursue a fairly normal existence — by Soviet standards.

The legislative "thaw" staged in 1954 was matched before long by a distinct change of tone in reference to the subject of statelessness. The type of general observation deploring the phenomenon of statelessness now gave way to sharper criticism of the institution. The new trend sought to emphasize that the Soviet government viewed statelessness as undesirable, so that, undoubtedly, one of the main tasks of legal regulation of questions of Soviet citizenship was said to be the reduction in the number of persons incurring statelessness,[38] and that statelessness resembled dual citizenship in the sense that, from an international law perspective, both figured as an evil that called for eradication and, hence, amounted to a juridical anomaly.[39] However, the indictment never went so far as to condemn statelessness in absolute terms nor did the pitch rise to the stridency of the average denunciation of the evils of double nationality. Though clearly negative, the attitude toward statelessness in informed Soviet circles is expressed in relatively moderate language, hedged with caveats about how the vexing problem might be tackled. The pros and cons are nicely deployed in the following statement:

> "The status of statelessness represents from the standpoint of the interests of the state a somewhat lesser evil than dual citizenship. But, it too can

cause definite inconvenience for states and even disputes between them, connected, for example, with the regulation of exit and entry of persons without citizenship, in particular with respect to their expulsion into other states, etc. If, on the other hand, one approaches the issue from the standpoint of the interests of the physical person, then statelessness rates as no less an evil than dual citizenship. In no state does the stateless person enjoy the plenitude of political and civil rights, that is, his general legal capacity is always in some degree diminished. A person with dual citizenship is not put in that position.

This does not mean that states are obliged to avoid statelessness at all cost. Instances are possible where some person consciously commits acts entailing loss of citizenship. In deciding the question of liquidation of statelessness one must, therefore, take into account the interests both of the state and the physical person with an appreciation of the concrete setting, and not by wrestling with statelessness per se as an abstract evil."[40]

Given the Soviet regime's record of reliance on deprivation of citizenship as a punitive measure, such reluctance to fault official conduct that spawns statelessness in toto is perfectly understandable. As for the perception of dual citizenship as worse than statelessness, the reason for this ranking probably lies in the fact that the former is more prone to be the source of difficulties at the international level than the latter and, although the person concerned may indeed suffer more from statelessness than from double citizenship, the Soviet agenda has always featured the state's stake ahead of that of the individual where the respective priorities diverge.

Even so, some strong anti–statelessness sentiments got an airing in the "liberalized" atmosphere of the sixties, with advocates of reform taking the position that

"very likely one ought to forswear the institution of statelessness. However, this question still requires further special investigation on the basis of detailed analysis of the practical situation brought about by the implementation of the resolution of the Presidium of the USSR Supreme Soviet of December 16, 1954."[41]

Or, to quote another local spokesman who sounded the same note of mixed optimism and prudence: "The reduction in cases of statelessness undoubtedly represents one of the important tasks of the legal regulation of citizenship questions. The question of the advisability of keeping the institution of stateless persons requires, of course, special study."[42] Clearly, the old policy on statelessness no longer commanded unanimous support within the Soviet legal community, but its opponents continued to act with a certain degree of caution since a formal decision on the subject had apparently not yet been reached and, until they sensed how the official wind was going to blow, Soviet scribes were just not willing to commit themselves unequivocally on a rather controversial issue.

Interestingly enough, the urge to prescribe a cure for statelessness was not limited to manifestations of that condition inside the USSR and at least one Soviet author with an academic penchant for the legal affairs of his native Armenia sought to focus attention on the pressing need to mount a rescue operation aimed at the thousands of stateless Armenians scattered over the face of the globe. His recommendation to return to the union republics the right to admit to their citizenship individuals located "overseas" was plainly motivated by the desire to enhance his own republic's ability to initiate appropriate measures on behalf of these unfortunates. Here is the picture he drew:

> "... the essential mass of Armenians living abroad, though wholeheartedly identified with the Motherland, in substance remains in a status of statelessness, has no juridical ties with the Motherland. The question arises whether it is not time to establish a firm legal link between the working Armenians abroad and their Motherland — Soviet Armenia, regardless of the concrete prospects for their repatriation?
>
> In contemporary circumstances where the entire Soviet country, including Soviet Armenia, is taking giant steps on the road to comprehensive development and has registered huge successes in all areas of life, the chances of gradual enlargement of the contingent of repatriated Armenians become a realistic matter.
>
> We believe that the Soviet legislator must proceed further in his undertakings in terms of the enormous attention he expends with respect to Armenians abroad and, perhaps, study the question of the possibility of admitting to Soviet citizenship working Armenians wishing to repatriate regardless of the actual possibility of repatriation at the present stage.
>
> The solution of this problem will, obviously, be fraught with difficulties, will require the consent of the authorities of those countries on the territory of which the Armenians provisionally reside, etc. However, its solution in the suggested manner would have a great political and moral significance, would save from their stateless lot a mass of workers, for the title 'Soviet citizen' would inspire them, instill in them a sense of faith and hope in their future and, in addition, they would forge political and juridical contact with the Motherland, with all the attendant consequences."[43]

The proposal came to naught.

The political climate in the USSR underwent a dramatic change between the early sixties and the late seventies — in the direction of a dominant mood of pronounced conservatism. Not surprisingly, then, the contents of the 1978 citizenship statute did not consecrate these "radical" schemes, although the influence of these ideas persisted to the extent that a serious effort was made on this occasion to shift to procedures that would have the effect of curbing the future incidence of statelessness associated with conflicts–in–law phenomena. This is not to say, as one Soviet analyst has, that "the Act makes it completely impossible for any stateless person to be automatically counted as a Soviet citizen while, at the same time, facilitating a substantial reduction in the number of such persons".[44] For, first, the law does in fact sanction unilateral assignment of Soviet citizenship in several designated contingencies and, second, its arrangements for containing the frequency of occurrence of statelessness apply only to minors and offer no relief to adults caught in the same predicament.

Thus, when Soviet writers choose to identify who benefits from these improvements, they are forced to refer to: children born on the territory of the USSR of stateless persons who permanently reside in the USSR; children residing on the territory of the USSR when one parent becomes a citizen of the USSR and the other remains a stateless person; a child of stateless parents adopted by citizens of the USSR, and so forth.[45] Stateless adults are conspicuously absent from the list. The revised format lets Soviet spokesmen claim that the government has taken positive steps to stamp out statelessness for which the regime has, of course, always professed intense dislike, while allowing the authorities to maintain their guard against "infiltration by undesirable aliens" by the bald expedient of limiting the whole operation to minor children who pose no danger to the country's security or the system's ideological and political antisepsis.

What next needs to be done is to evaluate the overall performance of Soviet law in the matter of statelessness both in terms of how it compares to the practice of other states in this field and of how well it lives up to whatever special virtues Soviet commentators tend to attribute to their government's policy here. The best way to tackle the job is to start by drawing a distinction between Soviet and foreign nationality legislation as it pertains to Soviet citizens and as it affects foreign nationals.

As regards the former case, it must be conceded that Soviet legislation does indeed accomplish what it is said to, in the sense that Soviet citizens cannot by accident of mere "collision" of national legal systems find themselves destined to statelessness. The sole exception to this hard and fast rule involves children under fourteen whose Soviet parents both expatriated themselves and acquired the nationality of a state which does not eo ipso confer its citizenship on the minor offspring of its freshly naturalized subjects. Otherwise, no amount of conflict of nationality laws can produce inadvertent statelessness on the part of the Soviet citizen trapped in such a situation.

This is not to conclude that Soviet citizens can never end up stateless, for that would not be true. But, if and when they do, that comes about either because the Soviet government has deliberately deprived them of their Soviet citizenship before they had a chance to acquire another nationality, as it may, or because they have themselves renounced Soviet citizenship in accordance with set procedure and then either failed to obtain a foreign citizenship or, having secured one, later managed to lose it. Statelessness of this genre, though, does not represent stricto sensu the outcome of blind inter- state collision of legal norms, but is rooted in a conscious choice of a definite course of action by the Soviet authorities with or without the consent of the party affected. Technically speaking, it does not therefore fall within the scope of the present inquiry, except in this respect that, if the Soviet regime really believes that statelessness is a misfortune that urgently demands a cure, one would expect it to offer effective remedy in a situation where a Soviet citizen has for some reason declined into that sad state.

Of course, if the Soviet government was itself the cause of the person's statelessness in that it had cancelled his citizenship outright, no facile solution would be forthcoming from that quarter, which is understandable. On the other hand, if other events had led to the individual's becoming stateless, in principle nothing would preclude the Soviet regime, given its avowed distaste for statelessness, from offering the victim a relatively easy way of returning to the fold, as it were. The 1978 citizenship statute does differ on that score from its 1938 antecedent by formally recognizing the possibility of reinstatement in Soviet citizenship of individuals who had previously lost it (whether on their initiative or also by fiat is not entirely clear) and, hence, sounds more progressive here than its predecessor. Subsequently issued instructions specified, however, that applications for restoration to Soviet citizenship were to be processed by the Presidium of the USSR Supreme Soviet in the manner prescribed for handling petitions for admission to the citizenship of the USSR,[46] which dispelled any illusion of routine entitlement by these people to privileged treatment in this matter regardless of how they came to be dropped from the membership rolls.

A plausible explanation for this singularly rigid attitude may lie in the maxim of "the impossibility of automatic loss of the citizenship of the USSR"[47] by which Soviet savants appear to set much store and the consequent fact that formal surrender of Soviet citizenship requires two things: a request to that end by the interested person and express approval by the Presidium of the USSR Supreme Soviet. In these conditions, it would seem that the rationale for refusing to subscribe to any simplified format for reinstitution of Soviet citizenship stems from the notion that the person in question had voluntarily and consciously relinquished his or her Soviet citizenship, not lost it owing to circumstances beyond his or her control, and therefore might just as well retrace the route in order to regain it. Note, however, that even when the regime had operated without benefit of a legislative mandate in this domain, it had occasionally relented and on an ad hoc basis sprung quick detours to expedite recovery of its citizenship by certain groups of erstwhile citizens, including those who in the interim had lapsed into statelessness.[48] Now that the practice is once again an established feature of the Soviet repertory, the competent organs will doubtless feel freer yet to accelerate the pace of readmission to Soviet citizenship whenever the situation, in their opinion, warrants fast service: at any rate, since the citizenship act sheds no light on the scheduled duration of regular naturalization proceedings, no statutory writ prevents the business of restoration to Soviet citizenship which is patterned on the same model from being attended to in a trice — if the officials in charge decide that they need to spend very little time on the task. Inasmuch as Soviet jurisprudes indicate awareness that the general tendency in modern international law has been to grant easier terms in connection with reintegration than those which apply to primary entry into citizenship,[49] resort to the more accommodating methods here may prove not to be uncommon in the long run.

In any event, looked at strictly from the technical vantage-point of whether it promotes or lessens the incidence of statelessness, this side of Soviet law must be adjudged to be markedly superior to that of most nations in that it virtually bars the prospect of a Soviet citizen unintentionally being sentenced to that sorry condition. There is another dimension to this whole problem, of course, which must also be kept in mind, and that is that the immunity is bought at the cost of the individual's liberty to decide his own fate. Some will balk at the price and prefer the risk of statelessness to the regimentation which in this case is offered as a panacea for it. Indeed, while a Soviet citizen cannot inadvertently become stateless, that insurance is purchased at the expense of his right to surrender his Soviet citizenship at will. He can only do so with the prior consent of the authorities, which may be denied to him.

By the same token, if he should happen to be abroad at the time and therefore have the opportunity to renounce his Soviet citizenship with impunity simply by describing himself as a refugee and asking the host country for asylum and the issuance of appropriate documents certifying him as an apatride, turning himself, then, into a de facto stateless individual (as did millions of Soviet citizens in the wake of the last war), this still would not, in the eyes of Moscow, affect the person's Soviet citizenship. Even today, for instance, the Soviet government continues to regard as Soviet citizens the mass of refugees and displaced persons of Russian origin who found themselves in the west after the Second World War, refused to go home, sought and received special identification papers and severed all ties with the USSR, on grounds, inter alia, that they had never secured a formal release from Soviet citizenship and had not been granted written permission to give up their Soviet passport.[50] Until they do, so runs the official thesis, they remain Soviet citizens. As has been aptly put, "c'est sans doute par cette conception [priorité du domaine publique] qu'il faut expliquer l'insistance dont a fait preuve l'Union soviétique pour exiger le rapatriement des exilés volontaires après la deuxième guerre mondiale: le lien rattachant les personnes à l'État serait uniquement un lien de droit public et objectif, ne dépendant que de la volonté de l'État".[51]

The treatment locally afforded foreigners who, caught in a conflicts–in–law web, wind up stateless presents a very different picture. Despite the recent reforms designed to shield minors from that experience, Soviet policy vis–à– vis adult aliens placed in that difficult position against their will because of discrepancies between the applicable norms of Soviet legislation and those of a competing foreign legal system essentially remains content not to interfere with the consequences and offers the victim of such an accident neither sympathy nor relief. Routine naturalization is its only answer to the mishap. However, if one is to believe Soviet lawyers, the scenario is far less austere than this statement would make it sound, for, according to them, a number of extraneous factors temper the severity of the rule.

They point out, for example, that Soviet legislation abjures any a priori quota scheme for the naturalization of aliens based on racial, religious or other criteria, so that ex principio no one is artificially excluded from obtaining Soviet citizenship on such contrived grounds.[52] They likewise contend that Soviet citizenship law far surpasses its bourgeois counterparts in that it does not insist on any special qualifications for naturalization (e.g., income) and does not impose any minimum residence requirement either.[53] Hence, they conclude, it is already so easy to acquire Soviet citizenship that further simplifications would serve no good purpose and, as it is, no stateless person need long remain stateless if he wants to become a Soviet citizen, unless he has something serious to hide or something in his past renders him ineligible for the "noble distinction of counting himself among the citizens of the USSR".

The 1978 citizenship statute (Art.15) is at pains to reenforce that flattering image by broadcasting that foreigners and stateless persons may at their request be admitted to Soviet citizenship irrespective of their racial and national extraction, gender, education, language, situs of residence, but, notably, fails to include in the list a person's "social origins". The omission was apparently deliberate and has been interpreted to mean that "the Soviet state is not indifferent to the social status of an individual petitioning for admission to the citizenship of the USSR, a citizenship of the working people".[59]

On paper, then, the whole operation looks quite simple and straightforward, except that in the Soviet Union especially political realities all too often run counter to juridical appearances. There is in fact no satisfactory assurance that an application for naturalization will be processed rapidly; nor is there any genuine guarantee that it will succeed, in which case the accidental statelessness may yet turn out to be permanent. Granted, the law erects no synthetic barriers here — aside from the "minor" test of suitable social origins — including no specific length of prior domicile in the country, but background factors and personal data nevertheless play a prominent role and are carefully taken into account when a petition for naturalization is being scrutinized by the competent agency. So, while the general formula sounds extremely permissive, Soviet spokesmen let it publicly be known that the mechanism does not function automatically and the official rapporteur for the 1978 citizenship bill himself took care to stress that "every person desiring to become a Soviet citizen must demonstrate by his actions that he is deserving of such a high calling and is ready to bear that calling with dignity, safeguard the interests and authority of our state". Only when "this fundamental condition is complied with", he added, is the question of admission to Soviet citizenship resolved without regard to the indicia mentioned in the corresponding provision of the statute.[55]

Thus, in the end, the process may turn out to be as protracted and as unsure as its counterpart in the despised "capitalist" countries, though no self-respecting Soviet lawyer would confess to any similarities between his own and the outside world, even on such a routine matter.

A healthy dose of scepticism is also called for in the face of the companion Soviet claim to the effect that should for some reason a person living in the USSR find his stateless condition unduly prolonged (despite the alleged facility of naturalization in the Soviet Union), that would still not represent a major disaster in view of the generosity of Soviet treatment of apatrides located on Soviet soil.[56] Indeed, Soviet sources regularly draw invidious comparisons between what they please to designate as the "rights-less" position of stateless individuals elsewhere in the world and the advantageous juridical status formally guaranteed these persons by Soviet law under which they occupy a place identical to that of any foreigner, with the sole exception that they do not enjoy the diplomatic protection of a home state. Again, it is a nice theory, but, given the record of the Soviet regime's past performance in this sphere, one is inclined to take it with a large grain of salt. Perhaps the future will yet bear out the optimism encountered in Soviet legal literature in this context, but if so the development will come as a welcome break with and in marked contrast to long-standing precedent and not, as contended, as an embodiment of a quality that has always here characterized Soviet policy, including during the Stalin period.

Aside from all that, what is it that has since 1938 prompted Soviet authorities to take such an intransigeant attitude toward foreigners who, thanks in part at least to Soviet law, found themselves stateless against their will? The answer, it is suggested, must be sought in the overall Soviet conception of the idea of citizenship itself. At the heart of that vision lies the axiom that citizenship is essentially an element of constitutional law, i.e. a facet of the domestic legal system of each state.

Soviet authors will concur that the question does betray what they will permit themselves to call "international moments", namely, a conjuncture where some issue pertaining to citizenship constitutes the object of an international agreement or where it legitimately attracts inter–state attention, in cases of dual or multiple nationality, for example.[57] But, apart from these marginal contingencies, citizenship, in their learned opinion, falls into the category of every state's own private business. Or, as an authoritative source puts it, "the regulation of citizenship, i.e. the conditions for its acquisition and loss, are the internal affair of each state, that is why there does not exist a uniform regulation of citizenship in international law".[58] Not only that, but Soviet writers further maintain that in our day citizenship is one of the most vital attributes of state sovereignty, one of the most precious and exclusive prerogatives of an independent nation that will brook no outside interference.[59]

All this logically leads to two conclusions, both of which Soviet spokesmen are quick to reach. First, since the problem of citizenship is perceived as a domestic one, it naturally follows that the responsibility for defining the criteria of citizenship in such a way as to avoid negative repercussions, like statelessness, rests on the shoulders of the respective state itself. In short, if foreign nationals suffer statelessness as a result of conflict between their country's laws and the laws of the Soviet Union, the home state, according to the Soviet view, bears the onus of adapting its laws in order to protect its subjects. The Soviet Union does as much for its citizens and obviously thinks other countries ought to take care of theirs. If not, they must live with the unfortunate consequences.

The pitch implies, of course, that the Soviet Union here expects other states to synchronize their citizenship legislation with its own if they wish, that is, to cease causing conflict–in–law situations generating, inter alia, statelessness. In any event, whether they do so by tailoring their legal system to the Soviet model or otherwise is immaterial. The central factor remains that, in Moscow's estimate, it lies with them to rectify the shortcomings in their law such as hold accidental statelessness in store for their unforewarned citizens, if they object to having it happen, and that it is not up to the Soviet Union to do the job for them by allowing their penalized nationals easy access to its citizenship. The Soviets may have a valid point here, but the policy is too dogmatic and leaves no room for the kind of compromise that might beget ecumenical consensus. What is required is a modicum of mutual adjustment to minimize the undesirable effects of the contemporary adherence by the world's states to opposing doctrines of nationality and that is an idea that the Soviet regime has so far refused to entertain, preferring instead to stay in its present inflexible position and work unilaterally.

Second, in light of the above it will come as no surprise to discover that the Soviet Union does not consider statelessness a fit subject for solution through international legal channels. True, it has, as noted, acceded to the 1957 Convention on the Nationality of Married Women, but this constitutes a lone departure from the established pattern to be explained only by the innocuous character of that treaty and the fortuitous fact that nearly everything it contains coincides with what Soviet law has to say on the matter. As against that, for instance, at its fifth and sixth sessions in 1953 and 1954 the International Law Commission of the United Nations had prepared draft conventions on the elimination of statelessness,

> "but the delegation of the USSR, basing itself on the fact that questions of acquisition and loss of citizenship refer to the internal competence of each state, voted against these projects, which, moreover, foresaw the creation of a special tribunal of the United Nations for handling complaints by persons concerning deprivation of citizenship and thereby allowed the possibility of interference in the internal affairs of a state."[60]

Procedural considerations probably figured as the principal reason for Soviet opposition to the Commission's recommendations, including curbs on the right of the parties to file reservations which, inter alia, barred them from refusing to accept the compulsory jurisdiction of the International Court of Justice where a dispute between the signatories concerning the convention's interpretation or application was submitted to that body by one of the sides. Interestingly enough, though, Soviet legal experts have also raised substantive issues in a bid to justify their country's refusal to endorse the 1954 treaty. In particular, they have claimed that:

> "... the legislation of the USSR contains norms that envisage wider rights for stateless persons than the provisions of the convention. Thus, with respect to receiving higher education stateless persons in the USSR enjoy the national regime, whereas the convention sanctions in this connection a regime not inferior to the common regime for foreigners in the designated country. So, participation by the USSR in the convention would practically do nothing for the stateless persons residing on its territory, but could inflict damage to its sovereignty."[61]

The Soviets gave the 1961 Convention on the Reduction of Statelessness even shorter shrift: the USSR neither attended the conference which labored to produce the document nor signed the convention. Soviet analysts reflect their government's views when they charge that "some of its provisions were in the nature of attempts to regulate questions which it is in the exclusive competence of a State to settle", ticking off the following items: "the Convention prescribes that a State should confer its nationality on any person born in its territory and even abroad; lays down rules under which no one may be deprived of nationality; allows the possibility for a person to appeal against refusal by a State to grant nationality, and so on".[62]

After that, to hear a Soviet spokesman declare that "in the international legal resolution of questions connected with the condition of statelessness, the Soviet Union always takes an active part",[63] strikes one as a piece of sheer effrontery. Although in empirical terms the statement is utter nonsense, the stylistic motif is nonetheless important and sets the tone for subsequent Soviet pronouncements that betray an awareness of the growing role of international law media in settling citizenship problems. Simply as a rhetorical matter, Soviet commentators find it no longer politic to slight the importance of international law artifacts relating to citizenship phenomena and now openly admit that "increased internationalization of economic and other sides of life, rapid expansion of international contacts and augmentation of movement of population from the territory of one state to the territory of another means that more questions constantly arise apropos the legal status of the population which require international solution".[64] The inevitable result of all this traffic is, they concede, a proliferation of norms of international law, both customary and conventional, designed to handle the awkward fall–out.

However, in a practical sense the Soviet response to these new developments has been to abstain from assuming formal obligations vis–à–vis other states in this area and yet maintain a chic international image by: 1) liberally sprinkling local speech with references to how much value the Soviet regime attaches to international agreements in looking for ways to eliminate causes of statelessness;[65] and, 2) modeling the language of a few clauses of the USSR's latest citizenship statute on the wording of the more innocuous dicta enunciated, say, in the 1961 Convention on the Reduction of Statelessness in order to be able then to claim that the Soviet citizenship agenda matches modern universal standards.[66] The facade may serve to deceive the unwary, but anyone who has ever bothered to consult the record will quickly see through the artifice.

The cruel irony of the game is that it undoubtedly is also calculated to distract public attention from the fact that these essentially cosmetic retouches plus a few genuine improvements on the margin of the main script coincide with a virtual explosion in the number of cases of statelessness intentionally occasioned by the policies pursued by the regime. While castigating "capitalist" states for stripping suspected "subversive elements" of their citizenship followed by deportation proceedings or summary imprisonment,[67] the Soviet authorities have in recent years resorted with increasing frequency to the technique of denaturalization by executive decree as a means of ridding the country of ideological dissidents and other individuals officially considered non gratae. On an even grander scale, the Soviet government is today responsible for saddling the world with thousands of new apatrides by making emigration largely contingent on prior renunciation of Soviet citizenship, leaving the host countries to grapple with the mass influx of stateless souls. A modest effort to curtail the incidence of statelessness spawned by accident is thus more than offset by greater proneness to churn out sizable amounts of the fabricated specimen, a performance which an outside observer is free to denounce as an act of hypocrisy or excuse as an example of fine discrimination between sympathy for innocent victims of historical circumstances and implacability toward "determined trouble–makers".

NOTES

1. B. Volin, *Grazhdanin SSSR*, Moscow 1938, p.18. In the same vein, A.I. Lepeshkin, *Kurs Sovetskogo gosudarstvennogo prava*, Moscow 1961, Vol.1, pp.461, 469; F.I. Kozhevnikov, *Sovetskoe gosudarstvo i mezhdunarodnoe pravo, 1917–1947 gg.*, Moscow 1948, p.166; *Diplomaticheskii slovar'*, Moscow 1960, Vol.1, p.405.
   For similar comments by non–Soviet authors, see D.V. Sandifer, "Soviet Citizenship", *American Journal of International Law*, 1936, No.4, p.624; T.A. Taracouzio, *op. cit.*, pp.90–91; R. Dufour, "La nationalité dans l'U.R.S.S.", *Revue Générale de Droit International Public*, 1930, pp.511, 516.
   F.I. Kozhevnikov, *op. cit.*, p.167, notes, too, that "the Soviet state was also the first in 1934 to submit to the League of Nations the question of marriage, seeking the adoption of a special international convention on the subject that contracting a marriage should not affect the citizenship of the bride". V.S. Shevtsov, *Sovetskoe grazhdanstvo*, Moscow 1965, p.49, refers to the same incident.
   For a contemporary commentary, see I.S. Pereterskii, "Sovetskaia initsiativa v Lige Natsii po voprosu ravnopravii zhenshchin", *Sovetskoe gosudarstvo*, 1934, No.6, pp.66–67.
2. Except that F.I. Kozhevnikov, *op. cit.*, p.167, implied that by special dispensation of the proper authorities, permission could in individual cases be given to marry a foreigner even then. For the text of the decree of February 15, 1947, see *VVS SSSR*, 1947, No.10, and for the text of the law of February 4, 1948, confirming the decree and repealing expressis verbis Article 5 of the 1938 statute, *ibid.*, 1948, No.6.
3. For the text of the edict of November 26, 1953, see *VVS SSSR*, 1953, No.49; and for the text of the law confirming it, *ibid.*, 1954, No.10.
4. I. Trainin, "K voprosu o grazhdanstve", *Sovetskoe gosudarstvo*, 1938, No.5, p.70.
5. E.g., M. Rusakov, "Sovetskoe grazhdanstvo (Praktika RSFSR)", *Administrativnyi vestnik*, 1930, No.3, pp.18–20; *idem*, "Brak i grazhdanstvo po sovetskomu zakonodatel'stvu", *ibid.*, 1927, No.10–11, pp.104–108; N.I. Palienko, "Pravo grazhdanstva v Soiuze SSR", *Vestnik sovetskoi iustitsii*, 1925, No.7, p.272; S.S. Kishkin, *Sovetskoe grazhdanstvo*, Moscow 1925, pp.44–47.
6. See A.G. Budanov, *Demokraticheskaia Respublika V'etnam, Osnovy gosudarstvennogo stroia*, Moscow 1975, pp.116–117.
7. Text in *Beijing Review*, 1980, No.40, pp.17–18. See, too, the comments by Gong Qiuxiang, "On the Nationality Law", *Beijing Review*, 1980, No.45, p.24, and the author's "The 1980 Nationality Law of the People's Republic of China", *American Journal of Comparative Law*, 1982, No.3, pp.459–498.
8. Texts in *VVS SSSR*, 1944, No.35, and No.38; texts of the edicts in English in V. Gsovski, *Soviet Civil Law*, Ann Arbor 1949, Vol.2, pp.302–304.
9. See, *Ukrainska RSR u mizhnarodnikh vidnosinakh*, Kiev 1959, pp.193–199; *Belorusskaia SSR v mezdunarodnykh otnosheniiakh*, Minsk 1960, pp.207–214; *Soviet Foreign Policy during the Patriotic War, documents and materials*, London, n.d., tr. by A. Rothstein, Vol.2, pp.138–139; L. Gelberg, *Prawo miedzynarodowe i historia dyplomaticzna, wybór dokumentów*, Warsaw 1960, Vol.3, pp.178–180.
10. *Izvestiia*, July 11, 1946; *Vneshniaia politika Sovetskogo Soiuza, 1946 god, dokumenty i materialy*, Moscow 1952, p.149. For text of the agreement, see *Sovetsko–chekhoslovatskie otnosheniia 1945–1960 gg., dokumenty i materialy*, Moscow 1972, pp.73–82.
11. *Izvestiia*, March 26, 1957; *VVS SSSR*, 1957, No.16, Art.418; *Sbornik deistvuiushchikh dogovorov, soglashenii i konventsii, zakliuchennykh SSSR s inostrannymi gosudarstvami*, Moscow 1960, Vol.19, pp.107–112.

12. For an analysis of these and other Soviet agreements on option and exchanges of population during this period, see the author's "Option of Nationality in Soviet Treaty Law: The War–Time and Post–War Record", *Iowa Law Review*, 1964, No.4, pp.1130–1176.
13. A.I. Denisov & M.G. Kirichenko, *Sovetskoe gosudarstvennoe pravo*, Moscow 1957, p.139.
14. *Ibid.*
15. *Laws Concerning Nationality*, United Nations Legislative Series, ST/LEG/SER. B74., New York 1954, pp.437–439. Also, R.W. Flournoy, Jr., & M.O. Hudson, eds., *A Collection of Nationality Laws of Various Countries as Contained in Constitutions, Statutes and Treaties*, New York 1929, pp.537–540.
16. Among other things, the provisions of the edict could only be carried out properly on the condition of close cooperation between the Soviet Union and Spain, yet, because diplomatic relations between them did not exist, domestic legislation had to be used, reenforced by understandings reached through various non–governmental agencies, in particular the Spanish Red Cross. See the report in the *New York Times*, July 29, 1956, p.5.
17. G.K. Dmitrieva, *Mezhdunarodnaia zashchita prav zhenshchiny*, Kiev 1975, p.113.
18. O.E. Polents, in E.A. Korovin, ed., *Mezhdunarodnoe pravo*, Moscow 1951, p.233; D. Gaidukov, *Grazhdanstvo SSSR*, Moscow 1940, p.31; Ia.N. Umanskii, *Sovetskoe gosudarstvennoe pravo*, Moscow 1960, p.218; I.D. Levin, in I.P. Trainin & I.D. Levin, eds., *Sovetskoe gosudarstvennoe pravo*, Moscow 1948, p.263.
19. D. Gaidukov, *op. cit.*, p.29. Also, I.D. Levin, in I.P. Trainin & I.D. Levin, eds., *op. cit.*, p.263, and "O proekte Zakona 'O grazhdanstve SSSR', Doklad deputata Bulganina, N.A.", *Pravda* and *Izvestiia*, August 18, 1938.
20. E.g. O.E. Polents, in E.A. Korovin, ed., *op. cit.*, p.233; Ia.N. Umanskii, *op. cit.*, p.219; A.I. Lepeshkin, *op. cit.*, p.471; editorial, "Zakon o grazhdanstve SSSR", *Izvestiia*, August 18, 1939.
21. See "Polozhenie o vidakh na zhitel'stvo dlia inostrantsev", enacted by resolution of the NKVD of June 15, 1927, published in *Izvestiia*, June 26, 1927.
22. D. Gaidukov, *op. cit.*, p.28.
23. A.A. Esaian, *Nekotorye voprosy sovetskogo grazhdanstva, Voprosy naseleniia v praktike Sovetskoi Armenii*, Erevan 1966, p.17.
24. I.D. Levin, in I.P. Trainin & I.D. Levin, eds., *op. cit.*, p.264; A.I. Lepeshkin, *op. cit.*, p.475.
25. See, M. Ruby, *L'Évolution de la nationalité allemande d'après les textes (1842 à 1953)*, Baden–Baden 1954, pp.665, 723.
26. To cite just one example, *Russkaia tikhookeanskaia epopeia*, Khabarovsk 1979, p.563, contains a statement to the effect that: "Immediately after the end of the war, almost half of the permanent inhabitants of this region (9,419 individuals out of 18,845) left from the southern portion of the Kurile islands to Japan. By the summer of 1949, virtually all the Japanese returned to their homeland, with the exception of 12 individuals who decided to stay in their former place of residence and acquire Soviet citizenship."
27. For example, E.Ia. Chernomordik, "K voprosu o dvoinom grazhdanstve v inostrannom i mezhdunarodnom prave", *Sovetskoe gosudarstvo i pravo*, 1947, No.1, p.57.
28. By contrast, the legislation of some of the other socialist countries has on occasion extended voting rights to non–citizens as well. For example, on December 31, 1956, the State Council of Poland granted suffrage to stateless persons permanently residing in Poland in connection with elections to the Sejm. The 1957 law on elections to the National Councils featured an analogous norm, mutatis mutandis. See, B.A. Strashun, *Izbiratel'noe pravo sotsialisticheskikh gosudarstv*, Moscow 1963, p.42.

29. D.L. Zlatopol'skii, *Gosudarstvennoe ustroistvo SSSR*, Moscow 1960, p.258. Cf., V.M. Safronov, *Ty — grazhdanin Sovetskogo Soiuza*, Moscow 1978, p.14; L.B. Kuzmenko, "Razvitie pravovogo regulirovaniia statusa lichnosti v novom zakone o grazhdanstve SSSR", *Vestnik Moskovskogo un–ta*, 1980, No.4, seriia 11: Pravo, p.31; V.S. Shevtsov, *Grazhdanstvo v sovetskom soiuznom gosudarstve*, Moscow 1969, p.112; S.V. Chernichenko, *Mezhdunarodno–pravovye voprosy grazhdanstva*, Moscow 1968, pp. 141–142; B.V. Shchetinin, *Problemy teorii sovetskogo gosudarstvennogo prava*, Moscow 1974, p.195.
30. Viz., *Sbornik zakonov SSSR i ukazov Prezidiuma Verkhovnogo Soveta SSSR (1938g. –noiabr 1958g.)*, Moscow 1959, p.75; S.S. Studenikin, ed., *Istoriia Sovetskoi Konstitutsii (v dokumentakh), 1917–1956*, Moscow 1957, pp.803–804; G.E. Vilkov, comp., *Zakonodatel'stvo SSSR i mezhdunarodnye soglasheniia po voprosam grazhdanstva*, Moscow 1964, pp.23–24; A.I. Lepeshkin, ed., *Sbornik ofitsial'nykh dokumentov (primenitel'no k kursu sovetskogo gosudarstvennogo prava)*, Moscow 1964, pp.210–211.
31. V.S. Shevtsov, *op. cit.* (note 29 above), p.112.
32. G.V. Ignatenko, in G.V. Ignatenko & D.D. Ostapenko, eds., *Mezhdunarodnoe pravo*, Moscow 1978, p.182.
33. A.I. Lepeshkin, *op. cit.*, p.471. Also, V. Shevtsov, *Citizenship of the USSR (A Legal Study)*, Moscow 1979, p.111: "There are not so many stateless persons residing in the USSR. The reason why this is so is that most persons of foreign descent habitually residing in the USSR have acquired Soviet citizenship and have become equal citizens of the Soviet Union."
34. S.V. Chernichenko, *op. cit.* (note 29 above), p.142. Likewise, V. Shevtsov, *op. cit.* (note 33 above), p.103: "As a result [of the 1954 decree], the number of stateless persons sharply dropped."
35. *Khronika zashchity prav v SSSR*, New York 1975, vyp.12, pp.50–51.
36. *Khronika tekushchikh sobytii* (Moscow 1979), New York 1980, vyp.53, p.139.
37. *Khronika zashchity prav v SSSR*, New York 1976, vyp.23–24, pp.54–67; *Khronika tekushchikh sobytii*, New York 1976, vyp.42, pp.63–64; V. Bukovskii, *"I vozvrashchaetsia veter ..."*, New York 1978, pp.365–368.
38. E.g., V. Shevtsov, *op. cit.* (note 33 above), p.111; *idem*, *Sovetskoe gosudarstvo i lichnost'*, Moscow 1978, p.17; L.B. Kuzmenko, *op. cit.*, p.31.
39. S.V. Chernichenko, *op. cit.* (note 29 above), p.99.
40. *Ibid.*, p.138.
41. D.L. Zlatopol'skii, *op. cit.*, p.261.
42. V.S. Shevtsov, *op. cit.* (note 1 above), p.45. Also, idem, *op. cit.* (note 44 above), p.112.
43. A.A. Esaian, *op. cit.*, pp.114–115.
44. V. Shevtsov, *op. cit.* (note 33 above), p.103.
45. L.B. Kuzmenko, *op. cit.*, p.31.
46. Federal edict of June 15, 1979, *VVS SSSR*, 1979, No.25, Art.436.
47. V. Durdenevskii, "Zakon o grazhdanstve Soiuza Sovetskikh Sotsialisticheskikh Respublik", *Problemy sotsialisticheskogo prava*, 1938, No.6, p.64. In similar vein, V.V. Polianskii, "Printsipy sovetskogo grazhdanstva", *Sovetskoe gosudarstvo i pravo*, 1980, No.5, p.128.
48. For example, the various decrees of 1945–1947 on the restoration of Soviet citizenship to certain persons abroad.
49. G.I. Tunkin, ed., *Mezhdunarodnoe pravo*, Moscow 1974, p.220.
50. See the author's "The Soviet Union and the Problem of Refugees and Displaced Persons, 1917–1956", *American Journal of International Law*, 1957, No.2, pp.344– 361.

51. J.-Y. Calvez, *Droit International et Souveraineté en U.R.S.S.*, Paris 1953, p.175, citing R. Ristelhuber, *Au service des réfugiés*, Paris 1950.

52. D. Gaidukov, *op. cit.*, p.28; A.I. Lepeshkin, *op. cit.*, pp.466–467; F.I. Kozhevnikov, *op. cit.*, pp.164–165; A.I. Denisov, in A.I. Denisov & M.G. Kirichenko, *Sovetskoe gosudarstvennoe pravo*, Moscow 1957, p.139.

53. I. Trainin, *op. cit.*, p.69; K.Ia. Chizhov, in F.I. Kozhevnikov, ed., *Mezhdunarodnoe pravo*, Moscow 1957, p.151.

54. V.V. Polianskii, *op. cit.*, p.128.

55. "O proekte Zakona SSSR o grazhdanstve SSSR", Doklad pervogo zamestitelia Predsedatelia Prezidiuma Verkhovnogo Soveta SSSR V.V. Kuznetsova, *Pravda*, Dec. 2, 1978, p.2.

56. E.g., O.E. Polents, in E.A. Korovin, ed., *op. cit.*, pp.233–234; K.Ia. Chizhov, in F.I. Kozhevnikov, ed., *op. cit.*, p.152.

With the enactment of the new civil codes, Soviet lawyers can now document their claims by pointing to Article 123 of the Principles of Civil Legislation of the USSR and union republics and Article 60 of the Principles of Civil Procedure of the USSR and union republics. The former provides that "stateless persons residing in the USSR shall enjoy civil legal capacity equally with Soviet citizens. Exemptions may be established by the law of the USSR". The latter states that "stateless persons resident in the USSR shall have the right to apply to the court and shall enjoy civil procedural rights equally with Soviet citizens".

Now, of course, there is the comprehensive Law on the legal status of foreigners in the USSR of June 24, 1981 (scheduled to enter into force on January 1, 1982), whose provisions, according to the official rapporteur of the bill, N.V. Talyzin, extend to stateless persons as well, unless otherwise prescribed by the legislation of the USSR. For text of the Law, the Resolution putting it into effect and the report by Talyzin, see *Pravda* and *Izvestiia*, June 25, 1981.

57. S.S. Kishkin, *op. cit.*, p.3; Report by the People's Commissar for Foreign Affairs, G.B. Chicherin, on Union Citizenship at the 2nd session of the 2nd convocation of the CEC of the USSR, morning meeting of October 24, 1924, *Stenograficheskii otchet 2 sessii TsIK soiuza SSR 2 sozyva*, Moscow 1924, p.496.

58. *Bolshaia Sovetskaia Entsiklopediia*, 2nd ed., Mocow 1952, Vol.12, p.421; *Malaia Sovetskaia Entsiklopediia*, 3rd ed., Moscow 1959, Vol.3, p.98.

59. See, for instance, the two articles by S.V. Chernichenko, "K voprosu o znachenii grazhdanstva v sovremennom mezhdunarodnom prave", *Vestnik Moskovskogo universiteta*, seriia X: pravo, 1963, No.3, pp.52–61, and "Pravo natsii na samoopredelenie i voprosy grazhdanstva", *Sovetskoe gosudarstvo i pravo*, 1964, No.1, pp. 110–114.

60. *Iuridicheskii slovar'*, 2nd ed., Moscow 1956, Vol.1, p.58. Likewise, V.I. Menzhinskii, in F.I. Kozhevnikov, eds., *Mezhdunarodnoe pravo*, Moscow 1964, pp.281–282: "These draft conventions, as well as the draft conventions on questions of dual nationality, in the main reflect the concept of primacy of international law over internal state law and fail to take into account that questions of regulation of citizenship primarily belong to the internal competence of the respective state." In similar vein, G.E. Vilkov, "Mezhdunarodno-pravovoe regulirovanie voprosov dvoinogo grazhdanstva", *Sovetskii ezhegodnik mezhdunarodnogo prava 1959*, Moscow 1960, pp.366–367.

For a critical survey of the record of the League of Nations and the United Nations in this field, see G.E. Vilkov, "Mezhdunarodno-pravovoe regulirovanie voprosov bezgrazhdanstva", *Sovetskii ezhegodnik mezhdunarodnogo prava 1963*, Moscow 1965, pp.260–270.

61. S.V. Chernichenko, *op. cit.* (note 29 above), p.147. For a general discussion of the

problem, see *ibid.*, pp.144–153.

62. V. Shevtsov, *op. cit.* (note 33 above), p.109. S.V. Chernichenko, *op. cit.* (note 29 above), pp.153–156.
63. V.S. Shevtsov, *op. cit.* (note 1 above), p.45.
64. G.I. Tunkin, ed., *op. cit.*, pp.215–216.
65. E.g., V. Shevtsov, *op. cit.* (note 33 above), p.111.
66. See, S.I. Rusinova, *op. cit.*, p.8.
67. *Idem*, "Voprosy grazhdanstva v evropeiskikh stranakh narodnoi demokratii", *Uchenye zapiski Leningradskogo gosudarstvennogo universiteta*, No.201, seriia iuridicheskikh nauk, vyp.7, 1955, pp.176–177.

ACQUISITION OF USSR CITIZENSHIP

The contents of Chapter II of the 1978 citizenship statute which deals with the subject of acquisition of USSR citizenship evince the most substantial changes consummated by the latest enactment in the existing law on Soviet citizenship.

1. Grounds for Acquiring USSR Citizenship

The 1978 citizenship act strikes a new note by featuring a general provision that lists the grounds for acquiring USSR citizenship.[1] Thus, according to Article 10, USSR citizenship is acquired by birth, as a result of being admitted to USSR citizenship, upon grounds determined by international treaties of the USSR, and upon other grounds recognized by the present Law. Soviet authors consider the innovation a material improvement over the previous script by virtue of the fact that the current formula

> "significantly supplemented the grounds for acquiring USSR citizenship compared with the 1938 Law, establishing norms: on the most common means of acquiring Soviet citizenship — by birth; on grounds determined by international treaties of the USSR; on other grounds recognized by the Law (like adoption)".[2]

Actually, the added text offers no real surprises and its chief contribution seems to be stylistic, namely, to spell out the principal ways by which people enter into possession of Soviet citizenship — all of which also operated under the old system, but without benefit of express legislative confirmation. The mention of treaties in this connection marks the only slight difference in tone: traditionally, Soviet analysts have been prone to look at citizenship questions essentially through the prism of municipal law. Willingness now to concede the role played by international accords reflects two recent developments that have tended to modify the original attitude: first, the Soviet government has in the past few years elected in several instances to resort to the medium of international agreements in order to take care of assorted citizenship problems which had arisen between the USSR and other states[3] and has acceded to various universal conventions which focus on sundry aspects of nationality from the human rights angle; second, Soviet legislation today frequently features references to the USSR's international stake in a bid apparently to underline the expanding scope of the Soviet diplomatic agenda and advertise Moscow's avowed intention to honor its foreign commitments.

Next, the statement has been made that the enumeration contained in Article 10 is "exhaustive", meaning that "no legislative or substatutory acts can prescribe any other grounds for acquiring Soviet citiznship as well as repeal or limit their application".[4] The claim is rather doubtful. Already on earlier occasions, for instance, while discussing proposed reforms in the citizenship legislation of the USSR, local writers had drawn up a far more comprehensive roster of the methods for obtaining Soviet citizenship, a catalogue that included the following contingencies: 1) birth; 2) adoption; 3) naturalization (admission to citizenship); 4) territorial changes (but not automatically); 5) repatriation; and, 6) option (choice of one particular citizenship).[5] It is fairly safe to assume that in the future Soviet citizenship may still be acquired in such eventualities, even though the 1978 act fails to list all of these cases: certainly, one cannot imagine the Soviet regime denying itself the opportunity, say, of assigning its citizenship to the permanent inhabitants of a territory that might some day be incorporated into the USSR simply because the relevant statute does not specify that transfer of territorial title can validly effectuate "conversion" to Soviet citizenship of the affected indigenous population.

A further item worth noting at this point is the absence from both the recommendations and the final version of any indication that the phenomenon of state succession likewise fits the bill as a viable mechanism for staging a "reception" into Soviet citizenship. What Soviet spokesmen have in mind here is not changes of ownership between socialist and bourgeois states, but inheritance "by a new state of the population and, hence, the territory of the old state on which it resides":

> "The method of succession rso understoodt is not an ordinary method of acquiring rights of citizenship and it cannot be placed on the same footing with the other methods. It may be characterized as a constitutive method sui generis of establishing the citizenship of a new state ..."[6]

The Soviet experience in Russia reportedly illustrates the above thesis in the sense that the victory of the Bolshevik revolution and the attendant "birth of a new state" set the scene for the Soviet regime to designate as its original citizens all physical persons who on November 7, 1917, were subjects of the former Russian empire and had not lost Soviet citizenship. The overwhelming majority of individuals who currently figure as Soviet citizens qualify by reason of the fact that Soviet citizenship was ascribed to their forebears pursuant to this concept of Soviet Russia as natural heir to Russia's national patrimony, including its people. By the same token, the present administration in the USSR may yet regard some elements now living abroad as inherently entitled to Soviet citizenship by virtue of this doctrine and vested with a latent claim to return to the ancestral fold waiting to be exercised at an opportune moment through a process of "summary reversion" keyed to the theme of the primacy of "native roots": this access route is not recorded in the 1978 citizenship act, but the oversight is not apt to prevent its official use for the sake of expediency, despite the contention that the pronouncements of Article 10 are dispositive on the issue.

2. Acquisition of USSR Citizenship by Birth

The copy of *Izvestiia* for April 10, 1968, carried on page 4 the full text of the draft of the "Basic Principles of Legislation of the USSR and Union Republics on Marriage and the Family".[7] Article 30 of the bill, incorporated without change in the final edition of the statute enacted on June 27, 1968 (and next reproduced as Article 160 of the RSFSR Code of Marriage and Family),[8] read:

> "Citizenship of children
>
> A child, both of whose parents are citizens of the USSR at the moment of its birth, is recognized as a citizen of the USSR, irrespective of the place of birth.
>
> If the parents hold different citizenship and one of them is a citizen of the USSR at the moment of the child's birth, the child is recognized as a citizen of the USSR if at least one of the parents was resident on USSR territory at the time. If, however, both parents were resident outside the USSR at the moment of birth, the child's citizenship is established by agreement between the parents."

With that, Soviet law here reverted in every detail but one to the formula featured in the first federal "Regulation on Union Citizenship" of October 29, 1924.[9] The lone exception lies in the latter's inclusion of an additional proposition to the effect that "on reaching majority this person [i.e., the one whose citizenship was established by agreement between the parents' whereupon they chose for their offspring a citizenship other than that of the USSR] could obtain the citizenship of the USSR by a simplified form of procedure", which the present version does not contain.

How much difference this makes is debatable in any case, since the proposed "simplified form of procedure" was never spelled out and the closest we get to finding out what the authors of the clause may have been contemplating is a suggestion de lege ferenda from the pen of a contemporary commentator that: 1) the mechanics of the matter should be defined by federal law; 2) probably the most feasible way of handling the question would be by acknowledging "a declaratory right of entry into Soviet citizenship on the condition that the de cujus at the moment of reaching majority reside on the territory of the USSR"; 3) further, the instructions ought to indicate that "the application of this simplified form of procedure may take place only during a designated period (let us say, during one year) after attaining majority"; and, 4) "in the event the corresponding persons resided abroad, they could be admitted to Soviet citizenship on a discretionary basis by the plenipotentiary representatives of the USSR abroad".[10]

The reason for omitting this item very likely stems from the Soviet leadership's overt rejection since 1938 of all devices, once quite common in Soviet administrative usage, routinely sanctioning the technique of "speeded–up" naturalization, renaturalization and denaturalization in various situations. Solely ad hoc dispensation engineered by medium of special decrees emanating from the central authorities henceforth operated to alter the criteria and tempo governing the acquisition or loss of Soviet citizenship on particular occasions.

At any rate, the important aspect for our purposes is that the key elements of the 1924 norm were thus revived, following a switch in the Regulations of June 13, 1930, and April 22, 1931,[11] to rigid adherence to the extreme concept of jus sanguinis pursuant to which an individual was "considered a citizen of the USSR by virtue of birth when at the time of birth both parents were citizens of the USSR or one of them was". Again, although the Law on the Citizenship of the USSR, promulgated on August 19, 1938, nowhere mentioned the subject of acquisition of Soviet citizenship at birth, most students of Soviet jurisprudence were nonetheless convinced that, despite the formal repeal of the 1931 statute by the edict of June 2, 1939,[12] the past (post–June 13, 1930) rule of ascribing Soviet citizenship by descent to a child even if just one of its parents was then a Soviet citizen, independently of where it was born, continued fully in force. As an eminent foreign observer of the Soviet juridical scene opined at the time:

> "The fact that in the Soviet practice this principle rof jus sanguinist has always been considered preeminent as compared with that of jus soli prompts an assumption that the principle of jus sanguinis is now regarded as self–understood and so firmly accepted in Soviet practice that there is no longer any need for referring to it in a legislative act."[13]

For many years, this thesis seemed eminently sound. True, most Soviet writers in analyzing the provisions of the 1938 law did not explain whether Soviet citizenship passed by descent and how: the text shed no light on the topic and they apparently did not feel called upon to remedy the oversight. Still, the few among them who chose to tackle the problem unanimously found that "at the root of acquisition of the citizenship of the USSR through birth lies the blood principle"[14] or endorsed the idea that a child born of Soviet parents was ipso jure a citizen of the USSR.[15] To the extent that these sources dealt with the legal status of the progeny of a Soviet father and mother, the accounts are accurate enough, as is, too, the companion statement that, in this instance, neither "an exercise of will on the part of the parents is required" nor "is the person's locus of birth (on the territory of the USSR or the territory of a foreign state) relevant" for the determination of Soviet citizenship.[16] What ensued when just one parent of the child was a Soviet citizen and the birth occurred abroad — precisely the type of contingency which produces innumerable complications — was left unuttered. However, in the absence of any intimations to the contrary from the people on the spot, outsiders tended to conclude that, as hitherto, a parent with Soviet citizenship could singly transmit his citizenship to the offspring at nativity, irrespective of the place of birth.

Yet, after 1965, a degree of confusion crept into this picture, which had looked so clear at the outset. The author of a brochure specifically devoted to the theme of Soviet citizenship, published in that year, unambiguously declared:

> "One of the most common instances of recognition of citizenship is acquisition of citizenship by birth.
>
> Said question was not settled by the Law on the Citizenship of the USSR of 1938. Thus, it does not say anything about the fact that children both of whose parents are Soviet citizens are recognized as Soviet citizens by birth. *The Law also maintains silence on the question of the citizenship by birth of a child in the event that only one of its parents is a Soviet citizen, although from the sense of the law it follows that in that case functions the principle of agreement by the parents*."[17]

The last sentence was not altogether correct, of course. Even if one were, for the sake of argument, prepared to concede the general validity of that assertion, it would still have to be substantially modified to stipulate that the parents' shared preference on this score dictated the outcome, at best, if the child was born abroad and if the father also was outside the confines of the USSR on the critical date. Failure to meet either condition entailed automatic acquisition of Soviet citizenship by the child at birth, the above contention notwithstanding. But that is a marginal detail; the significant ingredient was the claim that the rule of jus sanguinis in its most radical articulation did not monopolize the process of acquisition of Soviet citizenship by lineal devolution and that instead, under certain circumstances, the parents' joint wish reportedly played a decisive role here.

An equally explicit, and technically more accurate, treatment of this issue next surfaced in a 1966 booklet by an Armenian jurist,[18] in which he commended to the attention of the legislators a model of "A Regulation on the Citizenship of the Armenian SSR" and a project of "New Rules on Soviet Citizenship". Both samples purported to synthesize and refine pertinent past experience in this field and to build on existing practices, and by and large that is indeed an apt description of the writer's efforts. Nevertheless, this did not prevent him from frankly advocating a solution according to which the prospective republican statute would classify as citizens of the Armenian SSR, inter alios,

> "persons born on the territory of the USSR if at the moment of birth one of their parents possessed the citizenship of the Armenian SSR, and the other the citizenship of a foreign state, as well as persons even though born abroad if at the moment of birth one of the parents was a citizen of the Armenian SSR provided the father at the moment of the person's birth resided on the territory of the USSR.
>
> If one of the parents possessed the citizenship of the Armenian SSR and the other the citizenship of a foreign state and at the moment of the child's birth both parents resided outside the territory of the USSR, the citizenship of the child was determined by agreement of the parents."[19]

A similar approach was envisaged at the federal level:

> "3. Are deemed citizens of a Union Republic and thereby of the USSR persons whose parents are citizens of the given Union Republic regardless of where these persons are born.
>
> Are deemed citizens of a Union Republic and thereby of the USSR persons one of whose parents at the moment of birth was a Soviet citizen provided that at least one of them at that moment resided on the territory of the USSR.
>
> The citizenship of a person one of whose parents possessed Soviet citizenship at the moment of birth while both parents resided at that moment outside the territory of the USSR is determined by agreement of the parents."[20]

Finally, a collective volume on Soviet constitutional law, dated 1967 and approved by the Ministry of Higher and Middle Special Education of the USSR as a text for students of law institutes and faculties, in the section reserved for a summation of the highlights of recent Soviet citizenship legislation, plainly told its intended audience that

> "if the parents have different citizenship, one of them possesses the citizenship of the USSR and the other holds a foreign citizenship, provided at least

one of the parents at the moment of birth of the child resides on the territory of the USSR, the child is counted as a Soviet citizen. If, on the other hand, one of the parents was a citizen of the USSR at the moment of a child's birth, but both parents resided outside the frontiers of the USSR, the question of the child's citizenship is resolved by agreement of the parents."[21]

A footnote referred the reader to Articles 14 and 35 of the Ukrainian SSR and RSFSR codes of Laws on Marriage, Family, and Guardianship, respectively.

In view of these developments, the official modus operandi in this area may then very well have already been in the process of shifting from the initial commitment to the purist interpretation of the institution of jus sanguinis to the compound formula associated with the 1924 federal act. If so, the trend did not go entirely unchallenged. At least one Soviet lawyer rose to the defense of the old order. In a critique of a compilation of the laws of the USSR and international agreements concerning citizenship questions, the editor was roundly chided for having neglected to reproduce in his survey the Union law of April 22, 1931, in a tone suggestive of a deeper doctrinal cleavage rather than mere divergence over problems of scholarly methodology. To wit: "The Collection has certain shortcomings. Thus, in the first section there should have been included the Regulation on the Citizenship of the USSR of April 22, 1931. It is interesting in the respect that in it is precisely formulated the principle of blood on which also rests the Law on the Citizenship of the USSR of August 19, 1938, even though the latter contains no direct reference to that principle."[22]

The second incident involved a frontal encounter. When the draft of the Basic Principles of Legislation of the USSR and Union Republics on Marriage and the Family was disseminated through the press as an invitation to mass discussion, the same lonely voice was heard objecting to the contents of Article 30, insisting that "in practice the rule is applied whereby the child of a Soviet citizen is deemed a Soviet citizen independently of the place of birth" and urging that "it would be advisable to set that very rule in Article 30". In place of the published version, the following wording was proposed: "A child both of whose parents were Soviet citizens at the time of birth or one of whom was is recognized as a citizen of the USSR wherever he may have been born, unless otherwise provided by an international treaty to which the USSR is a party." The whole business of "agreement of the parents" was to be eliminated.[23]

As it turned out, the last–minute attempted parry was in vain. Moreover, one wonders both if the lack of overt comment itself on what was, after all, an important legislative step does not prove that the result was a foregone conclusion and whether ad hoc administrative enforcement of that procedure over the last few years had perhaps not converted most members of the Soviet legal profession to a position of supporting or simply acquiescing in the reform.[24]

The truth may never be known, but the available bits and pieces of information do suggest that, at some point in 1965 or shortly before, the functioning pattern changed and the Soviet regime again began implementing the 1924 norm in lieu of the substitute prescription introduced in the 1930 and 1931 regulations, without benefit of an official amendment of the statute to mark the transition. In fact, the historical record furnished excellent precedent for such behavior. Thus, while both the 1930 act and its successor of the next year unequivocally proclaimed jus sanguinis as the sole doctrine, the codes of Laws on Marriage, Family, and Guardianship of every Union republic save Georgia, Tadzhikistan, and Uzbekistan continued to contain a section modeled on the original provision of the 1924 federal citizenship charter. In the RSFSR collection, the relevant item — Article 35 — for instance, read: "If the citizenship of the parents is not the same, but at least one of them at the time of the birth of the child was a citizen of the RSFSR, and at least one of the parents at the time of the birth of the child was living on the territory of the USSR, the child shall be considered a citizen of the RSFSR. If one of the parents was a citizen of the RSFSR at the time of the child's birth, but at the time both parents lived outside the territory of the USSR, the citizenship of the child shall be determined by agreement of the parents."

To be sure, everyone has always acknowledged that this clause of the RSFSR compilation and its alter egos in the codes of the other republics were null and void from the moment that they conflicted with the later federal legislation. Yet the republics had never seen fit to bring the offending provisions textually into harmony with the directives of the central government. What is more, when the 1931 statute was in force and the discrepancy between the federal law, on the one hand, and most republican codes, on the other, could not possibly be overlooked, republican organs nevertheless went ahead and invoked their own legislation. Even a Soviet author was moved to observe at the sight of this astonishing spectacle that "it was quite hard to understand why the republican codes retained the norms of 1924 in the face of a contrary resolution of the federal legislation, *and yet practice leaned toward the use of republican codes*". And he illustrated this last remark by recalling a case which transpired in Moscow as late as 1936 where "a child born in Switzerland of a mixed marriage of a woman with a Soviet citizenship and a Swiss was going to be inscribed at the insistence of his father as Swiss on the basis of Article 35 of the Code on Marriage, Family, and Guardianship, the wording of which the leadership of the People's Commissariat of Justice of the RSFSR had not bothered to revise for eight years".[25]

Despite the criticism, the language of that article stayed unchanged until November 1, 1969. Now, if all that could happen when the federal law contained explicit instructions on the subject and the contradiction between the old republican statutes and more recent federal legislation was glaringly obvious, it is permissible to ask oneself whether the chances of such incidents then recurring in the teeth of the 1938 enactment's silence on the issue were not infinitely greater, ultimately perhaps crystallizing into a fixed policy. Of course, after recounting that revealing story, the source just quoted did hasten to add that the promulgation of the Stalin Constitution, "Article 19 of which established the absolute priority of federal over republican law",[26] cured this anomalous situation, but there is serious doubt that this particular problem lay at the root of the current trouble and that a general constitutional injunction per se would set matters aright. Indeed, it is symptomatic that the 1967 textbook on the state law of the USSR which offered an early hint of the probable administrative switch from the 1930/1931 rule to its 1924 counterpart documented the account precisely with reference to the aforecited Article 35 of the RSFSR Code of Laws on Marriage, Family and Guardianship and its clone in the

Ukrainian edition, Article 14.

At any rate, after October 1, 1968, the date when, pursuant to the law of June 27, 1968, the Basic Principles entered into force, the mechanics of acquisition of Soviet citizenship at birth were once again (as in the 1924–1930 interlude) governed by the following propositions: a child born of a Soviet couple was ipso jure vested with Soviet citizenship no matter where born; a child born on Soviet soil of parents only one of whom was a Soviet citizen was likewise immediately classified as a Soviet citizen by virtue of descent; a child born on foreign soil of parents only one of whom was a Soviet citizen and whose father at that moment resided on the territory of the USSR received Soviet citizenship at birth too; finally, the citizenship of a child born on foreign soil of parents only one of whom was a Soviet citizen and whose father at the moment of birth was also abroad was determined by agreement of the parents.

No official explanation for the return to this intricate formula has been furnished so far. Back in 1924, however, when this procedure was first devised, the bill's appointed rapporteur went to considerable lengths to acquaint the assembled delegates with the perceived merits of the scheme and his reasoning may still be largely valid for identifying the motives behind the decision. Noting that the concept of jus soli, if fully adhered to, would lead to endless conflicts with other states, the speaker qualified the solution adopted by the federal Council of People's Commissars as "somewhat more modest" for, in his words, it meant:

> "first, that if on our territory reside a husband and wife and one of them is a Soviet citizen, where we are concerned this will suffice for the recognition of their children as Soviet citizens. If the child was born abroad, though, i.e., the wife was abroad at that moment, while the father was located on our territory, in that case this child is nevertheless recognized as a Soviet citizen if one of the two — husband or wife — is a Soviet citizen. Two cases are thus possible: the wife was abroad, the child was born there; the father is a Soviet citizen. Quite clearly: since the father is a Soviet citizen and his wife and child are temporarily located abroad, the child will be a Soviet citizen. The second case is the reverse: the wife is a Soviet citizen and she went abroad, the child is born abroad; the father is a foreigner. And so again, since the father resides on our territory, consequently, is bound to our territory, is bound to our state and his wife is a Soviet citizen, then this will be enough for the recognition of their children as Soviet citizens. But one cannot, of course, hide the fact that from this principle may also develop, although in lesser degree, collisions with other states and we must, undoubtedly, conclude conventions in which we will have to resolve all these cases of definition of the citizenship of children one way or another.
>
> Further, a completely different case — if both parents reside abroad. The question of the citizenship of persons, one of whose parents was a citizen of the USSR at the moment of birth whereas both parents resided at that moment outside the territory of the USSR, is settled by agreement of the parents. For example, a German prisoner of war married a Soviet citizen and together with her went back home to Saxony or Bavaria and children are born to them there. Naturally, the local authorities consider the children of the former German prisoner of war as German citizens, but his wife is a

Soviet citizen and he perhaps contracted enough of a liking for our system, our state and desired that his children become Soviet citizens. How he will manage with the German authorities — that is his business; but when this child recognized as a Soviet citizen by agreement of the parents comes to our land, we will recognize him as a Soviet citizen.

Another case: if the father, a Soviet citizen, settled abroad and the wife is a foreigner. In foreign legislations, under these circumstances the citizenship of the children is dictated by the citizenship of the father, but we cannot share that point of view. The bourgeois states up till now stand on the grounds of the inequality of men and women, the inequality of husband and wife, and that is why in accordance with the legislation of bourgeois states the citizenship of the father determines the citizenship of the children. We cannot accept that attitude and that is why we must determine the citizenship of children by other methods. Meanwhile, since this family resides on foreign territory we must take into account this completely alien environment in which the parents may, despite the formal citizenship of one or the other, turn into elements entirely alien to us. That is why we must in this case rely on the agreement between the parents. What will happen if such an agreement is not forthcoming? The text of the law itself says nothing about that because the answer is self–evident: if no agreement exists, the question is resolved in conformity with the laws of the country where these citizens reside; agreement did not take place, we cannot meddle in the life of another country and mores utterly alien to us, if the unanimous decision of the parents does not give us a basis and one must reckon with the fact that the citizenship of the children in this instance is established by the legislation of the country where they reside."[27]

Two main themes are in evidence here: 1) the regime thereby sought to cut down on the incidence of dual or multiple nationality affecting individuals whom it claimed as its own citizens; 2) in granting its citizenship by lineal descent in the marginal situation of an issue of a mixed marriage born to a couple residing abroad, it fixed a minimum standard of effective relationship between the de cujus and the mother country as demonstrated by the freely expressed choice by the parents of Soviet citizenship for their progeny. Essentially the same objectives are pursued today.

In adopting its present policy, Moscow plainly intended further to reduce the frequency of incipience, through the international operation of the phenomenon of conflicts of laws, of dual/plural citizenship episodes involving persons already designated as Soviet citizens. The current solution, just as its 1924 ancestor, certainly serves to accomplish that end and will, without a doubt, henceforward significantly curtail, when compared with the previous experience, the volume of disputes arising out of rival attributions of citizenship status to persons eo ipso blessed (or cursed) with the citizenship of more than one state by grace of the asynchronous stipulations of the domestic legislation of the interested parties. For that matter, should dual citizenship still occur in a context where the parents have the opportunity to register a preference on behalf of their offspring, the USSR can tout its position by pointing out that on this occasion it is the other state's obtrusive confer-ment of its nationality on grounds of lex situ which acts to frustrate the parents' wish that their child enter the world strictly as a citizen of the Soviet Union. The Soviets themselves are not prepared to make any more "concessions" in order to avoid the confrontation and their spokesmen, after posing the question "whether the parents can select Soviet citizenship for the child if on the territory of the country where it is born the child automatically acquires the citizenship of the given state", categorically respond that "Soviet legislation by no means abrogates the rights granted to the parents to pick for their child the citizenship of the USSR even if the child acquires the citizenship of the other state by birth".[28]

The other aspect apparently reflects the bureaucracy's heightened awareness of the futility of trying to foist Soviet citizenship by fiat on the children of parents who, despite the Soviet citizenship of one spouse, have elected to live abroad and whose own contacts with the Soviet Union are tenuous at best, so that the children born and reared in an alien milieu promise to grow up with almost no feelings for the absent homeland. Blood ties seldom will, under these adverse conditions, compensate for the want of any emotional attachment to the "native sod" and the Soviet hierarchy now seems to appreciate the significance of this cultural estrangement and has here made a concession to reality by abandoning the erstwhile rigid approach which had led it to assign Soviet citizenship mechanically by reason of descent alone in circumstances where, through sheer lack of jurisdictional control over the people concerned, it could not possibly enforce its writ. In those terms, Soviet citizenship had a modicum of nuisance value, perhaps, but achieved very little else, and the very palpable loss of public credibility due to the obvious disparity between fact and fiction did not redound to the USSR's advantage. The latest reform has eliminated this cardinal defect.

The practice of automatic acquisition of Soviet citizenship at birth was preserved, then, in cases where the Soviet citizenship of both parents or the Soviet citizenship of one parent plus either birth on Soviet soil or the father's residence at that moment on Soviet territory offered secure guarantees that the bonds of allegiance to the USSR would be maintained in the future. In the last two variants, the maxim of jus soli, newly reintroduced into Soviet law after being banished in 1930, works to bestow Soviet citizenship on the subject from the instant of birth. The concept's enunciation may be highly unorthodox, but it does manage to dilute the previous total reliance on the principle of jus sanguinis and, in combination with elements of the latter, to afford a broader coverage than would be produced by exclusive dependence on the norm of jus soli or the common attenuated version of the jus sanguinis alternative (i.e., succession solely through the paternal line). Its range is narrower than that of its predecessor (which, in turn, was extreme), but, as noted, the resurrected formula gains commensurately by avoiding some of the inherent difficulties associated with the application of the preceding technique.

The obverse side of the coin cannot be ignored either, of course. The price of the anticipated reduction in the incidence of dual/plural nationality cases and the slight expansion of the radius of the individual's choice in one small corner of the administrative domain was paid for, as already admitted by the official spokesman for the 1924 bill, by the partial surrender of governmental authority over the legal fate of the people involved with a consequent freer interplay of national laws and a greater likelihood that statelessness might ensue. The lapse is partially compensated for by the fact that under the revised modus operandi, as hitherto, statelessness here can never advene involuntarily. It takes a conscious gesture on the part of the responsible adults to trigger a process that might culminate in their child incurring statelessness at birth, but they always have the initial opportunity to dispose of this contingency by deciding that the child shall be a Soviet citizen from birth. Put differently, the blind collision of national laws does not in this instance function to cause statelessness at birth: poor judgment by the parents may; or the parents' deliberate preference for statelessness for their progeny to the status of a Soviet citizen; or if the parents either cannot agree on the item or merely neglect to indicate their desire on that score.

The present solution is far from ideal in that it does not entirely bar the prospect of dual citizenship and makes statelessness possible;[29] this moved a domestic opponent of the experiment to criticize the draft text of Article 30 and urge that the proposed clause be dropped in favor of a straightforward endorsement of the pure rendition of jus sanguinis. The attempt failed, but his cogent arguments bear repeating:

> "It remains unclear whether Soviet citizenship is acquired by a child born at a time when both of its parents, possessing a different citizenship, also resided abroad, if they did not reach any agreement on the question. The citizenship of a child born abroad cannot always be determined by agreement of the parents. Such an agreement is effective when the parents have decided to choose Soviet citizenship for their child. But if they choose for it a foreign citizenship, then the effectiveness of the agreement hinges on the law of the state whose citizenship the second parent holds or the state on whose territory the child was born. Cases are quite possible when the legislation of the foreign state will categorically consider such a child its citizen, independently of whether or not the parents reached an agreement in that connection. For example, the child of a Soviet citizen and a woman who is an Argentinian citizen, born on the territory of Argentina, simultaneously acquires, even though the parents may have decided to choose Soviet citizenship on its behalf, the citizenship of Argentina inasmuch as all persons born in Argentina are deemed by its laws to be Argentinian citizens.
>
> In general, is it advisable to attribute decisive weight to the agreement between the parents on a question so important in a man's life? And if the agreement did not take place? Will the child really lose the right to be a Soviet citizen?"[30]

How many Soviet lawyers think the same way is hard to tell. The number may be considerable, even if none felt called upon to commit his views to print, with this one lone exception. For, quite obviously, not only does the new measure not cure all the related problems to everybody's satisfaction, but now Soviet law is once again saddled with a rule whose prototype often drew from local commentators the epithet of "excessively complex"[31] — a well– earned characterization, especially when contrasted in retrospect with the simple rule on the subject propounded by the 1930 and 1931 statutes.

The 1978 citizenship act follows the example set by the 1968 codification in this matter, but amends one notable detail of the preceding arrangement. To wit, instead of the reference in the context of a child of a mixed marriage (one parent being a Soviet citizen) born abroad to the test of the father residing on Soviet soil at the time of the child's birth — which, if met, caused the child forthwith to receive Soviet citizenship and, otherwise, meant that the parents were left to reach a decision — the law (Art.12) now speaks of parents here having "a permanent place of residence on USSR territory" which connotes a common legal artifact. In lieu, then, of letting the citizenship of the child in this type of situation be determined by the phenomenon of accidental presence of the father on Soviet soil on the critical date, a valid juridical criterion has been chosen, predicated on the maintenance of a stable linkage between the individual concerned and the country thereby identified as the "home" state. In that sense, the new rule is no doubt technically superior to its predecessor. Its effective radius is also greater: indeed, whereas the geographical location of the father alone spelled the difference according to the earlier modus operandi, today either parent's position can shape the outcome since the latter is no longer based on fulfilling the requirement of physical contact with Soviet soil (which obviously excludes the mother's role in a scenario calling for the offspring of a mixed marriage to be born outside the USSR), but on possessing a legal quality (a premise which either parent can satisfy even at a distance and do so more readily).

Under the current terms, the prospect of automatic assignment of Soviet citizenship to children of binational parentage (i.e., Soviet/foreign) born abroad is increased: if either parent retains a registered address back in the USSR, the couple's offspring is ipso jure classified as a Soviet citizen. In short, the mesh is so fine that the number of individuals allowed to slip through is bound to be minimal, which is probably what Soviet authors have in mind when they write that the ensemble of rules governing the acquisition of Soviet citizenship by birth attests to the "recognition by the legislator of the precedence of Soviet citizenship over the foreign one".[32] True, the process functions less arbitrarily than when the results hinged on the father's incidental presence on the Soviet scene at the right moment; however, since the attribution of Soviet citizenship under these circumstances is more routine and the mechanism is set in motion more easily than before, the weight attached to the will of the individual parties in this affair has been proportionately reduced. Looked at pragmatically, the adjustment was probably designed to take into account the experience of a growing corps of Soviet citizens posted abroad, often with their families, who remain Soviet citizens in good standing and presumably plan to return to the USSR upon completion, say, of their tour of foreign duty. Occasionally, Soviet emigrants might likewise wish to keep a foothold in the mother country in the event they would ever want to return. Asking these people to disrupt their normal lifestyle and stage a visit to the USSR just in order to convey their Soviet citizenship to a newborn child poses a logistical problem and, more important, may call for official accommodation to personal discretion by leaving undue room for the interested individuals to influence the results through their own behavior. The current formula avoids many of these distractions and, by focusing on the formal insignia of citizenship, manages to bypass the parents' desires by unilaterally pinning Soviet citizenship on the progeny at the time of birth, regardless of where the "blessed" event occurs.

Similarly, where consultation of the will of the parents is mandated, the 1978 modification of the 1968 diction from "resident" to "maintaining a permanent place of residence" (i.e., "where there is a difference in the citizenship of the parents, one of whom had USSR citizenship at the time of the birth of the child, and if at that time both parents *had a permanent place of residence* [instead of 'resided'] outside the borders of the USSR, the citizenship of a child born outside the borders of the USSR is determined by agreement of the parents") introduces an important refinement in the former wording. In effect, people can be resident abroad with no intention of terminating the association with their country of origin, while people who establish a permanent residence abroad generally end up sustaining only an ephemeral relationship with the "homeland" and lacking any real motive to saddle their children with their own nominal citizenship. Hence, the whole business amounts to the Soviet regime just accepting the logical consequence of its inability to direct the behavior of people who, though content to retain passive Soviet citizenship, have safely put themselves outside Moscow's reach and, by settling down elsewhere, have served plain notice on the Soviet authorities of the shadow character of any future allegiance they would still contemplate owing the USSR.

The script prompts two general observations. First, the record indicates an inconsistency between the Soviet regime's readiness to let the citizenship affiliation of a child born abroad to a couple in which one partner is a Soviet citizen and the other a foreigner be decided by parental consensus and its adamant refusal to sanction the individual's right to relinquish Soviet citizenship on his own initiative. The difference in attitude is probably due in part to stylistic considerations in that jus soli provides a convenient pretext for bowing graciously to a force majeure situation and drawing a technically plausible distinction between these cases and the treatment reserved for offspring born in the Soviet Union or otherwise validly connected to the USSR. No reasonable excuse can be offered for allowing a Soviet citizen abroad to divest himself (herself) of Soviet citizenship at will while denying the same opportunity to a countryman inside the USSR except by openly admitting that the former is beyond the practical control of the Soviet authorities and thus entitled to "privileges" that can safely be withheld from Soviet citizens to whom Soviet law effectively applies. Such a public formulation might be awkward. A possible further explanation is that psychologically it might be easier for the Soviet system to acquiesce in the notion of "non–acquisition" of Soviet citizenship on special occasions than in the concept of personal liberty to renounce Soviet citizenship by one already in formal possession of that status. Recognizing the freedom to repudiate what is officially pronounced to be a signal honor would raise a whole host of problems that the Soviet apparatus must prefer to avoid, which is not true in a context where entry into Soviet society is flatly said never to have occurred. Original non–inclusion as a consequence even of personal choice is doctrinally more tolerable than a subsequent bid to resign from existing membership.

Second, the current switch from the principle of "residence" to that of "permanent place of residence" brings up the item of the legal definition of the latter. The answer, however, is still far from clear, except for the view aired in Soviet literature that Soviet law alone is competent to set the relevant terms. On the other hand, a tone of uncertainty pervades local discussions about which branch of Soviet law should furnish the proper guidelines given that the criteria used for this purpose are not uniform. A Soviet author has noted, for instance, that in matters of inheritance the corpus of civil legislation mandates that the last permanent place of residence of the deceased be established by means of analysis of the factual circumstances which, in his opinion, does not coincide with the interpretation of permanent place of residence prevailing in citizenship practice. Here, he claims, other standards must operate which need not correspond to those followed in Soviet civil law. On the basis of earlier experience, the recommendation is then made that the issue be decided by reference to a broad range of administrative–legal questions relating to the de cujus, with particular importance attached to the document confirming the right of the designated individual to reside on the state's territory which usually indicates whether its owner is a permanent or a temporary resident of that particular country. Since the citizenship statute mentions permanent place of residence only in conjunction with the territory of the USSR — i.e., speaks of persons maintaining a permanent place of residence either on the territory of the USSR or outside the confines of the USSR — the conclusion is that the ruling must in each case be dictated by the documents procured by the appropriate Soviet organs.[33] The bottom–line, of course, is that the Ministry of Internal Affairs will be calling the shots.

Next, let us look at a number of technical aspects of these provisions of Article 12 the meaning of which is opaque. The initial point is whether the child for whom its parents did not record a choice of Soviet citizenship can on its own elect Soviet citizenship upon coming of age. In Soviet legal literature, the view seems to prevail that the right of registering a preference is here vested in the parents and not the offspring and so, if the parents failed to pick Soviet citizenship for their child, the latter can later change its citizenship strictly in accordance with established routine, i.e., by filing a petition for admission to Soviet citizenship with the federal or the proper republican Presidium.[34] The opinion was once expressed that this formula should apply only to cases where the parents actually selected a foreign citizenship for their progeny, and a different solution was proposed for instances where no evidence existed that the parents had decided on a particular foreign citizenship or, indeed, there was positive proof that no such agreement had ever been reached. In the latter situation, the argument ran, the assumption that the mere absence of a declaration in favor of Soviet citizenship was tantamount to choice of the citizenship of the foreign parent and consequent insistence that any future conversion to Soviet citizenship follow the standard modus operandi governing naturalization was unjustified and, instead, it was thought advisable to let the child itself pronounce for the desired citizenship upon attaining majority.[35]

If the bid was aimed at creating an "easy way" for children of mixed marriages born abroad whose parents were remiss in getting them recognized as Soviet citizens at birth to correct the oversight at achieving adulthood, the move did not succeed. Rather, the general tenor of Soviet writing on the subject would indicate a solid consensus behind the policy that whatever the reasons responsible for the original "lapse" — i.e., either the parents' wish that their offspring own a foreign citizenship or negligence of their part in fulfilling the procedural requirements or sheer inability to make up their minds — the approved treatment in each case now is for the de cujus to submit an official request for entry into Soviet citizenship upon coming of age.

Then, remember that the terms of Article 12 pertaining to the status of children of a binational couple born abroad in a context where their citizenship affiliation is left to be determined jointly by the parents never concern themselves with what significance, if any, the corresponding foreign law attributes to the agreement of the parents regarding the citizenship of the child. In this sense, the claim that Soviet law fully complies with the international legal canon by virtue of the fact that it is careful not to meddle in the relationship between these people and another state is sound. Namely,

> "if the parents chose Soviet citizenship, pursuant to Soviet law the child acquires it forthwith. If the parents settled on the citizenship of another state, the law of the USSR solely provides that the child does not obtain Soviet citizenship. The answer to the question of whether he acquires the citizenship of the foreign state must be supplied and is supplied not by Soviet law, but by the law of the foreign state."[36]

As noted previously, Soviet authorities appear equally ready to accept the end result though the final upshot may be a minor possessing a valid foreign citizenship or even more than one foreign citizenship, or certified as both a Soviet and a foreign citizen, or stateless.

The third item involves the whole matter of the administrative format which the parents would have to observe on this occasion in order to secure Soviet citizenship for their child born abroad. Note that neither the 1968 Basic Principles of legislation on marriage and the family nor the citizenship statute proper contained any instructions on that score. Secondary sources sought to fill the gap by suggesting that registration of the child as a Soviet citizen effected with the consent of both parents in the USSR consular office at the place of the child's birth or the place of residence of one of the parents would serve the purpose. The record, they add, would have to show that both parents chose Soviet citizenship for their offspring. If the parents registered the birth of the child not in the consulate of the USSR, but with the competent authorities of the country where they lived and if in that connection they informed the organs concerned in writing or orally of their choice of citizenship for the child, then one piece of evidence of their decision would be an affidavit confirming that such a declaration had been made.[37] Since the pertinent enactments also said nothing about applicable time-limits, local authors resorted to analogizing from other legal practices to find a plausible answer, tending to rely on the general rule that a statement regarding the birth of a child had to be entered no later than one month from the date of birth, save that where the parents were ill or for other reasons could not meet the prescribed deadline, the declaration could be filed by persons empowered by the parents to do so or persons who were taking care of the child, and always subject to the exception that even if the due date had expired, the registration of the child was still permitted.[38]

Only in mid-1979 was the speculation at last put to rest. The decree of the federal Presidium of June 15, 1979[39] mandated that the agreement of the parents concerning their choice of USSR citizenship for their child had to be submitted to the diplomatic or consular mission of the USSR in written form within one year from the date of the birth of the child. Nothing was said of the status of any similar acts performed before a foreign state institution, which does not necessarily mean that

Soviet officials may not yet grant legal recognition to such arrangements sanctioned by the lex situ. The grace period of one year certainly makes more practical sense than the one–month version referred to earlier and conforms to the pattern set, for example, in the USSR's past experience with international option operations.

Another innovation of the 1978 citizenship statute's provision dealing with the citizenship of children when only one of the parents was a citizen of the USSR compared to the corresponding clause in the 1968 Basic Principles of legislation on marriage and the family consists of an extra paragraph positing that a child one of whose parents at the time of its birth was a citizen of the USSR and the other was a stateless person or was unknown is a citizen of the USSR regardless of the place of birth. In short, none of the aforementioned qualifications stamping the mechanics of acquisition of Soviet citizenship at birth (place of residence, agreement of the parents) play a role when one of the parents is a Soviet citizen and the other either a stateless person (instead of a foreign national) or an unidentified person, for the child then receives Soviet citizenship at once irrespective of where it is born. If, in accordance with this scenario, the child is born on Soviet soil, the mix of jus sanguinis and jus soli offers at least a logical pretext for the summary imposition of Soviet citizenship. However, in circumstances where the child is born abroad and the parents (or parent–mother) do (does) not maintain a permanent place of residence in the USSR, the grant of Soviet citizenship by fiat strikes one as rather intrusive.

When Soviet glossators start churning out explanations for the salient features of the new statute, they will, in all likelihood, try to alibi the procedure by invoking the regime's "deep concern" for curbing the incidence of statelessness and to justify the intervention by pointing out that, in this frame, the child is in fact statistically more apt to contract statelessness than when the second parent is a bona fide foreign national from whom the offspring can "inherit" an alternate citizenship (by descent or by medium of agreement between the parents). Indeed, an initial step in this direction has now been made by a Soviet author who contends that the terms of the last section of Article 12 taken together with the rest of its contents succeed in guaranteeing "the maximum possible solution of the question in favor of recognition of the child as a Soviet citizen and are conducive to the reduction and prevention of cases of statelessness of children".[40] To begin with, the assertion is not quite accurate: a fuller coverage would have included extending Soviet citizenship automatically also to children born abroad to mixed couples where both partners maintained a permanent place of residence outside the USSR instead of letting the parents jointly determine the outcome or, in extremis, doing so when reliance here on parental consensus resulted in the offspring being stuck with statelessness — a special measure of relief which at least one Soviet spokesman had recently advocated, but in vain.[41] Then, valid doubts arise about whether or not the situation warrants peremptory action on this scale. The progeny might, for example, be born on the territory of a country following the principle of jus soli and thus be saved from a stateless lot as well. In any event, a more humane approach would have entailed furnishing the opportunity of acquiring Soviet citizenship, if so desired, and not unilaterally applying that brand to the minor, never mind how intensely committed Moscow professes to be to an agenda of protecting children from this fate. The cure is too harsh and some may think it as bad as the illness for which the medicine is prescribed.

Two further comments are in order. First, the legislators establish a pattern on this occasion of treating stateless parents as a nullity (or non–persons) for these purposes which is consistently observed throughout the balance of the statute and simply denies the parent who happens to be an apatride any voice whatever in the determination of the child's citizenship. A policy so draconic can hardly be excused, no matter how averse one claims to be to the phenomenon of statelessness and, of course, the whole business reeks of multiple discrimination in that persons with a valid foreign citizenship get to exercise a lesser quantum of rights than Soviet citizens under Soviet citizenship law and stateless individuals often fare even worse.[42] Second, in a case involving a Soviet parent and an unidentified parent, the regulations say nothing about the potential repercussions of subsequent discovery of the unknown parent's identity. Is the presumption in respect to the child's Soviet citizenship absolute or is it rebuttable if later access to fresh data shows that the information might have affected the initial outcome, e.g., if the unknown parent turns out to be a foreigner and neither parent possesses a permanent place of residence on Soviet soil, would they now be allowed jointly to decide the offspring's citizenship and perhaps choose a foreign citizenship in lieu of the current Soviet one? And, if the presumption is indeed controvertible, does the effect of the reversal run back to the point of origin or only count ex nunc? Unfortunately, the law sheds no light on these subsidiary, but nonetheless significant, technical issues. Past practice is equally unilluminating on the subject, so extrapolation from the record is not an answer either. Future experience alone will tell.

In closing, the preceding analysis requires a slight corrective. For the sake of convenience, the discussion so far has focused on the citizenship status of children whose parents are married to each other because where citizenship is transmitted by direct descent, the fact of a child's birth within wedlock serves as prima facie evidence of the existence of the crucial kinship link. According to some Soviet sources, however, Soviet citizenship may be relayed by natural parents as well. The relevant norms, they point out, refer to parents and not to parents–spouses and the former concept likewise embraces individuals who are not married to one another. An example of how the system works is when a woman who is a Soviet citizen gives birth to a child on the territory of the USSR — clearly, the child qualifies at once as a citizen of the USSR. If the mother is a foreign citizen and resides at the time of the child's birth on the territory of the USSR, then the child will also be considered a citizen of the USSR if the father was a Soviet citizen. In this case, though, supplementary steps have to be taken to establish the necessary blood connection that proves entitlement to Soviet citizenship which means resort to paternity procedures sanctioned by Soviet legislation, i.e., most commonly through the medium of an appropriate entry effected by a Soviet office of registry of acts of civil status on the strength of a joint declaration by the parents or, absent such a declaration, by court order.[43]

Here, the picture is fairly straightforward, which is less true where a child is born to a foreign mother abroad and the record later indicates that the father was a Soviet citizen. If the parents file the prescribed joint declaration in a Soviet office of registry of acts of civil status (to look just at the routine scenario),[44] the child may either have a primary claim to Soviet citizenship because the father or the mother happened to maintain a permanent place of residence on the territory of the USSR at the time of its birth or, if neither met that criterion, then the parents might still have the right to decide what citizenship they wanted for the child and pick that of the USSR. If the parents reside abroad, they have the further option of taking care of such business at the local Soviet consulate, with the same effect on the citizenship position of their offspring. Finally, Soviet law in force today confirms that documents issued by the competent organs of foreign states in authentication of acts of civil status performed outside the borders of the USSR under the laws of the corresponding states with respect to citizens of the USSR, foreign citizens and stateless persons shall be considered valid in the USSR given a consular legalization, as long as they do not contravene the basic principles of the Soviet system.[45] Should the foreign proceedings name a Soviet man as the father of a child born abroad to a foreign woman and the findings be recognized by the Soviet authorities, the child could be eligible for Soviet citizenship either by virtue of either parent maintaining a permanent place of residence in the USSR on the date of birth or, failing the residency test, the parents jointly choosing Soviet citizenship for their progeny.

Where a treaty of legal assistance operates between the USSR and another state the terms of which also cover matters pertaining to family law,[46] the expectation is that a ruling by a local court or other competent institution in a paternity hearing that pronounced a Soviet man the father of a particular child would be duly visaed by the proper Soviet organs and again thereby give the child a stake in Soviet citizenship or entitle the parents to determine the child's citizenship affiliation so that the latter might end up being nominated for Soviet citizenship.

3. Acquisition of USSR Citizenship by Children of Stateless Persons

The provisions of Article 13 of the 1978 citizenship statute represent an important additive to the Soviet legal canon. Pursuant to its terms, now a child born on the territory of the USSR of stateless persons who have a permanent place of residence in the USSR is ipso jure considered a citizen of the USSR. A number of Soviet commmentators had spoken in favor of this liberal sounding formula already before the 1978 law was enacted on the grounds that, although cases where both parents were stateless were infrequent, nonetheless, since the Universal Declaration of Human Rights proclaimed the right of each child to a nationality, refusal to recognize such children as citizens of the USSR would run counter to its pronouncements.[47] Heretofore, of course, these children had shared the parents' statelessness, but "because stateless individuals were placed in a less advantageous position than citizens, in the process of progressive development of international law a tendency emerged to institute conditions conducive to the reduction or even complete liquidation of the status of statelessness".[48] The 1948 Universal Declaration is said to have marked the first major step in that direction and the 1978 citizenship legislation gives further expression to that trend and thus is also praised for being "in perfect accord" with the norms of the International Covenant on Civil and Political

Rights and "the dictates of other international documents, e.g. the 1961 Convention on the Reduction of Statelessness".[49]

A few words about the technical aspects of the policy enunciated in Article 13 are next in order. First, note that while Soviet practice in ordinary circumstances plainly favors the criterion of jus sanguinis as a method of determining title to Soviet citizenship, in this instance the principle of jus soli takes precedence. Soviet authors attribute the switch to humanitarian motivations on the part of the Soviet regime and "concern for granting the human being an active role in the political life of the society and the state".[50] Second, the present measure is treated as but the latest move in a series of initiatives launched by the Soviet authorities designed to lower the statistics on statelessness in the USSR. Back in 1940 and in the post–war years, we are reminded, a mass of people were restored to Soviet citizenship by virtue of the special edicts then issued that sanctioned recovery of USSR citizenship by members of Russian emigré communities settled in various foreign countries. For that matter, attention is drawn to the fact that the decree of September 7, 1940, had established that persons belonging to national minorities who for political reasons could not obtain the local citizenship prior to the entry of the Baltic republics into the USSR, thereafter acquired Soviet citizenship in a simplified manner. Despite these efforts, a certain residue of stateless individuals remained on Soviet soil and the current clause, continuing the "traditional commitment" to the eradication of the problem of statelessness on home soil, amplified the older rules by arranging to eliminate yet another source of contagion.[51]

Third, as just mentioned, hitherto a child born to stateless parents on the territory of the USSR inherited their lot. Resort to common naturalization ultimately afforded a cure for this congenital handicap. A more radical solution was attempted in 1954 when the Presidium of the USSR Supreme Soviet directed that persons born abroad who had entered the USSR on different occasions (except political emigrants) and had not submitted documents attesting to their possession of a foreign citizenship, as well as their children, forthwith rated as Soviet citizens. Reportedly, that action brought the number of apatrides living in the USSR to a "minimum",[52] which meant that future chances of the "disease" being routinely transmitted to the offspring were likewise proportionately diminished. Fourth, an interesting feature of the new procedure is the fact that Soviet citizenship is scheduled to be assigned to children born on Soviet soil to stateless parents irrespective of how the parents fare in that regard — i.e., whether or not they seek Soviet citizenship for themselves.[53] Now, if the parents had in the past tried but had been unable to gain admission to Soviet citizenship (for whatever reasons), presumably they would have no objections to their progeny achieving a desired goal that had eluded them. If, on the other hand the parents were stateless by their own choice because they preferred not to be stuck with Soviet citizenship, the "involuntary conversion" of their minor child to Soviet citizenship could spell added hardship since the expedient gave the authorities means to exert extra leverage on the family unit. In that sense, the benefits of recognition of a child's right to a nationality are significantly offset by failure to take account of the parents' will on a key issue affecting the entire household. How, in the face of such prima facie evidence to the contrary, a Soviet writer can still maintain that the 1978 piece of legislation "makes it completely impossible for any stateless person to be automatically counted as a Soviet citizen while, at the same time, facilitating a substantial reduction" in the corresponding figures, is puzzling, unless he has in mind solely individuals who already bear the stigma and leaves out of the picture those who are prevented by executive fiat from incurring the affliction.[54] Lastly, such eligibility vests solely in "home"-born offspring of "sedentary" apatrides and the scheme does not propose to "salvage" either the locally born progeny of "guest" apatrides or the children of apatrides settled in the USSR who managed to be born abroad: only a combination of jus soli and family roots suffices in this case to abort "hereditary" statelessness.

The citizenship law shed no light on the way the terms of Article 13 were supposed to be administered. The decree of the federal Presidium of June 15, 1979, supplied the necessary information. The following procedure was devised. The mechanics of instant acquisition of Soviet citizenship by children of stateless persons operate in relation to individuals born subsequent to June 30, 1979. Minors who had not turned eighteen by July 1, 1979, could receive the citizenship of the USSR upon declaration by their legal representatives. In Soviet literature, the "retroactive effect" of the new legislation, as, for example, on this occasion, is billed as "genuinely humane".[55] It should be pointed out, however, that children born before the crucial date would appear to be treated less generously than those born after since an affirmative request must be filed on their behalf in order to obtain Soviet citizenship and the record does not indicate whether approval is a foregone conclusion or the petition may yet meet with rejection by the competent agencies. In any event, such applications had to be submitted at the place of residence to the organs of internal affairs before the minor reached majority, but not later than one year from the moment of the statute's entry into force, i.e., prior to July 1, 1980, with the further proviso that acquisition of Soviet citizenship here by children between the ages of fourteen and eighteen could occur only with their consent, expressed in writing. If all else failed, i.e., owing to the deadline having been missed (or the bid having been denied by the proper authorities?), the avenue of formal naturalization remained available for those young souls who wished (or, rather, for whom the decision was usually made) to trade their stateless condition for Soviet papers.

4. Foundlings

The Law on Citizenship of 1938 failed to regulate the matter of the status of foundlings discovered in the Soviet Union. In view of the official silence, a Soviet jurist once posed the question in this connection as to whether "the minor children of unknown parents found on the territory of the USSR (so- called 'foisted children', homeless minors)" should be included in the category of stateless individuals named in Article 8. His own belief was that "in this — practically ever rarer — event was permissible ... a presumption of Soviet extraction and, consequently, of Soviet citizenship".[56] In fact, this opinion was repeatedly echoed by other Soviet lawyers who dropped the tentative tone and flatly asserted that "children found on the territory of the USSR whose parents are unknown are recognized as Soviet citizens on the strength of the presumption that they are born of Soviet citizens".[57]

The doctrinal statements sounded definite enough, but as will be noted in a minute, some doubts have recently arisen about how accurately these accounts reflected the tenor of administrative practice here.

At any rate, let us first accentuate the positive by pointing out that the 1938 statute's oversight has now been corrected by its successor which pronounces, expressis verbis, that "a child located on the territory of the USSR, both of whose parents are unknown, is a citizen of the USSR" (Art. 14). Reportedly, the same rationale as before applies, to wit, the presumption that the child was born to Soviet citizens.[58] In this case, too, the concept of jus soli serves as a convenient substitute for the "missing" (at least in the sense of not proven) jus sanguinis link.[59] Finally, the law itself did not indicate how the terms of Article 14 were to be put into effect and once again the federal edict of June 15, 1979, was used to supply the necessary information. The familiar pattern was repeated. Thus, the rule on automatic acquisition of USSR citizenship by children whose parents are unknown refers only to persons born after June 30, 1979. Those among them who are born prior to that date and had not turned eighteen by July 1, 1979, could acquire Soviet citizenship by declaration of their legal representatives, which had to be filed at the place of residence with the organs of internal affairs before the child attained majority but in any event no later than one year following the statute's entry into force, i.e., by June 30, 1980. Acquisition of Soviet citizenship under these circumstances by children between the ages of fourteen and eighteen required their consent, certified in writing.

The decision to give the provision retroactive play may, as Soviet spokesmen maintain, have been prompted by "genuinely humane" considerations,[60] but the gesture is certainly hard to square with earlier claims that such a procedure had also operated up till then. If true, arrangements to clear a backlog would be surplus. Alternatively, the need to prescribe an antidote could be attributed to bureaucratic performance hitherto differing from jurisprudential theory in a way that caused statelessness to occur among foundlings located on Soviet soil, or administrative treatment of the phenomenon suffering from inconsistency due to absence of legislative instructions on the matter and these lapses occasionally resulting in failure to assign Soviet citizenship to children of unknown parentage discovered on Soviet territory, or the authorities adopting the policy just as a general precaution. Whatever the explanation, one is left with the distinct impression that, despite what Soviet sources say on that score, foundlings in the USSR might well have not in the past received Soviet citizenship in routine fashion and run into statelessness as a consequence.

A few additional observations will help round out the picture. Notice that where the "older" foundlings, i.e., of the pre–June 30, 1979, vintage, were concerned, acquisition of Soviet citizenship depended on affirmative motion, whereas their junior, post–June 30, 1979, counterparts come into possession of Soviet citizenship "passively". The record does not show whether a declaration by the proper legal representatives on behalf of a foundling younger than eighteen on July 1, 1979 (accompanied by his written consent, if need be) meant that the authorities would rubberstamp the application or that they retained the right to review it on the merits and perhaps reject the petition. Though the law does not deal with the question, it is probably safe to conclude that for those who either did not avail themselves of this opportunity to acquire Soviet citizenship in a simplified manner or were not entitled to do so (for example, because they were already over eighteen as of July 1, 1979), regular naturalization proceedings still held out hope for negotiating the transition to Soviet citizenship.

Lastly, what continues to remain unclear is whether the presumption which works to render a foundling immediately eligible to get Soviet citizenship is final or conditional, i.e., if once acted upon, it may not be subsequently refuted by fresh data as to the origins and/or locus of birth, or if it holds true only as long as the contrary has not been demonstrated. In the former case, foundlings in the USSR never face the risk of losing their Soviet citizenship. In the latter, that danger does exist if new evidence comes to light which, had it been known at the time, would have destroyed the raison d'être for the initial decision to award Soviet citizenship. Precedent offers no clue as to how the Soviet regime proposes to deal with this problem when it crops up — as it must at some point — and the current script is equally uninformative.

5. Admission to the Citizenship of the USSR

According to Article 15 of the 1978 statute, "foreign citizens and stateless persons may, upon their application, be admitted to the citizenship of the USSR pursuant to the present Law irrespective of race and nationality, sex, education, language, place of residence". The current language is more elaborate than that of the matching clause in the 1938 text. The latter had conveyed the same message, but the old catalogue of "non–conditions" boiled down to just "nationality and race". The verbal difference probably means very little anyway since we are told that the revision merely ratified a record of "established practice" spanning many years.[61]

Still, the latest formula is supposed to be much superior to its predecessor in both tone and substance. Even if the basic norm dating from 1938 has remained in force, its edited contents are said to be marked by greater detail and its pronouncements set forth in a more comprehensive manner.[62] As a result, Soviet authors claim, the new version "states precisely the grounds and procedure of acquisition of the citizenship of the USSR" and "significantly expands the democratic principles of admission to Soviet citizenship"[63] by, inter alia, consecrating the rule of the "legal parity of foreigners in the sphere of citizenship".[64] The second proposition is illustrated by contrasting the impressive list of criteria that cannot be invoked to discriminate among applicants for Soviet citizenship with pernicious "bourgeois" methods that resort to an array of "antidemocratic" indicia to deny their citizenship to "undesirable" elements — e.g., suitable life–style and mores, political reliability, familiarity with the local history and government system, literacy, fluency in the native tongue, permanent place of residence.[65] A further virtue attributed to Soviet policy on that count is that, by eschewing these artifices, it fully complies with the Universal Declaration of Human Rights which enunciates every individual's entitlement to a citizenship, whereas, of course, the "capitalist" countries are consistently adjudged to fall short of meeting the prescribed standards.[66]

Next, in line with earlier suggestions, the provision's terms have been modified to refer in this connection not only to "foreigners", as was the case in the 1938 act, but to "foreigners and stateless individuals", a semantic adjustment that amplified the coverage although, once again, reportedly no major change was thereby effected because administrative routine had long ago taken to equating stateless persons with foreigners in matters of admission to Soviet citizenship.[67] The script now confirms the uniform treatment, but presumably in the process nothing concrete was added to the existing picture. Note, however, that the final roster features fewer items than one Soviet analyst had seen fit to recommend for inclusion in this section in order plainly to express (in his words) the profoundly democratic complexion and humaneness of Soviet citizenship, to wit, sex, age, race and nationality, social origins, religion, education, and property status.[68] Particularly striking is the readiness voiced on that occasion to waive the qualification of social origins for such purposes. The legislators did not follow this bit of advice (as, far from accidentally, they also omitted to indicate the irrelevance of religion and property status in weighing the merits of an application for naturalization) and, indeed, the contrary view has since been asserted that the statute's silence on the subject of a person's social origins proves that the Soviet socialist state retains a vital interest in the social position of the individual petitioning to enter the citizenship of the USSR, "the citizenship of the working people".[69]

Certainly, the emphasis in Soviet literature on the absence of egregious barriers in Soviet law to the admission of aliens into Soviet citizenship is calculated to leave the impression that the business of naturalization is here conducted in prompt, smooth and reasonable fashion. At the same time, however, Soviet spokesmen are careful to dispel the notion that, just because the traffic (according to them) is handled in a sensible and straightforward way,[70] the whole operation tends to assume a mechanical quality. Thus, they point out that in this instance the legal relationship arises between the petitioner and the state when the former files papers requesting Soviet citizenship rights and that this stage of their liaison "is exhausted and is consequently terminated from the moment when a decree is issued granting or refusing Soviet citizenship to the person concerned".[71] Both sides, then, figure in the engagement and each retains an independent role in the transaction: the individual can set the procedure in motion by asking for admission to Soviet citizenship, but "this does not mean that everyone who submits an application for admission to the citizenship of the USSR receives it"[72] and the "union" is not consummated until the state exercises its sovereign prerogative to decide in favor of the petitioner.[73]

In sum, a negative outcome is clearly also possible, except that the law only says what considerations may not cause a petition for admission to Soviet citizenship to be turned down and mentions no valid grounds for rejecting such a bid. Other sources help fill the gap to some extent by keeping track of how the competent agencies tackle the job and the kind of information they seek in order to arrive at an official determination. For example, we are told that the proper authorities are charged with ascertaining if there is good reason for the petition[74] (an oracular refrain plainly intended to fit every contingency) and to take into account the presence of relatives in the USSR,[75] where the applicant resides and for how long he has done so and whether in the USSR or abroad, and what are his ties to the country of which he is a citizen.[76]

Coincidentally, the applicant "must by his actions show that he is worthy of this high title [i.e., Soviet citizenship] and is ready to bear this title with honor, to safeguard the interests and authority of our state".[77] Or, to quote a second opinion, the individual is tested on "his attitude toward the basis of the social structure and policy of the USSR, his sincere commitment to observe the Constitution of the USSR and Soviet law, to respect the norms of socialist communal life, protect the interests of the Soviet state, promote its power and authority, and bear with honor the high distinction of citizen of the USSR".[78] However, even surmounting these elastic hurdles will not guarantee success for, in the last analysis, the principle of state sovereignty is perceived in Soviet quarters as encompassing both the right unilaterally to fix the procedure and terms of naturalization and to deny any person's request for naturalization though the petitioner formally fulfills all the conditions required for naturalization in that country. The bottom–line, according to Soviet commentators, is that "the right to naturalization, and not just to apply to the competent organs of the state asking that they consider the question of possible naturalization, vests in the foreigner in the event that the laws of the corresponding state grant him that right".[79] Since Soviet law does not, the regime's power to veto an application for naturalization remains absolute.

A further indispensable factor in this connection is the existence of a practical link between the de cujus and the Soviet Union, or at least the desire on the candidate's part to forge the necessary link.[80] Finally, one must remember that the Soviet credo does not conceive of a state organ being independent of the state[81] so that, by definition, every state entity is presumed to be politically motivated in pursuing its assigned functions and the local institutions entrusted with evaluating applications for admission to Soviet citizenship are no exception to the rule. In the Soviet environment, then, the treatment afforded requests for naturalization will always evince the stamp of invidious political preferences, no matter how liberal the formal pitch may sound.

Thus, when all the statements and explanations are recorded, the picture that emerges is of a process that may take fully as long and prove just as difficult as in any of the "bourgeois" countries, theory to the contrary notwithstanding. And, when one adds to the scales the political realities of the Soviet experiment, with its traditional disregard for legal proprieties and its penchant for bureaucratic arbitrariness, much of the official roseate portrayal of a high–level administrative apparatus dedicated to handling personal requests for naturalization quickly, sympathetically and objectively threatens to vanish with hardly a trace. Possibly, the mechanism performs no worse than in other countries, but it surely does not work as wonderfully as the regime likes to pretend and would have us believe.

Switching now from the subjective to the technical side of the problem, four aspects of the prescribed modus vivendi invite attention. First, we have the express waiver of the residence test as an index of eligibility for acceptance into Soviet citizenship, amply demonstrated by the fact that a foreigner can obtain Soviet citizenship without ever setting foot in the USSR. The procedure therefore preserves the old Soviet tradition (which was also maintained during the tenure of the 1938 statute although the text was silent on that score) of sanctioning the naturalization of individuals living abroad, despite the evident absence of physical bonds that commonly constitute the prime rationale for such a "conversion". Why a Soviet citizenship thus acquired should not be dismissed by other nations as a mere "flag of convenience", so to speak, is not clear, unless one assumes that the interested parties would on these occasions have satisfied some further criteria denoting a will to owe "effective allegiance" to the USSR capable of compensating for the lack of material roots.

At any rate, the potential for conflict is obvious here and Soviet spokesmen are sufficiently aware of the situation to try to fend off the expected criticism. They start out by declaring that "the Soviet law on citizenship refutes the opinion of certain bourgeois jurisprudes that only a person customarily residing on the territory of the respective state can be naturalized". A qualification is then injected apropos arbitrary naturalization of foreign citizens resident abroad amounting to a violation of the sovereignty of the foreign state and, to boot, representing a veiled bid to regulate foreign citizenship which means additional encroachment on the sovereign rights of the other state. According to Soviet sources, a premier example of such abuse is the law enacted in West Germany on June 23, 1966, which authorized the Bonn government to waive jurisdiction over Germans living outside the sphere of application of the FRG Constitution, a formula which, the Soviets claim, operates on the assumption that in principle the FRG's jurisdiction does indeed extend to these people. An official protest was filed by Moscow on August 22, 1966,[82] which, inter alia, accused the West German political leadership of wantonly seeking to substitute for the concept of citizenship that of national membership in order to subject all Germans, no matter where they lived, to the laws and justice of the FRG, thereby in practice treating them as citizens of West Germany. The Soviet note went on to condemn the scheme as a direct infringement of the sovereign rights of other states and the rights of their citizens and a fresh instance of blatant violation of the Potsdam agreement and the universally recognized norms of international law.

The last word, though, is that bad cases do not signify that on particular occasions individuals residing abroad cannot be naturalized. We are again referred to the example of a foreigner residing abroad who can address the Presidium of the USSR Supreme Soviet through the local Soviet diplomatic mission with a request to be admitted to Soviet citizenship and told that granting Soviet citizenship to such a person will not run counter to international law since the decision entails a strictly individual act and is based on the request of the interested party. To deny now the right of the state to naturalize the designated person, so goes the argument, smacks of an attempt to limit the sovereignty of the state in citizenship affairs.[83]

Second, the item mentioned earlier concerning Soviet insistence that the process of naturalization marks a relationship in which both partners, i.e., the individual and the state, must concur[84] logically prompts the pronouncement that "an indispensable condition of the lawfulness of naturalization from the standpoint of international law is its voluntariness".[85] Pursuant to this dictum, the mandatory consent of the individual to naturalization is dictated by the sovereignty of the state whose citizen he is. Nor can the business of presuming acquiescence to naturalization be carried to unreasonable lengths,[86] since that practice would lead to forcible naturalization which, of course, is incompatible with state sovereignty and the principle of non–interference. On the question of the legitimacy of automatic naturalization of persons who have resided in a given country for a long time and fulfill other requirements laid down by the law, attitudes vary. One school of thought espouses the view that coercive or automatic naturalization is inconsistent with the contemporary international law canon, since the phenomenon calls for attribution of citizenship against the will of the affected persons and intrudes on the sovereign rights of the state with whose citizenship these souls happen to be endowed.[87] A second opinion counsels a more flexible approach and takes the position that automatic naturalization on these terms is not always considered coercive on the grounds that the element of voluntariness is observed by virtue of the opportunity available to the members of the "constituency" to leave the host country before the established deadline if they do not wish to become its citizens.[88] Other factors can likewise influence the picture. On balance, though, the issue is a controversial one since, stricto sensu, naturalization by fiat loses the flavor of naturalization and degenerates into mere imposition of citizenship on foreigners, at which point the whole routine is branded as a flagrant violation of the foreign state's sovereign domain.

Yet, measured by this general standard affirming that "the state cannot without the person's expressed desire enter into relations with him concerning admission to citizenship",[89] the USSR's own record here also falls far short of perfection. For example, one need only recall the 1954 decree whereby Soviet citizenship was unilaterally conferred on a congeries of individuals born abroad who had moved to the USSR on various earlier occasions and could not prove possession of a foreign citizenship, as well as their children, save for those in the lot classified as political emigrés. True, the fact that the experiment focused on stateless persons spared the Soviet regime the embarrassment of trampling on the sovereign rights of any other state in launching the conversion. However, the people involved were certainly not consulted on their desire in this context which hardly squares with the popular notion of voluntariness; nor is the ingenious alibi that the latter obligation is discharged where the projected "beneficiaries" can exercise the option to depart before the date set for the "baptism" credible apropos the USSR since, as is common knowledge, Soviet doctrine does not consecrate the institution of freedom of exit.

Much depends, too, on how naturalization is defined. If one goes beyond the prototype of the singular application for admission to citizenship and looks at some congeneric methods of acquiring citizenship, the Soviet Union's ratings on this scale drop even lower. What I am referring to now are the ad hoc arrangements that envision a sort of "collective naturalization" — e.g., through succession as an accompaniment to territorial gains, in the wake of programs of mass repatriation, etc. In Soviet literature, the theme recurs that "in a frame where the self–determination of nations and guarantee of fundamental human rights and liberties represent universally recognized principles of international law, option in connection with the passage of territory from one state to another must be considered a mandatory requirement"[90] or, in a slightly less peremptory tone, that "in contemporary international relations, option is used in preference" to transfer (i.e., automatic change of citizenship). The kind of treatment where the cession of territory included the inhabitants who, without being asked what they wanted, forthwith received a new nationality, is portrayed as a feature of the feudal and early capitalist phases of history, quite unsuitable for modern times.[91]

Still, closer examination reveals that Soviet writers on the subject often hedge their bets with a disclaimer that "not every automatic group grant of citizenship runs counter to international law".[92] Leaving a convenient loophole makes a great deal of sense in their case since past Soviet experience with option proceedings in an effort to settle the legal consequences of the territorial annexations staged at the beginning and at the end of the Second World War, attests to very limited reliance on option techniques on those occasions and a pronounced bias in favor of a policy of outright ascription of Soviet citizenship to the bulk of the local population. The whole operation in fact paid very little attention to the concept of voluntariness and perhaps a casual aside suggesting that resort to naturalization en masse at the sole discretion of the state might in some instances also be appropriate could be aimed at parrying possible criticism of the Soviet record in these matters. Large-scale repatriation ventures provide a similar setting and, again, Soviet practice here has tended to interpret the decision to "return to the mother country" as synonymous with a conscious choice of the "homeland's" citizenship, which is precisely how the status of the post-war Armenian immigrants to the USSR was resolved.[93] Of course, such repatriates did freely elect to go to the USSR, but having Soviet citizenship thrust upon them on arrival meant that the chances of changing one's mind and trying to leave were henceforth much reduced by virtue of the extra legal bonds created by the act of acquisition of Soviet citizenship which in no way reflected the affected individual's will.

Even then, Soviet spokesmen are not altogether at a loss for excuses. If the empirical evidence does not corroborate the official rhetoric, they are not averse to calling on metaphysics in defense of the national interests. Evoking the inherent "spiritual" superiority of Soviet citizenship is a fairly popular device in that the theme lets its exponents argue that membership in the Soviet polity is, by its very nature, always a blessing and never a burden, so that the question of how Soviet citizenship has in practice been obtained is dwarfed by the vital advantages that accrue from possession of the title, namely, full participation in the ensemble of rights and duties which the Soviet system formally guarantees to all its citizens and publicly advertises as the most progressive model in the world.[94]

The reason for concentrating on these special events is that their documented format betrays the frailty of the Soviet regime's professed commitment to the principle of voluntariness in connection with the dynamics of acquisition of the USSR's citizenship. Ordinary naturalization is an administrative routine and data about how the mechanism actually functions are hard to come by. The situation thus allows only tentative conclusions to be drawn on whether or not the same "lax" attitude also prevails in the latter sector. Nevertheless, occasional "leaks" lead one to believe that this kind of slippage may be a general phenomenon which afflicts every dimension of the traffic. The story of Ma Hun, recounted once before, comes to mind: the man fled from China to the Soviet Union and, at some point, was invited "to accept Soviet citizenship"; he declined the offer and was subsequently arrested, tried and sentenced to a long term in a forced labor camp as a standard method of reprisal, according to him, for, inter alia, refusing to undergo conversion to Soviet citizenship at the KGB's urgings.[95] The scenario may not always be so dramatic, but the likelihood plainly exists that the KGB will not hesitate to use such tactics in dealing with random displays of recalcitrant behavior.

Third, the 1978 statute, like its predecessor, is silent on the subject of the old citizenship of an individual applying for Soviet citizenship. By custom and treaty, the members of the "socialist Commonwealth" now seem to follow the practice of not granting naturalization to each other's citizens without coincidentally resolving the status of their current citizenship. Vis–à–vis other countries, though, the USSR apparently prefers to dispense with prophylactic measures, despite the fact that several of its associates pursue a different route. "The legislation of Poland, Bulgaria, Romania and Yugoslavia requires as a condition precedent to acquisition of citizenship by foreigners the severance of legal ties with the state whose citizens they are." Hungary does not mandate loss of the former citizenship as a prerequisite for admission to Hungarian citizenship, but in deciding on a request for naturalization looks favorably on evidence indicating that the petitioner is a stateless person or his citizenship will lapse upon admission to Hungarian citizenship or he will renounce his foreign citizenship or will seek to be released from it. By contrast, the law of both the USSR and the GDR simply ignores the issue which, of course, means that in those two countries dual nationality can easily occur as a result of naturalization. The perceived virtue of their approach is that it avoids undue delays in the naturalization process.[96]

In sum, Soviet publicists echo national policy when they assert that "the state is not obliged ... in naturalizing a person to take into account that person's possession of the citizenship of another state".[97] Where the formula produces dual nationality, that problem is "taken care of" by the bare expediency of refusing to recognize the validity of the initial citizenship, which perhaps offers cosmetic relief, but does not cure the malady. No explanation is volunteered as to why the competent organs will not institute more positive steps here, but my guess is that the reasons are probably quite petty: cult of the sovereign mystique, desire to retain a free hand in setting the terms of entry into Soviet citizenship, unwillingness as a matter of principle to accept the rival stake of the "capitalist" (or, at least, "non–socialist") states in this matter and then face the prospect of having to defer in some commensurate degree to their matching rights in operating the local naturalization system.

Finally, one must remember that the 1938 piece of legislation had effected a major change in past routine by failing to include the provision hitherto sanctioning, under certain designated circumstances, the acquisition of USSR citizenship "in a simplified manner" and, what is more, letting even local organs of government in these cases "speed up" the business of naturalization. "Foreign workers and peasants residing in the USSR for purposes of labor, ... foreigners enjoying the right of political asylum, as a result of prosecution for political activity", aliens married to Soviet citizens and wishing to obtain the nationality of their spouse, all had until then qualified for this special treatment, so long, that is, as the interested executive department had no objections on that score. For, the law gave the latter full discretion to determine in each instance whether to accede to such an application or refuse to follow this method and, instead, advise the petitioner to seek admission through the standard channels. Nor, as best one can judge, did the responsible agency have to state the motives for arriving at a negative conclusion.

The revision was justified in those days primarily with reference to intense concern for the Soviet Union's security needs in light of the worsening global situation and, hence, the wisdom of switching to a procedure that enabled the competent authorities to screen every individual applying for Soviet citizenship with appropriate thoroughness. With the gradual return, after Stalin's death, to a more normal atmosphere both on the domestic and in the international arena, a move to wean Soviet public mores away from these extremes of paranoia was soon afoot and the language reminiscent of those witch–hunting orgies fell into official disfavor. The improvement in the home climate prompted new interest in reviving an artifact with a fine doctrinal pedigree and a good track record in the local citizenship repertory, but there was no real sense of urgency in advocating reform because of a general feeling that the pace of naturalization in the USSR would be adequate already under existing conditions if perversions did not occur, since Soviet law did not erect any artificial barriers in the path toward gaining entry into Soviet citizenship.

Nonetheless, the sixties heard some calls for innovation on this front as well. An early bid along those lines proposed the adoption of rules that would materially facilitate the acquisition of Soviet citizenship by citizens of the "people's democratic countries" in order, allegedly, better to reflect "the development of the world socialist system as the beginning of the historical process of peoples generally drawing closer together". The same advocate recommended a more constructive approach to the item of admission to Soviet citizenship of "subjects of bourgeois countries persecuted for political, scientific, national–liberation activity, the struggle for peace", claiming that "the interests of proletarian solidarity presuppose that the fighters for democracy, peace and progress can enjoy priority rights for entry into Soviet citizenship by comparison with others".[98]

The notion of privileged treatment for citizens of the USSR's "satellites" in obtaining Soviet citizenship through naturalization ran into criticism from one of the author's colleagues on grounds that in these cases no "need existed to establish another type of procedure for admission to Soviet citizenship different from the common one". However, strong support was expressed for amending the pertinent rules in such a way as "clearly to convey the socio– political character and historical mission of the citizenship of the Soviet socialist state by sanctioning special preference with regard to its acquisition by certain categories of persons".[99] Accordingly, the suggestion was made that:

> "it be legislatively affirmed that in virtue of the international nature of the Soviet state, as well as owing to the spiritual affinity of the Soviet people with the activist figures of the revolutionary movement, with fighters for the social and national emancipation of oppressed peoples, these persons have first–priority right to receive Soviet citizenship. This advantage also accrues to persons who have performed great services for the people of the USSR in the revolutionary movement, in socialist construction, in the struggle for the freedom and independence of the USSR.
>
> Specifically, the following people could be eligible: individuals per-

> secuted by the governments of capitalist countries for participation in the struggle for peace, for revolutionary, national–liberation, scientific and anti–religious activity; individuals who have performed great revolutionary, military and labor services for the peoples of the USSR; individuals enjoying the right of political asylum on the territory of the USSR".[100]

None of this amounted to anything notably earth–shaking; yet, when the 1978 citizenship statute was enacted, the text contained no concession to these "liberal" views and the 1938 model's rejection of the concept of "easy" naturalization remained fully in force. The discussion seems to be over. Even so, the question may validly be raised as to why, if Soviet lawyers were indeed convinced that no extraneous criteria intruded to slow the tempo of the naturalization operation, did they still favor the restoration of the old exemption opening a "fast lane", as it were. One plausible explanation, of course, is that the gesture had a certain symbolic value, meaning that for the sake of public relations such a piece of plastic surgery looked fairly worthwhile. Or, to offer a more elaborate interpretation, the record may be read for evidence that Soviet experts in the field know that practice here does not correspond to the formal picture and thus a few of them had hoped, by extracting an explicit commitment from the authorities to handle at least some of the case–load in prompt fashion, to reduce this disparity and get the mechanism to function more in keeping with its official billing.

Now, where outside analysts are concerned, the available documentation shows that in point of fact the gist of the proposed reforms would not be amiss. The regime's contentions to the contrary notwithstanding, for many people access to Soviet citizenship has proved to be an elusive, and at times impossible, dream. Note, inter alia, that the terms of the 1954 decree which, we are told, succeeded in virtually ridding the USSR of statelessness, were expressly intended not to apply to foreign "political emigrés" residing in the USSR. True, Soviet authors like to claim that "the Soviet Union extends to individuals who are granted political asylum the status of political emigrant which in substance differs little from the legal status of Soviet citizen" and that, "if they so wish, political emigrants may acquire the rights of Soviet citizenship by the standard method".[101] How, then, account for the continued presence in the USSR of considerable numbers of individuals whom the authorities persist in classifying, and treating, as stateless persons: for example, those Greek and Turkish citizens and Iranian nationals from whom various restrictions regarding choice of place of residence were lifted by the secret decree of November 3, 1972;[102] or, the group of more than 200 Iranians living on the territory of the USSR with "residence permits" instead of passports and not considered Soviet citizens who were recently reported trying to get Moscow's consent to let them move to Iran.[103] Unless one assumes that these people themselves had defeated the government's every attempt to convert them to Soviet citizenship, the logical conclusion must be that the story about how simple it generally is to acquire Soviet citizenship deserves to be greeted with a good deal of scepticism.

NOTES

1. V. Zenin, "Gromadianstvo SRSR — velika chest' i velika vidpovidal'nist'", *Radianske pravo*, 1979, No.2, p.10.
2. L.B. Kuzmenko, "Razvitie pravovogo regulirovaniia statusa lichnosti v novom Zakone o grazhdanstve SSSR", *Vestnik Moskovskogo universiteta*, 1980, No.4, seriia 11: Pravo, p.31.
   Compare the tone of the following assessment by R.I. Kulik, *Zakon o grazhdanstve SSSR*, Moscow 1980, p.48, of the meaning of this added feature, which strikes one as highly exaggerated:
   "An enormous merit of the Law on citizenship of the USSR of 1978 lies in its consecration of an exhaustive enumeration of the grounds for acquisition of Soviet citizenship. The precise legislative regulation of such important politico– legal issues represents a big step in perfecting our legislation on citizenship. In deciding these questions, Soviet legislation relies on the terms of Art.33 of the USSR Constitution, takes into account the experience of other countries and the norms of international law."
3. Note that when I.G. Kebin, chairman of the Commission on Legislative Proposals of the Soviet of Nationalities, acting in the name of the commissions on legislative proposals of both chambers, submitted a recommendation on June 25, 1973, at a session of the Presidium of the USSR Supreme Soviet, for the drafting of a new Law on the citizenship of the USSR, he gave as one of the reasons for the project the fact that the Soviet Union had meantime signed some international agreements and conventions the provisions of which, in the opinion of the Commission on Legislative Proposals of the upper chamber, should be reflected in the statute. *Vedomosti Verkhovnogo Soveta SSSR*, 1973, No.26, p.396 (hereafter abbr. as *VVS SSSR*).
4. R.I. Kulik, *op. cit.*, p.48.
5. B.V. Shchetinin, *Problemy teorii sovetskogo gosudarstvennogo prava*, Moscow 1974, p.184, citing V.M. Safronov, in the book *Kurs sovetskogo gosudarstvennogo prava*, Moscow 1961, p.198.
6. B.V. Shchetinin, *op. cit.*, pp.184–185.
7. Also published in *Sovety deputatov trudiashchikhsia*, 1968, No.5, pp.14–22; English text in *Soviet News*, 1968, No.5442, pp.147–150.
8. *VVS SSSR*, 1968, No.27, Art.241; *Sovetskaia iustitsiia*, 1968, No.15, pp.2–7. *VVS RSFSR*, 1969, No.32, Art.1086.
9. *SZ*, 1924, No.23, Art.202; text in English in R.W. Flournoy, Jr., and M.O. Hudson, eds., *A Collection of Nationality Laws of Various Countries as Contained in Constitutions, Statutes and Treaties*, New York 1929, pp.511–514.
10. S.S. Kishkin, *Sovetskoe grazhdanstvo*, Moscow 1925, p.48.
11. *SZ*, 1930, No.34, Art.366; *SZ*, 1931, No.24, Art.196. For the text of the 1931 Regulation in English, see T.A. Taracouzio, *The Soviet Union and International Law*, New York 1935, pp.379–382.
12. *VVS SSSR*, 1939, No.22; *Sbornik zakonov SSSR i ukazov Prezidiuma Verkhovnogo Soveta SSSR (1938g–noiabr 1958g.)*, Moscow 1959, p.76.
13. T.A. Taracouzio, "The Soviet Citizenship Law of 1938", *American Journal of International Law*, 1939, No.1, p.18. This conclusion was likewise taken for granted by V. Durdenevskii, "Zakon o grazhdanstve Soiuza Sovetskikh Sotsialisticheskikh Respublik", *Problemy sotsialisticheskogo prava*, 1938, No.6, p.65.
14. D.T. Iakovenko, *Radianske gromadianstvo*, Kiev, 1960, p.16.
15. A.I. Lepeshkin, *Kurs sovetskogo gosudarstvennogo prava*, Moscow 1961, Vol.1, p.465; V.I. Menzhinskii, in F.I. Kozhevnikov, ed., *Mezhdunarodnoe pravo*, Moscow

1964, p.285; V.I. Menzhinskii, in F.I. Kozhevnikov, ed., *Kurs mezhdunarodnogo prava*, 2nd ed., Moscow 1966, p.294; *Kurs mezhdunarodnogo prava*, Moscow 1967, Vol.3, p.85; S.V. Chernichenko, *Mezhdunarodno–pravovye voprosy grazhdanstva*, Moscow 1968, p.58.

16. L.D. Voevodin, in S.S. Kravchuk, ed., *Gosudarstvennoe pravo SSSR*, Moscow 1967, p.179,
17. V.S. Shevtsov, *Sovetskoe grazhdanstvo*, Moscow 1965, p.47 (italics added).
18. A.A. Esaian, *Nekotorye voprosy sovetskogo grazhdanstva, Voprosy naseleniia v praktike Sovetskoi Armenii*, Erevan 1966.
19. *Ibid.*, p.92.
20. *Ibid.*, pp.101–102.
21. L.D. Voevodin, in S.S. Kravchuk, ed., *op. cit.*, p.184.
22. S.V. Chernichenko, review of G.E. Vilkov, ed., *Zakonodatel'stvo SSSR i mezhdunarodnye soglasheniia po voprosam grazhdanstva, sbornik*, Moscow 1964, in *Sovetskii ezhegodnik mezhdunarodnogo prava 1964–1965*, Moscow 1966, p.472 (hereafter abbr. as *SEMP*).
23. S. Chernichenko, "Nash grazhdanin", *Izvestiia*, June 15, 1968, p.5.
24. Cf., V.S. Shevtsov, *Grazhdanstvo v sovetskom soiuznom gosudarstve*, Moscow 1969, p.120; I.K. Gorodetskaia, "Grazhdanstvo detei", *Sovetskoe gosudarstvo i pravo*, 1971, No.4, p.39 (hereafter abbr. as *SGiP*).
25. V. Durdenevskii, *op. cit.*, pp.63–64. The author repeats the story in V.N. Durdenevskii, S.B. Krylov, eds., *Mezhdunarodnoe pravo*, Moscow 1947, p.183.
26. *Ibid.*
27. Report by the People's Commissar for Foreign Affairs, G.V. Chicherin, on Union citizenship at the 2nd session of the CEC of the USSR, 2nd convocation, morning meeting of October 24, 1924, in S.S. Kishkin, *op. cit.*, pp.81–82.
28. E.g., M. Shafir, *Grazhdaninom byt' obiazan*, Moscow 1972, pp.36–37; I.K. Gorodetskaia, *Mezhdunarodnaia zashchita prav i interesov detei*, Moscow 1973, p.38; *idem*, *op. cit.* (note 24 above), p.40.
29. I.K. Gorodetskaia, *op. cit.*, p.39.
30. S. Chernichenko, *op. cit.* (note 23 above).
31. Viz., V. Durdenevskii, *op. cit.* (note 13 above), p.60.
32. R.I. Kulik, *op. cit.*, p.49.
33. A.A. Rubanov, "Mezhdunarodno–pravovye voprosy zakonodatel'nogo regulirovaniia otnoshenii sovetskogo grazhdanstva", *SEMP 1978*, Moscow 1980, pp.157–158. See, too, the same author's *Zagranichnye nasledstva: Otnosheniia mezhdu sotsialisticheskimi i kapitalisticheskimi stranami*, Moscow 1975, pp.187–190.
34. M. Shafir, *op. cit.*, p.36; I.K. Gorodetskaia, *op. cit.* (note 24 above), p.40; *idem*, *op. cit.* (note 28 above), pp.37–38.
35. A.Ia. Pergament, review of Gorodetskaia's study cited in note 28 above, *SEMP 1974*, Moscow 1976, pp.320. Writing already after the enactment of the federal Basic Principles of Legislation on marriage and the family and polemicizing with the views expressed by S. Chernichenko (note 23 above), V.S Shevtsov, *op. cit.* (note 24 above), p.120, urged that, absent an agreement by the parents, the child still be recognized as a Soviet citizen provided that the national law of the parent who was a foreign citizen or the law of the country where the child was born does not recognize it as its citizen. Without increasing the prospects of incidence of dual nationality in these circumstances, such a solution would offer the advantage of reducing the chances of statelessness occurring, except that the procedure would, of course, indirectly act to overrule a possible conscious preference by the parents that their child even end up stateless rather than figure as a Soviet citizen. Obvi-

ously, though, the legislators here rejected the arguments of both Chernichenko and Shevtsov.

36. A.A. Rubanov, *op. cit.*, p.151.
37. I.K. Gorodetskaia, *op. cit.* (note 28 above), p.37.
38. *Idem*, *op. cit.* (note 24 above), pp.39–40.
39. *VVS SSSR*, 1979, No.25, Art.436.
40. R.I. Kulik, *op. cit.*, p.49.
41. See the passage by V.S. Shevtsov quoted in note 35 above.
42. A.A. Rubanov, *op. cit.*, p.143.
43. Cf., I.K. Gorodetskaia, *op. cit.* (note 24 above), p.40, and note 10; *idem*, *op. cit.* (note 28 above), p.38.
44. For special exceptions to the standard modus operandi, see text on pages 152–153 and 158–159 above.
45. Articles 38 and 39 of the federal edict of October 9, 1979, *VVS SSSR*, 1979, No. 42, Art.696.
46. The USSR has concluded such treaties with Czechoslovakia, the German Democratic Republic, Bulgaria, the Korean People's Democratic Republic, Poland, Romania, Albania, Hungary, Mongolia, Yugoslavia, Vietnam plus Iraq. The USSR's agreements with Austria, Greece and Finland on questions of legal aid do not provide for mutual recognition of judicial and other official decisions concerning paternity matters.
47. E.g., A.I. Pergament, *loc. cit.*; I.K. Gorodetskaia, *op. cit.* (note 28 above), pp.43–44.
48. G.I. Tunkin, "Zakon o grazhdanstve SSSR", *SGiP*, 1979, No.7, pp.25–26.
49. "The New Law on Citizenship", *Socialism: Theory and Practice*, 1979, No.8, p.62 (originally published in *Sovetskaia Latviia*, February 25, 1979). In similar vein, R.I. Kulik, *op. cit.*, p.48.
50. V.V. Polianskii, "Printsipy sovetskogo grazhdanstva", *SGiP*, 1980, No.5, p.128.
51. R. Kulik, "Pravovye nachala sovetskogo grazhdanstva", *Sovety narodnykh deputatov*, 1979, No.2, pp.37–38. Also, R.I. Kulik, *op. cit.* (note 2 above), pp.47–48; V. Shevtsov, *Grazhdanstvo SSSR*, Moscow 1980, pp.37, 39.
52. I.K. Gorodetskaia, *op. cit.* (note 28 above), p.44. Likewise, V. Shevtsov, *op. cit.* (note 51 above), p.36.
53. I.K. Gorodetskaia, *op. cit.* (note 28 above), p.44.
54. V.S. Shevtsov, *op. cit.* (note 24 above), p.113; *idem*, *Citizenship of the USSR (A Legal Study)*, Moscow 1979, p.103.
55. R.I. Kulik, *op. cit.* (note 2 above), p.36.
56. V. Durdenevskii, *op. cit.* (note 13 above), p.65. Also, *idem*, in V.N. Durdenevskii & S.B. Krylov, eds., *op. cit.* (note 25 above), p.187.
57. E.g., V.S. Shevtsov, *op. cit.* (note 17 above), p.50.
58. Cf., V. Shevtsov, *op. cit.* (note 51 above), p.41; *idem*, *op. cit.* (note 54 above), p.122; *idem*, in *Konstitutsionnyi status lichnosti v SSSR*, Moscow 1980, p.43.
59. V.V. Polianskii, *op. cit.*, p.128.
60. R.I. Kulik, *op. cit.* (note 2 above), p.36.
61. *Ibid.*, pp.49–50. Similarly, G.I. Tunkin, *op. cit.*, p.28.
62. G.I. Tunkin, *op. cit.*, p.27.
63. R. Kulik, *op. cit.* (note 51 above), p.37. *Idem*, *op. cit.* (note 2 above), p.50.
64. A. Arbuzkin, "Pravovoe polozhenie inostrantsev v SSSR", *Chelovek i zakon*, 1979, No.6, p.16.
65. R. Kulik, *op. cit.* (note 51 above), p.37.
66. N. Salishcheva, E. Koveshnikov, "Novyi zakon o grazhdanstve SSSR", *Sotsialisti-*

cheskaia zakonnost', 1979, No.3, p.11.

67. V.S. Shevtsov, *op. cit.* (note 24 above), p.140; G.I. Tunkin, *op. cit.*, p.28.
68. V.V. Polianskii, *op. cit.*, p.128.
70. Cf. V.S. Shevtsov, *op. cit.* (note 24 above), p.86: "The legislation on Soviet citizenship contains no discriminatory restrictions, onerous or complicated conditions and procedure of recognition, acquisition or loss of citizenship. This legislation is clear and universally easy to understand." Similarly, *idem*, *op. cit.* (note 54 above), p.142.
71. V.S Shevtsov, *op. cit.* (note 54 above), p.93.
72. M. Shafir, *op. cit.*, p.32. Also S.V. Chernichenko, *op. cit.* (note 15 above), p. 63.
73. V.S. Shevtsov, *Gosudarstvennyi suverenitet (Voprosy teorii)*, Moscow 1979, p.109.
74. *Idem*, *op. cit.* (note 54 above), pp.93, 141; *idem*, *Sovetskoe gosudarstvo i lichnost'*, Moscow 1978, p.15.
75. *Idem*, *op. cit.* (note 54 above), p.14.
76. M. Shafir, *op. cit.*, p.32.
77. V.V. Kuznetsov (official rapporteur of the citizenship bill), *Izvestiia*, December 1, 1978. See, too, V. Zenin, *op. cit.*, p.10.
78. R.I. Kulik, *op. cit.* (note 2 above), pp.50–51.
79. S.V. Chernichenko, *op. cit.* (note 15 above), p.61.
80. *Ibid.*, p.63.
81. *Ibid.*, p.155.
82. *Izvestiia*, August 23, 1966.
83. S.V. Chernichenko, *op. cit.* (note 15 above), pp.63–64.
84. V.V. Polianskii, *op. cit.*, p.124, fn.6; S.I. Rusinova, "Zakon o grazhdanstve SSSR", *Pravovedenie*, 1980, No.1, pp.8–9.
85. S.V. Chernichenko, *op. cit.* (note 15 above), p.64. In similar vein, V.S. Shevtsov, *op. cit.* (note 74 above), p.15.
86. Cf., S.V. Chernichenko, *op. cit.* (note 15 above), p.59: "Naturalization takes place at the request or with the consent of the interested person. In particular cases, such consent is presumed (for instance, in connection with the naturalization of minors). As a rule, consent to naturalization must be clearly expressed." The observation is repeated on p.60. See, too, V.S. Shevtsov, *op. cit.* (note 74 above), p.15.
87. G.V. Ignatenko, D.D. Ostapenko, eds., *Mezhdunarodnoe pravo*, Moscow 1978, p.182.
88. S.V. Chernichenko, *op. cit.* (note 15 above), pp.64–65.
89. V.S. Shevtsov, *op. cit.* (note 24 above), p.105; *idem*, *op. cit.* (note 74 above), p.15.
90. G.I. Tunkin, ed., *Mezhdunarodnoe pravo*, Moscow 1974, pp.219–220.
91. G.V. Ignatenko, D.D. Ostapenko, eds., *op. cit.*, p.183.
92. S.V. Chernichenko, *op. cit.* (note 15 above), p.70.
93. For an analysis of the legal relationship between citizenship, on the one hand, and option and repatriation, on the other, see *ibid.*, pp.60, 66–77.
94. E.g., V.S. Shevtsov, *op. cit.* (note 73 above), pp.115–120.
95. *Khronika zashchity prav v SSSR*, New York, October–December 1976, vyp.23–24, pp.58, 62.
96. V. Baiaki, "Obshchee i osobennoe v pravovom regulirovanii grazhdanstva v evropeiskikh sotsialisticheskikh stranakh", *SGiP*, 1976, No.11, pp.85–86.
97. S.V. Chernichenko, *op. cit.* (note 15 above), p.59.
98. A.Ia. Berchenko, "Voprosy sovetskogo grazhdanstva", in *Torzhestvo leninskoi natsional'noi politiki*, Moscow 1963, p.277.
99. V.S. Shevtsov, *op. cit.* (note 24 above), p.140 and fn.1.
100. *Ibid.*, pp.140–141.

101. B.V. Shchetinin, *op. cit.*, p.203.
102. *Khronika zashchity prav v SSSR*, New York 1975, vyp.12, November–December 1974, pp.50–51.
103. *Khronika tekushchikh sobytii*, Moscow, Samizdat, Aug.1, 1979, republished in New York 1980, vyp.53, p.139.

LOSS AND RESTORATION OF SOVIET CITIZENSHIP

1. Grounds for Losing USSR Citizenship

Unlike its 1938 predecessor, the new law contains a general provision (Art. 16) outlining how Soviet citizenship may be lost.[1] Such termination may occur: a) upon exit from USSR citizenship; b) upon deprivation of USSR citizenship; c) on grounds indicated by international agreements concluded by the USSR; and, d) on other grounds provided by the present statute. The last clause refers, we are told, primarily to situations involving minor children. For instance, the law recognizes that where both parents leave Soviet citizenship, the citizenship of their children younger than 14 changes accordingly. This treatment certainly applies to children "by blood", but learned opinions diverge on the question of whether it also extends to adopted children, some Soviet sources claiming that it does,[2] while others maintain that "change of citizenship by the adopting parents ... does not automatically entail change in the citizenship of the adopted children".[3] (The technical aspects of this problem will be discussed in greater detail in the next chapter.) In any event, the distinctive feature here is that change in the citizenship of the children does not require the issuance of a special act by the federal Presidium, as would be the case where a standard release from Soviet citizenship is staged. Additional examples concern loss of USSR citizenship by children sanctioned per agreement of the parents or adopting parents where the latter possess the citizenship of different states or authorization for release on occasions where children are adopted by foreigners or spouses of whom one is a foreigner.[4]

Basically, though, apart from the statement about the role of international accords in this setting which, as mentioned earlier, has the dual effect of broadcasting the Soviet Union's stake in the principle pacta sunt servanda and attesting to the growing significance of inter–state treaties in Soviet practice as a means of regulating such matters,[5] the script follows the old pattern, except for pulling it all neatly together in a single package. The closing paragraph cautions that loss of USSR citizenship incurs loss of the respective republican citizenship. The formulation offers further proof — if more is needed — of the primacy of the federal over the republican status, since not only is the reverse not true but, in fact, that possibility is ruled out by virtue of the formal exclusion of the republican agencies from the denaturalization process: the central apparatus alone can license divestiture of Soviet citizenship.

The picture prompts three doctrinal observations. To begin with, the position has been taken that within the compass of Art.16 the legislator has drawn up an exhaustive roster of the grounds on which Soviet citizenship may be lost and that no other laws can augment the list (in proof of which appeal is made to Art.33 of the USSR Constitution which says that "the grounds and procedure for the acquisition and loss of Soviet citizenship is determined by the Law on the citizenship of the USSR"). This approach reportedly excludes loss of citizenship through resort to some "formal, indefinite or insufficiently clear motive" and, in the words of local spokesmen, marks the superiority of Soviet policy in this domain over the matching practices of most bourgeois nations (pointing the finger specifically at lapses in the record of France and Great Britain).[6] Neither argument is completely convincing. First, unless the Soviet regime promptly develops a much stronger attachment to procedural proprieties than it has evinced in the past, the constitutional injunction is unlikely to operate as an insurmountable barrier to adoption of ancillary measures aimed at enlarging the range of circumstances leading to the loss of Soviet citizenship. Second, the faults here attributed to bourgeois law in the sense of its alleged partiality to mechanical and ambivalent criteria are avoided on the Soviet scene by the simple expedient of relying entirely on blanket pronouncements which really means that administrative discretion reigns supreme and not, contrary to what Soviet jurisprudes seek to imply, that bureaucratic abuses will consequently be foiled and the highest order of objectivity guaranteed. Where the law contains no concrete guidelines and, instead, confines itself to mouthing abstract platitudes, the ensuing performance by the responsible branch of the civil service usually turns out to be utterly random and, hence, inherently unfair rather than benign, as the official version would have us believe. Recent Soviet history in the realm of public affairs certainly warrants that conclusion.

The next item on the agenda relates to the views espoused in Soviet literature that question the existence of any international law norms dealing with loss of citizenship. In these conditions, every state is still held to be obligated to respect just the commonly recognized principles of international law and the treaties that bind it. Thus, mass deprivation of citizenship for racial or national reasons is seen as an infringement of international law because the deed violates the nation's right to self–determination and the prohibition against racial and national discrimination. More conceptually daring (in the Soviet political environment, that is) is the tandem notion that a state must not wholly exclude the possibility of loss of its citizenship since that would be at odds with fundamental human rights.[7] How tight these constraints can afford to be before the treatment crosses the limits of the permissible is not spelled out, so that one is left wondering if explicit "disenfranchisement" would be branded unacceptable while cumulative restrictions, never mind how severe their ultimate impact, would escape indictment or at least would be entitled to a hearing instead of earning instant condemnation. Meantime, the affected individual may discover to his chagrin that the difference in tangible terms is hardly worth talking about.

The last piece of business focuses on the broader theme of the generic nature of the rights enjoyed by Soviet citizens in the field of citizenship law. The conventional wisdom seems to be that citizenship as a particular legal linkage between the individual and the state figures where the person proper is concerned only as an objective fact. The Soviet state alone has the capacity to render a decision regarding change of citizenship by any individual vested with Soviet citizenship, as an intrinsic function of its sovereign power. That is why, we are told, the norms of the legislation on citizenship do not consecrate any subjective rights, except, of course, that in the process of applying these rules the individual exercises his legal competence as a subject of concrete legal relations pertaining to citizenship.

For example, the Soviet citizen cannot demand of his state that it deprive him of its citizenship inasmuch as the initiative to do so lies solely with the state. Granted, the Soviet citizen can approach his state with a request that he be allowed to change citizenship, by submitting a corresponding petition to the federal Presidium. However, the legal competence of the Soviet citizen in this case merely consists of the right to ask for release from Soviet citizenship and in no way entitles him to insist on the validation of his subjective right to switch citizenship. Given that premise, Soviet criticism of the 1948 Universal Declaration of Human Rights for indulging in the glorification of subjective rights at the expense of state sovereignty in proclaiming, inter alia, that everyone has the right to a nationality and that no one shall be arbitrarily deprived of his nationality nor denied the right to change his nationality sounds both logical and inevitable.[8] The fact that this line of reasoning undercuts the essential viability of those freedoms and runs counter to the thrust of contemporary efforts to amplify the scope of these liberties and fill them with substantive content less dependent on each state's unilateral preferences does not appear to trouble the Soviet regime and, for that matter, such an "anti–libertarian" vision squarely fits that system's ideological canon and fixed routine.

2. Exit from Soviet Citizenship

The first paragraph of Article 17 repeats verbatim the language of Article 4 of the 1938 edition in providing that "exit from the citizenship of the USSR is sanctioned by the Presidium of the USSR Supreme Soviet". The law thus establishes a so–called *"permissive procedure for exit from Soviet citizenship"*,[9] i.e., one whereby (1) the individual must obtain the government's consent in order formally to quit Soviet citizenship and cannot legally sever the ties on his own, and (2) the authorities can let the de cujus leave Soviet citizenship, but are not obligated to give their approval and, by withholding it, effectively veto the bid. Some Soviet authors applaud the formula for its organic congruence with the general principles of Soviet citizenship — which is fair enough since it does indeed partake of the dominantly conservative flavor of the statute as a whole — except that when they choose to stress the identity in such terms as shared "humanism" and "democratism",[10] we obviously no longer operate on the same wavelength.

The persistence of the old wording should not obscure the fact that the political climate has certainly changed in the interim, so that the tone of the pronouncement does not convey the sense of some recent doctrinal shifts in this area. For example, back when the draft of the Universal Declaration of Human Rights was being debated in the United Nations, the Soviet delegate did not mind going on record with the statement that "he could not accept the inclusion of the right to change nationality. That was not appropriate in the Declaration. The United Nations should not, in any case, encourage changes of nationality but should respect the relations between states and individuals."[11]

Such candor is no longer popular in Soviet official circles. Today, local spokesmen not only feign to recognize that a state cannot totally exclude the possibility of loss of its citizenship because that sort of action would impinge on basic human rights,[12] but take considerable pains to publicize how closely the norms of Soviet law here comply with the prescriptions featured in an array of international documents to which the USSR now subscribes.[13]

In similar vein, the very conception of the phenomenon of citizenship has been extensively redefined and the latest trend is to picture that status as a mutual association of an individual and the country to which he owes allegiance, a quasi–contractual arrangement that can be sundered only by joint agreement of the interested parties. Stylistically, the image of a two–way liaison looks far more progressive than the rendition prevailing in Stalin's day which in essence referred to citizenship as the legal quality that attached to a person by virtue of his "belonging" to a given state.[14] By current standards, that script suffered from twin major flaws: the choice of terminology put extreme emphasis on the state and relegated the individual to a frankly subordinate position; and, the mode of expression struck an unfortunate note in making the individual sound like an object of state property which, as far as Soviet (and East European) commentators are concerned, is fine when describing feudal or bourgeois mores, but quite unsuitable in talking about the kind of intimate rapport forged between the individual and the state in a socialist milieu.[15]

Most outside observers tend to dismiss these "revisions" as mere verbal artifice which, though propounding a more equal partnership between the citizen and his state entailing reciprocal rights and duties, still leaves the state free to checkmate any move by a Soviet citizen to exchange his Soviet citizenship for that of some other country. While Stalin was alive, the policy was voiced in the bluntest tone imaginable; the current approach is more subtle. Nevertheless, according to the sceptics, the new dressing has not altered the original gameplan and the net outcome remains the same: without official dispensation, a person cannot de jure divest himself of Soviet citizenship.

Looked at practically, the dichotomy is drawn too sharply and the actual record indicates a greater "mix" than credited by the critics. Renunciation of citizenship is not, at this stage, a stranger to the Soviet scene, even if cases of denaturalization do not yet rate as a quotidian affair. On an incremental scale, the individual's lot here has undoubtedly improved. However, one must also concede that the mechanism has only been adjusted, not redesigned, and replicates many of the features of the previous model. The element of continuity is unmistakable, for instance, in the treatment afforded the respective roles played by the individual and the state in the denaturalization process. The theoretical upgrading of the individual's status has not reversed the existing pecking order, and Soviet writers neither pretend otherwise nor try to deny that the state retains a primary stake in these matters.

In the local scenario, the state has sole power to determine the proper grounds for relinquishing its citizenship[16] and, though the statute is silent on that score, administrative routine has in fact narrowed down the viable choices to expatriation prompted by the desire of Soviet citizens married to foreigners to go abroad or of persons seeking to move to another country for permanent residence with an eye to reunifying family units that had been disrupted due to sundry circumstances.[17] Emigration for its own sake is seldom recognized as a valid enough reason to win the applicant an exit visa or permission to renounce Soviet citizenship as a prelude to departure and, indeed, if the individual fails to pass the pre–screening eligibility test operated by the authorities he may never be granted a chance to file a request in the first place and thus at least bring his wishes to the attention of the people in charge of the program.[18] Once the subjective criteria are satisfied, the candidate is allowed to enter a bid and then waits for the apparatus to reach a decision. Soviet spokesmen claim that, in this setting, the Soviet state "always carefully considers these applications and, in conformity with our legislation, approves them".[19] Statistics are cited to that effect. A 1976 account noted that, "in the past few years", all 5,500 Soviet citizens married to foreigners who had expressed the desire to emigrate with their spouses had accompanied their families to 110 different countries. Among them were 544 men. A further 2,000 Soviet citizens in a similar position had so far not informed the appropriate organs of their wish to settle elsewhere, although reportedly they were offered "every opportunity to do so". In addition, between 1945 and December 31, 1975, a total of 122,000 Soviet Jews were said to have left the USSR for Palestine/Israel.[20] By 1980, the figures released by Soviet media showed that 15,000 Soviet citizens had married foreigners and 10,500 of them had moved to more than 100 countries, while the number of emigrants (essentially by grace of the "family reunification" scheme) had meantime risen to around 300,000 and now included Germans, Spaniards, Greeks and Armenians, as well as Jews.[21]

The exodus is therefore fairly sizable, despite the regime's efforts to control the flow in a frame of mind that does not even remotely resemble the benign attitude which Soviet commentators picture as its stock in trade on these occasions. On the other hand, a related remark that in treating questions of emigration, the competent institutions take into account not just the interests of the family (in reunification cases) but foremost the interests of the state[22] is unlikely to get much in the way of argument. Nor is anybody prone to contest the accuracy of the observation that "any steps taken by a citizen with the intention to withdraw from Soviet citizenship without proper permission injure the sovereignty of the Soviet state"[23] in terms of how aptly if reflects the official view.

The conception of denaturalization as a bilateral rapport logically leads to endorsement of the individual's function as a separate party to the relationship. Soviet analysts see the connection too and, in fact, go so far as to posit that "exit from citizenship ... is sanctioned only upon personal petition".[24] Of course, the person's desire alone is not sufficient to end the liaison and the state's acquiescence is still required to dissolve the association,[25] but the initiative presumably must originate with the de cujus and the authorities then just respond to the bid. Two corollary propositions round out the picture: the state cannot on its own mandate renunciation of its citizenship; and, "*automatic loss of Soviet citizenship is not recognized*",[26] as purportedly evidenced by the various safeguards provided against such eventuality in cases of "mixed" marriages, transnational adoptions, etc. Objections come to mind on both counts.

Let us look at the second item first. While it is true that inadvertent lapse of Soviet citizenship can rarely occur due to a host of prophylactic measures instituted by the regime to prevent that contingency, the system is not as foolproof as Soviet commentators would have us believe. For example, children under 14 ipso jure lose Soviet citizenship if both parents leave Soviet citizenship: the minor has no option and the officialdom is not called upon to render an ad hoc decision and, in a technical sense, need only record the results in order to keep score. Next, the matter of voluntariness also raises questions. To begin with, we have historical precedent to show that a similar doctrinal stance in the past, i.e., that denaturalization always presupposed a petition for release from Soviet citizenship personally submitted by the de cujus, did not deter the regime on several occasions from acting affirmatively to license denaturalization of sundry categories of people possessed of particular qualifications. For example, the various treaties on "option" and "repatriation" concluded by the Soviet Union and a number of neighboring states after 1939 foresaw a simplified procedure for the surrender of Soviet citizenship by certain designated elements of the USSR's population, accompanied by their automatic acquisition of the citizenship of the corresponding contracting party. Interestingly enough, in a few instances like results were achieved by unilateral means as well, through the promulgation of domestic decrees billed as authorizing a given class of Soviet citizens to turn in their Soviet citizenship and obtain instead the citizenship of another (specified) country, e.g., an assortment of Soviet citizens of Polish extraction and others of Ukrainian and Russian nationality who had specially distinguished themselves during the war on behalf of the Polish and Czechoslovak cause, respectively, plus Spanish emigrés in the USSR.[27]

Those episodes indicate that the governing apparatus was quite capable then of both modifying the established rules concerning release from Soviet citizenship in terms of lowering in certain cases the usually stringent barriers against such exit and, in essence, inviting applications in that connection from "appointed" constituencies. Comparable exceptions can be made again, whenever convenience or expediency appears to warrant a different treatment of the problem. In fact, the current repertory is already marked by many of the same features. Thus, to the extent that present Soviet administrative practice has followed a pattern whereby relinquishment of Soviet citizenship is virtually bracketed with expatriation and the latter avenue is, to all intents and purposes, open solely to members of a few minority entities, the system operates in a discriminatory fashion and, in substance, means that the authorities tacitly serve notice that eligibility to apply for denaturalization/ expatriation is limited strictly to the people who belong to these fringe groups. The regime's positive role in setting the stage here hardly fits the advertised image of withdrawal from Soviet citizenship procured by random and spontaneous exercise of private will.

Another credibility gap develops over the claim that denaturalization is always the outgrowth of the individual's own overt choice. Consider, for instance, the course nearly all citizens of the USSR must travel today to divest themselves of

Soviet nationality. With rare exception, the loss occurs because a person wishing to leave the USSR is routinely required by the authorities to name Israel as the place of destination, whereupon he is told that he must ask for release from Soviet citizenship as part of the emigration package. To be sure, the de cujus is generally free to decide whether to go or stay and, consequently, to surrender or retain his Soviet citizenship, but it would be prima facie unfair to say that a request to give up Soviet citizenship under these conditions is not externally induced. After all, elsewhere a person can reside abroad and still keep his old citizenship affiliation; by common usage, expatriation does not inherently depend on prior denaturalization and, quite plainly, the opportunity to indulge one's personal preferences is severely curtailed when a potential emigrant must pay the price of waiving his citizenship in order to be let out of the country. To insist on keeping the citizenship at this cost does not rate as a viable option.

The point is not that prospective emigrants would want to remain Soviet citizens in their new homeland if given the chance, but rather that confronting them with the alternative of emigration–cum–denaturalization or continued sojourn in the USSR makes mockery of the original premise that exit from Soviet citizenship is governed by the person's own actions.

The situation is bad enough when individuals of Jewish ancestry figure in the emigration proceedings and verges on the absurd where non–Jews, with no link to Israel, have nevertheless been forced by the competent organs to state in their emigration documents that they intended to move to Israel and, on these grounds, compelled simultaneously to seek denaturalization. Even the flimsy "national" or "folk" rationale now vanishes and the punitive dimensions of the whole scheme become glaringly obvious. For example, that fate befell the late Andrei Amalrik and his wife. Though neither was Jewish and they had received invitations from the United States and Holland where they planned to go, they were officially instructed to declare that they were moving to Israel and, accordingly, were obliged to petition for exit from Soviet citizenship.[28] On occasion, the authorities skip the charade altogether and stage an expulsion in the guise of expatriation, complete with a ready–made set of emigration documents coupled with the standard denaturalization ritual. When Iosif Brodskii was told to leave the country, though he reportedly had never applied for emigration, the responsible agencies supplied the necessary papers (including invitations from fictitious foreign relatives), quickly rubber-stamped an exit permit and "lifted" his Soviet citizenship on the pretext that he was headed for Israel (he actually went to the United States).[29] A more recent incident involved Vladimir Borisov and his wife, Irina Kaplun (since deceased). Following a series of diverse detentions and after being taken into custody, on June 22 (1980) Borisov was

> "forcibly put on an Aeroflot plane flying to Vienna. In Vienna Borisov refused to leave the aircraft until the arrival of the Austrian police. His demand was met: his escort handed over to the Austrian police Borisov's visa for exit from the USSR, drawn up as in the case of citizens voluntarily leaving the USSR for permanent residence in Israel".[30]

A very important innovation, in the opinion of virtually every Soviet legal scholar, is the statutory affirmation of a list of "concrete circumstances when exit from

USSR citizenship can be denied".[31] Such refusal may be forthcoming when the applicant has "unfulfilled obligations to the state or material responsibilities connected with substantial interests of citizens and of state, cooperative, and other social organizations" (Art.17, para.2). Typically, the law cites no positive reasons for letting an interested party relinquish Soviet citizenship, since that might enable the de cujus to argue that he satisfies the criteria and so is entitled to have his wishes complied with. Instead, the legislators have reeled off a string of general conditions that can serve to justify disapproval of petitions for denaturalization. The office procedure, as explained by Soviet spokesmen, calls for the corresponding organs, acting on the authority of the federal Presidium, to study all the facts relating to a request for exit from Soviet citizenship and submit "an objective conclusion" on the merits of the case. If the investigation reveals that the petitioner has not performed certain duties vis-à-vis the state as prescribed by law, say, the obligation of a young specialist who has graduated from a higher institution of learning to work for three years in conformity with the postings on the assignment of specialists, the request for release from citizenship may be rejected. A similar policy applies to persons who have unfulfilled property or financial aid obligations (to children, dependents),[32] commitments owed to housing construction cooperatives, kolkhozes, outstanding bank loans, etc.

Note that the statute resorts here to permissive language, meaning that the law "does not prohibit the Presidium of the USSR Supreme Soviet from permitting a person to forfeit Soviet citizenship even if he has unfulfilled obligations and duties".[33] Indeed, Soviet commentators are prompt to point out that the law-makers did not in this instance have in mind just any unfulfilled obligation and they indicate that it would be unfair to refuse to decide on such a vital socio-political question as denaturalization simply on formal grounds. Reference in this context, we are told, focuses precisely on pending situations in which fundamental or essential interests of citizens or organizations are at stake.[34] What is not mentioned, however, is that the "magnitude" factor attaches only to the "interests of citizens or state, cooperative and other social organizations", but does not concern the state proper. In principle, the omission can, of course, be read either way: the state is not hobbled by considerations of "scale", is at liberty to drop any claim regardless of the latter's size and this total freedom of waiver is bound to profit the individual because a major liability can then be dismissed as easily as a petty one; or, the reverse, to wit, the state has consciously drawn no distinction based on the "gravity of the offense" in order to give itself ample room to stop someone no matter how trivial the charge. The historical record leaves little doubt that the second interpretation sounds far more plausible. Forgetting technicalities for a minute, all this other talk about appreciating the difference between "substantial" and "inconsequential" debits apropos citizens or state, cooperative and various social organizations still sheds no light on where the critical dividing line runs and offers no valid guarantee that reasonable standards will be adhered to in making that determination. Clearly, the local expectation is that the practical answer will be provided by ad hoc executive/administrative fiat and, once again, there is no cause for optimism that the job will be decently done, the sonorous contentions of our Soviet colleagues to the contrary notwithstanding.

The next paragraph of the same article (whose contents are equally new and are pronounced in Soviet circles to be as important as those of the preceding clause) lays down the rule that "release from USSR citizenship is not permitted if the person applying for release figures as a defendant or there is against him a sentence of a court of law that has entered into legal force and is subject to execution, or if renunciation by this person of USSR citizenship contradicts the interests of state security of the USSR". Several motives are cited for the move. First, in regard to the judicial side of the picture, the arrangement is characterized as a normal precautionary measure dictated by the thought that a person's exit from Soviet citizenship "markedly alters his legal status", which, in turn, can definitely affect the situation in all these cases.[35] The view among members of the Soviet legal profession is that "it would be unlawful and immoral to allow release from citizenship of a person who, for example, has been arraigned or is slated to serve sentence imposed by a court in accordance with established procedure for a crime he has committed". To act differently, they argue, would violate the tenets of current legislation (e.g., Art.3 of the Fundamental Principles of Criminal Procedure) requiring that state organs take all possible steps to uncover crimes, ascertain the relevant facts, apprehend the guilty parties and bring them to justice.[36]

Nor do Soviet authorities see anything strange in the desire of their government to prevent leaks harmful to national security by barring the denaturalization of persons privy to sensitive data. The official version is that the world still suffers from considerable tension, "despite the gigantic efforts of the Soviet state and the entire socialist commonwealth". The intelligence networks of the imperialist powers miss no trick in the book to extract valuable information from people leaving the USSR. Hence, local spokesmen maintain, "it would be an act of supreme naivete and irresponsibility toward the people, neglect of the elementary rules for protecting the safety of our state to sanction expatriation by persons with access to the state secrets of the USSR". The norms featured in the latest law on this subject are said to comply in full with the prescriptions of international law, especially Article 12 of the International Covenant on Civil and Political Rights,[37] and stem from the need to "ensure the defense capability of the USSR, its readiness to parry any aggression".[38]

Hard analysis of the Soviet record in applying the criteria pertaining to discretionary denial or automatic foreclosure of egress from Soviet citizenship is difficult for the simple reason that the competent agencies do not have to account for the decisions they reach here. We thus have no evidence by which to judge what causes the administrative apparatus to approve or reject a particular request for release from Soviet citizenship. On the other hand, the statutory language used in this connection matches the wording of the provision (Art.25) of the recently enacted Law on the legal status of foreign citizens in the USSR defining the terms of their departure from the USSR[39] and echoes the statements voiced by Soviet official spokesmen and legal scholars in discussing the indicia of eligibility for emigration from the USSR. What we have here, then, is a unified set of rules, a sort of mini–code, regulating all three curricula, which leads to the assumption that these activities further share a common repertory. To the extent that the policy in the sphere of emigration is well documented, extrapolating from that experience is likely to shed light on the practice followed with respect to denaturalization. (Both this topic and the relationship between this section of the statute and the precepts of international law will be dealt with in detail in subsequent chapters.)

Even so, a few general observations may now be in order. For example, Soviet writers often make the point that the government's intention in adopting this routine was to forestall the possibility that a person's exit from local citizenship might inflict injury on the state, its institutions and social organizations, as well as fellow citizens. That concept is not per se objectionable. Far more risqué, however, is the companion assertion that the elaboration of this "exhaustive list enables persons petitioning for withdrawal from Soviet citizenship to know precisely the grounds on which they may be denied such release".[40] Two counts of demurrer may be entered. First, the suggestion that the statute's catalogue of "disqualifying conditions" relating to denaturalization is preemptive is open to challenge. Soviet legal experts have always insisted that "different occurrences in life may bring about the request for exit from Soviet citizenship", so that "in all instances the decision of the question is preceded by a meticulous analysis and comprehensive examination of all the circumstances",[41] which plainly connotes a wider range of inquiry than just a look at whether certain technical pre–requisites have been met. Another theme that continues to recur is that the legislators were prompted to espouse the present modus operandi by concern not only for the welfare of the state, organizations and interested citizens, but also of the person seeking denaturalization himself.[42] Whenever the state casts itself in the role of custodian of the individual's rights, it is prone to expand the scope of its assignment and to assume unwarranted prerogatives in decreeing what is good for the ward without paying adequate attention to the latter's own desires. On the Soviet scene, such usurpation is a common enough phenomenon and no special immunity would accrue to this pocket of activity.

Second, the idea per se that the language of today's law can serve as an accurate signpost to someone contemplating renunciation of Soviet citizenship is not viable simply because the terms are too vague to pass any realistic reliance test. The cumulative effect of conscious resort to general pronouncements is virtually to destroy the legislation's meaning as a tool for shaping human behavior since the key element of predictability will then be lacking and legal culture does not readily accommodate the notion of a game played at random. Worse yet, a "fluid" relationship in essence tends to put the weaker partner at the mercy of the stronger associate and therefore to say that the individual's stake is amply protected in a rapport based on considerations of power rather than due process is to defy credibility. The utter frustration here experienced by ordinary Soviet citizens caught in the administrative maze is evidenced by repeated reports of bids for unilateral divestiture of Soviet citizenship.[43] The authorities consistently ignore these attempts, of course, but for a person to be willing to take that risk shows that he must have lost all faith in the fitness of the official canon.

In conclusion, one ought to mention that none of the criticisms and proposals for reform heard during the "liberal" sixties with reference to the former statute's treatment of the subject of denaturalization ultimately gained legislative acceptance. Thus, the old regulations had been adjudged defective for neglecting to spell out the minimum age at which an individual could ask to be relieved of his Soviet citizenship[44] and the opinion was expressed that a person should attain majority before being permitted to take so vital a step in order to make sure that the choice reflected a clear grasp of the seriousness of the occasion and its consequences.[45] They were likewise faulted for not requiring "submission by the de cujus of proof that, having lost his Soviet citizenship, he will be admitted to a foreign citizenship".[46] A more substantive recommendation favored changes in the existing law destined to facilitate "transfer into the citizenship of the people's democratic states by Soviet citizens". Again, the reason given for advocating the amendment was that such a solution would better convey the flavor of "the development of the world socialist system as the beginning of the historical process of peoples generally drawing closer together".[47] The gesture would still have marked no more than a small sacrifice on the altar of "proletarian internationalism", otherwise leaving unimpaired the inherent rigidity of the operating procedure in all standard cases. At any rate, even this agenda of modest revisions won no converts in high places, as the final text indicates.

3. Deprivation of USSR Citizenship

The penultimate article of the 1938 enactment dealt with the question of forfeiture of Soviet citizenship. This could take place either upon a decree of a court of law in instances prescribed by law,[48] or on the strength of a special decree in each case of the Presidium of the USSR Supreme Soviet. The concept of withdrawing a person's citizenship by court order dates back to the Fundamental Principles of Criminal Legislation of the USSR and the union republics, promulgated on October 31, 1924, which bracketed that "measure of social defense" with pronouncing the defendant "an enemy of the working class" and banishing him forever from the USSR. The Criminal Codes subsequently passed by the republics incorporated the composite formula, reserving that "dire" penalty for certain "counter-revolutionary" crimes. Actually, it was very rarely used, and by 1948 a textbook on Soviet criminal law could openly acknowledge that "in court practice this measure is almost never encountered".[49] The new Fundamental Principles of Criminal Legislation of the USSR and the union republics, enacted on December 25, 1958, no longer feature that sanction. So, although the Citizenship Law of 1938 for a while continued to speak of forfeiture of Soviet citizenship by sentence of a court, this section of the statute was a dead letter after that, until at last it was formally repealed by the decree of January 19, 1961.[50]

Loss of citizenship by ad hoc executive decree, however, remained very much a part of the Soviet legal scene. Even so, official and scholarly commentary on the subject was singularly sparse, presumably because the natives did not want to attract excessive attention to a phenomenon which they treated as a rare and extraordinary occurrence. What few remarks they made do deserve brief notice. In the international forum, for example, Soviet delegates felt called upon to state their mind in the course of the debates in the United Nations on the draft of the Universal Declaration of Human Rights in reference to a clause meant to prohibit the deprivation of nationality. The Soviet representative urged that the section be rewritten to read, inter alia, that "no one shall be arbitrarily deprived of his nationality, i.e., in any other manner or in any other case than provided for in the laws of the country concerned".[51] The suggestion was eventually rejected and the final version here featured the formula "No one shall be arbitrarily deprived of his nationality ...". The difference between the two versions is significant. The official copy contains a general injunction against arbitrary "disenfranchisement" of an individual, whereas the Soviet alternative sought to spare the law from any such test: as long as a person's nationality was "repealed" in compliance with the terms of existing legislation, the latter would be immune from scrutiny as to whether they too were free of any tinge of arbitrariness (substantive due process versus adjectival due process).

A similar reluctance to accept external limitations on the state's power to cancel the citizenship of one of its nationals sets the tone for the Soviet representative's observations during the International Law Commission's discussion of the Draft Conventions on Future Elimination (and Reduction) of Statelessness in response to a motion to add a provision mandating that no person could be deprived of his nationality except in pursuance of a decision by a competent authority in accordance with due process of law. The Soviet diplomat now took the position that:

> "The question of deprivation of nationality must be examined further, since it involves a number of general philosophical considerations. There were some states where moral and political identity between the individual and the state has been achieved, and clearly, sanctions must be brought to bear against individuals whose acts tended to destroy or undermine that identity."[52]

Again, the pitch is in favor of the state or, at least, those states in which reigns this supreme civic communion — the prime example being the USSR. Where full social consensus has been reached, loss of membership in the community is made to sound like a perfectly suitable punishment for public deportment that threatens to disrupt this unique rapport. The only trouble is that the script casts the state in the role of both party and judge in the case and not many people will trust that arrangement to produce an objective verdict.

Ultima ratio, the Soviets can still fall back on the technical argument that these principles have not attained the status of universally valid norms. The USSR never adhered to the Conventions, which would be enough to take care of this problem. The defense mounted against the Declaration is that it does not qualify as an international treaty and just as other such resolutions of the UN General Assembly constitutes a recommendation which is not legally binding on states. Furthermore, inasmuch as the subsequent practice of states did not follow this precept of the Declaration, it could not currently be regarded as a customary rule of international law. The conclusion was that general agreement prevailed to the effect that international law sanctioned the right of a state to deprive individual citizens of its nationality.[53]

Next, local sources also revealed that the socialist countries had developed an interesting intramural policy whereby a person deprived of citizenship by one socialist state was not accepted as a citizen by the other socialist states.[54] The assumption is that the synchronization was accomplished through administrative channels, since neither the legislative nor the treaty record yields an appropriate artifact. The affected individual's options are, of course, reduced by virtue of this "united front", but in all probability a person forcibly denaturalized by a socialist regime would look for relief outside the league rather than shop around within the system.

Another point which drew some attention was apropos the law's evident failure to specify which offenses incurred this "drastic" punishment.[55] Soviet analysts profess not to see anything strange in that situation and note the item without betraying any compulsion to explicate the matter, merely chronicling that:

> "Deprivation of citizenship can occur in some countries even if the grounds for so doing are not spelled out in routine or special legislation. In that event, it is staged by means of a resolution of the supreme organ of state power and concerns a particular person or persons. Thus, in the Soviet Union, the Presidium of the USSR Supreme Soviet has the right to deprive any person of citizenship despite the absence at the time of a special law sanctioning the deprivation of citizenship of a certain category of people."[56]

In short, the executive branch is granted absolute discretion in these affairs and yet Soviet scribes indicate no awareness of an anomaly between the ostensible gravity of the penalty and the lack of legislative guidelines governing its application.

Armed with this carte blanche, the regime did indeed publish several edicts over the years citing individuals whose Soviet citizenship was forthwith revoked. An extensive list of such names was issued in 1938 and the announcement did not even bother to say what these people had allegedly done to deserve retribution.[57] A second, somewhat shorter, roster put out in 1939 charged that the designated individuals had been guilty of acts "dishonoring the calling of Soviet citizen", but did not volunteer further details.[58] Much later, there was the case of Valerii Tarsis, the controversial author, who was permitted to travel to the United Kingdom and, while on the visit, watched his Soviet citizenship annulled by decree of the Presidium of the USSR Supreme Soviet again on grounds that the subject had committed "actions discrediting a citizen of the USSR".[59] In sum, that fate lay in store for persistent and troublesome opponents and critics of the Soviet government whom the latter thought it unnecessary or impolitic to repress by other, more direct, means. It disowned them and by this device attempted to bill them as "enemies of socialism, traitors to the Motherland, unworthy of bearing the title of citizen of a socialist state",[60] thus hoping to wreck their public image and take the sting out of their denunciations of various aspects of life in the Soviet Union.

The treatment of Tarsis raises an important ancillary question in the sense that, although he was not, strictly speaking, expelled from the USSR, nonetheless the cancellation of his Soviet citizenship in absentia operated to bar his return "home" and stranded him in exile. Now, Soviet students of international law claim to share the view of their colleagues elsewhere that

> "a state is obliged, in letting its citizens go abroad or in banishing them for whatever reasons beyond the borders of its own territory, to take into account the willingness of foreign states to receive those citizens. The duty of a state not to foist its own citizens on other states is an inevitable outgrowth of the principles of the sovereign equality of states and non-interference."[61]

How Tarsis' experience fits that scenario is totally unclear. True, the Soviet authorities would probably maintain that the "host" nation can still safeguard its sovereignty here by ridding itself of an unwanted "guest" that had been unceremoniously dropped in its lap through the expedient of re-exporting him to a third country, but that should not absolve the Soviet Union of blame for the original breach of international etiquette. (Today, very little effort is made to disguise these "dumping" practices, as will be shown in a moment.)

At any rate, the inconsistencies that marked the substantive side of the picture did not spill over into the procedural half where the pieces fell into a uniform pattern. Suddenly, beginning in 1970, precedent was abandoned and new "styles" were introduced in this department. The first innovation surfaced when, in a curt announcement printed on the last page (10) of *Vedomosti Verkhovnogo Soveta SSSR*, 1970, No.1, the Soviet government revealed that "in accordance with the Law of the USSR of August 19, 1938, 'On the Citizenship of the USSR' the Presidium of the USSR Supreme Soviet by Decree of December 19, 1969, for misconduct defaming the title of citizen of the USSR, deprived Svetlana Iosifovna Allilueva, born in 1924, native of Moscow, residing in the USA, of her Soviet citizenship".

The statute invoked as the basis for the action did, of course, permit the cancellation of Soviet citizenship in particular cases by executive fiat, in the manner just described. Moreover, a precise decree was identified as the means chosen for accomplishing the job, again in line with the established regulations. For some strange reason, however, the text of the edict itself was not released nor was it published in "Section Two" of the *Vedomosti* reserved for legislative measures not of a general normative character, in stark contrast, for example, with the procedure observed in stripping Tarsis of his Soviet citizenship a few years earlier, or, back in 1938 and 1939, in revoking the Soviet citizenship of a large group of individuals associated with the political opposition to Stalin's regime.

Why this sharp switch from the original track is a puzzle. On the other hand, the Soviet hierarchy might simply not have wished to dignify what it considered to be the dishonorable behavior of Stalin's daughter by promulgating a special edict to "punish" her for expressing anti-Soviet sentiments or perhaps hoped to avoid dramatizing and advertising the incident by burying the news in the portion of the *Vedomosti* devoted to miscellaneous business. Alternatively, the move may have been intended as a compromise solution induced by technical exigencies. In effect, Miss Allilueva has publicly asserted, in a story widely disseminated by the press, that she had burned her Soviet passport in the summer of 1967 before several witnesses.[62] Then, in July of 1969, pursuant to her testimony, her lawyers applied on her behalf to the Soviet consulate in Washington seeking legal renunciation of her Soviet citizenship. In a letter dated July 31st, her attorney informed the Soviet mission that:

> "She has renounced her Soviet citizenship and has asked us to inquire of you as to the appropriate procedure to be followed by her to receive a confirmation of that renunciation from the Soviet government."

Neither this communication nor the next, of November 24, 1969, elicited a reply.[63]

Under the circumstances, a decree unilaterally annulling the Soviet citizenship of a person who had already renounced it and has instituted steps to have that fact acknowledged might have seemed all–advised. In order possibly not to stir up vexing discussions about whether pride of place went to the act of renunciation or revocation and which of these enjoyed legal priority and hence was responsible for having engineered the denaturalization of the party concerned, an ambiguous formula was contrived which alluded to a formal decree but did not produce it, thereby fulfilling in principle the law's stipulation while circumventing it in practice, strictly for purposes of political convenience, one would guess.

All this speculation is really fueled by the family connections of the person involved which are sufficiently unusual to warrant perhaps a different political approach. It may very well be, though, that no elaborate diagnosis is required and the plain answer is that the apparatus is either ignorant of or insensitive to the virtues of administrative coherence. Certainly, A.A. Zinov'ev, who is a commoner, should have received routine treatment when he was relieved of his Soviet citizenship for systematically engaging in "actions incompatible with possession of the citizenship of the USSR ..., conduct detrimental to the prestige of the USSR, randt actions demeaning the calling of citizen of the USSR". Yet, he earned the same type of notice posted in the last part of the parliamentary gazette recording withdrawal of his Soviet citizenship, except that the message contained no reference to a specific decree on this occasion or even the date on which the ouster had allegely occurred.[64] The oversight serves to reenforce the impression of a generally lackadaisical attitude toward form within the bureaucracy running the operation.

The next permutation joined the repertory soon after the Allilueva episode. On December 13, 1972, while on a one–month trip to the United States, V. Chalidze was visited by an employee of the Soviet consulate who, in the course of the conversation, asked to see Chalidze's passport in order to check the visa. The official then pocketed the passport and told Chalidze that on December 12, 1972, the Presidium of the USSR Supreme Soviet had ruled to deprive Chalidze of his Soviet citizenship and that now he could not return to the USSR. No reply was forthcoming to Chalidze's letter addressed to the chairman of the federal Presidium where, inter alia, he objected to a procedure that penalized an individual without first indicating the concrete motives behind the move and listening to explanations and arguments he might be prepared to make in his own defense and called for a review of the decision and repeal of the corresponding decree.[65] In this instance, an exactly dated decree was cited as the medium for consummating the summary denaturalization (as per the original model), but the text of the edict was never published (or paraphrased) in the legislative bulletin.

The story was repeated in the case of Zh. Medvedev. During an authorized sojourn in England, he was invited to come to the London embassy on August 8 and to bring along his passport on the pretext of getting a permit to travel to the United States. Upon arrival, he was informed that on July 16, 1973, the Presidium of the USSR Supreme Soviet had withdrawn his Soviet citizenship.[66] Once again, there is no trace of the respective decree in the journal issued over the imprint of the national legislature. Less than a year later, we have the incident with A.I. Solzhenitsyn. On February 12, 1974, he was taken into police custody, detained, and the following morning escorted aboard an Aeroflot plane headed for Frankfurt–am–Main, West Germany. Shortly before the plane landed, the Soviet authorities alerted their West German counterparts to expect Solzhenitsyn and the latter expressed their willingness to receive him. Meantime, the Soviet press carried a TASS release with the news that by decree of the Presidium of the USSR Supreme Soviet A.I. Solzhenitsyn had been deprived of the citizenship of the USSR and on February 13 evicted from the territory of the USSR. His family was said to be free to rejoin him abroad whenever they wished and indeed did so soon after.[67]

Note that Solzhenitsyn's dossier further differs from the rest of the lot. First, the Soviet authorities here perpetrated a blatant act of expulsion and were saved from the potentially embarrassing consequences of "trespassing" on a foreign country's territory only by virtue of last–minute acquiescence on the other's part in "welcoming the surprise guest". How Solzhenitsyn would have fared had Bonn responded negatively and what alibi the Soviet regime would have mustered when thus caught in flagrante delicto is left to our imagination, but it is obvious that a gross violation of international law was just barely avoided thanks to the West German government's complaisance in the face of Moscow's impropriety. Second, the Soviet legal canon no longer featured the punishment of exile which meant that Solzhenitsyn's banishment either constituted a distinct violation of local law or fell into the category of those discretionary powers that the executive branch could exercise without benefit of a legislative mandate.[68] On the other hand, like the balance of the sample, the edict voiding Solzhenitsyn's citizenship did not grace the pages of the official record.

At this point, let me add that a technical rationale can be offered for the occasional decision not to publish such decrees. In Soviet legal doctrine, "a decree of the Presidium of the USSR Supreme Soviet on deprivation of citizenship will not have normative character" and "must be considered as an act of application of the law, an act of effectuation of the competencies entrusted to the Presidium by the Constitution of the USSR".[69] "Special bills" do not, then, have to be printed in the congressional gazette and items of no general interest to the mass of the population are frequently skipped. Criticism in this instance is not directed at the fact of omission per se, but at the erratic quality of the whole performance in which choice seems to be dictated by happenstance or caprice rather than logic.

For, resort to "deviant" procedures did not, of course, preclude reliance on the standard modus operandi as well. Between 1975 and December 1, 1978, i.e., the date of passage of the new citizenship statute, five decrees were published whereby six people were peremptorily stripped of their Soviet citizenship: V.E. Maksimov, N.D. Solzhenitsyna, P.G. Grigorenko, M.L. Rostropovich and G.P. Vishnevskaia, and O.Ia. Rabin.[70]

Under the provisions of Article 18 of the 1978 legislation, deprivation of Soviet citizenship can occur "in an exceptional case by decision of the Presidium of the USSR Supreme Soviet if the person committed acts discrediting the high calling of citizen of the USSR and harming the prestige or state security of the USSR". Despite the elaborate language (missing in the 1938 edition), the script has gained nothing in substance, for the clause merely repeats the grounds for indictment routinely intoned in the random edicts previously issued by means of which designated individuals were forthwith relieved of their Soviet citizenship. As before, the charges are couched in such vague terms that the formula can be stretched to meet any contingency — an aspect of the picture that must be attributed to policy calculations and not blind chance. Otherwise, the prime innovation resides in the fact that the motives traditionally adduced by the regime for lifting the citizenship of various individuals who had incurred its displeasure are now spelled out in the statute proper instead of, as hitherto, representing a product of executive improvisation. The law takes care to note, though, that the deprivation of a person of USSR citizenship entails no change in the citizenship of the spouse or children.

Hopes that the adoption of the new law would put some order in the procedural closet were soon dashed, however. On April 27, 1979, while in jail, E.S. Kuznetsov was summoned to appear before a three–man board and told that, "by decree of the Presidium of the Supreme Soviet of the USSR", he, as a state offender, was "hereby deprived of his Soviet citizenship and must leave the territory of the USSR within two hours".[71] The staging thus reverted to a combination of expulsion (still practiced without legislative license) and a decree the text of which was not released. Only on June 15, 1979, did the federal Presidium at last promulgate a decree explaining how the citizenship law was to be put into force which, inter alia, recognized that a person deprived of USSR citizenship in accordance with Article 18 could be evicted from the premises.[72] The regime was at least intelligent enough to use a permissive, and not imperative, turn of phrase, which left it with a facesaving device in the event no foreign country volunteered to host an individual stripped of Soviet citizenship. Furthermore, lip–service was paid to the dictates of international law and a technical defense mounted against potential charges that Soviet policy slighted the key concepts of sovereign equality of states and non–interference. Presumably, an individual officially deprived of Soviet citizenship and found to be "non–exportable" would be sentenced to lead a stateless existence on Soviet territory. An insight into how the refurbished system operates is afforded by the experience of T. Goricheva, N. Malakhovskaia and T. Mamonova who ran afoul of the KGB for editing an underground magazine *The Woman and Russia*. All three were arrested and reportedly were given 24 hours to get out of the Soviet Union or face imprisonment. When the trio chose exile, the authorities quickly divested them of their Soviet citizenship.[73] No notice to that effect appears in the primary sources.

Meantime, incidents of deprivation of USSR citizenship by decree in the routine manner multiply. From the tail end of 1978 to the onset of 1983, 13 edicts were published in the legislative bulletin revoking the citizenship of 14 persons: V.L. Korchnoi; V.P. Nekrasov; V.V. Sosnovskii; G.O. Rode; V.K. Lysenko; V.P. Aksenov; L.Z. Kopelev and R.D. Orlova (Kopeleva); V.N. Voinovich; B.V. Kovalenko; S.S. Strubbe; A.S. Glessner; E.M. Ulmann; and L.N. Miussigmann.[74] The wording of the decrees follows a stock formula, except that the one referring to Korchnoi mentions as an extra reason prompting the government's move "the opinion of the Soviet sports community and the Chess Federation of the USSR on this question". The populist theme is pure window–dressing.

A few last observations need to be made. The added clause proclaiming that the deprivation of an individual of USSR citizenship involves no change in the citizenship of the spouse or children is said to have its roots in the "principles of socialist humanism".[75] Nevertheless, a fact worth remembering is that the same results can easily be achieved by surreptitious means, especially where summary denaturalization happens to hit a person visiting abroad and accompanied by members of the immediate family: the latter can be made to share the common fate by the simple expedient of letting their passports lapse. When Zh. Medvedev, for example, was informed that his citizenship had been terminated, he sought to intercede on behalf of his wife and son who, by his account, "were threatened with loss of citizenship upon the expiration of the tenure of their Soviet passports".[76] Refusing to extend the duration of the travel passports handles the practical job of meting out collective punishment without attracting a lot of undesirable attention.

Then, Soviet authors contend that "deprivation of USSR citizenship figures, so to speak, as a force majeure act by the Soviet state and therefore this measure is used extremely rarely".[77] The number of people affected by the special decrees of divestiture is indeed not large, although the sample swells to impressive size if the emigrants who are forced to surrender their Soviet citizenship under circumstances closely approximating compulsory denaturalization are included in the roll call. Even without this increment, however, the scale of the operation should not be the sole criterion. If unilateral revocation of a person's citizenship by executive fiat is deemed a prima facie violation of human rights, a solitary case would still merit condemnation, — and the Soviet regime has more than one such malefaction to its credit.

Finally, Soviet analysts insist that revocation of a person's citizenship does not alter his status in the sense of buying the de cujus immunity from prosecution where his actions qualify as criminal or other types of liability where, for instance, the conduct that led to loss of citizenship also caused material damage or the culprit committed offences beside those that cost him his citizenship. By the same token, we are told, "application to the guilty party of criminal, administrative or civil sanctions does not exclude the possibility of withdrawing his citizenship if the acts committed by him justify doing so".[78]

One is struck by the discrepancy between the views aired on this occasion and the restrictions attached to the process of renunciation of Soviet citizenship. In the latter context, it will be recalled, a person wishing to relinquish Soviet citizenship may be or is barred from winning release if faced with charges similar to the above. The excuse is that access to denaturalization would enable the miscreant to escape justice. The thesis is valid only if voluntary exit from Soviet citizenship is treated as synonymous with expatriation and, inasmuch as the two phenomena are quite separable, an individual could be allowed to quit his citizenship and yet remain subject to local jurisdiction until his "home debts" are settled. Instead, what we have is a situation where the person's "privilege" to leave Soviet citizenship is suspended or denied on the strength of this spurious reasoning while, in an identical setting, the state retains the right to strip the "miscreant" of his Soviet citizenship without fear of thus forfeiting any of its power to chastise the villain. The scene confirms the dramatic asymmetry in the Soviet conception of the respective entitlements of the state and the citizen — if fresh corroboration of the warp be needed.

4. Restoration of USSR Citizenship

The 1938 Law on the Citizenship of the USSR contained no reference to the notion of restoring Soviet citizenship to an individual who once possessed it and then lost it. Or, in the words of a leading Soviet expert in the field, that text did not regulate the matter of "the grounds for and procedure of reinstating people in the citizenship of the USSR, union and autonomous republics".[79] By contrast, the preceding legislative act — the statute of April 22, 1931 — had featured an appropriate clause (Art.15), which read:

> "Persons who have lost the citizenship of the USSR or the union republic may be restored to the citizenship of the USSR by decree of the Presidium of the Central Executive Committee of the USSR or by decree of the Presidium of the Central Executive Committee of the union republic whose citizens they were.
>
> Persons whose citizenship of the USSR or of the union republic has been forfeited may be restored to their citizenship by the Presidium of the Central Executive Committee of the USSR or by the Presidium of the Central Executive Committee of the union republic by whose decree the citizenship had been forfeited."[80]

After the 1938 law was promulgated, though, its 1931 predecessor was formally repealed,[81] and the formula quoted above presumably dropped out of the Soviet legal repertory.

The law's silence on the subject was not construed to mean that reinstatement in Soviet citizenship could not take place, in the technical sense that an individual who had renounced or had been stripped of Soviet citizenship could not, ipso jure, regain that status. Rather, the occasional comments on the topic found in the legal literature simply explained that no special preferences now existed for persons wanting to revert to Soviet citizenship and that the "returnees" could be "admitted to the citizenship of the USSR on general terms".[82] Interestingly enough, advocacy of the principle of "naturalization de novo" paralleled explicit recognition by Soviet spokesmen of the fact that, "as a rule, in connection with reintegration [i.e., reinstatement in the citizenship of a given state of an individual who lost that citizenship] easier conditions are granted than those that control entry into citizenship".[83] The rule apparently did not extend to the USSR, for local law did not promise any concessions on that score and legal doctrine declared that none was forthcoming. Ideological pique may account for this reluctance to afford privileged treatment to individuals whose poor judgment had cost them their Soviet citizenship (either via release or divestiture) or perhaps the feeling that plain naturalization was already so facile that further relaxation of the regulations for the sake of reinstitution of Soviet citizenship was not warranted since the "prodigal son" would incur no extra burden by being asked to retrace the original access route.

The political nature of the beast next prompts a question of primary practical importance, namely, what kind of welcome a retrovert might expect if his past record exposed him to possible official reprisals. The issue's relevance is attested to by the decision of the Presidium of the CEC of the USSR to request a plenary session of the USSR Supreme Court to clarify whether "an act of reinstatement in rights of citizenship of individual persons returning from abroad figures as an act of application to them of amnesty for the counter–revolutionary deeds committed or as sanction of the right to enter the confines of the USSR". On January 16, 1925, the federal Supreme Court advised the executive branch that, in its opinion: 1) if the Presidium's resolution concerning recovery of citizenship came in response to a petition asking specifically for reinstatement, without any indication on the part of the suppliant of the crimes he had committed, it cannot be regarded as a concurrent act of private amnesty for all the counter–revolutionary and other crimes committed by the de cujus; 2) if the decision concerning recovery of citizenship followed upon a petition also for amnesty for the crimes committed by the candidate with exact indication of these crimes, the resolution must be considered a simultaneous act of private amnesty for the crimes indicated in the petition, as a consequence of which a person thus pardoned could be brought to trial only for more serious crimes about which he had knowingly kept silent or consciously lied in his petition. The pronouncement (listed as valid late in 1978 and presumably in force today) was assigned retroactive effect.[84]

Recoupment of Soviet citizenship by particular individuals may have occurred during the earlier tenure of the 1938 statute, but Soviet sources cite no illustrative cases. On the other hand, a major experiment in collective renaturalization was staged in the post–war years. Beginning November 10, 1945, a string of edicts, virtually identical in content, mutatis mutandis, authorized persons residing at the time in Manchuria, the province of Sinkiang, the cities of Shanghai and Tientsin, in France, Yugoslavia, Bulgaria, Japan, Czechoslovakia, and Belgium who on November 7, 1917, were subjects of the former Russian empire, as well as persons who, having possessed Soviet citizenship, lost it, together with their children, to recover Soviet citizenship.[85] Those among them who wished their Soviet citizenship resurrected had to submit an application to that effect with the local Soviet diplomatic mission, appending to it documents establishing their identity and the fact that they were once subjects of the old Russian empire or Soviet citizens. These papers would be examined on the spot and if they were found to satisfy the requirements of the law, a permis de séjour would forthwith be delivered to the petitioner. Anyone else who could ask for the return of his or her Soviet citizenship pursuant to these regulations and did not do so by the established deadline could subsequently seek admission to Soviet citizenship in the ordinary fashion.

The project displayed a number of unusual features. First, Soviet writers concede that the government had to resort to issuing ad hoc decrees because the 1938 legislation lacked a suitable provision. Adoption of these measures was allegedly necessitated by the "enlargement of the territory of the USSR, the addition of new union republics" and by the regime's desire to accommodate "the requests of subjects of the former Russian empire residing abroad to accept them into Soviet citizenship".[86] Second, the locals imply that, initially, the authorities contemplated sticking with the standard admission procedure, but, given the scale of the enterprise, that type of operation looked difficult and unfeasible and these considerations ultimately prompted the switch to this improvised method.[87] Third, despite statements that the tone of the 1938 score signified that restoration of Soviet citizenship would henceforth be performed strictly on "general terms", this packet of decrees introduced a simplified drill designed to facilitate and expedite the transaction. Routine restoration moved at a normal pace, but apparently the competent organs could always crank up the machinery by devising shortcuts for special occasions.

Fourth, re–acquisition of Soviet citizenship did not here depend on emigration to the USSR (although a sizable reflux did ensue)[88] nor in this instance did Moscow always press for immediate repatriation. In fact, a paradoxical aspect of the case is that these "revived" citizens of the Soviet Union could not even assert a right to go and live "back home" on the strength alone of the certificates they received, but had to secure extra visas from the administration if they wanted to transfer their abode to the USSR.[89] Lastly, in a technical sense, the expression "restoration" is only semi–correct in the present situation inasmuch as the "return" of Soviet citizenship was also offered to ex–subjects of the Russian empire who had never staked a valid title to Soviet citizenship as such and whose Russian juridical nationality had at some point after the Bolshevik revolution "atrophied in exile". In order to justify calling their conversion a reversion, the Soviet regime would have to rely on the concept of automatic succession whereby, at least as regards "ownership" of the native population of the Tsarist dominion, the Soviet system crowned itself universal heir to its predecessor's estate.

When the reform of Soviet citizenship legislation was being discussed during the sixties, the problem of restoration of Soviet citizenship got short shrift and the pertinent recommendations boiled down to the proposition that the future law must indicate that "restitution of Soviet citizenship is effectuated in the standard mode set for persons freshly entering Soviet citizenship".[90] No one sounded eager to champion the institution of special waivers in this connection, while everybody seemed to agree on the desirability of including an extra clause in the prospective statute dealing expressis verbis with the theme of "renaturalization".

It is ironic, in view of the professed aversion in Soviet scholarly circles to the whole idea of "easy reintegration" into the citizenship of the USSR, that the very next incident of resort to this practice had all the earmarks of a case sui generis. I refer to the Cherches affair. The reported facts are as follows. No.13 of *Vedomosti Verkhovnogo Soveta SSSR* for 1970 carried on page 140 a small item announcing that: "The Presidium of the Supreme Soviet of the USSR, having examined the request by Abram Lazarevich Cherches, residing in Israel, reinstated his Soviet citizenship and permitted him to return to the Soviet Union."[91] The Presidium purportedly acted in response to a letter from Cherches in which he had written:

> "I spent my whole life in the Soviet Union. The Soviet state gave me everything necessary for life. My sons and daughter received an education. On March 28, 1969, I made a terrible mistake and left the Soviet Union to live with my wife's parents (my sons refused to go).
>
> From the first days of my stay in Israel I saw that everything my wife had told me on the basis of letters from her parents proved to be false.
>
> For a person who had spent his whole life in the Soviet state it is difficult to get accustomed to life in a capitalist state where everything is subordinated to money alone. Only now have I fully realized that I made a mistake in leaving the country where I had been born and had spent my whole life.

My longing for the motherland and for my sons makes my state of mind even worse.

Knowing the humanity of the Soviet state, I ask you not to reject my request, to help me to return to my motherland and to restore my Soviet citizenship."[92]

The Kremlin's motives in publicizing the episode were clear enough. The pitch fitted well the Soviet regime's ongoing anti–Israel campaign and attempted to mount a rebuttal to the persistent Israeli charge that the Soviet Jews were suffering systematic repression in the USSR, the majority were bitterly dissatisfied with their lot there and dreamt of emigrating — to Israel or elsewhere — if granted the opportunity. The account of Mr. Cherches' experience and his alleged disillusionment with Israel and desire to go back to the Soviet Union was expected to help counter the thrust of the Israeli claims.

Whether the various details of Mr. Cherches' story were accurate or not is impossible to verify. From the legal point of view, however, the way in which the matter was handled raises some interesting questions. Indeed, Mr. Cherches' treatment differed from precedent in two respects. First, in the post– war venture analyzed above, the Presidium's directives had been addressed to a specific class of individuals, whereas in this instance the measure was solely meant to meet one man's needs, a classical resort to the device of lex specialis. Second, both under the terms of the 1931 norm and the provisions of the 1945–1947 expedition to recover the emigré elements currently domiciled in certain foreign countries, an appropriate edict was called for and used. Now this was dispensed with. The corresponding fascicle of *Vedomosti* did not reproduce an ukaz in reply to Mr. Cherches' petition and the language of the aforequoted official statement nowhere mentioned a concrete resolution or postanovlenie on the subject. At most, one got the impression that the Presidium had rendered a simple decision in re Cherches which was duly inscribed in the protocol of the minutes of the meeting. Extracted and published in the legislative journal, this routine administrative determination apparently sufficed to consummate the applicant's reversion to Soviet citizenship and open the door to his repatriation to the USSR.

The extreme flexibility of Soviet legislative procedures, as illustrated by this event, and the casual manner in which methods have been adlibbed in order to cope with random contingencies will hardly come as a revelation to any serious watcher of the Soviet scene. If the wayward Mr. Cherches' public vita taught a jurisprudential lesson it was that the Presidium of the USSR Supreme Soviet obviously considered itself competent de lege to restore Soviet citizenship on a singular basis to persons who had owned it and subsequently renounced it, even without benefit of an explicit mandate, but, due to the minor nature of the transaction, preferred to dispose of it by medium of an intramural ruling, afterwards suitably posted for common information, than by going through the elaborate ritual of adopting a full–fledged decree.

According to Soviet sources, Mr. Cherches' "round trip" was typical of the shuttle that took several hundred Soviet Jews to Israel and then later brought them back again to the preferable environment of the USSR. One would assume that all these people, just like our hero, relinquished their Soviet citizenship as a pre–condition to emigration to Israel and would have had to manage to recover it to qualify for repatriation. How this was accomplished remains a deep mystery, for Soviet official sources are innocent of evidence on when and by what means the alchemy occurred. To be sure, public notice of a private bill is not imperative in Soviet usage and this factor could explain the legislative silence surrounding these activities. So why thrust Mr. Cherches into the limelight and disrupt the pattern? A solitary specimen certainly did not prove that a mass reflux was in progress, if that is what the regime intended to demonstrate by producing a "live" trophy. On the contrary, a lone performer sparks legitimate questions about the real size of the rest of the cast. Furthermore, any incidental advantage to be gained from staging such a soliloquy would, in other systems, be more than offset by the stigma commonly attached to indulgence in procedural philandering, but in the Soviet political milieu formal decorum commands a low price and practical expediency rates much higher. The case of Cherches and his fellow–returnees testifies once more to the lack of esteem for organizational and stylistic uniformity intrinsic to the local bureaucratic outlook.

When enacted, the 1978 statute fulfilled expectations by housing a clause establishing that "a person who has lost the citizenship of the USSR may, upon his application, be reinstated in the citizenship of the USSR by decision of the Presidium of the USSR Supreme Soviet". The institution of restoration of citizenship was thus reintroduced in the Soviet legal repertory, although Soviet spokesmen note that the crop of post–war decrees had kept the policy from lapsing altogether. Nevertheless, these had been "episodic acts", whereas now the arrangement functioned on a permanent footing[93] and fitted into a "general format".[94] Even so, the language of the law shed no light on the administrative mechanics of restitution of Soviet citizenship. Insofar as the text did not here refer to any special norms, a Soviet scholar was moved to interpret the blank to signify that the rules pertaining to admission to USSR citizenship would operate in this instance. He added, however, that the law left room to prescribe, if it were thought advisable to do so, "a different routine for processing applications on matters of restoration in the citizenship of the USSR than the one that would be posted by the Presidium of the USSR Supreme Soviet or the Presidia of the Supreme Soviets of the union republics for dealing with applications for admission to the citizenship of the USSR (Art.28)".[95]

These pronouncements proved prophetic. The federal decree of June 15, 1979, explained that petitions for restoration of USSR citizenship were decided by the Presidium of the USSR Supreme Soviet in the manner set for considering applications for admission to USSR citizenship.[96] The rationale behind the choice of this solution, we are told, is that "the legal status of persons who previously lost the citizenship of the USSR is regarded as the status of foreigners or stateless persons",[97] implying that, like the latter, the exes can acquire Soviet citizenship only through regular naturalization channels. In terms of the office modus operandi in this department, the speculation that certain adaptations might have to be made in the system followed in handling original entry applications has turned out to be equally valid. Indeed, another source has since confirmed that

> "by reason of the distinct nature of the circumstances concerning this form of acquisition of citizenship [i.e., through restoration] somewhat different

rules can apply here than in respect to admission to citizenship. However, there cannot be framed conditions in this context that would render the process of recovery of citizenship either easier or more difficult. All the peculiarities of reinstatement in citizenship can relate just to the persona itself of the prospective reentrant as a former citizen of the USSR and cannot run counter to the uniform order of acquisition of Soviet citizenship".[98]

According to Soviet writers, awareness of these variances prompted the legislators to assign restoration a separate slot instead of filing the concept under the broader heading of naturalization, so as better to take into account the special position of the de cujus as a past citizen of the USSR. For example, this extra factor dictated recourse to the principle that restoration of citizenship is effected only by the federal Presidium. Apparently, the premise is that, since the citizenship of the USSR was originally at stake, the competent national organ would have to approve the reversion and the idea makes good sense for the future, given that loss of Soviet citizenship at present can be visaed solely by the central Presidium: what the USSR Presidium has wrought, it alone can undo. Remember, though, that applications for restoration in Soviet citizenship can likewise emanate from people who had lost that status prior to 1938 and, under the terms of the 1931 norm quoted earlier both federal and republican presidia were each fully entitled to sanction renunciation and forfeiture of Soviet citizenship.

Granting the USSR Presidium monopoly authority to permit reinstatement in Soviet citizenship overlooks the possibility that a republican presidium may have been responsible for the applicant's old predicament and, in a sense, constitutes an usurpation of a union republic's right to review its own ruling. The anomaly might have generated enough of a feeling of malaise in some circles to induce the regime to try to accommodate the republics' role in this affair by drawing them into the picture in roundabout fashion anyway. For, secondary sources inform us that:

"in practice, when the question of restoration of Soviet citizenship to a person residing abroad is being decided, the Soviet diplomatic or consular representatives abroad who prepare the documentation for consideration in the Presidium of the USSR Supreme Soviet of the question of restitution of Soviet citizenship request the consent of the Presidium of the Supreme Soviet of the union republic whose citizenship the designated person previously had. After receiving such consent, all the documents are forwarded to the Presidium of the USSR Supreme Soviet for final decision on the question of reinstatement of the person in Soviet citizenship. This practice, in our opinion, exactly squares with the right consecrated in the new USSR Constitution of participation by the union republic in the resolution of questions referred to the jurisdiction of the USSR".[99]

Despite the focus in the preceding passage exclusively on the treatment here afforded to persons domiciled abroad, nothing in the script suggests that a different procedure, mutatis mutandis, would be followed vis-à-vis a person living on Soviet territory who had lost his Soviet citizenship and now desired to recoup it. One might recall that the federal decree of June 15, 1979, which indicated that a person who was stripped of his Soviet citizenship could be evicted from the USSR made expulsion optional so that an individual could conceivably be divested of his

Soviet citizenship and yet continue to live on Soviet soil and, at some point, perhaps wish to recover his Soviet citizenship and be eligible to do so. By the same token, renunciation of Soviet citizenship is not per se contingent on expatriation and, again, a person might win release from Soviet citizenship, remain in the USSR and eventually seek to recover Soviet citizenship and officially qualify for "reintegration". In either situation, resort to an analogous formula sounds quite plausible.

The last bit of technical analysis tackles the ambiguity created by use of the generic expression "loss of Soviet citizenship" in connection with the business of restoration, since from the wording one cannot tell whether the draftsmen had in mind a termination occasioned by release or deprivation or both. An early comment concluded that "a person who for some reason renounced Soviet citizenship may apply to the Presidium of the USSR Supreme Soviet and regain his citizenship on its decision".[100] In this version, renunciation was singled out as the juridical precur sor of the subsequent bid for renaturalization. More recently, that view has been challenged and the opposite thesis has been propounded that "the law stipulates no exceptions whatever for certain categories of persons on issues of restoration of citizenship" and, "consequently, restoration occurs independently of the grounds for loss of citizenship, if the Presidium of the USSR Supreme Soviet judges the particular person to be worthy of it".[101] Knowing the way Soviet law operates, one can safely assume that even deprivation would not preclude a subsequent "pardon", as long as the party concerned had adequately "redeemed" itself in the eyes of the authorities. What these services would have to involve is left to the imagination and the official rapporteur of the bill only alluded mysteriously to the "existence of sufficient reasons"[102] to warrant a step of such magnitude.

NOTES

1. See V. Zenin, "Gromadianstvo SRSR — velika chest' i velika vidpovidal'nist'", *Radianske pravo*, 1979, No.2, p.10.
2. R.I. Kulik, *Zakon o grazhdanstve SSSR*, Moscow 1980, p.64.
3. E.g., *Kommentarii k zakonodatel'stvu o registratsii aktov grazhdanskogo sostoiania*, Moscow 1977, p.185, citing *Kommentarii k Kodeksu o brake i sem'e RSFSR*, Moscow 1971, p.230.
4. R.I. Kulik, *op. cit.*, pp.64–65.
5. *Ibid.*, pp.19–20.
6. *Ibid.*, pp.54, 65.
7. S.V. Chernichenko, *Mezhdunarodno–pravovye voprosy grazhdanstva*, Moscow 1968, p.80.
8. V.S. Shevtsov, *Grazhdanstvo v sovetskom soiuznom gosudarstve*, Moscow 1969, pp.37–38. *Idem*, *Gosudarstvennyi suverenitet (voprosy teorii)*, Moscow 1979, p. 112.
9. V.V. Polianskii, "Printsipy sovetskogo grazhdanstva", *Sovetskoe gosudarstvo i pravo*, 1980, No.5, p.129 (hereafter abbr. as *SGiP*), (italics in original).
10. *Ibid.* See, too, S.I. Rusinova, "Zakon o grazhdanstve SSSR", *Pravovedenie*, 1980, No.1, p.7.
11. A/C.3/SR. 123, at 350, cited by H.–J. Uibopuu, "Soviet Nationality: Privilege or Burden? An International Lawyer's View", *Israel Yearbook on Human Rights*, 1977, Vol.7, p.55.
12. Cf., S.V. Chernichenko, *op. cit.*, p.80. At the international level, the same concept has found expression in the proposition that "option in connection with the passage of territory from one state to another must be considered a mandatory obligation". G.I. Tunkin, ed., *Mezhdunarodnoe pravo*, Moscow 1974, p.220. The idea is enunciated in less absolute terms in G.V. Ignatenko, D.D. Ostapenko, eds., *Mezhdunarodnoe pravo*, Moscow 1978, p.183, which refers to option as the principal means of handling this problem in current international relations, whereas automatic transfer here is viewed as characteristic of the feudal period.
13. E.g., R. Kulik, "Pravovye nachala sovetskogo grazhdanstva", *Sovety narodnykh deputatov*, 1979, No.2, p.39; *idem*, *op. cit.* (note 2 above), pp.56, 58; N. Salishcheva, V. Koveshnikov, "Novyi zakon o grazhdanstve SSSR", *Sotsialisticheskaia zakonnost'*, 1979, No.3, p.12; "The new Law on Soviet citizenship", *Socialism: Theory and Practice*, 1979, No.8, p.63.
14. D. Gaidukov, *Grazhdanstvo SSSR*, Moscow 1940, p.7; Ia.N. Umanskii, *Sovetskoe gosudarstvennoe pravo*, Moscow 1960, p.216; *Iuridicheskii slovar'*, Moscow 1953, p.142.
15. For instance, A.Ia. Berchenko, "Voprosy sovetskogo grazhdanstva", in *Torzhestvo leninskoi natsional'noi politiki*, Moscow 1963, pp.278–280; D.T. Iakovenko, *Radianske gromadianstvo*, Kiev 1960, pp.4–6;V.Ia. Boitsov, "K voprosu o poniatii grazhdanstva kak gosudarstvenno–pravovogo otnosheniia", *Sbornik uchenykh trudov* (Sverdlovskii iurid. in–t), vyp.9, Sverdlovsk 1969, pp.18–26; N.V. Vitruk, "Grazhdanstvo kak pravovaia sviaz' lichnosti s gosudarstvom", *Problemy gosudarstva i prava*, Moscow 1977, No.12, pp.16–17; Iu.A. Petrov, "Sootnosheniia poniatii grazhdanstva, pravosposobnosti, pravovogo polozheniia grazhdan", *Vestnik Leningradskogo universiteta*, 1974, No.5, p.117; V.S. Shevtsov, *Grazhdanstvo* ... (note 8 above), p.14; V. Baiaki, "Obshchee i osobennoe v pravovom regulirovanii grazhdanstva v evropeiskikh sotsialisticheskikh stranakh", *SGiP*, 1976, No.11, p.80.
16. V.S. Shevtsov, *Gosudarstvennyi suverenitet* (note 8 above), p.109.
17. V.M. Safronov, *Ty — grazhdanin Sovetskogo Soiuza*, Moscow 1978, p.25. Also, R.

Kulik, *op. cit.* (note 13 above), p.38.

18. Consider the following episode, reported in *Khronika tekushchikh sobytii*, vyp.60 (Moscow, Samizdat, 1980), New York 1981, p.77:
On November 18, Igor Gerashchenko and Irina Ratushinskaia, who want to leave the USSR, were summoned to the militia. In the office, they were seated on two chairs placed in the middle rof the roomt. Five people sitting around them (three in mufti and two in militia uniforms) questioned Gerashchenko and Ratushinskaia: "What harm did the Soviet system do to you? Why did these two non–Jews want to go to Israel? What are you going to do there? Who needs you there? They maltreat even Jews from the Soviet Union, so they will treat you like negroes? How can anybody lose touch with our life to this extent and sell himself to the enemy?" The whole conversation, lasting 20 minutes, ended with the statement that emigration was denied to them. To the question "By whom?" after some confusion the answer was given: "The Commission on emigration of the passport section of the Leningrad raion department of internal affairs". To the question of how they could be refused if they had not yet submitted the documents (the forms are not being issued to them to submit the documents), they received the answer: "And you won't submit them — forget about it".

19. V.M. Safronov, *op. cit.*, p.24. See, too the USSR Report to the Human Rights Committee, General Assembly Official Records, 33rd session, Supplement No.40 (A/33/40), New York 1978, p.74: "All those wishing to leave the Soviet Union had left, with a few exceptions which were justified for the protection of state security, public order, property and family rights. There were no restrictions in respect of persons intending to leave the USSR. In fact, many people wanted to enter the USSR but encountered obstacles in the countries in which they lived."

20. Interview with Boris Shumilin, USSR Deputy Minister of Internal Affairs, *Soviet News*, 1976, No.5819, p.35.

21. Interview with Konstantin Zotov, head of OVIR in the USSR Ministry of Internal Affairs, *Soviet News*, 1980, No.6024, p.183.

22. V.M. Safronov, *op. cit.*, p.26.

23. V.S. Shevtsov, *Grazhdanstvo ...* (note 8 above), p.52. *Idem*, *Citizenship of the USSR (A Legal Study)*, Moscow 1979, p.48.

24. E.g., R. Kulik, *op. cit.* (note 13 above), p.38. Likewise, S.I. Rusinova, *op. cit.*, p.8; V.S. Shevtsov, *Sovetskoe gosudarstvo i lichnost'*, Moscow 1978, p.15, and *idem*, in *Konstitutsionnyi status lichnosti v SSSR*, Moscow 1980, p.41.

25. Cf., R.I. Kulik, *op. cit.* (note 2 above), p.55.

26. V.V. Polianskii, *op. cit.*, p.128 (italics in original).

27. For more detail, see the author's *Soviet Citizenship Law*, Leiden 1968, pp.41–42, and the sources cited therein.

28. *Khronika zashchity prav v SSSR*, April–June 1976, vyp.20–21, p.43.

29. The authorities dealt the same way with Gesia Pinson, Viktor Shtern and Anna Vudka. See *Khronika zashchity prav v SSSR*, January–March 1976, vyp.19, p.46.

30. *Khronika tekushchikh sobytii*, vyp.57 (Moscow, Samizdat, 1980), New York 1981, p.28.

31. R. Kulik, *op. cit.* (note 13 above), p.38. Also, N.Salishcheva, E. Koveshnikov, *op. cit.*, p.12; G.I. Tunkin, "Zakon o grazhdanstve SSSR", *SGiP*, 1979, No.7, p.28; L.B. Kuzmenko, "Razvitie pravovogo regulirovaniia statusa lichnosti v novom Zakone o grazhdanstve SSSR", *Vestnik Moskovskogo universiteta*, seriia 11: pravo, 1980, No.4, p.32.

32. R. Kulik, *op. cit.* (note 13 above), p.38.

33. "The New Law on Soviet Citizenship", *loc. cit.*

34. R.I. Kulik, *op. cit.* (note 2 above), pp.56–57.

35. G.I. Tunkin, *op. cit.*, p.28.
36. R.I. Kulik, *op. cit.* (note 2 above), p.57.
37. *Idem, op. cit.* (note 13 above), p.39; N. Salishcheva, V. Koveshnikov, *op. cit.*, p.12.
38. R.I. Kulik, *op. cit.* (note 2 above), pp.57–58.
39. Text in *Pravda*, *Izvestiia*, June 25, 1981; *Vedomosti Verkhovnogo Soveta SSSR*, 1981, No.26, Art.836. The law entered into force on January 1, 1982 *(ibid.*, Art. 837).
40. L.B. Kuzmenko, *op. cit.*, p.32.
41. V.S. Shevtsov, *Sovetskoe grazhdanstvo*, Moscow 1965, p.61. *Idem*, *Grazhdanstvo SSSR*, Moscow 1980, p.57.
42. V.V. Polianskii, *op. cit.*, p.129.
43. For just the more recently reported cases, see *Khronika tekushchikh sobytii*, vyp.57, pp.72, 77.
44. Cf., V.S. Shevtsov, *Sovetskoe grazhdanstvo* (note 41 above), p.61.
45. *Idem*, *Grazhdanstvo* ... (note 8 above), p.159.
46. *Idem*, *Sovetskoe grazhdanstvo* (note 41 above), p.61, and *Grazhdanstvo* ... (note 8 above), p.159.
47. A.Ia. Berchenko, *op. cit.*, p.277.
48. As T.A. Taracouzio, "The Soviet Citizenship Law of 1938", *American Journal of International Law*, 1939, No.1, p.157, points out: "From the Statute of 1931 (Article 17) this differs in that now the courts of law are again authorized to act upon the issue." On the other hand, he also observes that: "As a matter of record, it must be noted that in this the new law merely reintroduces the provision found in Article 12 of the Statute of 1924, which was later omitted from the Statute of 1931 without, however, actually affecting the old practice." For further comments on the subject, see H. Freund, "Das neue Staatsangehörigkeitsgesetz der UdSSR", *Zeitschrift für Ostrecht*, 1930, p.708; W.N. Durdenevski (V.N. Durdenevskii), "Die Sovetstaatsangehórigkeit und ihre Neuregelung im Jahre 1930", *Zeitschrift für Ostrecht*, 1931, p.351; *idem*, "Das Staatsangehörigkeitsgesetz der UdSSR", *ibid.*, 1931, pp.519–520.

    It should be noted that the law of November 21, 1929, *(SZ SSSR*, 1929, No.76, Art.732), pursuant to which any Soviet official abroad who refused to come home when summoned by the authorities could be declared an outlaw, did not entail loss of citizenship. As V. Durdenevskii, "Zakon o grazhdanstve Soiuza Sovetskikh Sotsialisticheskikh Respublik", *Problemy sotsialisticheskogo prava*, 1938, No.6, p.63, explains: "In this manner, there was retained the possibility of demanding the surrender of the person refusing to come back if, in addition to a political act, he had committed an act regarded as criminal."
49. V.D. Menshagin, ed., *Ugolovnoe pravo, Obshchaia chast'*, Moscow 1948, p.500. To the same effect, M.D. Shargorodskii, *Nakazanie po sovetskomu ugolovnomu pravu*, Moscow 1958, p.74; I.T. Goliakov, "K proektu Ugolovnogo kodeksa RSFSR", *Sovetskaia iustitsiia*, 1957, No.2, p.31.
50. *VVS SSSR*, 1961, No.4, Art.35.
51. *A/C.3/286/Rev.1*, as quoted by H.–J. Uibopuu, *op. cit.*, p.55.
52. [1952/1] *Yearbook of the International Law Commission*, p.111, *ibid.*, p.56.
53. G.I. Tunkin, *op. cit.*, p.29.
54. V. Baiaki, *op. cit.*, p.83.
55. E.g., V.S. Shevtsov, *Grazhdanstvo* ... (note 8 above), p.156.
56. S.V. Chernichenko, *op. cit.*, p.79. Interestingly enough, the author recognizes (p.155) that states following this policy would find it difficult to adhere to the 1961 Convention on the Reduction of Statelessness in that they could not file a reservation about retaining the right to deprive of their citizenship even in the instances indicated in Art.8 because their

legislation established no special conditions for deprivation of citizenship.

57. *VVS SSSR*, 1938, No.12.

58. *VVS SSSR*, 1939, No.9.

For purposes of the following analysis of the procedural pattern in this area, the two edicts of 1938 and 1939 will not be taken into account as being atypical: because a single decree was apparently used in each case to denaturalize a large group of people (several hundred and 67, respectively), the texts were not published under the appropriate sub–heading and the actions were merely reported in the corresponding "Chronicle" section.

59. *VVS SSSR*, 1966, No.8, Art.135. See, too, *New York Times*, February 22, 1966, p.5.

60. V. Baiaki, *op. cit.*, p.83. Likewise, V.S. Shevtsov, *Grazhdanstvo* ... (note 8 above), p.156, and M. Soloviov, "Pozbavlennia gromadianstva — zasib borot'bi z iavishchami, shcho zavdaiut shkodi radianskii derzhavi", *Radianske pravo*, 1975, No.3, pp.78–81.

61. S.V. Chernichenko, *op. cit.*, p.84.

62. S. Alliluyeva, *Only One Year*, New York 1969, p.340.

63. *New York Times*, January 22, 1970, p.3.

64. *VVS SSSR*, 1978, No.37, p.599.

65. *Khronika zashchity prav v SSSR*, 1973, vyp.1, pp.23–26.

66. *Ibid.*, 1973, vyp.3, pp.36–40.

67. *Ibid.*, 1974, vyp.7, pp.11–12.

68. *New York Times*, February 14, 1974, p.5.

69. S.V. Chernichenko, *op. cit.*, p.80.

70. *VVS SSSR*, 1975, No.44, Art.713; 1977, No.11, Art.194; 1978, No.8, Art.125–No.12, Art.208–No.26, Art.412.

71. E.S. Kuznetsov, "Flight from the Gulag", *New York Times Magazine*, April 27, 1980, p.106.

72. *VVS SSSR*, 1979, No.25, Art.436.

73. *Time*, August 4, 1980, p.41.

74. After the citizenship statute was enacted, but before it entered into force: *VVS SSSR*, 1979, No.1, Art.30, and No.18, Art.358. After the citizenship statute went into effect: *ibid.*, 1980, No.6, Art.119–No.15, Art.287–No.34, Art.711; 1981, No.2, Art.74–No.3, Art.106–No.25, Art.818–No.27, Art.882; *VVS SSSR*, 1982, No.3, Arts.60 and 61; No.12, Art.212.

75. L.B. Kuzmenko, *op. cit.*, p.32.

76. *Khronika zashchity prav v SSSR*, vyp.3, p.40.

77. S.S. Kravchuk, ed., *Sovetskoe gosudarstvennoe pravo*, Moscow 1980, p.222. Likewise, R.I. Kulik, *op. cit.* (note 2 above), p.59.

78. *Ibid.*, p.61. Not at all surprisingly, the author pronounces the deprivation of Solzhenitsyn, Korchnoi et alios of USSR citizenship an "act of absolute justice" (p. 62). Note, too, his claim (p.61) that the decrees of deprivation of Soviet citizenship "always enjoy the support of public opinion, the political endorsement of the people" and that the publication of these edicts is designed to reach a mass audience so as to exert important political–educational influence since loss of status of Soviet citizen "is connected with state and civic censure of the anti–Soviet activity of the individual concerned".

79. V.S. Shevtsov, *Grazhdanstvo* ... (note 8 above), p.148.

80. *SZ*, 1931, No.24, Art.196;English text in T.A. Taracouzio, *The Soviet Union and International Law*, New York 1935, pp.379–382.

81. Decree of June 2, 1939, *VVS SSSR*, 1939, No.22.

82. G.I. Tunkin, ed., *op. cit.*, p.224.

83. *Ibid.*, p.220.

84. Text in *Sbornik postanovlenii Plenuma Verkhovnogo Suda SSSR 1924–1973*, Moscow 1974, pp.364–365; *Sbornik postanovlenii Plenuma Verkhovnogo Suda SSSR 1924– 1977*, Moscow 1978, Vol.2, pp.80–81.
85. *VVS SSSR*, 1945, No.78; 1946, No.2; 1946, No.21; 1946, No.36; 1946, No.37; 1947, No.18. *Sbornik zakonov SSSR i ukazov Prezidiuma Verkhovnogo Soveta SSSR (1938g.–noiabr 1958g.)*, Moscow 1959, pp.78–84.
86. L.B. Kuzmenko, *op. cit.*, p.32. Likewise, D.L. Zlatopol'skii, *Gosudarstvennoe ustroistvo SSSR*, Moscow 1960, p.263, citing archival materials.
87. S.S. Kravchuk, ed., *Sovetskoe gosudarstvennoe pravo*, Moscow 1975, p.164.
88. For example, according to *Izvestiia*, January 6, 1946, in Manchuria alone from the middle of November to the end of December 1945, Soviet consulates received requests for reinstatement in Soviet citizenship: in Harbin — nearly 7,000; in the city of Dal'nyi (Dairen) — more than 1,000; in the city of Manchuria — around 3,000.
89. See A.I. Lepeshkin, *Kurs sovetskogo gosudarstvennogo prava*, Moscow 1961, Vol. 1, p.478.
90. V.S. Shevtsov, *Grazhdanstvo* ... (note 8 above), p.148.
91. Also published in *Pravda*, Mar. 27, 1970.
92. *Soviet News*, 1970, No.5535, p.126. See, too, *Izvestiia*, Aug. 1, 1970.
93. G.I. Tunkin, *op. cit.*, p.29.
94. L.B. Kuzmenko, *op. cit.*, p.32.
95. G.I. Tunkin, *op. cit.*, pp.29–30.
96. Article 6, *VVS SSSR*, 1979, No.25, Art.436.
97. R.I. Kulik, *op. cit.* (note 2 above), p.63.
98. V.V. Polianskii, *op. cit.*, p.128.
99. S. Kosakov, "Konstitutsionnye osnovy kompetentsii soiuznoi respubliki po voprosam grazhdanstva", *Izvestiia Akademii nauk Kazakhskoi SSSR*, 1980, No.5, seriia obshchestvennykh nauk, p.62.
100. "The New Law on Soviet Citizenship", *loc. cit.*
101. R.I. Kulik, *op. cit.* (note 2 above), p.63.
102. Report by V.V. Kuznetsov, *Izvestiia*, Dec.2, 1978.

STATUS OF MINORS

Soviet authors like to point out that "in contrast with the law of 1938 which only briefly referred to the citizenship of children in case of change of citizenship of parents and did not regulate at all the question of citizenship of children in case of adoption, the new law on citizenship devotes to said questions a whole section consisting of 6 articles". The contents of the package, we are told, reflect "on the whole the practice that had crystallized in the USSR on the designated questions".[1] Despite the alleged element of continuity, the decision itself to give administrative routine proper statutory sanction ostensibly attests to the regime's "particular concern for the fate and interests of children"[2] which, Soviet spokesmen add, "fits the humane principles of development of our state as well as the international law act — the Covenant on civil and political rights".[3] Hyperbole aside, this chapter does tackle some of the thorniest issues of citizenship law, at times with singular results; even so, the current piece of legislation comes fairly close to fulfilling the local claim that it procures "precise answers to the questions encountered in life"[4] — especially when compared with the treatment afforded these complicated matters by its laconic predecessor.

1. When Both Parents Change Citizenship

Least troublesome of the lot is the principle enunciated in the lead article to the effect that, "upon change in citizenship of the parents, as a result of which both become citizens of the USSR or both leave the citizenship of the USSR, the citizenship of their children under the age of fourteen changes accordingly". The formula follows the earlier pattern, and also retains the problematic feature whereby the age of discretion in this context is set uncommonly low by universally accepted standards. Why a minor between the ages of fourteen and eighteen should have a right to arrive at a crucial conclusion regarding his citizenship affiliation on his own and perhaps in opposition to the parents' wishes has never been satisfactorily explained by Soviet sources, and one suspects that behind the "liberal" sounding policy lies the bare fact that youngsters are more susceptible to external influences and, by manipulating them, the regime can induce the parents to alter their plans for the sake of keeping the family cell intact. The Soviet contention, then, that the operative concept here is preservation of the *"unity of citizenship of members of the family"*[5] is accurate enough where it applies to offspring in the pre–fourteen age group, except that because the compass is drawn more narrowly than is the general custom the professed concern for the homogeneity of the family's citizenship denomination rings hollow.

Incidentally, the Russians are prone to raise a loud outcry whenever resort by others to similar tactics is perceived to affect adversely the Soviet Union's stake. A recent example is the fierce controversy that erupted over the decision by American authorities to let twelve–year–old Walter Polovchak remain in the United States by choice and against the parents' wish that the boy accompany them back to the Soviet Union. The family had emigrated from the Ukraine and, after a six–month sojourn in the United States, the parents expressed the desire to return, whereupon Walter ran away from home to move in with relatives in Chicago. Court hearings were held that resulted in Walter being allowed to stay and the parents eventually went back to the USSR with another son (a six–year–old), leaving Walter behind as well as his seventeen–year–old sister who also elected to remain, but retaining the services of the Soviet consular staff to press for Walter's reversion to their custody and repatriation to the Soviet Union. So far, these efforts have been thwarted, but the views now advanced by the competent Soviet officials indicated none of the erstwhile sensitivity for the welfare of the child and stressed instead the primacy of maintaining the integrity of the family unit coupled with the duty to defer in this instance to parental will. Or, to quote a statement attributed by the press to a Soviet embassy employee: "Our position is that a 12–year–old should not be able to tell his parents what he wants to do. He does what they say."[6]

Granted, twelve is not fourteen, although what magical property attaches to the latter will not be evident to everybody. Furthermore, Soviet law occasionally dips even below that level in order to consult a child's preference. Thus, in connection with the proposed adoption of a minor who has reached the age of ten, the law requires that the de cujus give his formal consent.[7] The inconsistency is quite plain and, to be blunt about it, simply betrays recourse to the old double–standard — a technique for which the Soviets have a definite knack, but by no means a monopoly.

2. When One Parent Acquires USSR Citizenship

Here comes the first surprise. According to the opening paragraph of Article 21, if one parent becomes a citizen of the USSR and the other remains a foreign citizen, the child may acquire USSR citizenship upon a request to that effect by the parent acquiring USSR citizenship. Thus, just the will of the one parent applying for Soviet citizenship is now enough to confer Soviet citizenship on the couple's minor children. The previous statute had managed to skirt the issue by declaring that where a couple "split" and one partner received or withdrew from Soviet citizenship "change in the citizenship of children who had not attained the age of eighteen could ensue only in virtue of general procedure". By consulting secondary sources, one learns that administrative practice subsequently took the route of interpreting the dictum to mean that on such occasions a petition for naturalization (or de–naturalization) had to be filed on behalf of each minor offspring (i.e. under eighteen) pursuant to a prior agreement between the parents concerning their progeny's fate and, absent the required unanimity, the child ended up keeping its original citizenship. For that matter, when the reform of Soviet citizenship legislation was discussed in local legal circles in the sixties and early seventies, voices were heard essentially favoring "codification" of the established modus operandi in the future statute (with a few nuances). The version recommended would have read, inter alia:

> "if as a result of change in citizenship of the parents only one of them will be a citizen of the USSR, the citizenship of minor children under 14 years of agreement of the parents. In the absence of such agreement, the minor children retain their former citizenship". [Citing V.S. Shevtsov, *Grazhdanstvo v sovetskom soiuznom gosudarstve*, Moscow 1969, p.124.]
> "... [C]hange of citizenship of children between the ages of 14 and 18 may take place in virtue of general procedure, i.e., upon application by the person itself whose citizenship changes and on the basis of a decision of the Presidium of the USSR Supreme Soviet or Presidium of the Supreme Soviet of the union republic in each single case."[8]

By comparison, the latest norm utterly ignores the legitimate rights of the parent who elects to stay a foreign citizen to share in determining the child's status and vests exclusive authority in this context to the parent who is obviously attracted to Soviet citizenship. On that scale, the policy can be regarded as constituting an act of gross discrimination against foreign nationals on an issue of critical importance to the respective individuals and is bound to lead to serious confrontations. For one can hardly imagine that other states will be content passively to watch as their citizens are denied the exercise of a prime attribute of parenthood, namely, participation in picking the national identification of their offspring — a choice that can radically affect the person's whole life, especially in a situation (like the one involving the Soviet scenario) where the individual has only a limited opportunity to recoup by later switching allegiances. Contracting a citizenship under these circumstances could well prove an irreversible experience, and summarily depriving a parent of an equal voice in a case where the child's welfare is clearly at stake runs counter to the most elementary sense of fairness.

The blanket explanation for the tenor of the entire chapter is, as has already been mentioned, that the provisions of the act devoted to questions of the legal position of the children in conjunction with the change of citizenship of the parents are imbued with "profound concern" for their interests. Here, a conceivable justification is that the present solution eliminates all possibility of a minor being involuntarily doomed to statelessness: in the past, assuming the father requested Soviet citizenship for himself, the parents could not agree on what citizenship the children ought to have and the state of which the mother was a citizen called on minor children to match the citizenship of the father, statelessness would befall the couple's under–age offspring. However, the prospects are just as good or, indeed, better under the current scheme for the minor children to incur dual nationality: take the same set of facts, except that the law of the country of which the foreign parent is a citizen does not mandate that the minor children accompany the father in the citizenship transfer, and the under–age children in this instance will be saddled with dual nationality. Furthermore, since few countries provide for the minor children to share the mother's citizenship, recognizing the latter's right to acquire Soviet citizenship and, in addition, obtaining it for the under–age offspring significantly increases future chances of the children being burdened with dual citizenship next to how often they had been apt to "catch" statelessness under the previous system.

Even an intense desire to prevent minors from experiencing statelessness, though, does not furnish valid grounds for unilaterally voiding a parent's rights with respect to the children and ex parte letting the other parent convey Soviet citizenship to the offspring as lone arbiter of their destiny. A much less drastic cure could be prescribed for the ailment, if the urge to eradicate statelessness were the real motive, without having to resort to treatment that many might pronounce considerably worse than the malady. Certainly, the new formula has great potential for causing human hardship and generating both family dissension and international conflict. To the outsider, the tangible gains seem minimal by comparison, when all that zeal in waging war on statelessness has managed to elicit an unwarranted extension of state authority into the realm of family affairs and flagrant disregard of the parents' freedom jointly to select among the options available for their children.

True, the formal script also lends itself to a more charitable interpretation, in the light of which the same evidence is seen as a solid reaffirmation of the Soviet commitment to the tenet of full equality of the adult partners. In essence, when one parent has decided to convert to Soviet citizenship, why should the other parent enjoy the luxury of sole possession of veto power over what citizenship their children should have? By just withholding consent, the children would be forced to retain the existing citizenship and the parent seeking a different citizenship for him(her)self could not singlehandedly alter the status quo where the minor offspring of the couple are concerned. Under the revised rule, the parent petitioning for admission to Soviet citizenship can at least superimpose a second citizenship on the children's initial nationality and thus maintain a bond with the children. The phenomenon of dual nationality itself can, of course, be viewed as a minor evil and even perhaps be endowed with some ancillary virtues: multiple affiliations mean alternative sources of diplomatic protection and a possibility of registering a preference from among the available stock.

Note that the notion of parity was not carried to its logical extreme by endowing the parent who kept his (or her) foreign citizenship with an equivalent right independently to seek Soviet citizenship for the minor children where the spouse who did convert to the citizenship of the USSR decided, for some reason, not to do so. Soviet authors are cognizant of the asymmetry and concede that in this setting "the law vests Soviet citizens with particular rights, but does not grant the same rights to foreign citizens". Their quite candid (and plausible) response to the anomaly is that "Soviet citizenship binds its bearer to the Soviet state much more tightly than those relations that exist between that state and a person belonging to the citizenship of another state". That consideration presumably swayed the legislators to postulate that if one parent becomes a citizen of the USSR and the other remains a foreign citizen, the child may obtain the citizenship of the USSR at the request of the parent acquiring the citizenship of the USSR, while "the second parent in this case does not exercise an analogous right".[9] Practically speaking, the likelihood that the foreign parent would push for the children's conversion to Soviet citizenship when the parent who is a naturalized Soviet citizen refuses to take that initiative is remote, which may be why the regime has not bothered to anticipate this contingency and accepted to absorb the loss if it should occur.

The law establishes no deadline for submitting such petitions and leaves the impression that the lone parent who has acquired Soviet citizenship can apply for the children to follow his example at any time until they reach fourteen and is still entitled to take this sort of action on behalf of children from the ages of fourteen to eighteen as long as the latter acquiesce in written form in the proposed naturalization. After that, the request must emanate from the de cujus proper.

The record prompts two further observations. First, whichever sampling of intentions one chooses to impute to the Soviets on this occasion, the picture we get is of a Soviet policy that is now markedly more assertive in certifying candidates for receipt of USSR citizenship and facilitating their access to USSR citizenship, under the official guise of reducing the incidence of statelessness and in the spirit of spreading around the superior advantages accruing from Soviet citizenship in order to benefit a wider audience. Second, equally noteworthy is the curious divergency between the principle enunciated here and the solution proposed for the situation involving a Soviet parent and a foreign parent of a child born abroad when neither owns a permanent place of residence in the USSR. In the latter case, it will be remembered, despite one parent's claim to Soviet citizenship, the child's citizenship is left to be determined by common agreement of the parents, while in the event only one parent is naturalized a Soviet citizen, the solitary will of this parent is enough to secure Soviet citizenship for children under the age of fourteen. The discrepancy is quite plain and is probably due to the fact that an application for naturalization rates as a positive gesture to which is consequently attributed a capacity to exert a broader impact than is afforded the insignia of passive possession of title to USSR citizenship.

Less controversial, albeit still intrusive in animus, is the concept articulated in the next two paragraphs according to which: 1) if one parent becomes a citizen of the USSR and the other remains a stateless person, the child residing on the territory of the USSR becomes a Soviet citizen; and, 2) if one parent becomes a citizen of the USSR and the other remains a stateless person, the child residing abroad may acquire Soviet citizenship at the request of the parent acquiring the citizenship of the USSR. Once again, the implied rationale behind these moves is a desire to spare the children the stigma of statelessness, and the above procedure largely succeeds in achieving that end.[10] True, a bit more finesse would not be remiss, especially in the treatment dispensed to stateless persons who are simply excluded from the equation, but on that point the text is consistent with the statute's earlier prescriptions for like contingencies whereby a parent's statelessness is used as an alibi to classify him (or her) as a legal nullity, and the phenomenon itself features as a convenient justification for taking vigorous measures "to fill the incipient vacuum" with Soviet citizenship. In short, the tactic is aimed at conveying a rather simplistic picture of Soviet citizenship selflessly riding to the rescue of beleaguered minors threatened with a stateless lot. How much substantial profit the Soviets derive from the operation — in terms of inflating the number of nominees for USSR citizenship — is not discussed.

In this instance, though, the stateless parent does not suffer a greater circumscription of his rights than his foreign counterpart, except in the case where the child happens to reside on the territory of the USSR. Were the non–Soviet parent a foreign citizen here, the "convert" parent would have to file an application to secure the minor's admission to Soviet citizenship, whereas that formality is skipped when the non–Soviet parent is an apatride and Soviet citizenship is then unilaterally assigned to the under–age offspring located on Soviet soil. Otherwise, both the foreign parent and the stateless parent can safely be ignored by the parent who enters Soviet citizenship and wants the minor children to partake of his (her) new status.

While all the older norms governing the mechanics of change in citizenship of minor children in conjunction with change in citizenship of one parent entailing acquisition of Soviet citizenship have thus been recast, the business of automatic extension of Soviet citizenship to minors under certain conditions probably figures as the most innovative element in the package. Despite the formula's potential for vitally affecting the future of the individuals to whom it applied, the statute said nothing about the manner in which its authors intended it to be implemented. The oversight was corrected by the federal decree of June 15, 1979,[11] which spelled out how the citizenship law was to be put into effect and indicated, inter alia, that only persons born after June 30, 1979, were eligible for such involuntary induction (a general rule also appertaining to children of stateless parents (Art.13), children of unknown parents (Art.14), and special occasions of adoption to be discussed below (Art. 23, paras.1, 2, and 3). If the de cujus had not attained eighteen by July 1, 1979, he (she) could acquire Soviet citizenship by petition of his (her) legal representatives,[12] which had to be filed at the place of residence with the organs of internal affairs before the child reached majority, but no later than one year from the time the statute entered into force, i.e., prior to July 1, 1980. With respect to children between the ages of fourteen and eighteen acquisition of Soviet citizenship could occur solely with their consent, expressed in written form. The imposition of a cut–off date suggests that the authorities were in principle prepared to rubber-stamp these requests for admission to Soviet citizenship and waive the usual routine followed in handling applications for naturalization. By the same token, if the individual who qualified for this preferential treatment missed the grace period, he (she) could still bid for Soviet citizenship through regular naturalization channels.

3. When One Parent Leaves USSR Citizenship

Nothing illustrates better the curious cast of the official Soviet mind than the content of the new clause (Art. 22) which provides that, in the event one parent quits Soviet citizenship and the other retains USSR citizenship, the child keeps its USSR citizenship. The local solons show not the slightest compunction here against violating the principle of reciprocity: whereas, in the reverse case, the foreign parent converting to Soviet citizenship can also obtain it on his (her) own initiative for the couple's minor children, an analogous right is not extended to the parent exiting from Soviet citizenship and the other (Soviet parent) commands precedence in preserving the status quo where the children are concerned, an opportunity similarly denied to the foreign counterpart in kindred circumstances. The accent, then, is on the absolute primacy of Soviet citizenship in this setting and the net inferiority of any foreign citizenship in a competitive relationship.

Of course, the Soviet hierarchy cannot prevent another government from taking a leaf out of the Soviet book and, in line with the Soviet example, allowing the Soviet parent entering its citizenship unilaterally to engineer the concurrent naturalization of his (her) minor children. The key difference is that since the Soviet system refuses to recognize double citizenship, the competent organs there would continue to list these children as Soviet citizens and, hence, in all probability would not let them out of the country. Most other societies display a more ambivalent attitude toward the issue of dual nationality and hesitate to insist that they will attach no legal significance whatsoever to its occurrence, thus encouraging Soviet hopes of successful diplomatic intervention on behalf of its "protégés" abroad, while denying this comfort to foreign agencies put in the same spot, mutatis mutandis.

Incidentally, the present formula is even less liberal than its 1938 "Stalinist" predecessor which, in theory, endorsed the proposition that, when one parent quit Soviet citizenship, the children could follow suit by agreement of both parents and only when such unanimity could not be attained, the progeny's existing citizenship stayed in force. Now, the parents' wishes on the subject appear to be irrelevant, as long as one of them counts as a Soviet citizen. Note, though, that the law is silent on the reasons that had led to the "split" family. Whether the parent with the Soviet citizenship freely chose to retain that status or was not permitted by the responsible institutions to surrender it makes not practical difference for these purposes, giving the administrative apparatus maximum opportunity to influence the outcome. Indeed, by putting enough pressure on one parent to desist from seeking denaturalization or refusing to honor one parent's application for denaturalization, the regime insures that the Soviet citizenship of the minor children remains intact. The device enables the authorities to drive a solid legal wedge between the parent who persists in wanting to shed Soviet citizenship and the offspring and, by raising the specter of separation, increase the chances of convincing the "maverick" to abandon his (her) plans to "cancel" membership in the Soviet community. A further consideration is that the latest norm is evidently intended to have general relevance — defining the position of offspring of Soviet citizens when one parent has asked to be relieved of Soviet citizenship both at home and abroad. Even if the whole family is on foreign soil when one parent proceeds to stage a "legal defection" from the USSR, the continued allegiance of the other parent to the USSR will have the effect of preserving unimpaired the Soviet citizenship of the children which, in turn, will serve as valid grounds for the government to claim a right to exercise the usual brand of extra-territorial jurisdiction over the brood.

The sole virtue of the new arrangement lies in the fact that all possibility is excluded that minor children might inadvertently stumble into a condition of statelessness as a consequence of a parent's improvident behavior in connection with a bid to shed Soviet citizenship. Some people, however, will conclude that the "safety net" carries an excessive price–tag in terms of the degree of control imposed by the bureaucracy over the individual's freedom of choice here on the road to achieving this "immunization".

The implications of this "hardline" formula have been assessed by a knowledgeable observer of the Soviet scene from the standpoint of its relationship to Soviet emigration practice since denaturalization in the USSR occurs today mostly in the context of expatriation. Appraising the policy as a potentially serious obstacle to emigration, the analyst reads the latest script to mean that

> "in the case of divorced or separated parents, if one of them wishes to emigrate and for that reason renounces citizenship, but the other parent does not, the children cannot leave with the emigrating parent even if they live with that parent or if he or she is their legal guardian, unless the children, too, go through a separate process of relinquishing their citizenship. However, the question arises from what age is a child entitled to make a renunciation and who makes it on behalf of the child prior to that age? According to Article 18 of the Fundamentals of Soviet Legislation on Marriage and the Family 'parents shall enjoy equal rights and bear equal duties in relation to their children also in cases where the marriage has been dissolved'. It would thus appear that both parents would have to institute the procedure for renunciation of citizenship — in other words, also the parent who does not wish to emigrate."[13]

The interpretation is tenable, but needs to be set in a broader framework. Actually, the language of Article 22 is not very forthcoming and the clause seems to pursue a rather limited objective, namely, to establish that Soviet law does not sanction the right of a parent who has won release from Soviet citizenship while the other parent still possesses it to stage single–handedly the minor children's corollary exit from USSR citizenship. On the other hand, the terse pronouncement neither states that the status quo is unalterable nor indicates how to go about it in order to perform the transition. Logic commends the following bill of possibilities: 1) the existing situation is immutable; or, 2) the parent relinquishing Soviet citizenship can try to get the permission of the proper Soviet authorities to have the minor children follow in his (her) footsteps; or, 3) agreement by both parents in favor of the minor children's exit from USSR citizenship is sufficient to achieve that goal; or, 4) even the consent of both parents to the loss of Soviet citizenship by their minor children requires the approval of the competent state agencies.

We can tell, from looking at the record, that no absolute bar has operated against the release of minors from Soviet citizenship when the parents no longer shared that citizenship. The authorities may be reluctant to let the minors leave Soviet citizenship in the company of the "apostate" parent and against the wishes or at least without the express sanction of the "loyal" parent, but the Soviet regime has amply demonstrated its ability in the past to bend the rules when the lure of egregious profit beckons. So, this scenario ought not to recur too often and yet feature as part of the active portfolio. Parental consensus might strike most people as adequate to determine the citizenship affiliation of the family's minor children, except that hard experience has shown that in the Soviet system "private" preference is rarely allowed to play a decisive role even in what elsewhere would be considered a personal matter (there are exceptions, of course, and we find a few of these in the field of citizenship law). A more likely alternative is that the denaturalization of minor children coupled with that of just one parent will call for the consent of both parents plus official acquiescence — the optimal combination to surmount at the de facto level the statute's silence on that score.[14]

A contingency not yet mentioned deserves a moment's notice. In Soviet literature, we come across the commentary that, "although under the terms of Soviet legislation adopted children have exactly the same rights and duties as children who are related by blood ties to their parents, change of citizenship by the adoptive parents ... does not automatically result in change of citizenship of the adopted child".[15] The doctrine sounds fine, but it lacks legislative corroboration and its execution poses a problem. Indeed, Soviet law mandates secrecy of adoption and, reportedly, to preserve this confidentiality "the adopters at their request are inscribed in the birth certificate of the child as blood parents and from the documents issued it is impossible to determine whether the given child is natural or adopted".[16] If that is true, one wonders by what logistical means an adopted child both of whose parents withdraw from Soviet citizenship will be screened out and realistically prevented from tagging along when its papers contain no clue to the "suspect" origins of the kinship. In sum, the theoretical proposition may not be procedurally viable, though it may still be a fixture of the legal canon.

4. Adoption and Acquisition of USSR Citizenship

By a strange oversight, the 1938 Law on Soviet citizenship failed to address itself to the matter of how the experience of adoption might affect the citizenship of the de cujus. Secondary sources were unanimously of the opinion that a child possessing Soviet citizenship kept it upon adoption by foreign citizens. On the question of whether a child vested with a foreign citizenship automatically acquired Soviet citizenship in the wake of its adoption by Soviet citizens, local spokesmen plainly disagreed, each school of thought implying that current practice supported its views. One faction maintained that a foreign child adopted by Soviet citizens forthwith acquired the citizenship of the parents,[17] and random voices were even heard claiming that "a child under the age of fourteen who does not have Soviet citizenship when adopted by a Soviet parent becomes a citizen of the USSR".[18] Somewhat more cautiously, another wing only wrote that if the child permanently resided on the territory of the USSR and had no citizenship, it acquired Soviet citizenship upon adoption and, if the child had a valid foreign citizenship, then in connection with its adoption the prior approval of the diplomatic mission of the corresponding state was required.[19] At the opposite extreme, their critics insisted that the act of adoption of a foreign child by Soviet parents per se entailed no change in the child's citizenship status and that the sole way in which Soviet citizenship could be acquired in these circumstances was through the routine of naturalization.[20]

Again, without challenging the conceptual authenticity of the latter position the practical question was raised as to how a foreign child adopted by a Soviet couple could help being recognized as a Soviet citizen when, pursuant to the principle that the secrecy of adoption was protected by law, the adopting parents by their own choice are entered in the birth certificate of the child as blood parents and the documents procured offer no grounds for deciding whether the child is natural or adopted.[21] With all the official papers indicating that the child's parents are Soviet citizens, the logical consequence would be for the child also to figure as a Soviet citizen by virtue of descent.[22]

Obviously, these discordant voices produced a confused picture. The 1978 statute tries to set the record straight. Henceforth, a child who is a foreign citizen or a stateless person becomes a USSR citizen upon adoption by USSR citizens — inter alia, fulfilling thereby the advertised desideratum of *"unity of citizenship of members of the family"*.[23] The same rule (minus, however, the incidental effect just mentioned) applies to a child who is a foreign citizen when adopted by a couple where one spouse is a Soviet citizen and the other is a stateless person and to a child who is a stateless person when adopted by a couple where one spouse is a Soviet citizen. In short, the results on such occasions hinge on a combination of factors. First, for a foreign child to acquire Soviet citizenship through adoption requires either a Soviet pair or its equivalent, to wit, a Soviet citizen plus a stateless person since the latter is not recognized as an independent element and the former acts in lieu of both. (In this situation, the stateless parent is discriminated against compared to a foreign counterpart, whereas both are equally "disenfranchised" in "split" naturalization cases where the other parent gains admission to Soviet citizenship and is single-handedly capable of obtaining USSR citizenship for the minor offspring as well.[24]) Second, for a stateless child to be converted in this manner one prospective Soviet parent suffices, even if the other spouse should prove to be a foreign citizen: a further instance of gratuitous neglect of the will of the foreign partner, extenuated perhaps by reference to the need to find a prompt solution for the minor's stateless lot through simplified enrollment in Soviet citizenship that would avoid the extra pitfall of having to rely on an entente between the parents on the subject of the child's future citizenship.

A separate paragraph then deals with the final scenario involving a child who is a foreign citizen and faces adoption by a couple where one spouse is a Soviet citizen and the other is a foreign citizen. In the presence of a mix of so many different full-fledged citizenships, the law opts to extend Soviet citizenship to the de cujus only by agreement of the adopting parents. Notice that where naturalization is at stake, one parent is able to alter the status of minor children, whereas in this context the decision must emanate jointly from the parents: greater weight is apparently attached to the wishes of a natural parent vis-à-vis underage offspring than an "artificial" one, which is why the "consent quota" is now upped to two.

Although the 1978 statute has, as Soviet sources claim, "corrected the substantial gap which existed in Soviet legislation on questions of citizenship of children in the event of adoption",[25] its fairly cryptic instructions were obviously not intended to blanket the terrain. A number of ancillary issues were left unresolved and the relevant answers must be sought in the contents of other pieces of legislation or the pages of specialized literature. Thus:

a. The federal decree of June 15, 1979, added that the norms regarding automatic acquisition of USSR citizenship in connection with adoption — i.e., in all cases except when a child with a foreign citizenship is adopted by a binational couple (one Soviet citizen and one foreign citizen) whereupon its citizenship is left to be determined by parental consensus — apply solely to children born after June 30, 1979. Those born earlier and not yet eighteen as of July 1, 1979, may acquire Soviet citizenship by request of their legal representatives,[26] to be filed at the place of residence with the organs of internal affairs before the child attains majority, but not later than one year following the citizenship act's entry into force (i.e., prior to July 1, 1980). Such petitions concerning children between the ages of fourteen and eighteen had to be accompanied by the latter's written consent to the proposed "naturalization". Presumably, these solicitations received favored treatment (hence the deadline), while those who missed the cut–off date could still gain admission to Soviet citizenship through the regular channels.

b. The same edict next elaborated that the agreement of adopting parents on the acquisition by the child of USSR citizenship — i.e., where a foreign child is adopted by a Soviet citizen and a foreign citizen — must be submitted in writing to the organs of internal affairs or, if the adopting parents reside abroad, to the nearby diplomatic or consular mission of the USSR within a year from the day of adoption.

c. The decree of the Presidium of the USSR Supreme Soviet of October 9, 1979,[27] amended Article 34 of the 1968 Fundamentals of legislation of the USSR and union republics on marriage and the family[28] (in the process renumbering it to 35) by inserting, inter alia, a clause to the effect that "the adoption of children who are foreign citizens and reside in the USSR takes place in conformity with Soviet legislation". A leading Soviet authority on the citizenship repertory of the USSR sheds further light on the subject with the explanation that:

> "The adoption of children who are foreign citizens or stateless persons on the territory of the USSR is performed in accordance with common standards. The law envisages no special rules for such adoption. In practice, the organs of guardianship and trusteeship in all cases where this is possible first request consent for the adoption from the corresponding organ of the state of which the adoptee is a citizen."[29]

We also learn that this preliminary clearance has an extra meaning in the USSR's relations with certain sister socialist countries to which it is linked by pacts designed to abort the occurrence of double nationality by paving the way for a simultaneous citizenship transfer. The system apparently operates as follows:

> "Although the conventions on the prevention of incidence of cases of dual citizenship concluded by the USSR with Bulgaria, Hungary, Poland and the GDR do not feature provisions directly regulating questions of citizenship of children upon adoption, these treaties establish the duty of each contracting party not to admit to its citizenship persons possessing the citizenship of the other side without the consent of the latter's competent organs. This rule likewise finds application in practice in deciding questions of adoption. For example, spouses M. who are Soviet citizens, while temporarily in Hungary, took Teresa M., a Hungarian citizen, from a children's home for upbringing and then wanted to adopt her. The competent Hungarian organs responded positively to this request by citizens M. They were granted per-

> mission to adopt her and permission was also granted for Teresa M. to leave Hungarian citizenship."[30]

Elsewhere, the transition may be less smooth, but a valid premise here is that when the home government signals through the proper channels that is has no objections to a minor vested with its citizenship being adopted by citizens of a foreign country, acquiescence in the corollary conversion of the de cujus to the latter's citizenship will be duly forthcoming.

d. Lastly, Soviet scholars tell us that

> "in those cases where the adopted child resides on the territory of the USSR, the Soviet court has the right to rescind the adoption performed abroad in the organs of the state on whose territory the child resided at the time of adoption. The Soviet court has the right to decide these cases both when the adoptee is a Soviet citizen and when he is a foreigner."[31]

Two ways have been recommended for dealing with the effects of such a revocation on the citizenship of a child who "contracted" Soviet citizenship by virtue of adoption: 1) if, for instance, the act of adoption is set aside by the Soviet court at the request of the parents who are foreign citizens and before the child reaches the age of fourteen, then the child automatically reverts to the citizenship of the natural parents; the primary reason is that "the grounds for acquisition of Soviet citizenship — adoption — is pronounced void"; or, 2) upon turning fourteen and if he (she) wants to retain the citizenship of the USSR, the minor must through his (her) legal representatives apply to the Presidium of the USSR Supreme Soviet asking to conserve his (her) Soviet citizenship, while, upon attaining adulthood, the de cujus becomes entitled to submit a corresponding petition to the federal Presidium in his (her) own name.[32] The first version sounds more plausible, whereas the second suffers from the further technical defect of referring to preservation of Soviet citizenship when judicial cancellation of an adoption should operate ab initio — so that nullification of the adoption ex tunc would also mean that the attendant "naturalization" was never consummated either.

Insofar as foreign and stateless minors can be adopted on Soviet soil as well and the local courts have general authority to countermand domestic adoption proceedings, the same scenario would fit the home setting.

5. Adoption of Soviet Children by Foreign Citizens

Comprehensive rules have likewise been formulated to cover the present situation. Thus, a child owning USSR citizenship, if adopted by foreign citizens or by a couple of whom one is a USSR citizen and the other a foreign citizen, retains its USSR citizenship. At the request of the adopting parents, however, such a child may be allowed exit from Soviet citizenship by the Presidium of the USSR Supreme Soviet.

To begin with, let it be noted that, notwithstanding vehement Soviet professions of commitment to the doctrine of unity of citizenship of members of the family, this concept is flatly repudiated on the occasion when a minor with Soviet citizenship is adopted by a foreign couple and yet does not undergo a routine switch to the parent's citizenship. The inferior treatment of foreigners adopting Soviet children compared to that afforded Soviet citizens adopting foreign children is lamely excused by invoking the goal of "defense of the interests of the under–age citizens of the USSR, premised on common principles of humanism".[33] Curiously enough, this view of humanism dictates that the Soviet child adopted by foreign parents not immediately share their citizenship, while the foreign child adopted by Soviet parents forthwith partake of the citizenship of the latter.

Next, the rule featured in Article 24, para. 1, bars automatic loss of Soviet citizenship by adopted children where the adopting parents are foreigners or at least one of them is a foreigner and "denaturalization" here requires express approval by the Presidium of the USSR Supreme Soviet.[34]

Then, the proposed solution sanctions additional inequalities. For example, a binational couple (Soviet/foreign partners) adopting a minor with a foreign citizenship need only agree inter se to accomplish the adoptee's conversion to USSR citizenship, while a similar "mixed" pair adopting a Soviet child and wanting to transfer it to a foreign citizenship would have to record a joint decision to that effect plus get the federal Presidium to accept their wish. Nor does the law differentiate for these purposes between a foreign couple with a single citizenship and a foreign couple holding distinct citizenships, mandating parental consensus in either eventuality in order to be able to file a valid petition with the central Presidium, whereas the criterion of unanimity applies solely when a Soviet parent and a foreign parent seek to adopt a foreign minor, but not when Soviet spouses perform an identical function (i.e., their views on the adoptee's future citizenship are not solicited and the child is assigned ex parte the citizenship of the USSR upon enrollment in a homogeneous Soviet household).

Further, the above procedure once again vividly attests to the theme of the evident primacy attached by the Soviet regime to the matter of maintaining the child's entitlement to Soviet citizenship.[35]

Finally, under the terms of the federal decree of October 9, 1979, which, inter alia, amended Article 34 of the Fundamentals of legislation of the USSR and union republics on marriage and the family (and coincidentally renumbered it to 35), "the adoption in the USSR by foreign citizens of children who are Soviet citizens ... takes place in accordance with Soviet legislation". Presumably, this operation too is governed by "the secrecy of adoption" postulate in which case the old question recurs of how, in fact, can a child who is a Soviet citizen and is adopted in the USSR by foreign nationals who are now inscribed in the child's official papers simply as his (her) parents retain Soviet citizenship in light of reports that it is practically impossible under those conditions to monitor the adoptee's antecedents and the prima facie image created by the personal documents that the de cujus is the offspring of two aliens and, hence, also vested with a foreign nationality. Obviously, the legislators had something different in mind or they would not have insisted that the adoptee's Soviet citizenship remained valid and lapsed by grace alone of the central Presidium's fiat, but mystery stamps the logistical side of the affair.

The statute at least stays consistent by stipulating that a child endowed with Soviet citizenship, if adopted by stateless persons or by a couple where one spouse is a Soviet citizen and the other a stateless person, retains its Soviet citizenship. The ostensible rationale, once again, is to safeguard the child from incurring statelessness and the current act is deemed to have done the job well.[36] Parenthetically, the latest legislation does not consider the prospect of a minor vested with Soviet citizenship being adopted by a couple where one spouse is a foreign citizen and the other a stateless person. Where the roles are transposed a foreign child is ipso jure scheduled to end up with Soviet citizenship. Going by the established pattern, however, it is highly improbable that the regime would let a minor with Soviet citizenship experience comparable treatment, mutatis mutandis: at a minimum, the occasion would seem to call for a regular petition by both candidate parents or, say, the potential foreign parent for approval of the child's exit from Soviet citizenship, subject to endorsement by the federal Presidium.

Several organizational questions to which the citizenship law omitted to pay attention were dealt with elsewhere. For instance, the federal Fundamentals on marriage and the family (Art.34) took time to explain that the adoption of a child who is a Soviet citizen and lives outside the confines of the USSR shall be performed in the embassy or consulate of the USSR (revised by the decree of October 9, 1979, by deleting the reference to embassy and substituting "consular institutions" for "consulate"). Where the adopting parent (singular!) is not a Soviet citizen, the permission of the competent organ of the union republic is necessary for the adoption. Technically, this last clause only seemed to address itself to the situation where a minor possessed of Soviet citizenship faced adoption by a "mixed" couple consisting of a Soviet citizen and a foreign partner, but one assumes that the same routine a fortiori applies when the adopting spouses are both foreigners (nothing indicates that Soviet law bars in principio the adoption of a minor child owning Soviet citizenship and living abroad by a foreign pair and certainly sanctions such activity on Soviet soil).

Another point is that the process of adoption must in these circumstances "meet all other requirements set by law",[37] since the phenomenon of adoption is still understood in these special circumstances in the sense attributed to it by the Soviet legal system. In particular, if the prescribed permission for the adoption of the child was not procured, the staged adoption will not qualify as an adoption under Soviet law and will not give grounds for resort to the device of "denaturalization" of the de cujus by federal edict upon the request of the "adopting" parents.[38] The mandatory approval by the proper republican office emanates from: in the Lithuanian and Azerbaidzhan SSRs — the Presidium of the republic's Supreme Soviet; in the Georgian, Armenian and Tadzhik SSRs — the republican Council of Ministers; in the RSFSR, BSSR, UkSSR, and the Estonian, Latvian and Uzbek SSRs — the Ministry of Education; in the Moldavian, Kirgiz and Turkmen SSRs — the Ministries of Public Education; in the Kazakh SSR — the executive committees of the corresponding oblast Soviets of people's deputies.[39]

Next, the Fundamentals of legislation on marriage and the family introduce an "exception to the general rule" pertaining to the adoption of children vested with Soviet citizenship and living abroad by conceding that such an adoption is also recognized as valid if performed in the organs of the host state as long as permission is received beforehand from the competent organ of the union republic (i.e., the appropriate institution among those just listed). The motive, we are told, is to serve the interests of the child in those special cases where adoption cannot be carried out in the prescribed manner,[40] presumably because the respective state considers adoption rites administered in a local foreign consulate null and void.[41]

Lastly, the decree of October 9, 1979, spells out that "adoption in the USSR by foreign citizens of children who are Soviet citizens is effectuated in accordance with Soviet legislation". Paraphrasing this clause, a secondary source modifies the above wording to refer to foreign citizens *and* stateless persons and adds that these adoptions follow "the general rules"[42] which, in turn, are established by the legislation of the union republics. The latter, however, again choose to feature the extra safeguard that a transnational adoption affecting a minor with a stake in Soviet citizenship be formally approved by a designated republican agency, namely: in the Lithuanian SSR — the Presidium of the Supreme Soviet of the republic; in the Estonian, Armenian, Kirgiz, Tadzhik and Turkmen SSRs — the local Council of Ministers; in the Georgian and Azerbaidzhan SSRs — the Council of Ministers of the republic, the Council of Ministers of the Autonomous SSR or the executive committee of the Soviet of people's deputies of the autonomous oblast; in the RSFSR, UkSSR, BSSR and Uzbek SSR — the Council of Ministers of the Autonomous SSR or executive committees of krai, oblast, city (cities of republican subordination) Soviet of people's deputies; in the Latvian SSR — the Ministry of Education; in the Moldavian SSR — the Ministry of Public Education. The Kazakh SSR figures as the sole maverick in the lot by waiving the need for prior sanction in order for a child with Soviet citizenship to be adopted by foreigners on its territory.[43]

The "licensing" procedure obviously guarantees the regime ample control over the operation and since Soviet policy reportedly looks askance at juvenile adoption[44] except where a husband or wife adopts the other spouse's offspring by a previous marriage, the attitude makes sense. On the other hand, once official authorization for an adoption of this sort is secured, chances are excellent that approval will be equally forthcoming for release of the adoptee from Soviet citizenship — if and when the adopting parents do indeed ask for that dispensation.

In closing, a theme not broached in Soviet literature calls for brief notice. What I have in mind is the problem of how the citizenship status of a minor originally possessed of Soviet citizenship and later duly converted to foreign citizenship in the wake of adoption by a foreign couple or spouses of whom one is a citizen of the USSR and the other a foreign citizen is apt to be affected if a Soviet court thereafter decides to rescind the adoption. Soviet legal experts claim that the courts in the USSR are entitled to do so even apropos adoptions concluded abroad in the organs of the state on whose territory the de cujus was then domiciled if the adopted child now lived on the territory of the USSR.[45] The likelihood of this combination of factors occurring is quite small, but the possibility is, of course, not entirely excluded and thus the question of how the contingency might be handled is not strictly academic.

Inasmuch as loss of Soviet citizenship by a minor in connection with adoption calls in each instance for an affirmative ruling by the central Presidium in response to a suitable request from the adopting parents (and can never happen "egregiously"), no direct link exists between the event of adoption and the act of denaturalization: the two experiences are juridically discrete. Should a Soviet court nullify such an adoption, its order would neither destroy the grounds for the denaturalization (i.e., the national Presidium's edict) nor, for that matter, be capable of invalidating a decree issued by the executive branch. The only viable remedy would be for the de cujus to apply for restoration of his (her) former Soviet citizenship or, in extremis, for the federal Presidium on its own initiative to reverse itself by invoking the nullity ab ovo of the transaction which served as the sole justification for sanctioning the subject's release from Soviet citizenship. Both routes are feasible and plausible: one may prefer the first because it enjoys statutory imprimatur; but the Presidium does exercise extensive discretionary powers and can easily improvise an ad hoc solution along the proposed lines without fear of "precipitating a constitutional crisis".

The current law likewise maintains the old norm mandating that any change in the citizenship of children between the ages of fourteen and eighteen in the event of change in the citizenship of their parents or adoption take place solely with the consent of the children, except to add that the choice must be expressed in writing (Art.25). Soviet spokesmen attach a "significance of principle"[46] to the practice of letting fourteen–year–old youngsters decide their citizenship affiliation, but ulterior motive probably had more to do with the design of the game–plan than ethical or esthetic considerations. In effect, giving minors of that tender age a right to assert a private preference on a matter of vital importance to them as well as their immediate family allows the state maximum opportunity to maneuver the various parties to its own advantage, since, as observed earlier, the junior members of a household are more prone to be swayed by external blandishments or pressures and, through their response, will manage to affect the status of their near kin.[47] The Soviet hierarchy is no doubt fully aware of the prospect, and its "liberal" stand in favor of the children's role in determining their future is, one is morally certain, in fact primarily shaped by the desire to augment the available means of control over or manipulation of people's behavior in this domain (as in others) in order to get them ultimately to act in a manner consonant with the official wishes.

NOTES

1. G.I. Tunkin, "Zakon o grazhdanstve SSSR", *Sovetskoe gosudarstvo i pravo*, 1979, No.7, p.27 (hereafter abbr. as *SGiP*). The same idea is expressed by S.I. Rusinova, "Zakon o grazhdanstve SSSR", *Pravovedenie*, 1980, No.1, p.7, namely that the 1978 law concentrated "all the experience of resolution of questions of citizenship of children accumulated by Soviet legislation". See, too, N. Salishcheva, E. Koveshnikov, "Novyi zakon o grazhdanstve SSSR". *Sotsialisticheskaia zakonnost'*, 1979, No.3, p.11.

2. V. Zenin, "Gromadianstvo SRSR — velika chest' i velika vidpovidal'nist'", *Radianske pravo*, 1979, No.2, p.10.

   In similar vein, R.I. Kulik, *Zakon o grazhdanstve SSSR*, Moscow 1980, p.67, writes that "in situations which entail change of citizenship of children, these principles [i.e., jus sanguinis and jus soli] are applied by the Soviet legislator in various versions, but with the object of solving the problem in the manner most favorable to the child". He then adds that, "in the interests of the child", a further principle is invoked, to wit: "in disputed situations, when different solutions of the problem are possible, the law gives preference to maintaining the Soviet citizenship of the child or else to the child's acquisition of the citizenship of the USSR".

3. S.I. Rusinova, *loc. cit.*

4. N. Salishcheva, E. Koveshnikov, *loc. cit.*

5. V.V. Polianskii, "Printsipy sovetskogo grazhdanstva", *SGiP*, 1980, No.5, p.128 (italics in the original).

   According to R.I. Kulik, *op. cit.*, pp.68–69, the unity is here preserved by resort to the concept of jus sanguinis "which has become traditional in international practice, has acquired the character of a customary norm of international law. This humane principle contains the basis of all premises for guaranteeing the child the special care and protection of the parents which is indispensable at an early age". Reference is also made in this connection to Art.6 of the Declaration of the Rights of the Child with which Soviet policy is, of course, pronounced to be fully congruent.

6. See, inter alia, *New York Times*, July 21, 1980, p.A9; July 22, 1980, p.A12; August 5, 1980, p.A8; October 18, 1981, p.44. Likewise, I. Konstantinova, "Amerikanskaia Femida protiv prav roditelei i detei", *Chelovek i zakon*, 1981, No.1, pp. 120–123.

7. Cf., I.M. Kuznetsova, "Spornye voprosy usynovleniia", *Problemy sovershenstvovaniia sovetskogo zakonodatel'stva*, Moscow 1980, Trudy 17, p.129.

8. E.g., I.K. Gorodetskaia, "Grazhdanstvo detei", *SGiP*, 1971, No.4, p.42. *Idem*, *Mezhdunarodnaia zashchita prav i interesov detei*, Moscow 1973, p.43.

   Reference is also made to the fact that this question was handled in analogous fashion in connection with option projects. For instance, apropos option of Polish citizenship on the basis of the federal decree of June 22, 1941, (*VVS SSSR*, 1944, No.35), the formula adopted was that the choice of citizenship by the parents forthwith determined the citizenship of their children younger than fourteen. All children between the ages of fourteen and eighteen had a right of independent choice of citizenship. In the event the parents selected different citizenship, the citizenship of children under fourteen was decided by agreement of the parents and, if no agreement was reached, it depended on the territory of which of the two states the minors would reside.

   Note that the option scheme's solution whereby in the absence of agreement between the parents their minor children ended up with the citizenship of the contracting state in which they resided differs from what the majority of Soviet spokesmen tell us was the administrative practice on this question, namely, that no parental agreement meant that the minor children kept their former citizenship. See the author's *Soviet Citizenship Law*,

Leiden 1968, pp.46–48, and the sources cited therein. Yet, even then a number of Soviet jurists claimed that the outcome was in fact determined by reference to the territorial principle. Cf., K.Ia. Chizhov, in F.I. Kozhevnikov, ed., *Mezhdunarodnoe pravo*, Moscow 1957, p.151; N.T. Samartseva, in D.B. Levin & G.P. Kaliuzhnaia, eds., *Mezhdunarodnoe pravo*, Moscow 1964, p.159; L.A. Aleksidze & G.I. Tunkin, in G.I. Tunkin, ed., *Mezhdunarodnoe pravo*, Moscow 1974, pp.225–226.

Whether the policy here gradually changed or its application was not uniform and vacillated between these two models or one of the factions was in error or tried to pass off wish for deed is impossible to tell without access to primary evidence, — so far unavailable.

9. Cf., A.A. Rubanov, "Mezhdunarodno–pravovye voprosy zakonodatel'nogo regulirovaniia otnoshenii sovetskogo grazhdanstva", *Sovetskii ezhegodnik mezhdunarodnogo prava 1978*, Moscow 1980, p.143. Note that, according to R.I. Kulik, *op. cit.*, p. 69, situations involving the question of the citizenship of children in families where parents have different citizenships are not rare and the "legislator must take them into account".

10. Thus, R.I. Kulik, *op. cit.*, pp.70–71, who, after confirming that the primary objective here was to "overcome the statelessness of the children", adds:
"Such a decision is humane. It corresponds to the recommendation of Principle 3 of the international Declaration of the Rights of the Child. In this instance, the question of the opinion of the other parent does not arise inasmuch as owing to his rsict statelessness he rsict cannot offer the child another variant for resolving the problem. In favor of this decision is also the fact that the child [under 1) above] resides on the territory of the Soviet Union. Consequently, we are now talking about a situation where the child automatically, without any application and special Edict, acquires citizenship. The child on this occasion, as the Law says, 'becomes a citizen of the USSR'."
With respect to the case described under point 2) above, the author notes that the question of acquisition by the child of USSR citizenship is decided by Decree of the Presidium of the USSR Supreme Soviet and that in this setting too "there is no need for the consent of the other parent, who remains a stateless person".

11. *VVS SSSR*, 1979, No.25, Art.436.

12. R.I. Kulik, *op. cit.*, p.71, makes the interesting point in this connection that where the legislator, under the terms of the decree of June 15, 1979, gives retroactive effect to the rules of acquisition by minor children of USSR citizenship, he makes the results depend entirely on the desires of the parents or other legal representatives of the child. First, of course, this confirms that the "easy" — in the sense of fully automatic — method of acquisition of Soviet citizenship in these cases was only meant to operate prospectively. Second, it suggests that where the relevant facts predated the statute's entry into force and a formal application was mandatory to engineer the minor child's conversion to Soviet citizenship, both parents' animus was required — the foreign parent and the stateless parent alike.

13. S.J. Roth, "The New Soviet Citizenship Law and Jewish Emigration", *Research Report* USSR/79/3 (July 1979), Institute of Jewish Affairs, London, p.5.

14. R.I. Kulik, *op. cit.*, pp.70–72, makes it sound as though loss of a minor child's citizenship in connection with loss of citizenship by one of the parents depends on the availability of a duly certified statement of concurrence by the other parent who is a citizen of the USSR. This latter condition reportedly "corresponds to the principle of the primacy of USSR citizenship". However, the author fudges on the issue by discussing the problem solely in the context of the right of the parent who left Soviet citizenship and acquired the citizenship of another country to submit a petition to grant the child the right to exit from USSR citizenship, *if the child permanently resides with this parent outside the confines of the USSR*. By extrapolating, one may conclude that even before expatriation both the other spouse's consent and official permission would have to be secured in order to con-

summate the denaturalization of the minor children in conjunction with that of one parent.

The writer adds a valuable bit of information by observing that the question of the consent of the parents or one of them to change in the citizenship of the child lapses in cases of deprivation of parental rights or recognition that the parent(s) is (are) missing or has (have) been declared dead.

15. *Kommentarii k zakonodatel'stvu o registratsii aktov grazhdanskogo sostoianiia*, Moscow 1977, citing *Kommentarii k kodeksu o brake i sem'e RSFSR*, Moscow 1971, p.230.
16. A.Ia. Pergament, in *Sovetskii ezhegodnik mezhdunarodnogo prava 1974*, Moscow 1976, pp.320–321.
17. E.g., V.I. Menzhinskii, in F.I. Kozhevnikov, ed., *Mezhdunarodnoe pravo*, Moscow 1964, p.285.
18. See, L.A. Aleksidze & G.I. Tunkin, in G.I. Tunkin, ed., *op. cit.*, p.224.
19. V.M. Safronov, *Ty — grazhdanin Sovetskogo Soiuza*, Moscow 1972, p.21; B.V. Shchetinin, *Problemy teorii Sovetskogo gosudarstvennogo prava*, Moscow 1974, p.185.
20. Cf., A.A. Esaian, *Nekotorye voprosy Sovetskogo grazhdanstva, Voprosy naseleniia v praktike Sovetskoi Armenii*, Erevan 1966, p.94; V.I. Menzhinskii, in F.I. Kozhevnikov, ed., *Kurs mezhdunarodnogo prava*, 2nd ed., Moscow 1966, p.294; I.K. Gorodetskaia, *Mezhdunarodnaia zashchita prav i interesov detei*, Moscow 1973, pp.44–45; *Kommentarii k zakonodatel'stvu o registratsii aktov grazhdanskogo sostoianiia*, p.185; *Kommentarii k kodeksu o brake i sem'e RSFSR*, p.230.
21. A.Ia. Pergament, *loc. cit.*
22. As R.I. Kulik, *op. cit.*, p.72, observes:
"At present no special procedure whatever for recognition of the adoptee as a Soviet citizen is required. Acquisition of Soviet citizenship by the child follows from the act of its adoption. Obviously, the adoption must be effected in full conformity with the existing law, i.e., formalized by the competent state organs and in the prescribed manner. In particular, there must be the consent of the child to the adoption if it has reached the age of ten (para.3 Art.24 of the Fundamentals of legislation on marriage and the family)."
23. V.V. Polianskii, *op. cit.*, p.128 (italics in the original). See, too, V. Baiaki, "Obshchee i osobennoe v pravovom regulirovanii grazhdanstva v evropeiskikh sotsialisticheskikh stranakh", *SGiP*, 1976, No.11, p.82.
24. A.A. Rubanov, *op. cit.*, p.143.
25. V.I. Menzhinskii, in F.I. Kozhevnikov, ed., *Mezhdunarodnoe pravo*, 4th ed., Moscow 1981, p.225. Similarly, R.I. Kulik, *op. cit.*, p.72.
26. The comments by R.I. Kulik, *op. cit.*, p.71, quoted in note 12 above are fully applicable here too, mutatis mutandis.
27. *VVS SSSR*, 1979, No.42, Art.696.
28. *VVS SSSR*, 1968, No.27, Art.241.
29. V. Shevtsov, *Grazhdanstvo SSSR*, Moscow 1980, p.44.
30. I.K. Gorodetskaia, "Grazhdanstvo detei", p.43.
31. V. Shevtsov, *op. cit.*, p.46.
32. R.I. Kulik, *op. cit.*, pp.72–73.
33. V.V. Polianskii, *op. cit.*, p.128.
34. *Ibid.* Also, R.I. Kulik, *op. cit.*, p.74.
35. Cf., R.I. Kulik, *op. cit.*, pp.67, 74.
36. *Ibid.*, p.74.
37. V. Shevtsov, *op. cit.*, p.45.
38. A.A. Rubanov, *op. cit.*, pp.156–157.
39. *Kommentarii k zakonodatel'stvu* ..., p.193.

40. *Ibid.*
41. V. Shevtsov, *op. cit.*, pp.45–46.
42. *Ibid.*, p.45.
43. *Kommentarii k zakonodatel'stvu* ..., pp.193–194.
44. See David K. Shipler, "Russian Orphans, Though Well Tended, Have Sad Eyes", *New York Times*, January 18, 1979, p.A2. V. Shevtsov, *op. cit.*, p.45, writes: "This rule [i.e., concerning mandatory prior permission by the authorities for the adoption to be consummated] is introduced with the object of reliable protection of the interests of the child who is a citizen of the USSR."
45. V. Shevtsov, *op. cit.*, p.46.
46. R. Kulik, "Pravovye nachala sovetskogo grazhdanstva", *Sovety narodnykh deputatov*, 1979, No.2, p.37.
47. See, for instance, the episode recounted in *Khronika tekushchikh sobytii* (Moscow, Samizdat, 1979), New York, 1979, vyp.52, pp.111–112, concerning the KGB's bid to split the Kunitsa family and pit the children against the father in connection with the latter's attempts to win permission to emigrate. In this case, the stratagem reportedly backfired.

PROCEDURAL FORMAT

1. Background

A major additive to the 1978 citizenship statute consists of a lengthy subheading (Section V) devoted to the organizational modus operandi framing the consideration of applications and petitions concerning citizenship. The innovation marks a substantial improvement compared to past practice, for the 1938 law was notably remiss in providing almost no or, at best, a bare minimum of information about what routine was followed in handling citizenship affairs. Secondary sources contributed a few shreds of evidence, but the office record remained virtually terra incognita until just a couple of years ago. Now, new data have come to light and our picture of the inner workings of the responsible administrative apparatus, while by no means complete, is fuller than it has ever been. To appreciate the magnitude of the change here, let us first sum up the situation that existed prior to December 1, 1978.

An important revision effected by the 1938 legislation in the preceding system entailed the abrogation of the simplified method of entry into citizenship, whereupon the step was also taken to repeal the right of local Soviets and the supreme organs of state authority of the autonomous republics to admit individuals to Soviet citizenship. Jurisdiction over admission to citizenship was henceforth vested exclusively in the Presidium of the USSR Supreme Soviet and the Presidia of the Supreme Soviets of the union republics. Simultaneously, the principle enunciated in Article 12 of the 1931 Regulation permitting appeal from the decisions of the supreme organs of state authority of the union republics denying admission to citizenship to the matching supreme organs of state authority of the USSR was rescinded. This last stroke was interpreted by some Soviet authors as a bid to enlarge the sovereignty of the union republics by excluding the possibility of seeking review of the conclusions of republican organs refusing admission to citizenship.[1] The technical rationale offered for the switch was that "the Constitution of the USSR of 1936 does not envisage the right of the Presidium of the USSR Supreme Soviet to set aside the decrees of the Presidia of the Supreme Soviets of the union republics".[2]

While the 1938 act postulated that "foreigners, irrespective of their nationality and race, are admitted to the citizenship of the USSR upon their request by the Presidium of the USSR Supreme Soviet or the Presidium of the Supreme Soviet of the union republic in which they reside", the dividing line (if any) between the particular competence of the corresponding federal and republican institutions in these matters was never clearly drawn. The wording of the applicable clause did not pinpoint what role was assigned to the central Presidium and the interested republican Presidium, respectively, in treating an alien's petition for naturalization. From the explanations volunteered on the floor of the legislature by the bill's official rapporteur, one difference between their relative positions seemed fairly certain: when the question arose of granting Soviet citizenship to a foreigner domiciled abroad at the time the request was received, only the national Presidium had the right to act; an alien residing on Soviet soil and desiring naturalization, on the other hand, could file the requisite documents either with the Presidium of the Supreme Soviet of the union republic in which he lived or with the federal Presidium, both, ostensibly, being equally competent to do the job.

Nevertheless, Soviet commentators subsequently managed to cast doubt even on the validity of this apportionment scheme. Thus, statements occasionally cropped up in Soviet literature suggesting that departures from the basic formula were also possible in the sense that an alien residing abroad could request that his application for admission to Soviet citizenship be forwarded by the appropriate organ of the Soviet state abroad for consideration by the Presidium of the Supreme Soviet of the union republic in which he wanted to reside after his admission to Soviet citizenship.[3] In similar vein, another source observed that "petitions for admission to Soviet citizenship are examined by the Presidium of the USSR Supreme Soviet if the foreigner resided abroad or by the Presidium of the Supreme Soviet of the union republic within whose borders the foreigner resides or intends to reside".[4] From these rather tentative pronouncements, one might infer that in special instances the writ of the republican presidia likewise extended to naturalization requests emanating from individuals residing abroad, the tone of the statutory text notwithstanding. The net result would amount to shared authority between the responsible federal and republican agencies in this domain since the national Presidium could along with its republican counterparts entertain applications from locally domiciled aliens while foreigners residing abroad could submit their naturalization papers either to the federal Presidium or its equivalent in the republic of their choice. According to the Consular charter of the USSR (1976), the consul is empowered to accept applications from people living in his consular district concerning questions of USSR citizenship (Art.40), for transmission upward through designated channels.[5]

Admission to Soviet citizenship was formalized by the issuance in each case of a decree of the Presidium of the USSR Supreme Soviet or a decree of the Presidium of the Supreme Soviet of the union republic involved. Since these acts qualify as private bills, their posting in the legislative gazette is not mandatory and, as far as one can tell, none has been published in the federal record. Official reports do confirm, however, that the topic of admission to the citizenship of the USSR featured on the agenda of a few sessions of the federal Presidium, without indicating either the nature of the problem or the outcome of the deliberations:[6] whether the minute sample of three available references reflects how rarely the Presidium is called upon to deal with the subject or evinces a policy of advertising only the weightier items of business cannot be determined. The scenario for treating questions of admission to USSR citizenship purportedly looked as follows:

> "Preparation for considering petitions for admission to the citizenship of the USSR takes place in the department of the Presidium of the USSR Supreme Soviet that makes the necessary inquiries and formalizes the materials. As a rule, the consular administration of the Ministry of Foreign Affairs of the USSR expresses its opinion in the case of admission of foreigners to the citizenship of the USSR, and it maintains contacts with the petitioners residing abroad. Account is taken of the motives for submitting the application, the existence of kinship ties in the USSR, etc.
>
> The Commission formed by the Presidium of the USSR Supreme Soviet for preliminary consideration of citizenship questions gives its views on applications, and the decisions are adopted by the Presidium of the USSR Supreme Soviet in the form of Decrees, while resolutions of the Presidium are adopted where applications are rejected."[7]

The union republics have behaved less consistently in regarding these edicts as private bills and so giving them no public notice, and both the Estonian and Lithuanian SSRs, for instance, have published in their respective legislative bulletin ad hoc decrees each serving to confer the particular republican citizenship on the individual named therein. In the Georgian SSR, we are told, such decrees have been adopted as well, but they have been too numerous to publish.[8] Indeed, Soviet spokesmen portray naturalization at the republic level as a common phenomenon and the figures they cite are quite sizable. Until the passage of the 1978 citizenship law, admission to the citizenship of the union republics was governed by the Regulation on the procedure for consideration of applications concerning admission to the citizenship of the union republic enacted in each republic: e.g., the Regulation of November 29, 1961, in the Kirgiz SSR; of November 4, 1961, in the Uzbek SSR; of November 24, 1961, in the Georgian SSR. Although these measures were said to require up-dating in that the definition of the conditions for admission to republican citizenship needed perfecting pursuant to the terms of the USSR Constitution, the constitutions of the union republics, and the Law on the citizenship of the USSR, they could continue in force until the scheduled synchronization of republican legislation with the prescriptions of the 1978 statute insofar as they did not contradict the latter's norms.[9]

By virtue of the Regulations, the union republics, functioning within their range of competence, routinely engaged in admitting into their citizenship foreigners and stateless persons residing on their territory in response to requests submitted by such individuals. These applications were processed by the Commission on admission to the citizenship of the union republic, established by the local Presidium, which looked into the grounds for filing the application, evidence of family relations, the true commitment of the petitioner to becoming a citizen of the USSR. The final decision on admission to citizenship was rendered by the Presidium of the republic Supreme Soviet in the form of a decree and resolutions of the Presidium dealt with rejected applications. Preparatory work in connection with the consideration of petitions for naturalization was performed in the Legal department of the Presidium of the republic Supreme Soviet which made inquiries and organized the relevant data. The process of formal arrangement of the materials was regulated by special acts of the republic Presidium.

In practice, foreigners and stateless persons who wished to acquire the citizenship of the republic submitted a statement to that effect at the civil police (militsiia) headquarters in their precinct, expressly indicating in the applications if they had children (those between the ages of fourteen and eighteen had to give their written consent for conversion to Soviet citizenship). Citizens of socialist countries requesting admission to Soviet citizenship had to furnish affidavits on the attitude of the organs of state authority of their current homeland toward the proposed switch to Soviet citizenship. If these documents could not be procured, the omission had to be duly noted in the application, in line with the existing agreements on the prevention of dual citizenship between the USSR and its fellow socialist regimes. The materials relating to applications for admission to citizenship received by the civil police were then forwarded to the Legal department of the republican Presidium. Generally, the republican Ministries of Internal Affairs and Foreign Affairs likewise expressed their opinion concerning the admission of foreigners to republican citizenship.

The allotted time for formally drawing up the materials referring to applications and submitting these applications to the republic Presidium was not to exceed three months from the moment the applications and documents were received. Ordinarily, a year had to elapse before a reapplication following an earlier rejection of a petition for naturalization was accepted. Applications from foreigners and stateless persons on which there had previously been a decision of the federal Presidium were forwarded to that body for its determination.

By official computation, the volume of traffic at the republic level is quite impressive: the Presidium of the Kirgiz SSR had occasion to admit 1,462 persons to local citizenship between 1955 and June 1961; the Presidium of the Kazakh SSR fared even better — approving the naturalization of 669 persons in 1957, 811 in 1958, 1,025 in 1959, 852 in 1960, 896 in 1961, 937 in 1962, and 476 in 1963; and the Presidium of the Uzbek SSR sanctioned the acquisition of republican citizenship by 627 individuals between 1968 and 1971.[10]

In mid–1980, the head of OVIR publicly claimed that "over the past few years more than 300,000 people came to the Soviet Union from various countries and were granted citizenship".[11]

According to Article 4 of the 1938 statute, "denaturalization of the citizens of the USSR may take place by permission of the Presidium of the Supreme Soviet of the USSR". The formula differed from the corresponding provision in the 1931 regulations chiefly in that it vested the right to release a person from his or her Soviet citizenship solely in the federal Presidium. Previously, a republican Presidium too could exercise that authority where the individual seeking to shed Soviet citizenship resided within its confines, while only the central Presidium could deal with any such petitions activated by Soviet citizens located abroad. The assignment of exclusive competence to the supreme organs of the state to consider applications on admission to citizenship and withdrawal therefrom allegedly attested to the "harmoniously coinciding interests of the socialist state and the individual"[12] (a theme we shall return to shortly).

How release from Soviet citizenship occurred is not clear. If a decree was required to pronounce renunciation of Soviet citizenship, none has been published in the official journal. A sample of correspondence between the Consular division of the USSR embassy in Washington, D.C., and an individual who asked to be released from Soviet citizenship, apprising the de cujus that the request had been granted, simply informed the addressee that "your petition for release from Soviet citizenship has been approved".[13] Apparently, this is all that particular person got to indicate that he had been formally relieved of his Soviet citizenship: no reference to a decree or decision of the federal Presidium which could be adduced in case of need, no subsequent publication of a notice certifying this major change in the person's status, nothing more than this cryptic memorandum on a leaf of diplomatic stationary which, to make matters worse, omitted even to state the date on which the ruling entered into force.

The mass of recent emigrants from the USSR who are compelled to divest themselves of Soviet citizenship in order to be let out of the country have still less proof of loss of Soviet citizenship. In fact, going by an eye–witness account, they have none at all:

> "In 1973--1974, when I submitted to OVIR a request for an exit visa, the following procedure operated. Immediately upon accepting my application, I was warned that, if my request were fulfilled, I would lose my citizenship at the moment of crossing the frontier. When my application was approved, I was instructed to pay a tax for the right to quit Soviet citizenship, which I did. I don't remember exactly, but it seems to me, in the exit visa which I was issued figured the statement that I was 'stateless'. Everything, then, looks perfectly clear. The problem, however, is that OVIR which issued me the visa and concurrently took back the receipt for payment of the tax for exit from citizenship is not competent to decide questions of relinquishment of citizenship. As for the decision of the competent organ — the Presidium of the Supreme Soviet of the USSR — its decision was never communicated to me. Yet, release from citizenship is a rather important legal act and each Soviet emigrant has the right to count on receiving at least in exchange for the receipt for payment of the tax for renunciation of Soviet citizenship which was taken away from him an official document indicating when exactly the Presidium of the USSR Supreme Soviet sanctioned his release. I don't know if the procedure just described remains in force. It would be interesting to hear about this from latter–day emigrants. Maybe someone could send me for publication in the paper a copy of the form for applying for emigration, of a receipt for payment of the tax for release from citizenship or of an exit visa. In any event, as of now I do not have on hand any document confirming that the Presidium of the USSR Supreme Soviet permitted me to leave [Soviet] citizenship and I intend to request an appropriate affidavit through the Soviet embassy in Canada with the assistance of the Canadian Ministry of Foreign Affairs."[14]

By Soviet estimate (circa mid–1980), "over the past few years" approximately 300,000 people had left the USSR to be reunited with their families, — in the main, Jews, Germans, Spaniards, Greeks, plus Armenians. Meanwhile, more than 15,000 Soviet citizens married foreigners and 10,500 of them left the USSR to reside in more than 100 countries. Expatriation generally entailed denaturalization. Even so, we have only a single clue to show that the problem of renunciation of Soviet citizenship has formally figured on the national Presidium's calendar.[15]

Under the terms of the 1938 legislation, deprivation of Soviet citizenship could take place, inter alia, on the strength of a special decree in each instance of the Presidium of the USSR Supreme Soviet. Again, the union republics which, by virtue of the provisions of the 1931 Regulation had shared the right to stage forfeiture of their respective citizenship (which eo ipso meant the annulment of the citizenship of the USSR) were excluded from the picture in favor of a federal monopoly. The concentration of that power in the hands of the central authorities was justified by invoking the extraordinary character and particularly grave consequences of this penalty (more so since a person stripped of citizenship by one socialist state was in practice ineligible for admission to the citizenship of its fellow regimes).[16] The Consular charter of the USSR (1976 edition, Art.41) mandates that "a consul may, with the consent of the head of the diplomatic mission of the USSR in the host country, initiate a petition to deprive of USSR citizenship persons who had committed acts besmirching the high calling of USSR citizen and causing harm to the prestige or state security of the USSR".

In contrast to the failure of the law to specify the means for consummating release from Soviet citizenship, in this case the chosen instrument was precisely identified — to wit, an ad hoc edict of the national Presidium. However, since such decrees were not regarded as possessing normative status, but counted as acts of implementation of the law, acts of exercise of the competence vested in the Presidium by the USSR Constitution,[17] official publication was treated as optional and the record shows that some of them were indeed printed in the legislative bulletin, others were merely mentioned there, and many more were never entered in the public ledger. The one principle adhered to with remarkable constancy was that where revocation of citizenship fell within the jurisdiction of the supreme organs of state authority, the matter could not be the object of judicial hearings.[18]

The 1938 statute completely ignored the concept of restoration to Soviet citizenship, unlike its predecessor which had allowed both the federal and republican presidia to engage in that activity by resort to decrees (the same routine, incidentally, as then employed in sanctioning voluntary denaturalization). Nonetheless, the regime did on occasion license reinstatement in Soviet citizenship and elected to do so either by promulgating appropriate decrees in the name of the federal Presidium or, as in the Cherches case, by reporting a decision of the executive branch to that effect.

A number of reforms in the established modus operandi, relating to aspects of organization as well as style, were proposed in the sixties, much of the animus stemming from the wish to reverse the preceding trend and correct a phenomenon that was now castigated as "the unwarranted restriction of the sovereign rights of the union republics in the sphere of legislative activity, which occurred during the period of the cult of the personality and resulted in the principal functions in this sphere being aggregated in the national organs".[19] With reference to the process of admission to Soviet citizenship, for example, preference was expressed for a system where the right to grant naturalization would be exercised by the presidia of the autonomous republics along with their federal and union republic counterparts.[20] In order to enhance the importance of the union republics in citizenship affairs, the recommendation was made that every individual petitioning for admission to Soviet citizenship distinctly state the citizenship of which union or autonomous republic he desired.[21] By the same token, it was urged that the jurisdiction of the presidia of union republics be expanded so as to enable them to admit to the corresponding republican citizenship aliens residing elsewhere on the territory of the USSR and even foreigners (stateless persons) living abroad.[22] Suggestions were likewise heard advocating the simplification and acceleration of the method of naturalization maintained for citizens of other socialist states[23] and/or for active members of oppressed peoples, individuals who had rendered signal services to the nations of the USSR in the revolutionary cause, in socialist construction and in the struggle for the freedom and independence of the USSR.[24]

The mechanics of release from Soviet citizenship were felt to be in need of overhaul as well, — primarily in the sense of letting the union republics once more be associated with the decision to allow individuals to leave Soviet citizenship, as under the 1931 Regulation;[25] and, a few Soviet authors ventured so far as to argue the advisability of restoring the concurrent competence of federal and republican institutions in dealing with occasions of deprivation of Soviet citizenship.[26] (The issue of "liberalizing" the practice of recovery of Soviet citizenship seems to have been overlooked.) To match the projected "relaxation" of the rules applied to the conversion of citizens of socialist countries to Soviet citizenship, a further change was envisioned aimed at facilitating the "transfer into the citizenship of the people's democratic states by Soviet citizens", as a way of marking the gradual rapprochement afoot on the community scene.[27]

Finally, in tune with the bid to shift the center of gravity in the field of citizenship from the federal peak closer to the republican level, the view was propounded that the national government tackle the job of enacting the Bases of legislation on Soviet citizenship, perhaps suitably amplified to "codify" all the norms pertaining to citizenship relations,[28] while leaving to the union republics the task of adopting their own legislation in this domain.[29]

How these plans fared will be noted below in analyzing the relevant provisions of the 1978 statute and appraising the novel elements they incorporated.

Compared to the fairly open access we enjoy to the Soviet legislative repertory, insights into administrative policy are rare and fragmentary — and the observation is true for citizenship questions as well. What follows, then, is a collation of the random bits of pertinent evidence leaked by the local media which, of course, only represents the bare tip of the iceberg. Thus, in 1977, the regime was considerate enough to release the text of the Instruction of the Ministry of Finance of the USSR of December 31, 1976, No.95, on the state tax,[30] which, inter alia, tabulated the fees charged for various services connected with citizenship operations. The scale included an impost on applications for admission to and withdrawal from the citizenship of the USSR (Art.1). The amount of the duty was subject to reimbursement if the citizen who paid the tax dropped the request to the state organ that levied the tax for performance of the designated act or receipt of the document, and also if the state organ which levied the tax refused to perform the designated act or issue the document for which the tax had been paid. Similarly, full reimbursement of the tax was slated in case of rejection of a petition for release from the citizenship of the USSR. The sum due is refunded on condition that the application for refund be filed with the state organ which collected the tax or the finance organ no later than one year from the day the amount was entered in the budget (Art.11). The rates were set as follows: application from foreigners or apatrides for admission to USSR citizenship — five rubles; application for renunciation of Soviet citizenship from persons residing abroad — 50 rubles, from persons residing in the USSR and intending to move to a socialist country — 50 rubles and from those intending to move to a capitalist country — 500 rubles; applications from political emigrants, members of their family and persons equated with political emigrants for admission to USSR citizenship — 50 kopeks, and no cost attached to applications from such persons for renunciation of Soviet citizenship (Art.56).[31]

Very little is known of the office routine for handling the paper work relating to citizenship business. One of the assigned speakers for the bill of the 1978 citizenship statute told his audience that in recent years several steps had been initiated to facilitate and expedite the desk traffic and, in particular, claimed that the "consideration and formalization of applications from people regarding the right rsict to receive the citizenship of the USSR had become more effective [*operativnye*]".[32] Nothing was said about improving or easing the flow in the opposite direction, i.e., as concerns the procedure for treating applications purporting to exercise the "right to renounce the citizenship of the USSR", — which is not in the least surprising.

2.Current Legislation

A. Certification of Soviet Citizenship

The new statute omits to mention the matter of establishing a person's legal entitlement to the citizenship of the USSR, leaving the Presidium of the USSR Supreme Soviet to fill the gap which the latter proceeded to do in the decree of June 15, 1979. Its Article 7 read:

> "In the case where a question arises whether a person belongs to the citizenship of the USSR, the determination of this fact is effected in accordance with the rules established by the Presidium of the USSR Supreme Soviet. If the circumstances which relate to the person's connection with the citizenship of the USSR occurred before the Law's entry into force, then the rules of the legislative acts of the USSR and union republics operating at the time these facts occurred are applied.
>
> Determination of a person's belonging to the citizenship of the USSR is entrusted to the organs of internal affairs, and with respect to persons residing abroad — to the corresponding diplomatic or consular missions of the USSR.
>
> Appeals from decisions on questions of affiliation with the citizenship of the USSR are submitted to the Presidium of the USSR Supreme Soviet."

The mere elaboration of this normative setting already marks a step forward compared to the pre–1978 situation. Virtually all we know of previous practice here is that the courts had no competence to hear such cases. Directive No.9 of the People's Commissariat of Justice, dated 1937, noted that the people's court of the Kiurda–Mirskii district of the Azerbaidzhan SSR had rendered a decision on the citizenship (nationality) of a certain Gussein Murid Ogly and pronounced him to be an Iranian national. By so doing, the court was now reminded, it had violated the norms of the resolution of the USSR Central Executive Committee of November 1, 1930, whereby the right to issue affidavits of possession of a given state's citizenship was vested in city Soviets or executive committees equipped with special departments or offices. To avoid further incidents of this sort, the local authorities were summoned to explain to the republic's courts that the present item did not fall within their jurisdiction.[33] The same general principle is followed today.

Useful light has also been shed recently on the treatment afforded in the Soviet legal environment to the conflict–of–law dimensions of the problem. First, we learn that the citizenship law's clause (Art.8) specifying that a person who is considered a citizen of the USSR is not recognized as belonging to the citizenship of a foreign state, means that the Soviet regime will not acknowledge the right of a foreign state to take action in the manner prescribed by public international law in defense of the interests of an alleged bipatride whenever he happens to qualify as a citizen of the USSR. Second, a person in that position cannot cite his obligations vis–à–vis the foreign state in his dealings with the appropriate Soviet institutions, nor will similar assertions by the foreign government be taken into account. Third, the point is made that it is up to Soviet law alone to fix the procedure for resolution by the responsible Soviet organs of instances requiring determination of the fact of a person's status as a citizen of some foreign state. This conclusion presumably derives from the universally accepted precept that the modus operandi of a state's organ is, in essence, laid down by that state's law — which would logically extend to this contingency as well. Insofar as most other countries tend to spell out their own grounds for attributing citizenship to constituents, collisions between rival claimants are common.

To break the impasse, the Soviet legal canon has enunciated a series of propositions. To begin with, Soviet legislation maintains that only those people residing on the territory of the USSR can seek to prove their title to a foreign citizenship who are not citizens of the USSR: hence, a person who figures as a Soviet citizen is a priori ineligible to approach the competent Soviet organs to even "take the test". Next, Soviet law indicates what means can be used to prove possession of the citizenship of a foreign state, i.e., what documents and data can serve as evidence of the putative relationship. Then, Soviet law grades the probative value of the documents and data submitted in support of the assertion that the de cujus belongs to the citizenship of a foreign state and, inter alia, defines what foreign documents or data will suffice to let the proper Soviet organ make up its mind that the petitioner is indeed the citizen of a foreign country. Lastly, Soviet law regulates the entire evidentiary process, especially the various deadlines, who bears the onus probandi, etc., but may, on certain issues, permit referral to foreign law. In the opinion of one local spokesman, for example, resort to the technique of renvoi would be theoretically quite justified on the subject of the term of duration of a passport issued by foreign authorities. If, according to Soviet legislation, the responsible Soviet organs may accept a foreign passport as evidence of the fact of possession of foreign citizenship, a suitable proviso would be that the passport fulfills that function solely while valid and that question is answered by the law of the country of origin.[34]

The script is remarkable in two ways: 1) it strives to reduce to a minimum the extent to which cognizance has to be taken of foreign law by unilaterally dismissing the other state's stake in all cases of binationality in which Soviet citizenship is coupled with that of another country, thus dramatically curbing the volume of business involving certification of citizenship affiliation and cavalierly brushing aside the toughest part of the problem; and, 2) it plainly stacks the deck in favor of maximum reliance on Soviet law in arriving at a solution while relegating the relevant principles of the competing foreign legal system to a strictly peripheral role. The pattern is familiar to those who have studied Soviet responses to the phenomenon of "contest" between their law and that of the "opposition".

A distinctive element of the relationship forged between the individual and the state in reference to certification of citizenship affiliation is the fact that on this occasion the petitioner possesses specific rights sanctioned by Soviet legislation and either seeks to exercise them or vindicate a right that has been violated. The initiative to start proceedings in these matters rests, we are told, with the interested person or his representative or a Soviet official figure. The most common item in the basket features a request to establish title to Soviet citizenship, i.e., not to change a person's citizenship, but to clarify his juridical status and determine whether the de cujus is a Soviet citizen or a foreigner or an apatride. Such uncertainties regarding citizenship identity can arise, for instance, as a consequence of prolonged residence abroad. Disputes of this sort most frequently concern the citizenship of children. Thus, the legal representative of a minor petitions the Soviet consul in the foreign country where the child is located to have the child recognized as a Soviet citizen on the grounds that at the time of its birth one of the parents was a Soviet citizen and the other a stateless person (Art.12, para.5). The consul, after checking the evidence and ascertaining that it substantiates the claim forthwith authenticates the child in the name of the Soviet state as a citizen of the USSR. Another example of this procedure occurs when the local organs of internal affairs consider the application of parents who are stateless individuals to have their offspring born on the territory of the USSR certified as a Soviet citizen in accordance with Article 13.

As mentioned earlier, Article 7 of the federal edict of June 15, 1979, indicates that determination of a person's belonging to the citizenship of the USSR is effected in conformity with rules prescribed by the Presidium of the USSR Supreme Soviet. An important addendum here, in the opinion of Soviet lawyers, is the proviso that the decision regarding a person's stake in Soviet citizenship must be based on the legislative norms in force at the time from which date the relevant circumstances. For example, if an individual received Soviet citizenship under the terms of the federal decree of March 30, 1948 (now lapsed) "On the procedure for acquisition of the citizenship of the USSR by citizens of the Lithuanian, Latvian and Estonian republics and natives of Bessarabia residing in Latin American countries" and did not subsequently lose it, then he continues to count as a Soviet citizen irrespective of his current homeland.

The same clause of the federal edict of June 15, 1979, assigned the business of determining title to Soviet citizenship to the organs of internal affairs and, in relation to persons residing abroad, to the corresponding diplomatic and consular institutions of the USSR. Reportedly, the competent agencies are obliged to extend to the applicant the necessary assistance with establishing his legal position, performing the required legal acts, drawing up the official documents, etc.

The crucial ingredient in this context, though, is the point that this category of cases involves recognition or non–recognition of the fact of acquisition by the designated person of a right enunciated by law. The dispute, therefore, is over entitlement to a legal right and not, say, over warranted or unwarranted denial of a privilege. As a result, the decisions of the responsible functionaries on citizens' applications for certification can be duly appealed to the higher organs of state administration and, ultimately, to the Presidium of the Supreme Soviet of the respective union republic and the federal Presidium. This profile of the review procedure emerges from the language of Article 7 of the federal decree of June 15, 1979, which speaks expressly of such appeals to the national Presidium and the implied meaning of the clause in Article 26 of the 1978 statute referring to the right of the USSR Presidium to rule on "other petitions on questions of Soviet citizenship, adopted for consideration" by writ of certiorari, as it were. The intermediate stages of the appellate system lack a statutory stamp, but if Soviet secondary sources are to be believed, apparently operate as a matter of standard practice.[35]

B. Admission, Renunciation, Restoration and Deprivation

According to the first paragraph of Article 26:

> "The Presidium of the USSR Supreme Soviet adopts decisions on:
>
> applications for admission to USSR citizenship from foreign citizens and stateless persons residing abroad;
>
> applications for admission to USSR citizenship from foreign citizens and stateless persons residing in the USSR if with respect to their citizenship a decision of the Presidium of the USSR Supreme Soviet had previously been rendered;
>
> applications for restoration in USSR citizenship, withdrawal from USSR citizenship, as well as motions for deprivation of USSR citizenship;
>
> other applications on questions of Soviet citizenship taken up by the Presidium of the USSR Supreme Soviet for consideration.
>
> Decisions on applications for admission to the citizenship of a union republic and thereby to the citizenship of the USSR from foreign citizens and stateless persons maintaining a permanent place of residence on the territory of the union republic are adopted by the Presidium of the Supreme Soviet of the union republic."

The wording of the passage prompts several observations.

i. The style here is said to be superior to that of the matching clause in the 1938 statute in that now the respective spheres of competence of the federal and republican presidia in matters of admission to Soviet citizenship are "more precisely demarcated". Whereas the 1938 edition gave the impression of parallel jurisdiction in treating of naturalization, the new version establishes that decisions on requests for admission to the citizenship of a union republic and thus to the citizenship of the USSR received from foreign citizens and stateless persons residing on the territory of that union republic are passed by the latter's Presidium. The primary power in this case seems to rest with the corresponding republic Presidium and where the federal authorities fit into the picture is not clear from the letter of the legislation. Even so, a local author indicates that the federal Presidium still retains the right to take charge of such petitions,[36] presumably by virtue of the blanket license entitling it to direct that any application on questions of Soviet citizenship be rerouted to it for final disposition. The novelty, then, would be that the federal Presidium might henceforth issue this preemptive writ only in extraordinary circumstances, whereas in the past concurrent jurisdiction was the norm in these affairs and the central apparatus could put these items on its own agenda at any time (and, indeed, generally did). How deferential the federal branch is likely to be under the present system, technical nuances notwithstanding, is impossible to predict, but, in any event, whatever balance will be struck in this domain will in practice be the result of discretionary auto– limitation by the national government and will not be dictated by some compartmentalization scheme propounded in the text of the law.

ii. The latest accent on the role of the union republics in this sector probably explains why the institution of administrative review has been revived on the naturalization circuit. True, the same rationale was once offered to account for the exact opposite phenomenon. Remember that when the 1938 act failed to reproduce the formula featured in its 1931 antecedent recognizing that "the decree of the Presidium of the Central Executive Committee of the union republics refusing to admit to citizenship of the USSR may be protested before the Presidium of the Central Executive Committee of the USSR", the move was interpreted as significantly enlarging the sovereignty of the union republics. The story is not credible. In effect, it would look perfectly natural to have a similar proviso in the successor law too, since, as hitherto, an adverse republican verdict turning down the petitioner's request for republican citizenship eo ipso served to deny him the citizenship of the USSR. Given the unmistakable trend toward administrative centralization reflected in the 1936 Constitution and the companion social and economic programs connected with Stalin's rise to power, the absence of any visible check on republican performance in an area of some national importance plainly runs counter to the whole contemporaneous tenor of Soviet public behavior and the then dominant pattern of political development inside the country.

The prospect that, in 1931, when central constraints were far less stringent, the regime should see fit to furnish in naturalization cases a ready avenue of appeal to the very apex of the governmental pyramid against an unfavorable ruling on the republican plane and, seven years later, when the drive to concentrate all authority in the hands of the federal agencies was mounting to a climax, such a safeguard was cashiered without a murmur, simply taxes credulity. The only reason it was done, as far as one can tell, is that at this juncture nobody in the Soviet Union seriously conceived of the republics from then on doing anything in this province on their own, official contentions to the contrary notwithstanding. Consequently, Moscow could easily forego the luxury of instituting a special mechanism to guarantee routine monitoring of republican decisions in order to ensure uniform interpretation of federal naturalization rules.

In the light of reports recording that several union republics have, for instance, actively engaged in administering the rules concerning admission to Soviet citizenship starting in the mid–fifties, the return to a situation where the federal regime could maintain supervision over how these operations were handled makes eminent sense. The existence of an audit procedure is a better index here to the reality of the republic's footing than the ostentatious waiver of all superior control. In fact, when in the sixties some Soviet authors urged that the union republics again share equal status with the federal establishment in the citizenship field,[37] they were smart enough to couple these recommendations with a proposal to revive the review system, knowing full well how slim the chances in their environment of the republican units gaining a bigger role without the top brass making certain that it had ample opportunity to police their drill.

As a final bit of irony, a point worth recalling is that the technical excuse for abolishing the appellate format in 1938 was that the 1936 Constitution did not sanction the USSR Presidium's right to set aside the decrees of republican presidia.[38] Neither does the 1978 charter, and yet the practice is back in business, which could lead one to conclude that the earlier explanation was bogus, namely, constitutional silence on this issue was not meant to estop such oversight, or that the legal analysis was (and still is) sound, but the injunction is now conveniently ignored.

iii. All of the projects of reform looking to the assignment (or reassignment) of competency to the autonomous republics in naturalization questions and to the union republics apropos the naturalization of persons residing abroad, withdrawal from and deprivation of Soviet citizenship aborted. In particular, federal jurisdiction over the entire package relating to loss of Soviet citizenship remained absolute and, furthermore, officially reposits in the Presidium of the USSR Supreme Soviet which crowns the state edifice. The arrangement is supposed to have many advantages. For example, the Minister of Justice of the USSR speaking in his capacity of parliamentary delegate on behalf of the citizenship bill stressed the theme that "in contrast with certain western countries where questions of exit from citizenship are decided by individual functionaries, in the draft of the Law under discussion it is determined that decisions on these questions are reached collegially and by such a high organ of state authority as the Presidium of the USSR Supreme Soviet".[39] In comparable vein, the claim is often made that "the procedure whereby decisions on these questions may be taken solely by the Presidium of the USSR Supreme Soviet serves as a guarantee of observance of the Law and preclusion of arbitrary actions",[40] — inter alia, allegedly because the "supreme organ of the Soviet state embarks on the resolution of these questions with great care and maximum attention to all the circumstances".[41]

Or, the pitch is that "such a high state level of treatment of questions of exit from Soviet citizenship matches the political, legal and moral significance of the act of exit from citizenship", for, regardless of the animus, "a person's exit from citizenship always cuts his ties with his people, his state" while, of course, "protection of the interests of the state and its security is also a prime concern".[42] Or, on a more technical note, the position has been espoused that, "since exit from citizenship can affect the interests of not just one union republic, but possibly even several union republics and the whole USSR", the legislator wisely opted to let the federal Presidium corner the market.[43] Overlooked in the shuffle is the minor matter that because in most cases renunciation of USSR citizenship automatically terminates a republic's citizenship as well, an equally cogent argument would be that the latter has as valid a stake in policing the operation as the federal authorities.

The logistical side of the picture presents an added complication. In effect, granting the federal Presidium a formal monopoly over the withdrawal from and deprivation of Soviet citizenship in principle means that no appeal from its decisions lies elsewhere since it perches at the top of the government hierarchy. The Supreme Soviet of the USSR does have the residual power to exercise any right assigned by the Constitution to the central regime but the odds against its intervening in these affairs run tall. On the other hand, we know that the routine work of processing citizenship applications is in fact done by lower administrative agencies, so, in organizational terms, a review mechanism could function within the bureaucratic structure.

The tone of the statutory language, incidentally, is rather non–committal. After identifying the national Presidium as the decision–making organ, the citizenship act establishes that applications in reference to citizenship matters are submitted, correspondingly, in the name of the Presidium of the USSR Supreme Soviet or the Presidium of the Supreme Soviet of a union republic, with persons residing abroad filing through the appropriate diplomatic or consular mission of the USSR (Art.27). The decree of the federal Presidium of June 15, 1979, sheds a little more light on the subject by explaining that the organs of internal affairs are charged with formalizing petitions on questions of admission to, restoration in and withdrawal from the citizenship of the USSR, as well as issuing documents or entering changes in documents confirming the acquisition or loss of USSR citizenship and, with respect to people living abroad, these duties are entrusted to the diplomatic or consular institutions of the USSR.[44] The script gives the impression, though, that these subordinate echelons merely engage in checking to see that the papers are in order, the portfolio is complete and the information is up to date and then serve as a passive communication channel for forwarding the dossiers through the vertical chain of command or registering the upshot of their superior's deliberations.

Reality, we learn from Soviet writings, diverges markedly from the book version. The requirement that these petitions be addressed to the federal Presidium does not exclude their submission through the local state organs — the executive committees of Soviets of people's deputies. Upon receipt of such applications from individuals domiciled in a foreign country, the diplomatic or consular mission of the USSR transmits them to the national Presidium along with its conclusions, the necessary data concerning the de cujus, etc. The opinion of the organs of the respective state regarding the person's intent to leave its citizenship is also passed on where mandated by an existing treaty or convention (e.g., between the USSR and the majority of its socialist partners): otherwise, further inquiries would have to be launched at the preparatory stage, which would drag out the proceedings.[45] Forfeiture of USSR citizenship obviously follows a slightly different route since the affected individual's desire is not taken into account here and the initiative emanates from outside sources: Soviet consular agencies abroad, for example, may recommend to the home government that a designated individual be stripped of his Soviet citizenship; civic organizations can likewise chime in on the domestic scene, as the Soviet sports community and the Chess Federation of the USSR were credited with instigating the move against V.L. Korchnoi.

Additional input is forthcoming at the Presidium's own level. All applications for admission to, recovery of and withdrawal from Soviet citizenship are first studied by the Commission of the Presidium of the USSR Supreme Soviet on questions of citizenship, which is a standing auxiliary of the Presidium. If need be, the Commission consults the interested ministries and departments, farms out specific tasks and invites their spokesmen to its sessions to present their findings. On special occasions, the Commission may perform other functions as well. The organizational–technical and legal services connected with readying citizenship cases for final scrutiny are provided by the staff of the federal and republican presidia, respectively.[46] Thus, the Legal Department of the Presidium of the USSR Supreme Soviet is responsible for much of the original paperwork. The Consular Department of the Ministry of Foreign Affairs of the USSR usually expresses its views concerning the admission of aliens to USSR citizenship and keeps in touch with applicants residing abroad.[47] The republican presidia have a similar set–up.[48]

Despite this elaborate scheme, the sort of internal verification that is practiced and the avenues available for mounting an external challenge to the bureaucratic will fall far short of the normal review standards, in part because the Presidium's immunity extends downward and shields the lower ranks. For example, dissident sources have long complained that the OVIR/ UVIR offices which handle petitions for emigration and commonly also end up performing the denaturalization ceremony, do not observe the general deadline fixed for considering applications by the public (two months) or ever furnish legal reasons in the event of rejection.[49] The exemption presumably stems from association with the Presidium's special status, as witness the following thesis propounded by the local legal experts.

The activity of the federal and republican presidia relating to the consideration and settlement of citizenship questions, they claim, represents a species of supreme executive and administrative competency and is exercised in accordance with the interests of the state and those of the individual within the frame of valid legislation. These powers have a sovereign–evaluative character, which boils down to saying that in analyzing the treatment of cases of admission to, reinstatement in and withdrawal from citizenship, the key element is that no dispute over a right can occur here. Hence, the organ rendering a decision is not bound, inter alia, to justify its ruling. By the same token, the decisions in these cases have final force and are not subject to appeal. Inasmuch as their resolution does not involve conflict over a right, appeal does not enter the picture for the simple reason that appeal is, by definition, nothing more than a procedure sanctioned by law for dealing with a request for the restoration of a violated right.

The statements filed by a person with the corresponding organ which rejected his solicitation for exit from Soviet citizenship regarding the nature of his property obligations toward the state or other persons do not qualify as a complaint either, but figure only as a notification of facts which the de cujus asks the supreme organ of authority to take into account and then look again at his petition or, rather, examine his new petition in the light of this additional evidence. A decision of the federal Presidium to adopt for consideration a case previously passed on by a republican organ likewise does not constitute appellate review.

The routing of citizenship traffic is free of all procedural time constraints, since the supreme organ of state authority is pronounced not to be bound by temporal phenomena. Indeed, the flavor of utmost discretion imbues the entire official repertory in this domain. Seized of a situation calling for approval of a change in citizenship affiliation, the presidium may instruct the petitioner to supply more information, such, for example, as evidence of the attitude of the children or dependents of the applicant toward the substance of his request. Action on the petition may be postponed if, independently of the organ handling the affair, appreciable time has elapsed since the applicant's original inquiry and the matter has not been pursued further. In practice, the early stages of the processing of a dossier concerning citizenship status may reveal lack of clarity on some questions pertinent to the final decision or other shortcomings in how the papers were drawn up. If these deficiencies cannot be corrected on the spot and the competent presidium may be inclined to consent to the request, formal determination may be delayed until the petitioner fulfills the necessary conditions.[50]

iv. The cryptic reference in the statute to the federal Presidium's exclusive right to receive applications for admission to USSR citizenship when the rolls show that the topic had already been the object of a prior decision by the same body is stylistically awkward and so a trifle misleading. What is meant, of course, is not that the Presidium of the USSR Supreme Soviet stricto sensu must previously have had occasion here to attend to the problem, but that a ruling emanating from a federal instance duly featured in the record and a fresh decision on the subject would be reserved for the appropriate federal agency in order to avoid the embarrassment of a republican organ reversing a determination made by a superior federal unit. Soviet sources offer the following hypothetical case to illustrate the relationship. By resolution of the Central Executive Committee and Council of People's Commissars of November 13, 1925, persons located abroad who missed the deadline for registration fixed by the legislation of the union republics, were deemed to have lost their Soviet citizenship. Even if a person with this kind of background resided on the territory of the USSR, his application for naturalization (or, better yet, reentry) would still have to be submitted to the national Presidium and not to the Presidium of the union republic in which he now lived.[51]

v. Mention was made earlier of the catch-all provision in the 1978 act which empowered the federal Presidium, inter alia, to hand down decisions on other applications regarding questions of Soviet citizenship which it chose to put on its agenda. As noted, the clause lets the central Presidium review by certiorari findings by its republican counterparts on applications for admission to Soviet citizenship, although the law does not expressly visa an audit system. The formula's net effect is to guarantee the federal Presidium jurisdiction of a universal scope in the area of citizenship practice, since it can unilaterally assume control over any such matter or issue an appropriate assignment to any state organ of the USSR or union republic.[52]

vi. Within their respective jurisdictional sphere, the federal and republican presidia issue decrees on affirmative decisions involving change of citizenship and adopt resolutions upon denying such petitions. These acts, Soviet authors add, "bear a personal character", i.e., they display the name of each person to whom the measure is addressed.[53] Where the edicts have been published, the accuracy of that statement can be verified and the available sample substantiates the claim; edicts stamped for "internal circulation only" and resolutions which are never reproduced textually and seldom reported cannot be checked for evidence of compliance with the stated standard. Nor is it true that it would make little difference apropos resolutions since they purportedly just memorialize the preservation of the status quo, for in some instances they have served as vehicles for consummating change in citizenship liaisons — legislative literalness to the contrary notwithstanding.

vii. As observed before, decrees and resolutions concerning admission to, recovery of and withdrawal from citizenship are generally treated as private bills and, "as a rule, are not published". The policy is simply to "notify the interested persons of the action taken".[54] One may recall that in the case of the majority of recent emigrants from the USSR who are compelled to surrender their Soviet citizenship in connection with departure abroad, no documentary proof of exit from Soviet citizenship is left in the possession of the expatriates and failure to publish the relevant information compounds the air of uncertainty surrounding the experience. Even in more routine circumstances, the practice of not publishing an official account of the transaction may have serious consequences for the de cujus if the terms of the personal communication are not sufficiently precise on an array of technical points germane to pinning down the individual's future position.

viii. An example of this type of slippage involves the timing of the change occurring in an individual's citizenship status which, according to the citizenship law, falls on the day the decree is issued, unless the latter specifies otherwise. The statute says nothing about resolutions in this connection and yet it would seem that, for instance, A.A. Zinov'ev was deprived of his Soviet citizenship without benefit of an ad hoc decree (at least none was ever identified), A.L. Cherches was restored to Soviet citizenship in the same surreptitious manner and thus neither could refer to the effective date of the event since the printed notices written in second–hand tense neglected to calendar the occasions. However, even if formal edicts are in fact resorted to here, the bulk of them, as already mentioned, do not stage a debut in commonly accessible media and cannot be directly cited should a dispute afterwards develop as to when a particular citizenship conversion allegedly took place, leaving the affected individual at the mercy of whatever message the authorities saw fit to send him to apprise him of his lot and the language of such correspondence, as the record indicates, tends to be enigmatic, — to put it kindly. Of course, we are now talking about "petty" details, except that the human being caught up in the official machinery often finds that these few solid toeholds offer the only slim margin of security he can hope for.

ix. The 1978 act is equally remiss in explaining what happens once the competent presidium reaches a conclusion that alters existing citizenship relations. The federal decree of June 15, 1979, corrects the oversight to some extent by establishing that the organs of internal affairs are charged with issuing documents or amending documents to confirm acquisition or loss of USSR citizenship, and in regard to people residing abroad this job is entrusted to the local Soviet diplomatic or consular agencies. Legal literature adds a footnote: upon admission to citizenship, the de cujus receives a Soviet passport and a minor collects a birth certificate; a person leaving Soviet citizenship gets a residence permit for apatrides; an alien residing abroad who acquires Soviet citizenship by writ of the central Presidium procures a Soviet passport from the nearby consul.[55]

x. The legislative script (on the national scale) is blank on what a petitioner is supposed to do if his application meets with formal rejection. Scholarship comes to the rescue with the revelation that this contingency does not exclude the possibility of filing the request anew and that administrative usage at both the federal and republican levels has settled on a one–year waiting period before a return engagement.[56]

xi. Academic literature also sheds light on another item which does not receive statutory treatment, namely, the material form which the parties must follow in transacting citizenship business. Reportedly, the procedure calls for the operations to be conducted in writing: the requirement extends both to the petitions lodged by individuals and the conclusions of state organs which the Presidium commissions for each application. Pursuant to the law, officials are bound to accept written as well as oral communications from the public and citizenship problems are no exception to the rule. In the latter case, however, an oral application can only set off certain preliminary moves, such as assistance to the de cujus with the necessary paperwork (a task performed by the local organs of internal affairs or the consul), but will not instigate consideration of the citizenship issues proper.[57]

xii. The last paragraph of Article 27 reaffirms that applications concerning questions of citizenship of persons younger than eighteen are submitted by their legal representatives. The formula raises no difficulties, save for the manner of its interpretation in a conflict–of–law situation, since it is clear from the terms of the statute that such petitions can also be filed by persons residing abroad, including aliens. As a Soviet author rightly points out, the problem then comes up as to which legal system should determine whether a particular individual qualifies as the minor's legal representative. His own line of reasoning is that:

> "Under Soviet law, parents are the legal representatives of their minor offspring, with the father and mother possessed of equal rights and duties vis–à–vis their children (Arts.53 and 54 of the Code on marriage and the family of the RSFSR). Under the law of Spain, Argentina, Brazil and some other countries, on the other hand, 'parental authority' over the child (which includes the right to act as legal representative) is exercised by the father and, only in his absence, by the mother.
>
> From the basic conflict principle of Soviet legislation on citizenship it follows that all questions of Soviet citizenship (and, hence, likewise the question of the content of concepts employed by the norms of Soviet legislation on citizenship) are decided by Soviet law. That is why the question of who figures as the legal representative of a person less than eighteen years of age is established by Soviet law. The content assigned to this concept by the norms of law of foreign states plays no role here, independently of any circumstances whatever — for example, citizenship or place of residence of the

persons lodging the application regarding questions of USSR citizenship."[58]

xiii. A theme recurs in Soviet writings to the effect that the union republics have an important stake in citizenship affairs. To quote directly:

> "The existence not only of all–union, but also republican, legislation on citizenship makes it possible to implement a uniform legislative policy on questions of citizenship and, at the same time, paves the way for development of the initiative of the republics in the sphere of legislation. On the basis of all–union law, the union republics have the right to elaborate and adopt republican legislative acts on citizenship."[59]

We now have samples of republican "creativity" in this field, with the recent publication of the decree of the Presidium of the Supreme Soviet of the Armenian SSR of August 26, 1981, "On the procedure for admission to the citizenship of the Armenian SSR", and identical edicts, mutatis mutandis, in the RSFSR (June 29, 1981), the Moldavian SSR (August 13, 1981), the Kazakh SSR (August 28, 1981) and the Kirgiz SSR (September 22, 1981).[60] If the contents indicate the range of entrepreneurship the republics are willing (or able) to evince in these matters, the claim that they contribute something substantial to the repertory is plain nonsense. A quick summary of the Armenian edict's pronouncement will show what I mean.

Foreign citizens and stateless persons permanently residing on the territory of the Armenian SSR, irrespective of their race and nationality, sex, education and language, may at their request be admitted to the citizenship of the Armenian SSR and thereby to the citizenship of the USSR. Consideration of the question of admission to the citizenship of the Armenian SSR takes place per written application of the interested person. Petitions for admission to the citizenship of the Armenian SSR from persons under the age of eighteen are submitted by their legal representatives. In the case of submission of a petition for admission to the citizenship of the Armenian SSR of children between the ages of fourteen and eighteen, their consent expressed in written form is mandatory. Applications for admission to the citizenship of the Armenian SSR are addressed to the Presidium of the Supreme Soviet of the Armenian SSR. Decisions concerning applications for admission to the citizenship of the Armenian SSR are adopted by the republic's Presidium. Petitions from foreign citizens and stateless persons residing on the territory of the Armenian SSR whose citizenship had been the object of an earlier decision by the federal Presidium are forwarded to the latter for its consideration.

The republic's Presidium issues decrees when approving admission to local citizenship and adopts resolutions when turning down applications for naturalization. The citizenship of the Armenian SSR is acquired on the day of issuance of the respective decree. The formalization of applications for admission to the citizenship of the Armenian SSR as well as the issuance of documents and the entry in documents of changes confirming the acquisition of the republic's citizenship are entrusted to the organs of internal affairs. Renewed applications from individuals for admission to the citizenship of the Armenian SSR are examined when a year has expired since the decision was rendered on the preceding petition. The procedure for considering applications relating to questions of admission to the citizenship of the Armenian SSR, preparing and formalizing the corresponding materials as well as executing the decisions of the republic's Presidium on these questions is determined by the Presidium of the Supreme Soviet of the Armenian SSR.

Even a cursory glance will reveal that this package merely reproduces the relevant features of the federal model. The only noticeable additions are the references to the applications for naturalization having to be in writing and the one-year moratorium before a fresh application can be lodged after a previous bid had proved unsuccessful. Neither "extra" earns high marks for substantive originality. Simply put, the venture is congruent with the official portrayal of the union republics as members of the cast in the game of administering citizenship policy, but leaves no doubt that they have no voice in shaping the agenda. Our author's further observation that "the practice of considering applications for admission to the citizenship of the union republics shows that the definition of the conditions for admission to the citizenship of the union republics requires improvement in accordance with the Constitution of the USSR, the constitutions of the union republics and the Law on the citizenship of the USSR"[61] is quite valid from a stylistic point of view: consistency and symmetry are desirable qualities. But, in real terms, shifting the scenery around makes very little difference to the story's denouement.

xiv. Article 28 of the federal statute (and its counterpart in the decree of the Armenian SSR — Article 7) provides that the procedure for considering applications and motions concerning questions of citizenship, preparing and formalizing materials on these questions, as well as establishing title to the citizenship of the USSR is determined by the Presidium of the USSR Supreme Soviet, and with regard to questions of citizenship assigned to the jurisdiction of the union republics, by the Presidium of the Supreme Soviet of the union republic. Thus, the procedural rules enunciated by the parent law (in itself a major plus compared to the 1938 version) await further "concretization and refinement" in the normative acts slated to be issued in the near future. This organizational frame, we are told, sets the foundation for the continued "democratization of the state and social life of the country, the strengthening of legality and protection of the rights and interests of the person in a community of developed socialism".[62]

One has reason to greet these self-congratulatory speeches with scepticism. What information about the administrative modus operandi has been disclosed through the contents of the national citizenship act, the federal decree of June 15, 1979, and the Armenian piece consists of general dicta which cannot per se impose effective constraints on the behavior of the responsible functionaries and do not offer the affected individual tangible means for mounting a viable defense of his rights against bureaucratic abuse. The routine regulations that are scheduled to be enacted will, in all probability, not be released to the lay public and so, once again, will be of no avail to the person concerned in the event he is ever drawn into a dispute with the authorities over citizenship claims. Until and unless the office rules are made sufficiently specific and accessible to equip the ordinary citizen with adequate artifacts to assert his "entitlements" versus the political system, all talk of the current script's "humanistic essence",[63] the aura of "profound respect and trust, paternal care of the state for the Soviet man" which it radiates,[64] its embodiment of the "tendency toward the steady amplification of the real rights and freedoms of the citizens"[65] can safely be dismissed as twaddle. Hence, when the late MVD General chose to caution his fellow delegates that the "adoption of the Law will require of all law enforcement state organs, including the organs of internal affairs, single–minded and concrete work to guarantee its precise and undeviating implementation" and went on to assure his listeners that, "appreciating the full measure of responsibility and importance of the work in store ... the personnel of the organs of internal affairs will exert maximum effort, energy, and skill to fulfill this important state task",[66] his statement was not apt to instill confidence in anyone planning to run the citizenship gauntlet. A police promise of strict adherence to the regulations when their exact terms are unknown to the man in the street puts the latter at dire disadvantage in pleading his case.

Ironically, true salvation lies in precisely the reverse course of action, i.e., a "lax" approach to the letter of the law with the objective of profiting the "consumer". Recent history shows that the Soviet apparatus has been quite adept at this sort of game of "selective observance of the law" in modulating its citizenship practices and emigration strategies when swayed by supervening policy calculations. Let us hope that today's citizenship legislation will be similarly liberalized through the operation of administrative discretion more sensitive to the advantages liable to accrue to Soviet diplomatic initiatives if the regime's treatment of its own population can be presented to the world in a kindlier light.

The thought applies to the concept espoused in the final article of the federal statute as well, namely, that if principles other than those laid down here are set by an international agreement to which the USSR is a party, the treaty's postulates prevail. For, as has repeatedly been noted, at home the regime alone decides which standard to invoke vis–à–vis a particular individual and though a person may feel eligible to enjoy the benefits procured by some international accord, he cannot challenge the authorities so as to compel them to live up to the commitments contracted in relation to foreign states. In this instance, too, one can only count on the local hierarchy's sporadic willingness to bend its domestic rules in order to project a benign image to a global audience.[67]

NOTES

1. E.g., F.Sh. Shabanov, *Razvitie sovetskoi gosudarstvennosti v Azerbaidzhane*, Moscow 1959, p.122.
2. Cf., V.S. Shevtsov, *Sovetskoe grazhdanstvo*, Moscow 1965, p.52.
3. A.I. Lepeshkin, *Kurs Sovetskogo gosudarstvennogo prava*, Moscow 1961, Vol.1, p.466.
4. N.T. Samartseva, in D.B. Levin and G.P. Kaliuzhnaia, eds., *Mezhdunarodnoe pravo*, Moscow 1964, pp.157–158.
5. *Vedomosti Verkhovnogo Soveta SSSR*, 1976, No.27, Art.404 (hereafter abbr. as *VVS SSSR*).
6. *VVS SSSR*, 1971, No.13, p.211, and No.27, p.371; 1972, No.21, p.276.
7. V.S. Shevtsov, *Grazhdanstvo v Sovetskom Soiuznom gosudarstve*, Moscow 1969, p.139.
8. H.–J. Uibopuu, *Die Völkerrechtssubjektivität der Unionsrepubliken der UdSSR*, Vienna–New York 1975, p.67 and footnote 8.
9. Decree of the Presidium of the USSR Supreme Soviet of June 15, 1979, on the procedure for putting into force the Law on the citizenship of the USSR, Article 1, *VVS SSSR*, 1979, No.25, Art.436.
10. S. Kosakov, "Konstitutsionnye osnovy kompetentsii soiuznoi respubliki po voprosam grazhdanstva", *Izvestiia Akademii nauk Kazakhskoi*SSR, 1980, No.5, seriia obshchestvennykh nauk, pp.64–65.
11. *Soviet News*, 1980, No.6024, p.183.
12. V. Baiaki, "Obshchee i osobennoe v pravovom regulirovanii grazhdanstva v evropeiskikh sotsialisticheskikh stranakh", *Sovetskoe gosudarstvo i pravo*, 1976, No.11, p.83 (hereafter abbr. as *SGiP*).
13. See the author's "Soviet Citizenship Law: New Light on Administrative Procedure", *Osteuropa–Recht*, 1971, No.1, p.6.
14. Iu. Lurii, "Sovetskii zakon o grazhdanstve i emigranty", *Russkaia Mysl'*, May 31, 1979, p.6.
15. *Soviet News*, 1980, No.6024, p.183; *VVS SSSR*, 1972, No.21, p.276.
16. V. Baiaki, *op. cit.*, p.83.
17. S.V. Chernichenko, *Mezhdunarodno–pravovye voprosy grazhdanstva*, Moscow 1968, p.80.
18. *Ibid.*, pp.155–156.
19. A.A. Esaian, *Nekotorye voprosy sovetskogo grazhdanstva, Voprosy naseleniia v praktike Sovetskoi Armenii*, Erevan 1966, p.96.
20. V.S. Shevtsov, *op. cit.* (note 7 above), p.139, giving credit to D.L. Zlatopols'kii for first championing the idea in his doctoral dissertation *Osnovnye problemy sovetskoi federatsii*, pp.19–20.
21. A.A. Esaian, *op. cit.*, pp.103–104, 111.
22. *Ibid.*, pp.92–93, 103, 109.
23. A.Ia. Berchenko, "Voprosy sovetskogo grazhdanstva", in *Torzhestvo leninskoi natsional'noi politiki*, Moscow 1963, p.277. Per contra, V.S. Shevtsov, *op. cit.* (note 7 above), p.140, fn.1.
24. A.Ia. Berchenko, *op. cit.*; V.S. Shevtsov, *op. cit.* (note 7 above), pp.140–141.
25. D.L. Zlatopol'skii, *Gosudarstvennoe ustroistvo SSSR*, Moscow 1960, p.260; A.A. Esaian, *op. cit.*, pp.104, 109; V.S. Shevtsov, *op. cit.* (note 7 above), p.156.
26. A.A. Esaian, *op. cit.*, pp.105, 109.
27. A.Ia. Berchenko, *op. cit.*
28. S.N. Bratus', I.S. Samoshchenko, eds., *Teoreticheskie voprosy sistematizatsii so-*

vetskogo zakonodatel'stva, Moscow 1962, p.278.

29. V.S. Shevtsov, *op. cit.* (note 7 above), p.165.
30. *Biulleten' normativnykh aktov ministerstv i vedomstv SSSR*, 1977, No.7, pp.3–40.
31. See, too, "Market Laws and Soviet Citizenship", *Radio Liberty Research* RL 246/77 (October 24, 1977), and "Soviet Emigration Fees", RL 273/77 (November 23, 1977).
32. V.S. Paputin, *Izvestiia*, December 3, 1978.
33. S.S. Askarkhanov, A.N. Iodkovskii, comps., *Spravochnik po voprosam sudebnoi praktiki*, Moscow 1937, pp.145–146.
34. A.A. Rubanov, "Mezhdunarodno–pravovye voprosy zakonodatel'nogo regulirovaniia otnoshenii sovetskogo grazhdanstva", *Sovetskii ezhegodnik mezhdunarodnogo prava 1978*, Moscow 1980, pp.153–154.
35. R.I. Kulik, *Zakon o grazhdanstve SSSR*, Moscow 1980, pp.81–82.
36. G.I. Tunkin, "Zakon o grazhdanstve SSSR", *SGiP*, 1979, No.7, p.28. See, too, F.I. Kozhevnikov, ed., *Mezhdunarodnoe pravo*, 4th edition, Moscow 1981, p.223.
37. F.Sh. Shabanov, *op. cit.* Cf., A.A. Esaian, *op. cit.*, pp.95, 104.
38. V.S. Shevtsov, *op. cit.* (note 2 above), p.52.
39. V.I. Terebilov, *Izvestiia*, December 3, 1978.
40. "The New Law on Soviet Citizenship", *Socialism: Theory and Practice*, 1979, No.8, p.63.
41. V. Shevtsov, *Grazhdanstvo SSSR*, Moscow 1980, p.57.
42. R.I. Kulik, *op. cit.*, pp.55–56.
43. V.V. Polianskii, "Printsipy sovetskogo grazhdanstva", *SGiP*, 1980, No.5, p.129.
44. V. Shevtsov, *Citizenship of the USSR (A Legal Study)*, Moscow 1979, p.157; *idem*, in *Konstitutsionnyi status lichnosti v SSSR*, Moscow 1980, p.49.
45. R.I. Kulik, *op. cit.*, pp.76–77.
46. *Ibid.*, p.79.
47. V. Shevtsov, *Citizenship* (note 44 above), p.141.
48. *Idem*, *Konstitutsionnyi status* ... (note 44 above), p.49.
49. *Khronika tekushchikh sobytii* (Moscow, Samizdat, 1980), New York 1981, vyp.60, p.77.
50. R.I. Kulik, *op. cit.*, pp.77–79.
51. *Ibid.*, p.38.
52. *Ibid.*, p.37.
53. *Ibid.*, p.79.
54. *Ibid.*, p.80.
55. *Ibid.*
56. *Ibid.*, p.79.
57. *Ibid.*, p.76.
58. A.A. Rubanov, *op. cit.*, p.156.
59. S. Kosakov, *op. cit.*, p.63.
60. *Vedomosti Verkhovnogo Soveta Armianskoi SSR*, 1981, No.16, Art.174; *VVS Mol davskoi SSR*, 1981, No.8, Art.66; *VVS Kirgizskoi SSR*, 1981, No.18, Art.150; *VVS RSFSR*, 1981, No.26, Art.903; *Sbornik zakonov Kazakhskoi SSR i ukazov Prezidiuma Verkhovnogo Soveta Kazakhskoi SSR 1938–1981*, Alma–Ata 1981, Vol.2, pp. 348–349.
61. S. Kosakov, *op. cit.*, p.66.
62. R.I. Kulik, *op. cit.*, pp.74–75.
63. V.I. Prokhorov, *Izvestiia*, December 3, 1978.
64. V.S. Paputin, *ibid.*
65. A.V. Gitalov, *ibid.*
66. V.S. Paputin, *ibid.*
67. See, for instance, R.I. Kulik, *op. cit.*, pp.19–20.

EMIGRATION AND IMMIGRATION

Emigration/immigration and citizenship are discrete phenomena: entering or leaving a country need not affect the citizenship status of the migrant. Soviet law recognizes the dichotomy by serving notice that the residence of a citizen of the USSR abroad does not per se ensue in loss of the citizenship of the USSR (Art.5). In practice, however, movement across state frontiers frequently sets the stage for subsequent changes in the citizenship affiliation of the expatriate and so a common connection between the two experiences does exist. An individual settling in a new homeland generally seeks to convert to local citizenship. He may accomplish the transition smoothly by first formally renouncing his old nationality; or, he may neglect to take that precaution or not receive the proper permission from the authorities of his former country and then end up as a bipatride. Or, he might not wish to or not be able to acquire the citizenship of the state in which he now lives and yet refuse to maintain relations with his ex–country and thus turn into a de facto stateless person without technically terminating the juridical association with the country of origin. All these routine permutations apply to people who have gone to live in the USSR or left the USSR to live elsewhere. Of course, a state may also follow a policy of establishing a direct link between the two concepts, either on a special or on a permanent basis. The USSR falls into the category of those regimes which prefer to operate here in ad hoc fashion.

Before looking at the cases, let us review the legal frame of the process of emigration from and immigration to the Soviet Union. The stock of statutory hardware is remarkably meager. Its centerpiece is the Regulation on entry into and departure from the USSR approved by the USSR Council of Ministers on September 22, 1970 (in force from January 1, 1971), which supersedes a namesake dated June 19, 1959.[1] The enactment provides, inter alia, that entry into the USSR of foreign citizens and stateless persons is permitted on the strength of valid foreign passports or substitute documents accompanied by a Soviet entry visa, unless a different entry procedure has been sanctioned by agreement between the USSR and the corresponding country. Such entry visas are issued abroad by Soviet embassies, missions and consulates or, in particular instances, by specially authorized Soviet representatives.

An ordinary Soviet citizen going abroad on private business requires a civilian external passport (or, for lack thereof, a certificate of reentry). Exit from the USSR of foreign citizens and stateless persons calls for valid foreign passports or substitute documents accompanied by an exit visa, except where other arrangements operate by virtue of an agreement between the USSR and the respective country.

Exit visas are issued by the Ministries of Foreign Affairs of the USSR and the union republics, diplomatic agencies of the Ministry of Foreign Affairs of the USSR, the Ministries of Internal Affairs of the USSR and the union and autonomous republics, the departments of internal affairs of executive committees of krai, oblast, and city Soviets in the prescribed manner. Civilian external passports for USSR citizens going abroad are issued by the Ministries of Foreign Affairs of the USSR and the union republics, the Ministries of Internal Affairs of the USSR and the union and autonomous republics, the departments of internal affairs of executive committees of krai, oblast and city Soviets. In order for stateless persons residing on the territory of the USSR to leave the country, they must obtain the necessary documents containing an exit visa. These documents are issued in accordance with set routine by the Ministries of Internal Affairs of the USSR and the union and autonomous republics, the departments of internal affairs of the executive committees of krai, oblast and city Soviets.

Civilian external passports are issued to Soviet citizens going abroad on service, social and private matters, as well as to Soviet citizens permanently residing abroad. Wives, children under eighteen and unmarried daughters over eighteen going abroad with or to join a person traveling with a civilian external passport receive their own passports, while children under sixteen may be inscribed in the passport of one of the parents or a person they escort. The proper documents are issued in response to applications filed by citizens desiring to go abroad on private business, who are also expected to get whatever foreign visas they may require themselves by applying directly to the foreign missions.

Note that the instructions do not treat entry into or departure from the USSR as a right vested in the individual and exercised at the latter's discretion. Rather, the impression one gets is that movement in either direction occurs by the grace of executive and administrative indulgence and, of course, the record confirms that the official apparatus seeks to and usually manages to maintain tight control over such traffic. To be sure, the mere adoption of these rules serves to imply that immigration to and emigration from the USSR are both possible and legitimate — as long as the competent institutions approve a personal request to that effect. The last word, however, rests with the authorities and, without their consent, the application must fail. What is more, the Regulation does not indicate what criteria govern these activities, meaning that the average soul wanting to enter or leave the USSR is stranded without a single clue on how the system is supposed to operate, what type of response his bid might elicit and what results he can expect. Hence, even though considerable numbers of people have, over the years, crossed the frontiers of the USSR, these migrations have duly been viewed as unique concessions and not symptomatic of any public recognition of the inherent freedom of the individual to come or go. Inasmuch, then, as Soviet practice has condoned the ingress and exodus of population on a certain scale as of late, the occasion represents, and locally has always been perceived as, an incidence of political dispensation constituting a special privilege conferred on the interested party by the organs of the state and not something that a person can claim unilaterally oblivious of or in opposition to the regime's express wishes.

Another point worth mentioning is that stateless persons residing on the territory of the USSR and wishing to leave the country need documents with an exit visa that are procured exclusively by the agencies of internal affairs, whereas the foreign affairs branch shares that jurisdiction in the case of all other would–be emigrants. Since the great majority of the people currently leaving the USSR must first relinquish their Soviet citizenship and reach foreign soil as apatrides, the emigration project verges on a monopoly run by the police whose status and style are sufficiently different to ensure the waiver of whatever institutional safeguards are available to the Soviet citizen to counter abuse at the hands of the common bureaucracy.

Along with the Regulation, the USSR Council of Ministers passed a bill featuring a series of supplements and amendments to the resolution of the Council of People's Commissars of the USSR of April 29, 1942, on the rates of state tax, which listed the fees to be charged for various administrative services connected with foreign travel.[2] A certificate of invitation to relatives and friends abroad to visit the USSR now cost a Soviet citizen five rubles and for an invitation to persons residing in capitalist countries the price was fifteen rubles. The fee for civilian external passports for persons going abroad on private business was one ruble apiece. To obtain exit permits (excluding diplomatic passports), citizens of the USSR, foreigners and stateless persons permanently residing in the USSR (except political emigrés) were slated to pay 30 rubles if they were headed for a socialist country for temporary or permanent residence and 400 rubles if their temporary or permanent destination was another country. The sum of five rubles was levied for entering changes in exit papers issued to Soviet citizens, foreigners and stateless persons permanently residing in the USSR (except political emigrés) and for issuing a certificate of invitation received by a Soviet citizen from abroad. The charge for an application by foreigners and stateless persons for admission to USSR citizenship amounted to five rubles and 50 kopeks in the case of political emigrés. The price of renouncing Soviet citizenship was fixed at 50 rubles for persons living abroad, 50 rubles for persons residing in the USSR and intending to relocate to a socialist country and 500 rubles if contemplating a move to a capitalist country.

On December 31, 1976, the Ministry of Finance of the USSR issued an Instruction on state tax[3] which confirmed some of the figures quoted in the 1970 directive, revised some others and added a few entries. The one–ruble fee for civilian external passports was dropped and instead a uniform 30–ruble rate was established for issuance of a civilian external passport granting Soviet citizens the right to travel abroad on private business to socialist countries and for issuance of documents granting stateless persons that same right and in both instances the price tag was upped to 300 rubles where the destination was another country (though down from the 400–ruble mark on the 1970 scale). Making changes in exit documents issued to Soviet citizens and stateless persons costs five rubles, as before, but foreigners were now charged 50 kopeks instead of five rubles for alterations and corrections in the visa affixed to a foreign passport or substitute exit papers. Corrections in the visa appended to exit documents issued to stateless persons also cost 50 kopeks. A Soviet citizen was scheduled to pay five rubles for a certificate of invitation from abroad of relatives and friends and fifteen rubles where Soviet citizens, foreigners and stateless persons permanently residing in the USSR extended such an invitation to persons residing in capitalist countries (as hitherto). In case several persons from a capitalist or socialist country were invited to the USSR, the tax was to be levied from each invitee older than sixteen, regardless of the number of people involved, but had to be paid only if the decision was favorable. The tax for issuing certificates of invitation from socialist countries is collected from Soviet citizens alone, and no charge applies to foreigners who receive these certificates.

Citizens of countries that do not maintain diplomatic relations with the USSR pay five rubles and citizens of other countries 1.50 rubles for the issuance or prolongation of their permits of residence in the USSR, for the registration of foreign passports or substitute documents and the extension of their registration date. Stateless persons pay one ruble for a local residence permit and, in case of loss of a local residence permit, a new one cost a foreigner or stateless person ten rubles. Extension of local residence permits for stateless persons is performed gratis.[4] As heretofore, the fee for filing an application for admission to USSR citizenship is five rubles for foreigners and stateless persons and 50 kopeks for political emigrés, members of their family and persons equated with political emigrés, and the assessment for renunciation of Soviet citizenship follows the previous breakdown of 50 rubles/50 rubles/500 rubles. Payment of the tax is waived in connection with issuance to political emigrés and persons so treated as well as members of their families of documents for travel abroad and with respect to applications for exit from Soviet citizenship (the exemption includes the children of political emigrés and people with similar status and their spouses and children). In order to be excused from paying the surtax, these people must submit appropriate affidavits from the competent organizations.

Where persons younger than sixteen are inscribed in exit permits, the tax is levied only on the person to whom the documents are issued and when children under sixteen receive their own exit permits, they pay the tax like everyone else. When issuing exit visas from the USSR to foreign citizens, the tax is due from every person who has reached the age of sixteen regardless of whether each person gets a separate visa or several persons share a common visa. The tax for the issuance and extension of residence permits for foreign citizens must be paid regardless of the duration of the permit or the extension. Upon applying for civilian external passports for travel abroad on private business, citizens deposit 10% of the tax amount owed. The balance is paid upon receipt of the civilian external passport. If the document is not issued because the citizens themselves decide to cancel their trip abroad, the deposit is not refunded. The tax is waived for issuance and extension of residence permits, registration, extension of the date of registration and inscription of foreign passports (or substitute documents) for citizens of socialist countries coming to the USSR for temporary sojourn, inter alia, on private business. The same privilege is granted on the basis of reciprocity to the citizens of all other countries. Likewise, no fee is charged for the issuance of documents for travel abroad when the trip is connected with the death of close relatives or a visit to the graves of close relatives (a spouse, parents, children, and brothers and sisters are eligible).[5]

A significant aspect of the 1970 Regulation, as mentioned earlier, was its failure to indicate what, if any, consideration prompted the responsible agencies to grant or refuse requests for entry or exit permits. Publicly, however, Soviet spokesmen took the position that the focus in some foreign circles "on cases of persons who wished to leave the USSR was not justified. All those wishing to leave the Soviet Union had left, with a few exceptions which were justified for the protection of State security, public order, property and family rights. There were no restrictions in respect of persons intending to leave the USSR. In fact, many people wanted to enter the USSR but encountered obstacles in the countries in which they lived".[6]

Without going at this point into the veracity of these claims, let it at least be noted that certain factors were now listed as affecting the freedom of expatriation, i.e., concern for safeguarding state security, public order, property and family rights. Compared to the statutory silence on that count that made it sound as though egress was virtually unimpeded while the record showed the contrary to be true, the admission that some controls operated in this area marked a step forward — in general candor, if not yet in the accurate reporting of the facts. The standards cited still lacked enough specificity to satisfy most people's sense of due process, but the "open door" myth was thereby dispelled.

Further corroboration that the same set of indicia is widely used by the Soviet administrative apparatus in its dealings with related activities is furnished by the formulas featured in the 1978 citizenship act and the 1981 law on the legal status of foreigners in the USSR. The former also referred, inter alia, to unfulfilled duties to the state and property obligations connected with substantial interests of citizens or state, cooperative and other social organizations and the interests of state security of the USSR as a bar to relinquishment of Soviet citizenship. The latter imposed similar conditions (among others) apropos the entry into and departure from the USSR of foreign citizens, whether residing abroad or locally.[7] In short, a uniform code seems to apply here so that the administrative interpretation of these principles with respect to emigration matters (about which we have a modicum of information) should then shed light on the likely meaning of these rules for denaturalization cases (on which such data are lacking).

To the extent that the 1981 statute is designed to regulate the entry into and exit from the USSR of foreign citizens on both a permanent and transient basis which may have an effect on the citizenship status of the de cujus, a closer look at the relevant provisions may be warranted. The measure confirms that foreign citizens (the concept includes stateless persons unless otherwise specified) may enter the USSR on the strength of valid foreign passports or substitute documents upon receipt of permission from the competent Soviet organs. Admission may be denied in the interests of maintaining state security or public order, if required for the protection of the rights and lawful interests of USSR citizens and other persons, if during a previous sojourn in the USSR known instances occurred of violation by the individual concerned of the legislation on the local status of foreign citizens, or customs, currency or other Soviet legislation, if in filing the application for an entry permit the petitioner gave false information about himself or did not submit the necessary documents, or on other grounds established by the legislation of the USSR. Foreign citizens can leave the USSR on the strength of valid foreign passports or substitute documents if they have permission to do so from the competent Soviet organs. Departure is not authorized if there are grounds for instituting criminal proceedings against the petitioner — until the case is closed, if he is found guilty of having committed a crime — until sentence is served or he is released, if going abroad runs counter to the interests of state security — until the circumstances causing the problem have lapsed, or if there are other obstacles to travel abroad established by the legislation of the USSR. In addition, the departure of a foreign citizen from the USSR may be delayed until he has discharged property obligations connected with substantial interests of USSR citizens and other persons, state, cooperative and sundry social organizations.

A foreign citizen violating the legislation on the legal status of foreign citizens in the USSR may see the duration of his stay in the country cut short and this can also happen when the grounds for his continued presence have lost their raison d'être. The decision to curtail the stay is taken by the organs of internal affairs. A foreign citizen may be evicted from the USSR if his actions contradict the interests of guaranteeing state security or defending public order, if ejection is necessary for the protection of the health and morals of the population, the defense of the rights and lawful interests of citizens of the USSR and other persons, or if he has grossly violated the legislation on the legal status of foreigners in the USSR, customs, currency or other Soviet legislation. The decision on expulsion is adopted by the competent Soviet organs and the affected party must quit Soviet soil by the prescribed deadline. Evasion of the order entails apprehension with the sanction of the procurator and forcible ouster, with interim detention in custody until the expulsion can be staged.

The legislative picture would not be complete without mention of the notorious resolution of the federal Presidium of December 16, 1954, which conferred Soviet citizenship on persons who were born abroad and arrived in the USSR at different times (with the exception of political emigrés) and did not produce documents to show possession of a foreign citizenship (nationality), as well as their children.[8] The directive illustrates the link that Soviet practice drew on this occasion between immigration and citizenship affiliation in that Soviet citizenship was assigned to this contingent because of prolonged residence inside the USSR which had eventually resulted in the termination or expiration of the original nationality (unless, of course, the de cujus already arrived as an apatride). True, the treatment only afforded ad hoc relief in that it proposed to cure the existing backlog of such phenomena without offering a solution for similar incidents in the future, but the experiment could set a precedent for how the problem might be tackled again when the need next arises. At any rate, the occurrence indicates that extended residency by a stateless immigrant on the territory of the USSR can end in naturalization by fiat as though the mere act of physical transfer to Soviet jurisdiction plus atrophy (or initial absence) of juridical ties with a foreign country equaled a silent vote for Soviet citizenship.

Our knowledge of the common administrative routine observed by the Soviet regime in processing immigration and emigration affairs is scant. (The information is somewhat more plentiful on the manner of handling a particular strain, say, the exodus of Jews.) Official pronouncements on the general policy followed here are rare. Thus, we have been told that "with the objective of further development of contacts between Soviet and foreign citizens on the basis of family and personal liaisons and the simplification of the procedure for travel abroad and entry into the

USSR on private business, the time allotted for considering these applications has recently been halved".[9] A parliamentary spokesman for the citizenship bill used the occasion to reveal that "a number of steps have been taken by us aimed at facilitating the further development of contacts between people", to wit: "the procedure for formalizing foreign trips has been streamlined, the deadlines for considering applications for going abroad or entering the USSR have been shortened, consideration and formalization of petitions by individuals for the right to acquire the citizenship of the USSR has become more effective".[10]

A fuller account was provided in an interview granted the Soviet media in 1976 by the USSR Deputy Minister of Internal Affairs, Boris Shumilin.[11] According to him, when would-be emigrants were involved, for instance, in family disputes, the competent agencies defer giving an answer "until close relatives have settled their relations, and in particular, material ones". Similarly, "the decision to grant an exit visa can be delayed if the person concerned possesses information constituting a state secret or has recently undergone training in major military spheres". As for exit duties, they could be waived in respect to those who had low incomes or were in financial straits. A person once refused permission to leave reportedly was eligible to have the case reopened — "after a certain period, linked with his possession of state secrets, has expired ... or after settling his relations with close relatives". The reply to the question of whether the fact of applying to emigrate affects a person's job or social status was:

> "As a rule, no. Applicants employed in defense enterprises and offices linked with state secrets do constitute a small exception to this. In such cases, on the basis of an arrangement with their trade union organizations and in keeping with the labor code, they can be relieved of their jobs and given jobs of lesser importance. However, such persons usually take steps to change their jobs beforehand, prior to submitting their applications. There is a shortage of manpower in our country and changing one's job does not present any problem."

Finally, the point was made that "the wish of some persons to leave the country in order to be 'reunited with relatives' actually leads to the disintegration of existing families and relations between relatives: children leave parents, parents leave children, husbands divorce wives, and vice-versa". Confronted with this dilemma, the Soviet authorities concede that they are primarily motivated by the desire to "protect ... the interests of Soviet citizens who are remaining in the country", even though, by their own admission, "it is not easy to find the right criterion of objectivity and justice in settling such complicated and delicate questions as family relationships and relationships between relatives".

Statements made by K. Zotov, head of OVIR, to the Soviet press in 1980,[12] recited the government's initiatives to "liberalize" freedom of international movement in the spirit of the Helsinki accords. Pursuant to these recommendations, he claimed, local regulations were extensively amended as follows:

> — the time limit for the consideration of requests concerning entry into and departure from the USSR has been reduced by 50 percent; entry visas to foreign citizens for a temporary visit to the USSR are now issued not later than ten days after the submission of the necessary documents to Soviet con-

sulates, and foreign passports for the departure of Soviet nationals abroad within the time limit of 15 to 30 days;

— the duty for the issue of documents has been reduced by 50 percent (in two stages — in 1975 and in 1978), and local financial bodies have been given the right to free some citizens from paying the duty on account of their material circumstances;

— the time limit for the revision of negative decisions on departure from the country has also been reduced by 50 percent (this is now done at the request of the applicant in not more than six months);

— the payment of the duty in the event of a repeated consideration of applications has been repealed;

— the registration of departure from the USSR has been simplified, in particular, the number of documents to be submitted by citizens has been reduced;

— customs formalities have been simplified during the moving away of household or personal belongings, including durables (cars, furniture, refrigerators, etc.), irrespective of when they were purchased.

The speaker then repeated earlier assertions that the "negligible" number of refusals of permission to leave amounted to a mere postponement owing to unresolved family problems, access to state secrets and important military training, to which he now added investigation in progress or serving a term of imprisonment imposed by verdict of a court.

That is the sum total of official disclosures about how the system of processing emigration and immigration traffic supposedly functions. Eye–witness reports and records compiled by outside observers shed a lot more light on particular immigration and emigration experiences, which will be analyzed in greater detail below.

To put the legal picture in perspective, a quick sketch of the physical dimensions of the phenomenon should prove useful. By Soviet computation, between 1945 and December 31, 1975, i.e., in a 30–year span, 122,000 Soviet Jews emigrated to Israel (Palestine). As of that last date, local accounts put at 5,500 the number of Soviet citizens married to foreigners who had relocated with their families to 110 different countries "in the past few years" (among them 544 men), with another 2,000 eligible to follow suit who had not yet expressed the wish to do so.[13] A mid–1980 tally supplied a new set of data here. Immigration was now mentioned and the size of the influx "over the past few years" pegged at more than 300,000 people arriving from assorted other countries and promptly granted Soviet citizenship. The level of emigration for purposes of family reunification during that (indeterminate) period was about the same and the outflow featured mostly Jews, Germans, Spaniards and Greeks. The official source failed to mention Armenians, although the record shows that they constituted a significant proportion of the exodus. In addition, the contingent of Soviet citizens married to foreigners that had opted to settle abroad had by then grown to 10,500, with 4,500 still waiting to make up their mind.[14]

The bulk of recent emigrants from the USSR consists of individuals of Jewish origin (and accompanying family members). Estimates on the size of the lesser components vary since no organized book–keeping system exists.[15] Hence, only approximate statistics can be offered. For example, available tabulations indicate that over 2,000 Spaniards were repatriated (plus non–Spanish spouses and children).[16] Up to June 1, 1977, eleven thousand Armenians had emigrated and the U.S. emerged as the principal destination of Armenians currently leaving the Soviet Union: 3,000 American entry visas were issued from 1976 to 1979, the quota was expected to top 7,000 for 1980 (smaller groups sought to rejoin relatives in Canada, Lebanon and France), but due to a sudden clamp–down by the local authorities 4,334 Armenians in all managed to get out in the first nine months of 1980 and the trickle was reduced to 1,826 for the corresponding three–quarters of 1981.[17] Around 85,000 ethnic Germans were allowed out of the USSR in the seventies (the mass of them headed for West Germany), and a further 180,000–300,000 were said to be eager to leave: by 1981, the emigration had fallen to a ten–year low — 3,117 Germans left in the first nine months of 1981, compared to 5,097 during the same months of 1980.[18] Nearly 22,000 Greek political refugees returned to Greece from Eastern Europe since 1974; 15,000 remain in the USSR, 13,500 in Czechoslovakia, and 9,000 in Poland, where they are listed as being "without nationality". At the moment, repatriation is snarled in political dispute and few people are able to make their way back home.[19]

A. The Chinese Case

As of 1945, according to the better estimates, there were 60,000 to 70,000 persons of Russian origin living in Sinkiang (some of these settlements dating back to the 19th century when Old Believer peasant groups made the trek)[20] and nearly 200,000 Russians scattered over the whole of China.[21] In addition, Sinkiang contained a large number of people of non–Russian ethnic stock, principally Kazakhs and Uighurs, who at different times had left their homes in Russia or the Soviet Union and moved to China's neighboring province. Thus, in 1916, approximately 300,000 Kazakh tribesmen from Russian Central Asia sought asylum in Sinkiang; then, in the nineteen–thirties, thousands of Kazakhs again fled to Sinkiang from the Soviet Union to escape a forced farm– collectivization drive.

Not surprisingly, the nationality status of this motley crew mirrored its heterogenous composition. A number of these people still owned papers issued by the old (pre–Soviet) Russian state institutions (or Church records). The documents had either lapsed or had been renewed by an assortment of self–appointed emigré organizations established on Chinese soil after the Bolshevik revolution and tolerated by a succession of Chinese central governments or local regimes and, later, by the Japanese and Manchukuo authorities in the areas under their control as well. At any rate, these "passports" served to identify their bearers as "Russian" nationals, even though currently many of them were in fact stateless by virtue of the doubtful validity of such certification. A second element had been in possession of Soviet citizenship when it managed to cross the frontier (outward bound) and was subsequently stripped of that citizenship by operation of a set of special decrees promulgated by the Soviet regime in the twenties and thus officially rendered stateless. Yet a third faction which quit the USSR after the publication of these edicts never formally lost its Soviet citizenship: however, to the extent that the great majority of these expatriates refused to maintain their past association with the USSR, their Soviet nationality in practice remained a dead letter. If any of these individuals became naturalized Chinese (or foreign) citizens without having first duly divested themselves of Soviet citizenship (assuming they figure in the category of those who had retained it), they henceforth qualified as dual citizens; by the same token, children born of mixed marriages between Soviet emigrés in China and Chinese citizens often ended up being ascribed both citizenships.

The war took a heavy toll of the Russian community in China. When the northern regions were overrun by the Soviet army after the USSR joined the fight against Japan, many of the local Russian residents were rounded up and summarily deported to the USSR. Thousands more relocated southward and eventually were evacuated from China and resettled elsewhere under the auspices of assorted international programs of aid to refugees. A residue either chose to stay put or had no opportunity to get out and lived to see the Nationalist regime replaced on the mainland by its Communist rival. On the legal scene, the main feature was the Soviet edict of November 10, 1945, which announced that "persons residing on the territory of Manchuria who on November 7, 1917, were subjects of the Russian Empire, as well as persons who had possessed Soviet citizenship and lost it, and their children, may recover the citizenship of the USSR". They could do so by "submitting a declaration to that effect to a USSR consulate on the territory of Manchuria not later than February 1, 1946, together with documents establishing their identity and the fact that they had in the past been subjects of the former Russian Empire or Soviet citizens". The applications would be examined on the spot and, if approved, led the consulate to issue the petitioner a Soviet permis de séjour. Persons who failed to make the necessary overtures aimed at regaining Soviet citizenship by the prescribed deadline could subsequently acquire it through the regular channels. A supplementary directive of January 22, 1946, prolonged the time limit for filing applications until April 1, 1946. On January 20, 1946, a second edict of the federal Presidium extended the provisions of this act to such persons domiciled in the province of Sinkiang and the cities of Shanghai and Tientsin, giving them until April 1, 1946, to contact the nearest Soviet consulate. The cut-off date was later moved back first to July 1, 1946, and after that to December 31, 1946, for those living in Sinkiang, and to July 1, 1946, for those residing in Shanghai and Tientsin.

It should be noted, though, that the new legal concept of residence permit meant something quite special. On the one hand, the persons who received these documents were thereby recognized as citizens of the USSR and ipso jure fell under the legal protection of the Soviet Union. On the other hand, mere possession of such certificates did not entitle their owners to enter the Soviet Union at will and the question of the admission of these individuals into the USSR was left to a separate decision in each single case, quite independently of the initial issuance of these "limited" nationality papers. The technical rationale for this rather unusual procedure was that appropriate arrangements first had to be made to find suitable shelter and employment for potential returnees, a difficult task given the wartime devastation of the Soviet Union. Stringent security calculations probably also played a role in instituting this additional verification mechanism.

Even so, the response was gratifying. Fired by wartime patriotism and eager to terminate the uncertainties of a stateless condition, Russian exiles accepted the offer of "restoration in Soviet citizenship" with considerable alacrity. According to official Soviet figures, in Manchuria alone from the middle of November to the end of December 1945, Soviet consulates received requests for reinstatement in Soviet citizenship: in Harbin — nearly 7,000; in the city of Dal'nyi (Dairen) — more than 1,000; in the city of Manchuria — around 3,000.[22] The next step frequently entailed petition for permission to take up residence in the Soviet Union and in the following years several thousand people were in fact repatriated from China to the USSR pursuant to this scheme.

The advent of the Chinese Communists to power on the mainland did not affect the status of the Russians remaining on Chinese soil. Apart from those who had chosen to move to the USSR, a large contingent of local Russian emigres harboring anti–Soviet (or at least not pro–Soviet) attitudes were evacuated from China by various international refugee organizations before the Communist troops overran the country. Many of the people who did not manage to get away in time congregated in Shanghai and a significant portion of them was soon after "liberation" allowed to leave by the Chinese Communist authorities under the auspices of different aid programs from abroad. The small residue was on occasion threatened with expulsion, either on an individual or mass basis. Indeed, the corresponding orders were published, but they were not enforced, while efforts to relocate the rest continued.[23]

The emigration trickle then slowed, partly due to the impact of the Korean war and the worsening international situation and partly, one suspects, because the Russians exerted significant pressure on their Chinese ally to keep members of the local Russian contingent from migrating to the "capitalist" world. Soviet sources reported in 1954 that over 100,000 Russians still lived in China,[24] the majority of them concentrated in the northeastern provinces and the large cities (Shanghai, Tientsin, Peking, etc.). Around 2,000 were engaged in agricultural pursuits in Sinkiang in the environs of Kuldja and Urumchi. As long as relations between Moscow and Peking stayed cordial, the fate of these people seems to have caused no concern. Thus, the shift in Chinese policy in the mid–fifties toward letting people of Russian origin leave the mainland may be read in either of two ways: as an early sign of Sino–Soviet estrangement and, hence, a gesture of independence on the part of Peking vis–à–vis its senior partner; or, as a symptom of the post–Stalin process in both countries which, inter alia, might have prompted Moscow to drop its opposition to the exodus.

In any event, protracted efforts by foreign Jewish circles to extricate the remnants of the Jewish community in China finally met with success in 1956. The group numbered 543 souls, of whom 402 were recorded as Soviet citizens (207 resided in Harbin, 105 in Tientsin, and the balance in Shanghai). After reports indicating that the Soviet government had changed its position towards the Jews in China, these people quickly received exit permits from the competent Chinese organs and by March of 1957, they were nearly all gone.[25] However, the "thaw" benefited not only the Russian Jewish colony and other Russian nationals (including many who technically qualified as Soviet citizens) now also managed to joint the efflux. Since 1956 more than 20,000 of them (drawn from all corners of China, Sinkiang among them) have passed through Hongkong en route to permanent abodes in South America, Australia, the United States, Switzerland and New Zealand. A 1980 account estimated that, on any given month, about 200 "White Russians" were in Hongkong waiting for final clearance to migrate to a new homeland. With recently relaxed emigration procedures, many more were expected to follow suit. In the beginning, exit visas were granted just to individuals of Russian extraction, but later their Chinese spouses and children born of mixed marriages were allowed to leave too, once they had been accepted by another country.[26]

As the Sino–Soviet rift widened, the status of the "Russian" minority in China became a serious bone of contention between the two capitals. Random pieces of evidence tend to confirm that legal questions connected with citizenship were intimately involved in these conflicts at a fairly early stage, suggesting that the subject itself spawned controversy and that the difficulties then encountered in dealing with these issues further aggravated existing tensions. For example, Soviet spokesmen charge that the preparations for the signature of the Sino–Soviet consular treaty which finally took place in June, 1959, were dragged out by the Chinese for more than two years. Meanwhile, the Chinese supposedly refused outright to sign an agreement on citizenship and the legal protection of citizens of both countries. In sum, the conclusion that citizenship matters were at stake in the growing Sino–Soviet dispute and were adding to the list of items over which the two regimes could not come to terms looks obvious in retrospect.[27]

The situation here rapidly got worse. The Russians now claim that the wholesale purge of native cadres and intellectuals waged in the late fifties and sixties hit particularly hard those individuals in Sinkiang who were born in the Soviet Union and especially those among them who claimed Soviet citizenship. For their part, the Chinese have accused their Russian comrades of using their organs and personnel in Sinkiang in April–May 1962 to carry out extensive subversive activities in the Ili region and of enticing and coercing several tens of thousands of Chinese citizens into going to the Soviet Union. Although the Chinese government reportedly lodged repeated protests and made numerous representations, the Soviet authorities declined to repatriate these Chinese citizens on the pretext of "the sense of Soviet legality" and "humanitarianism".

As one might expect, Moscow has its own version of the incident. According to its story, in the spring of 1962 the inhabitants of Sinkiang staged a mass exodus to Soviet territory to escape from economic hardships and national persecution from which they were suffering as a result of the policies initiated by the Maoist authorities. At first, the Russians say, the PRC Deputy Foreign Minister called the phenomenon an "unfortunate event", but subsequently Peking changed its tune and blamed the whole thing on "the subversive activities of the Soviet authorities". The Russians trace the roots of the problem to the local presence of a large community of expatriates from Russia and the Soviet Union with a somewhat ambiguous legal status. By virtue of the post–war decrees referred to earlier, circa 120,000 eligible individuals had formally registered as Soviet citizens and received Soviet permits to live abroad; but many of their compatriots for different reasons did not procure proper documents, although under the terms of Soviet legislation they had not lost Soviet citizenship.

In the beginning, the attitude of the PRC officialdom toward this contingent was friendly; however, conditions subsequently deteriorated. Starting in 1958–1959, Soviet citizens permanently residing in Sinkiang saw their property, legal and other rights curtailed, dismissals from jobs in state institutions and enterprises became commonplace, persecutions for insignificant infractions increased in frequency. The personnel of Chinese institutions treated Soviet citizens rudely, rejecting the simplest requests, ridiculed their national mores and customs, prohibited the use of their mother tongue. Simultaneously, with the onset of 1962, the local authorities in Sinkiang ceased almost entirely to issue exit permits to the USSR to Soviet citizens wanting to return home.

As a result, we are told, in the spring of 1962 a swarm of people who were no longer able to put up with the harsh living conditions, famine, national discrimination, persecution and anti–Soviet debauchery fled spontaneously to the safety of Soviet territory, and just between April 22 and early June 1962, 67,000 souls illegally crossed the frontier. The Chinese tried to blame the Soviet authorities for "welcoming those who violated" the border. In reply, the Soviets sent a note on April 29, 1962, which rejected the Chinese charges and pointed out that the crossings of the frontier occurred from the Chinese side, under the eyes of the Chinese authorities who therefore ought to take appropriate measures to stem the tide. Indeed, Soviet sources have since embroidered on the theme by contending that the Chinese officials, realizing that recourse to force in this case would only compromise them, soon switched to a different tactic and actually abetted the departures. The authorities in Kuldja and Chuguchak, in this version, informed the citizens demanding permission to leave for the USSR that they did not require visas and could simply cross the frontier. A system was even organized for the sale of tickets for highway travel to border points and the dispatch of luggage by postal conveyances. Toward the end of May 1962, some 10–20 trucks loaded with 40–50 persons each left daily from Kuldja alone. The passengers descended a few kilometers from the border and continued their trip on foot. While so engaged, the Chinese allegedly insisted that the Soviets employ physical force against persons seeking to cross the frontier in the expectation that if the refugees were met with bullets and bayonets and compelled to return to the PRC, the Soviets would incur the eternal hatred of these unfortunate folk.

Reportedly, the Soviet government persistently sought ways of amicably resolving the ensuing problem. The fugitives were urged to return to the PRC and, if they then still wanted to emigrate to the USSR, to do so through established channels. The Soviet government repeatedly invited the competent PRC agencies to send representatives to talk to the refugees, but they refused, presumably because they understood full well that not many individuals would care to go back. A few did express such a wish, chiefly people who had left numerous relatives behind. Nevertheless, the Chinese insisted that all the inhabitants of Sinkiang who had escaped to the USSR be forcibly returned to the PRC, even under threat of resort to arms, and at the same time they would not accept those who had volunteered for repatriation. The Soviet government said it could not consent physically to expel to the PRC people who had fled for their lives, the bulk of them old folk, women and children.

Diplomatic messages, larded with mutual recriminations, flew back and forth.

The PRC Ministry of Foreign Affairs asserted that the Soviets had "prepared and organized the mass crossing", that Sinkiang was in imminent danger of "serious subversive activity by the Soviet Union", and the like. The Soviet government denied the truth of these statements and spelled out its own position on the course of events in Sinkiang, especially in connection with the widespread flight of the local population to Soviet soil. The Chinese leadership reiterated its earlier claims and added that the Russians were also responsible for having provoked the bloody incidents in Kuldja in the spring of 1962 (Moscow, in turn, maintained that the Chinese had here deliberately staged a pogrom of the non–Han elements among the population which entailed heavy loss of human life). Peking demanded once again that all the refugees forthwith be restored to Chinese jurisdiction while continuing to reject suggestions that it dispatch representatives to persuade the fugitives to retrace their steps.

According to Soviet spokesmen, the Chinese then proceeded to mount a vicious campaign against the personnel of Soviet consulates in Sinkiang: these provocative actions included the arrest and search of Soviet diplomats. The associations of local Soviet citizens were closed and their directors taken into custody on charges of anti–government activity and violation of the laws. Anti–Soviet propaganda was stepped up in Sinkiang and in these impossible circumstances the Soviet government decided to shut down the consulate– general in Urumchi and the consulate in Kuldja. Next, at the insistence of the Chinese, the branch of the Soviet trade mission in Urumchi was likewise liquidated.

Similar incidents occurred in Harbin in 1962 when the premises and facilities belonging to the association of local Soviet citizens were sealed. The members of the governing board and the staff in the city as well as the suburbs were arrested. They underwent humiliating interrogations and were subjected to physical abuse: two men reportedly died in confinement. Concurrently, the Chinese police blockaded the Soviet consulate–general in Harbin and barred Soviet citizens from access to it. In view of the existing situation, the Soviet government moved in the fall of 1962 to close its remaining consulates and branches of the trade mission in China.[28]

Eventually the Chinese themselves were obliged to acquiesce in the desire of Soviet citizens and people born in Russia to leave for the Soviet Union. In September, 1962 (already after the liquidation of the Soviet consular installations in Sinkiang), the PRC Ministry of Foreign Affairs asked the Soviet government to allow entry into the USSR through a simplified procedure by individuals who wanted to move there. Acceding to the request, the Soviet authorities introduced a temporary program of visa–less immigration to the USSR from China of Soviet citizens and members of their families. From October 15, 1962, to May 1, 1963, more than 46,000 souls availed themselves of this opportunity to quit Sinkiang for the Soviet Union. In the end, the Soviet government found it necessary to propose to the PRC authorities that the normal visa regime be restored, for the flow of repatriates continued unabated and measures had to be taken to provide them with living space and employment.[29]

By 1966, according to one account, there was only a handful of Russians left in Sinkiang, mostly around Kuldja, and some estimates put at no more than 800 the number of Russians still remaining in the whole country, including possibly 300 in Sinkiang.[30] As usual in these affairs, however, the figures are based essentially on guess–work and cannot be treated as hard data. In 1980, for instance, a Hongkong source reported that 2,000 "White Russian" refugees were poised to leave the mainland, implying that many more were waiting in the wings and indeed mainland Chinese data for 1978 refer to a concentration of 600 Russians residing just in Sinkiang, a number upped without any further explanation in 1983 to 2,935.[31] The statistical disparity cannot be resolved given the scarcity and unreliability of the material evidence and, of course, the gap in assessment may very well be simply due to how the sample is initially defined, e.g., whether the term Russian connotes ethnic origin or territorial provenance so that persons hailing from Russia but not of Russian nationality would also fit the bill.

What is fairly certain, though, is that a strikingly similar pattern developed during the Cultural Revolution. The Soviet press announced that in the last months of 1966 several hundred thousand Uighurs and Kazakhs had crossed the border from Sinkiang and taken refuge in the Soviet Union. The efflux was prompted by fear of the Cultural Revolution and the hunt for Soviet sympathizers which accompanied it, the mass settlement of Chinese in Sinkiang, and the alleged persecution of national minorities. Illegal border crossings by the flow of refugees precipitated a rash of incidents and raised tensions along the Sino–Soviet border. However, by February 1967, the Chinese authorities had managed to reassert control and complete an evacuation of the civilian population from the border zone, — particularly thorough in Sinkiang, with the result that the flight of refugees into the Soviet Union had been almost brought to an end. It is reckoned that more than 100,000 individuals migrated from China just to Kazakhstan and gradually they were resettled within the republic. Soviet sources contend that the competent official agencies made a concerted effort to get some of the refugees to return to China and record that a few hundred people did in fact consent to being repatriated. Their departure could have marked the beginning of a gradual evacuation of a considerable proportion of the refugees, but the Chinese flatly refused to readmit them and so the newcomers have put down roots in the USSR. By now, the individuals concerned seem to have acquired Soviet citizenship.

In 1969, the Soviet authorities moved to interdict further crossings of the frontier and those caught in doing so have been summarily arrested and sent to penal colonies for illegal entry. Attempts have also been made to recruit some of these people for spying missions in China on behalf of the Soviet intelligence apparatus, although it is impossible to say with what success this project has met. Suffice it to note that since the 1969 clashes the frontier is heavily guarded on both sides and the clandestine passage of people across the line in either direction, although it occasionally occurs, is both extremely difficult and hazardous. The status quo is therefore likely to remain undisturbed in the foreseeable future.

Meanwhile, the minute colony of Russians residing in China also had to bear the brunt of the Cultural Revolution. Soviet citizens permanently domiciled in China suffered, according to Soviet spokesmen, from hooligan raids, searches, beatings, outrages to human dignity. Their property was unlawfully seized, they were ejected from their homes, dismissed from jobs, expelled from educational institutions, forbidden to correspond with relatives in the USSR and contact the Soviet embassy. Many of them were reportedly arrested, without the USSR embassy staff being notified of that fact. The experience again led to a round of diplomatic exchanges and to fresh efforts to extricate the tiny Russian enclave in China, leaving only a few stray souls behind as mute reminders of what had once been a large flourishing Russian community in the Far East.

A brief legal footnote will ring down the curtain on this curious (and unique) episode which single–handedly is responsible for the bulk of the USSR's post–war immigration repertory. Whatever the juridical status of many of these fugitives from China in the sense of the validity of their title to Soviet citizenship (and, obviously, the latter was often clouded), the mass had apparently not bothered formally to acquire Chinese citizenship either. In their case, the problem of dual citizenship did not arise when they subsequently received (or reactivated) Soviet citizenship. On the other hand, a certain percentage among them were considered dual citizens already while they resided in China by virtue of local naturalization on top of the existing Soviet citizenship or possessed Chinese citizenship when they fled to the USSR and their switch to Soviet citizenship without prior divestiture of their PRC citizenship then turned them into bipatrides. The citizenship policies of both countries which render difficult withdrawal from their respective nationality produced an impasse, the only practical relief from which seems to lie in the provision of the PRC's 1980 nationality statute mandating that "any Chinese national who has settled abroad and has been naturalized there or has acquired foreign nationality there of his own free will automatically loses Chinese nationality" (Art.9).[32] The formula, as far as one can tell, is intended to operate retroactively as well as prospectively and thus would in principle apply to those among the refugees who were deemed to possess Chinese citizenship — causing them to forfeit it by reason of this new rule. Such a denouement would cure the present headache, except that the Chinese side has also publicly reserved the right not to recognize the "involuntary conversion" to foreign citizenship of its nationals located "overseas" and on that convenient (and, indeed, not implausible) pretext, may yet refrain from sanctioning the lapse of the Chinese nationality of this particular lot,[33] — effectively keeping the issue alive.[34]

B. The Korean Question

A by–product of the Soviet entry into the war against Japan was that large quantities of Koreans serving in the Japanese armed forces and assorted para– military units were captured by the Red Army in the course of the campaign or fell into Russian hands at the time of the Japanese surrender and were promptly shipped off to POW camps in Siberia. Civilian personnel frequently suffered the same fate and in several instances plain ordinary folk of Japanese or Korean ancestry in the local population were also rounded up and shifted to the USSR. In the early post–war period, a quota of Koreans from the Soviet zone of occupation in Korea joined the stream: people who has collaborated with the Japanese, native representatives of the "enemy classes", prominent anti–Communist and non–Communist political figures, including leaders of diverse "bourgeois–nationalist" factions and organizations, etc. Furthermore, by conquering and annexing South Sakhalin and the Kurile Islands, the USSR forthwith inherited the people inhabiting these territories which happened to comprise a sizable contingent of Koreans in their midst.[35]

An early order of business, then, was the issue of what to do with the crop of Korean POW's and civilians in the custody of the Soviet authorities or merely located within their sphere of jurisdiction. The Potsdam Proclamation defining the terms for Japan's capitulation had provided that "the Japanese military forces, after being completely disarmed, shall be permitted to return to their homes with the opportunity to lead peaceful and productive lives". Pursuant to that pledge, an agreement was concluded between the USSR and the Supreme Commander for the Allied Powers in Japan on December 19, 1946, spelling out the procedures for the expeditious repatriation of Japanese prisoners of war and Japanese nationals from the territory of the USSR and the territories under the control of the USSR to Japan, as well as of Korean nationals from Japan to Korea north of the 38th parallel.[36] The first part of the arrangement applied to: 1) Japanese prisoners of war; 2) Japanese nationals, with the added safeguard that the evacuation of Japanese nationals from the territory of the USSR be made on a voluntary basis. In a practical quid pro quo, the signatories next concurred that "subject to repatriation from the territory of Japan are Koreans numbering 10,000 persons, who previously resided in Korea north of the 38th degree north latitude and who were born in the aforementioned part of Korea". The rate of movement of Japanese from designated Soviet ports was established at 50,000 per month; the movement of Koreans from Japan to northern Korea would be carried out simultaneously, by means of shuttle operations, after 10,000 Japanese had been repatriated from northern Korea to Japan.

From this rather meager fund of data, several conclusions can nonetheless be drawn. To begin with, it is clear from the context that the USSR was expected to return to Japanese soil without delay all Japanese prisoners of war whom it was still detaining. The formula would certainly appear to embrace persons in this category who were ethnic Koreans and who did not originate in the portion of Korea situated north of the 38th parallel. As regards these people, the Soviet government undertook an unconditional commitment to effectuate repatriation without further ado. By contrast, the return of the other Japanese nationals was predicated on the free choice of the persons eligible for the program, but again, those among them who were of Korean stock and who did not hail from the segment of Korea north of the 38th parallel presumably could exercise this right too.

Less clear is the position of their kinsmen, both within the ranks of the POW's and in civilian circles, who were for these purposes considered "natives of North Korea". The companion clause on the mandatory exchange repatriation of 10,000 Koreans from this section of the country and now living in Japan back to their "birthplace" constitutes quite positive evidence that the interested parties openly recognized "North Korea" as the legal homeland of such individuals. By logical extension, one would think that the same rule would hold for their compatriots (ex-military men or civilians) who were currently subject to Soviet authority. With respect to them, the USSR had consequently incurred no international obligation to ensure their repatriation to Japan proper or was, at best, just morally bound either to allow their return to North Korea by raising no objections to their departure or to negotiate a suitable deal with the North Korean regime for the voluntary resettlement of the individuals concerned.

Even so, the actual implementation of the project has generated much controversy and, indeed, some of it has not been dispelled to the present day. Thus, on April 22, 1950, TASS issued a special communique announcing that the competent Soviet agencies had to date completed the scheduled repatriation of Japanese war prisoners from the Soviet Union to Japan.[37] The sole exception were 1,487 Japanese war prisoners sentenced or under investigation for war crimes committed by them, 9 Japanese war prisoners who qualified for repatriation after undergoing medical treatment and 971 Japanese prisoners of war who had committed serious crimes against the Chinese people and who had been turned over to the government of the People's Republic of China. The TASS statement of June 9, 1950, featured an essentially identical version, based on a similar set of statistics indicating that a total of around 500,000 Japanese POW's had been repatriated from the Soviet Union to Japan since the end of the war, in addition to 70,880 men captured during the fighting and immediately released in 1945 in the zone of combat operations.[38] The Soviet claim was promptly challenged by the Japanese, Americans, British and Australians who demanded a full accounting of what had befallen a further 300,000–370,000 Japanese presumed still to be located in the "areas under Soviet influence (including Siberia, Sakhalin, North Korea, Dairen and Chinese Communist areas)" whose fate was unknown. The démarche was in vain, however. The Russians insisted that their data were correct, each side thereafter stuck to its position and the "dialogue" aborted on that note. A tangible proportion both of those returned and those remaining behind consisted of former Japanese nationals of Korean extraction.

A somewhat different picture emerges concerning the situation of the Korean admixture to the USSR's population in the wake of the Soviet Union's territorial gains in the Far East upon Japan's defeat. When the Soviets occupied South Sakhalin in August, 1945, they inherited around 45,000 Koreans employed in the local coal-mines, most of them recruited from the southern provinces of Korea. Though technically the members of this complement should have fitted within the scope of the 1946 repatriation agreement and qualified for evacuation to Japan along with fellow Japanese civilians, few of their numbers in fact followed this exit route. Remember that on this occasion repatriation had not been mandatory, but was predicated on the freely expressed desire of the competent individuals to choose to go or stay put: thus, either this group of Koreans almost unanimously decided not to "return" to Japan in light of past experience with the Japanese or they were never given an adequate chance to air a preference and their "silence", however obtained, was forthwith assumed to indicate no wish to join in the proposed exodus.

For the majority, the latter seems to have been the case and citizenship law played a very curious role in this episode. Accounts by several recent Korean returnees from Sakhalin offer interesting new insight into what happened here. For example, according to the published story of one such fresh repatriate from Sakhalin, Kim Chin-hoe, he was "registered as a North Korean national since the Soviet seizure of the island", although he had been born in South Korea.[39] The inference is that, in order to avoid the possibility of international pressure at the close of World War II in favor of the repatriation of Koreans from the southern half of the country who found themselves in Soviet custody in territories captured from the Japanese, the Soviet authorities unilaterally recorded them as North Korean nationals, thereby aiming to "internalize" the problem by reducing it to the status of a private matter between the Kremlin and its North Korean ally. At that time, the Russians had no reason to expect any difficulties from their North Korean satellite and, even if questions were to arise, they could be handled amicably in camera without causing an international fuss. By this stratagem, the legitimacy of the interest of other countries in the fate of these people could be denied and the whole issue could be confined to intramural channels.

From the legal point of view, the incident is highly unusual. The idea of the Soviet Union summarily bestowing the citizenship of another political entity, North Korea, on a large batch of individuals native of South Korea is strange, to say the least, and can hardly be squared with the tenor of established international law practice in this field. Was North Korea consulted in this connection? Did it formally concur or just tacitly acquiesce or did the Kremlin take it for granted that whatever it decided to do in these circumstances would automatically enjoy the approbation of its loyal puppets in Pyongyang?[40]

In retrospect, a probable "redeeming" factor on this occasion was the element of coincidence between Soviet and North Korean policies in the legal treatment afforded this constituency. True, the evidence is not conclusive owing to Pyongyang's strange reluctance until as late as 1963 to promulgate any statutory regulations setting forth the norms defining North Korean citizenship and governing the mechanics of its acquisition and loss. In the meantime, no formal guidelines existed as to whom the North Korean regime considered a citizen of North Korea and what legal criteria determined the decision. When on October 9, 1963, the North Korean authorities did enact the appropriate legislation,[41] some of the uncertainties were resolved. In particular, an answer of sorts was furnished to the crucial question of what system of initial classification of individuals as citizens of the Democratic People's Republic of Korea prevailed on the local scene. The new Citizenship Law recognized qua citizens of the DPRK: 1) those who had Korean citizenship before the establishment of the DPRK and had retained it up to the day of publication of the 1963 statute, and their children; and, 2) foreigners who acquired the citizenship of the DPRK in accordance with legal procedure. Of course, what was meant by the expression "those who had Korean citizenship before the establishment of the DPRK and had retained it up to the day of publication of the present statute" was not entirely clear. Read literally, the proposition could well apply to just about every Korean abroad. All the emigrants had once possessed some form of Korean citizenship or other or were descended from individuals who fit this description; few had officially renounced Korean citizenship, and the procedure for renunciation was elusive; even during the Japanese conquest, Koreans had been ascribed a separate identity as subjects of the Empire and continued to function as a distinct nationality group.

Though enunciated in 1963, the rule undoubtedly reflects the North Korean regime's attitude in this domain from its inception. In principle, then, virtually the whole of the Korean community in the USSR could thus by unilateral fiat have been assigned the citizenship of the DPRK, including the Sakhalin contingent, and since the Soviet apparatus seemed inclined to attribute to the latter group that same status, the parties presumably found themselves in perfect harmony, at least on this one item.

At any rate, some 43,000 Koreans were reportedly living on Sakhalin in 1967. According to one recent account, "the majority have taken North Korean (65 percent) or Soviet (25 percent) citizenship, but 10 percent or about 4,000 are still stateless and demand repatriation to Japan or South Korea".[42] It is worth recalling that Soviet citizenship was never imposed outright on the inhabitants of the areas won from Japan in the closing stages of the Second World War nor was any special provision made, as far as we know, for the easy bulk naturalization of those who remained in these territories, by choice, the accident of fate or compulsion, after the initial post–war repatriation project had been officially completed. A valid premise is that admission to Soviet citizenship in the regular manner in response to a personal application was open to this category of people too and some of the persons involved did elect to resort to that solution during the next several years. Indeed, should the story of the peremptory wholesale post–war enrollment of the Korean civilian population of South Sakhalin into North Korean nationality be true, it would not be at all surprising if a sizable proportion of its members subsequently petitioned to acquire Soviet citizenship instead, in the hope, inter alia, of thereby improving their material lot.

Whether only those who "adapted" had access to the temporary "option" route instituted by the 1957 "dual citizenship" convention between the USSR and the DPRK, or a total inventory was conducted to get a full headcount without first investigating if the individuals concerned did or did not have dual citizenship stricto sensu, is more guess–work. However, from the 65%– 25%–10% breakdown, it looks as though either in conjunction with the 1957 "option" scheme or on some other occasion, a poll was in fact executed which ascertained the citizenship affiliation to which each such person seemed to aspire. The responses apparently even reflected miscellaneous claims of possession of a stateless status coupled with a tacit or overt preference for residence abroad and recovery or revival of title to Japanese or South Korean nationality advanced by a fringe element of those consulted in the matter.

This latter phenomenon will be examined in detail shortly. At this point, let me just note that the 65% "vote" in favor of the citizenship of North Korea has not, as far as one can tell, entailed any commensurate efflux to the DPRK of those whose preference reputedly ran in this direction. The Korean population of the Sakhalin oblast did drop from the estimated 43,000 to the 35,369 souls featured in the 1970 census tabulation and some of the decline may be due to a modest repatriation effort, but even so the difference comes nowhere near matching the sum of the inhabitants of the region theoretically eligible to leave for their "native homeland". Again, either the paper "wish" was not tantamount to a practical impulse to relocate or the Soviet authorities tolerated a nominal "choice" but took precautions to see to it that it was not translated into corresponding action, perhaps, inter alia, for fear of worsening the perennial shortage of manpower in these remote outposts. What the attitude of the North Korean regime was toward this strange state of affairs is a big question mark. If the episode has generated any friction between Moscow and Pyongyang, the affair has been carefully kept private by both parties up till now. On the one hand, the DPRK is known to suffer from an acute labor deficit and extra working hands ought to be a welcome commodity. On the other hand, the entry of an uncontrolled mass of individuals who had been exposed to alien influences into the hermetically sealed environment of North Korea is probably not calculated to appeal to the ideological tastes of the DPRK leadership.

Outside interest in the fate of the Japanese and Koreans stranded in the USSR in the aftermath of World War II has waxed and waned depending on the political weather, but the topic never completely disappeared from the diplomatic agenda. Stalin's death sparked renewed hope that the Soviet authorities might hereafter prove more accommodating in resolving the problem of the human debris spewed by the last global conflict. Thus, on August 24, 1953, the Japanese Ministry of Foreign Affairs revealed that, on the basis of evidence it had collected from returned prisoners, about 56,000 Japanese remained in China and the USSR, of whom 12,700 (both prisoners of war and civilians) were believed to be in Russian hands. On October 12, 1953, the Soviet Red Cross consented to meet with a delegation from the Japanese Red Cross in Moscow to discuss the repatriation of Japanese hitherto held as war criminals. The Japanese Red Cross mission arrived in Moscow on October 29 and on November 19 agreement was reached for the release of 1,274 Japanese prisoners — soldiers and civilians — who were serving sentences as war criminals or for other offenses. A further 1,047 were to be set free when they had completed their sentences.[43] The outcome of the talks conceivably also benefited a tiny fraction of ex–Japanese subjects of Korean nationality who formed part of this contingent. The difference of 10,000 individuals between the Japanese estimates and the slightly more than 2,000 men who the Soviets confirmed were in their custody was left unaccounted for: the Japanese representatives cited the data they had gathered and their Soviet opposites simply insisted that the arithmetic was inaccurate and that all eligible Japanese had already quit Soviet soil, save for the criminal segment that had now been attended to.

The next step had to wait until 1956, when by virtue of the comprehensive joint Soviet–Japanese declaration on the political situation concluded on October 19 the USSR bound itself to repatriate all Japanese citizens serving sentences in the Soviet Union on that document's entry into force. On December 12, 1956, the compact went into effect and on the morrow the Soviet government promulgated an edict directing that all Japanese citizens be set free from places of confinement and be permitted to return to their homeland.[44] Nevertheless, "in 1957 the Japanese stated that 8,069 Japanese citizens continued to be detained in the Soviet Union and Outer Mongolia, 2,629 in North Korea, and 1,392 in Sakhalin and the Kurile Islands".[45] The figures may have included a sprinkling of former Japanese subjects of Korean extraction.

The latest chapter of the odyssey dates to the fall of 1973.[46] At that juncture, Tatsuya Tabuchi, a Japanese legislator who had just returned from a visit to Russia as the head of a Japanese parliamentary mission, disclosed that a high-ranking

Soviet Foreign Ministry official had informed him that the Soviet government was willing to repatriate Koreans in Sakhalin, if Japan issued entry permits for them. The Soviet source had allegedly admitted that many Koreans in Sakhalin had no nationality, but claimed that they were not discriminated against in any way. The Soviet authorities were reportedly prepared to allow the Koreans to depart from the island whenever Japan issued the necessary entry permits. Japan's cooperation in the scheme seemed to be a sine qua non since the USSR did not maintain diplomatic relations with the Republic of Korea and apparently did not wish to establish liaisons with Seoul even through private channels.

The theme recurred during the visit of Japan's Prime Minister Tanaka to the USSR in October, 1973. During his conversations with Soviet leaders, Tanaka was said to have asked them to return as soon as possible the Koreans in Sakhalin who wanted to go home and forthwith submitted to the Russians a list of Koreans seeking repatriation. Although the question was not formally solved on that occasion, Tanaka subsequently did describe it as a pending problem between Japan and the USSR. According to newspaper accounts, Brezhnev had promised that the Russians would do their best to settle the repatriation matter. The communique adopted at the end of the meeting only mentioned that the two countries proposed to study methods of returning Japanese who lived in Soviet territory. The repatriation of Koreans had, however, been discussed and the omission of any reference to this item in the published statement was solely due, we are told, to the fact that Korea was a third country. At any rate, the media concluded, if the problem of repatriating the Japanese was settled, the question of Koreans would likewise be resolved.

Soon after, the chairman of the Association of Koreans in Japan for the Repatriation of Compatriots in Sakhalin announced that a total of 201 Koreans in Sakhalin had filed applications for repatriation to South Korea with the Japanese Embassy in Moscow. Another 1,630 Koreans on the island had supposedly expressed a desire to move to Japan or South Korea (1,565 in the contingent had picked Seoul as their ultimate destination). The Japanese envoy in Moscow had received specific instructions to approach the Soviet authorities with the object of getting the evacuation under way with a minimum of delay. Separate arrangements were scheduled to be worked out between Seoul and Tokyo to enable the interested individuals to proceed to South Korea after a brief stop in Japan en route. A note of caution was sounded in the meantime not to expect quick results, for Moscow's attitude had not yet crystallized into a policy commitment and, it was revealed, North Korea had at once voiced strenuous objections to the whole business.

Nevertheless, South Korean political circles have since tried by various means to crank up the machinery of repatriation. The Seoul regime has confirmed its eagerness to conduct direct negotiations with the competent Soviet agencies with a view to expediting the operation. The Korean National Red Cross attempted to make contact with the Soviet Red Cross Society, while the South Korean government both pressed the Japanese to take swift action on behalf of the Korean minority in Sakhalin and searched for opportunities to engage in bilateral discussions with the Russians with the same purpose in mind, although its efforts here have all proved in vain. Gradually, new data on the subject came to light. For example, South Korean spokesmen currently quote a figure of at least 7,000 Koreans in Sakhalin who had staunchly refused to accept Soviet citizenship and insisted throughout that they had a right to leave. In fact, a roster of 7,197 Koreans who wished to return to Korea had been supplied to the Japanese government back in 1969 and, because the Japanese authorities had originally been responsible for the presence of these people in Sakhalin, South Korean quarters contended that Tokyo was technically and morally obligated to secure their early repatriation.

A few South Koreans would have preferred to by–pass Japan altogether and, if possible, deal strictly with the Russians, claiming that, in the past, the Japanese had pursued their own set of priorities in this area. Of the more than 40,000 Koreans living in Sakhalin, 1,500 had indicated a wish to resettle in Japan. The Japanese had previously restricted themselves to facilitating the repatriation of those Koreans alone whose wives were Japanese on grounds that they could be treated as members of Japanese families and, indeed, had already managed to bring out a small number of individuals who fit that description. In some cases the legal status of the people concerned was quite complex. One episode, for instance, involved a 46–year old Korean male who had spent 30 years on Sakhalin where he had been taken during World War II as a laborer at the age of sixteen by the Japanese. He arrived in Japan in February, 1973, on a travel certificate issued by the Russians in which he was marked down as having "no nationality" and accompanied by his Japan– born wife and two daughters, all identified as Russians. In July, he finally got back to South Korea with assistance from the Japanese government.

The North Korean nationality which many of these individuals officially possess has occasioned further difficulties. Reports about the emigration experience of Kim Chin–hoe, to which reference has already been made, note that he renounced his North Korean nationality along with six other Korean families who were also allowed to leave the Soviet Union, and claim that "the Soviet authorities are known to have defied North Korea's tenacious opposition to their repatriation".[47] Again, we have the curious spectacle of the Russians apparently acting unilaterally in permitting or probably even requiring members of the Korean community in Sakhalin who had North Korean nationality and sought to emigrate first to surrender the nationality of another country, contrary to the recognized canon of international law governing these procedures.

What the account leaves unclear is whether Pyongyang ever demanded that these families be "repatriated" to North Korea since its "nationals" were at stake or merely opposed them going elsewhere and if the Soviets where thus faced with a double or triple alternative: 1) to let these people stay in the USSR or go to Japan; or, 2) to let them stay in the USSR or freely chose between going to North Korea or Japan. In any event, both the phenomena of summary relinquishment of North Korean nationality at the behest of the competent Soviet agencies and Soviet willingness to risk North Korea's displeasure in sanctioning the departure of ostensibly former North Korean nationals to Japan give extra credence to the view that this nationality was acquired in the same "irregular" fashion and that the reason the Russians were now behaving in this manner may well stem from their attitude that a situation which they themselves had been instrumental in creating should likewise be resolved by them alone (and with an equally cavalier disregard for the established rules, one might add).

By contrast with the modest gains posted by the continuing efforts to extricate "Japanese Koreans" from the USSR, their Korean kinsmen who did not fall into this "mixed" category fared poorly and no tangible progress was recorded in the matter of winning them an analogous right of exit from the Soviet Union. South Koreans blamed the bottle–neck on Japan, charging that the Japanese authorities hesitated to issue the requisite entry visas under the pretext that they did not want the prospective recipients to establish residence in Japan. The outlook improved slightly with the advent of 1974. In January, the Japanese government announced that it had drawn up a list of Koreans who wished to be repatriated from Sakhalin to Japan or Korea and planned on submitting it to Soviet Foreign Minister A. Gromyko during his impending visit to Japan. The roster was expected to be much shorter than the one the South Koreans had compiled and which had featured over 7,000 names. The Japanese had instead assembled their own index based on petitions filed with the Foreign Ministry and the Japanese Embassy in Moscow and, in an apparent policy switch intended to appease the South Koreans, now proposed to negotiate first for the repatriation of Koreans who wished to return to South Korea and then launch talks on the repatriation of those who wanted to resettle in Japan, the latter consisting essentially of Koreans with Japanese wives. The news story also disclosed that the original list which Tanaka had supplied to the Russians during his 1973 trip to the USSR contained 104 Korean families that desired to be evacuated to Japan and of these households 80 Koreans had Japanese wives. Muted optimism was expressed about the chances of springing the Koreans married to Japanese women and getting them back to Japan in the foreseeable future, but serious difficulties were anticipated in tackling the problem of Koreans in Sakhalin who were classified as stateless.

April struck an upbeat note, when it was reported that Japan and the Soviet Union had agreed to repatriate 201 Koreans under detention in Sakhalin and that around 1,000 additional detainees on the island counted on being repatriated soon. Meantime, available scattered accounts of those who did trickle out spotlighted exclusively Koreans with Japanese wives, as if the Japanese still adhered to precedent in this respect and, despite recent promises made to the South Koreans to give primacy to the repatriation of ordinary Koreans, quietly stuck to the routine of first obtaining the release of Koreans with Japanese matrimonial connections. Otherwise, the intervening years witnessed no major new developments in this sector: the door swung slightly ajar, a handful of people have slipped out, an occasional letter brings information of a long missing relative who had been given up for lost, families keep alive the dream of being reunited some day soon, but the harsh reality is that no significant exodus has so far materialized.

Many of these hardy individuals who have made no secret of their desire to leave the USSR and relocate to Japan or Korea have met the same kind of systematic harassment and persecution as have other folk who in the last few years had declared their aspiration to quit the USSR and move elsewhere. The 7,000 or so Sakhalin Koreans who persist in wanting to "go home" were reputedly being treated as "stateless" by the Soviet Union. Moscow's contentions to the contrary notwithstanding, circumstancial evidence indicates that "they are discriminated against in jobs and in education for their children, and as noncitizens they are sharply limited in their right of travel even within the country that holds them against their will".[48] The would-be emigrants face the familiar pattern of endless delays. In 1977, for example, the Japanese government announced that it had decided to allow 339 members of 108 Korean families detained on Sakhalin to enter Japan as a preliminary step to returning them to Korea. The sources claimed that the Soviet authorities had also agreed in principle to repatriate the Koreans to Japan, but North Korean obstruction was said to have hindered the final repatriation.[49] Simultaneously, a story was circulated to the effect that on the previous November a group of Korean residents on Sakhalin had staged a wildcat demonstration demanding their repatriation to Korea which was quelled by Russian soldiers: at least one Korean was reported killed, 30 arrested and some were rumored to have been forcibly sent to North Korea.[50]

In March 1978, Japanese officials again publicly confirmed their readiness to accept the Koreans detained on Sakhalin who had requested repatriation to Japan: 437 individuals had filed such applications and the Japanese authorities had already issued entry visas for 391 Koreans.[51] However, in September, these hopes were dashed — owing to Soviet refusal to issue exit visas to some 400 Korean residents of Sakhalin although they had duly procured permission from the Japanese to land in Japan. The accounts of Soviet bureaucratic duplicity sound sadly familiar. One of the people seeking to emigrate told how he had submitted a proper request to the competent institutions in Moscow asking for an exit permit, along with an entry visa issued by the Japanese Embassy in Moscow in 1975, but his petition was rejected on grounds that he should return to Sakhalin and apply from there since that was his place of residence. The Russian brass on Sakhalin then denied his request on the pretext that "Koreans are not allowed to land in Japan".[52] By February 1979, Japanese Prime Minister Ohira openly conceded that his government had tried without success to talk with the Soviet regime to settle the problem of the Korean community on Sakhalin, but vowed that the matter would not be left unsolved.[53] Once in a while references still appear in the press to a family unit that managed to get out of the USSR and travel to Japan; yet, nearly every case mentioning a person of Korean origin has featured a "mixed" household so that the old pattern seems to persist where Koreans "escape" from the USSR essentially by virtue of their Japanese connection.

By perseverance through further suffering, the more venturesome members of the Korean component will in time probably also join the dribble of emigrants of assorted nationalities whom the Soviet system grudgingly lets out. The obstacle course they must run is tougher than the one confronting most people in a similar position. The potential Korean emigrants face a double hurdle: first, the Soviet bureaucracy; and, second, the North Korean regime which claims that they are citizens of the DPRK and presses Moscow either to preserve the status quo or, in extremis, turn the Koreans over to North Korea, but not, by allowing them to move to Japan or South Korea, to advertise the superior attraction exercised by the DPRK's ideological competitors. This additional term in the equation is certainly not calculated to ease the lot of the prospective Korean applicant for a Soviet exit visa.[54]

Nor is the fact that the whole affair must follow the circuitous channel of Soviet–Japanese contacts likely to help matters any. Despite repeated assurances, the Japanese do not seem, at least so far, to have interceded as energetically on behalf of their former Korean subjects as they have in favor of their own nationals or Koreans married to Japanese. There is a glimmer of hope, however, that Tokyo's conduct on that score may gradually improve, if one can set stock by recurrent reports that the Japanese authorities have bowed to outside pressure and relented to the point of sending a sizable batch of visa application forms to the Koreans in the USSR who wished to be repatriated (2,000 copies, according to one account).[55] This procedural detail in the past proved a major stumbling block in the way of the proposed repatriation program. What remains for the Japanese diplomatic corps to do now is to act in good faith in also vigorously championing the right of the Korean minority in the USSR to avail itself of these documents to extract exit permits from the Soviet administrative apparatus by overcoming the latter's feigned aversion to letting people emigrate to countries with which the USSR does not maintain normal relations, i.e., South Korea. Were Japan to push hard enough its role as the staging area for Koreans who desire to leave the USSR, such a policy might finally clear the chronic bottle–neck and initiate the long overdue process toward the piece–meal extrication of a portion of the Korean community in the USSR from its present bondage.

C. The Jewish Problem

In the case of Jewish emigration from the USSR, a direct connection exists between citizenship status and expatriation.[56] Because here we have the best documentation of both the relevant legal artifacts and administrative routine, the record warrants close scrutiny for insights into the relationship between "foreign exile" and nationality in Soviet practice. An analysis of these emigration procedures offers a glimpse into how the Soviet regime treats the tandem question of denaturalization and interprets the rules applicable to the latter institution where the local repertory otherwise tends to shed little light on the "resignation" mechanism per se. The collage looks as follows.

a. Restrictions on Emigration

Soviet spokesmen have, in several instances, maintained that today no obstacles stand in the path of those who, for valid motives, seek to emigrate from the USSR and that, on such occasions, permission to leave is quickly forthcoming. In an article printed in the chief government paper, for example, its two authors wrote:

> "In principle, Soviet law decides the question of the exit of those desiring to emigrate with maximum democracy. When some Soviet Jews (these were principally elderly people) wanted to leave the USSR and join their relatives abroad, including in Israel, they received and are receiving permission."[57]

Or, to quote another Soviet source "... the fact that individual citizens, for a variety of reasons, mainly on family grounds, wish to live in another country does not contradict Soviet legislation. Requests for exit are examined by the Ministry of the Interior and as a rule are granted".[58] In similar vein, a Deputy Minister of the Interior even cited statistics to support that argument, announcing to the mass media that "permission to go was given to 95.5 per cent of the people of Jewish nationality who applied to go to Israel" during 1972.[59] Outside observers conclude otherwise. No evidence supports the assertion that applications for emigration are handled by the competent Soviet agencies with sympathy, dispatch and "maximum democracy". On the contrary, both the formulation of the relevant rules (insofar as it is known) and the technique of their routine enforcement seem calculated to hinder the process of emigration as much as possible by compounding an air of uncertainty, arbitrariness and abuse and interposing endless obstructions along the route of those who wish to go abroad. Admittedly, the Soviet Union is not alone in hedging in the mechanism of emigration with assorted restrictions. The essential element in this context is whether the attached conditions are reasonable and if the manner of their application conforms to the accepted standards of justice and fairness. It is precisely on this count that the Soviet regime's record of performance fails to meet the acid test.

The Soviets themselves concede that sundry restrictions affect individuals with advanced military training or who, by nature of their profession, are employed on jobs with a national security risk or fulfill an important social need so that the community can ill-afford to dispense with their services. (In addition, according to western reports, emigration has been denied to "persons living in the so-called 'closed areas', — i.e., geographical locations where alleged secret military-related activities are carried out — such areas as Angarsk, Perm', Krasnoiarsk, and so forth".)[60] Departure is then either barred a priori or delayed until the secret information in these people's possession has lost its potential value to foreign powers (e.g., the President of the USSR Academy of Sciences claimed in 1972 that any scientist who has been engaged in "secret" work would be refused permission to emigrate "for a period of five years after termination of his classified activities");[61] those who have met their military obligation are ineligible to apply for exit papers until at least three years have elapsed after they completed their tour of duty.[62] That is, formally, the common status, but in the case of emigration to Israel Soviet government spokesmen have reinterpreted the original qualification by extending the prohibition to persons who might significantly bolster Israel's military capacity vis-à-vis its enemies in the region. Whereas, previously, prospective emigrants, at least in theory, only had to worry whether their background and training might prove an impediment to departure because of the USSR's own external objectives and international rivalries, the latest crop of potential emigrants to Israel must also figure on the impact the Kremlin might attribute to them on the sensitive military equilibrium in the Middle East.

In this context, the universal military service clause becomes important. It is by no means peculiar to the Soviet system, but how it is implemented in the present situation has been adjudged by many to be severely deficient. Inducting individuals of military age into the armed forces because they or their families have registered a desire to leave the USSR amounts to nothing less than gross political chicanery designed to exert pressure on prospective emigrants and their kin and muzzle their protests against the violation of their right to petition for an exit permit pursuant to the provisions of the written law. Drafting someone with this end in mind and then appending another three–year "quarantine" period after his return to civilian life before the person is deemed eligible to file for exit papers merely compounds the offence.

Worse yet, according to eye–witness accounts and reports of first–hand experiences, the rules are invoked in totally arbitrary fashion: some people have been arrested and imprisoned for having tried to evade the summons, others have not been molested and have been allowed to emigrate; in some cases compliance with the three–year post–discharge waiting period has been exacted in full, in others the requirement has been summarily waived; possession of special military expertise has operated to bar some individuals from leaving the USSR within the foreseeable future, while others in a comparable position have run the bureaucratic gauntlet subject only to token interference. The net impression is that no discernible principle governs the entire mechanism and that administrative caprice or momentary political impulse alone animates the whole procedure.

Using the allegedly secret character of a person's work as a pretext to reject his application to emigrate fits into the same pattern. The definitions of what constitutes a secret have ranged from the specious to the inane, but, once again, the device has furnished the regime with an effective weapon to harass those who dare to express a preference for living elsewhere, no less so by virtue of the fact that it too has been applied quite arbitrarily.

The attempt to keep people back on the grounds that they perform a vital social service of which the community should not suddenly be deprived, though perhaps characteristic of a socialist ethic which favors the exigencies of the collective over the aspirations of the individual member of the group, nonetheless equally makes sense in certain circumstances. Conversely, such subordination of the goals of the individual to the corporate needs of his peers, while justifiable on a temporary basis and in emergency conditions, cannot be permitted to last indefinitely and one would expect some kind of an arrangement to supply a replacement in order to relieve the ministrant of his special duties. Thus far, the Soviet government has shown no disposition to explore these alternative solutions and, instead, has simply insisted that those whom it considers non–expendable stay at their posts. Nor has administrative conduct been consistent in this respect either, and the official response to demands from the people affected by this classification scheme that the extraordinary limitations imposed on the separate category to which they have been unilaterally consigned be lifted, has fluctuated between flurries of permissiveness and bouts of repression.

However, the authorities' efforts to restrict emigration by conjuring up a list of legal interdictions seem to have backfired. Aware of these technical barriers, people have ignored draft notices, switched from high priority jobs to menial occupations, abandoned employment in which they might inadvertently come into contact with "secret" data and provisionally found innocuous ways of earning a living so as to enhance their chances of slipping through the bureaucratic dragnet. If the Soviet leadership's concern for these matters was genuine, its approach to the problem has accomplished little and still meant the professional loss of the very personnel whose particular services it was interested in preserving. The brave attempt by Soviet spokesmen, quoted earlier, to portray the situation as one in which the authorities, the trade unions and the would–be emigrants normally teamed up to find "safe" positions that would let the latter pursue their departure plans with a minimum of disruption is pure fiction. Unwittingly, of course, the bid shows that the phenomenon is common enough to require an official explanation, but the proposed version has no bearing on how people strive to buy themselves immunity from charges of being privy to state secrets by quitting their careers and engaging in makeshift work to win the desired release.

b. Possibility of Appeal

While, according to reliable accounts, appropriate directives have indeed meantime been issued to the government offices entrusted with emigration affairs, instructing them on how to perform their assigned duties, the members of the general public have had no access to the text of these regulations and so can neither refer to them to press their case, nor invoke them to refute an administrative ruling, nor consult them to check the accuracy of a bureaucratic assertion prejudicial to the petitioner's interests. Such devices are by no means rare in the Soviet administrative repertory and they conspire to put the individual in a precarious position where the defence of his presumed rights is concerned.[64] Not surprisingly, this is precisely the way non–publication of the regulations was perceived by the victims of the artifice, some of whom have since openly called for publication of a Soviet emigration law and the establishment of regular emigration procedures which would clearly spell out the terms on which exit permits might be procured.

A related source of aggravation is the absence of any effective means of obtaining an independent review of an unfavorable administrative decision on grounds of its incompatibility with a superior legal norm or its fundamental inequity. "Appeals" can, of course, be taken to higher administrative instances, but experience confirms that in emigration matters resort to these channels has, at least up this point, not accomplished very much. After all, the efforts of the lower rungs of the bureaucracy to block the avenues of emigration mirror the attitude of the central leadership. In the occasional case of an appeal to a higher level being successful, reasons for the decision are not stated and, consequently, the episode cannot truly serve as a reliable precedent for future cases or an accurate index to the regime's subsequent intentions.

Furthermore, the courts offer no relief whatever in this respect. An examination of the 1977 Constitution reveals that it contains no omnibus grant of a mandate to the regular court system or any special tribunal to review the validity of legislative or sub–legislative enactments. What rights the courts possess to sustain or deny the legality of an administrative act, they owe entirely to explicit statutory authorizations to that end. An ad hoc legislative recognition of the power of the courts to check on the legal propriety of diverse manifestations of the rule–making activity of the administrative branch has always characterized Soviet policy in this area. Article 4 of the Principles of Civil Procedure of the USSR and the union republics, approved by the USSR Supreme Soviet on December 8, 1961, makes that abundantly clear by enunciating that "the courts shall have jurisdiction over suits upon complaints concerning incorrect entries in electoral rolls, acts of administrative organs in connection with the imposition of fines and other cases arising out of administrative legal relations referred by the law to the jurisdiction of juridical organs".[65] The impression is reenforced by the conclusions of an authoritative commentary on that clause holding that

> "Part 3 of Article 4 [just quoted] speaks of cases arising out of administrative legal relations which fall within the jurisdiction of the courts. Here is formulated the principle that, as a general rule, this type of case is processed by administrative organs and only in special instances expressly stated by law, by the courts. Article 4 of the Principles indicates that the jurisdiction of the courts extends to suits on complaints concerning incorrect entries in electoral rolls and acts of administrative organs in connection with the imposition of fines. But this enumeration is not exhaustive. The Principles foresee that the law may also make the courts competent with respect to other matters arising out of administrative legal relations. Proceeding from the legislation in force, among such cases may be named suits on complaints against actions of notarial offices and other organs fulfilling notarial functions."[66]

The subsequent adoption of the new republican Codes of Civil Procedure left the situation virtually unchanged. Article 231 of the RSFSR statute,[67] for example, simply notes that the courts have jurisdiction over suits arising out of complaints against errors in electoral rolls and against actions of administrative organs, and suits concerning the collection of arrears from citizens on state and local taxes and duties, compulsory wage insurance and voluntary assessments.

Nothing in the law prevents the government from adding emigration matters to the list of items over which the courts may exercise appropriate supervision. To date, it has not seen fit to do so, which means that the topic of emigration falls outside the jurisdiction of the courts, as presently defined. Of course, there is no assurance that, if Soviet courts were indeed injected into the picture, they would necessarily behave otherwise and provide a more viable vehicle for the protection of civil rights against naked Party fiat. Today, however, those whose efforts to emigrate have been vetoed by the administrative apparatus are left no choice but to resort to extra–judicial methods of advertising their plight and assume all the serious risks that such a contravention of the written rules entails.

In fact, even an attempt at court litigation when deemed "improper" by the hierarchy may be fraught with grave consequences and the danger incurred is graphically illustrated by a recent incident reported from the local scene where, according to accounts in the western press, "a 36–year–old auto mechanic who sued the KGB paid for his temerity ... when a Moscow court sentenced him to a year in jail for parasitism and forbade him to live in Moscow for five years after he is released".[68]

> When the suit came up for hearing in a Moscow court three months ago [dating back from March 10, 1982], the mechanic, Viktor Tomachinsky, said he was the first person ever to bring a civil action against the KGB. In his suit, Mr. Tomachinsky said the KGB had reneged on a promise to obtain visas for him and his family to emigrate to the United States. He sought 13,400 rubles in damages, the equivalent of $20,000, the sum he said he

would have earned if he had spent nine months working as an auto mechanic in the United States.

Shortly after a three-judge panel ruled that it had no jurisdiction in that case, Mr. Tomachinsky was arrested at home.

He was held in custody until today [i.e., March 10, 1982], when a court in suburban Moscow convened in a basement room of an apartment block to try him on the parasitism charge. After an eight-hour hearing from which foreign reporters were barred, he was found guilty and sentenced to the maximum penalty for citizens who refuse to work.

The conviction appeared to bring an end to Mr. Tomachinsky's battle against the KGB ... His wife, Lena, 30, told reporters after today's hearings that she had no doubt that the parasitism charge was a "technicality" to put her husband behind bars.

"Viktor has been fighting the KGB for years now and they have had enough", she said. "This is their way of punishing him".

Judging from the testimony of individuals who had occasion to deal with Soviet emigration procedures, the agencies involved initially insisted on the observance of a one-year waiting period following the rejection of an application for exit papers before a new petition could be filed. No directive can be discovered sanctioning this practice. On the other hand, as attested to by the language of the RSFSR decree of January 2, 1928, a similar modus operandi was once in force in regard to repeated requests for admission to the citizenship of the RSFSR and the responsible institutions were then instructed that petitions may be initiated by persons whose petitions were previously rejected by decrees of the All-Russian Central Executive Committee not earlier than one year from the day of rejection.[69] (The 1978 citizenship statute is silent on that score, but Soviet writers insist that administrative usage at both the federal and republican levels continues to abide by the one-year moratorium before a return engagement;[70] the latest citizenship law enacted in the Armenian SSR now features a norm to that effect.[71]) For all we know, this injunction perhaps was used as a formal model for the handling of successive applications for emigration documents or by analogy was extended to cover this latest contingency.

Official and dissident sources agree that periodic review of rejected petitions for exit permits occurs, presumably in response to importunate requests from the disappointed suppliants. Where they differ by a very wide margin is in estimating the frequency of original refusals and subsequent reversals. Private accounts claim that the percentage of first-time rejections of emigration applications runs high and that the ratio of approvals on reconsideration is comparatively low. Government spokesmen argue the contrary: e.g., that as of January 1, 1976, the decision was "postponed" for only 1.6 percent of the total number of applications for emigration filed by Soviet Jews, whereas in 1975 alone more than "300 people who had earlier been refused permission to emigrate, did receive permission".[72] On balance, students of Soviet affairs abroad tend not to set much store by the regime's published statistics in this field either.

c. Nationality Criterion

In the past, measures adopted by the Soviet authorities licensing the emigration of particular groups of individuals have, in a majority of instances, employed national indicia to define candidacy. The present scheme, in theory inspired by the theme of family reunification, ostensibly eschews that criterion. In fact, however, emigration has been virtually restricted to certain national minorities, whereas their fellow Soviet citizens, even if they happened to fulfill the formal requirements, have not been able to avail themselves of this avenue because they lacked the "proper" national affiliation. To be sure, isolated exceptions do occur. In general, though, reports filtering out of the Soviet Union agree that where incidences of sizable exodus from the USSR have been observed in recent years they have invariably involved national groups, e.g., Greeks, ethnic Germans, Armenians, to cite just a few of those who have featured in the news lately. Today's "mass" efflux of Soviet Jews is guided by similar considerations and the experience acts to confirm once again their enjoyment of a tacitly recognized status as a distinct national entity in this connection. Essentially, the situation is far from novel: suffice it to remember that, back in the forties, the option projects with Poland had designated persons of Polish Jewish stock as a separate component entitled ipso jure to seek transfer from the USSR to Poland pursuant to these arrangements.

An interesting question thus arises. The 1977 Soviet Constitution reiterates the right of every union republic freely to secede from the USSR — a supreme embodiment of the Marxist–Leninist thesis on national self–determination. Might not, then, a lesser right of free emigration for a certified national minority be deduced from an identical premise? To be sure, the concept would require devising suitable techniques to ascertain the will of the majority of the adult members of the nationality concerned. The vague hints occasionally dropped suggest that a few people in the Soviet upper crust may well be thinking along these lines. For instance, Deputy Minister of the Interior, Major–General B.T. Shumilin, when outlining the different conditions on which emigration to Israel purportedly depended, supposedly made the remark: "But certainly some changes will be possible if 50% of Soviet Jews wish to go to Israel."[73] To be sure, no further effort was made to pursue the matter; yet, the soupcon of a quasi–referendum geared to a particular constituency strikes an intriguing note and, parenthetically, tends to legitimize the idea that such a special "electorate" indeed exists.

d. Family Reunion Principle

In keeping with the notion that the current relaxation of exit controls vis– à–vis Soviet Jewry was prompted by the desire to facilitate the reunification of families separated by war and geopolitical changes in Europe, the first step in the process has entailed the procurement of a written certified invitation *(vyzov)* from close relatives abroad to join them. The responsibility for securing such an invitation lies with the individual himself. The document must be mailed to the de cujus directly, and not to any government institution.

For the most part, the Soviet officialdom made no effort to verify whether the invitations really emanated from "close relatives" as prescribed by the regulations:

some of them did; the bulk did not, simply because nobody thought it mattered. But, whenever the Soviet government has seen fit, it has invoked also this requirement in order to curb or disrupt the flow of emigration. The style has varied. At times, petitions for an exit visa have been refused specifically on the grounds that the invitation did not originate with a relative who was close enough. In similar vein, on multiple occasions charges have been publicly levelled that the Soviet authorities were intercepting letters sent to Soviet Jews and confiscating any invitations; thus the regime has effectively prevented aspiring emigrants from even initiating the laborious process of applying for an exit permit.

Alternatively, when for some reason the Soviet apparatus has made up its mind that the expatriation of a certain individual is desirable, technicalities have not been allowed to stand in the way. Official invitations to come to Israel, devoid of any personal element or any pretense of familial sentiment, have in several instances been accepted at face value by the competent agencies in lieu of the usual attestations. A number of invitations mistakenly addressed to government offices have elicited quick and positive action. Episodes are known where people were summoned by administrative organs dealing with emigration affairs, formalities were waived, including the exigency of producing a suitable invitation from near kin, they were instructed to fill out the requisite application immediately (often on threat of unpleasant consequences if they did not comply), the papers were rubber-stamped and the people were literally hustled out of the country on short notice.

This special treatment has so far been reserved primarily for "troublesome" characters of whom the authorities have been eager to rid the local scene — vocal critics of the regime, an occasional soul who had become personally objectionable but could not be suppressed without sparking a vexing outcry in foreign quarters. In the case of the poet Iosif Brodsky, we are told, he was called before the proper officials, supplied with an utterly fake invitation from alleged relatives in Israel, directed to fill out the relevant application blanks which were approved without delay and then, in a matter of days, was virtually expelled from the country. By his account, he had never sought to leave the USSR, had never made any attempt to obtain an exit permit, had never been contacted by relatives in Israel with a view to supplying him with the mandatory invitation and, in fact, had no intention of becoming an expatriate from the Soviet Union.

e. Character Reference and Family Permission

Whereas the *vyzov* at least has the color of practical relevancy, the *kharakteristika* can scarcely be explained in those terms. Character references are, of course, commonplace to the Soviet milieu, but heretofore they were required by law strictly in connection with job opportunities. Hence, when the authorities first demanded that such documents be produced for emigration purposes, the result was utter consternation, for the management of the factory or institution where the applicant was employed had no experience in these matters and in the standard bureaucratic fashion refused to do what was not prescribed in the existing regulations. Apart from uncertainty as to precisely what was expected of them, the whole business posed a serious corollary problem for the managerial staff involved: a negative response might lead to embarrassing inquiries as to why a person without proper qualifications featured on the payroll to begin with; a positive reply might call for explanations as to why the directors were willing to assist so valuable a man to leave the USSR. Under the circumstances, the safest solution was again to ignore the issue and dismiss the importunate solicitor without an answer.

Furthermore, in this way the person's desire to emigrate immediately became known and, given the climate of opinion in the USSR, seldom missed exposing him to a string of thoroughly unpleasant consequences: ostracism and public condemnation, dismissal, harassment, intimidation, and pressure tactics intended to make him change his mind, inability to find another occupation coupled with threats of arrest for "parasitism", and so forth. Often, the same methods were tried on other members of the family in an attempt to split the household and make emigration more difficult by influencing the weakest link and raising the specter of having to leave part of the family behind, with no assurance as to its subsequent fate or the chances of proximate reunion.

The net effect of the *kharakteristika* requirement was to throw a roadblock in the path of the prospective emigrant by capitalizing on the bureaucracy's natural proclivity to avoid taking the initiative, so that, by sheer procrastination and red–tape, the entire mechanism could be brought to a halt, all the while without saddling the regime with the odium of having to resort to an overt refusal. Fittingly enough, in those few cases where, according to reports, an emigration office did choose to contact the person's employer on its own, the *kharakteristika* was immediately forthcoming which merely confirms that the scheme represented an egregious delaying bid and lacked any conceivable juridical rationale. Moreover, the contents of the testimonial had no bearing whatever on whether the accompanying application for an exit visa would succeed. From the above, it is obvious that the *kharakteristika* was solely meant as an extra obstruction to emigration.

Of equally dubious legal pedigree is the stipulation whereby an applicant for an exit permit must furnish a written statement from parents, dependents, children or ex–spouse remaining in the Soviet Union that they have no objections to his or her departure and no past, present or future material claim against the potential expatriate. The dictum runs counter to every canon of Soviet legal doctrine, establishes a form of wardship for adults that is virtually unprecedented in modern legal practice and pegs it not only to a recognized claim but to the mere possibility of such a contingency arising at some later date. With no parallel in Soviet civil and family law to serve as a guide, small wonder that people approached for a document of the sort hesitated to commit themselves for fear of adverse repercussions or simply out of ignorance of what the waiver might entail.

Once the situation was clarified and those involved came to realize that no juridical encumbrances attached to the act, securing the requisite paper turned into a mere formality. Nevertheless, from a strictly legal point of view, no valid justification can be found for this procedure. And, law apart, one must always remember that the device does give the regime an additional fulcrum for exerting leverage against an individual whose emigration it wishes to prevent by prevailing upon a person whose consent is mandatory to withhold it. For example, in the case of Valery Panov, a member of the Kirov ballet company in Leningrad, the official reason cited for denying him an exit permit was precisely that his wife's mother had not expressed agreement with the couple's plan to emigrate.

To be sure, this is little more than a convenient excuse that lends an air of legality to the government's opposition to Mr. Panov's going abroad, for we know that in other more routine instances the authorities have been prone to overlook the technicality. The nub of the matter thus always seems to be what the official attitude is vis–à–vis a particular episode: the letter of the law may be totally disregarded when the authorities do not want to create a fuss over someone's emigration application or, conversely, every sinuosity of the law will be utilized to stop the departure of an individual whom the leadership had decided to keep at home.

In the latter eventuality, resort to the pretext of "family opposition" frequently lends a surreal quality to the scene. A sampling will convey the sense of Grand Guignol that marks the administrative repertory. For instance, as long as the Soviet leadership was against the departure of E. Alekseeva, the Sakharovs' protegée, her invalid father's and sick mother's "categorical objection" to her emigration ostensibly vetoed her wish to move to the United States. When the Sakharovs staged a hunger–strike and the regime developed second–thoughts about the whole affair and concluded that letting Ms. Alekseeva leave would be the wiser alternative, the parents promptly changed their mind (or so we are asked to believe) and the main obstacle to her departure disappeared.[74] Or, to mention a different, but equally balky, setting which afflicts divorced couples and can lead to the kind of desperate plight into which one 47–year old woman was plunged when she tried in vain for two years (by last count) to convince her former husband, with whom she had not lived for 21 years, to sign the necessary papers allowing their 22–year– old son to leave with her for the west.[75] Such dramas are legion and while some may reflect sincere emotions in a society where family units are still relatively close–knit and foreign exile is looked upon with trepidation, all too often deep–seated human sentiments are coldly manipulated by the ruling apparatus for its own ends.

f. Reimbursement for Higher Education

Rivulets of ink have been spilled over the topic of the so–called educational tariff since its introduction in the summer of 1972. The texts of the relevant laws were eventually released and can be examined in the flesh, so to speak, instead of having to rely on paraphrased accounts as to the nature of their contents. We will focus here on analysis of the legal ingredients of the scheme alone, and skip those aspects of the problem which pertain primarily to its economic and social logistics.

On August 3, 1972, the Presidium of the USSR Supreme Soviet resolved that citizens of the USSR departing for permanent residence abroad (except those going to socialist countries) were obliged to reimburse state expenses for higher education and receiving various advanced academic degrees. The size of the refund and the conditions on which the money had to be repaid were to be spelled out by the USSR Council of Ministers.[76] A directive[77] was accordingly issued by the latter body on the same day which, in addition to endorsing a corresponding price scale drawn up by the competent Ministries, approved the following procedure.

The USSR Ministry of Finance, together with the USSR Ministry of Internal

Affairs, was authorized in special cases where valid reasons existed to excuse Soviet citizens going abroad from repaying the tax in whole or in part. The rules further provided that invalids of the first and second group and men and women who had reached the statutory pensionable age (60 and 55 years, respectively) would be totally exempt from having to reimburse the state, invalids of the third group might be excused to the extent of 50% of the designated sum, and a graduated discount was also allowed to those who had worked a specified number of years, who had earned their diplomas without interruption from work or without having been formally enrolled in a graduate program. Curiously enough, individuals who married citizens of foreign countries were likewise entitled to a 25–50% rebate, depending on their financial situation, while those who had married prior to August 3, 1972, owed nothing at all. In similar vein, Soviet citizens who wished to leave the USSR in order to establish permanent residence in developing countries could be granted an exception in excess of the one foreseen by these instructions to the amount of 70% and persons married to the citizens of these countries — up to 80%, and in individual cases — 100%. The formalization and issuance of exit visas to persons emigrating abroad for permanent residence was entrusted to the organs of the USSR Ministry of Internal Affairs after the persons concerned submitted receipts from the USSR State Bank confirming that the money due in reimbursement for state expenses for education had been paid. An end clause stipulated, expressis verbis, that these regulations did not apply to citizens of the USSR emigrating for permanent residence to socialist countries.

The Soviets put forth a two–fold justification for this measure: first, that rules governing the conditions of emigration from a country lie exclusively within the sphere of domestic jurisdiction and, hence, every state has the sovereign right to adopt in this realm whatever definitions suit its purposes; second, where a country spends a great deal of money on offering its citizens free education, it has the inherent right to protect itself by appropriate means from the consequences of a prospective major "brain drain".[78]

Both contentions are quite plausible. They do, however, run counter to the currently prevailing view in international law that an individual's freedom to decide where he wants to live forms part of the modern code of human rights and its exercise should not be unreasonably circumscribed by state agencies. That the Soviet educational surtax, whatever its official rationale, would in fact and indeed was meant to operate precisely in such a way as to render nugatory the chances of certain classes of individuals to emigrate from the Soviet Union, is beyond doubt. And, to that extent, the argument of domestic jurisdiction and economic convenience would have to fail in the face of the overriding exigencies of the international norms on the protection of fundamental civil liberties. The "brain drain" thesis is further weakened by the policies which the Soviet authorities meantime pursued in this connection. For, the moment a highly qualified Soviet citizen of Jewish extraction indicated a desire to seek exit papers, he was dismissed from his post and otherwise prevented from utilizing his special skills, so the anticipated damage was actually done even without physical expatriation.

At a more prosaic level, the legislation in question suffered from various technical defects that, ultima ratio, were perhaps even more crippling. To begin with, the tone of the regulations was nakedly discriminating. The Soviets have always been extremely sensitive to the slightest sign of differential treatment at the hands of foreign legal systems and have not hesitated to retaliate against what they perceived to be artificial distinctions deliberately aimed at the interests of the USSR and calculated to place the Soviet Union in an inferior status compared, say, to a member of the "capitalist" club. Yet, in this case, gross favoritism was shown the socialist and developing countries, at the expense of the rest of the global community, which is difficult to square either with customary international legal standards or how the Soviet leadership expects others to behave vis–à–vis the USSR. Under the circumstances, other countries might well be entitled to react in kind, in areas where they enjoy a net advantage, and the Russians would have no one to blame but themselves for the unpleasant results.

The legal script was likewise hopelessly flawed in juridical terms since the formulas it featured were so riddled with exceptions that the latter thorougly destroyed its value as a normative statement of the attendant rights and duties. Instead, what we have here is an example of flagrant abdication of legislative responsibility and a sweeping delegation of authority to the administrative apparatus which is vested with full discretion to interpret and enforce the rules and plug the countless interstices of the law in whatever manner it deems best. The aggrieved private party has no access to any independent institutional media enabling him to challenge the validity of an adverse administrative decree, either by judicial or other means, except, of course, through appeal to the higher echelons of the bureacracy, usually a futile gesture in that the entire mechanism functions in sync. The subsequent record of Soviet administrative performance amply corroborated the impression of the regime's utter reliance on administrative power in this domain, operating behind a thin veil of legislative sanction: newspaper reports and personal accounts unanimously concurred in painting a picture of political arbitrariness and unpredictability, of pervasive proneness to disregard the letter of the law out of supervening pragmatic considerations either to the profit or the detriment of the individual, contingent on what the occasion seemed to call for.

The random flavor of the levy scheme can be gauged from the following:

> "While in effect (from August 3, 1972, to March 19, 1973), Soviet official sources maintain that only some nine hundred out of a total twenty thousand Jewish emigrants (or 4.5 percent) actually paid the required tax. However, one high–ranking Soviet official, Vladimir S. Alkhimov, Vice– Minister of Foreign Trade, has stated that '10 percent' of the total Jewish emigration during that period was obliged to pay the tax. This corresponds with most Western estimates that between 10 and 15 percent paid."[79]

g. Renunciation of Citizenship

The question of renunciation of Soviet citizenship in connection with the ongoing exodus of Soviet Jews from the USSR also raises its quota of technical problems. To start with, there is nothing in the relevant Soviet statutes or ministerial directives that specifies that an individual seeking to emigrate from the USSR must first formally surrender his Soviet citizenship. Indeed, the entire thrust of Soviet legal experience runs exactly to the contrary and the present feature spells a major innovation in the Soviet record in this domain, apparently motivated by sundry political considerations. Note, for example, the aura of ambiguity which surrounds the phenomenon: the hefty fee which is collected for relinquishing Soviet citizenship is not always separately itemized in the receipt issued to the applicant. Some individuals who insisted on getting a receipt for each transaction have since reported that both papers showed that the fee for the exit visa had been paid, with no mention anywhere of the surtax levied for denaturalization.

The inference (supported by the pronouncements of the 1978 citizenship statute) is that the authorities have, at least so far, decided against the wisdom or advisability of elevating renunciation of Soviet citizenship to the rank of an express prerequisite for emigration from the USSR and have been content with letting the matter be handled at the administrative level without having to tamper with the fabric of the law and without committing the government to a fixed rule. The legal status of the experiment thus remains cloudy.

The contention that the increment charged for renunciation of Soviet citizenship amounts to just another excuse for extracting money from the prospective emigrants does not make much sense. The same end could readily be accomplished by simply increasing the visa fee and, moreover, without introducing new elements into the Soviet legal system over which a bitter controversy reputedly has been raging among Soviet leaders. The story is that one faction, which eventually won out, was determined that those who demanded the right to emigrate from the USSR be suitably penalized. Forcing the aspiring expatriates to renounce their Soviet citizenship beforehand and to pay for so doing was deemed an effective means of alerting them to the full gravity of the proposed step. By relinquishing Soviet citizenship, the person concerned knew that his chances of ever returning to the USSR, even for a brief visit, were very slim and that his ties with relatives who remained behind might be severed for good.[80] Meantime, the heavy fee was added to the script in order to dramatize the theme that emigration marked the consummation of an irreversible estrangement between the individual party and his erstwhile homeland — a violent break that neither reconciliation nor accommodation could mend.

How big a wrench this "detour" is from the traditional Soviet habit of thought on that score may be judged from the fact that considerable sympathy is still occasionally expressed among Soviet cognoscenti for the old principle whereby an individual would not be released from Soviet citizenship until he could prove that he would forthwith acquire the citizenship of another state.[81] Soviet adherence to this policy in the past ostensibly stemmed from profound aversion to the concept of a status of rampant statelessness on the world scene. If the explanation is accepted at face value, then the Soviet treatment of Soviet Jews applying for emigration indeed strikes an ominous note. For, the Soviet regime has apparently not hesitated in this case to vacate a position which it has staunchly defended over the years and to incur international responsibility as a potential source of stateless souls who might become a serious legal and material burden on the rest of the global community, all for the sake of either deterring Jews from emigration or meting out punishment to those who despite everything succeed in emigrating.

That the provisions of the Israeli law on naturalization have worked to rescue a sizable proportion of the emigrants from this fate in no sense frees the USSR from original liability for the consequences of its actions. Besides, as growing numbers of Soviet Jews refuse to settle in Israel and seek admission to third countries, incidences of statelessness in their midst will proliferate.

h. Returning to the USSR

In the light of what has been said above, it is a foregone conclusion that the Soviet authorities are reluctant to reinstitute in Soviet citizenship those who a short while earlier accepted the supreme sanction of its loss. However, in this respect the Soviet attitude has not been consistent, apparently due again to the intrusion of extraneous political calculations. We have already had occasion to refer to the well-publicized "redemption" of Mr. Cherches whose recovery of Soviet citizenship even warranted a notice in the legislative gazette, but his "notoriety" has not since been repeated and mystery surrounds what befell other ex-Soviet Jews who, like our hero, relinquished their Soviet citizenship and went to live abroad and then decided that they wanted to repatriate to the USSR. Their numbers are computed at the "hundreds" by Soviet spokesmen, with one source going as high as 1,500,[82] while Jewish and Israeli circles mention a far smaller figure. Hard data are, of course, extremely elusive in these matters and yet a third report, circulated in 1977, noted that:

> "A group of Soviet Jews who emigrated to Israel and now want to return to the Soviet Union asked the Kremlin today to forgive them for leaving their homeland. A committee of Soviet Jews here [in Vienna] says it represents 700 Soviet Jews in Austria who are seeking to return to the Soviet Union. The Soviet Government has refused them re-entry visas."[83]

Quantity is not the principal issue from the legal point of view. The real problem is the current legal status of these people, especially those who have in the meantime left Israel and moved to other countries, and the future in store for them. Technically, they have shed their Soviet citizenship, have virtually repudiated Israeli citizenship and either verge on de facto statelessness or plainly fit into that category, depending on how one interprets their position from the perspective of the evolving principles of modern international law.

In theory, the precedent enunciated in the Cherches case should squarely apply to the latter group, especially since the 1978 citizenship act has finally dispelled the statutory silence on the subject of restoration of Soviet citizenship maintained by its 1938 predecessor which had necessitated resort to ad hoc procedures during the previous four decades to accomplish the reintegration of ex-Soviet nationals (such as Mr. Cherches) into the citizenship of the USSR. Between the special measures employed prior to 1978 and the formal recognition of the concept of re-admission to Soviet citizenship by virtue of the terms of the latest citizenship law, Cherches' lot should have been shared by others who, Soviet authorities claimed, were eager to atone for their error in deserting the Motherland and begged to be allowed to come back. Indeed, according to Soviet testimony, Soviet embassies and missions abroad are besieged by former Soviet citizens pleading for permission to repatriate.

A pamphlet recently published (one of many samples of this genre of literature) identifies by name fifteen individuals who emigrated to Israel and subsequently returned to the Soviet Union.[84] How did all these people reacquire their Soviet citizenship? Why, if the business is handled through departmental channels without requirement of official posting, was Mr. Cherches nominated for unique treatment while his fellow–returnees were not so favored? The record simply attests once again to the amazing lack of coherence in Soviet administrative practice and the singular nonchalance with which the responsible apparatus disregards its own organizational rules.

As for those among the emigrés who have had a change of heart, but have not managed to convince the Soviet authorities to relent (the majority of that particular lot), they have ceased to be the concern of the Soviet regime. Even if the competent Soviet agencies deign to reply to their petitions, the unsuccessful candidates will likely have received just a routine notification from the local Soviet embassy or mission that their applications have been denied, without any explanation of the grounds for the refusal, and have no alternative than to try again and again in the hope that at some point their entreaties will strike a responsive chord.

i. Detente and Emigration

The preceding narrative about how the exodus of Soviet Jews has unfolded since its inception should leave no doubt about the intimate connection between law and policy in this field of activity both in the sense of the elaboration of a loose matrix of legal norms that fosters excessive reliance on administrative initiative to fill the many gaps in the system and the prevalence of a "flexible" manner of enforcement of the regulations in response to tactical dictates. Not surprisingly, then, the warming of international temperatures in the early seventies coinciding with the latest spurt in East–West rapprochement had a direct effect on Soviet emigration practices — the substance of the rules framing the operation and the style of their routine implementation by the institutions supervising the traffic.

At the beginning of 1973, the Soviet authorities suspended the collection of the education surtax introduced in 1972 in conjunction with the ongoing Soviet–American negotiations for a comprehensive trade and economic package which, inter alia, would have guaranteed the USSR large credits from US banking and industrial circles and important additional commercial privileges. Hopes soared at the time that emigration procedures would be appreciably relaxed and even that a definite annual quota scheme might be established that would at least ensure the departure from the USSR of a designated number of individuals each year, with a regular monitoring screen keeping track of the flow and making sure that the commitment was duly honored. The project ultimately foundered over Soviet objections to the bracketing of the economic agreement with concessions to freer emigration, but the education levy has not been reimposed. However, the decree itself remains on the books and, presumably, can be invoked if and when desired, thereby perpetuating the uncertainty which seems a favorite Soviet technique in this sphere. The entire scene is steeped in legal ambiguity, when it is not just a legal wasteland, and this incident conforms to the prevalent official stamp.

The collapse of these efforts to strike a modus vivendi in which various economic inducements would convert the Soviets to adopting a more "open door" policy on questions of emigration put an end to earlier optimism. Press accounts emanating from the USSR during 1974 reported that

> "bureaucratic restrictions have ... been tightened. The formidable paperwork must now be typed rather than handwritten, a difficult chore that some find impossible. A further requirement is that applicants must now check in with the local police before proceeding to the Visa Office, further intimidating some applicants from even beginning.
>
> Among the documents needed to apply are a letter of invitation from a relative, permission from parents if they are not going and a reference from the employer.
>
> Because employers have tended to protect themselves by giving out poor references, some Jews were quitting their jobs with a good reference before applying to emigrate. This practice has been frustrated in some areas by a new regulation that the reference must date back six months. Anyone unemployed for more than four months faces prosecution for 'parasitism'."[85]

These innovations were not, however, translated into statutory propositions accessible either to the population at large or, at a minimum, to those whose interest in leaving the USSR brought them within the purview of these rules. This, in turn, left ample room to the relevant agencies to "improve" the procedure as they saw fit and, in fact, to invent new bottlenecks to block the path of individuals seeking to go through the pipeline.

Other signs of a downtrend followed. Thus, a decree of the Presidium of the USSR Supreme Soviet of May 23, 1975, supplementing the decree of April 10, 1942, "On state taxes", directed that a state tax be introduced from January 1, 1976, on payments to USSR citizens of money transmitted from abroad.[86] However, the USSR Ministry of Finance was forthwith empowered to exempt individual recipients and groups of recipients from payment of the aforementioned tax. On the same day, the USSR Council of Ministers issued ancillary instructions[87] pegging the tax at 30 percent of the amount transferred. Concurrently, the USSR Ministry of Finance was ordered to waive payment of the tax on sums involving alimony, inheritance, author's honoraria, reparations for injury caused, proceeds from the sale of property abroad owned by citizens and in other property cases, including money belonging to reemigrants and repatriates, remittances from employees of Soviet institutions abroad and employees temporarily posted abroad, remittances from military personnel, employees and workers of military units and organizations of the USSR Ministry of Defense, and pensions.

Outside the Soviet Union, the measure was understood as being aimed principally at cutting funds sent from abroad to succor individuals who had incurred the authorities' displeasure and were being economically penalized.[88] Prominent among those upon whom the burden of the extra impost fell most heavily was, of course, that element which had expressed the desire to emigrate. As a consequence, its members became the target of systematic official harassment, with economic persecution featuring high on the list of pressures brought to bear.

Granting the Ministry of Finance blanket authority further to excuse any individual or group of individuals receiving such sums from payment of the special tax merely underscored the infinite elasticity of the scheme, which permitted the bureaucracy to decide at its own discretion who would and would not be subject to the levy.

Another nail was hammered into that coffin soon after in the shape of fresh instructions providing for a steep rise (up to tenfold) in the tariff rates on packages forwarded to Soviet citizens from abroad. The measure went into effect on June 15, 1976, together with sundry limitations on the quantity of certain items that could be included in a single parcel.[89] Although routine economic grounds were cited in explanation of the move, a number of observers of the Soviet scene saw the episode as another attempt by the regime to reduce traffic between the local population and the outside world. And, while a broad category of persons was bound to suffer from the "freeze", the hardest hit would again be those who were experiencing material straits as a result of a dispute with the regime, self–announced candidates for emigration among them.

j. Helsinki and After

The "Final Act" of the Helsinki Conference, signed on August 1, 1975, rekindled hope for a spell, but the substantive results have so far amounted to a mixed bag. Repeatedly criticized in the West for failing to abide by the principles embodied in that document calling for steps which would facilitate wider travel by citizens of the particular states, the Soviet leadership gradually staged a few modifications in the technical norms heretofore governing the mechanics of emigration from the USSR. Reports reaching the outside world in January 1976 noted several steps instituted around the turn of the year which eased to a degree the complex emigration procedures enforced until then. For instance, a reduction of the exit fee from 400 to 300 rubles was verified by a number of applicants, which meant a cutback equivalent to $133.[90] However, emigrants to Israel were still expected to pay 500 extra rubles ($665) to renounce their Soviet citizenship, which Moscow allegedly insisted on because it did not maintain diplomatic relations with Israel.[91]

A further change in the rules stipulated that upon subsequent denial of issuance of a general foreign passport the tax paid had to be reimbursed in full, which apparently referred to the 40–ruble fee which previously had to accompany each fresh application, no matter how often an individual had his petition rejected and filed anew. Emigrants of Jewish origin were probably not affected by this clause in any event since, as stateless persons following the mandatory surrender of their Soviet citizenship, they traveled abroad on the strength not of a civilian foreign passport but of a special substitute travel certificate. Thus it is unclear whether or not they qualify for this "bargain" at the moment and the corresponding edict does indeed mention solely general foreign passports in this connection. The prevalent feeling abroad was that both concessions seemed intended to display formal compliance with the Helsinki Declaration's provisions on increased human contacts which, inter alia, contained specific pledges to "lower, where necessary, the fees charged for these applications to insure that they are at a moderate level", and to see that fees for renewed applications "will be charged only when applications are granted".

Other innovations in a similar vein, aimed at simplifying the maze of paperwork previously required to submit a valid request for emigration, included this array: instead of the character reference which had had to be signed by the applicant's boss, trade union chief and party leader at his place of employment, a plain affidavit testifying to his work place and signed by his boss was now sufficient; visa applications would henceforth be handled by local visa offices rather than forwarded to superior authority for approval or rejection; appeals against refusals could be submitted to higher visa offices and those whose appeals were denied could in the future have their cases reviewed every six months, as against a year formerly.[92]

Whether these measures will offer significant relief from the procedural difficulties which plagued aspiring emigrants in the past or amount to little more than token gestures remains an open question. At the risk of sounding repetitive, let me point out that, with the exception of the amendment sanctioning reimbursement of the fee in the case of an unsuccessful application for an exit visa (which, as suggested, may not be relevant to what we are concerned with here anyway) and the 100–ruble discount on the exit visa fee, the rest of these practices have not received statutory confirmation. Thus, they can, at this juncture, only be viewed as samples of tentative, de facto administrative dispensation, inspired by pragmatic, ad hoc considerations. How long these "revised guidelines" will be observed by the competent authorities, and how consistently the new norms will be applied nobody can tell. The legal terrain is, as usual, terra incognita and until these developments are reduced to legal language and their contents published and publicized, the individual whose fate is at stake cannot count on them to vindicate his rights, but must continue to hope that bureaucratic discretion will favor his lot, strictly on a "one–shot" basis.

However, in concrete terms one should remember that these changes can hardly be described as revolutionary. Furthermore, their actual impact may be double–edged in the sense that the individual involved may find that his own emigration prospects are on the whole likely to be both positively and negatively affected by these shifts. It is hard to say what the effects of the "repeal" of the character reference will be. On the other hand, the situation with regard to the collective responsibility of the petitioner's relatives, stemming from the applicant's obligation to obtain the consent of the members of his family and dependents remaining behind to his departure (itself a legal phenomenon sui generis, one might recall) has worsened in the meantime:

> "thus, in Kiev and Vilnius, it has been officially announced that permissions from parents for the emigration of their children will be attested exclusively at the parents' place of employment [which] means that the parents may anticipate the same difficulties at work as someone who has applied for an exit visa."[93]

Finally, it has been estimated that the 100–ruble rebate in the cost of a visa avails little to the potential emigrant: adding all the expenses connected with the acquisition of the necessary travel documents, customs duties, tickets, etc., this sum amounts to no more than five to seven percent of the total cost.

If the legal performance looks disappointing, so does the actual policy record. The Soviet contention is that from 1945 to December 31, 1975, a total of 122,000 citizens of Jewish nationality emigrated to Palestine/Israel and that "those who wanted to leave the country did so". By Moscow's tabulations, the efflux comprised approximately 5 percent of the Soviet Union's Jewish population. The Russians pointedly noted that in 1975 emigration to Israel fell by 67 percent as compared with 1973 and by 50 percent as against 1974, and that in 1975 it amounted to a mere 11,700 individuals. The Soviet press continued to report a steady drop in the rate of applications for exit permits (for example, in January 1975, the competent agencies were said to be processing less than 1,500 requests),[94] while a growing contingent of individuals who had already received visas had "reconsidered their decision and declined to use them".[95] Official sources explained the phenomenon not by any "artificial restrictions" imposed by the Soviet government, but rather the widespread sense of uncertainty and disillusionment with conditions encountered in Israel engendered by letters from earlier emigrants from the USSR to Israel received by many members of the Jewish community in the Soviet Union and stories told of their harsh experiences there by increasing numbers of repatriates from Israel. Hundreds of such people, thoroughly disenchanted with life in the capitalist environment, were allegedly now clamoring to be allowed to return and bombarding Soviet embassies abroad with requests for re-entry visas and pleas for reinstatement in Soviet citizenship.[96]

In the opposing camp, the evidence has been interpreted quite differently. Responsibility for the ebb in the recorded flow of immigrants — from 32,049 in 1973, to 20,634 in 1974, to around 13,000 in 1975 — was put squarely on the shoulders of the Soviet authorities who were accused of using every means at their command to slow down and, if possible, reduce the rate of exodus. The picture painted by these observers of the Soviet scene was of a consistent campaign waged by every cog of the Soviet official machinery to harass, cow and, where necessary, physically coerce aspiring emigrants in order to compel them to cease their exertions. Individuals who expressed a desire to emigrate have been summarily dismissed from jobs and prevented from finding new employment. Men of draft age have been summoned to military service: if they balk at reporting for duty, they are often arrested and sentenced to long terms in labor camps;[97] if they comply, they are then denied exit visas on grounds that they came into possession of state secrets during their stint in uniform and must wait an undetermined number of years until this confidential information is pronounced obsolete. Meantime, their families must either decide to stay to preserve the family unit or choose to emigrate and leave the inductee behind in the hope that he will follow later.

People active in the emigration movement have been arrested, prosecuted[98] and sent to remote places of detention for protracted periods; others have been forcibly committed to psychiatric institutions for prescribed treatment. Weaker members of families have occasionally succumbed to threats, pressures or the lure of sundry rewards and raised objections to the prospective departure of their relatives on various pretexts. Families have been split, with some members allowed to leave and others kept back, frequently on the assurance that the necessary authorization for the rest would soon be forthcoming. If all else fails, the administrative apparatchiki may simply refuse to grant an exit visa, never communicating the reason for the rejection in writing[99] and either intoning a stock formula (e.g., access to state secrets) without further explanation or not even bothering to produce any valid reason.

Contrary to the Soviet claim that most petitions succeed, statistics are quoted to show that in anywhere between 14 and 30 percent of these cases the requests meet with rejection and only by dint of repeated submission does a proportion of the initial negative rulings eventually manage to get reversed. Thus, an estimated backlog ranging from 140,000 to 175,000 Jews seeking to emigrate from the USSR had gradually built up by the beginning of 1975.[100] On the other hand, as previously mentioned, Soviet spokesmen have acknowledged the existence of a tiny residue of hard–core "ineligibles" and insisted that fresh applications had dwindled to a trickle.

The initial phase of the post–Helsinki era was maked by an encouraging rise in the volume of Jewish emigration from the Soviet Union: around 14,000 in 1976; circa 17,000 in 1977; approximately 29,000 in 1978; and 51,320 in 1979. The fact that more people now got out of the USSR, while gratifying, did not mean that the regime ceased causing grief to most of the lot: true, the "liberalized" legal script was left untouched, but the apparatus still could, and did, indulge in various administrative games designed to make life difficult for those bent on quitting the country — and the technique offered the further advantage of being invisible and hard to document, while being just as effective a deterrent or punishment as legislated sanctions. Evidence mounted, for instance, during 1976 that emigrants traveling overland were subjected to methodical humiliation and harassment at the railroad depot at Chop close to the Soviet–Czechoslovak frontier where they underwent their final clearance procedures: pilfering, badgering, search and rough treatment by customs guards and policemen were common experience. Those who reached the west by air from Moscow and Leningrad also had complaints, particularly about Leningrad airport that had earned a special reputation for losing the checked luggage of emigres.[101] In addition, it was noted that "most of the long–standing 'refuseniks' who have been waiting six, seven or even more years, were unable to get a favorable reconsideration even in the peak year of 1979. Only 12.3% of these hard–core cases succeeded in obtaining exit visas in 1979, and in the first half of 1980 only 8.5% of the long–standing 'refuseniks' were successful. And in 1979, 539 'new' families were added to the list of known 'refusenik' families, and in the first half of 1980, about 400 families were added".[102]

At least the quantitative picture looked positive for a while, except that as the international situation then began deteriorating the Soviet leadership abruptly reversed gears here too and the bottom fell out of the market: in 1980, 21,471 Jews left the USSR and in 1981 such departures totaled a mere 9,249 (other emigrant groups posted a similar dramatic decline, with the exodus of Armenians and ethnic Germans likewise dropping to its lowest level in recent years). The decapitation was accomplished essentially without tampering with the legal scaffolding, by the plain expedient of routine reinterpretation of the existing rules and intramural introduction of fresh conditions in the frame of administrative practice. Local "refinements" conspired to create extra obstacles. In 1980, for example, the officials in Minsk reputedly "improved" on the old tactic whereby young couples usually had to obtain their parents' permission to leave by extending the requirement even to couples who "were in their 40's and their parents in their 80's".[103] The general result was a systematic trend toward applying bureaucratic brakes at every turn in order to bring the outflow to a virtual halt. As a comprehensive survey of the latest incarnation of the tough line noted:

> "Reports have been received that various OVIR offices have reduced their working hours roccasionally to as little as one hour per weekt. For instance, at the beginning of 1980 it was reported that the offices in Baku, Kishinev, Chernovtsy and Minsk were open to the public only once a week, while the office in Samarkand was closed altogether.
>
> However, the most serious difficulty is the demand that the invitations [*vyzovy*] from Israel for 'family reunification', which serve as the basis of applications for exit permits, must come from relatives of 'first degree kinship', i.e., spouse, parents, or children. This new policy was practiced first in the Ukraine, Moldavia and Uzbekistan, but later also spread to other regions. On the basis of this 'close kinship' principle, applications are not accepted if the invitiations do not meet the OVIR's requirements.
>
> No information is available on the number of families which were prevented in this way from submitting an application. In the main cities of the Ukraine their number is probably very high. Moreover, because of the new policy, many Jews are afraid even to try to submit their papers to the OVIR. As a result we have now three categories of unsuccessful would–be Jewish emigrants: (1) the 'refuseniks', whose applications were rejected, (2) those whose applications were not even accepted, and (3) those who did not even dare to apply.
>
> In the past, 'refuseniks' could re–apply after a certain period. But it is rumored that since 1 September 1980 the OVIR office in the city of Kharkov has started a new practice of issuing 'final refusals'."[104]

The regime's primary reliance on sub rosa departmental constraints as a means of choking off the stream of emigration from the USSR has induced would–be emigrants in the Soviet Union to step up a round of agitation demanding the adoption of appropriate legislation defining emigration procedures and a public explanation of the laws and rules by which OVIR is guided in handling requests from Soviet citizens for permission to leave for permanent residence in other countries.[105] Their motive, obviously enough, is to bring the matter out into the open, recognizing that if the corresponding regulations are accessible, grounds exist for arguing with the bureaucracy about the correctness of its decision whereas no effective challenge can be mounted to administrative acts per se in the absence of superior standards by which they can be judged. The campaign has made no headway as yet and, given the prevailing political climate, no progress on this front is apt to be forthcoming.

To sum up the present state of affairs here, one can do no better than quote from the eleventh semiannual report (for June 1, 1981 — November 30, 1981) on compliance by the USSR, inter alia, with the terms of Basket III of the Helsinki Conference. It draws a grim balance–sheet of how these human rights currently fare in the

USSR and the following salient points amply chronicle its keynote theme that "the Soviet record in the areas of emigration and family reunification significantly worsened during the review period", namely:

"Most citizens have little or no chance to emigrate. No Soviet law exists on emigration. Authorities recognize family reunification as the only acceptable grounds for emigration ... During the reporting period ... the number of exit visas has dropped precipitously.

All applicants for emigration from the Soviet Union encounter some degree of official harassment. The Soviet Government regards a desire to leave the Soviet Union as tantamount to treason or evidence of insanity and subjects applicants to whatever form of discrimination it deems appropriate to the individual case. Unsuccessful applicants face harassment at the workplace or actual loss of jobs; they are accosted on the street by 'hooligans' and tend to lose friends at a rapid rate. Successful applicants face lengthy and costly procedures and the loss of much of their personal property as the price of emigration. Soviet authorities have made the application process even more difficult during the reporting period. Jewish applicants, especially, have experienced problems in receiving required letters of invitation through the international mails. The number of petty bureaucratic obstacles has also risen. Restrictions on travel of emigrants have also progressively tightened ...

Soviet performance on family reunification has sharply deteriorated during the reporting period ... The Soviets have defined 'family' in increasingly strict terms. Only the closest of relatives — spouses, parents, children — meet that definition. Reports indicate that Soviet authorities are using a 'pre–application questionnaire' to weed out those without immediate relatives abroad; in that manner, the Soviets are able to claim that a high percentage of 'applications' are granted. The fact is that uncles, aunts, cousins, and even brothers and sisters are rarely considered 'family' and are therefore not even allowed to apply. But even those with 'first degree' relatives abroad find it difficult to emigrate.

.....

The number of Jews allowed to emigrate in 1981 continued to drop sharply. Only 8,047 have left in the first 9 months of 1981 compared to 17,734 during the same period of 1980 and 38,678 in the first 9 months of 1979. Many Soviet Jews attribute this decline to the deterioration of East–West relations in the last several years and to Soviet reluctance to lose skilled manpower. Jewish sources estimate that more than 200,000 Soviet Jews possess the letters of invitation [*vyzovy*] from Israel necessary for applications to emigrate. Some Soviet Jews have waited for more than 8 years for permission to emigrate."[106]

* * *

This dismal tale notwithstanding, the fact remains that, except for state succession, immigration and emigration have served as the main conduit for the acquisition and loss of Soviet citizenship. The thing to remember, however, is that the mechanism has consistently operated under tight control, has always been heavily politicized, never gained an adequate legal shell, runs essentially on executive–administrative fiat, and, hence, functions in utterly random fashion. In entry cases, official discretion determines both who shall be let into the USSR and, once in, will be allowed admission to Soviet citizenship: arbitrariness may be less pronounced in this connection than it was in Stalin's day, but the system still works in mysterious ways. Immigrants may, for instance, find themselves unilaterally classified as political emigrés because Moscow pursues an ulterior objective vis–à–vis their country of origin and they are held in reserve for a key role in the revolution abrewing in their homeland. Such status bars them from local naturalization, for that would spell the end of their value as prospective returnees primed to execute their master's will, help spread the word and physically enlarge the Kremlin's sphere of influence. The exiles' own desires regarding these matters rarely figure in the treatment they receive while "guests" of the USSR. In exit cases, the Soviet authorities can turn the tap on and off as they please and thus dictate who will be eligible to shed the citizenship of the USSR: some are required to do so before going abroad and their choice boils down to staying or facing life on foreign soil as stateless persons (at least provisionally); others will be told that sojourn "overseas" does not affect the validity of their title to Soviet citizenship, that prolonged absenteeism will not cause it to lapse, but they will also be urged to register periodically with the Soviet embassy or mission in the host country in order to keep the record straight and prevent their sovzagranvidy from expiring. With respect to this contingent, though, the Soviets can only count on voluntary cooperation on the part of the people involved to preserve the viability of the old citizenship link: true, even a seasoned expatriate cannot single–handedly dissolve the juridical bond between himself and the Soviet Union, but, by the same token, the liaison retains little practical purpose if the emigrant ceases to maintain relations with his former state and here the Kremlin can no longer exact obedience by the usual resort to brute force.

NOTES

1. Text of the 1970 Regulation in *Sobranie postanovlenii pravitelstva SSSR*, 1970 No.18, Art.139 (hereafter abbr. as *SP SSSR*); English translation in UN Economic and Social Council, Commission on Human Rights, Periodic Reports on Human Rights, E/CN.4/1098/Add.25 (January 9, 1974), pp.33–36. Text of the 1959 Resolution in *SP SSSR*, 1959, No.13, Art.80, and A.G. Khazikov, comp., *Sbornik normativnykh aktov po sovetskomu administrativnomu pravu*, Moscow 1964, pp. 449–502.
2. *SP SSSR*, 1970, No.18, Art.140.
3. *Biulleten' normativnykh aktov ministerstv i vedomstv SSSR*, 1977, No.7, pp.3–40.
4. Malicious violation by foreigners and stateless persons of the rules of sojourn in the USSR and transit travel through the territory of the USSR entails administrative liability the first time around and, if repeated within a one–year span, is criminally punishable. Thus, under the terms of the latest act, i.e., the federal decree of Dec.4 1981, which supersedes the federal edict of July 23, 1966 (in force from Jan.1, 1982), such behavior, namely, sojourn without proper residence permits or while in possession of invalid documents, infringement of the established procedure for registration or inscription or for relocation and choice of place of residence, evasion of departure upon the expiry of the set deadline for staying as well as nonobservance of the rules regarding transit travel through the territory of the USSR, if committed a second time within the space of one year after a previous infraction had drawn an administrative penalty, ensues in deprivation of freedom for up to one year or corrective labor for the same period or a fine of up to 200 rubles. *Vedomosti Verkhovnogo Soveta SSSR*, 1981, No.49, Art.1285 (hereafter abbr. as *VVS SSSR*).
5. Interesting light on how the system actually works is shed by the recently circulated story, not officially confirmed, that General Konstantin I. Zotov, head of the bureau responsible for issuing emigration permits (OVIR/UVIR) was dismissed in January, 1982, for "his failure to halt subordinates who were selling the permits at black market prices said to run as high as 3,500 rubles, or more than $4,700". Apparently, the trafficking in documents was stimulated by the new restrictiveness of emigration policies and "the opportunities for profiteering in the sale of permits widened. It has been an open secret that money passes under the table at the Department of the Internal Affairs Ministry, which issues the permits. Under General Zotov, who had headed the department since 1977, the practice gained ground. Soviet sources said investigators had found no evidence of personal profiteering by General Zotov, who had been dismissed for failing to curb the corruption".
   New York Times, Feb.27, 1982, p.3.
6. Report of the Human Rights Committee, General Assembly Official Records: 33rd session, Supplement No.40 (A/33/40), United Nations, New York, 1978, p.74. The report filed by the Belorussian SSR repeated the gist of this statement, recited the same reasons for a "rare" denial of an emigration request and added that "there were no other restrictions and there were no sanctions in connexion with applications for permission to leave the country" *(ibid.*, p.92).
7. Text in *Pravda*, *Izvestiia*, June 25, 1981; *VVS SSSR*, 1981, No.26, Art.836. The Law was scheduled to enter into force from Jan.1, 1982.
8. Cf., D.L. Zlatopol'skii, *Gosudarstvennoe ustroistvo SSSR*, Moscow 1960, p.258.
9. V. Itkin, "Myl'nye puzyri i real'nye fakty", *Izvestiia*, Jan.23, 1977, p.4.
10. V.S. Paputin, *Izvestiia*, Dec.3, 1978.
11. *Soviet News*, 1976, No.5819, pp.35–36.
12. *Ibid,*, 1980, No.6024, p.183.

13. *Ibid.*, 1976, No.5819, p.35.
14. *Ibid.*, 1980, No.6024, p.183.
15. For additional details, see Th.E. Sawyer, *The Jewish Minority in the Soviet Union*, Boulder, Colo., 1979, pp.182–184.
16. *New York Times*, December 19, 1956, p.7.
17. *Ibid.*, May 25, 1980, p.6; July 6, 1980, p.2E. U.S. Department of State, Bureau of Public Affairs, *Implementation of Helsinki Final Act*, 11th semiannual report, June 1, 1981 — November 30, 1981, Special Report No.89, p.19.
18. *New York Times*, November 8, 1981, p.12; November 17, 1981, p. All. Radio Liberty Research, "Ethnic Germans Maintain Pressure to Emigrate", RL 121/77, July 14, 1977. *Kleine Zeitung* (Graz, Austria), August 23, 1981, p.5. *Implementation of Helsinki Final Act*, 11th semiannual report, p.19.
19. *New York Times*, February 14, 1982, p.17. Note that the figure for the Greek population in the USSR refers only to the post–civil war political emigrés, for the 1970 census reported 336,869 Greeks in the USSR. *Itogi Vsesoiuznoi perepisi naseleniia 1970 goda*, Moscow 1973, Vol.4, p.10.
20. *Kitai*, Moscow 1954, p.40.
21. For background information on the Russian presence in China, including the refugee community, see C.H. Peake, "Refugees in the Far East", *The Annals of the American Academy of Political and Social Sciences*, May 1939, pp.55–62, and several other contributions to that volume, and J. Vernant, *The Refugee in the Post–War World*, New Haven, 1953, pp.55–56, 771–772.
22. *Izvestiia*, January 6, 1946.
23. J. Vernant, *op. cit.*, p.773.
24. *Kitai*, p.40.
25. J. and L. Silverstein, "David Marshall and Jewish Emigration from China", *China Quarterly*, 1978, No.75, pp.647–654.
26. Paul Loong, "White Russians Still Wandering", *The Korea Herald*, June 5, 1980, p.5.
27. The following account is, unless otherwise specified, based on: A.Ia. Kriazhev, "Izvrashchenie maoistami leninskoi natsional'noi politiki", *Izvestiia Sibirskogo otdeleniia Akademii nauk SSSR*, seriia obshchestvennykh nauk, 1976, No.1, vyp.1, pp.99–105; O. Borisov, B. Koloskov, "Politika Sovetskogo Soiuza v otnoshenii KNR — sotsialisticheskii internatsionalizm v deistvii (sovetsko–kitaiskie otnosheniia v 1948–1967 gg.)", in *Leninskaia politika SSSR v otnoshenii Kitaia*, Moscow 1968, pp.208–210; O.B. Borisov, B.T. Koloskov, *Sovetsko–Kitaiskie otnosheniia 1945–1970, kratkii ocherk*, Moscow 1971, pp.274–277; *Vneshniaia politika i mezhdunarodnye otnosheniia Kitaiskoi Narodnoi Respubliki 1959–1963*, Moscow 1974, Vol.1, pp. 232, 239–240; S.G. Iurkov, *Pekin: Novaia politika?*, Moscow 1972, p.60; M.S. Kapitsa, *Levee zdravogo smysla (O vneshnei politike gruppy Mao)*, Moscow 1968, pp.70–71; *idem*, *KNR: dva desiatiletiia — dve politiki*, Moscow 1969, pp.195–197. Likewise, *New York Times*, February 21, 1967, p.8; *Asian Recorder*, 1963, p.5459; and *Facts on File*, Sept.12–18, 1963, p.324.
28. Cf. the author's *The Legal Framework of Trade between the USSR and the People's Republic of China*, The Hague 1976, p.83.
29. See G. Ginsburgs, C.F. Pinkele, *The Sino–Soviet Territorial Dispute, 1949–1964*, New York 1978, pp.70–72.
30. An interesting vignette by Fox Butterfield, "Reporter's Notebook: Chinese Mud House Gets TV", *New York Times*, May 7, 1980, p.A7, recounts the experiences of David Rosenberg, born in China of a father who was a refugee from Poland in 1939 and a mother who migrated from the Soviet Union. A Chinese citizen, he continues to reside in the

PRC. At one time, there was a sizable group of European Jewish immigrants in Gulja (Yining) in Sinkiang, where Mr. Rosenberg was born, and others of his generation have had a similar history.

31. P. Loong, *loc. cit.*; *Beijing Review*, 1980, No.9, p.17; *Beijing Review*, 1983, No.21, p.20.

32. Text in *Beijing Review*, 1980, No.40, pp.17–18.

33. In principle, the observation applies equally well to the cluster of 25,781 Chinese which the 1959 Soviet national census identified as forming part of the USSR's population, some of whom arrived in Russia before the 1917 revolution. *Itogi Vsesoiuznoi perepisi naseleniia 1959 goda, SSSR (svodnyi tom)*, Moscow 1962, p.186. The published accounts of the 1970 Soviet census no longer listed this category.

34. The prime precedent for the Chinese phenomenon is, of course, the Armenian experience. According to estimates, since 1962 about 30,000 Armenians came to Soviet Armenia from beyond the Soviet borders, the majority from Iran. "The net influx was apparently about 5,000 a year until a sharp decline in recent years", noted a 1978 survey. At that point, a reverse trend set in and the Armenian SSR was now said to be losing more people than it was gaining by repatriation. Soviet sources claimed that about 1,000 people a year were still coming back to the homeland and about 600 were leaving each year, but western accounts put the latter figure much higher and reported a migration deficit. *New York Times*, June 26, 1978, p.A2.

Worth mentioning is the fact that in the wake of the adoption of the 1978 citizenship statute, the decree of October 19, 1946, which granted Soviet citizenship to Armenian "repatriates" upon arrival in the USSR was pronounced to have lapsed, effective July 1, 1979 (*VVS SSSR* 1979, No.25, Art.437). The move may have indicated that the inflow of Armenians had dropped to a level where the operation no longer warranted the maintenance of a special naturalization policy here or may have reflected a more general desire to standardize naturalization procedures and do away with some of the older ad hoc improvisations associated with Stalin's public style.

35. On the subject of the citizenship status of Koreans in pre– and post–revolutionary Russia, see V.V. Grave, *Kitaitsy, koreitsy i iapontsy v Priamur'e*, St. Petersburg 1912; G. Ginsburgs, "The Citizenship Status of Koreans in Pre–Revolutionary Russia and the Early Years of the Soviet Regime", *Journal of Korean Affairs*, 1975, No.2, pp.1–19; Kim Syn Khva, *Ocherki po istorii Sovetskikh Koreitsev*, Alma–Ata 1965, pp.37–43, 140–142. Some information for the thirties can be found in J.J. Stephan, "The Korean Minority in the Soviet Union", *Mizan*, 1971, No.3, p.142, citing A.N. Petrov, "Koreans and their significance in the economy of Far Eastern region", *Severnaia Aziia*, I, 24 (1929), p.45.

For general background on the history of the Korean minority in Tsarist and Communist Russia, see, too, W. Kolarz, *The Peoples of the Soviet Far East*, New York 1954, pp.32–42.

36. Department of State, *Bulletin*, 1950, No.584, pp.431–433.

37. *Izvestiia*, April 22, 1950; *Vneshniaia politika Sovetskogo Soiuza, 1950 god*, Moscow 1953, pp.154–155.

38. *Izvestiia*, June 9, 1950; *Vneshniaia politika Sovetskogo Soiuza, 1950 god*, pp.177–178.

39. *Korea Newsreview*, November 22, 1975, pp.4, 8.

40. The treatment accorded the Korean component in the territories acquired from the Japanese as a result of the Second World War falls midway between standard Soviet practices observed in the case of "friendly" and "enemy" population increments gained through the mechanics of state succession. In respect to the former, for example, the Ukrainian, Belorussian and other East European elements whose incorporation into the

USSR was actively sought by the Kremlin, the norm has been automatic wholesale conversion to Soviet citizenship in the wake of the extension of Soviet dominion over the regions inhabited by these "kin–folk". Vis–à–vis the latter, for instance the German, Finnish and Japanese communities in areas annexed by the USSR in the aftermath of World War II, the basic policy has been general expulsion coupled with official neglect to define by appropriate statutory means the legal status of those who remained under Soviet jurisdiction, leaving them uncertain as to whether they validly retained their old citizenship or had been reduced to statelessness or had become candidates for routine application for admission to Soviet citizenship. By contrast, the Korean community on Sakhalin was neither expelled as a hostile faction nor experienced blanket conversion to Soviet citizenship as a "desirable" group, but summarily acquired en masse the nationality of an alien, but allied, political entity — North Korea.

41. For text in German translation, see *Osteuropa–Recht*, 1971, No.1, pp.11–12, and E. Tomson, *Das Staatsangehörigkeitsrecht der ostasiatischen Staaten, China–Japan–Korea–Mongolei*, Frankfurt/Main–Berlin 1971, pp.267–268. The official Korean text was published in *Minju Choson*, October 10, 1963.

For additional information on the earlier period, see Yoshio Tameike, "Nationality of Formosans and Koreans", *Japanese Annual of International Law*, 1958, pp.55– 65, and for analysis of the provisions of the 1963 statute, see E. Tomson, *op. cit.*, pp.257–266.

42. J.J. Stephan, *op. cit.*, p.144.

43. P. Calvocoressi, *Survey of International Affairs 1953*, London–New York–Toronto 1956, p.275, citing *Nippon Times*, August 25, 1953, and December 5, 1953, and *The Japan Annual 1954*, p.97.

44. *Pravda* and *Izvestiia*, October 20, 1956; *VVS SSSR*, 1956, No.24, Art.525.
For text of the edict of December 13, 1956, *VVS SSSR*, 1956, No.24; P.S. Romashkin, *Amnistiia i pomilovanie v SSSR*, Moscow 1959, p.78.

45. *Notes — Soviet Affairs*, No.233, p.13 (August 10, 1959).

46. The following information is culled from: *Korea Newsreview*, 1973, No.38, p.9; No.42, p.5; No.43, p.24; No.44, pp.4, 11; No.51, pp.6, 25–26; 1974, No.17, p.8; No.43, p.9; 1975, No.1, p.21; No.2, p.26; No.5, p.4; *The Korea Herald*, October 26, 1973, p.1; October 30, 1973, p.1; November 2, 1973, p.3; November 6, 1973, p.1; January 13, 1974, p.1.

47. *Korea Newsreview*, November 22, 1975, pp.4, 8.

48. *New York Times*, February 27, 1977, p.10.

49. *The Korea Herald*, July 29, 1977, p.1.

50. *Ibid.*, August 26, 1977, p.8.

51. *Ibid.*, March 5, 1978, p.1.

52. *Ibid.*, September 13, 1978, p.1.

53. *Ibid.*, February 23, 1979, p.1.

54. It is interesting to note that a similar kind of problem has now arisen vis–à–vis the PRC. South Korean sources estimate the number of Koreans living in China to total between 1 and 1.5 million, more than half of whom, they claim, want to be repatriated for reunion with their families. The tone of South Korean dispatches on the subject sounds more sanguine than in the case of the USSR. Reports note that China has set at least one favorable precedent in which an aged Korean was allowed to return home to the Republic of Korea and has as of late permitted the delivery of mail from Koreans in China to their kin in Japan and South Korea. In 1979, there were further reports that the PRC was discussing possible means of repatriating two Korean households, numbering 9 persons, in Manchuria with a Tokyo–based public organization representing the South Korean government. Cf., *Korea Newsreview*, 1975, No.12, p.26, and *The Korea Herald*, May 17,

1979, p.1.

55. *Korea Newsreview*, 1975, No.36, p.4.

56. Accounts in the western press have occasionally claimed that most emigrants from the USSR to capitalist countries must renounce Soviet citizenship in order to get permission to leave. These reports seem to be in error. A recent study indicates, for example, that, "with one known exception, both Jewish and non–Jewish families immigrating to the United States, Great Britain and other such Western countries, are excused from both paying the fee [for denaturalization] and of the need to renounce their Soviet citizenship". In fact, the author adds, "individual Jewish immigrants to the United States have been advised prior to their departure from the USSR of the 'necessity' later to contact the Soviet Embassy in Washington, D.C., in order to retain their Soviet citizenship status". Th.E. Sawyer, *op. cit.*, p.191.

57. L. Berenshtein, M. Fridel, "Pod chiu dudku pliashut sionisty", *Izvestiia*, December 14, 1969.

58. V. Katin, in *New York Times*, September 16, 1972, p.27. Mr. Katin is identified as "political correspondent of the Novosti Press Agency in Moscow".

59. *New York Times*, December 30, 1972, pp.1–2.

60. Th.E. Sawyer, *op. cit.*, p.192.

61. *Ibid.*, p.193. This source notes, however, that "the experiences of individual Jewish emigrants ... indicate considerable fluctuation in the required time interval — some who had possessed a 'first degree' *dopusk* (security clearance) had been allowed to emigrate after two years and in some cases after less than two years; others were obliged to wait the full five years".

62. Again, though, a 1974 *samizdat* publication attests to the discretionary manner in which these regulations operate by recording that "these cases are periodically reviewed and denials may be revoked after one, two, or more years, depending on the circumstances". Cited by Th.E. Sawyer, *op. cit.*, p.192.

63. Interview with Boris Shumilin, in *Soviet News*, 1976, No.5819, p.35. See, too, E.C. Scheetz, "State Secrets and the Right to Emigrate", Radio Liberty Research RL 82/77, April 13, 1977, and "Vyezd Evreev iz SSSR i emigratsionnaia politika Sovetskikh vlastei (obzor za iun' 1975 — ianvar' 1976), *Khronika zashchity prav v SSSR*, 1976, vyp.19, pp.36–42.

64. Cf., D.A. Loeber, "Legal Rules 'For Internal Use Only', A Comparative Analysis of the Practice of Withholding Government Decrees from Publication in Eastern Europe and Western Countries,", *International and Comparative Law Quarterly*, January 1970, pp.70–98.

65. *VVS SSSR*, 1961, No.50, Art.526; *Soviet Civil Legislation and Procedure, Official Texts and Commentaries*, Moscow n.d., pp.146–175. See the author's "Judicial Controls over Administrative Acts in the Soviet Union — The Current Scene", *Osteuropa–Recht*, 1968, No.1, pp.1–33, and D.D. Barry, "Administrative Justice and Judicial Review in Soviet Administrative Law", in D.D. Barry, G. Ginsburgs, P.B. Maggs, eds., *Soviet Law After Stalin, Part II: Social Engineering through Law*, Alphen aan den Rijn 1978, pp.241–269 *(Law in Eastern Europe* No.20).

66. P.I. Bardin, ed., *Nauchno–prakticheskii kommentarii k Osnovam grazhdanskogo sudoproizvodstva Soiuza SSR i soiuznykh respublik*, Moscow 1962, p.23. In the same vein, Iu.M. Kozlov, ed., *Sovetskoe administrativnoe pravo (Obshchaia chast')*, Moscow 1962, p.279.

67. Text in *Zakony RSFSR i postanovleniia Verkhovnogo Soveta RSFSR, priniatye na tret'ei sessii Verkhovnogo Soveta RSFSR shestogo sozyva (10–11 iiunia 1964g.)*, Moscow 1964, pp.201–355.

68. *New York Times*, March 11, 1982, p.A4.

Mr. Tomachinsky may well be the first individual to try to sue the KGB while residing in the USSR. An interesting earlier case in which a person of Armenian origin who migrated to the Soviet Union from France in the post–war euphoria and was then falsely imprisoned in the Soviet Gulag system for eight years before being released and allowed to return to France attempted to file suit in a Soviet court demanding "compensation for damages brought on by an action of the defendant" is reported in the *International Herald Tribune*, May 4, 1979, p.6, by Leopold Unger, "When a Gulag Victim Sues the Kremlin".

69. Cited in D.L. Zlatopol'skii, *op. cit.*, p.252.
70. R.I. Kulik, *Zakon o grazhdanstve SSSR*, Moscow 1980, p.79.
71. *Vedomosti Verkhovnogo Soveta Armianskoi SSR*, 1981, No.16, Art.174.
72. *Soviet News*, 1976, No.5819, p.35.
73. Quoted by L. Schroeter, "How They Left: Varieties of Soviet Jewish Exit Experience", *Soviet Jewish Affairs*, 1972, No.2, p.5.
74. L. Grigor'ev, V. Nilin, "Ocherednaia provokatsiia", *Izvestiia*, December 5, 1981, and *New York Times*, December 13, 1981, p.11.
75. M. Rosenwasser, "Traumas of Emigration Embitter Russian Families", *The Korea Herald*, January 6, 1981, p.5. See, too, *Khronika tekushchikh sobytii* (Moscow, Samizdat 1979), New York 1980, vyp.53, pp.141, 144–145.
76. *VVS SSSR*, 1972, No.52, Art.519.
77. *SP SSSR*, 1973, No.1, Art.4.
78. Cf. V. Katin, "Just Measure and Zionist Insinuations", *New Times*, 1972, No.38, pp.10–11; V. Aleksandrov, "The Latest Anti–Soviet Fulminations", *International Affairs*, 1972, No.11, pp.79–81.
79. Th.E. Sawyer, *op. cit.*, p.197. The educational surtax did not apply to Jewish emigrants only and, while it was enforced, ethnic German emigrants, for instance, were also subject to the assessment. See *Khronika zashchity prav v SSSR*, 1973, vyp.3, p.35. Likewise, *ibid.*, p.33.
80. The lengths to which the Soviet regime can carry the vendetta may be judged from the press accounts of the funeral of Judith Lerner, widely recognized as a matriarch of Moscow's troubled Jewish community. A refusenik of ten–years' standing, together with her husband, Mrs. Lerner died in 1981 at the age of 65 and the officials denied permission for her body to leave the country for burial in Israel. "Instead, the authorities allowed the Lerner's 31–year–old daughter, Sonya Levin, who emigrated with her husband and child in 1973, to return for the funeral." *New York Times*, July 14, 1981, p.A2.
81. E.g. V.S. Shevtsov, *Grazhdanstvo v Sovetskom soiuznom gosudarstve*, Moscow 1969, p.159.
82. Quoted in *New York Times*, January 28, 1972, p.4.
83. *Ibid.*, April 29, 1977, p.A5.
84. *The Deceived Testify, Concerning the Plight of Immigrants in Israel (Letters, Statements, Diary Notes, Interviews)*, 2nd edition, Moscow 1972.
85. Christopher S. Wren, "Emigration of Soviet Jews Declines, but Reasons are Disputed", *New York Times*, May 26, 1974.
86. *VVS SSSR*, 1975, No.23, Art.358, ratified by the Law of July 9, 1975, *VVS SSSR*, 1975, No.29, Art.438.
87. *SP SSSR*, 1975, No.14, Art.82.
88. E.g., *Khronika zashchity prav v SSSR*, 1976, vyp.19, p.47.
89. Steven Rattner, "Higher Soviet Duty Stirs Flurry of Gift Packages", *New York Times*, June 15, 1976. Also, *Current Abstracts*, November 10, 1977, p.11.
90. Duly confirmed upon publication of the text of the Instructions on state tax of

December 31, 1976, No.95, issued by the Ministry of Finance of the USSR, *Biulleten' normativnykh aktov ministerstv i vedomstv SSSR*, 1977, No.7, p.24. See, too, "Market Laws and Soviet Citizenship", Radio Liberty Research RL 246/77, October 24, 1977, and "Soviet Emigration Fees", *ibid.* RL 273/77, November 23, 1977.

91. This rationale has apparently not been used on home ground to justify Soviet policy on this issue to prospective Jewish emigrants, but seems to be intended for foreign consumption to blunt Western criticism as inconsistent with the Helsinki pledges. The implications here (and I am guessing) may be that the Soviet Union must require the surrender of its citizenship by individuals who seek to emigrate to a country where, having no diplomatic representation, the Soviet government is in no position to offer them the necessary diplomatic protection it inherently owes its citizens abroad or to ensure that they abide by the proper standards of international behavior for breaches of which the USSR itself might be held responsible.

Incidentally, the Soviet authorities claim that they also moved to facilitate ordinary travel to and from the USSR. According to K. Zotov, head of OVIR (in 1980), thanks to these reforms, "the number of foreigners coming to the Soviet Union has increased considerably and during the four years which have passed since the signing of the Final Act has reached about 16 million (from 154 countries). Over the same period more than 12 million Soviet citizens have visited 135 countries". He then added that Soviet officials "dealing with these matters favorably considered the requests of foreign nationals concerning entry to the USSR and of Soviet citizens wishing to make trips abroad to meet members of their families and also relatives. In recent years the total number of such trips has increased by more than one–third and amounts to about a million a year". *Soviet News*, 1980, No.6024, p.183.

92. Christopher S. Wren, "Soviet Revising Bureaucratic Procedure for Would–Be Emigrants", *New York Times*, January 21, 1976; Robert C. Toth, "Soviet Said To Relax Rules on Emigration", *New York Post*, January 17, 1976.

According to V. Shevtsov, *Grazhdanstvo SSSR*, Moscow 1980, p.60, in 1976, 737 citizens whose previous requests had been turned down received permission to leave and, in 1977 and 1978, around 2,000 persons who applied for the second time to go to Israel received a visa.

93. *Khronika zashchity prav v SSSR*, 1976, vyp.19, p.54, notes 1, 2 and 3.

94. James S. Clarity, "Moscow Says It Is Processing 1,500 Emigration Applications", *New York Times*, February 26, 1975.

95. Ibid.

96. *New York Times*, June 8, 1975.

97. See, for instance, the case of A.V. Malkin, *Khronika zashchity prav v SSSR*, 1975, vyp.17, pp.47–53; also, *ibid.*, 1976, vyp.19, pp.40–44.

98. *Ibid.*, 1976, vyp.19, pp.42–45; also case of S.G. Miuge, *ibid.*, 1973, vyp.2, p.13.

99. The first instance of a written refusal of permission to emigrate was reported in 1979 when V. Nekipelov received the following notification from the department of internal affairs of the Vladimirsk oblast executive committee:

"On instruction of the corresponding institutions you are informed that your request to leave for permanent residence in the state of Israel and withdraw from the citizenship of the USSR cannot be fulfilled because your relative living in the state of Israel is not a member of your family and exit from the citizenship of the USSR runs counter to the interests of the USSR."

In substantive terms, the communication still said nothing and put the applicant in no better position to contest the administrative decision than the standard oral refrain he would have heard at the police quarters. *Khronika tekushchikh sobytii*, (Moscow, Samizdat, 1979), New York 1980, vyp.53, pp.139–140.

100. *New York Times*, February 15, 1975.

101. *Ibid.*, January 19, 1977, p.A9.

102. "The Decline of Soviet Jewish Emigration in 1980", *Research Report* No.17 (October 1980), Institute of Jewish Affairs (London), p.3.

103. *New York Times*, January 4, 1981, p.15.

104. "The Decline of Soviet Jewish Emigration in 1980", *loc. cit.* Likewise, *New York Times*, June 8, 1980, p.3, and *Philadelphia Inquirer*, April 13, 1980, p.27–A. In similar vein, Ph. Baum, Memorandum from American Jewish Congress, September 22, 1980: "This decline in emigration rin 1980t has resulted from Soviet action that no longer permits Jews applying to leave the USSR to submit letters of invitation from relatives in Israel unless those relatives are of first–degree consanguinity, that is, unless they are parents, children, or siblings.

Since large numbers of Soviet Jews have left over the last decade, the Soviet government can often ask that letters of invitation come from first–degree relatives; however, since many of those emigrants are not living in Israel, and only Israeli–based letters of invitation are acceptable, the Soviet government is declining to consider such letters from relatives who are of more distant consanguinity than would be the case if Soviet Jewish emigrants had, in fact, gone to Israel.

This device has virtually cut off emigration from the Ukraine and other major centers. It has stopped the application process for many thousands of Soviet Jews at the initial phase. It is discouraging Soviet Jews from making use of letters of invitation that have already been received. And it is discouraging many other Soviet Jews from even requesting letters of invitation."

The item apropos "final refusals" in Kharkov is attributed to *Financial Times* (London), September 19, 1980.

105. *Khronika tekushchikh sobytii* (Moscow, Samizdat, 1980), New York 1981, vyp.60, pp.76–77, and vyp.61 (Samizdat, 1981), New York 1981, pp.58–59.

106. U.S. Department of State, Bureau of Public Affairs (Washington, D.C.), *Special Report* No.89, "Implementation of Helsinki Final Act", pp.18–19.

THE NEW SOVIET CITIZENSHIP LAW AND HUMAN RIGHTS

An interesting aspect of the circumstances surrounding the adoption of the new Law on Citizenship of the USSR was the recurrent emphasis by the official rapporteur of the bill[1] and three of the five delegates picked to speak on its behalf[2] on the legislation's complete concordance with the USSR's treaty commitments in general and the provisions of various conventions dealing with human rights issues to which the USSR is a party in particular. The same note was sounded in two editorial commentaries on the latest law: "Grazhdanin Sovetskogo Soiuza",[3] and "Grazhdanin strany Sovetov".[4] In light of these official assertions, a brief inquiry into how valid these claims really are should be instructive.

1. Universal Declaration of Human Rights

One of the deputies who addressed the congregation in support of the draft, V.I. Terebilov, referred twice in his statement to the Universal Declaration of Human Rights in order to make the point that the proposed legislative measure fully complied with the spirit and the letter of that landmark pronouncement. Such willingness to invoke the Declaration effectively disposes of the technical question concerning the binding nature of a General Assembly resolution for our purposes.[5] The speaker's recorded attitude in this instance leaves no doubt as to his conviction that the Declaration enunciated principles which states were expected to observe,[6] that their municipal legislation could be required to comply with its formulations and that its dicta therefore possessed ample normative potency in terms of prescribing proper standards governing state behavior in the present context. Where a party freely submits itself to a test, argument over the applicability of the corresponding criteria becomes redundant. The fact that Terebilov happens to occupy the post of USSR Minister of Justice adds, of course, legal weight to his testimonial.

Thus, citing the Declaration's words that "all human beings are born free and equal in dignity and rights" (Article 1) and "everyone has the right to a nationality" (Article 15–1), Terebilov went on to assure his audience that Article 10 of the projected statute which "established comprehensive grounds for the acquisition of Soviet citizenship" duly matched these desiderata. I am not quite certain what the first proposition has to do with the mechanics of acquisition of Soviet citizenship, except insofar as the language of the statute takes special care to convey the impression that "egregious" insignia play no role in determining a person's eligibility to possess Soviet citizenship.[7] The law does not peg ownership of USSR citizenship to fulfillment of any prior "artificial" attributes and, indeed, positively denies the relevance of considerations of the sort to the whole business. For example, the new regulations feature a clause (Article 1, para.3) affirming that "the citizenship of the USSR is equal for all Soviet citizens regardless of the bases for its acquisition". Similarly, Article 15 specifies that "foreign citizens and stateless persons may, at their request, be admitted to USSR citizenship in accordance with the present Law irrespective of racial and national affiliation, gender, education, language, place of residence". On a formal scale, then, the tone of the statute may be said to square with the Declaration's theme here.

What meaning to attach to the sentence propounding the notion that "everyone has the right to a nationality" raises a different problem. Sweeping proclamations are notoriously difficult to interpret and this case is no exception. In a passive sense, the formula may be read as intended to obligate the state to furnish adequate means for granting its nationality to individuals, because they either routinely qualify by virtue of the customary sample of indicia or deliberately seek to obtain that certification. For that matter, in public law the initial step usually entails getting the state to recognize the existence of a right and thereby create the "objective conditions" for its consequent implementation. Seen as a bid to ascribe to the competent state authorities a duty to guarantee a fair opportunity for individuals to gain possession of its nationality, the experiment boils down to instructing the state to define the substantive and procedural terms for acquiring its citizenship in a style sufficiently inclusive to offer a reasonable quantum of people the practical prospect of attaining that status.

The idea of reducing a right to the level of a state responsibility has always appealed to the Soviets who view rights as a political phenomenon — conceived, maintained and safeguarded by the will of the state (or the organized society). This logic accounts for the thrust of Terebilov's remarks inasmuch as he professes to find the right to a nationality aptly redeemed in the tenor of the provisions elaborating the official policy on the subject of acquisition of Soviet citizenship through birth, naturalization, the operation of international agreements, and the like.[8] In this version, then, the essence of the right to a nationality now ends up totally identified with the profile of the institutions devised by the state pertaining to the methods of its acquisition, resulting in a scenario where, if the medium looks complex enough, the value associated with it is forthwith presumed to be faring very well.

On the other hand, the libertarian school of thought assumes a more adversary relationship between the individual and the state on that score. In the belief of its adherents, once a right is properly recognized, liability for its further preservation must rest primarily with the individual and the measure of viability of a right in a given legal system lies in how effectively a private person is able to defend his stake vis–à–vis the power of the state and what tools are put at his disposal to tackle the job successfully. The goal can be achieved only if two prerequisites are met. First, the right must be spelled out in suitable detail, so that the prospective beneficiary can adduce solid reasons when alleging that his interests have been violated and, by pointing to specific standards, document the discrepancy between the script and the performance. Failure to invest a right with concrete shape can amount to its practical nullification in that the individual is left without substantive recourse against official abuse because he is helpless to show that the objectionable conduct runs counter to any explicit requirement featured in the relevant legal text. Second, the aggrieved party has to have access to appropriate channels that can afford him bona fide protection in his efforts to press for a vindication of his claim against the acts of the state apparatus and, if need be, have the authority to compel the offending agency to make fitting amends. In a nutshell, an autonomous arbiter must function on the public scene to settle disputes pitting the individual against the state in a way calculated to make the confrontation a true contest where the opponents both have motive to expect that they will receive even treatment.[9]

On each count, the Soviet experience falls far short of the mark. To be sure, the statute is quite informative in identifying the grounds on which Soviet citizenship is summarily assigned to individuals by sheer force of law, — for example, in connection with the circumstances of birth or adoption. However, where the situation involves a decision by an individual to seek Soviet citizenship, the regulations shed no light on what criteria will be applied by the offices in charge of these affairs to determine whether the petition will be approved or rejected. Without cognizance of what guidelines the administrative staff relies upon here and what defects in his record ostensibly prompted the refusal, the person concerned is deprived of the wherewithal to impugn the validity of the proceedings by demonstrating his eligibility with reference to some designated list of prior qualifications. Total silence on the rules of the game leads to total discretion in how it is played, leaving the weaker competitor, — i.e., the individual — at the mercy of the stronger rival, — i.e., the state.

Nor should one harbor any illusion that, since the law does not mention conditions on which Soviet citizenship shall be granted, the omission evidently signifies that the procedure is automatic. Indeed, recent history confirms that the Soviet regime has consistently maintained the position that title to USSR citizenship represents a high honor that must be affirmatively earned by those wishing to rate membership in the Soviet community, although nothing is said about how a person goes about meriting the distinction except for the obvious premise that the candidate must please the authorities in every particular. We do know, for instance, that all requests for admission to or restoration in Soviet citizenship are carefully screened. According to Soviet spokesmen, the time required to process applications for entry into the USSR has now been reduced and the method of examination of and completion of the paperwork in connection with petitions filed by individuals to acquire USSR citizenship has been streamlined.[10] Still, the reported reforms have occurred at the departmental level and, since they cannot be verified, outside observers cannot tell how rigidly or leniently the whole business is run. That the competent officials do not simply rubberstamp the documents crossing their desks is, I think, already clear from the fact that a special organization has developed to monitor the traffic, despite lack of data on the way the mechanism routinely functions. Equally unsatisfactory is the picture with respect to institutional safeguards that might permit the individual to enter the arena against an arm of the state in defense of a right: in citizenship matters, the system provides for no independent source of review of its findings and, except for allowing intramural appeals against a negative ruling, excludes all possibility of lateral intercession on behalf of the individual affected by these actions.[11]

In light, then, of the extreme vagueness of formulation of the right to a nationality that effectively incapacitates the person seeking to exercise it and the absence of an institutionalized modus operandi that would let the individual challenge the state's handling of his case with adequate faith that justice will be forthcoming, the only reasonable conclusion one can reach is that under present Soviet law a right to a nationality does not exist in the strict sense of a right that an interested person can practically assert versus the will of the state.

Terebilov next shifted to the second paragraph of Article 15 of the Universal Declaration which postulates that "no one shall be arbitrarily deprived of his nationality nor denied the right to change his nationality" and again reminded his colleagues that these propositions fully corresponded to the text of Articles 17 and 18 of the bill. Whether or not the claim is credible can perhaps best be ascertained by analyzing each component in turn.

"Arbitrarily" is a tricky concept, susceptible of several interpretations. In one guise, such criticism has often been prompted by incidents where the state behaves in a manner incompatible with its own established procedures or fixed standards. Transgressions of the sort are committed in the course of policy implementation and the bare letter of a statute cannot give rise to a charge that, by definition, stems from a recorded discrepancy between word and deed. A second aspect of the problem figures in a situation where the prescribed norms themselves strike the average person as inherently unfair. The third — and probably most common — variant features an occasion where the rules are so loosely structured that the ordinary individual cannot with sufficient certainty predict the type of phenomenon to which their sanctions are intended to apply and the treatment in store for particular contingencies. Here, lack of due notice fosters the feeling of arbitrariness since the individual who might run afoul of the law cannot tell in advance if he is guilty of wrongdoing or what punishment his actions could incur so that he may be master of his fate through awareness of the alternatives. Where consequences cannot be anticipated, the opportunity for intelligent choice disappears and the element of chance assumes a disproportionate role in shaping a person's encounter with the law.

Fourthly, a quality of arbitrariness marks a set–up in which the individual is offered no organizational route to pursue an appeal from an administrative verdict which affects his status through separate channels not so closely associated with the institution responsible for the original decision as to impair their ability impartially to evaluate the case on its merits. Final ex parte determination of culpability and pronouncement of sentence reduces the individual to the size of a humble pawn in the hands of the governing elite, doomed passively to suffer his lot and precluded from mounting a legal protest against official conduct that, he claims, infringes on his rights. Unilateral and unlimited power is generally perceived as an irresistible invitation to abuse and a system fraught with potential for excessive state control over the individual's life instinctively conveys to many people a picture of "licensed arbitrariness".

Using the last two yardsticks to check whether the formula for depriving an individual of Soviet citizenship contained in the statute passes the test of the Declaration's injunction against arbitrariness leaves one no option but to disagree categorically with Terebilov's optimistic assessment concerning their essential congruence. According to the present regulations (which in this respect merely ratify past practice), an individual may be stripped of USSR citizenship in an exceptional case by decision of the Presidium of the USSR Supreme Soviet if he committed acts discrediting the high calling of citizen of the USSR and harming the prestige or state security of the USSR.[12] What constitutes discreditation of the high calling of citizen of the USSR or harm to the prestige of the USSR seems to depend on subjective factors alone. If recent history serves as a reliable guide on that score, when the regime takes umbrage at a citizen's attitude toward some facet of the Soviet experience, the maverick may end up accused of such intangible offenses and lose his Soviet citizenship by executive fiat.

Not only are the grounds for these retaliatory measures vague to an extent that allows the authorities absolute discretion in countering so-called deviant behavior and, by the same token, keeps the individual ignorant of what is likely to befall him, but the latter is also denuded of means to instigate a review of the treatment he receives. Vesting jurisdiction to terminate a person's Soviet citizenship in the federal Presidium may, as Soviet authors contend, lend a special aura of solemnity to the event; however, the arrangement eliminates even the logistical possibility of applying to a higher instance for a reappraisal of the case since the Presidium crowns the state pyramid. Under the circumstances, no doubt remains that the annulment of a person's Soviet citizenship by decree is conceived of and designed as a punitive weapon to which the authorities can and do resort at will: motive, opportunity, method and technique are contrived in a way that guarantees the state apparatus complete freedom and impunity in the use of this form of "retribution" while affording the subject no footing to engage in a defense of his interests.[13]

The third assigned rationale for lifting an individual's Soviet citizenship is in response to acts causing harm to the state security of the USSR which, on the whole, has a more solid ring than honor and prestige. In principle, the relevant criteria here can be spelled out with enough precision to produce a rule that would match accepted standards of legal craftsmanship. Unfortunately, Soviet legislators have never bothered to do so and, as a consequence, the individual is not better informed on when he runs the risk of incurring loss of Soviet citizenship for allegedly inflicting injury to the state security of the USSR than on the other two counts. The state's own ad hoc assertion that a given episode amounts to a breach of state security settles the issue, and to most people this kind of partisan conduct again smacks of arbitrariness.

The new law's provisions dealing with the mechanics of formal renunciation of Soviet citizenship can be faulted on similar grounds. First, the federal Presidium has sole power to authorize exit from Soviet citizenship, which means no vertical supervision, — to say nothing, of course, of the usual absence of alternative fora where the private party could seek redress. Second, at no point does the statute explicitly recognize an individual's right to quit Soviet citizenship and, instead proceeds on the clear assumption that without the prior consent of the central Presidium an individual cannot sever his legal ties to the USSR.[14] Third, the law does not contain the slightest indication that the Presidium is normally obliged to acquiesce in a person's request to be allowed to leave Soviet citizenship, but rather treats the matter as the state's exclusive prerogative, so that the competent organs can grant or withhold approval on such items just as they see fit. Fourth, no qualifications are ever mentioned which a person wishing to divest himself of Soviet citizenship might fulfill in order to be entitled to a denaturalization permit and the omission — obviously deliberate — bars the individual from asserting the right in question vis–à–vis the officialdom by furnishing affirmative proof of eligibility. Fifth, the alternative thesis that would deduce the existence of a general right of denaturalization in the USSR from the law's silence, figuring that what is not expressly prohibited is ipso facto allowed, overlooks both the Soviet legal canon which happens not to subscribe to that principle and the Soviet record in this area which shows consistent adherence to the reverse formula, namely, the concept according to which an act, unless specifically validated, lacks legal sanction.

Note that the authors of the current piece of legislation have included a set of conditions pertaining to the practice of renunciation of Soviet citizenship. Thus, an application to that effect may be denied if the petitioner has undischarged obligations toward the state or property obligations involving significant interests of citizens or state, cooperative and other social organizations. Furthermore, exit from Soviet citizenship is forbidden whenever the applicant figures as a defendant or is slated to serve a court sentence that has entered into force or waiver of Soviet citizenship would be detrimental to the interests of state security of the USSR. Enumerating the terms is plainly intended to convey the impression that only the intrusion of special considerations will lead to the refusal of a proper request to shed Soviet citizenship. Even so, no observer of the scene should forget that: 1) the preceding list betrays every sign of being illustrative, and not exhaustive, so that other reasons can always be adduced by the regime to justify rejection of petitions for denaturalization;[15] and, 2) the reservations featured in the statute are already so broad in scope and ill–defined in substance that the responsible agencies will have no difficulty classifying an individual under one of these headings for purposes of refusing him permission to relinquish Soviet citizenship. Either way, a right whose very content is vitally dependent on incidental bureaucratic interpretation might more aptly be described as a unique privilege or occasional favor, since the person's access to its benefits is entirely predicated on ad hoc official discretion. In sum, Minister Terebilov's claim notwithstanding, objective inquiry fails to reveal any material similarity between Article 15 of the Universal Declaration and the related provisions of the 1978 citizenship charter.[16]

Interestingly enough, our source makes no reference to paragraph 2 of Article 13 of the Universal Declaration which enunciates the rule that "everyone has the right to leave any country, including his own, and to return to his country". A likely explanation is that the Soviets have always been critical of efforts to get the right of departure recognized as a principle of international law and have openly resisted such attempts.[17] Another possibility is that "freedom to travel abroad" is not automatically linked to nationality status and, in theory, need not be discussed in a law devoted to the theme of citizenship. Meanwhile, even though shying away from a formal commitment on this issue, Soviet spokesmen commonly maintain that, as a practical matter, exit from the USSR is a comparatively routine affair.[18] Indeed, one of the deputies who backed the proposed enactment (Paputin) reported to his fellow delegates that the procedure for handling the formalities with reference to foreign trips had been simplified and the time required to examine applications to go abroad had now been shortened. According to him, the overwhelming majority of citizens who apply to the organs of internal affairs for visas to travel abroad with the object of family reunification or for other motives — tourism, excursions, medical treatment — receive such permission in the prescribed manner.[19]

The aforementioned reforms involve internal administrative operations and, since the relevant instructions are not published, the truth of these statements cannot be verified. Nor can we, by consulting the appropriate departmental files, check what percentage of applications for foreign travel meet with success and whether the ratio of approvals versus rejections would warrant the conclusion that, indeed, the average Soviet citizen has a right to leave the country, subject perhaps to certain reasonable restraints, or, on the contrary, the experience occurs too rarely and unpredictably to testify to the existence here of a right in the normal sense of that word.[20] From the accounts of those who have had a taste of how the system functions, the latter seems to convey a truer picture of the policy followed in this sector thus far.

To be sure, people are currently being allowed to leave the USSR and the exodus has, on occasion, even assumed rather impressive proportions. The point that needs to be made in this connection, though, is that the size, composition and mechanics of the efflux continue to depend, to the best of our knowledge, entirely on administrative dispensation and are not governed by legal routine, so that one cannot really peg the practical phenomenon of emigration to effective exercise by the individual concerned of a personal right to travel abroad at will. By the same token, nothing in the Soviet record to date justifies the idea that a given course of action, sustained over a period of time, can eventually acquire precedential value and lock the regime into observance of a particular pattern of behavior. The authorities may encounter a few snags in a bid to reverse a policy that has managed to generate certain expectations among different sectors of the population, but their final decision in such a case will be determined by considerations of expediency and not by fears that they might be violating a normative relationship developed through prescription if they instituted changes in the rules of the game in mid–stride.[21]

To complicate the situation further, the concept that citizenship status and freedom to travel are separate entities is for the most part not valid in the Soviet context. Remember that the bulk of the present traffic from the USSR consists of people (primarily Jews) who must obtain permission to "resign" from Soviet citizenship before the regime will let them emigrate. And, as was noted earlier, the process of renunciation of Soviet citizenship operates in accordance not with the preferences of the interested private party but those of the state apparatus. Under these circumstances, where no prior right to relinquish Soviet citizenship exists, the corollary right of departure is hopelessly compromised too. The individual's "right ... to return to his country" confirmed in the Universal Declaration turns out to be equally ephemeral when measured by these standards. A person who is required to surrender his Soviet citizenship as the price for getting an exit visa cannot then assert a right to reenter the USSR — having forfeited that claim upon agreeing to give up his Soviet citizenship as a precondition to be allowed to expatriate himself.[22]

On a number of recent occasions, the Soviet government has also used an alternate tactic with similar results: an individual will be authorized to travel outside the USSR on the strength of his Soviet passport and, while abroad, his passport will be lifted or his citizenship revoked by decree of the federal Presidium (pursuant to the broad terms of the statute), leaving him stranded in some foreign land and unable to return to the Soviet Union. Since both deprivation of and reinstatement in Soviet citizenship work by executive discretion alone, one can hardly speak of a bona fide "right to return" when a person can be summarily (and randomly) stripped of Soviet citizenship and thereby barred from recrossing the frontiers of his country of origin and kept in exile as long as his ex–Motherland wishes by the simple medium of unilaterally refusing to restore his Soviet citizenship.[23]

2. International Covenant on Civil and Political Rights

Soviet spokesmen also like to emphasize the compatibility of the various clauses of the new statute with corresponding dicta of the International Covenant on Civil and Political Rights. Save for one instance, the latter document does not directly deal with the topic of citizenship. However, Article 12 proclaims, inter alia, that "everyone shall be free to leave any country, including his own". Furthermore, this right is not to be "subject to any restrictions except those which are provided by law, are necessary to protect national security, public order *(ordre public)*, public health or morals or the rights and freedoms of others, and are consistent with the other rights recognized in the present Covenant". The last paragraph adds that "no one shall be arbitrarily deprived of the right to enter his own country".

Of course, a link can — and, in the Soviet case, does — exist between the phenomena of emigration, repatriation and citizenship which, in effect, is how Soviet commentators choose to look at the situation. According to them,[24] the foremost area of coincidence of the statute and the Covenant resides in the full conformity of the latest law's instructions concerning the manner of loss and deprivation of Soviet citizenship with the above propositions. To that end, they point out that exit from Soviet citizenship is permitted solely by the Presidium of the USSR Supreme Soviet, recite the specific reasons named in the current legislation as grounds for refusing a request for denaturalization and underline that termination of Soviet citizenship can occur only in extraordinary circumstances.

The wording of the Covenant here closely approximates that of the Universal Declaration. Thus, the theme has already been explored in that context and the doubts expressed then regarding the validity of the Soviet position on the inherent similarity of the 1978 citizenship act and the Declaration on these questions extend to the statute–Covenant relationship as well.[25] One difference between the Covenant and the Declaration in this sector is the former's reference to the limitations which can be imposed on the exercise of the designated rights. Although the language used in this connection is of the most general kind and obviously requires detailed elaboration at the municipal level, plain logic dictates that such qualifications cannot be so broadly conceived as to allow the destruction of the right itself. Outwardly, the reservations formulated in the statute can be squared with the common tenor of the Covenant's pronouncements on that score.[26] As noted earlier, however, the way in which the regime has in the past seen fit to interpret and apply these rules has in practice amounted to a negation of the right per se and its replacement by a decision–making procedure marked by systematic administrative manhandling of human aspirations with respect to choice of national domicile and the associated matter of citizenship affiliation.

More problematic is the issue of what meaning ought to be ascribed to the Covenant's clause (Art.24–3) postulating that "every child has the right to acquire a nationality" — the text's single express mention of the citizenship item. Again, Soviet analysts see the intent of this dictum duly realized in the provisions of Articles 12, 13, 14 and 21 of the current law which define the status of children when one of the parents is a citizen of the USSR, when both parents are stateless or their identity is unknown, and when just one parent acquires Soviet citizenship.[27] A glance at the record shows that, if by acquisition is meant the peremptory assignment of Soviet citizenship to a minor by virtue of fulfillment of certain objective criteria, the conclusion is warranted that Soviet legislation now endorses comprehensive and fairly generous standards for conferring Soviet citizenship on children adapted to assorted contingencies. On the whole, the coverage is sufficiently inclusive for these purposes to forestall most of the risk of the minor contracting statelessness through the blind operation of conflict–of–law principles. Assuming for the sake of argument, then, that the concept of a right to a nationality in this instance equals unilateral state intervention in order to institute adequate protection from an unwilling brush with statelessness, the Soviet contention that the present statute meets the Covenant's expectations on that account makes considerable sense.

On the other hand, in the event that the "right to a nationality" is understood as affording the individual an opportunity to assert title to citizenship on his own behalf or, as in this affair, on behalf of a dependent minor even against the contrary desires of the competent state agencies, Soviet experience categorically demonstrates that the interested individual has no prospect at all of making the official apparatus defer to his wishes in this type of case. Hence, where a child's possession of Soviet citizenship hinges not on automatic classification in that capacity by the grace of the Soviet authorities but on the outcome of a personal initiative to obtain the child's acceptance into Soviet citizenship, the naturalization mechanism functioning in the USSR today does not, as previously indicated, offer any assurance that the petition for admission will in fact succeed. Quite the reverse, the state enjoys exclusive jurisdiction in this domain and whatever the individual can still do in such a situation to further his cause does not rate as a "right" in any normal parlance.

Characteristically, by addressing themselves to the subject of a "right to a nationality" solely within the framework of Articles 12, 13, 14 and 21 of the citizenship act, Soviet glossators manage to confine the discussion to one aspect of the agenda alone — namely, the viability of the means available for letting minors attain Soviet citizenship, with further emphasis on the effectiveness of acquisition through ex parte assignment rather than in conjunction with an individual's expression here of free choice. What is never mentioned, of course, is the right to a nationality in terms of a minor's right to trade Soviet citizenship for a different status. The omission is a curious one. Soviet law contains strict safeguards against the likelihood that minors owning the citizenship of the USSR could somehow end up as stateless persons and elaborate technical precautions are taken to perpetuate their Soviet citizenship in circumstances where it might otherwise be forfeited. Whether this policy stems from a genuine concern to spare children the adversities of statelessness or an urge to retain maximum control over the fate of the younger generation (and through the latter influence the attitude of the parents as well) is open to debate.[28] The fact nonetheless remains that the child's freedom to transfer from Soviet to foreign citizenship is rigidly circumscribed, allegedly to guarantee that the minor does not lose the benefits of Soviet citizenship as a consequence of the responsible adults' lack of foresight or by falling into the empty spaces which often develop when the corresponding norms featured in the competing legal systems do not match.

Hence, if one proceeds from the premise that the right to a nationality should encompass not only suitable protection from unintentional occurrence of statelessness in the wake of lapse of the original citizenship, but also the affirmative right to switch valid nationalities, the latter version cannot be said to be a recognized part of the Soviet repertory. The reason why Soviet commentators choose to ignore it thus becomes quite clear and, in turn, their silence on this score casts added doubt on the existence of such a right in either Soviet legal theory or practice.

3. Convention on the Nationality of Married Women

Our attention is next drawn to the total congruence between the new statute and the 1957 Convention on the Nationality of Married Women, which the USSR has ratified. Article 4 of the latest legislation which stipulates that "acquisition or loss of the citizenship of the USSR by one spouse does not entail any change in the citizenship of the other spouse" is singled out as an "important guarantee of the full independence of each spouse".[29] Equally relevant, however, is the preceding paragraph of the same clause which explains that entry into marriage by a male or female citizen of the USSR with a person possessing a foreign citizenship or a stateless person, as well as the dissolution of such a marriage, involves no change in the citizenship of the spouses.

Both formulas echo the language of the Convention, designed to insulate the juridical position of the woman in the area of citizenship from possible adverse effects arising out of matrimony with or divorce from a foreign partner or the husband's subsequent change of nationality. In this respect, the woman enjoys full security under Soviet law and, inasmuch as she is barred from automatically following in her husband's footsteps, her quality as a separate juridical entity in this sphere is unassailable.

However, in this case too, Soviet spokesmen concentrate on one facet of the problem and willfully disregard another that is as significant. Note that Article 3, para. 1 of the Convention goes on to affirm that "each Contracting State agrees that the alien wife of one of its nationals may, at her request, acquire the nationality of her husband through specially privileged naturalization procedures", adding that "the grant of such nationality may be subject to such limitations as may be imposed in the interests of national security or public policy". Despite this provision, the present citizenship act (like its predecessor) nowhere authorizes an easing of the regular modus operandi that would amount to the implementation of the proposed "specially privileged naturalization procedures".

To be sure, Soviet law does not attach any specific conditions for the acquisition of Soviet citizenship through naturalization: no fixed waiting periods, economic requirements, or personal qualifications, except that the candidate must satisfy sundry "moral" criteria attesting to eligibility for membership in the Soviet community. From the standpoint of material attributes, then, naturalization can be literally instantaneous and the regime can bestow Soviet citizenship on an applicant whenever it chooses to, thereby ostensibly dispensing with the need to relax the relevant regulations in order to institute the extra "privileges" called for by the Convention. In principle, this may all be true, but, at the same time, the absence of any formal commitment to abide by a defined code of conduct also means that the official apparatus is free to do as it pleases and to decide on its own when an individual deserves to receive Soviet citizenship and when he has not earned that signal honor. Under the circumstances, naturalization can be incredibly swift — if the competent organs set their mind to expedite matters — or the affair can drag on forever because the appropriate agencies are bound by no hard rules or deadlines and can both reject a petition and delay an answer at will without openly violating any prescribed standard. Plainly put, the theoretical prospect that practice here will follow a simplified route is no real substitute for concrete assurances that the authorities are prepared to perform routinely in this manner and that a style which, stricto sensu, is only optional will in fact be treated as mandatory, with due regard to the reasonable limitations sanctioned by the Convention.

Another side of the problem must now be considered. Inasmuch as the parties to the Convention have formally recognized that the alien wife of one of their nationals could, at her request, acquire her husband's nationality "through specially privileged naturalization procedures" the logic of the situation requires that each of them adopt a policy enabling these "simplified procedures" to operate properly. When one state accepts that a second state has the right forthwith to grant its nationality to the former's citizen in certain designated cases, a natural consequence would be for the first state to facilitate the arrangement by letting the citizen in question leave its citizenship in similar uncomplicated fashion, else the original acquiescence will really have achieved very little. Note, too, that while the Convention was, in all likelihood, primarily motivated by the desire to protect the married woman from incurring statelessness, its concern extended to other issues arising out of conflicts in law as well. For example, the preamble expressly referred to Article 15 of the Universal Declaration and, inter alia, its clause to the effect that "no one shall be arbitrarily deprived of his nationality nor denied the right to change his nationality".

In sum, difficulties stemming from the inception of dual nationality would also seem to be a legitimate object of interest in this connection and, coupled with reiteration of the right to change nationality, the reasonable conclusion would be that the Convention further had in mind acceptance by the signatory states of a suitable method of prompt denaturalization to coincide with the principle of "easy" naturalization they were henceforward expected to apply in their mutual relations. Soviet law makes no such accommodation. Under Soviet conditions, even regular denaturalization is, as already mentioned, conceived as the exclusive prerogative of the state and does not in practice amount to an affirmative right vested in the individual, so that to speak of "special privileges" on this occasion sounds rather far-fetched. Of course, since Soviet law contains no blueprint of the process of denaturalization, the point can validly be made that the existing mechanism is geared to function rapidly enough to render additional concessions redundant. In the absence of a set routine, the business can be handled virtually at a moment's notice, provided the authorities favor a quick solution. By the same token, however, the regime can take as long as it wants and technically still not contravene any of its own rules. Again, practice, no matter how potentially benign, is not the equivalent of a prescribed modus operandi that establishes a fixed pattern on which the individual can rely to figure his options.

According to official reports, several thousand Soviet citizens have recently married foreigners, many have sought permission to join their spouse abroad and have been allowed to do so, and the rest have not yet indicated a desire to emigrate.[30] The story cannot be verified. Well worth remembering, though, is the fact that, pursuant to the regulations now in force, the cost of expatriation/denaturalization varies dramatically depending on whether the individual involved intends to relocate to a "socialist–Third World" or "capitalist" destination.[31] Such flagrant discrimination runs counter to the letter and the spirit of the Convention. Just in absolute terms — disregarding for an instant the invidious distinctions instituted here by the relevant directives — the price alone of moving to a "capitalist" country cannot be squared with the notion of "privileged procedures", leaving one to wonder at how selective the vision of Soviet commentators must be if, despite all the evidence to the contrary, they can nonetheless pronounce the new citizenship act in total harmony with the Convention.

4. Convention on the Reduction of Statelessness

The Soviet Union never signed the above Convention, allegedly because its text featured "certain discriminatory articles".[32] Yet, we are told, the general thrust of the Convention aimed at curbing statelessness conforms to the Soviet view of the problem. In particular, our attention is drawn to Article 13 of the 1978 citizenship law which declares that "a child born on the territory of the USSR of stateless persons who maintain a permanent place of residence in the USSR is a citizen of the USSR".

Normally, one would not spend much time analyzing the degree to which Soviet citizenship legislation does or does not comply with the contents of this Convention, since the latter does not bind the USSR. However, since Soviet spokesmen themselves have seen fit to engage in comparison, perhaps a closer look at the record would be warranted. Needless to say, singling out Article 13 does not convey the whole picture and, indeed, gives an entirely wrong impression of the extent to which the language of the statute resembles that of the Convention.

To begin with, it must be admitted that the claim concerning Article 13 and its essential correspondence to the Convention's position on this issue is correct. For that matter, careful examination of the substance of the Soviet citizenship act reveals an evident appreciation by its authors of the value of prophylactic measures designed to control the occurrence of statelessness. Thus, little room is left for the accidental inception of the phenomenon of statelessness under the existing provisions of Soviet law, especially where the status of children is at stake. The observation holds for both children of foreign origin brought into contact with Soviet citizenship law and children of Soviet origin confronted with the experience of "converting" from Soviet citizenship to a foreign nationality. Ample protection is offered in either situation against an unexpected encounter with statelessness.

However, on most other counts Soviet performance in this domain falls short of the standards advocated by the Convention. For example, the latter also attaches a great deal of importance to the question of availability of sufficient remedies to deal with registered cases of statelessness: prevention is fine, but an effective cure is no less necessary. Here, Soviet law fails to meet the test. The only solution it underwrites is common naturalization and, as we know, that procedure is fraught with too many uncertainties to furnish a satisfactory answer to the present problem. To repeat an earlier remark, as long as naturalization is purely a function of executive–administrative discretion, the key element of predictability is missing and the interested individual cannot safely count on the rules being applied in a way that would afford him fair treatment.

The sin of omission is bad enough, but it is overshadowed by other flaws in Soviet practice in this area of a far more critical nature. For instance, the Convention recommends that individuals be allowed to retain their current nationality while seeking to acquire a different one until they have managed to gain a new identity or are guaranteed that their efforts in this connection will succeed. Soviet law sticks to the opposite view and takes the attitude that the individual who wants to shed his citizenship does so at his own risk — in short, once the person has formally expressed preference for another citizenship and the competent agencies have given their approval, the individual is abandoned to his private devices and, to all intents, and purposes, is cast adrift by the Soviet authorities to fend for himself. If the venture results in statelessness, the individual alone is responsible for the mishap and the Soviet government assumes no obligation to bail him out by keeping his Soviet citizenship alive until such time as he finds escape from a predicament for which he has only himself to blame.

Similarly, no reconciliation is possible between official Soviet policy on the subject of deprivation of individuals of their Soviet citizenship and the tenor of the Convention's pronouncements on that score. Unilateral revocation of a person's citizenship is, of course, a prime source of statelessness in our times and the Convention, quite rightly, tries to restrict the use of this power by the state. By contrast, the Soviet regime has turned a deaf ear to all such appeals and continues to inflict statelessness on former citizens of the USSR on a greater scale than ever before. Specific individuals whose behavior displeases the Soviet authorities are either allowed or pressured to go abroad and, once outside the USSR, they learn that their Soviet citizenship has been annulled: the decision is final and the victim is given no opportunity to file a protest or argue his case. In addition, thousands of people have been required to surrender their Soviet citizenship in order to receive exit permits and this mass of emigrés crosses the Soviet frontier stripped of Soviet citizenship and left to be taken care of by others, with the Soviet government shrugging off any further responsibility for their fate. Obviously, for as long as the Soviet apparatus feels free to indulge in the wholesale manufacture of stateless exiles to satisfy its ideological and political preconceptions, the USSR's contribution to the task of reducing the number of stateless persons floating around in search of a permanent home will be distinguished principally by its negative qualities.

5. Final Act of the Helsinki Conference

Lastly, Soviet contentions[33] that the new citizenship statute incorporates the principles adopted at the Helsinki Conference and included in the Final Act's chapter addressed to the theme of cooperation in humanitarian and other fields call for a brief assessment.

The Helsinki text does not explicitly mention the topic of citizenship. Instead, it concentrates on problems connected with contacts and regular meetings on the basis of family ties, the reunification of families, marriage between citizens of different states and travel for personal and professional reasons. A fair assumption, though, is that if any of the foregoing activities entail changes in the citizenship status of the persons concerned, the ancillary issue will be handled in the same generous spirit which the participants promised to display with respect to the items featured on the primary agenda. Otherwise, much of the latter's purpose could be defeated through the expedient tactic of raising technical obstacles at the secondary level whose net effect would be to bar expeditious access to the main benefits spelled out in the master script.

Logic may dictate such a conclusion, but the Soviet law–makers seem to be tuned to a different wavelength. Even though the citizenship statute does not expressly refer to the topic of expatriation — presumably on the grounds that sojourn abroad and denaturalization are discrete concepts — the fact remains that emigration from the USSR today is, in the main, contingent on prior denaturalization. The official fiction thus makes little sense in practice, except that the scenario lets the Soviets pretend that each affair is a relatively simple matter since neither is unduly complicated by association with the other. The real linkage between the two means, of course, that travel abroad is ordinarily subject to the vagaries of Soviet policy on denaturalization which, as repeatedly indicated earlier, follows the principle that the individual does not have a personal right to divest himself of Soviet citizenship and that administrative fiat alone determines who will be allowed to take that step, and when, and under what conditions.

Ultimately, the easing of departure procedures for purposes of family reunification in accordance with the recommendations of the Helsinki Conference therefore depends in virtually all cases on the regime evincing a more benevolent attitude toward the issue of denaturalization. Since the process of denaturalization is governed by no specific rules and is premised on the supremacy of ad hoc dispensation, the award or denial of that favor normally decides the fate of the application for foreign travel as well. After looking at the record, one can only end up with the impression that the Soviet authorities have used the requirement of antecedent denaturalization to make a mockery of the humanitarian clauses of the Helsinki charter: indeed, the machinery of denaturalization runs so unpredictably that its operation effectively stymies the international community's attempts to open channels for human traffic motivated by the impulse to bring divided families together again.

To be sure, people are now leaving the USSR in significant numbers and the efflux is technically credited to the Soviet Union's successful management of a program of family reunification in conformity with the letter and the spirit of the USSR's diplomatic commitments, among which the Helsinki protocols. Physical proof of emigration of a certain quantum of individuals is not the bottomline, however. Equally important here is the quality of the bureaucracy's performance and, as far as we can tell, on that score the general picture is bleak: the waiting period tends to be long (contrary to the Final Act's call for speeding up the system); requests for exit permits are often turned down and either no reason is given for the refusal[34] or some stock formula is recited which sheds no light on the situation; no institution is available to serve as a review board before which the interested party can plead his cause; the competent agencies claim the executive right to certify when the relatives abroad are, in their opinion, sufficiently close kin to the petitioner to constitute a sample of "family reunification" and to figure when the blood– ties are too loose to exert the necessary attraction;[35] the opportunity to emigrate itself, ostensibly designed to promote family unity, has frequently been extended on terms that have occasioned fresh rifts in existing family entities — children have been allowed to leave and their parents kept behind, and vice versa; spouses have been separated.[36] Even when prior denaturalization is not treated as a prerequisite to departure from the USSR, households have been split, with many known instances of a wife and children being prevented from joining the husband and father abroad, or the other way around.[37]

At the prosaic level of administrative routine, one discovers a similar style. For example, the Final Act expects the parties to lower where necessary the fees charged in connection with applications to go abroad with family reunification in mind, in order to ensure that the amount due is moderate. Though some adjustments have recently been made in the local price–list, the expense of the paperwork for the average Soviet petitioner is still sizable and, when the cost of relinquishing Soviet citizenship is added to the bill, the outlay puts a serious strain on the typical native's financial resources. The result is an extra hurdle to be surmounted by those seeking to quit the USSR and a further stumbling–block in the path of the freer movement of individuals for reasons recognized as legitimate by the states assembled at Helsinki.[38]

* * *

To make a long story short, after weighing the objective evidence, one can but marvel at the official speakers' bravado performance in the august chambers of the Supreme Soviet, for they managed to deliver a script whose most notable feature lies in its glib disregard of the truth in attributing virtues to the latest piece of Soviet citizenship legislation in reference to human rights which must remain invisible to independent students of the record.

NOTES

1. V.V. Kuznetsov, *Pravda* and *Izvestiia*, Dec.2. 1978.
2. V.I. Prokhorov, V.I. Terebilov, and V.S. Paputin, *Izvestiia*, Dec.3, 1978.
3. *Pravda*, Dec.4, 1978.
4. *Izvestiia*, Dec.5, 1978.
5. Soviet legal analysts have, of course, raised objections on these grounds, maintaining, inter alia, that "the declaration of the UN General Assembly is not equivalent to an international treaty and, like other resolutions of the UN General Assembly, represents a recommendation which is not juridically binding on states". G.I. Tunkin, "Zakon o grazhdanstve SSSR", *Sovetskoe gosudarstvo i pravo*, 1979, No.7, p.29 (hereafter abbr. as *SGiP*).
6. For example, N.V. Vitruk, "Grazhdanstvo kak pravovaia sviaz' lichnosti s gosudarstvom", *Problemy gosudarstva i prava*, Moscow 1976, vyp.12, p.18, refers to Art.15 of the Declaration as reflecting "the progressive ideas that found embodiment in an international law document" and whose effectuation wholly depended on legal regulation by the corresponding propositions of national legislation on citizenship. The reliance on domestic jurisdiction does not deny the model role of the Declaration which, furthermore, is here phrased in legal terms.
7. Note, for instance, that B.V. Shchetinin, *Problemy teorii sovetskogo gosudarstvennogo prava*, Moscow 1974, pp.179–180, claims that the central idea expressed in Art.15 of the Declaration was first incarnated in Lenin's Decree on the abolition of estates and civil ranks and that subsequent Soviet legislation and practice on questions of citizenship invariably adhered to this principle.
8. Thus, G.I. Tunkin, *op. cit.*, p.26, associates with the same progressive trend the new statute's featuring of a clause prescribing that a child born on the territory of the USSR to stateless persons permanently residing in the USSR counts as a citizen of the USSR (Art.13).
9. The notion of a separate institutional "arbiter" between the state and the individual does not fit Soviet public doctrine. Typically, S.V. Chernichenko, *Mezhdunarodno–pravovye voprosy grazhdanstva*, Moscow 1968, pp.155–156, criticizes the concept incorporated in Art.8 of the 1961 Convention on the Reduction of Statelessness of entrusting consideration of the question of deprivation of citizenship to some sort of "independent" organ. In his words: "There are no state organs independent of the state. Furthermore, in those states where deprivation of citizenship falls within the competence of the supreme organs of state authority, this question cannot be the object of judicial proceedings".
10. V.S. Paputin, *loc. cit.* The delegate has been identified as First Deputy Minister of Internal Affairs of the USSR with the rank of Lieutenant General and his death in Afghanistan on December 28, 1979, was linked to the events surrounding the coup that deposed President Amin. See *New York Times*, Feb.3, 1980, p.10.

    The claim that the administrative routine had been simplified and speeded up is not new and could merely be confirming organizational changes made earlier. Already in January 1977, a newspaper story reported that "for purposes of further development of contacts between Soviet and foreign citizens on the basis of family and personal ties and to ease the procedure of travel abroad and entry into the USSR for personal matters, the time–limits for considering applications relating thereto have recently been cut in half". V. Itkin, "Myl'nye puzyri i real'nye fakty", *Izvestiia*, Jan.23, 1977.
11. The courts were excluded long ago from deciding questions of entitlement to Soviet citizenship. See Order of the USSR Ministry of Justice No.9/1937, referring to a 1930

directive whereby the right to issue certificates of possession of the citizenship of this or that state was vested in the city Soviets or executive committees whose staff included special departments or sections. *Spravochnik po voprosam sudebnoi praktiki*, comp. by S.S. Askarkhanov and A.N. Iodkovskii, Moscow 1937, pp.145–146. Under the terms of the federal decree of June 15, 1979, *VVS SSSR*, 1979, No.25, Art.436, these affairs are now entrusted to the organs of internal affairs and, in respect to people residing abroad, the corresponding diplomatic or consular representatives of the USSR. Appeals from their decision may be filed with the national Presidium.

Admission to Soviet citizenship can be sanctioned by federal or republican presidia and, presumably, a negative decision at the republican level may be reexamined by the federal Presidium by virtue of its residual power to adopt for consideration any "other applications on questions of Soviet citizenship". Only the USSR Presidium can sanction deprivation and renunciation of Soviet citizenship which excludes all prospect of higher review, except by the USSR Supreme Soviet itself — possible, but most unlikely. In the case of renunciation, however, since the OVIR/UVIR system that handles emigration must also take into account denaturalization that accompanies much of the expatriation program the question has been raised as to whether the USSR Presidium has delegated the actual decision–making authority to the OVIR/UVIR apparatus and the conclusions of the latter's local branches can be protested in accordance with general procedure for dealing with citizens' complaints or petitions. The impression, though, is that OVIR/UVIR has thereby inherited the mantle of the Presidium's own immunity since even in its processing of exit applications it does not seem to be bound to observe the standard 2–month deadline which the law sets for deciding petitions filed by citizens. (See *Khronika tekushchikh sobytii* (Moscow, Samizdat, 1980), New York, 1981, vyp.60, p.77.) Renunciation not being a right, the citizen concerned has no juridical grounds on which to submit a formal protest requiring an official response and privileges receive discretionary treatment by the interested administrative institutions who operate on the basis of unilateral dispensation and not from any sense of obligation.

12. Overlooking, of course, the fact that the so–called denaturalization practiced in connection with the majority of cases of expatriation verge on deprivation, despite efforts to paint a different picture. In a statement dated Dec.29, 1973, and addressed to the UN Secretary General, Waldheim, the Presidium of the USSR Supreme Soviet and the Soviet committee on human rights, a group of Russian Jews seeking to emigrate, pointed out, inter alia, that: "In the TASS release of December 25 of this year it is asserted that several hundred Soviet Jews who left the USSR for Israel and want to come back will not receive permission to return on the grounds that nobody ostensibly forced them earlier to renounce Soviet citizenship.

This assertion is a lie. Every Jew over 16 years of age leaving the USSR for Israel is compelled by the Soviet authorities to pay 500 rubles tax for divestiture of citizenship even though none of the emigrants requests to be relieved of the citizenship of the USSR and fills out the documents required by law for exit from citizenship." *Khronika zashchity prav v SSSR*, 1974, vyp.7, pp.33–34.

13. The doctrinal underpinnings for resort by the Soviet state to the artifact of unilateral revocation of an individual's citizenship were provided by the Soviet representative to the International Law Commission in the course of debates on the Draft Conventions on the Future Elimination (and Reduction) of Statelessness, when he stated:

"The question of deprivation of nationality must be examined further, since it involved a number of general philosophical considerations. There were some states where moral and policital identity between the individual and the State had been achieved and clearly sanctions must be brought to bear against individuals whose acts tended to destroy or undermine that identity."

[1952/1] *Yearbook of the International Law Commission*, p.111, as quoted in H.–J. Uibopuu, "Soviet Nationality: Privilege or Burden? An International Lawyer's View", *Israel Yearbook on Human Rights*, 1977, Vol.7, p.56.

The appeal to some metaphysical communion lets the state decide when and how the spirit of unity has been disrupted and mete out appropriate punishment to the transgressor who may be hard put to figure out, given the vagueness of the terms, wherein lies his guilt, except for incurring the regime's displeasure.

14. Cf. the statement by the Soviet delegate on the occasion of the discussion of the draft of the Universal Declaration on Human Rights to the effect that

"he could not accept the inclusion of the right to change nationality. That was not appropriate in the Declaration. The United Nations should not, in any case, encourage changes of nationality, but should respect the relations between States and individuals."

A/C.3/SR.123, at 350, as quoted in H.–J. Uibopuu, *op. cit.*, p.55.

15. According to official Soviet sources, for instance, the self–same list of "disqualifications" applies to the emigration process, yet we have the following examples here of bureaucratic "creativity". When A.A. Galich was trying to get permission to go abroad, he was suddenly informed at one point that refusal to let him leave was motivated by "fears of an ideological character", a novel theme that immediately drew dissident criticism for opening the door to rampant administrative capriciousness in dealing with exit applications (*Khronika zashchity prav v SSSR*, vyp.7, pp.20–21). Equally new and unenlightening was the formal explanation furnished to V. Nekipelov who was told that

"your request to emigrate for permanent residence in Israel and renounce the citizenship of the USSR cannot be fulfilled since your relative residing in Israel is not a member of your family and exit from the citizenship of the USSR runs counter to the interests of the USSR".

Khronika tekushchikh sobytii (Moscow, Samizdat, 1979), New York, 1980, vyp.53, pp.139–140.

16. It is therefore ironic to hear Soviet spokesmen pontificate that the Declaration is correctly perceived by bourgeois lawyers as an act establishing limits not to be crossed by the omnipotent machine of state power in its relations with its own citizens, but that such a vision would simply be inappropriate in reference to the socialist states "since the very nature of socialist state power excludes any manifestation of usurpation of rights of citizenship". B.V. Shchetinin, *op. cit.*, pp.180– 181.

17. Curious euphemisms are sometimes used to mask this aversion. One account notes, for instance, that:

"Soviet authorities adamantly refuse to recognize the right of emigration but attempt to obscure this fact by arguing — as a high Soviet official in charge of emigration did on the eve of the Madrid CSCE Meeting — that the USSR 'lacks objective conditions for the development of emigration as a social phenomenon'."

Country Reports on Human Rights Practices, Report submitted to the Committee on Foreign Relations US Senate and Committee on Foreign Affairs US House of Representatives by the Department of State, February 2, 1981, p.904.

For a good analysis of the Soviet record in this area, see M.A. Robin, "Soviet Emigration Law and International Obligations under United Nations Instruments", *Journal of International Law and Economics*, 1979, pp.403–431.

18. Viz. the reports by the USSR and BSSR, *Report of the Human Rights Committee*, General Assembly, Official Records: 33rd session, Supplement No.40 (A/33/40), New York 1978, pp.74, 92; in 1972 Soviet sources claimed that all applications for the departure of Jews to Israel were or would be approved and that "only considerations of state security

or family response could serve as an obstacle to issuance of permits to emigrate", *Khronika zashchity prav v SSSR*, 1973, vyp.1, p.21; "The Law and the Rights of Man in the USSR", in *Human Rights: International Documents*, ed. by J.A. Joyce, Alphen aan den Rijn, The Netherlands, 1978, Vol.2, pp.1137–1138.

19. See V.S. Paputin, *loc. cit.* Likewise, V. Itkin, *loc. cit.*

20. For concrete data documenting that the Soviet government does not recognize the general right of its citizens to emigrate and that those who apply to leave "often find the process costly, lengthy, complicated, arbitrary, and uncertain in its results", plus occasionally fraught with personal hardship due to official penalization of attempts to emigrate, see *Implementation of the Helsinki Accord*, semiannual reports issued by the US Department of State, Bureau of Public Affairs, of which ten numbers have appeared so far. For an excellent analysis and critique of Soviet emigration practices, see M.Z. Novikov, "Pravovye voprosy repatriatsii", *Khronika zashchity prav v SSSR*, 1978, vyp.29, pp.35–42.

21. The precipitous decline in the volume of Jewish emigration from the USSR is a good indication of the regime's ability to reverse previous trends with virtual impunity. The level recorded for 1981 — 9,249 — was the lowest for the past decade: 21,471 Jews left the USSR in 1980 and 51,320 in 1979 (the record high) and since 1970 no fewer than 13,000 Jews had left the Soviet Union in any single calendar year. For current coverage, see *New York Times*, Feb. 22, 1980, p.A3; June 7, 1980, p.7; July 11, 1980, p.A2; Nov. 4, 1980, p.A9; Nov. 12, 1980, p.A3; Jan. 4, 1981, p.15; Feb. 14, 1981, p.24; Mar. 19, 1981, p.A9; Apr. 9, 1981, p.A6; Sept. 2, 1981, p.A5; Dec. 15, 1981, p.A3; Dec.31, 1981, p.A3. Also, *Philadelphia Inquirer*, Apr. 13, 1980, p.27–A; *The Korea Herald*, Oct. 9, 1980, p.4, and "The Decline of Soviet Jewish Emigration in 1980", Institute of Jewish Affairs *Research Report* No.17, October 1980.

In mid–1981, the US Department of State reported that the emigration of Armenians from the USSR was leveling off because no new applications for emigration had been accepted since May 1980 "on purportedly technical grounds" and the processing time for those who applied for exit permission before May 1980 had lengthened. Meantime, ethnic German emigration had also declined. *Implementation of Helsinki Final Act, Dec. 1, 1980 — May 31, 1981*, 10th semiannual report, Special Report No.85, p.16.

22. See footnote 12 above. On March 16, 1978, Hodding Carter III, the Department of State's Spokesman was asked to comment on the Soviet actions to strip Soviet citizenship from M. Rostropovich, G. Vishnevskaia and P.G. Grigorenko who were in the United States at the time on nonimmigrant visas. He replied:

"On Rostropovich and his wife, we regret that the Soviet Union has seen fit to take this unnecessary action. In our view, this is in conflict with internationally accepted standards of human rights as set forth in such documents as the Final Act of the Helsinki Conference on Security and Cooperation in Europe, which states that 'Everyone has the right to leave any country, including his own, and to return to his country'.

...[I]n relation to General Grigorenko ... while we don't know of any relationship between the two actions, we believe that the same principles of human rights are applicable and, therefore, the general statement would have to be the same."

Quoted in *Digest of United States Practice in International Law 1978*, Department of State Publication 9162, Washington, D.C., December 1980, pp.368–369.

23. For the recent cases of Aksenov, Kopelev and Orlova, see *New York Times*, Jan. 23, 1981, p.A5.

24. E.g., V.V. Kuznetsov, *loc. cit.*; editorial in *Izvestiia*, Dec. 5, 1978.

25. M.A. Robin, *op.*cit., pp.418 ff.

26. A fact constantly emphasized by Soviet authors. See, for instance, V.M.

Chkhikvadze, "Prava cheloveka i ideologicheskaia bor'ba", *SGiP*, 1977, No.4, p.102. Per contra, S.J. Roth, "The New Soviet Citizenship Law and Jewish Emigration", Institute of Jewish Affairs *Research Report* USSR/79/3, July 1979, p.4, who concludes that some new burdens have been imposed on the would-be emigrant, namely: lack of forum to appeal for redress since the power to approve renunciation of Soviet citizenship vests in the central Presidium; the extension of the clause on prior fulfillment of material commitments to those owed to "state, cooperative and other public organizations"; the unlimited opportunity for restrictive policies and bureaucratic chicanery created by the provision on the duty to satisfy "unfulfilled commitments to the state".

27. V.I. Terebilov, *loc. cit.*

28. At the same time, however, the Soviet authorities strenuously object to other states following a similar practice where the interests of the USSR are affected. The most recent incident has involved a twelve-year old boy, Walter Polovchak, who has been granted permission to stay in the United States at his request and against the will of his parents who have returned to the Soviet Union. See, *New York Times*, July 21, 1980, p.A9; July 22, 1980, p.A12; August 5, 1980, p.A8; October 18, 1981, p.44. A strident campaign has been waged by Soviet spokesmen, accusing the United States of virtual kidnapping of the boy. Cf., I. Konstantinova, "Amerikanskaia femida protiv prav roditelei i detei", *Chelovek i zakon*, 1981, No.1, pp.120–123. Yet, Soviet citizenship requires a fourteen-year old minor to express his (her) own preference in matters of citizenship affiliation and, according to Soviet family law, a child who has reached the age of ten must give its consent to a proposed adoption. I.M. Kuznetsova, "Spornye voprosy usynovleniia", *Problemy sovershenstvovaniia sovetskogo zakonodatel'stva*, Moscow 1980, Trudy 17, p.127.

29. V.I. Terebilov, *loc. cit.*

30. According to "The Law and the Rights of Man in the USSR", *loc. cit.*, as of the beginning of 1976, almost 8,000 Soviet citizens (mainly women) married foreigners and more than 5,500 Soviet citizens then followed their husbands or wives to 110 countries of the world. B. Shumilin, Deputy Minister of Internal Affairs, also spoke of 5,500 Soviet citizens moving with their foreign spouses to 110 different countries, among them 544 men. A further 2,000 Soviet citizens married to foreigners had, according to him, not yet expressed any wish to emigrate "although they have every opportunity to do so". *Soviet News*, 1976, No.5819, p.35. In 1980, K. Zotov, head of OVIR, put at 15,000 the number of Soviet citizens married to foreigners and claimed that 10,500 of them left the USSR to reside in more than 100 countries. *Ibid.*, 1980, No.6024, p.183.

Official US sources estimate that about 20 percent of US–Soviet binational marriages run into some sort of difficulty, both before and after the weddings. See *CSCE Digest*, June 26, 1981, pp.7–8. Additional data are provided in the semiannual reports on the implementation of the Helsinki Accord issued by the US Department of State.

31. "Market Laws and Soviet Citizenship", *Radio Liberty Research* RL 246/77, Oct. 24, 1977, and "Soviet Emigration Fees", RL 273/77, 1977.

32. V.I. Terebilov, *loc. cit.* For a detailed critique of the provisions of the Convention, see S.V. Chernichenko, *op. cit.*, pp.154–156.

33. V.I. Prokhorov, V.S. Paputin, *loc. cit.*

34. The only known case where a written answer (negative) was given to an applicant for emigration/naturalization (V. Nekipelov, see note 15 above), it cited no substantive reason for the refusal. Similarly, the spouses Stezhko reported being told by the competent authorities that they could not leave "because they had no valid reason for migrating". *Khronika zashchity prav v SSSR*, 1973, vyp.4, p.34. The US State Department, in its 7th semiannual report on the *Implementation of Helsinki Accord*, June 1 — November 30, 1979, Special Report No.62, p.14, had occasion to note that "there has been no improve-

ment in the Soviet practice of refusing to reveal the grounds for rejection of their [refuseniks'] applications".

35. In the article by V. Itkin, *loc. cit.*, he cites examples of the Chernobylskii couple who wanted to emigrate to Israel to live with the sister of the husband's grandmother, while leaving behind in the USSR his own father, mother and sister and the wife's parents. Similarly, a certain Polishchuk was described as seeking to rejoin his aunt in Israel, leaving parents and a sister in the USSR. The Sakharovs were likewise accused of pushing E. Alekseeva to emigrate to the US to rejoin E. Bonner's son, A. Semenov, while spurning the human rights of Alekseeva's old, invalid parents to receive assistance from their daughter. L. Grigor'ev, V. Nilin, "Ocherednaia provokatsiia", *Izvestiia*, Dec. 5, 1981. See, too, *New York Times*, Dec. 13, 1981, p.11, on the eventual policy shift that let Alekseeva leave the USSR. In 1980, new reports reached the west that the Soviet authorities had again stiffened the rules on invitations from relatives abroad in the case of Jewish would–be emigrants: only letters from relatives of first–degree consanguinity, i.e., parents, children, or siblings, residing in Israel were now accepted. *New York Times*, June 8, 1980, p.3, and American Jewish Congress *Memorandum*, Sept. 22, 1980, 2 pp.

36. F. Mehl, S.E. Rapoport, "Soviet Policy of Separating Families and the Right to Emigrate", *International and Comparative Law Quarterly*, 1978, No.4, pp.876–889.

A notorious case has been that of the Lozanskys: Mrs. Lozansky divorced her husband in 1976 because, she said, Soviet emigration officials told her it was the only way he could be allowed to leave. "We don't split up families", she said the officials told her. But when she tried to join him in the United States, the officials said that was impossible because "he is not your husband anymore", *New York Times*, Feb. 1, 1981, p.37. The US Department of State's 10th semiannual report on the *Implementation of Helsinki Final Act, Dec. 1, 1980–May 31, 1981*, Special Report No.85, lists 89 nuclear and nonnuclear divided family cases involving 271 persons still unresolved.

37. The reunification of family principle only occasionally applies when the relative abroad had defected from the USSR. The experience of V. Korchnoi, separated from his wife and son, is a case in point. *New York Times*, Aug. 7, 1980, p.B20; June 10, 1982, p.A7.

38. Official Soviet spokesmen claim that in the four years since the signing of the Helsinki Final Act more than 12 million Soviet citizens had visited 135 countries, and that to facilitate such movement, the time limit for consideration of requests for departure from the USSR had been reduced by 50 percent so that foreign passports for the departure of Soviet nationals abroad were currently issued within the time limits of 15 to 30 days. K. Zotov, in *Soviet News*, 1980, No.6024, p.183. In its 10th semiannual report on the implementation of the Helsinki Accord, the US Department of State paints a different picture of a situation where the Soviet Union does "not permit personal or professional travel abroad by [its] citizens except under conditions of strict governmental control and monitoring" (p.18).

SELECTIVE BIBLIOGRAPHY

A. Books

Alliluyeva, S., *Only One Year*, New York 1969.
Askarkhanov, S.S., Iodkovskii, A.N., comps., *Spravochnik po voprosam sudebnoi praktiki*, Moscow 1937.
Avakov, M.M., *Pravopreemstvo Sovetskogo gosudarstva*, Moscow 1961.

Bardin, P.I., ed., *Nauchno–prakticheskii kommentarii k Osnovam grazhdanskogo sudoproizvodstva Soiuza SSR i soiuznykh respublik*, Moscow 1962.
Bar–Yaacov, N., *Dual Nationality*, London 1961.
Beliaev, N.S., Shargorodskii, M.D., eds., *Kurs Sovetskogo ugolovnogo prava, chast' obshchaia*, Leningrad 1968, Vol.1.
Belorusskaia SSR v mezhdunarodnykh otnosheniiakh, Minsk 1960.
Borisov, O.B. Koloskov, B.T., *Sovetsko–Kitaiskie otnosheniia 1945–1970, kratkii ocherk*, Moscow 1971.
Bratus', S.N., Samoshchenko, I.S., eds., *Teoreticheskie voprosy sistematizatsii Sovetskogo zakonodatel'stva*, Moscow 1962.
Bukovskii, V., *"I vozvrashchaetsia veter ..."*, New York 1978.

Calvez, J.–Y., *Droit international et souveraineté en URSS*, Paris 1953.
Calvocoressi, P., *Survey of International Affairs 1953*, London 1956.
Černý, J., Červenka, V., *Státní občanství ČSSR*, Prague 1963.
Chernichenko, S.V., *Mezhdunarodno–pravovye voprosy grazhdanstva*, Moscow 1968.
Chkhikvadze, V.M., ed., *Sovetskoe ugolovnoe pravo, obshchaia chast'*, Moscow 1959.

Deklaratsii, zaiavleniia i kommiunike Sovetskogo pravitel'stva s pravitel'stvami inostrannykh gosudarstv 1954–1957 gg., Moscow 1957.
Denisov, A.I., Kirichenko, M.G., *Sovetskoe gosudarstvennoe pravo*, Moscow 1957.
Digest of United States Practice in International Law 1978, Department of State

Publication 9162, Washington, D.C., December *1980.*

Diplomaticheskii slovar', Moscow 1960, Vol.1.

Diplomaticheskii slovar', Moscow 1971, Vol.1.

Dmitrieva, G.K., *Mezhdunarodnaia zashchita prav zhenshchiny*, Kiev 1975.

Dogovory ob okazanii pomoshchi po grazhdanskim, semeinym i ugolovnym delam, zakliuchennye Sovetskim Soiuzom v 1957–1958 gg., Moscow 1959.

Dogovory ob okazanii pravovoi pomoshchi po grazhdanskim, semeinym i ugo lovnym delam, zakliuchennye SSSR s drugimi sotsialisticheskimi gosudarstvami, 2nd. enl. ed., Moscow 1973.

Dokumenty i materialy po istorii Sovetsko–Polskikh otnoshenii, Moscow 1974–1976, Vols.8 and 9.

Durdenevskii, V.N., Krylov, S.B., eds., *Mezhdunarodnoe pravo*, Moscow 1947.

Egor'ev, V.V., Lashkevich, G.N., Plotkin, M.A., Rozenblium, B.D., *Zakonodatel'stvo i mezhdunarodnye dogovory Soiuza SSR i soiuznykh respublik o pravovom polozhenii inostrannykh fizicheskikh i iuridicheskikh lits*, Moscow *1926.*

Entsiklopedicheskii slovar' pravovykh znanii (Sovetskoe pravo), Moscow 1965.

Esaian, A.A., *Nekotorye voprosy Sovetskogo grazhdanstva (Voprosy naseleniia v praktike Sovetskoi Armenii)*, Erevan 1966.

Esaian, A.A., *Nekotorye voprosy teorii i istorii mezhdunarodnogo prava*, Erevan 1977.

Feldbrugge, F.J.M., ed., *Encyclopedia of Soviet Law*, Dobbs Ferry, N.Y., and Leiden 1973, Vol.2.

Flournoy, R.W., Jr., Hudson, M.O., eds., *A Collection of Nationality Laws of Various Countries as Contained in Constitutions, Statutes and Treaties*, New York 1929.

Gaidukov, D., *Grazhdanstvo SSSR*, Moscow 1940.

Geilke, G., *Das Staatsangehörigkeitsrecht der Sowjetunion*, Frankfurt–am–Main/Berlin 1964.

Geilke, G., *Das Staatsangehörigkeitsrecht der Sowjetunion*, Frankfurt–am–Main/Berlin 1964.

Gelberg, L., ed., *Prawo miedzynarodowe i historia dyplomaticzna, wybór do-* York 1978.

Ginsburgs, G., Slusser, R.M., *A Calendar of Soviet Treaties 1958–1973*, Alphen aan den Rijn, The Netherlands and Rockville, Maryland, 1981.

Gorodetskaia, I.K., *Mezhdunarodnaia zashchita prav i interesov detei*, Moscow 1973.

Grave, V.V., *Kitaitsy, koreitsy i iapontsy v Priamur'e*, St. Petersburg 1912.

Gsovski, V., *Soviet Civil Law*, Ann Arbor, 1948–1949, 2 vols.

Iakovenko, D.T., *Radianske gromadianstvo*, Kiev 1960.
Ignatenko, G.V., Ostapenko, D.D., eds., *Mezhdunarodnoe pravo*, Moscow 1978.
Il'inskii, I.P., Shchetinin, B.V., *Gosudarstvennoe pravo stran narodnoi demokratii*, Moscow *1964*.
Iuridicheskii slovar', Moscow 1953; 2nd. ed., Moscow 1956, 2 vols.
Iurkov, S.G., *Pekin: Novaia politika?*, Moscow 1972.

Kapitsa, M.S., *KNR: dva desiatiletiia — dve politiki*, Moscow 1969.
Kapitsa, M.S., *Levee zdravogo smysla (O vneshnei politike gruppy Mao)*, Moscow 1968.
Kersten, K., *Repatriacja ludności polskiej po II wójnie światowej (studium historyczne)*, Wroclaw 1974.
Khazikov, A.G., comp., *Sbornik normativnykh aktov po sovetskomu administrativnomu pravu*, Moscow 1964.
Kim Syn Khva, *Ocherki po istorii Sovetskikh Koreitsev*, Alma–Ata 1965.
Kishkin, S.S., *Sovetskoe grazhdanstvo*, Moscow 1925.
Kolarz, W., *The Peoples of the Soviet Far East*, New York 1954.
Kommentarii k Kodeksu o brake i sem'e RSFSR, Moscow 1971.
Kommentarii k zakonodatel'stvu o registratsii aktov grazhdanskogo sostoianiia, Moscow 1977.
Konstitutsiia (Osnovnoi zakon) Rossiiskoi Sovetskoi Federativnoi Sotsialisticheskoi Respubliki, Konstitutsii (Osnovnye zakony) Avtonomnykh Sovetskikh Sotsialisticheskikh Respublik, vkhodiashchikh v sostav RSFSR, Moscow 1979.
Konstitutsionnyi status lichnosti v SSSR, Moscow 1980.
Korovin, E.A., ed., *Mezhdunarodnoe pravo*, Moscow 1951.
Kotliarevskii, S.A., *SSSR i soiuznye respubliki*, Moscow 1924.
Kozhevnikov, F.I., ed., *International Law*, tr. from the Russian by Dennis Ogden, Moscow n.d.
Kozhevnikov, F.I., ed., *Kurs mezhdunarodogo prava*, 2nd. ed., Moscow 1966.
Kozhevnikov, F.I., ed., *Mezhdunarodnoe pravo*, Moscow 1957.
Kozhevnikov, F.I., ed., *Mezhdunarodnoe pravo*, Moscow 1964.
Kozhevnikov, F.I., ed., *Mezhdunarodnoe pravo*, 4th ed., Moscow 1981.
Kozhevnikov, F.I., *Sovetskoe gosudarstvo i mezhdunarodnoe pravo, 1917–1947 gg.*, Moscow 1948.
Kozlov, Iu.M, *Sovetskoe administrativnoe pravo (Obshchaia chast')*, Moscow 1962.
Kravchuk, S.S., ed., *Gosudarstvennoe pravo SSSR*, Moscow 1967.
Kravchuk, S.S., ed., *Sovetskoe gosudarstvennoe pravo*, 2nd. ed., Moscow 1975.
Kravchuk, S.S., ed., *Sovetskoe gosudarstvennoe pravo*, Moscow 1980.
Kuchinskii, V.A., *Osnovnye prava i obiazannosti grazhdan Belorusskoi SSR*, Minsk 1978.
Kulik, R.I., *Zakon o grazhdanstve SSSR*, Moscow *1980*.
Kurs mezhdunarodnogo prava, Vol.3, Moscow 1967.

Laws Concerning Nationality, United Nations Legislative Series, ST/LEG/SER. B/ 4, New York, 1954; *Supplement*, New York 1959.

Lepeshkin, A.I., *Kurs Sovetskogo gosudarstvennogo prava*, 2 Vols., Moscow 1961–1962.

Lepeshkin, A.I., ed., *Sbornik ofitsyal'nykh dokumentov (primenitel'no k kursu-Sovetskogo gosudarstvennogo prava)*, Moscow 1964.

Levin, D.B., Kaliuzhnaia, G.P., eds., *Mezhdunarodnoe pravo*, Moscow 1964.

Lisovskii, V.I. *Mezhdunarodnoe pravo*, Kiev 1955; 2nd ed., Moscow 1961.

Livre blanc sur les procédés agressifs des Gouvernements de l'URSS, de Pologne, de Tchécoslovaquie, de Hongrie, de Roumanie, de Bulgarie, et d'Albanie envers la Yougoslavie, Belgrade 1951.

Loeber, D.A., *Diktierte Option, Die Umsiedlung der Deutsch–Balten aus Estland und Lettland 1939–1941*, Neumünster 1972.

Meder, W., *Das Staatsangehörigkeitsrecht der UdSSR und der Baltischen Staaten*, Frankfurt–am–Main 1950.

Meliksetian, O.U., *Deportatsiia zapadnykh armian i repatriatsiia zarubezhnykh armian v Sovetskuiu Armeniiu 1915–1940*, Erevan 1975, in Armenian.

Menshagin, V.D., ed., *Ugolovnoe pravo, Obshchaia chast'*, Moscow 1948.

Mironov, N.V., *Pravovoe regulirovanie vneshnikh snoshenii SSSR 1917–1977 gg.*, Moscow 1971.

North Korea: A Case Study in the Techniques of Takeover, Department of State Publication 7118; Far Eastern Series 103, Washington, D.C. 1961.

Novaia Mongoliia, Ekonomiko–politicheskoe i kul'turnoe stroitel'stvo strany, Protokoly pervogo Velikogo Khuruldana Mongol'skoi Narodnoi Respubliki, Ulan–Bator–Khoto 1925.

Protokoly zasedanii Vserossiiskago Tsentral'nago Ispolnitel'nago Komiteta 4–go sozyva (stenograficheskii otchet), Moscow 1920.

Ravin, S.M., *Printsip federalizma v sovetskom gosudarstvennom prave*, Leningrad 1961.

Refugees, The Annals of the American Academy of Political and Social Science, 1939, Vol.203.

Reikhel, M.O., *Soiuz Sovetskikh Sotsialisticheskikh Respublik, Ocherk konstitutsionnykh vzaimootnoshenii sovetskikh respublik, Chast' I: Obshchaia*, Kharkov 1925.

Reikhel, M.O., ed., *Sovetskii federalizm, sbornik*, Moscow–Leningrad 1930.

Ro'i, Ya., *From Encroachment to Involvement, A Documentary Study of Soviet Policy in the Middle East, 1945–1973*, Jerusalem 1974.

Romashkin, P.S., *Amnistiia i pomilovanie v SSSR*, Moscow 1959.

Rubanov, A.A., *Zagranichnye nasledstva. Otnosheniia mezhdu sotsialisticheskimi i kapitalisticheskimi stranami*, Moscow 1975.
Ruby, M., *L'Évolution de la Nationalité Allemande d'après les textes (1842 à 1953)*, Baden–Baden *1954*.
Russkaia Tikhookeanskaia epopeia, Khabarovsk 1979.

Safronov, V.M., *Ty — grazhdanin Sovetskogo Soiuza*, Moscow 1978.
Sawyer, Th.E., *The Jewish Minority in the Soviet Union*, Boulder, Colo., and Folkestone, England 1979.
Sbornik postanovlenii Plenuma Verkhovnogo Suda SSSR 1924–1973, Moscow 1974.
Sbornik postanovlenii Plenuma Verkhovnogo Suda SSSR 1924–1977, Vol.2, Moscow 1978.
Sbornik zakonov Belorusskoi SSR i ukazov Prezidiuma Verkhovnogo Soveta Belorusskoi SSR za 1938–1955 gg., Minsk 1956.
Sbornik zakonov Kazakhskoi SSR i ukazov Prezidiuma Verkhovnogo Soveta Kazakhskoi SSR (1938–1957), Alma–Ata 1958.
Sbornik zakonov SSSR i ukazov Prezidiuma Verkhovnogo Soveta SSSR za 1947 god, Moscow 1948.
Sbornik zakonov SSSR i ukazov Prezidiuma Verkhovnogo Soveta SSSR za 1948 god, Moscow 1949.
Sbornik zakonov SSSR i ukazov Prezidiuma Verkhovnogo Soveta SSSR (1938 g.–noiabr' 1958 g.), Moscow 1959.
Shabanov, F.Sh., *Razvitie sovetskoi gosudarstvennosti v Azerbaidzhane*, Moscow 1959.
Shafir, M., *Grazhdaninom byt' obiazan*, Moscow 1972.
Shakhmatov, V.P., Khaskelberg, B.L., *Novyi kodeks o brake i sem'e RSFSR*, Tomsk 1970.
Shargorodskii, M.D., *Nakazanie po sovetskomu ugolovnomu pravu*, Moscow 1958.
Shargorodskii, M.D., Beliaev, N.S., eds., *Sovetskoe ugolovnoe pravo, chast' obshchaia*, Leningrad 1960.
Shchetinin, B.V., *Problemy teorii sovetskogo gosudarstvennogo prava*, Moscow 1974.
Shevtsov, V., *Citizenship of the USSR (A Legal Study)*, Moscow 1979.
Shevtsov, V.S., *Gosudarstvennyi suverenitet (Voprosy teorii)*, Moscow 1979.
Shevtsov, V., *Grazhdanstvo SSSR*, Moscow 1980.
Shevtsov, V.S., *Grazhdanstvo v Sovetskom soiuznom gosudarstve*, Moscow 1969.
Shevtsov, V.S., *Sovetskoe gosudarstvo i lichnost'*, Moscow 1978.
Shevtsov, V.S., *Sovetskoe grazhdanstvo*, Moscow 1965.
Shevtsov, V.S., *Suverenitet Sovetskogo gosudarstva*, Moscow 1972.
Simons, W.B., ed., *The Soviet Codes of Law*, Alphen aan den Rijn, The Netherlands 1980.
Slusser, R.M., Triska, J.F., *A Calendar of Soviet Treaties 1917–1957*, Stanford 1959.

Sovetskii Soiuz — Narodnaia Pol'sha 1944–1974, dokumenty i materialy, Moscow 1974.
*Sovetsko–Chekhoslovatskie otnosheniia 1945–1960 gg., dokumenty i materi*aly, Moscow 1972.
Sovetsko–Mongol'skie otnosheniia 1921–1966, Sbornik dokumentov, Moscow 1966.
Sovetsko–Mongol'skie otnosheniia 1921–1974, dokumenty i materialy, Vol.I, Moscow–Ulan Bator 1975.
Soviet Civil Legislation and Procedure, Official Texts and Commentaries, Moscow n.d.
Soviet Foreign Policy during the Patriotic War, documents and materials, tr. by A. Rothstein, London n.d., 2 *vols.*
Stenograficheskii otchet 2 sessii TsIK Soiuza 2 sozyva, Moscow 1924.
Studenikin, S.S., ed., *Istoriia Sovetskoi Konstitutsii (v dokumentakh), 1917– 1956*, Moscow 1957.
Strashun, G.A., *Izbiratel'noe pravo sotsialisticheskikh gosudarstv*, Moscow 1963.
Sverdlov, G.M., *Semeinoe pravo evropeiskikh stran narodnoi demokratii*, Moscow 1961.
Sverdlov, G.M., *Sovetskoe semeinoe pravo*, Moscow 1958.

Taracouzio, T.A., *The Soviet Union and International Law*, New York 1935.
Tomson, E., *Das Staatsangehörigkeitsrecht der ostasiatischen Staaten*, Frankfurt–am–Main/Berlin 1971.
Trainin, I.P., Levin, I.D., eds., *Sovetskoe gosudarstvennoe pravo*, Moscow *1948.*
Tretii s"ezd Mongol'skoi Narodnoi Partii, Urga 1924.
Tunkin, G.I., ed., *Mezhdunarodnoe pravo*, Moscow 1974.
Tunkin, G.I., *Teoriia mezhdunarodnogo prava*, Moscow 1970.

Uibopuu, H.–J., *Die Völkerrechtssubjektivität der Unionsrepubliken der UdSSR*, Vienna–New York *1975.*
Ukrainska RSR u mizhnarodnikh vidnosinakh, Kiev 1959.
Umanskii, Ia.N., *Sovetskoe gosudarstvennoe pravo*, Moscow 1960.

Vernant, J., *The Refugee in the Post–War World*, New Haven 1953.
Vikharev, S.R., *Suverenitet Belorusskoi SSR v sostave Soiuza SSR*, Minsk 1958.
Vilkov, G.E., comp., *Zakonodatel'stvo SSSR i mezhdunarodnye soglasheniia po voprosam grazhdanstva, sbornik*, Moscow 1964.
Vneshniaia politika i mezhdunarodnye otnosheniia Kitaiskoi Narodnoi Respubliki, Moscow 1974, *Vol.1.*
Vneshniaia politika Sovetskogo Soiuza, 1950 god, Moscow 1953.
Volin, B., *Grazhdanin SSSR*, Moscow *1938.*
Vot ona, ikh "pravda", Kharkov 1972.

Whiteman, M.M., *Digest of International Law*, Department of State Publication 8290, Washington, D.C., September 1967, Vol.8.

Zakony RSFSR i postanovleniia Verkhovnogo Soveta RSFSR, priniatye na tret'ei sessii Verkhovnogo Soveta RSFSR shestogo sozyva (10–11 iiunia 1964g.), Moscow 1964.

Zlatopol'skii, D.L., *Gosudarstvennoe ustroistvo SSSR*, Moscow 1960.

B. Articles

Aleksandrikov, D., "Do vregulirovania pitannia pro gromadianstvo osib z podviinim gromadianstvom mizh SRSR i krainami narodnoi demokratii", *Radianske pravo*, 1958, No.6, pp.107–112.

Arbuzkin, A., "Pravovoe polozhenie inostrantsev v SSSR", *Chelovek i zakon*, 1979, No.6, pp.12–18.

Avakov, M.M., "Oktiabr'skaia Revoliutsiia i Sovetskoe grazhdanstvo", *Uchenye zapiski* (Belorusskii gosudarstvennyi institut narodnogo khoziaistva im. V.V. Kuibysheva), Minsk 1957, Vol.4, pp.291–318.

Baiaki, V., (Bajáki), "Obshchee i osobennoe v pravovom regulirovanii grazhdanstva v evropeiskikh sotsialisticheskikh stranakh", *Sovetskoe gosudarstvo i pravo*, 1976, No.11, pp.80–86.

Berchenko, A.Ia., "Voprosy sovetskogo grazhdanstva", in *Torzhestvo leninskoi natsional'noi politiki*, Moscow 1963, pp.267–280.

Boim, L., "The Soviet Law of Nationality and its Application to Jews", *Israel Yearbook on Human Rights*, 1973, Vol.3, pp.173–201.

Boitsov, V.Ia., "K voprosu o poniatii grazhdanstva kak gosudarstvenno–pravovogo otnosheniia", *Sbornik uchenykh trudov* (Sverdlovskii iuridicheskii institut), vyp.9, Sverdlovsk 1969, pp.18–26.

Borisov, O., Koloskov, B., "Politika Sovetskogo Soiuza v otnoshenii KNR — sotsialisticheskii internatsionalizm v deistvii (sovetsko–kitaiskie otnosheniia v 1948–1967 gg.)", in *Leninskaia politika SSSR v otnoshenii Kitaia*, Moscow 1968.

Butkevich, V.G., "Pravovye voprosy grazhdanstva i statusa inostrantsev v pervye gody Sovetskoi vlasti", *Problemy pravovedeniia*, vyp.35, Kiev 1977, pp.67–78.

Chernichenko, S.V., "K voprosu o znachenii grazhdanstva v sovremennom mezhdunarodnom prave", *Vestnik Moskovskogo universiteta*, seriia X, Pravo, 1963, No.3, pp.52–61.

Chernichenko, S.V. "Pravo natsii na samoopredelenie i voprosy grazhdanstva", *Sovetskoe gosudarstvo i pravo*, 1964, No.1, pp.110–114.

Chernomordik, A.Ia., "K voprosu o dvoinom grazhdanstve v inostrannom i mezhdunarodnom prave", *Sovetskoe gosudarstvo i pravo*, 1947, No.1, pp. 57–62.

Chkhikvadze, V.M., "Prava cheloveka i ideologicheskaia borba", *Sovetskoe gosudarstvo i pravo*, 1977, No.4, pp.100–108.

F.D., "Sovetskoe grazhdanstvo (Dissertatsiia T.I. Zhukovoi)", *Sovetskoe gosudarstvo i pravo*, 1951, No.1, pp.76–77.

Dmitrieva, G.K., "Mezhdunarodnyi god zhenshchin", *Sovetskoe gosudarstvo i pravo*, 1975, No.3, pp.3–10.

Dmitrieva, G.K., "Nekotorye aspekty mezhdunarodnoi zashchity prav zhenshchin", *Pravovedenie*, 1969, No.6, pp.109–117.

Dmitrieva, G.K., "O mezhdunarodnoi zashchite prav zhenshchin", *Pravovedenie*, 1975, No.6, pp.7–13.

Dufour, R., "La nationalité dans l'U.R.S.S.", *Revue générale de droit international public*, 3ème série, 1930, Vol.4, pp.511–520.

Durdenevskii, V.N., "Die Sovetsstaatsangehörigkeit und ihre Neuregelung im Jahre 1930", *Zeitschrift für Ostrecht*, 1931, pp.332–352.

Durdenevskii, V.N., "Das Staatsangehörigkeitsgesetz der UdSSR vom 1931", *Zeitschrift für Ostrecht*, 1931, pp.518–522.

Durdenevskii, V.N., "Zakon o grazhdanstve Soiuza Sovetskikh Sotsialisticheskikh Respublik", *Problemy sotsialisticheskogo prava*, 1938, No.6, pp. 47–65.

Emelianova, K.L., "Nekotorye voprosy sovershenstvovaniia deiatel'nosti organov ZAGS", *Pravovedenie*, 1968, No.4, pp.101–103.

Evseev, P.N., "Ispolnenie sudebnykh poruchenii i reshenii inostrannykh sudov", in L.A. Lunts, ed., *Problemy mezhdunarodnogo chastnogo prava*, Moscow 1960, pp.182–207.

Freund, H., "Das neue Staatsangehörigkeitsgesetz der UdSSR", *Zeitschrift für Ostrecht*, 1930, pp.706–710.

Ginsburgs, G., Pomorski, S., "A Profile of the Soviet Constitution of 1977", in F.J.M. Feldbrugge, ed., *The Constitutions of the USSR and the Union Republics: Analysis, Texts, Reports*, Alphen aan den Rijn, The Netherlands and Germantown, Maryland 1979.

Goliakov, I.T., "K proektu Ugolovnogo Kodeksa RSFSR", *Sovetskaia iustitsiia*, 1957, No.2, pp.30–33.

Gorodetskaia, I.K, "Grazhdanstvo detei", *Sovetskoe gosudarstvo i pravo*, 1971, No.4, pp.37–43.

Ignat'ev, V., "Soiuznoe grazhdanstvo", *Sovetskoe stroitel'stvo*, 1930, No.3 (44), pp.1–9.

Ivanov, F., Volodin, S., "Piataia sessiia Komissii mezhdunarodnogo prava OON", *Sovetskoe gosudarstvo i pravo*, 1953, No.7, pp.88–100.

Kartashkin, V.A., "Uvazhenie prav cheloveka i nevmeshatel'stvo vo vnutrennie dela gosudarstv", *Sovetskoe gosudarstvo i pravo*, 1974, No.6, pp. 113–119.

Kirichenko, M., "Grazhdanstvo Soiuza SSR", *Sotsialisticheskaia zakonnost'*, 1972, No.11, pp.9–12.

Klesment, J., "New Soviet Position on the Nationality of Estonians Abroad", *Highlights of Current Legislation and Activities in Mid–Europe*, 1959, No.9, pp.347–348.

Konstantinova, I., "Amerikanskaia Femida protiv prav roditelei i detei", *Chelovek i zakon*, 1981, No.1, pp.120–123.

Korovine, E., "La République des Soviets et le droit international", *Revue générale de droit international public*, 2ème série, 1925, Vol.7, pp.292–312.

Kosakov, S., "Konstitutsionnye osnovy kompetentsii Soiuznoi Respubliki po voprosam grazhdanstva", *Izvestiia Akademii nauk Kazakhskoi SSR*, seriia obshchestvennykh nauk, No.5, 1980, pp.60–66.

Kotliarevskii, S.A., "Voprosy soiuznogo grazhdanstva i grazhdanstva soiuznykh respublik", *Vestnik Verkhovnogo Suda SSSR*, 1927, No.2, pp.14–17.

Kriazhev, A.Ia., "Izvrashchenie maoistami leninskoi natsional'noi politiki", *Izvestiia Sibir'skogo otdeleniia Adakemii nauk SSSR*, seriia obshchestvennykh nauk, 1976, No.1, vyp.1, pp.99–105.

Kulik, R., "Pravovye nachala Sovetskogo grazhdanstva", *Sovety narodnykh deputatov*, 1979, No.2, pp.33–39.

Kuzmenko, L.B., "Razvitie pravovogo regulirovaniia statusa lichnosti v novom Zakone o grazhdanstve SSSR", *Vestnik Moskovskogo universiteta*, seriia 11: Pravo, 1980, No.4, pp.27–33.

Kuznetsova, I.M., "Spornye voprosy nasledovaniia", *Problemy sovershenstvovaniia sovetskogo zakonodatel'stva*, Moscow 1980, Trudy 17, pp.125–136.

Lepeshkin, A.I., "Konstitutsionnoe razvitie Sovetskogo soiuznogo gosudarstva", *Sovetskoe gosudarstvo i pravo*, 1962, No.12, pp.26–36.

Loeber, D.A., "Legal Rules 'For Internal Use Only', A Comparative Analysis of the Practice of Withholding Government Decrees from Publication in Eastern Europe and in Western Countries", *International and Comparative Law Quarterly*, January 1970, pp.70–98.

Lurii, Iu., "Sovetskii zakon o grazhdanstve i emigranty", *Russkaia Mysl'*, New York, May 17, 24, and 31, 1979.

Luryi, Yu., "Soviet Family Law", *Manitoba Law Journal*, 1980, No.2, pp. 117–209.

Makarov, A., "Le droit d'option en cas de double nationalité dans les conventions internationales", *Varia Juris Gentium*, Leiden 1959, pp.194–202.

Matveev, G.K., "Voprosy sovetskogo kollizionnogo semeinogo prava", *Pravovedenie*, 1972, No.2, pp.99–105.

Mehl, F., Rapoport, S.E., "Soviet Policy of Separating Families and the Right to Emigrate", *International and Comparative Law Quarterly*, October 1978, pp.876–889.

Motas, M., "Niektore kwestie dotychczasow przesiedlienie ludnosci polskiej z USSR do Polski w Iatach 1944–1946", *Z dziejow stosunkow Polsko–Radzieckich, studia i materialy*, Warsaw 1975, Vol.11–12, pp.221–234.

Nepesov, B., "'Dvoinoe grazhdanstvo': chto eto takoe?", *Chelovek i zakon*, 1979, No.11, pp.12–18.

Novikov, M.Z., "Pravovye voprosy repatriatsii", *Khronika zashchity prav v SSSR*, New York 1978, vyp.29, pp.35–42.

Osakwe, C., "Recent Soviet Citizenship Legislation", *American Journal of Comparative Law*, 1980, No.4, pp.625–643.

Palienko, N.I., "Pravo grazhdanstva v Soiuze SSR", *Vestnik sovetskoi iustitsii*, 1925, No.7(41), pp.270–273.

Pereterskii, I.S., "Sovetskaia initsiativa v Lige Natsii po voprosu o ravnopravii zhenshchin", *Sovetskoe gosudarstvo*, 1934, No.6, pp.66–67.

Petrov, Iu.A., "Sootnosheniia poniatii grazhdanstva, pravosposobnosti, pravovogo polozheniia grazhdan", *Vestnik Leningradskogo universiteta*, 1974, No.5, pp.115–120.

Polianskii, V.V., "Printsipy sovetskogo grazhdanstva", *Sovetskoe gosudarstvo i pravo*, 1980, No.5, pp.123–129.

Pusylewitsch, T., "Das neue Staatsangehörigkeitsgesetz der Sowjetunion", *Osteuropa–Recht*, 1979, No.4, pp.247–255.

Robin, M.A., "Soviet Emigration Law and International Obligations under United Nations Instruments", *Journal of International Law and Economics*, 1979, Vol.13, pp.403–431.

Roth, S.J., "The New Soviet Citizenship Law and Jewish Emigration", *Research Report* USSR/79/3 (July, 1979), Institute of Jewish Affairs, London.

Rubanov, A.A., "Mezhdunarodno–pravovye voprosy zakonodatel'nogo regulirovaniia otnoshenii sovetskogo grazhdanstva", *Sovetskii ezhegodnik mezhdunarodnogo prava 1978*, Moscow 1980, pp.141–161.

Rubanov, A.A., "Osnovnye kollizionnye voprosy sovetskogo zakonodatel'stva o grazhdanstve", *Sovetskoe gosudarstvo i pravo*, 1979, No.7, pp.48–55.

Rusakov, M., "Brak i grazhdanstvo po sovetskomu zakonodatel'stvu", *Administrativnyi vestnik*, 1927, No.10–11, pp.104–108.

Rusakov, M., "Sovetskoe grazhdanstvo (Praktika RSFSR)", *Administrativnyi vestnik*, 1930, No.3, pp.12–20.

Rusinova, S.I., "Voprosy grazhdanstva v evropeiskikh stranakh narodnoi demokratii", *Uchenye zapiski Leningradskogo gosudarstvennogo universiteta*, seriia iuridicheskikh nauk, vyp.7, 1955, No.201, pp.176–207.

Rusinova, S.I., "Zakon o grazhdanstve SSSR", *Pravovedenie*, 1980, No.1, pp.3–9.

Salishcheva, N., Koveshnikov, E., "Novyi Zakon o grazhdanstve SSSR", *Sotsialisticheskaia zakonnost'*, 1979, No.3, pp.9–13.

Samore, W., "Statelessness as a Consequence of the Conflict of Nationality Laws", *American Journal of International Law*, 1951, No.3, pp.476–494.

Sandifer, D.V., "Soviet Citizenship", *American Journal of International Law*, 1936, No.4, pp.614–631.

Schroeter, L., "How They Left: Varieties of Soviet Jewish Exit Experience", *Soviet Jewish Affairs*, 1972, No.2, pp.3–30.

Schroeter, L., "Soviet Jews and Israeli Citizenship: The Nationality Amendment Law of 1971", *Soviet Jewish Affairs*, 1971, No.2, pp.25–34.

Shevtsov, V.S., "Sovetskoe grazhdanstvo i gosudarstvennyi suverenitet", *Sovetskoe gosudarstvo i pravo*, 1970, No.6, pp.39–47.

Silverstein, J. and L., "David Marshall and Jewish Emigration from China", *China Quarterly*, 1978, No.75, pp.647–654.

Sipkov, I., "Settlement of Dual Nationality in European Communist Countries", *American Journal of International Law*, 1962, No.4, pp.1010–1019.

Soloviov, M., "Pozbavlennia gromadianstva — zasib borot'bi z iavishchami, shcho zavdaiut' shkodi radianskii derzhavi", *Radianske pravo*, 1975, No.3, pp.78–81.

Stephan, J.J., "The Korean Minority in the Soviet Union", *Mizan*, 1971, No. 3, pp.138–150.

Tameike, Yoshio, "Nationality of Formosans and Koreans", *Japanese Annual of International Law*, 1958, pp.55–65.

Taracouzio, T.A., "The Soviet Citizenship Law of 1938", *American Journal of International Law*, 1939, No.1, pp.157–159.

"The Decline of Soviet Jewish Emigration in 1980", *Research Report* No.17 (October 1980), Institute of Jewish Affairs, London.

"The New Law on Soviet Citizenship", *Socialism: Theory and Practice*, 1979, No.8, pp.60–63.

Trachtenberg, B., "La législation soviétique sur la nationalité", *Revue de droit international privé*, 1931, pp.150–163.

Trainin, I., "K voprosu o grazhdanstve", *Sovetskoe gosudarstvo*, 1938, No.5, pp.51–70.

Tunkin, G.I., "Zakon o grazhdanstve SSSR", *Sovetskoe gosudarstvo i pravo*, 1979, No.7, pp.22–30.

Uibopuu, H.–J., "Soviet Nationality: Privilege or Burden? An International Lawyer's View", *Israel Yearbook on Human Rights*, 1977, Vol.7, pp.53–65.

Vilkov, G.E., "Mezhdunarodno–pravovoe regulirovanie voprosov bezgrazhdanstva", *Sovetskii ezhegodnik mezhdunarodnogo prava 1963*, Moscow 1965, pp.260–270.

Vilkov, G.E, "Mezhdunarodno–pravovoe regulirovanie voprosov dvoinogo grazhdanstva", *Sovetskii ezhegodnik mezhdunarodnogo prava 1959*, Moscow 1960, pp.360–372.

Vitruk, N.V., "Grazhdanstvo kak pravovaia sviaz' lichnosti s gosudarstvom", *Problemy gosudarstva i prava*, Moscow 1976, No.12, pp.12–19.

Vondracek, Th.J., "Sowjet–staatsburgerschap", *Themis*, 1966, Vol.1, 14 pp.

Zenin, V., "Gromadianstvo SRSR — velika chest' i velika vidpovidal'nist'", *Radianske pravo*, 1979, No.2, pp.9–11.

INDEX

GPSR Compliance

The European Union's (EU) General Product Safety Regulation (GPSR) is a set of rules that requires consumer products to be safe and our obligations to ensure this.

If you have any concerns about our products, you can contact us on ProductSafety@springernature.com

In case Publisher is established outside the EU, the EU authorized representative is:

Springer Nature Customer Service Center GmbH
Europaplatz 3
69115 Heidelberg, Germany

Batch number: 10830943

Printed by Printforce, the Netherlands